THE MAKING OF HOMERIC VERSE

MILMAN PARRY, 1902–1935

THE MAKING OF HOMERIC VERSE

THE COLLECTED PAPERS OF
MILMAN PARRY

Edited by Adam Parry

NEW YORK OXFORD
OXFORD UNIVERSITY PRESS
1987

Oxford University Press

Oxford New York Toronto
Delhi Bombay Calcutta Madras Karachi
Petaling Jaya Singapore Hong Kong Tokyo
Nairobi Dar es Salaam Cape Town
Melbourne Auckland
and associated companies in
Beirut Berlin Ibadan Nicosia

First published in Great Britain in 1971 by
Oxford University Press

First published in paperback in 1987 in the United States by
Oxford University Press, Inc.
198 Madison Avenue, New York, New York 10016-4314

Library of Congress Cataloging-in-Publication Data
Parry, Milman.
The making of Homeric verse.
Includes bibliographical references and indexes.
1. Homer—Style. 2. Greek language—Style.
3. Greek language—Metrics and rhythmics.
I. Parry, Adam. II. Title.
PA4175.P37 1987 883'.01 87-14702
ISBN 0-19-520560-X

4 6 8 10 9 7 5 3

Printed in the United States of America
on acid-free paper

CONTENTS

LIST OF PLATES

ABBREVIATIONS

THE abbreviations used for Milman Parry's own works are shown in the List of Contents.

Other abbreviations:

AJA	*American Journal of Archaeology*
AJPh	*American Journal of Philology*
BICS	*Bulletin of the Institute of Classical Studies*
CPh	*Classical Philology*
CQ	*Classical Quarterly*
HPh	*Harvard Studies in Classical Philology*
PMLA	*Proceedings of the Modern Languages Association*
TAPhA	*Transactions of the American Philological Association*
YClS	*Yale Classical Studies*

INTRODUCTION[1]

MILMAN PARRY, who died at the age of 33 years on 3 December 1935, when he was Assistant Professor of Greek at Harvard University, is now generally considered one of the leading classical scholars of this century. His published work was entirely concerned with the epic tradition which is represented for us by the *Iliad* and the *Odyssey*. This published work, together with Parry's University of California Master of Arts thesis, selections from the notes he made in Jugoslavia during the winter of 1934–5 on Serbocroatian poetry and its relation to Homer, and an article descriptive of his field-work written by his student and assistant Albert Bates Lord, is here reprinted in its entirety.[2]

The first two works are the doctoral dissertations, or *thèses*, which Parry wrote to obtain the degree of Docteur-ès-Lettres at the University of Paris in 1928. This degree, the highest awarded by the French university system, is usually obtained by French scholars who have established themselves in university or *lycée* positions; most of those who get it do not do so until their mid thirties or later; it does not lead to academic position: it is designed to follow it, and it represents a kind of final initiation in the society of the learned. In 1923, Parry had spent four years of undergraduate and one of graduate study at the University of California in Berkeley, and had earned the degrees there of Bachelor of Arts and Master of Arts. In the following year, at the age of 23, with a wife and newly-born child and a most imperfect knowledge of French, he arrived in Paris. He spent his first year there in mastering the language, and only then devoted himself to his work for the doctorate. At the end of his four years in Paris, he had written the required major and minor *thèses* in French, and had had them published in book form, according to the requirements of that time. These books, now long out of print, have been translated into English for this volume by the editor. Parry then underwent the public *soutenance de thèse* with conspicuous success, and shortly afterwards, in the spring of 1928, returned to America, a young and

[1] To the following people, who offered valuable suggestions to him in writing this introduction, the editor wishes to express his gratitude: E. A. Havelock, G. S. Kirk, Hugh Lloyd-Jones, J. H. Moore, J. A. Russo, and not least to his wife, Mrs. Anne Amory Parry.

[2] The papers Parry left behind at his death include twenty-eight pages, double spaced, of typewritten notes for a course on Homer and Virgil to be given at Harvard. The misspellings and lacunae in these notes show them to have been typed by someone not familiar with Greek from imperfect recordings of dictation. The state of the text dissuaded me from reprinting them; but I have referred to them several times in the notes to this introduction, and have quoted many of the more interesting fragments there.

virtually unknown scholar, who had completed and published work which was to change the aspect of Homeric studies. He began his teaching career in the following autumn at Drake University in Iowa, and after a year moved to Harvard University, where he remained on the faculty until his accidental death six years later. While he was at Harvard, he published a series of articles in American classical journals, elaborating the arguments of the French *thèses*. These articles are all collected here, in chronological order.

Between the years 1933 and 1935, under the auspices of the American Council of Learned Societies and of Harvard University, Parry made two trips to Jugoslavia, the first in the summer of 1933 and the second in the academic year 1934–5. His purpose was to check and confirm the conclusions he had drawn from close analysis of the Homeric texts by observing a living tradition of heroic poetry. Some of his later published articles reflect much that he learned in Jugoslavia. But the work he had undertaken there was to be carried on by his assistant, A. B. Lord, who accompanied him on the second and longer trip. The concrete results of his investigations in Jugoslavia were, first, the Milman Parry collection of records and transcriptions of Serbocroatian heroic poetry, now in Widener Library in Harvard University, a small part of which is in the public domain in the form of the published volumes of *Songs from Novi Pazar*, edited by A. B. Lord,[1] and second, the volume of notes mentioned above, which was roughly arranged by Parry into book form and entitled *Ćor Huso: A Study in Serbocroatian Poetry* (here CH). Lord's article in volume 52 of the *American Journal of Archaeology*, 'Homer, Parry and Huso' (here HPH), reprinted at the end of this book, describes Parry's purposes and methods of work in Jugoslavia. The same article quotes the few introductory pages Parry had completed of a projected book on epic poetry.

§ 2

The Homeric Question[2] is a modern phenomenon, although we can trace some of its roots, and discern adumbrations of some of its notions,

[1] These are the first two volumes of a projected series of *Serbocroatian Heroic Songs* by Lord, published by the Harvard University Press (Cambridge, Mass.) and the Serbian Academy of Sciences (Belgrade) in 1953 and 1954. The first volume contains English translations by Lord, some musical transcriptions by Béla Bartók, and prefaces by John H. Finley, Jr. and Roman Jakobson; the second, the Serbocroatian texts.

[2] The following pages do not attempt to give a comprehensive summary of the Homeric Question, but only to sketch some of the lines of thought which helped to determine the direction of Parry's own study. Good recent accounts of the history of the Homeric Question can be found in: M. P. Nilsson, *Homer and Mycenae*, London 1933, 1–55 (the most thoughtful account); J. L. Myres, *Homer and his Critics*, edited by Dorothea Gray, with a continuation by the editor which contains good comments on Parry's own contribution, London 1958; J. A. Davison, 'The Homeric Question' in Wace and Stubbings, *A Companion to Homer*, London

in ancient times. Ancient scholars and men of letters, that is to say, sometimes showed hints of an awareness that Homer was not like later authors, and that the Homeric poems had origins more mysterious and more complex than later poetic compositions; but these intimations and conjectures amounted to little. Throughout the duration of the Ancient World, and in a dimmer way through the Middle Ages, and on through the Renaissance, Homer remained the primordial great poet, the truest expression of the divine inspiration of poetry, one who (as the eighteenth century would put it) 'perused the book of Nature', and during most of this time the works chiefly associated with his name, the *Iliad* and the *Odyssey*, remained the most popular and the most exemplary works of literary art the world possessed. The analogy of the Bible—the *Iliad* and the *Odyssey* together as a secular Bible—is not inappropriate.[1] If the Homeric poems never had the binding theological authority the Bible once enjoyed in our culture, they were throughout antiquity read and known far better than the Bible is read and known now, or has been for some time. Lacking our historical sense, and possessing the *Iliad* and *Odyssey* too much as part of themselves, the ancients never envisaged, let alone accomplished, anything like a scientific investigation of the origins of Homeric poetry.

The two references most often made to ancient anticipation of the Homeric Question show how casual and isolated such speculation was. Cicero's account of a 'Pisistratean Recension'[2] does not imply a theory of the Homeric poems as an amalgam of traditional songs, but the contrary: it assumes the existence, previous to Pisistratus, of the established text of a literary creation. Josephus' suggestion[3] that Homer could not write was made revealingly by a Hebrew author arguing the superiority of Hebrew culture, and it led to no genuine theory of the composition of the *Iliad* and the *Odyssey*. A line of approach potentially more fruitful than either of these, because it derived from actual observation of Homeric diction, was that of the Alexandrian scholars who distinguished between significant adjectives and ornamental epithets:[4] but the implications of this observation for the origins of Homeric poetry were never guessed then, and can only be seen clearly now because we have Parry's work behind us.

1962, 234–65 (the most detailed account); A. Lesky, 'Die homerische Frage' in his *Geschichte der griechischen Literatur*², Berne and Munich 1957–8, 49–58 (contains a good discussion of the importance of Parry's work); and now the fuller account in 'Homeros, II. Oral Poetry' and 'III. Mündlichkeit und Schriftlichkeit' in Lesky's new article for Pauly–Wissowa–Kroll, *Real-Enzyklopädie*, printed as a separate monograph, Stuttgart 1967; see also H. L. Lorimer, 'Homer and the Art of Writing', *AJA* 52, 1948, 11–23.

[1] Cf. Myres, op. cit. (p. x, n. 2 above), 14 and 20.

[2] Cf. J. A. Davison, 'Pisistratus and Homer', *TAPhA* 86, 1955, 1–21; C. H. Whitman, *Homer and the Heroic Tradition* (Cambridge, Mass. 1958), 71 f.

[3] *Contra Apionem* I. 12. See esp. Davison in Wace and Stubbings, op. cit. (p. x, n. 2), 246.

[4] See in this volume TE 148 f., and the references there.

A vain and irascible Frenchman of the seventeenth century, the Abbé d'Aubignac, has the best claim to be the originator of the Homeric Question. Reacting against the reverence for Homer of his day, and drawing on criticisms of Homeric poetry that had been uttered earlier by Erasmus, Scaliger, and others, he composed a polemic.[1] The poetry, the construction of plot, the characterization in Homer, he claimed, are poor, its morality and theology odious.[2] So far we have but an unimportant literary attack, without historical potentialities. But d'Aubignac went further: Homer, he argued, cannot be a standard for poetry, because there was in fact no man Homer, and the poems handed down to us in his name are no more than a collection of earlier rhapsodies. Individual perversity and awakening historical sense, the former in greater measure than the latter, mingle strangely in this first explorer of the question of what the Homeric poems are.

The same can be said of the freewheeling opinion of Richard Bentley: '[Homer] wrote a sequel of Songs and Rhapsodies, to be sung by himself for small earnings and good cheer, at Festivals and other days of Merriment; the Ilias he made for the men and the Odysseis for the other Sex. These loose songs were not connected together in the form of an epic poem till Pisistratus' time about 500 years after.'[3] Bentley is less extreme than d'Aubignac, in that he sees as author of the *Iliad* and *Odyssey* a man named Homer: but that author lived far earlier than the formation of the epic poems ascribed to him, while the processes both of transmission and formation are left obscure.

[1] François Hédelin, Abbé d'Aubignac et de Meimac (1604–76), *Conjectures académiques ou Dissertation sur l'Iliade*, written apparently shortly before 1670, but kept by friends of the author and not published till 1715 ('incertum amici an veterum amore' is Wolf's Tacitean comment [*Prolegomena*, n. 84; see below, p. xiv, n. 1]). Edited with a good introduction by V. Magnien, Paris 1925. Modern accounts of d'Aubignac's purposes and arguments vary curiously. See, in the works cited p. x, n. 2 above, Lorimer 12, n. 6; Myres 47; Davison 243; Lesky 51. Miss Lorimer (who is specifically concerned with the use of writing, on which d'Aubignac has not much to say) dismisses him as of no importance, although he obviously anticipated much of Wolf's far more learned argument, and his work was known to Wolf. On the other hand, Myres speaks with absurd extravagance of 'd'Aubignac's scholarship and real sense of literary art'. Magnien shows conclusively that he did not read Homer in Greek, and a glance at almost any page shows that he had no understanding of Homeric art whatever. Lesky's description of the Abbé's work as a defence of Homer is hard to understand. Davison's account is reasonably accurate.

For earlier criticism of Homer used by d'Aubignac, see, e.g., pp. 19 and 81 of Magnien's edition.

[2] Parry comments in his lecture notes: 'It is significant that it was a contemporary of Corneille and Racine who was first shocked by the literary form of the Homeric poems. To a mind habituated to the classical conception of literature of the time with its rigid sense of form, its exclusion of all which was not strictly relevant, Homer when regarded frankly, must have been the most slovenly of poets.'

[3] See the excellent discussion of this famous remark by Lorimer, *AJA* 52, 1948, 11–12. Bentley's dates are 1662–1742, and the remark occurs in a treatise (*Remarks upon a Late Discourse of Free Thinking*) of 1713.

A third view of the question was suggested by the Italian philosopher Giambattista Vico (1668–1744).[1] He was with d'Aubignac on the matter of the one poet: there was no such man. But this assumption led him to a judgement very different from d'Aubignac's, a judgement at once more romantic and more deeply historical. He declared that the Homeric poems were the creation not of one man, but of a whole people, and that they owed their greatness to this origin. They are the true expression of the Greek genius in one age of its history.

It was another Englishman who, however, in this early and speculative period of the Homeric question, set forth in essence the view that even today appears to have the best claim on our acceptance. A diplomat, one of the great travellers, an archaeologist, a man with a sober historical sense and a true lover of Homer, Robert Wood (*c.* 1717–71) set out to demonstrate the historical reality of the scenes and events in Homer. He had some success in this endeavour, travelling about and observing with a good eye the places we read of in the *Iliad* and *Odyssey*. This work, published in his *Essay on the Original Genius of Homer* in 1767, was to be confirmed by the excavations of Schliemann and Dörpfeld more than a century later. But Wood's sense of the poet Homer, as he considers the question in the last chapter but one of his *Essay*, is yet more interesting. He accepts, on historical grounds, the impossibility of a literate Homer. But this leads him to renounce neither the individuality of Homer nor his greatness. The problem forces him rather to a new concept. Homer was a different kind of poet from the later, literate masters. The mechanisms of literary craftsmanship were absent in him, so was the learning of a more refined civilization; but in their place was the power of unlettered memory. 'As to the difficulty of conceiving how Homer could acquire, retain, and communicate, all he knew, without the aid of Letters; it is, I own, very striking', he says (p. 259 of the second edition, London 1775), and goes on (pp. 259–60):

> But the oral traditions of a learned and enlightened age will greatly mislead us, if from them we form our judgement on those of a period, when History had no other resource. What we observed at Palmyra puts this matter to a much fairer trial; nor can we, in this age of Dictionaries, and other technical aids to memory, judge, what her use and powers were, at a time, when all a man could know, was all he could remember. To which we may add, that, in a rude and unlettered state of society the memory is loaded with nothing that is either useless or unintelligible; whereas modern education employs us chiefly in getting by heart, while we are young, what we forget before we are old.

Of course Wood gives us no clear picture of how an unlettered poet

[1] See B. Croce, *The Philosophy of Giambattista Vico*, translated by R. G. Collingwood, London 1913, 183–96; and G. Perrotta, 'Le Teorie omeriche di Giambattista Vico', in *Italia e Grecia*, Florence 1940.

operates. Yet even this he manages to suggest, though dimly. His Homer is above all the poet of Nature. Besides making him *veracious* (Wood exaggerates his historicity), this means that his knowledge is both more circumscribed and more distinct than that of later poets. As his knowledge was more distinct, so was his language, for 'the sense was catched from the sound' (281), and 'If his language had not yet acquired the refinements of a learned age, it was for that reason not only more intelligible and clear, but also less open to pedantry and affectation' (285–6). And 'this language [which] was sufficiently copious for his purposes . . . had . . . advantages more favourable to harmonious versification, than ever fell to the lot of any other Poet.' Wood then proceeds to speak of the usefulness of the free use of particles in hexameter verse in a way that anticipates Parry's own demonstration of the role of convenience of versification in Homeric diction.

For all its generality and its dependence on an unexamined concept of Nature, Wood's insight was in many ways the most valid conception until modern times of what sort of poet Homer was, and of how the *Iliad* and *Odyssey* came into being. Yet we can observe how this insight became obscured in the age of more exhaustive scholarship and more scientifically searching investigation that followed him. This was the age when men became conscious of the Homeric Question as such.

The nineteenth century, in so many fields of endeavour the laborious age of mankind, saw the full development of the Higher Criticism of Homer. The dominant movement of this period of scholarship was that of the Analysts, that is, of those who, in one way or another, saw our texts of the *Iliad* and *Odyssey* as combinations of earlier poems or fragments of poems. Their theories all rested on one assumption, an assumption which, because it was so fundamental, and in their eyes challenged by no alternative assumption, was never clearly stated by any of them. This was that there existed, previous to Homer, an 'original' text, or 'original' texts, of the Homeric epics, which either were written, or were possessed of the fixed form which only a written text can provide.

That this assumption could have so controlled, and (in the opinion of this writer) so vitiated, the work of so many men of learning and acumen appears all the more ironic when we consider the work which began their line of enquiry: the *Prolegomena* of Friedrich August Wolf (1759–1824), published in Halle in 1795[1]. Wolf, the first professor of *Philologie*, proved, or seemed to have proved, with a rigour and scholarly authority hitherto

[1] 3rd edition by R. Peppmüller, Halle 1884. The full title, exhibiting its author's *copia dicendi*, is *Prolegomena ad Homerum sive de Operum Homericorum Prisca et Genuina Forma Variisque Mutationibus et Probabili Ratione Emendandi*. For discussion, see, in addition to the works listed above (p. x, n. 2), Mark Pattison's biographical essay of 1865, in *Essays by the late Mark Pattison*, collected and arranged by Henry Nettleship, Oxford 1889, 2 vols., pp. 337–414 of vol. 1, esp. pp. 377–91).

unseen in the controversy, that Homer must have lived at a time when the alphabet was not yet in use. Homer therefore could not have been *read* by his audience, and so could not have composed, and would have had no occasion to compose, works of the length of the *Iliad* and *Odyssey*. This last point Wolf regarded as the keystone of his theory.[1] The texts, the original pieces of the poems, unwritten, composed around 950 B.C. orally for recitation by rhapsodes, were handed down by oral transmission until the 'Pisistratean Recension' in the sixth century B.C. In the course of transmission they were much changed and probably expanded. The unity of the poems as we now have them is due not so much to Homer, the original creator of most of them, as to the later editors who fused them, not always successfully, into whole works.

Wolf saw, more clearly than his successors, that there were difficulties in this account, chiefly deriving from the coherent structure of our texts, and in particular, as he saw it, of the *Odyssey*.[2] And unlike his successors, he avoided precise conjecture regarding the shape of the original ingredients of the Homeric poems, or the manner of their formation into the poetic unities which he clearly saw.[3] The intent of the *Prolegomena* made it easier for him to avoid committing himself in this way. The work was to explain the critical principles which would guide his establishment of a text of Homer. The acquaintance with Alexandrian criticism which the recent publication (by Villoison in 1788) of the scholia of Venetus A afforded him, had persuaded him that the textual problems of Homer were fundamentally different from those of other authors, and that there was no possibility of approaching, in his case, a hypothetical original manuscript. The *Prolegomena* sought to explain this state of things. The theory that nothing of Homer was written down until the time of Solon or Pisistratus, and that there already existed at that time a large number of variants, provided the explanation. There was no necessity to conjecture in detail what preceded the creation of the written text, although Wolf's general comments on this matter were what made his treatise so important an intellectual document.

[1] 112–13: 'Eodem pacto si Homero lectores deerant, plane non assequor, quid tandem eum impellere potuisset in consilium et cogitationem tam longorum et continuo partium nexu consertorum Carminum. Saepius eadem repeto: sed identidem repetendum est illud *posse*, cuius ex ipsa humana natura vis tanta est et firmamentum causae nostrae, ut, nisi illud tollatur, nemo aliis difficultatibus, quibus ea fortasse laborat plurimis, angi et sollicitari debeat.'

[2] 114: 'Difficultates illas, quas mirifica forma et descriptio horum ἐπῶν partiumque dispositio obiicit'; 117–18: '. . . de Odyssea maxime, cuius admirabilis summa et compages pro praeclarissimo monumento Graeci ingenii habenda est.' Elsewhere he speaks of the remarkable unity of style in the Homeric poems: 138: 'Quippe *in universum* idem sonus est omnibus libris, idem habitus sententiarum, orationis, numerorum.'

[3] He does, however, occasionally anticipate the later tendency to seize on certain passages as *late* or *inferior* or *unhomeric*; e.g., about the fourth book of the *Odyssey* from l. 620 on, he says (133): '. . . neque hic Homerum canentem audimus.' Cf. 137–8 on the last six books of the *Iliad*.

Like his successors, Wolf lacked any clear concept of what an oral tradition is like. He does not distinguish between the rhapsode, like Plato's Ion, who memorizes, and the bard or minstrel, like Phemius and Demodocus in the *Odyssey*, who, as Parry was to show, improvises from a poetic store of formulae, themes, and tales. He argues in general terms that the original poems would not have changed completely in the course of oral transmission, but that they would have received some modifications, additions, and subtractions.[1] He cannot imagine the actual fluidity of an oral tradition of song, which makes it inconceivable that a passage of poetry sung in 950 could have been preserved without the use of writing until the sixth century. While arguing vehemently against the use of writing by Homer, Wolf has to assume the kind of fixity of form which is only possible when writing exists. Yet his very uncertainty on this matter reveals an intuition of the inherent difficulties which was lost in the generations of work that followed his.[2] In the course of the nineteenth century, the unlettered poet was largely accepted. But his work, apart from the accidents which for better or for worse befell it between first composition and the final formation of our texts, was conceived as not fundamentally different from the pen product of a later poet. Lachmann (1793–1851) reverted somewhat to the Viconian concept of a *Volkspoesie* by suggesting that the *Iliad* was an amalgam of popular *Lieder*, leaving little place for a dominantly creative Homer. But this theory, it was reasonably held, failed to account for the actual unity of the poems,[3] and on the whole, nineteenth-century Homeric speculation, following the lead of G. Hermann (1772–1848),[4] played itself out in a series of hypotheses of an original nucleus by a single poet, which might as well have been a written text, and which underwent various expansions and transformations

[1] e.g. 104: 'Haec autem reputanti mihi vehementer errare videntur ii, qui putant litteris non usum Homerum statim totum immutari et sui dissimilem reddi necesse fuisse.' Then a few lines below (104): 'In primis vero recitatio ipsa, vivido impetu et ardore animi peracta, infirmaverit oportet memoriam, multisque mutationibus causam dederit, &c.' In 264 and 265, this uncertainty becomes, in Wolf's mind, an irresoluble tension between the logic of his historical conclusions and his experience of the poems: 'Habemus nunc Homerum in manibus, non qui viguit in ore Graecorum suorum, sed inde a Solonis temporibus usque ad haec Alexandrina mutatum varie, interpolatum, castigatum et emendatum. Id e disiectis quibusdam indiciis iam dudum obscure colligebant homines docti et sollertes; nunc in unum coniunctae voces omnium temporum testantur, et loquitur historia.' Then, beginning a new chapter: 'At historiae quasi obloquitur ipse vates, et contra testatur sensus legentis. Neque vero ita deformata et difficta sunt Carmina, ut in rebus singulis priscae et suae formae nimis dissimilia esse videantur.'

[2] Parry comments in his lecture notes: 'Wolf was strong by his very vagueness. He made possible the large number of different theories concerning the composition, which appeared in the 19th century.'

[3] Parry comments in his lecture notes: '. . . the laws of mathematical probability should have prevented the first conception of Lachmann's theories.'

[4] *Opuscula* v, 1832, 52 f.

at the hands of editors and 'reworkers'. First just the *Iliad*, then it and the *Odyssey* as well were treated in this way. For both poems the problem essentially reduced itself to the discovery of early and late *layers* of composition.

This was done by analysing the texts in order to establish discrepancies of plot, of historical and archaeological reference, of language, and of style. Thus G. Grote (1794–1871) in chapter XXI of his *History of Greece* of 1846[1] argued that of the *Iliad*, *B–H*, *I–K*, and *Ψ–Ω* were later additions to Homer's original *Achillêis*. (We note that from Wolf's point of view, the length of that *Achillêis* would have made it scarcely more conceivable as Homer's work than the whole *Iliad*: but the problem of illiteracy is of no real concern to Grote.) *B–H* must be intrusive because Achilles does not appear in them, and they are not connected with the story of his Wrath. *I* is inconsistent with the passages of *Λ* and *Π* where Achilles appears not to know that he has already been offered compensation. *K* is alien in tone, and again unconnected with the Wrath, and likewise *Ψ* and *Ω*.[2]

One of the most influential of the discerping critics of Homer, and one of the last in their line[3] was Ulrich von Wilamowitz-Moellendorff (1848–1931), whose *Die Ilias und Homer* of 1916[4] is described by E. R. Dodds,[5] in what may be an excessively generous estimate, as 'one of the great books on Homer', although Dodds himself finds the pattern of Wilamowitz's dissection unconvincing. Lesky's comment on this work could apply to most analytic Homeric scholarship since Wolf: 'No one who reads the concluding pages of Wilamowitz's *Die Ilias und Homer* (Berlin 1916) with their summary of his intricate theory of the origins of the *Iliad* can conceive a process of such complexity without making the assumption of widespread literacy.'[6]

In his essay on Wolf of 1865,[7] Mark Pattison said, in pointing out the immense influence of the *Prolegomena*, that 'no scholar will again find

[1] Edition of 1883, vol. 2, pp. 119–209.

[2] Despite this fierce analysis, Grote is so impressed with the coherence of the whole that he wonders (202) if the additions were not made by Homer himself. Grote expressed the prevailing opinion of his day in contending that the *Odyssey* is a unity. It was not until Kirchhoff's *Die homerische Odyssee und ihre Entstehung* of 1859 that the *Odyssey* became in its turn a victim of dissection.

[3] Not that the line has died out: see, e.g., Denys Page, *History and the Homeric Iliad* (Berkeley 1959), appendix on 'Multiple Authorship in the Iliad'.

[4] Wilamowitz dealt with the *Odyssey* in two books, *Homerische Untersuchungen*, 1884, and *Die Heimkehr des Odysseus* in 1927.

[5] In his valuable article 'Homer' in *Fifty Years of Classical Scholarship* (Oxford 1954), 1–37, esp. 5.

[6] 'Wer etwa in dem Buche von Wilamowitz *Die Ilias und Homer* (Berlin 1916) die letzten Seiten mit der Übersicht über die so komplizierte Entstehungstheorie der *Ilias* liest, kann sich so verwickelte Vorgänge nur unter der Voraussetzung reicher Schriftlichkeit vorstellen' (*Geschichte der griechischen Literatur*², 53–4).

[7] See p. xiv, n. 1 above.

himself able to embrace the unitarian thesis'. Pattison also speaks (p. 381) of a 'crudity of conception' in Wolf's great work: 'The Homeric problem was too complicated to be capable of being thought out by the first mind which grappled with it. The question has been wrought out with much greater precision and fullness of detail since by Lachmann, Lehrs, Nitzsch, . . . &c.' We can easily see one hundred years later that Pattison was looking into a very clouded crystal ball when he made the first of these comments. But the second may have been equally misconceived. Wolf's sense of the limitations of his own knowledge and his feeling for Homeric poetry, together with superior powers of logic, combined to keep him from making the errors of his successors. If he had little conception of what an oral tradition is, he did not at any rate put forth any theory of the poems which, by essentially assuming a literate tradition, would have undone the bases of his own theory. Nor would he ever have argued as Wilamowitz does, e.g. that the scene in the first book of the *Iliad* where the Greeks go to make amends to Chryseus must be a 'later addition', because the tone in that scene differs from the tone in the quarrel between Achilles and Agamemnon, as if the poet of the *Iliad* could command only a single tone or mood.

The assumption that in retrospect seems to have been common to all the analyst scholars, underlying all the erudition and ingenuity of their constructions, that Homeric poetry was essentially poetry like ours, only subject to peculiar distortion and development in its transmission, was more harmful finally to their work than the qualities for which they have been frequently taken to task: their dogmatic presentation of guesswork, their revealing disagreements with each other. But this assumption, implicit in their conjectures, became the avowed principle of their opposition. For there was, by the 1920s, a substantial reaction to the criticism of the previous century. E. R. Dodds says in his review of Homeric scholarship of 1954:[1] 'It is now more than thirty years since the old logical game of discovering inconsistencies in Homer was replaced in public esteem by the new and equally enjoyable aesthetic game of explaining them away.' The simple argument of the Unitarians, which had not replaced the old business of layer-hunting, but was much in the air when Parry was a student and was forming his own explanations, was this: The Homeric poems are works of art too great, their dramatic structure is too perfect, their characterization too consistent, to have been the more or less random conglomeration of a series of poets and editors. Moreover, those who attempt to assign different parts of them to different periods show their weakness by their inability to agree. Therefore each of the two poems is the unique and individual product of a great poetic mind. Such was the feeling of men of letters from Goethe onwards,

[1] See p. xvii, n. 5 above.

throughout the nineteenth century,[1] and such was the fundamental argument of those scholars who took up the unitarian cause in the years before Parry wrote.

Their work, of which J. A. Scott's *The Unity of Homer* (Berkeley 1921) was the most eloquent, if not the soundest, example, was more satisfying to our sense of poetry than any of the edifices of the analysts. But its superficiality was most apparent in the fact that it took largely the form of refuting individual analyst arguments. It provided no concept of epic poetry that could explain the difficulties which the analysts exploited. As Parry says succinctly: 'Yet those who have thus well refuted the theories which broke up the poems have themselves given no very good explanation of how they were made.' 'What reasons', he adds, 'have they had for passing over the fact pointed out by Wolf that a limited use of writing for literary purposes, which is the most that one can suppose for Homer's age, must have made for a poetry very unlike ours?'[2] Ignoring the problem of literacy, omitting any close study of Homer's language and diction, and unable to conceive clearly of the formation of the poems they prized, they wished to cancel the Homeric Question and return to the naïve view of antiquity, that Homer was a poet like Aeschylus (or Virgil or Dante), and that the *Iliad* and *Odyssey* were unique single creations of an original poetic mind. The essential insight, that Homer was a different kind of poet from the literary masters of a later age, an insight which had been offered the world by Robert Wood in 1767, was at least as absent from these men as it was from the analysts whose want of poetic and literary sensibility they justly deplored.[3]

But there was a third strain of Homeric criticism for Parry to draw on, one more technical and less prominent than the other two, but in the end perhaps more valuable. This strain consisted of close study of the language of the Homeric poems, and of its relation to the verse-form. Those who began this study, notably Ellendt and Düntzer,[4] were themselves analysts, at a time when hardly any serious Homeric scholar was anything else; but both men were able to forget their divisive study of the text long enough to establish what became for Parry the fundamental axiom of Homeric study: the dependence of the choice of words and word-forms on the shape of the hexameter line. Düntzer in particular not only pointed out that, out of a whole array of epithets, that particular

[1] e.g. Andrew Lang, who argued the point in three books. See M. Nilsson, op. cit. (p. 10, n. 2 above), 22–3.

[2] HS 75.

[3] A quite different, and not at all polemical, work of unitarian cast was C. M. Bowra's *Tradition and Design in the Iliad*, which appeared in 1930 (Oxford), too late to influence Parry's work, too early to have been influenced by it. Bowra more or less assumes a single author of the *Iliad*, but stresses, as most unitarians did not, that author's dependence on a long poetic tradition. Parry's work made it possible to give precision to Bowra's conception.

[4] See the references in TE 5 nn. 1–6.

one would be chosen which satisfied the metrical need of the moment, regardless of its particular meaning, but also noted the more striking phenomenon that, of a group of words and word-forms which in meaning could replace each other, there would exist only one for each metrical use. Thus of the epithets of wine, he remarks: 'All these forms are metrically distinct . . . and it is never the sense that determines the choice of one or another of them.'[1]

This observation of the economy of Homeric diction, elaborated and confirmed with a methodical rigour of which Düntzer never dreamed, was to become the core of Parry's explanation of Homeric poetry. But its relevance to the larger questions of Homeric criticism was missed by both Düntzer and his contemporaries. Nor did the slightly later scholars who examined the dialect-mixture of the poems perceive any such large relevance. A. Fick and his follower F. Bechtel,[2] observing correctly that the amalgam of early and late Aeolic and Ionic word-forms in the language of the Homeric poems precluded its ever having been spoken speech, tried to show that an original poem in Aeolic Greek had been translated into Ionic, only those Aeolic forms remaining in the final version which would have had to be replaced by forms metrically different. Metrical convenience thus made for conservatism, and conservatism made for the amalgam. But Fick and Bechtel, like Ellendt and Düntzer before them, were analysts, and they carried on their investigation in the service of analysis. They wanted to show that certain portions of the poems as we have them were composed at certain relative or absolute dates. Their work has been judged a failure, and Bechtel admitted this, because the dialect-mixture of Homeric poetry goes too deep: it is pervasive in the poems, and like Anaxagoras' elements, it seems to be found in the smallest units of them.[3] An attempt to find chronological layers in this way would lead to atomization. Yet these scholars were contributing to a body of knowledge about the language of Homer which would one day suggest a new insight. The failure of what they attempted showed the wrongness of assumptions they shared with other scholars of their time. What they themselves did not do, but helped others later to do, was to conceive of the kind of poetry which would use such a language as they described.

Meanwhile the effect of linguistic examination was the reverse of what had been intended by those who practised it: instead of discernible layers

[1] *Homerische Abhandlungen* (Leipzig 1872), 514: 'Alle diese Formen sind metrisch verschieden; dass bei der Wahl nie der Sinn den Ausschlag gab, lehrt genaue Betrachtung des betreffenden Gebrauches . . . &c.'

[2] See Nilsson, op. cit. (p. x, n. 2 above), 9 and n. 1; also HL 2–4.

[3] Cf. Nilsson 9; HL 40 ff., esp. 41, n. 1; now G. S. Kirk, *The Songs of Homer* (Cambridge 1962), 192–210, although Kirk does, at the end of this chapter, try to reintroduce a kind of linguistic criterion for 'post-Homeric' passages.

of language which would correspond to fixed stages of composition, they succeeded in demonstrating the homogeneity of the dialect-mixture. Thus K. Witte, who wrote the article on the language of Homer for the Pauly–Wissowa *Real-Enzyklopädie* (1913), thought that linguistic criteria would show 'early' and 'late' passages; but at the same time drew the famous conclusion that 'the language of the Homeric poems is a creation of epic verse'.[1] The two notions are not compatible. For if the tradition created an artificial language, that language, with its forms of diverse date and diverse place, could have been used at one time by one poet to create one work.[2]

In the early 1920s, when Parry wrote at the University of California in Berkeley the Master of Arts dissertation (reprinted in this volume) which contains in essence his new image of Homer, there was an established, yet monotonous and infertile, school of analyst critics; there was a growing unitarian reaction which shared with analysis the assumption that the stages of composition, whether one or many, represented the original wording of a fixed text; and there was a body of linguistic examination which had demonstrated the dependency of Homer's language on the verse-form in which he composed. No scholar had succeeded in imagining any better than Robert Wood in 1767, or even so well, the kind of poet who would sing the kind of song we have in the *Iliad* and *Odyssey*.

This was Parry's great accomplishment. It explains and justifies his present influence among scholars of Homeric poetry and of all poetry in the improvising style. He ignored the barren controversy between analyst and unitarian, and concerned himself instead with the implications of the linguists' work. He saw that it presupposed a different kind of poetry from all that we are familiar with. This was for him no vague intuition. To a romantic feeling for another kind of world and art he joined a strong and sober historical sense, and with this a strict method of procedure. Hence he was able to conceive with some precision what kind of poetic tradition made a Homer possible, and to give his conception considerable dramatic force.

[1] Pauly–Wissowa viii. 2214.

[2] The foregoing remarks are not intended to suggest that the attempt to investigate the formation of the language of Homer is a waste of time, or that relatively early and late forms and constructions cannot usefully be discerned in that language. Scholarship since Witte which has done exact and illuminating work of this kind includes J. Wackernagel, *Sprachliche Untersuchungen zu Homer*, Göttingen 1916; K. Meister, *Die homerische Kunstsprache*, Leipzig 1921; Pierre Chantraine, *La Formation des noms en grec ancien*, Paris 1933; id., *Grammaire homérique*, 2 vols., Paris 1948 and 1953; Manu Leumann, *Homerische Wörter*, Basel 1950; G. Shipp, *Studies in the Language of Homer*, Cambridge 1953; A. Hoekstra, *Homeric Modifications of Formulaic Prototypes*, Amsterdam 1965. But I believe that it is almost always the easier and more reasonable hypothesis (it is explicitly that of Hoekstra) to regard the inferred changes in Homeric language as having occurred before the composition of the Homeric poems. In holding this view, I very much agree with G. S. Kirk's comments on the studies of Shipp (*The Songs of Homer* [p. xx, n. 3 above], 202–3), but not with Kirk's own attempts (ibid. 204 f.) to discover 'post-Homeric phraseology'.

§ 3

It could fairly be said that each of the specific tenets which make up Parry's view of Homer had been held by some former scholar. Thus the dependence of the given word, especially of the ornamental adjective, on necessities of metre rather than considerations of meaning, had been observed by Heinrich Düntzer; Antoine Meillet had stated, though he had not set out to prove, that all Homeric poetry is made up of formulae; while the formulary structure of contemporary illiterate poetry had been stated by earlier researchers (e.g. A. van Gennep); so had the unfixed nature of illiterate poetry, its freedom from any true sense of verbatim repetition (M. Murko). Even the term 'oral' as applied to a kind of poetry, and a sharp differentiation of that kind of poetry from anything composed in writing, is to be found in Marcel Jousse.[1]

Parry's achievement was to see the connection between these disparate contentions and observations; to form from them a single consistent picture of what Homeric poetry was and of the conditions that allowed it to come into being; and to give substance to that act of imaginative understanding by demonstrating, with precision and the power of repeated proof, that it must be so. But this statement may give a misleading impression of the order of events in Parry's scholarly history. When we read his Master of Arts dissertation we discover that the initial impulse in his work was not the insights and suggestive theories of earlier scholars, but the text of Homer itself. There is no evidence that at the time he wrote that short thesis he had so much as heard of the scholars named above; yet it contains in essence his whole vision of Homeric poetry.

The historical positivism toward which Parry was himself inclined, and which would find the sources of intellectual creation in external environment, does little to explain the origin of the ideas in this remarkable essay. It sets forth with a clarity so quiet that apparently little notice of the work was taken at the time (and how can a Master of Arts thesis say anything important?) the view of Homer which, when developed in Parry's subsequently published works, was to render so much of earlier scholarship obsolete. The view itself was apparently arrived at by the reaction of an unusual mind to the text of Homer: nothing in Parry's background (middle-class, not particularly intellectual, Welsh Quaker origins), nor in the place where he was born and lived until he went to France in 1923 (Oakland and Berkeley, California, and the University of California in Berkeley) makes that reaction likely.[2] Parry's teachers in

[1] Düntzer, see above, pp. xix f.; Meillet, TE 8–9; van Gennep, Murko, and others, HL 6 f.; Jousse, see below, p. 23.

[2] Perhaps this is as good a place as any to correct a few errors in the perceptive and moving tribute to Parry, written shortly after his death, by his pupil Harry Levin, now Professor of Comparative Literature at Harvard University ('Portrait of a Homeric Scholar', *Classical*

Greek at the University of California included two of the finest Hellenists of their generation, George Calhoun (1886–1942) and Ivan Linforth (b. 1879). Both men knew Homer well and had a sensitive understanding of his poetry. But they were not the source of any of Parry's specific ideas. His work was as much a surprise to them as to the rest of the world. The mind that presented Homer to the world as the singer of traditional poetry was itself the product of no traditions.

The idea once conceived, Parry was quick to see how the work of earlier scholars related to it; and in this way he broadened and deepened his vision. His French *thèses* take full account of the work of strictly Homeric scholarship, and in particular, of the students of Homeric language whose work sometimes anticipated his own, sometimes provided an analogy to it: Düntzer, Ellendt, Fick, Witte, Meister. He had gone to Paris to study with Victor Bérard. Bérard's notions of Homer turned out to be far from Parry's own, and he did not wish to direct his work. The *thèses* were in fact written under the supervision of Aimé Puech, who was of great help to him in the composition of his work and who, after Parry's death, published a brief but affectionate testimonial to him.[1] He was supported and encouraged by M. Croiset (1846–1935), the author (with A. Croiset) of the famous *Histoire de la littérature grecque*. The professor at Paris whose ideas were most in harmony with Parry's own was Antoine Meillet (1866–1936), who was primarily a linguist, and as such more disposed to see the language of Homer as the product of a tradition than most straight Homerists. Meillet gave Parry confidence in following out his intuition that the structure of Homeric verse is altogether formulary; but he cannot be said to have vitally affected the direction of his thought. Nor did another scholar of note, who knew Parry in his Paris days and was one of the first to appreciate his work, Pierre Chantraine.[2]

Two other writers in French were of importance in Parry's thought at this time. The first was an anthropologist and student of psycholinguistics named Marcel Jousse, the influence of whose long essay 'Le Style oral rythmique et mnémotechnique chez les Verbo-moteurs',[3] marks the change of emphasis in Parry's thought from seeing Homer as a *traditional*

Journal 32, 1936–7, 259–66). Parry did not 'cross the bay' to go to the University of California, since he was born and brought up in Oakland, which is contiguous to Berkeley. Nor did he come to Berkeley to study chemistry. His first science course, in his second year there, was Zoology. His adolescence was no more burdened, or 'overburdened', than is that of most of us. And while he was much impressed by Harvard, he did not 'recoil . . . from the tawdriness of California'.

[1] *Revue des études grecques* 49, 1936, 87–8.

[2] Chantraine's review of TE and FM in *Revue de philologie* 3, 1929, contains an admirable summary of the arguments of these books, and shows him to have been the first scholar to acknowledge in print the value and importance of Parry's work. Parry's reference to the review in HS 74 makes it sound adversely critical of his own work; but that is far from the case.

[3] *Archives de philosophie* 2, 1924, cahier IV, 1–240.

poet to seeing him as above all an *oral* poet. A second decisive intellectual encounter was at the end of his stay in Paris when Meillet introduced him to Mathias Murko, a collector and student of Jugoslav poetry. It may have been Murko and his work that first suggested to Parry the possibility of finding in a living poetry an observable analogue to the poetry of Homer.[1]

These influences helped to show Parry the implications of his perception of the nature of Homeric verse, and may have suggested to him directions of further study. But the perception itself seems simply to have been Parry's direct reaction to the text of Homer, as it appears in his Master of Arts thesis, here published for the first time. The arguments of that document are too clear to need any summary; but a firm grasp of their central point is important, even essential, to an understanding of the whole range of Parry's work. It is from an aesthetic perception of the quality of Homeric verse that the whole thesis develops. What Parry later speaks of as the *historical method*, i.e. the attempt to explain the specific product of an age by the unique conditions of life in that age,[2] is necessary to the development. But the first thing is the reader's experience of the style of the poem.

Parry first describes this as the 'traditional, almost formulaic, quality of Homer' ('formulaic' here has not yet the technical meaning, which Parry was later to assign to it). He adds that only investigation, i.e. statistical investigation, shows how pervasive this quality is; and the M.A. thesis does provide a little of the careful statistical study which is set forth with such copious exactitude in TE. But the point is that the reader's experience precedes the counting, just as it precedes the historical explanation; and throughout Parry's work the appeal to the experience of the reader is over and again the strongest argument which he can adduce.[3]

In this, Parry's work differs from the most famous document of modern Homeric criticism, Wolf's *Prolegomena*, which applies arguments of a historical kind to the Homeric poems. Because such and such conditions, notably the absence of the art of writing, were true at the time of the composition of the Homeric poems, therefore the poems themselves must be of a certain nature. Parry's work moves from the tangible quality of the words of Homer to a whole vision of an art and even of a society.

The essentially aesthetic vision of Parry's work is more evident in the M.A. thesis than in most of his later pages. He here compares Homeric poetry to a kind of sculpture, and specifically to the Lemnian Athene of Phidias as he read of it in the appreciation of Furtwängler, where Furtwängler's own vision appears to derive from Winckelmann's *edle Einfalt*

[1] CH i–ii. [2] See TE 1, HM, and below, pp. xxx ff. [3] e.g. TE 126 f.

und stille Grösse.[1] The beauty of the poetry, like that of its statue, is simple, clear, calm, and traditional. It is almost impersonal in its freedom from striving after originality or individual expression. It is designed to realize what appears, in these early pages, as the concept of a whole people elevated to an almost Platonic Ideal. '[The repeated words and phrases] are like a rhythmic motif in the accompaniment of a musical composition, strong and lovely, regularly recurring, while the theme may change to a tone of passion or quiet, of discontent, of gladness or grandeur' (MA 427).

Parry nowhere else speaks in so extended and unguarded a fashion of the aesthetic basis for his judgement of Homer. But neither did he abandon the perception. In his latest printed work, the posthumously published article 'About Winged Words' (here WW), where he takes strong issue with his former teacher Calhoun on the meaning of the well-known recurrent line

τὸν (τὴν) δ' ἀπαμειβόμενος (-ένη) ἔπεα πτερόεντα προσηύδα,

he says that the principal issue is how we read Homer and criticizes (417) Calhoun's concept as 'too little Phidian'.

Parallel to the Platonic notion of an art which can, e.g., describe Athene not as she is 'on [a] particular occasion, but as she is immutably', (426) and to the romantic notion of an art which was 'the perfection . . . of the popular ideal' (425), is Parry's sense of the directness and swiftness of Homer. He refers to Matthew Arnold's judgement of Homer's 'rapidity of movement' (428), an idea which in TE (126 f.) he develops into a definition of the essential indifference of the audience to the single word, and in HS (306) to a definition of the traditional metaphor which 'found its place in the even level of this perfect narrative style, where no phrase, by its wording, stands out by itself to seize the attention of the hearers, and so stop the rapid movement of the thought . . .' In HG (241) he refers to 'the direct and substantial nature of Homeric thought'.

The experiential and aesthetic insight remains at the centre of Parry's thought, although it is expressed more briefly and guardedly in his later works. Corollary to that insight, at first sight at odds with it, and appearing already in MA (427 f.) is the practical and objective judgement of the utilitarian nature of Homeric style. Words and even phrases, he showed us (for to this aspect of his work he was able to give incontrovertible demonstration), are chosen for their metrical convenience, rather than for their appropriateness to the particular context in which they appear. This

[1] See now the most recent edition in English of Furtwängler's *Masterpieces of Greek Sculpture*, ed. A. N. Oikonomides, Chicago 1964. Parry is presumably referring to the first chapter on Pheidias, in the original English edition of 1895. Here Furtwängler gives an account of his 'discovery' of the statue, and a careful description of it. He stresses both the traditional (13 f.) and the original (26) quality of the statue. It was his remarks on the former that caught Parry's attention.

observation he could find in Düntzer (above, p. xx), although he does not seem to have derived it from him. In any case, nothing in Düntzer's rather chaotic essays suggests the extent of what Parry calls the 'schematization' (HS 314) of Homeric style. When our examination of Homeric style reaches the level of the individual word, Parry suggested (and demonstrated in the case of the epithet), convenience is the operative determinant in choice.

This, along with the emphasis on Homeric poetry as *oral*, is the best-known feature of Parry's work on Homer, and the one that has aroused most disagreement, even antagonism, for it has seemed to many to deny the poetry the possibility of artistic expression. Such is the thrust of the oft-repeated remark of Wade-Gery, that Parry, by removing the controlling hand of the individual artificer, became the 'Darwin of Homeric scholarship'.[1] To Parry himself, the opposition between art and convenience was unreal. Both the rapidity and the rituality of Homeric verse, the qualities he most loved, were, as he saw it, directly dependent on the utilitarian nature of the diction. From a negative point of view, it is only because the single word in Homer does not hold up the mind with an ingenious pregnancy of thought that 'the . . . heroic language . . . ever sweeps ahead with force and fineness . . . (and) also with an obviousness which . . . may deceive . . . the best of critics' (WW 418). But there is a positive point of view also: the inappropriateness, the ritually repetitive quality, of the single word or phrase, because it is not chosen for its context, instead illuminates the whole heroic world. The fixed metaphor is a part of the completely utilitarian nature of Homeric diction because (TM 373) 'a phrase which is used because it is helpful is not being used because of its meaning'. But this traditional diction as a whole is 'the work of a way of life which we may call the heroic', and so the fixed metaphor is 'an incantation of the heroic' and 'every word of it is holy and sweet and wondrous' (TM 374).

We can see here that the historical scholar is the child of his own age. In a sense Parry is one of the lovers of the exotic of our century, and his admiration for a language formed by the clear exigencies of singing and directly expressive of heroic ideals reminds us of Hemingway finding courage and beauty in the vision of the Spanish bullfighter, or of T. E. Lawrence (one of Parry's favourite authors) finding a more satisfactory theatre of self-realization in the austere simplicities of Arab life. But from a purely aesthetic point of view, if we remember that the tens of this century, when Parry was growing up, and the twenties when he formed his ideas and began to write, were the years in which in the visual arts the concept of the 'functional' as a positive value became established, we can better appreciate his assessment of Homeric language. His historical sense

[1] *The Poet of the Iliad*, Cambridge 1952, 38.

led him to distinguish sharply between Homeric poetic style and that of his own era; but what he found in Homer was not only the romantic possibility of a poetry expressive of a whole people, but also a quality of purposive directness which spoke strongly to the artistic sense of his own time.

Almost all of Parry's ideas on Homeric poetry can be found in the M.A. thesis, but his emphasis there is mainly aesthetic. The emphasis of the doctoral thesis is on demonstration. The imaginative grasp of Homeric style here recedes, though it does not disappear, to make way for a stringently scientific and objective examination of the use of the ornamental epithet in Homer. Of the scholarly level of the argument, one can do no better than cite the estimate of Denys Page:

> It is not easy at first to grasp the full significance of Milman Parry's discovery that the language of the Homeric poems is of a type unique in Greek literature —that it is to a very great extent a language of traditional formulas, created in the course of a long period of time by poets who composed in the mind without the aid of writing. . . . That the language of the Greek Epic is, in this sense, the creation of an oral poetry, is a fact capable of proof in detail; and the proofs offered by Milman Parry are of a quality not often to be found in literary studies.[1]

Not every point in the long *thèse* commands unquestioning assent, and some have argued that the total picture of Homeric poetry which it suggests is wrongly coloured; but the principal arguments themselves have never effectively been challenged. It is hard to imagine that they will ever be, since there are several of them, all crossing and reinforcing each other, each carefully worked out with accuracy and logic. The cumulative weight of all of them is overwhelming. They show that beyond a doubt the operative principle of Homeric style, at least in regard to the recurrent epithet, was a traditional pattern of metrical convenience rather than any sense of choosing the adjective appropriate to the immediate context. That this was so had been suggested earlier. Parry himself had argued it with some force in his M.A. dissertation. But the doctoral *thèse* demonstrated it beyond question and, what was more of a revelation, showed that there were whole systems of noun–epithet phrases fashioned with such *complexity* and with such *economy*[2] that it was all but inconceivable that the diction of the poems could be the creation of a single man, while the difference in this respect between Homeric style and that of literary epic, such as Apollonius and Virgil, was complete. The term 'traditional' had in the M.A. thesis represented an

[1] *History and the Homeric Iliad* (see above, p. xvii, n. 3), 222–3, where Page gives a concise summary of the nature of Parry's proof.

[2] See TE 7, 16, etc. Parry varies his terms. In HS 276, he speaks of *length* and *thrift* in the same sense.

intuitive and aesthetic perception. In the French *thèse*, it became an inescapable scientific inference. Only many singers, over at least several generations, could have produced the poetic language whose finely adjusted complexities these analyses revealed for the first time in an author whom men had known and read for two and a half millennia.

Those who discuss Parry's work, even those who have published comments on it, have rather rarely had a good knowledge of TE. This is partly because the work was written in French, while those who are naturally drawn to Parry's work are mostly in the English-speaking world; partly because it has long been out of print, and has been unavailable in many libraries; and partly because the thoroughness of the argumentation makes the work less attractive than many of the later articles,[1] and in particular the two long articles in *HPh* (HS and HL), which have been the source of Parry's thought for most scholars. Yet it remains Parry's basic work, and all the others are more or less specific applications of the conclusions which it works out.

A characteristic example of the subtlety of analysis which Parry in this work brought to bear on the problem of Homeric diction is the chapter on equivalent noun–epithet formulae. That in some cases there appear two or even three ways of expressing what Parry defines as an *essential idea* seems at first sight to show an incompleteness in the whole structure of formulary diction, and therefore might point to an area where individual style and particular choice operate. Parry shows that the contrary is true, since in most cases these apparent deviations from the economy of the system are themselves best explained by the sense of analogy which controls the system as a whole and indeed created it in the first place.[2]

The first work to apply the conclusions of TE was the supplementary French *thèse*, FM. Here, as in a number of later English articles, Parry took up an old Homeric problem and showed how the concept of the bard working entirely within a traditional poetic language set it in a new light, and for all practical purposes offered a solution. Departures from the standard metrical pattern of the hexameter in Homeric verse had previously been put down to the carelessness of early poetry or had been justified by the vague notion of poetic license. Since such metrical flaws appear most often at certain distinct places in the line, descriptive 'rules' had been set up, and were represented as the 'causes' of the metrical deviations. Parry first applies his vigorous sense of language to the modern term itself, showing that the so-called rules were merely an incomplete set of observations, and could not meaningfully be spoken of as 'causes'. He then shows how most of the metrical flaws in Homer can be explained as

[1] Chantraine says of TE in his review (p. xxiii, n. 2 above): 'On serait tenté de reprocher à son livre sa sobriété, si cette sobriété n'en faisait aussi la force.'

[2] See pp. 173ff. below.

uncommon juxtapositions of traditional formulae, or analogous formations where a change of grammatical form introduces a variation in metre, and shows that the flaws could only have been avoided if the poet had been willing to abandon his traditional diction. What had seemed inexplicable aberrations of style were revealed as phenomena natural to the living operation of a complex, but not infinitely adjustable, system.

When, in the spring of 1928, having completed his work for the doctorate, Parry made ready to return to America with his wife and daughter and son, he had no position and no notion of where he was going to go, until at the last minute, by the offices of George Calhoun, an offer of a job arrived from Drake University in Des Moines, Iowa, which Parry instantly accepted. One of his colleagues there, 35 years later (and 28 years after Parry's death), remembered him as the man who had built the Classics library into something respectable. But Herbert Weir Smyth of Harvard University, as Sather Professor at the University of California, had taught Parry when he was an undergraduate. On learning that he was once more in America, Smyth suggested that Parry read a paper at the American Philological Association meeting in New York at the end of 1928. At that meeting Parry was offered and accepted a position at Harvard, on whose faculty he remained until his death in December 1935.

The paper which Parry read at that meeting, and which was printed in the *TAPhA* of that year, was HG. It was Parry's first published article in English, and it sets the pattern for a number of articles to follow: DE, TM (of which HM appears to be an early summary), and TD. In all these articles, as in FM, Parry took up an old Homeric problem and looked at it in the light of his demonstration of the traditional character of Homeric diction. The method followed in HG is typical. Parry begins by making, between the terms *signification*, *meaning*, and *sense*, a distinction which is a good example of his lively, and twentieth-century, sense of what language is, and how the force of words is a function of their usage and context. He has an instinctive feeling for the operative definition. He then brings up the problem of the word of unknown definition in Homer, reduces it to its simplest terms, refers to the false philological method which had been used in an attempt to solve it, and then looks at the problem from the point of view of his own notion of two distinct kinds of poetry. The notion provides the solution to the problem: the gloss in Homer came into being because words were retained in formulae where the meaning of the entire formula was important for the narrative, but that of the single adjective in it was not. What the gloss possessed was not a relevant definition, but 'a special poetic quality': it added 'the quality of epic nobility' to the noun-epithet phrase. The conclusion of the article is characteristically aesthetic as well as scholarly: the decisive factor is the way the auditor reacts to the word as he hears it; his thought passes 'rapidly over the ornamental glosses, feeling in them only an element which ennobles the heroic style'. To ask the old question of the signification of these words, it is implied, is to ask the poet and audience alike to 'perform an etymological exercise of the mind' which is alien to the essential style of the poetry.

In TM and TD similarly, an old question is answered from a new point of view, so that the old formulation of the question is shown to be irrelevant. TD is the most purely linguistic piece Parry wrote, but here too the insight at the centre of the argument is the way in which 'the traditional formulaic diction must have trained the ears of the singers and their hearers . . .'; that is to say, the historical discussion is marshalled round an aesthetic perception of style. TM, with its brilliant comparison of Homeric style to that of English Augustan verse, is perhaps the single most elegant statement Parry made of the way words are used in Homer and the way in which they should properly be understood by us. At the conclusion of this article, Parry appeals, as he so often does elsewhere, to the value of the historical method of criticism, which he feels can give us a true picture of the art of the past, free from the kind of misunderstanding of forms of art different from their own which men have made, especially in the case of Homer, from Aristotle onwards. Our greater understanding of Homer is due to the growth of this historical spirit. But the historical spirit itself, he adds somewhat surprisingly, has accomplished so much in our own day 'through a study of the oral poetries peoples outside our own civilization'.

At the time he wrote these words, Parry's growing interest in oral poetry had caused him to modify his earlier concept of the historical method as a way of overcoming directly the barrier of time, as it is expressed in the quotation from Renan with which TE begins, and to conceive the possibility of returning to the world of Homer by studying at first hand the singing of living bards in another tradition. Of course the two ideas are not contradictory. Attainment of knowledge of the past by observation of living peoples who carry on a way of life which has disappeared elsewhere is a device exploited in one of the earliest applications of the historical method, the opening chapters of Thucydides' *History.*[1] For Parry it was a natural development, but a significant one. The emphasis on Homeric style as *traditional* shifts to the emphasis on Homer as an *oral* poet. The sense that by an imaginative perception of style and scholarly rigour of research one can free oneself from the presuppositions of the present and seize something of the different world of the past is modulated into the belief that there are two kinds of poetry, literary and

[1] Thucydides 1. 6. 2: *σημεῖον δ' ἐστὶ ταῦτα τῆς Ἑλλάδος ἔτι οὕτω νεμόμενα τῶν ποτὲ καὶ ἐς πάντας ὁμοίων διαιτημάτων.*

illiterate, corresponding to two kinds of civilization, and that one can still move from one of these to the other.

This change in emphasis is first clearly discernible in the two long articles which Parry wrote for *HPh.* They have been the most widely read of Parry's writings, and they are in an important way central in his work, because they look back to the detailed study of the formula in TE and FM, and at the same time point the way to the preoccupation with modern improvising poetry which marked Parry's last years. They also represent the most complete summary Parry gave of his work on Homer.

In the first, Parry answers some of the critics of TE.[1] Their objections help him to define his own position. They had argued that the fixity and traditional use of the noun–epithet formula was an exceptional feature in Homeric verse, so that the originality of Homer, lying in the remaining elements of style, was equal to, and essentially of the same kind with, that of later poets. Therefore Parry in this article widens the scope of his discussion. In a comparative section he shows that in later Greek poetry and in Elizabethan verse, there is nothing like the recurrent and functional element of the formula in Homeric verse. *Formula* here extends far beyond the most obvious example of it in the noun–epithet expression. In Homer, Parry demonstrates whole systems of, e.g., conjunction–verb phrases used over and again in the same way in the same part of the line to express a like idea, systems which in their length and in their thrift have no counterpart in any literary verse.

As Parry saw as early as the M.A. dissertation (426), no other system can reveal the traditionally elaborated pattern so well as that of noun–epithet formulae. The reasons for this are fairly obvious. No single element recurs in a heroic narrative with the same frequency as the names of the principal persons and of common objects. The proof of the traditional character of Homeric style depends on the length and thrift of the systems of formulae in it. But the length and thrift of a system depends on the poet's need for it. The need for systems of formulae capable of disposing frequently occurring proper names and common nouns in the line will be greater than for any other class of word, so that the systems involving these words will have greater length and thrift than those involving other words. At the same time, these names and nouns themselves occur more often, and so the evidence attesting the systems in which they occur is greater. Both factors made Parry's case more impregnable for the noun–epithet formula. Hence the arguments for the pervasiveness of the formula in general, which had been touched on in TE, but are given extended discussion only in HS and HL, are at once more telling in their implications and more open to criticism than the analyses of TE. Significantly, those who have tried to argue against the central thesis of

[1] See HS 266–7.

Parry's work (viz. that the style of Homer is so traditional throughout that originality of phrasing, as we understand the term, is a negligible factor (HS 137–8)) have been likely to concentrate their fire on HS.

The matter is clearly still open to debate, and a dogmatic pronouncement is futile here. It can be said, however, that at the date of writing of this introduction, the balance of scholarly and informed critical opinion finds Parry's central arguments convincing. This does not make them the last word on Homer: if we accept them, we have still agreed only that the poetry, in the narrowest sense of the way single words are put together within units of thought, is traditional and not the work of a single mind. Yet this is enough to determine our view of Homer in a radical way.

The wider scope with which Parry treats the formulary structure of Homeric verse in HS entails one other important factor: that of analogy.[1] This was a factor which had already been dealt with in TE, but again the discussion there is more confined to the noun–epithet formula than in HS. Analogy, the formation of new formulary expressions on the model of particular words and of the sound-pattern of old formulary expressions, is, Parry argued, the creative force in the formation of the epic style. Its importance in Parry's work has been much overlooked. Parry showed that the operation of analogy, while it exists in all poetries (HS 321), observably plays a vastly greater role in Homer. In later poetry, the poet either consciously borrows a phrase (HS 290), or attempts to create a style peculiar to himself and so to avoid the close modelling of phrase upon phrase which is the very life-force of the traditional language of the oral poet who, in order to attain fluency of improvisation, must yield himself entirely to this sort of play on word and sound. If we accept Parry's evidence on this point, we not only have a further dramatic manifestation of the traditionality of Homeric style; we have also significantly extended the concept of what a *formula* is. Parry's original and tight definition (TE 13, repeated in HS 272) had been 'a group of words which is regularly employed under the same metrical conditions to express a given essential idea'. The remarks on analogical formation in HS suggest that patterns of grammar, word-length, and pure sound are themselves 'formulaic', so that two examples of a given 'formulaic element' may, in the extreme case, have no words in common at all. Such a view of what is 'formulaic' goes far beyond the discussion of analogy in TE. It suggests a greater flexibility for the epic language, but a flexibility always controlled by the tradition. At the same time, the mobility of such a concept of the formula has displeased some, who insist that only phrases consisting of the same words can meaningfully be said to repeat each other and so to attain formulary status. Debate on the

[1] See HS. 323 and n. 1.

subject continues;[1] but possibly the most important aspect of the evidence of analogy in HS is not the minor problem which it raises of the definition of the formula, but the suggestion it makes of a poetry controlled by patterns of sound to a degree far beyond that with which we are familiar.[2]

The much more extended discussion of the effects of analogy in HS as compared with TE derives from Parry's increased awareness of the importance of sound in Homeric poetry, that the character of its style depended on its being a poetry of the spoken word. In HL he reviews the linguistic structure of Homer from this point of view. It was the linguists

[1] The broad view of the formula is now best represented by J. A. Russo: see especially 'A Closer Look at Homeric Formulas', *TAPhA* 94, 1963, 235–47; also 'The Structural Formula in Homeric Verse', *YClS* 20, 1966, 219–40. A narrower and more sceptical view is that of J. B. Hainsworth, 'Structure and Content in Epic Formulae: The Question of the Unique Expression', *CQ* (N.S.) 58, 1964, 155–64; see also A. Hoekstra, *Homeric Modifications of Formulaic Prototypes*, Amsterdam 1965, esp. chapter 1. Russo wants to regard structural patterns (or 'structural formulae'), such as τεῦχε κύνεσσιν and δῶκεν ἑταίρῳ (verb, – ∪, followed by noun, ∪ – ⏓, at the end of the line), the similarity of which was noted as significant by Parry himself, as formulary in much the same sense as the noun+ornamental epithet phrases analysed in TE. Hainsworth would restrict the word 'formula' to groups of words frequently repeated in like conditions. W. W. Minton, 'The Fallacy of the Structural Formula', *TAPhA* 96, 1965, 241–53, has challenged Russo's analyses directly on the grounds that the patterns Russo finds in Homer also occur in writers of literary hexameter verse, such as Callimachus. G. S. Kirk, 'Formular Language and Oral Quality', *YClS* 20, 1966, 155–74, has challenged J. A. Notopoulos' extension of the term 'formulaic' to the Homeric Hymns and the fragments of the Cyclic epics (see below, p. 83) on much the same grounds. Russo, in an as yet unpublished paper, answers Minton's objection by pointing out that Homeric poetry set the pattern for later Greek poetry in this metre.

One question here is the definition of the word 'formula' in Greek hexameter poetry. It is a question of nomenclature, and therefore of limited interest. Parry in HS was careful to speak of 'formulaic element' rather than 'formula', where actual repetition does not occur, and some such distinction is undoubtedly useful. Another, and more important, question is how far Parry's 'formulaic elements' and Russo's 'structural formulas' are uniquely characteristic of Homer, and so, presumably, of early Greek oral poetry. A still more important question is whether examination, such as Russo's, of structural and grammatical patterns within the framework of the hexameter line will shed light on the composition of Homeric verse. In being sceptical about the pervasiveness and regularity of such patterns, Hainsworth and Hoekstra seem to want to reserve some originality or spontaneity of style for the epic poet, although they do not make it clear how such originality might express itself. By stressing them, Russo wants to do the same thing, but in a different, and possibly more fruitful, way. Thus Russo, in his *TAPhA* paper, shows that the first two words of the *Iliad*, μῆνιν ἄειδε (noun, – ∪, verb ∪ – ⏓) belong to a pattern common at the end of the line, rare elsewhere. The third word, θεά, is also unusual from this point of view. He concludes (242): 'What we have, then, in μῆνιν ἄειδε θεά is a rather unusual expression . . . created . . . specifically and almost self-consciously to open this carefully wrought prologue.' In the unpublished paper referred to above, Russo gives other examples of departure, for special effect, from the normal patterning of the line.

[2] A number of the peculiarities of Homeric *language* (as opposed to *diction*) become more explicable if we conceive of the poetry as something existing as *sound*, not as writing. So, e.g., the derivation of ἀταλός from ἀταλάφρων, pointed out by Manu Leumann (*Homerische Wörter*, Basel 1950, 139 f.); or ὀκρυόεις from ἐπιδημιόο κρυόεντος (Boisacq, *Dictionnaire étymologique de la langue grecque*[4], Heidelberg 1950, s.v. ὀκρυόεις). Such processes of formation occur constantly in all languages, e.g. English *adder* from *a nadder*. Language in general even now consists fundamentally of *speech*. What is peculiar in the cases noted above and others like them is that the formation appears to have taken place within a body of poetry.

who had first established that the language, i.e. the dialect-mixture and the morphology of Homer, was the 'creation of the hexameter', an artificial poetic language which was created over the course of generations for heroic song. In TE Parry saw his work on diction, i.e. the combinations of words, as paralleling this earlier work of the linguists. Now, in HL, he explains the formation of the artificial language as the product of an oral technique of poetry, in this way synthesizing his own and earlier work on Homeric language. At the same time, even more than in HS, there is a strong emphasis on living oral poetry as an observable manifestation of the processes by which Homeric language and diction came into being. Here for the first time he quotes Murko and Dozon on Jugoslav poetry, Radloff on Kara-Kirghiz, and others on Berber, Finnish, Russian, and Afghan poetry (329 f.). The process of improvisation itself begins to dominate his mind. All this makes HL a somewhat curious article, since it mixes a new concern with what we might call Comparative Epic Poetry and a largely traditional and philological approach to the problems of Greek dialects in Homer.

Plato says of music (*Republic* 401d) that of all the arts it is 'the one which plunges furthest into the depths of the soul'. If we can extend the idea of music to include the art of the spoken (or sung) poetic word, we can say that a like conviction informs Parry's ideas on the character and value of oral poetry. Parry's work on the diction of Homer put the whole Homeric Problem in a new light and has significantly changed the way we read the lines of the *Iliad* and the *Odyssey*. But this is not the aspect of his work which has most caught the imagination. What has made him best known, and has most aroused interest in his writing, is his sense that all poetry is divided into two great and distinct realms, the literary and the oral, that each of these realms has its own laws of operation and its own values, so that each is almost a way of looking at the world; and finally that, of these two realms, the oral is in some way the more natural and the more satisfactory.

That the rhythms of oral poetry may be more natural in themselves because they correspond more closely to fundamental physiological rhythms of the human body Parry was willing to accept from Jousse (see HS 270); and the idea clearly matched his own inclinations. But what most interested him in oral poetry, and what he was able so well to describe, one might even say to dramatize, in his later work, is the close connection between the specific form of oral poetry and the way of life that surrounds it and allows it to exist. In the preface to CH he speaks of the possibility a careful study of Jugoslav song offered him of seeing 'how a whole oral poetry lives and dies'. And then: 'Style, as I understand the word and use it, is the form of thought: and thought is shaped by the life of men.' The same is presumably true of the style, or styles, of written poetry; but it is clear that Parry felt the relation between word and life to be more direct, and more observable, in the realm of oral song.

The best example of this belief is WF, which Parry wrote after his first summer in Jugoslavia. In this article he states simply and clearly that (377) 'the one part of literature is oral, the other written'. Homer belongs to the category of poetry which is, in a clearly defined way, *primitive*, *popular*, *natural*, and *heroic*. Parry defines these terms as they apply to oral poetry, and shows how they all, like the qualities of the *formulaic* and the *traditional*, depend on the oral nature of this kind of poetry. It follows that Homer could never be understood by those who looked at his poetry from a conventionally literary point of view. '[The] proper study [of the heroic element in early poetry] is . . . anthropological and historical, and what Doughty tells us about cattle-lifting among the Bedouins is more enlightening, if we are reading Nestor's tale of a cattle raid into Elis, than is the mere knowledge that the theme occurs elsewhere in ancient poetry' (377).

Having then, so to speak, taken Homer out of the conventional context of 'Greek Literature', and placed him in company with singers of other lands who tell of the heroic way of life, Parry turns to his own special interest, Jugoslav poetry. 'When one hears the Southern Slavs sing their tales he has the overwhelming sense that, in some way, he is hearing Homer.' Most of the rest of the article sets out to give specific illustration to those romantic words. Parry shows that large numbers of the most common whole-line formulae in Homer, those introducing speeches, marking the movements of the characters, or indicating the passage of time, have remarkably close parallels in Jugoslav verse. They are not only like in themselves: they also have a like function in the narrative. Then, at the end of the article, Parry tells from his travels in Jugoslavia an anecdote which is an epiphany of his own feeling for this kind of poetry. It is a simple story of an old Jugoslav singer who in telling the tale of his own life slips into the old formulae of his poetry (389–90). One senses in Parry's own careful words the excitement he felt at this example of a man who with a natural and unselfconscious pride saw his own life in terms of the traditional poetry which he sang. The slowness of change and the firm laws of the traditional formulary language, which could only exist in a culture of oral poetry, offered a closeness between life and art, and a satisfactoriness of self-expression, which struck Parry as a revelation.

Parry spent the summer of 1933 in Jugoslavia, and returned to that country in the early summer of 1934, to stay there until the end of the summer of the following year. During that time he travelled about the country, met singers and collected songs, some recorded on phonograph discs, some taken down by dictation. The article by his assistant, Albert Lord, who accompanied him on the second trip, originally published in the 1948 volume of *The American Journal of Archaeology* and included in this volume (HPH), tells much of his purposes in going and of his field methods there. That article also includes the first few pages, all that Parry was able to write, of a book which was to be entitled *The Singer of Tales*, and was to report on his work in Jugoslavia and to apply its results to the study of oral poetry generally.

Dubrovnik, where Parry took a house and where his family stayed while he and his assistants travelled into the more remote lands where singing still flourished, was then, as it is again now, a popular seaside resort. But the country itself was wild in comparison with most of America and Europe. The language was difficult and little known. Costumes and manners were strange. Roads were poor. Milk had to be boiled to be safe for drinking, a source of distress to Parry's children (aged 6 and 10 in 1934). There were no rules laid down for Parry's investigation. He had to learn the language, which meant getting to know a good deal of dialect; to choose his assistants; and to evolve the best methods of approaching singers and prevailing on them to sing. The recording equipment, involving aluminium discs, he had built by a firm in Waterbury, Conn., and for power he depended on the battery of his Ford V-8 (1934), which he brought over to Jugoslavia with him. Banditry was not uncommon in the inland valleys, and an air of risk and adventure always accompanied Parry's several trips into the interior.

Often Parry brought his assistants to the house in Dubrovnik to work with him there. His principal Jugoslav assistant, Nikola Vujnović, was a dashing and intelligent (though occasionally irresponsible) man whose abilities as an interpreter and interviewer of singers (he could himself sing somewhat) proved invaluable to Parry and, after his death, to Albert Lord, who returned several times to the country to continue Parry's work. Nikola became a familiar figure in the household and a great favourite with Parry's children. Other helpers were more awesome to them. Once Parry announced that one of them, a Turk, would come for dinner that night. In response to his children's eager questions, Parry said that the Turk was 'a real hero', a man of immense strength and ferocity, whose hands were 'as large as dinner plates'. 'Did he ever kill a man?' Parry's daughter asked. Yes, many times he had killed men. The Turk was anticipated with fearful excitement, and actually turned out to be tall, but stoop-shouldered and exceedingly gentle, with a scraggly black moustache.

From his children's point of view, the sojourn in Jugoslavia (even if the milk did have to be boiled in a great blue pot, and thus rendered unpalatable, and ginger ale was hard to come by) was a great adventure. This picture was not wholly due to childish imagination. Parry himself loved to dramatize what he was doing. The photograph of him in native dress costume (which he may have worn only on the occasion when the picture was taken) reveals a romantic and even histrionic side of himself which reminds one of T. E. Lawrence. Part of this was pure game; but part also derived from his convictions about poetry. Poetry, at least this kind of poetry, was valuable because it embodied life. To know it, to apply the true historical method in this modern but exotic setting, meant the ability to enter into the life of which the Jugoslav song was the expression. Parry was in a way romantic, but in another way, logical. If he had not been able to learn the language as well as he did, and to drink with the singers and their audiences in coffee-house and tavern, if he had not been able to take part in this society and win the respect of its members, he could not have carried on the work itself.[1]

Parry used to improvise stories to his children, and did it rather well.[2] In CH (448), he uses his own experience as a story-teller in this way as an analogy to the use of recurrent themes by the narrative poet. Can one say he was mistaken in seeing this kind of parallel? He sought and attained, in his own life, something of the connection between art and living which made heroic song itself so valuable to him.

What his family were in no position to observe, and what is made so clear by the descriptions of his methods in HPH and CH, is the care and the scholarly control which Parry exerted over his interviews[3] and his field-work generally; and the discrimination, as we see it in CH, with which he drew from his knowledge of Jugoslav singers and singing conclusions applicable to Homer. The desire in some manner to relive the world of Homer did not detract from the sobriety of his scholarly judgement.

The concrete result of Parry's study in Jugoslavia was the collection now named after him, which has been of uncommon interest to students

[1] Harry Levin (see p. xxii, n. 2 above) says well: 'He loved to meet the contingencies of travel, to tinker with his recording machine, to visit the local pashas and exchange amenities, to ply his *gouslars* with wine and listen to their lies. He attained a native shrewdness in apportioning their pay to the jealous canons of village renown and in detecting stale or contaminated material when it was foisted on him. He not only spoke the language, he produced the appropriate gestures and inflections. He respected the hierarchical nicety with which his hosts handed out the different cuts of meat. Their outlook seemed invested with an order that he had not encountered among the schools and movements of the civilization that had formed his own.'

[2] I recall one episode in a favourite series in which the setting was Paris, especially the sewers of Paris, and Mickey Mouse was always the hero and Winnie the Pooh the villain. Two of Winnie the Pooh's henchmen had been captured by Mickey Mouse, who told them that he would count to ten, and then, if they had not revealed some vital bit of information, he would shoot them. 'One of Winnie's men smiled to the other. *They knew Mickey was only kidding.*' Mickey then counted to ten, and shot one of them through the heart. The other straightway 'talked', enabling Mickey once more to vanquish the Pooh.

[3] In *Serbocroatian Heroic Songs* (see above p. x, n. 1), A. B. Lord records from the Parry Collection a number of interviews between Nikola Vujnović and various singers. The kind of questions Parry instructed Nikola to ask reveals something of the skill of his field methods.

of music, folklore,[1] and Comparative Literature as well as of Homer. It consisted of nearly 13,000 Serbocroatian texts, including those on more than 3,500 phonograph discs.[2] It has since been augmented by the assiduous work of A. B. Lord in the field. None of these texts were available to the public until 1953, when the songs from Novi Pazar were published by Lord.

What Parry himself regarded as the prize of the collection, the *Wedding Song of Smailagić Meho* by Avdo Međedović, has not yet been published. The importance of this song (taken down by dictation) lies partly in its quality, for Međedović was in many ways a superior singer, but mostly in its length: it is a single song telling a single story and has over 12,000 lines. Another song by Avdo, *Osmanbey Delibegović and Pavičević Luka*, was recorded on discs and comes to 13,331 lines.[3] The length of these songs (even if we make allowance for the shorter Serbocroatian line), sung in a series of creative performances in the traditional formulary style by an unlettered singer, seemed to Parry to offer the most striking proof he had yet found that the *Iliad* and *Odyssey*, poems of not much greater magnitude, could be the products of similar oral tradition in Greece in the eighth century B.C. He had of course earlier argued from their style that they must be the products of such a tradition.

Judgement on the quality and coherence of these songs will have to await their publication. Such a judgement will be important, because it will affect the now debated question of the validity of the analogy between Jugoslav and Homeric poetry.[4] To Lord, possibly even more than to Parry, the analogy is clear and certain, although Lord admits freely the superiority of the Homeric poems.[5] To others, for example G. S. Kirk and A. Parry,[6] the analogy is far less sure. In the case of the long works of Avdo, Kirk points out that they were very much *tours de force*, being 'elicited by Parry's *specific and well-paid request* for the longest possible song' (Kirk's italics).[7] The real question may not be so much the occasion of the

[1] See, e.g., *Serbocroatian Folk Songs* by Béla Bartók and A. B. Lord, New York 1951.

[2] See *Serbocroatian Heroic Songs*, I, xiii.

[3] Lord, *Singer of Tales* (see below, p. xxxix), 288. In *TAPhA* 67, 1936 (see below, p. xxxix, n. 1), Lord says (107): 'But one singer at Biyelo Polye in the Sanjak, Avdo Medjedovitch, though only a peasant farmer, is a veritable Homer; and he gave us songs of twelve and even fifteen or sixteen thousand lines.' Presumably Lord had not yet made a careful count.

[4] Cf. A. Lesky, *Geschichte der griechischen Literatur*[2] (above, p. x, n. 2), 34: '. . . wie stehen die homerischen Epen selbst zu dieser Welt von *oral composition*? Damit ist die homerische Frage unserer Zeit Formuliert . . .'

[5] He believes the finer songs in the Parry Collection to be comparable in quality to the *Chanson de Roland*.

[6] G. S. Kirk, *The Songs of Homer*, Cambridge 1962, esp. 83 f.; A. Parry, 'Have We Homer's *Iliad*?', *YClS* 20, 1966, 177–216, esp. 212 f.

[7] Op. cit. 274. Cf. p. 329, 'One can see a limited degree of novelty even in the expansions of an Avdo Međedović, although the chief basis of these is the extreme and in my view often tiresome elaboration of detail.'

songs (for who can know the occasion of the composition of the *Iliad* and *Odyssey*?) as their coherence and unity, which is certainly less than that of the Homeric poems, though how much less, and how significantly less, remains to be seen. Meanwhile, one can learn much of these and other songs and of the epic traditions of Jugoslavia in general from A. B. Lord's detailed and informative book *The Singer of Tales* (Cambridge, Mass. 1960). The title of that book is that of Parry's unfinished work.

The theoretic results of Parry's Jugoslav study exist only in the notes which he made on his researches in the winter of 1934 and 1935 and which he organized into a kind of unity and entitled *Ćor Huso* (here CH). Considerations of space have made it impossible to reprint these in their entirety, and so they are represented here by extracts. Being notes only, they have not the refinement of thought we find everywhere in Parry's published work; and as a record of his investigations in the field, they certainly contain much that he would later have modified: the more interesting singers, for example, such as Avdo Međedović, Parry only came to know after the date of writing of the last of these notes.

In CH, Parry tells us much of how he came to know various singers, what they were like as persons, and how they sang. He discusses in detail different versions of the same song, both from different singers and from the same singer. Throughout this chronicle and this minute examination of texts we see always the generalizing power of his mind. He constantly searches in the Jugoslav data for material which will illuminate the nature of Homeric, and of all oral, poetry. He touches on many topics of the broadest interest within the study of this poetry: the relation between poetry and social conditions; the effect of the encroachment of literate civilization upon a society in which oral song has flourished; how songs, and themes within songs, change as one singer learns a song from another, or as one singer sings the same song on different occasions, and in different circumstances.

He sees some aspects of Jugoslav poetry as directly applicable to Homer. Thus from the point of view of what he observes in Jugoslavia, he argues forcefully against the notion that the 'books' into which the *Iliad* and *Odyssey* are now divided, or any other divisions which one might make, represent any intended divisions in the composition of the poems.[1] But again, his observations at many points make him aware of the distinctions to be made between the Homeric and the Jugoslav traditions:

[1] 6. 75 f. These arguments were to be the basis of the article of which the title and the summary, reprinted here, appear in *TAPhA* 66: HH. After Parry's death, Lord put forward some of these ideas in an article of the same title in *TAPhA* 67, 1936, 106–13. Some of the arguments are repeated, with illustrations from Cretan heroic poetry, in James A. Notopoulos, 'Continuity and Interconnexion in Homeric Oral Composition', *TAPhA* 82, 1951, 81–101.

he finds he must posit a far greater degree of professionalism in Greece of the Homeric era in order to account for the unity of style and for the transmission of the Homeric poems (especially 444 f.). He also remarks on the differences in the verse itself. The hexameter, he argues, was a far more rigorous prosodic form than the Serbocroatian decasyllable.[1] And the far greater use of enjambement in the former makes for a different kind of poetry, as Parry shows in a postscript on this subject.[2]

In reading the pages of CH one can share Parry's intellectual excitement as the idea becomes vivid to him that much of Homer which formerly could only be the subject of scholarly conjecture can now be understood by direct observation. What he actually says on many topics is often inconclusive. He clearly was waiting for more evidence and more time to work out its application to Homer. In what we have, we can appreciate the range of Parry's mind and the flexibility with which he regarded each question, a flexibility which contrasts somewhat with the almost rigid certainty of conviction of much of his published work. Any one of a dozen subjects adumbrated in the midst of his observations in these notes could have been the theme of an extended study which might have brought it to the level of cogent conclusion.

To speak of one such example, Parry deals in CH, as he had not since MA, with some of the aesthetic criteria of oral poetry. He talks (e.g. 453) of the 'fullness' of detail which is so characteristic of Homer, but distinguishes (446) 'real fullness' from 'empty fullness', a distinction one wishes he had developed and illustrated. Detail, he argues elsewhere (454), is never included in oral poetry for its own interest. He speaks on the same page of the first four books of the *Odyssey* as an extended theme which has, however, no independence, but is entirely subordinate to the single plot of the poem. And he speaks generally (450) of *concision* and *diluteness* as aesthetic criteria, and wonders (461) about the social conditions which make for 'a more or less noble tradition'.

Many of his incidental remarks represent the distillation of his best thought; and some have a general critical authority: 'A popular poetry rises to greatness only in the measure that it shows a full understanding of the life which is portrayed or symbolized in its verses (and then, of course, only as that life itself is admirable), and it is the natural ability of oral poetry to show such an understanding that explains the high quality of

[1] 445 f. On this point, Parry seems to agree with the impressions of Sir Maurice Bowra, 'The Comparative Study of Homer', *AJA* 54, 1950, 184–92, esp. 187, and G. S. Kirk, *The Songs of Homer*, 89 ff., as against those of A. B. Lord, review of Kirk, *Songs*, *AJPh* 85, 1964, 81–5, esp. 84. The trouble here is that those who have uttered opinions on the subject have so far failed to define what they mean by expressions such as 'the far greater rigour of the hexameter as a verse form' (Parry, CH 445), 'the formal looseness of the South Slavic decasyllable' (Kirk, *Songs*, 90).

[2] These observations too were published by Lord, in one of his better articles, 'Homer and Huso III: Enjambement in Greek and Southslavic Heroic Song', *TAPhA* 79, 1948, 113–24.

so much of it' (441). Or: 'the mind, since it cannot think in a vacuum, must necessarily carry over to its comprehension of the past the notions of the present, unless a man has actually been able to build up from the very details of the past a notion which must necessarily exclude the application of his habitual notions' (454. 5).

The very fact that one can disagree with many of his unsupported and unqualified statements in these notes, such as that 'no parts of the *Iliad* and *Odyssey* have any unity in themselves' (461), shows how fully Parry let his mind range in these notes. They give us a tantalizing sense of the value which full development of the ideas touched on here would have had, if he had lived to provide it.

§ 4

It is impossible to know for sure exactly what direction Parry's work would have taken, if he had not been killed instantly, in Los Angeles, California, by an accidental gun-shot only a few months after his return from Jugoslavia in 1935. His close friend, Professor John H. Finley, Jr. of Harvard University, states in the introduction to Lord's *Serbocroatian Heroic Songs I* (p. x, n. 1 above) that Parry would never have done such detailed editing as *Serbocroatian Heroic Songs* represents, since 'he had said that he gathered the material "least of all for the material itself" '. Had he lived, Finley thinks, he would have gone on to 'the wider comparative studies that he planned'. On the whole, this seems right: the evidence is not only the generality of interest that we find in CH, but also the title and the opening pages of the unfinished *Singer of Tales*, quoted in full in HPH in this volume. On the other hand, his interest, despite his reported disclaimer, in the Jugoslav poetry itself is great, as again CH amply attests. We must remember that the finer singers, especially Međedović, and the longer songs were unknown to Parry when he wrote CH. His concern with Jugoslavia and its oral poetry would hardly have diminished.

The principal theoretic change in Parry's work, to judge from CH, in the last year of his life is the emphasis on the *theme* in oral poetry at the expense of the *formula*. The *theme* is a sort of basic unit of narration in an oral poem. It may be a unit of action: a single combat, the calling of an assembly, the arrival at a palace; or it may be a description, of arms, or a chariot, or a feast. It is clear that such themes recur often in the *Iliad* and *Odyssey*, indeed that the poems are to some extent made up of them. Parry, as we can see clearly in his review of Walter Arend in this volume (WA), and others after him, saw this as a distinguishing characteristic of oral poetry. Lord later took up the subject in an article, defining the theme as 'a recurrent element of narration or description in traditional oral poetry',[1] and his *Singer of Tales* devotes a chapter to the subject.

Parry had apparently worked out a kind of morphology of themes, for in CH (CF. p. 446 below), he refers to *major* themes, *minor* themes, *simple* themes, *essential* themes, and *decorative* themes. These categories were clearly not mutually exclusive, and we can get some idea of their relation to each other: thus the *essential* and *decorative* themes were different kinds of *simple* theme. But unfortunately, Parry nowhere gives us a real definition of these terms.[2] None the less, concern with the idea of *themes* pervades CH. On p. 445, he speaks of 'the problem of the technique of the themes, of which much must be said later' as 'a . . . way of getting at the problem of the authorship of the Homeric poems through the Southslavic epos'. On p. 446, he suggests a kind of equivalence of *theme* and *formula*. There can be little doubt that, as Lord has indicated in conversation with me, this subject would have absorbed some of Parry's scholarly energies.

The reasons for his concern with *themes* and relative lack of concern with *formulae* in CH lie somewhat in the material itself. The study of a living tradition of oral poetry offered virtually an infinite number of songs. Therefore the amount of repetition of theme that could be observed was vastly greater than what can be found in the limits of the *Iliad* and *Odyssey*. On the other hand, one of the striking facts which emerge from the study of Jugoslav poetry is the variation in phrasing of simple expressions. Even within the songs of one singer there does not appear to exist the same close economy of formula which Parry was able to demonstrate for Homer. And from singer to singer, and region to region, the

[1] 'Composition by Theme in Homer and Southslavic Epos' in *TAPhA* 82, 1951, 71–80. It is uncertain how far the *theme*, as Parry and Lord use the term, can be said to be unique to oral poetry. It would not be difficult to illustrate 'composition by theme' in the 19th-century English novel; or still more in the modern detective story. Anyone who has read more than two or three of the works of Rex Stout or Ross Macdonald will recognize that these writers compose more completely in standard scene types, most of them fairly traditional at that, than either the *Iliad* or *Odyssey*. Of course this observation does not invalidate what Parry says in WA of the reasons for the dominance of typical themes in poetry from an improvising tradition.

In analysing thematic patterns, however, one must be careful not to overlook the individual qualities of the single scene. Lord, in the article cited, lists the appearance thrice of the theme of feasting in the *Odyssey*, implying that we have three appearances of the same thing, although the wording varies. Actually the three passages (1. 146–51, 3. 338–42, 21. 270–3) differ in content: only the first describes a feast, the other two describe drinking only; and the additional line which distinguishes the second from the third is an addition of content, occasioned by the unique situation of Book Three, where it occurs. The analyses in chapters seven and eight of *The Singer of Tales* are still more impaired by a tendency to blur differences. E.g. 195: 'In fact, Patroclus' mission to spy out the situation for Achilles is strangely like the mission of Diomedes and Odysseus in the Doloneia.'

[2] Lord refers to them in 'Homer and Huso II: Narrative Inconsistencies in Homer and Oral Poetry', *TAPhA* 69, 439–45, esp. 440, but postpones their definition. In *TAPhA* 82 (n. 1 above), he has reduced the system to *essential* and *ornamental* themes, which he tries to distinguish and illustrate.

variation is far greater. It was partly his perception of this that led him (especially in the digression beginning p. 451) to pose somewhat different conditions for the composition and transmission of the *Iliad* and *Odyssey* from anything in Jugoslavia, and to reflect on the differences, in the two traditions, of metrical structure and poetic form.[1] Possibly the whole problem of the formula in a tradition like the Jugoslav is one with which Parry would have dealt separately at a later point.

§ 5

Parry's reputation has risen steadily since his death. Even those who at the time of his death knew him best and admired his work most could hardly have augured the high repute in which he stands today. There has even been a temptation to regard him as a misunderstood genius, a prophet not without honour save in his own time. This is really not true. Parry's ideas and the force and clarity with which he set them forth won him considerable recognition in the 1930s, both before and after his death. The Second World War was a natural distraction from the problems of Homeric scholarship, but from the late 1940s onwards there is a continual increase of interest in Parry's published writings and their implications.[2]

But Parry's true reputation rests on his influence among scholars and readers of Homer, and of other heroic poetries. Much of the most valuable work on such poetry since Parry's death and even before has been influenced by his theories, its direction even determined by them. They appeared at a time when the old Homeric Question, deriving from the doctrine of Wolf, had worn itself out and become a repetitive and futile debate. Parry's work gave the whole study of Homer a new life. Its fertility was bound to become more and more evident as more and more of the dialogue concerning Homer was involved with his name and his published arguments. The position which his theories and the whole

[1] The degree of formulary thrift in Jugoslav poetry is itself a matter for further study. Lord in the third chapter of *Singer of Tales* argues that it is very great and that apparent departures from it, in the case of a single singer, can be explained by considerations of rhythm and syntax. But even if one accepts the whole of Lord's explanations, we are still left with a freedom of word-order within the formulary expression which far exceeds the usage of Homer.

[2] Today, his name has almost won popularity, since Marshall McLuhan, on the first page of the Prologue to his *Gutenberg Galaxy* (Toronto 1962), has hailed him as one of the first to explore the different states of the human mind entailed by the use of different media of communication. McLuhan seems to know Parry's work from the references in Lord's *Singer of Tales*, and there is no evidence that he has actually read Parry. Cf. also Walter J. Ong, S.J., 'Synchronic Present: The Academic Future of Modern Literature in America', *American Quarterly* 14, 1962, 239–59, esp. 247–8, who joins the names of Parry, Lord, and H. Levin (who wrote the preface to Lord's *Singer of Tales*) to that of McLuhan, and argues, not very convincingly, that 'Parry's special type of interest in Homer was made possible by the fact that he lived when the typographical era was breaking up'.

problem of oral poetry occupy in the Homeric chapters of the latest edition of Lesky's *Geschichte der griechischen Literatur*, and in his new Pauly–Wissowa article,[1] is as good an index as any of his now established importance.

The influence of Parry's work has taken roughly five different lines of development. The first, in point of date, is the historical. Apart from the reviews of TE and FM by Shorey, Bassett, and Chantraine (HS 266–7), the first published notice of the significance of Parry's work by a scholar of international reputation was that by Martin Nilsson, whose astute judgement recognized its value in his *Homer and Mycenae* (London 1933), when Parry was virtually unknown outside Harvard and the University of California. When he wrote his book, Nilsson had been able to read TE, FM, and HG. He speaks (179) of Parry's 'able and sagacious work' and finds in it 'the final refutation of the view that the poets composed their epics with the pen in the hand'. But Nilsson's special interest in Parry's arguments lies in the evidence they provided of the antiquity of the epic language. Parry had argued that Homer (or the Homeric poet) was entirely dependent on the tradition and that he added little or nothing of his own to the stock of epic formulae. Parry was not concerned with the dating of the tradition, but merely with the mode of its formation; but it followed from his arguments that that formation was exceedingly slow, so that much of the language itself of the poems must go back to an extremely early date. On the other hand, the preservation of ancient formulae immediately appeared as the best explanation of the bard's memory of artefacts, of political conditions, possibly even of religious and mythological beliefs, which had ceased to exist long before his own birth. The memory of these things was embedded in formulary expressions which the bards retained from generation to generation because such expressions possessed, as Parry explained it, both nobility and convenience in versification. There is a danger that this sort of argument may be unjustifiably generalized: the hypothesis of the antiquity of formulae offers an explanation of cases where Homer's memory of things before his own time is guaranteed by external evidence. Because this is possible, the presumed antiquity of the formulae is itself used as evidence of the historicity of certain phenomena mentioned in Homer where no undisputed external evidence is available.

Nilsson cited Parry's work as one support among many for his theory of the possibility of extracting genuine knowledge of the Mycenaean world from the text of Homer. Denys Page, in his *History and the Homeric Iliad* (Berkeley 1963) takes the argument for the historicity of the Homeric epics as far as it can reasonably go. Some of his conclusions concerning historical material preserved in ancient formulae derive from the precise

[1] See p. x, n. 2 above.

studies of Miss Dorothea Gray.[1] The case for the documentary value of Homeric expressions is perhaps strongest when it is applied to artefacts. When it is applied to the Catalogue of Ships, which Page wants to be a 'Mycenaean battle order', it is weaker. Parry's arguments lay the foundation for the historical case, since they stress the antiquity and stability of the formulary expression. But the conclusions of Page must ignore Parry's many arguments for the generality and interchangeability of the Homeric epithet. It is unlikely, that is to say, that Parry would have been sympathetic to the view that such adjectives in the Catalogue as 'steep' or 'stony' or 'many-doved' actually described any specific place at all.[2]

Other arguments of interest deriving from formulary analysis for the possibility of gleaning historical information from Homer's language can be found in T. B. L. Webster, *From Mycenae to Homer* (London 1958), especially 183, 287. We must remember that Parry himself was quite unconcerned with the question of the historicity of information in the *Iliad* and *Odyssey*. Or rather, it was another kind of historicity which held his imagination: the way of life of the poet and his audience as it was reflected in the content and even more, in the style, of the poetry. What existed before Homer was of interest to him only in so far as it had become part of the living tradition which was a thing of Homer's own time. While there is no reason to think that Parry would have denied that fragments of information pertinent to the ages before Homer could be found in our texts, he clearly felt that the world depicted in these texts was, almost by the definition of poetry, that of Homer and his contemporaries. The implications of his view would run counter, for example, to the hypothesis of M. I. Finley, *The World of Odysseus* (London 1954, revised 1965) (which discusses Parry's work in its second chapter), that the *Odyssey* depicts a society somewhere between the Mycenaean and Homer's own.[3]

These historical arguments have been, implicitly or directly, criticized from a number of points of view. C. M. Bowra, in 'The Comparative Study of Homer' (see p. xi, n. 1 above), and at greater length in *Heroic Poetry* (London 1952), especially chapter 14, exploits his impressive knowledge of other heroic and oral poetries to show just how small the degree of historical accuracy to be expected from such poetry is. (That these other poetries—the *Chanson de Roland*, the *Edda*, Achin poetry, etc.—can be seen in Bowra's book so clearly as belonging to a like genre with the *Iliad* and *Odyssey* is itself due in no small measure to Parry's work.)

1 See D. Page, *History and the Homeric Iliad*, ch. 6 and notes.

2 See especially TE 126 ff., 191 ff.; and cf. A. Parry and A. Samuel, review of D. Page, *History and the Homeric Iliad*, *Classical Journal*, December 1960, 84–8.

3 Parry says in his lecture notes: 'It is not possible that the [poetic] tradition should have kept the details of the social existence of man at another epoch.'

The scholarly validity of historical argument from Homeric language was subjected to a characteristically strict and sober review by G. S. Kirk in 'Objective Dating Criteria in Homer'.[1] A more recent criticism which is especially germane to Parry's own arguments is A. Hoekstra's *Homeric Modifications of Formulaic Prototypes*, Amsterdam 1965, especially the first chapter, in which it is forcefully argued that the linguistic structure of the poetic tradition changed more rapidly, and achieved the form in which we have it at a time much closer to Homer, than Parry wished to allow.

In the category of historical applications of Parry's work fall also the books of R. Carpenter and E. A. Havelock. Carpenter was one of the earliest scholars outside the Harvard circle to see the importance of what Parry had done, and he pays him a handsome tribute in the opening chapter of his *Folk Tale, Fiction and Saga in the Homeric Epics* (Berkeley 1946). Carpenter applies the historical argument of the long 'memory' of Homeric language to his attempt to find in Homer not only hitherto unseen archaeological information, but also patterns of European folklore underlying the *Odyssey*. If his book is, as E. R. Dodds in *Fifty Years of Classical Scholarship*[2] has said of it, 'a work which suffers from an excessive preoccupation with bears', it is also one of the most lively and entertaining books of our time on a Homeric subject.

E. A. Havelock's *Preface to Plato* (Cambridge, Mass. 1963) is the work of a philosopher as well as an historian, and belongs properly in the domain of intellectual history. Starting from Parry's concept of a specific way of life which corresponds to the peculiar form of oral poetry, Havelock develops with great insight and much illustration the idea of what he calls the 'Homeric state of mind'. He sets out to analyze the implications, psychological as well as social, of oral poetry as the central vehicle of communication in early Greek culture. His boldest stroke is then to go on to suggest that even after the waning of the epic tradition and the rise of specifically literary forms of poetry, this 'oral culture' substantially prevailed in Greece until the time of Plato, whose 'war against the poets' in the *Republic* and elsewhere is to be explained as an attack on the bases of this older civilization of the spoken word by the greatest representative of the new age of prose, science, abstract thought, and writing. Havelock's book has been much attacked, but many of the criticisms made of it seem trivial in comparison with the energy and scope of the work itself. It is a work which could hardly have existed without Parry,[3] although its conclusions certainly go beyond any held by Parry himself, who would hardly have admitted that an 'oral culture' could exist without the living tradition of oral poetry which determined its character. Havelock is aware of this difference and ably disputes this and other points in Parry's theory.

[1] *Museum Helveticum* 17, 4, 1960, 189–205, see also his *Songs of Homer*, especially 179 f.
[2] See p. xvii, n. 5 above.
[3] Op. cit., x.

Another line of development from Parry's work is the *comparative*. Of course the studies of Parry himself and later of Lord concerning Serbocroatian oral poetry and its relation to Homer are the origin of all such comparison. But it has been extended, in a less thorough and more hypothetical way, to include other bodies of poetry too numerous to mention. Bowra's *Heroic Poetry* remains the best general study of this field. Lord has always been a student of Comparative Literature, and he includes useful comments on several kinds of medieval epic poetry from the viewpoint of formulary analysis in his *Singer of Tales*. J. A. Notopoulos has sought to do for modern Greek oral poetry, both by research in the field and by scholarly study, what Parry and Lord did for Serbocroatian.[1] He has at the same time tried to extend the purview of oral poetry within ancient Greece to include Hesiod, the *Homeric Hymns*, the Epic Cycle, and other poetry.[2]

§ 6

The remaining lines of development from Parry's work comprise studies which deal more or less directly with the problems which concerned Parry himself, and in particular with the criticism of Homer. It can itself be divided into three parts. First there are Parry's disciples, those who have bent their scholarly efforts to defending, expanding, and publicizing his theories. They are A. B. Lord and J. A. Notopoulos. The mantle of Parry has especially fallen on Lord, who was his assistant in Jugoslavia, and who since his death has worked with the material collected by him, material which has been kept in the Harvard University Library and increased by Lord himself. In a series of articles which have been mentioned above, as in his book, *The Singer of Tales*, Lord adopted titles proposed by Parry himself and tried to follow out lines of investigation as he would have done. Lord is also engaged in editing a series of volumes of Serbocroatian texts from what is now called the Parry Collection.

Like Notopoulos, Lord is an active and creative scholar in his own right. He has had more Jugoslav material to work with than did Parry,

[1] See especially 'Homer and Cretan Heroic Poetry', *AJPh* 73, 1952, 225–50.

[2] 'Homer, Hesiod and the Achaean Heritage of Oral Poetry', *Hesperia* 1960, 177–97; 'Studies in Early Greek Oral Poetry', *HPh* 68, 1964, 1–77; 'The Homeric Hymns as Oral Poetry: a Study of the Post-Homeric Oral Tradition', *AJPh* 83, 1962, 337–68. Strong criticism of this procedure is to be found in G. S. Kirk, 'Formular Language and Oral Quality', *YClS* 20, 1966, 155–74.

Individual studies of other poetries as they are illuminated by Parry's concept of oral poetry include Francis P. Magoun, Jr., 'Bede's Story of Caedmon: the Case History of an Anglo-Saxon Oral Singer', *Speculum* 30, 1955, 49–63; and, with criticism of the analogy, W. Whallon, 'The Diction of Beowulf', *PMLA* 76, 1961, 309–19. How useful the analogy can be for literary judgement of epic poetry may be seen in Stephen G. Nichols, Jr., *Formulaic Diction and Thematic Composition in the* Chanson de Roland, *University of North Carolina Studies in the Romance Languages and Literatures*, Chapel Hill 1961.

and of course more time, so that, in his book especially, he has been able to take the detailed study of Serbocroatian texts in directions which Parry can only have had in uncertain contemplation at the time of his death. This is clearly true, for example, of a section like that on pp. 56 ff. of *The Singer of Tales*, where he attempts to find complex alliterative patterns in certain passages of Serbocroatian heroic verse. Lord's work on the function of the *theme*, adumbrated by Parry, is developed with many comparisons and examples, and applied to the *Iliad* and *Odyssey*. His concept of the theme there is in several places marked by anthropological speculation of a kind that never appears in Parry's work.[1]

Notopoulos in his studies of Cretan improvising poetry has significantly extended the base of the comparative study of orally composed verse. He has also[2] sought to revise the notion suggested by Parry's work that Homer is virtually our only source of ancient Greek poetry. His interests have moreover embraced certain philosophical and critical concepts related to the idea of oral poetry.[3] It remains true, however, that the primary action of both Lord's and Notopoulos's scholarship has been a reassertion of the fundamental theses of Parry's own work. They have insisted on the correctness and the revolutionary usefulness of Parry's views, have reiterated and publicized these views to student and scholarly audiences, and have zealously defended them against doubters and unbelievers. In the history of Homeric scholarship since 1935, they must appear largely as the Defenders of the Faith. A notable feature of Lord's book, *The Singer of Tales*, is its apparent assumption much of the time that the reader knows nothing of Parry's concept of oral poetry and consequently must be sedulously indoctrinated.

If Parry has thus found a succession of champions, he has also had his attackers. The earliest of these, apart from what criticism there was in the reviews of his *thèses*,[4] was Samuel Bassett's decorous but energetic criticism in his posthumously published *The Poetry of Homer* (Berkeley 1938). Parry seems so much to have won the field, that Bassett's counter-arguments are little regarded today. It is true that the *originality* which Bassett wanted to save for Homer from Parry's doctrine appears in Bassett's own exposition to be of a conspicuously modern kind.[5] He appears to have

[1] e.g. 88.
[2] See pp. xlvii, n. 2 above.
[3] 'Mnemosyne in Oral Poetry', *TAPhA* 69, 1938, 465–93; 'Parataxis in Homer', *TAPhA* 80, 1949, 1–23.
[4] See p. xliv above.
[5] Discussing the influence of Parry's work in the introduction (xvii) to his valuable edition and commentary on the *Odyssey* (London, 1959), W. B. Stanford says: '. . . one last warning: the reader must lay aside all contemporary prejudices on the subject of "originality", that specious legacy from romanticism . . .; otherwise he may rashly conclude that Homer's rank as a great poet is being impugned when it is shown how much he owes to his predecessors.' This statement contains much truth. Only 'originality' is surely more than a 'specious legacy of romanticism'. The difficulty with many statements on this matter is that

had little notion that the originality of a poet working within the tradition which Parry exposed would have to be something rather different. But it is also true that the principles which Parry formulated, taken at their face value, seem to offer virtually no room for poetic originality of any kind or, for that matter, for any real development of the tradition itself; so that Bassett's objections ought perhaps not to have been set aside so lightly.

When Bassett wrote, Parry's ideas could still be considered radical. More recent critics have felt that they are challenging what has become an orthodoxy. A spirited statement of this point of view can be found in M. W. M. Pope, 'The Parry–Lord Theory of Homeric Composition',[1] an article which attacks Parry's central theses directly, and combines some valid points of argument with others more dubious. Pope's essay suffers besides from his restricted knowledge of Parry's own work, which appears to be limited to the two articles in *HPh.*[2] But in the present state of Homeric studies, it is hard not to feel some sympathy with such protests as that of Pope against the acceptance as established doctrine of all the conclusions of Parry and his successors.[3]

those who make them do not bother to clarify what they mean by 'originality'. When Macbeth says (2. 2),

No; this my hand will rather
The multitudinous seas incarnadine,

part of the beauty and dramatic force of the line derives from the two protracted Latinate words, and the unexpectedness of their choice and collocation here. Antony says, of himself, (*A & C.* 4. 8),

he hath fought today
As if a god in hate of mankind had
Destroyed in such a shape.

Again the power of the words depends on our hearing them in this place for the first and last time and as a way of speech unique to the speaker. (We are meant to admire Antony's own imaginative use of words, and at the same time sense a hollowness in his hyperbole.) The effect of *Iliad X* 132 is quite different—

Ὣς ὅρμαινε μένων, ὁ δέ οἱ σχεδὸν ἦλθεν Ἀχιλλεὺς
ἶσος Ἐνυαλίῳ, κορυθάϊκι πτολεμιστῇ—

but not less powerful. Each word occurs in a traditional and expected position; cf., e.g., *A.* 187, *Σ* 309, *X* 314, *E* 602, and, for the rhythm in the last part of the line (– – – πτολεμιστῇ), *Z* 239; and the image in the line is one central to the experience of heroic poetry. The compound third word does not appear elsewhere in our texts, and may conceivably be rare: but it is clear that the force of the line does not depend on any such rarity, or rare use, of the single word; it is due rather to the slow and relentless concentration on the image of destruction at this turning-point in the action. To have composed (or simply *used*) such a line at just this point certainly shows *originality*, i.e. words used uniquely well in poetry, but originality of a very different kind from Shakespeare's.

[1] *Acta Classica* 6, 1963, 1–21.

[2] Thus the argument on pp. 12–13 concerning χρυσέη Ἀφροδίτη could certainly be answered by the chapter on *equivalent formulae* in TE.

[3] Other recent publications offering either challenge or qualifying criticism of Parry's concept of the formulary quality of Homeric poetry are: G. E. Dimock, Jr., 'From Homer to Novi Pazar and Back', *Arion*, Winter 1963; T. G. Rosenmeyer, 'The Formula in Early Greek Poetry', *Arion*, Summer 1965; two mathematically concentrated articles by J. B. Hainsworth, 'The Homeric Formula and the Problem of its Transmission', *BICS* 9, 1962, 57–68, and 'Structure and Content in Epic Formulae: The Question of the Unique

The debate over the specific tenets of Parry's studies of Homeric style and their reassertion and extension by Lord, Notopoulos, and others—that is, over such matters as the proper definition of the *formula*, the extent to which Homeric diction as a whole is *formulary*, to what degree formulary means *traditional*, and *traditional* in turn means *oral*, and if *oral*, how far this justifies close analogy with other oral improvising poetries—is now a lively one, and far from settled. The works cited of Lord and Notopoulos themselves, of Hainsworth, Hoekstra, Russo, Pope, and Kirk, are among the more valuable contributions to it. But to the scholar with literary interests, or to the student or lover of literature in general, the whole argument may well appear to be so narrowly technical as to miss somehow the fundamental issue, which is the poetry of Homer, and how Parry's work, and that of his successors, both its champions and its critics, will affect our reading of it. Criticism, in short, in the wider sense of the attempt to understand and evaluate works of art which for almost three millennia have aroused men's admiration and love, and have seemed to make the world more beautiful and more comprehensible, has throughout so much of the controversy taken second place; and the question which is of real interest to most intelligent and educated persons—what does all this tell us about the *Iliad* and *Odyssey*?—receives little answer, or none.

The work of criticism, in this humane sense, has not altogether been assisted by the efforts of philology. In the nineteenth and early twentieth centuries, in the age when the Analysts, those who looked for layers of composition, held sway, any attempt to find meaning in the relation to each other of different parts of the Homeric poems fell under the shadow of the possibility that these parts had found a place together in our texts by accident. For one need not be particularly an Aristotelian to realize that a work of art can present a clear vision of life only if one can assume it to be the product of deliberate human design. To believe this of the *Iliad* and *Odyssey* will not mean that one must believe every part of these poems to be equally with every other integral to the whole: any intelligent assessment of the *Iliad*, for example, will have to keep open the possibility that some parts of it, perhaps portions as substantial as the Tenth Book, have been added from an alien source. But if we are to conceive of the *Iliad* as a work of art, we shall have to be able to regard it as in the main the complex construction of the designing artistic mind. This was precisely what Analytic criticism, by

Expression', *CQ* (N.S.) 14, 1964, 155–64, and now his book, *The Flexibility of the Homeric Formula* (Oxford 1968), which shows by careful examination how much the formula could be modified, both in length and in its position in the hexameter line; and especially Hoekstra's *Homeric Modifications of Formulaic Prototypes* (see p. xxxiii, n. 1 above). The first chapter of this last-named work contains what may well be the best criticism that has yet appeared of Parry's work on its own terms.

direct statement or by implication, denied; and as a result, humane criticism, rather than being helped by the work of the philologists, was so hindered by it that one could say that it existed, during this period of Homeric studies, in spite of them.

It was not the smallest accomplishment of Parry's Homeric theory that it made the whole Unitarian–Analyst controversy, at least in its older and best-known form, obsolete.[1] The idea of distinct layers of composition, or of poetic 'versions' of diverse provenience imperfectly welded together, makes no sense in the fluid tradition of oral improvising poetry. 'Naïve' Unitarianism, as Dodds calls it, becomes equally untenable in the light of Parry's theory, since the poetic tradition, however much it changed, and however recently in relation to Homer's lifetime it took its final shape, was now shown to be the product of many men over many generations, and the dependence of the poems on the tradition was in turn shown to be so great as to rule out the kind of individual creation which some Unitarians, such as Scott,[2] were looking for. Parry himself was by instinct a Unitarian, and his observation supported his instinct, because he saw how the individual bard could, without anything like deliberate manipulation of pre-existent versions, be the repository of a whole tradition. Moreover, he was in Jugoslavia impressed by the unity of style in the *Iliad* and *Odyssey* as opposed to Serbocroatian poetry. This seemed to him strongly to suggest single composition of the Greek poems as we have them. Yet his Unitarianism, if it should be called that, was far indeed from the earlier concept of individual creation, for to him the tradition was more important than the poet who at any moment embodied it. That poet's virtue lay not in the ability to create, as the modern world conceives it, but in the ability to focus and transmit what is, in a sense more precise than Vico had imagined, the creation of a people.

Parry's Lecture Notes (see p. ix, n. 2 above) show that he had not finally made up his mind on the matter of single composition of the poems. He presents in them a number of arguments in favour of unity, notably (1) the lack of repetition of character and incident in the *Iliad*: not only is each person given his proper place, actions also are not repeated: the duel between Ajax and Hector in *H* is quite different from that between Paris and Menelaus in *Γ*; (2) the use of what he calls 'conscious literary devices', as an example of which he gives the return of Hector to Troy in vi, where the ostensible reason is Hector's desire to tell his mother to appease Athena, the real reason, the poet's desire to present a colloquy between Hector and Andromache; (3) the fact that, out of the vast body of oral poetry, only the *Iliad* and *Odyssey* survived, which shows these

[1] Cf. Dodds in *Fifty Years of Classical Scholarship* (Oxford 1954), 16–17; C. H. Whitman, *Homer and the Heroic Tradition* (Cambridge, Mass. 1958), 4 f.

[2] See p. xix above.

poems to have been far superior to all others, and therefore probably the creation of one great poet (or conceivably of some closely organized guild). But then, at the end of the lecture, as if he were afraid that the conception of unity would detract from the importance he wished to assign to the Tradition, he says, 'I have spoken of a unity of conception of the story of the *Iliad*, but it would be wrong to suppose that this conception came to being in the mind of an individual poet. I do not think we shall ever know just how much of the *Iliad* was the work of Homer and just how much of his master and of the Singers who were his predecessors', and concludes by reverting to the traditional nature of the *style*: '... One who studies the traditional style . . . comes to see that it is a device for expressing ideas such as could never have been brought into being by a single poet. One's admiration of the poems increases as one realizes that we have here the best thought of many poets.'

The poet, then, is essentially subordinate to the tradition; and it never occurs to him to depart from it, or even to fashion it so as to produce any personal vision of the world (HS 323–4). This belief, which is at the very heart of Parry's thinking about Homer, led to a kind of paradox in the relation between his work and the critical understanding of Homeric poetry. He himself, unlike many, if not most, of his followers, possessed an acute sensitivity to the poetic values of Homer. His ideas on Homer, as we see from MA,[1] derive from an aesthetic insight; and his sense of the quality of the poetry, and of the relevance of that quality to our own lives, informs all his work, and is possibly the greatest factor in the indelible impression he has made on all his readers. But the strength of his feeling for the tradition as opposed to any single manifestation of it was such that we shall look in vain through all he wrote for any comment on the *Iliad* and *Odyssey* as poems.[2] If they have a unity, it is because the use of formulary diction in them is consistent, not because they have a beginning, a middle, and an end, or because they as dramatic narratives reveal any vision, or embody any attitude, which we shall find of value today. Nor is there anywhere any suggestion of the criteria by which we might distinguish a more effective portion of the Homeric poems from one less effective, or in general distinguish good epic poetry from indifferent or bad.

An example may serve to illustrate this judgement. At the end of HS, his best-known article, after urging that 'the question of originality in style means nothing to Homer', he says: '. . . in certain places in the poems we can see how very effective phrases or verses were made. The wondrously forceful line:

Π 776 = *ω* 40 κεῖτο μέγας μεγαλωστὶ λελασμένος ἱπποσυνάων

is made up of verse-parts found in other parts of the poems: κεῖτο μέγας

[1] See pp. xxi f.

[2] If we except the few remarks in LS.; see p. li, above.

(*M* 381); μέγας μεγαλωστί (*Σ* 26); λελασμένος ὅσσ' ἐπέπονθεν (*ν* 92); λελάσμεθα θούριδος ἀλκῆς (*Λ* 313).' The quotation of what is indeed a 'wondrously forceful line' makes for a moving conclusion to Parry's own essay; and we may think we have here, if in a detailed perspective, some hint of the artistic construction of the *Iliad* and *Odyssey*. But it becomes clear on consideration that Parry is by no means committing himself to the notion, may not even be suggesting, that the combination of parts which made this line is Homer's own work. It too, if we follow Parry's logic, is more likely to be a product of the tradition. Moreover, we are given no indication of what is in fact the case, that this line, like so many others which are repeated in our texts, may be far more 'wondrously forceful' in one passage than in another, because of the context in which it appears. The power of *Π* 776 depends first on the structure of the small scene (765–76) which it concludes. Here we find a simile and description in the first ten lines which combine free energy with marked symmetry—there are five lines of simile and five matching lines of description, each group beginning with ὡς—so as to catch the precarious balance of violent forces in battle. This is enhanced by the repetition of the reciprocal pronoun ἀλλήλων (765, 768, 770, followed by οὐδ' ἕτεροι 771) and the anaphora πολλὰ δὲ . . . πολλὰ δὲ . . . in 772 and 774. The tremendous but frozen turbulence continues till the middle of 775,

μαρναμένων ἀμφ' αὐτόν· ὁ δ' ἐν στροφάλιγγι κονίης,

where we abruptly leave the multitude of living men in turmoil for the sudden still vision of the single man in the eye of the storm who has left it all behind. It is because of its position in this scene that the line acquires its condensed pathos, and becomes a kind of symbolic representation of death in battle. Nothing matches this power in the passage of the Twenty-fourth Book of the *Odyssey*, where the slight inappropriateness of the image can hardly lead us to suspect interpolation or the like, but will almost certainly prevent us from finding the line in question memorable; especially since, unlike Cebriones, Achilles is not chiefly noted for his horsemanship.[1]

What holds Parry's attention in all his writing is the tradition, never the poems in themselves. His ideas concerning the tradition were new and exciting, and he clearly felt that it was his business in life to present these ideas to the world. So that there is no cause to blame him for the limitations of his view. Yet it is strange that those limitations have been so

[1] The more determined traditionalist may conceivably want to argue that *Π* 765–76 as a whole was given to the poet of the *Iliad* by the tradition. Proof of such an argument lies afar. It would not in any case account for the obviously effective position of the passage immediately before the lines that signal the shift in the battle and Patroclus' own death. Such argumentation will lead to the absurd conclusion that the whole of *Π*, and even of the *Iliad*, was ready to hand in the tradition.

little remarked by his admirers and followers. They have often cheerfully adopted his limitations along with his constructive arguments, and the result has been a further inhibition of intelligent criticism of the Homeric poems. Freed from the shadow of Multiple Authorship, the critic now finds his way darkened by the all-embracing Tradition and by the alleged rules of oral style. If he now tries to present an interpretation of the *Iliad* or the *Odyssey* involving the relation between one passage and another, he will have to fear the objection that the oral poet plans no such coherent structures, and that the occurrence of the passages in question is due to the fortuitous operation of the Tradition. It thus turns out that Parry's own sensitivity to the quality of Homeric poetry led ultimately to the erection of barriers to the understanding of the Homeric poems.

This was not so much the doing of Parry himself as of his followers. Parry avoided comment on the *Iliad* and the *Odyssey* themselves. He did speak more than once of the necessity of establishing an *aesthetics* of traditional or oral style.[1] But the readers of this volume will, I think, agree that his efforts in this direction were inconclusive. In fact the two places where he comes closest to confronting the problems of aesthetic criteria and literary judgement are the M.A. dissertation and some of the scattered remarks of CH, the two unpublished works in this collection. He himself took such pleasure in the idea of a noble diction created by a great popular tradition[2] that he never really troubled to define this nobility, much less to show how it operates in the monumental artistic structures of the *Iliad* and *Odyssey*.

He was, moreover, so concerned to urge his discovery of the functional role of noun–epithet combinations and of other formulary units, that he was inclined to see the meaning of such expressions as equivalent to the 'essential idea' to which he reduced them. Thus the essential idea of

ἦμος δ' ἠριγένεια φάνη ῥοδοδάκτυλος 'Ηώς,

which is the standard way of introducing a new day, is 'when dawn came' (TE 13), and Parry implied that the Greek expression had no imagistic power, no wealth of connotation, to distinguish it from the English paraphrase other than the undefined quality of 'nobility'. Therefore (it was implied) there is no valid distinction to be made between this phrase and a formula of like function from another tradition of heroic song (WF 383):

Kad u jutru jutro osvanulo.

[1] e.g. TE 21 ff.

[2] A pleasure which, of all his essays, TM perhaps communicates most directly. Parry sent an offprint of this article to A. E. Housman, who replied in a letter dated 16 February 1933: 'Dear Sir, I am much obliged by your kindness in sending me your paper on Metaphor. I agree with what you say about the diction of Homer and the 18th century, only I do not admire it so much as you do. Yours very truly, A. E. Housman.'

(Parry's translation in WF, *When on the morn the morning dawned*, is quite literal.) The richness of this and other Greek expressions, rarely paralleled by anything in Serbocroatian poetry, is thus removed from critical discussion.[1]

Again, to express the essential idea 'Hector answered', Homer gives us

τὸν (τὴν) δ' ἠμείβετ' ἔπειτα μέγας κορυθαίολος Ἕκτωρ.

Having once uttered the standard expression for 'answered' in the first half of the line, Parry showed, the poet had virtually no choice in naming the subject in the last half. Hector had to be μέγας κορυθαίολος. No one can deny this; but Parry's implied conclusion, that μέγας and κορυθαίολος mean nothing in themselves, does not follow of necessity; and is certainly restrictive to the critic who tries to explain the effect of Homeric verse.[2]

The negative case for any criticism of Homer dealing with the single word has been well put in the thoughtful article of F. M. Combellack, 'Milman Parry and Homeric Artistry'.[3] Combellack concludes: 'For all that any critic of Homer can now show, the occasional highly appropriate word may, like the occasional highly inappropriate one, be purely coincidental—part of the law of averages, if you like, in the use of the formulary style.' Whether this statement is open to challenge or not (the 'highly inappropriate' words in Homer seem considerably more 'occasional' than the 'highly appropriate'), it is much in the spirit of Parry's own argument, as we can see in WW. Parry's followers, especially Lord and Notopoulos, however, went considerably beyond this restriction on the criticism of the single word. Thus Notopoulos in 'Parataxis in Homer:

[1] Whitman, op. cit. (p. li, n. 1), 7, rightly objects to this procedure in the case of the phrase 'winged words' (see WW).

[2] There are really two distinct questions here. (1) Parry seemed to believe that the ornamental epithet had virtually no meaning at all: it was a sort of noble or heroic padding in the noun–epithet formula (see especially TE 145 f.). Accordingly, he never concerned himself with the problem of what individual epithets mean, and was content, for example, to accept the time-honoured, but essentially indefensible, translation of ἀμύμων as *blameless* (TE 122). See the forthcoming monograph of A. Amory, *Blameless Aegisthus*, which, accepting the formulary nature of such epithets, argues cogently that they, like other words in Homer, had none the less precise and ascertainable meanings. (2) κορυθαίολος is what Parry called an *épithète spéciale*, or *distinctive epithet*: the poet awards it only to Hector. Parry recognized a class of such epithets (TE 152 f.), but attributed little importance to them. It took independence of judgement on the part of W. Whallon ('The Homeric Epithets', *YClS* 17, 1961 ,97–142) to argue that there is a significant connection between this epithet of Hector and the scene at the Scaean Gate in *Z*, where Hector's helmet plays so dramatic a rôle. Parry was willing to see κορυθαίολος as *distinctive*, because it is never, in our texts, used of any hero other than Hector. He was unwilling to put, e.g., ἄναξ ἀνδρῶν into this category (TE 149) or to see in it any meaning besides 'hero', or any dramatic function at all, because, although principally used of Agamemnon, it occasionally qualifies the names of other heroes, including some of little note. Here again, the critic will have to assert himself to insist on what the good reader recognizes without meditation, that ἄναξ ἀνδρῶν is particularly appropriate to Agamemnon, and underlines the public role he plays in the *Iliad*. (See Whallon, op. cit., 102–6.)

[3] *Comparative Literature* 1959, 193–208.

A New Approach to Homeric Literary Criticism'[1] argues that Parry's placing Homer in the category of oral rather than of literary poetry makes it possible and even necessary to understand Homer in a new way. The old standards of poetic art, deriving from Aristotle and his philosophic predecessors, must be replaced by new aesthetic standards appropriate to this kind of poetry. For Homeric poetry is 'inorganic' and 'paratactic', as is oral verse in general, and must be judged as such.

The difficulty is that these new standards of art appear to be mainly negative: one must not look for any real coherence in the Homeric poems, because they are by nature episodic; nor, by the same token, for any relevance of part to whole, or of part to larger part, either in the case of single words, or in that of entire scenes. At the end of Notopoulos's article we may wonder what we are left with that could enable us to make an intelligent criticism of the *Iliad* or *Odyssey*.[2]

The effect of Lord's 'Homer and Huso II: Narrative Inconsistencies in Homer and Oral Poetry'[3] is much the same. Lord (like Notopoulos) argues against those who would dissect the *Iliad* and *Odyssey* into shorter poems on the basis of inconsistencies of narrative. For the poet composes in *themes* as well as *formulas*, and both of these are fixed. When the poet has embarked on a *theme*, he must go through it in the traditional manner, whether or not its content makes good sense in relation to other themes in the poem. The poet does not care whether or not he makes sense in this way, because his attention is wholly taken up with the theme he is composing at the moment. Lord closes his argument with the example of the alleged inconcinnity in the depiction of Diomed in the fifth and sixth books of the *Iliad*. In the former, mist is removed from his eyes so that he can perceive the gods, and at Athene's instigation he does battle with two of them. In the latter, he meets Glaucus son of Hippolochus, and tells him that he will not fight with him if he is a god, 'since I would not battle with the gods of heaven'. The critic, or indeed the simple reader, unless warned away from it, might be inclined to understand this change by the course of the narrative in books Five and Six, and the difference in tone between them. Diomed rises to momentary greatness only with the direct help of Athene; without her, he is a fairly ordinary hero.[4] Book Five is one of the most martial and clangorous in the *Iliad*; Six, with the

[1] See p. xlviii, n. 3 above.

[2] Cf. the thoughtful remarks of Norman Austin in 'The Function of Digressions in the *Iliad*', *Greek Roman and Byzantine Studies* 7, 1966, 295–312, esp. 295: 'An important result of the studies of Milman Parry on the nature of oral composition is that scholars are more cautious about imposing their own aesthetic bias on Homer and making anachronistic demands of him. . . . A danger of this new receptive attitude, however, is that while Homer may be vindicated as a historical personage, as an artist he may be merely excused. . . . The suggestion implicit in the oral approach is that we must recognize that there is after all no artistic unity in Homer, just as many Analysts claimed; moreover, we must learn not to look for any.'

[3] See p. xlii, n. 2 above.

[4] Cf. Whitman (p. li, n. 1 above), 167–8.

conversation between Diomed and Glaucus, and then between Hector and Andromache, one of the most explicitly peaceful. The contrast is characteristic of Homer, and to have made it through the medium of a Diomed placed in two different situations, and behaving, as is his wont, with perfect correctness in each, might seem a result of the poet's deliberate art— if the extension of the Parry theory to criticism did not tell us that this is wrong, and that we should instead recognize that the poet is dealing successively with two themes, of which 'the first is used, completed, and forgotten, and then the second comes in. This is just the sort of thing we found in [Serbocroatian] oral poetry.'[1]

It is quite impossible to know how Parry would have reacted to this extension of his theories to the criticism of the *Iliad* and *Odyssey* themselves by his successors. We can only say that his own work provided the impetus for theirs and that, although one may miss in their publications the intense feeling for the *style* of Homer which pervades his work, no explicit statement of his runs counter to their contentions. We must recognize, at all events, that the effect of these contentions has been to form a barrier to the sophisticated attempt to explain the greatness of the Homeric poems. Hence while formulary analysis and the concepts of traditional diction and oral improvisation have of recent years seemed to offer exciting new approaches to poetry other than Homeric, application of these methods and concepts to Homer himself has become increasingly technical, and what poetic criticism we have had of Homer has often ignored, for practical purposes, the implications of Parry's work.

[1] Lord, op. cit., 444. Parry himself could be averse to seeing obvious relationships in the poems. He says in his lecture notes, '. . . because of the circumstances of oral recitation [the] story must be told in episode[s] . . . When the poet within a certain episode makes some reference to another part of the legend, it is not one of the previous lays of the Singer, which occurs to the mind of the public, but rather the simple legend. For instance, when Pandarus is slain by Diomedes in the fifth book of the *Iliad*, Homer makes no mention of the fact that this was the man who but recently was responsible for the breaking of the truce; the evidence of course has been taken as showing that the poet of the fifth book was not that of the fourth book, but Homer, when he told of the slaying of Pandarus, though he only a few hundred lines before had been dealing with him at length, treats him simply as a well-known character of the legend, not as one of the personages who had a place of especial sort in his own particular poem.' Parry's observation that Homer is likely not to make cross-references, and that this reticence is characteristic of his style, is correct. But he appears to assume further that the proximity of Pandarus' death in *E* to his actions in *Δ* is a coincidence, unless he wanted to suggest that the connection was in the mind of the poet, but would not exist for the audience. In either case, the assumption is based on an undemonstrable theory of the circumstances of composition of our *Iliad*, and, like theories of Lachmann (see p. xvi, n. 3 above), should have been 'prevented [by] the laws of mathematical probability'. The death of Pandarus in *E* is no more the effect of chance than is the death of Euphorbus in *P*, where the connection with that hero's role in *Π* is equally implicit.

Cross-references are by no means entirely absent from the Homeric poems. Those in the *Iliad* are well examined by W. Schadewaldt, *Iliasstudien*, *Abhandlungen der sächsischen Akademie, Philologisch-historische Klasse* 43, 6, Leipzig 1938. For the *Odyssey*, see, e.g., K. Reinhardt, 'Homer und die Telemachie' and 'Die Abenteuer der Odyssee' in *Tradition und Geist*, Göttingen 1960.

This is certainly true of non-academic criticism, such as that of Simone Weil, in her justly celebrated essay 'L'*Iliade* ou le Poème de la Force'.[1] But it is largely true as well of such a work as C. Whitman's *Homer and the Heroic Tradition*,[2] the most ambitious work on Homer in recent years, and one of the few to treat Homer, with seriousness and imagination, as a poet. In a somewhat abstract chapter, 'Image, Symbol and Formula', Whitman discusses the artistic function of the formula, and tries to work out an aesthetics of Homeric style. But much of the critical examination, some of it most perceptive, of the *Iliad* which follows this chapter has little to do with formulary analysis, or with any concern for Homer as a composer of oral verse. On the other hand, like all work in German until recently, Karl Reinhardt's subtle and illuminating *Die Ilias und ihr Dichter*[3] knows nothing of Parry or his work. The most balanced and scholarly recent treatment of Homeric poetry, G. S. Kirk's *The Songs of Homer*,[4] is more concerned with historical than poetic matters. Where it does concern itself with poetic criticism, it seems to accept the prohibition imposed by Parry's successors. Thus Kirk states (337) that the *Iliad* would have greater dramatic impact if it were considerably shorter, but adds: 'Yet one cannot say that such a contraction would seem desirable by the *completely different canons of oral poetry* . . .' (italics mine). The finest critical passages of Kirk's own book (e.g. his eighth chapter, 'Subjects and Styles') owe their merit partly to his willingness to examine the poetry without regard to this principle, which would seem to render any literary discussion impossible.

There will always be criticism of the *Iliad* and *Odyssey* that treats these texts as if they were contemporary poems, and some of this, like Simone Weil's essay, may be of the very best. But for the more scholarly- and historically-minded critic, the revelations of Parry, and the attempt by some of his successors to derive from them principles of criticism, will pose a problem as well as offer an insight. The problem is really one manifestation of the fundamental problem of all historical method. If the historical method requires that we try to abandon our own natural judgement in order to grasp the conceptions, and adopt the standards, of a culture essentially different from ours, then the question of the value, or the relevance to us, of that culture, or of any product of it, arises. And together with the question of the value of the undertaking will be that of its feasibility: if the other culture is so thoroughly *other* as the historical approach appears to insist, will it ever, in any meaningful way, become comprehensible to us? The almost uniformly negative character of the

[1] *Cahiers du Sud* 1940–1, and again 1947; reprinted in *La Source grecque*, Paris, Gallimard 1953).

[2] See p. li, n. 1 above.

[3] Edited by Uvo Hölscher after Reinhardt's death, Göttingen 1961.

[4] See p. xx, n. 3 above.

artistic principles enunciated by Parry's successors appears to make an affirmative answer to this question doubtful in the case of Homer.

That Parry himself was aware of these problems, which his successors have mostly ignored, we know from his subtle if inconclusive article, originally a speech to the Overseers of Harvard College, in the Harvard Alumni Bulletin of 1936, 'The Historical Method in Literary Criticism', here HC. Parry there states: 'I can . . . see nowhere in the critical study of literature anything to check this ever accelerating concern with the past as the past. But when one trained in this method, . . . while still staying in the past, turns his eyes back to his own time, he cannot prevent a certain feeling of fear—not for the fact that he has become a ghost in the past, but because of what he sees in the person of his living self. For in the past, where his ghostly self is, he finds that men do the opposite of what he has been doing: they by their literature turn the past into the present, making it the mirror for themselves, and as a result the past as it is expressed in their literature has a hold upon them which shows up the flimsiness of the hold which our past literature has upon ourselves.' Parry's discussion, which follows this statement, of Robert Wood's anecdote about the 1st Earl Granville illustrates the dilemma, and perhaps reveals an excessive strictness in Parry's own conception of the historical method, since one may wonder if Lord Granville's situation in eighteenth-century England was after all utterly different from that of Sarpedon in the world of the *Iliad.* In this very strictness, we can again see, together with the relentless logic which was characteristic of him, Parry's sensitivity to the spiritual directions of his own time: for it is observable in HC that he stresses the historical approach partly as a defence against the propagandistic treatment of past literature as it was being practised by the political extremists of the 1930s. Nor does he quite succeed in resolving the dilemma which he formulates so accurately. He says in his conclusion: 'In the field with which I have been particularly concerned here, that of the literatures of the past, unless we can show not only a few students, but all those people whose action will determine the course of a whole nation, that, by identifying one's self with the past, with the men, or with a man of another time, one gains an understanding of men and of life and a power for effective and noble action for human welfare, we must see literary study and its method destroy itself.' Possibly there was a quality in Parry's own life and in his use of words which goes some way toward realizing this requirement. But no explicit statement of his shows how it can be done, nor did he ever fulfil his stated wish to articulate a distinct aesthetics of traditional improvising poetry.

A distinguished scholar of Medieval History[1] once said that the historian must ideally possess the Then and the Now, and must at the same

[1] The late Ernst Kantorowicz, in conversation with the writer.

time sit at the right hand of God. To interpret the past to the present, that is, he must understand what is unique, and uniquely valuable, in the past; he must know and be able to respond to his own time, both so that he can prevent the concerns of the present from distorting the image of the past, and so that he can know what the present needs and can use from the past. But with all this, he must be able to conceive an Olympian perspective which embraces them both; or in less theological terms, he must maintain a sense of what is in some measure universally human.

Such a thought can be applied with particular relevance to the current state of Homeric studies. It is because we now, as others have done for so many centuries in the past, respond with such directness, such instinctive immediacy of understanding, to the greatness of the Homeric epics, that all this work of archaeology and scholarship continues to take place. It would be perverse if the effect of our scholarship were to deny the validity of the spontaneous judgement which provided the impetus for that scholarship in the first place. One of Parry's strongest arguments for the central point of his Homeric theory—the ornamental nature of the epithet—was, we remember, the reader's own experience of the way words are used in the poems. In developing this kind of argument, Parry was making criticism fulfil its truest purpose: that it should tell us what we already know, only we did not know that we knew it; or less paradoxically put, that it should make clear and articulate what we had apprehended dimly and intermittently. The historical weight of his Homeric studies, their emphasis on differences that lie between the poetry of the *Iliad* and *Odyssey* and poetry deriving from later and literate traditions, has changed our picture of Homer and increased our understanding of his verse: we shall never read it in quite the same way. But the historical argument can only illuminate our understanding if it derives from, and eventually adds to, a conception of Homer itself not based on a purely historical perspective, but on a recognition, in the *Iliad* and the *Odyssey*, of an artistic order and a human significance not limited to any time or any place.

It has been stated by more than one scholar that Milman Parry's work began a new era in Homeric studies. That there is a large measure of truth in this judgement few would now deny; and I have tried here to show why and how this is so. It is equally true that some of the limitations of his work still need to be clearly recognized, while some of its positive value has yet to be perceived. It is unlikely, although some of his followers appear to make this claim, that his approach alone will ever provide the basis of a full criticism of Homer's art. He himself, it must be repeated, almost never discussed Homer, that is, the author or authors of the *Iliad* and the *Odyssey*, as opposed to the tradition in which Homer worked; nor did he ever demonstrate, although at times he seems to assume it, that Homer was himself an oral poet.[1] His discoveries about the style which Homer employed will perhaps be best exploited when we learn how to combine them with ways of criticism which we know already. His work has suffered from the attempt to make it an exclusive key to the understanding of the epic.

One thing that is surely needed is criticism which can use Parry's insights into Homeric style to understand more of how the Homeric poems are put together. It may be sobering to our belief in scholarly progress to note that one of the few essays which answer this need is the short monograph published in 1933 and entitled 'Homeric Repetitions' by Parry's teacher at the University of California, G. M. Calhoun.[2] Here Calhoun makes use both of Parry's three earliest publications (TE, FM, HG) and of the much earlier work of C. Rothe.[3] By way of explaining how Homer is able to vary some of the traditional elements at his disposal to produce the proper emotional effect of a given scene, Calhoun notes (6 f., especially 9) that the epic poet composes in formulae and whole lines as '. . . freely [and] readily as does the modern poet in words'.

[1] Parry manages generally to avoid stating this assumption; but in his lecture notes he says: '. . . it can be shown from the style of Homer himself that the poet composed orally.' The text on this page of the lecture notes, however, is lacunose, and it is not absolutely certain what is meant by 'the poet'.

Dorothea Gray puts the matter with characteristic neatness and accuracy in her edition of J. L. Myres, *Homer and his Critics* (see p. x, n. 2 above), 241, where she speaks of 'Milman Parry's proof that Homer's style is typical of oral poetry'. This is in fact what Milman Parry proved. That Homer himself, i.e. the composer or composers of the *Iliad* and *Odyssey*, or of either of these poems, or of any substantial connected part of either of them, was an oral poet, there exists no proof whatever. Otherwise put, not the slightest proof has yet appeared that the texts of the *Iliad* and *Odyssey* as we have them, or any substantial connected portion of these texts, were composed by oral improvisation of the kind observed and described by Parry and Lord and others in Jugoslavia and elsewhere. Hence the statement of Nilsson quoted above (p. xliv) is, strictly speaking, false; so is that of Dodds (*Fifty Years* [see p. xvii, n. 5 above], 13): 'the decisive proof that the [Homeric] poems are oral compositions'; and of Lord (*Singer* [see p. xxxix above], 141): 'There is now no doubt that the composer of the Homeric poems was an oral poet.'

What has been proved is that the style of these poems is 'typical of oral poetry', and it is a reasonable presumption that this style was the creation of an actual oral tradition. But it is still quite conceivable, for example, that Homer made use of writing to compose a poem in a style which had been developed by an oral tradition. This notion, first argued at length by H. T. Wade-Gery (*The Poet of the Iliad* [Cambridge 1952], 39 f.), was challenged by Dodds (*Fifty Years*, 14), on insufficient grounds, in my opinion, and has more recently been defended as a possibility by Lesky (*Geschichte*[2] [see p. x, n. 2 above], 56–7), and A. Parry ('Have We Homer's *Iliad*?' [p. xxxviii, n. 6 above], especially 210 f.). Cf. Whitman, op. cit. (above, p. li, n. 1), 79–80. Such an argument would hold that the composer, or composers, of the *Iliad* and *Odyssey* made use of writing (either directly or through a scribe), but did so at a time when no literary tradition had been able to develop; that the products of this composition are dependent on the oral tradition not only for their diction, but for many other distinctive features as well, such as the reticence in cross-reference noted above (p. lvii, n. 1); but that they owe to their use of writing both their large-scale coherence and their subtlety, qualities in which no known oral poem has begun to equal them.

[2] *University of California Publications in Classical Philology*, volume 12.

[3] *Die Bedeutung der Wiederholungen für die homerische Frage*, Berlin 1890.

Calhoun's essay thus began a kind of criticism which could show in a precise way how the poet was free to manipulate the materials given him by the tradition in which he so closely worked.

But criticism such as this, which tried to grasp both the existence and the poetic effect of the formula, and then to show how it becomes part of an artistic construct, has been rare since Calhoun's essay.[1] Among the few examples of it are J. Armstrong, 'The Arming Motif in the *Iliad*;[2] N. Austin, 'The Function of Digressions in the *Iliad*' (above p. lvi, n. 2); some of the remarks of C. Whitman in the tenth chapter of his book on Homer;[3] A. Parry, 'The Language of Achilles',[4] and 'Have We Homer's *Iliad*?'[5] In this last article, an attempt is made to show how the poet (of the *Iliad*) can choose the disposition of traditional formulae, how the quality of a scene can depend on this disposition, and how such organization in detail is related to the larger economy of the poem.

The rarity of this kind of criticism, now more than thirty years after Parry's death, should remind us not only that our knowledge of Homer is far from complete, but also that the implications of Parry's own work are in many ways yet to be realized. We want to see ever more clearly Homer in his own time, to grasp more fully the sense of language, the rhythms of thought, in which he composed. We want also to understand better what we have always known, that the poet (or poets) of the *Iliad* and *Odyssey* was not the representative of his tradition merely, but its master. By continuing the work of Parry, and of other scholars and critics who have extended his discoveries, with some such goal as this, we shall be taking heed of Parry's own warning (HC 413): 'I have seen myself, only too often and too clearly, how, because those who teach and study Greek and Latin literature have lost the sense of its importance for humanity, the study of those literatures has declined, and will decline until they quit their philological isolation and again join in the movement of current human thought.'

[1] So A. Amory, in the introduction to her monograph on Homeric epithets (see p. lv, n. 2 above): 'Parry had not the time and most of his successors have lacked the inclination to take up the task of analyzing the interplay between formula as a device for oral composition and formula as a vehicle of meaning.'

[2] *AJPh* 79, 1958, 337–54.

[3] See p. li, n. 1 above.

[4] *TAPhA* 87, 1956, 1–7; reprinted in G. Kirk, *The Language and Background of Homer*, Cambridge 1964.

[5] See p. xxxviii, n. 6 above.

I

The Traditional Epithet in Homer*

FOREWORD

THE idea of this book first occurred to me on the day when I became aware of the similarity of the styles of the *Iliad* and *Odyssey*, the fragments of the *Epic Cycle*, and the oldest of the *Homeric Hymns*. My explanation of this similarity of style is in agreement with that generally given, with this difference: it follows a distinct method. It is not enough to know that the style of Homer is more or less traditional; we must know which words are traditional, which expressions. The method of analysis which I offer here provides us, I believe, with that precise and substantial knowledge. Working within the limits of the texts of the *Iliad* and the *Odyssey*, I have applied this method of analysis to one part of Homeric diction: to formulae which contain epithets. Then I have attempted to show the importance of the results of this analysis to our understanding of Homeric thought. And finally, I have considered the relation of these results to the problem of the composition of the *Iliad* and the *Odyssey*.

I have not added a bibliography at the beginning of this volume. It would only have repeated the titles which I had occasion to cite in their proper place within the work itself. Except for two studies by Heinrich Düntzer (see TE, p. 124), I know of no book which deals in serious fashion with the technique of the use of the fixed epithet. I should however mention M. Victor Bérard's *Introduction à l'Odyssée* (Paris 1924). The bibliographies contained in that work were a chief source of material to me, and helped me greatly to define the framework of my subject. |

As I finish this book, I understand how much my work has been influenced by the advice and the example of the teachers who guided me. May MM. Maurice Croiset, Antoine Meillet, and Aimé Puech find herein my acknowledgement of respect and gratitude. M. P.

* *L'Épithète traditionnelle dans Homère* | *Essai sur un problème de style homérique* | Thèse pour le doctorat ès lettres presentée à la Faculté des Lettres | de l'Université de Paris | (Société Éditrice Les Belles Lettres, Paris 1928).

The texts of this and the following *thèse* (FM) have been translated and are here published by the kind permission of La Société d'Éditions *Les Belles Lettres*.

I

INTRODUCTION: THE STUDY OF HOMERIC STYLE

1. *The Study of Homeric style.* 2. *The study of Homeric language.* 3. *The general character of formulary diction.* 4. *The method of analysis of traditional diction.* 5. *Tradition and the poet's freedom of choice.*

'How can we grasp the physiognomy and the originality of a primitive literature', writes Ernest Renan, 'unless we enter into the personal and moral life of the people who made it; unless we place ourselves at the point of humanity which was theirs, so that we see and feel as they saw and felt; unless we watch them live, or better, unless for a moment we live with them?'[1] That is the central idea which we propose to develop in this volume; and, to do so, we shall select one of the many subjects which comprise the study of Homer: style; and within the realm of style we shall confine ourselves to the use of the epithet.

§ 1. THE STUDY OF HOMERIC STYLE

The literature of every country and of every time is understood as it ought to be only by the author and his contemporaries. Between him and them there exists a common stock of experience which enables the author to mention an object or to express an idea with the certainty that his audience will imagine the same object and will grasp the subtleties of his idea. One aspect of the author's genius is his taking into account at every point the ideas and the information of those to whom he is addressing his work. The task, therefore, of one who lives in another age and wants to appreciate that work correctly, consists precisely in rediscovering the varied information and the complexes of ideas which the author assumed to be the natural property of his audience. |

What I have just said is obviously no more than one of the countless ways of expressing a great truth of scholarship. But if the principle is only too evident, its application is rare in the extreme, is in fact so complex as to be impossible of realization in an entirely satisfactory manner: the goal of scholarship is nothing less than perfection itself. It is now generally recognized, for example, that those who have used the methods of comparative grammar to look for the meaning of certain Homeric

[1] *The Future of Science*, 292.

γλῶτται, have frequently lost sight of this fundamental principle, and that this has impaired the value of their conclusions.[1] What is true of the meaning of words is true likewise of certain abstract concepts. How much we must learn, for example, about the beliefs and prejudices which Homer shared with his audience on the subject of property and marriage, before we understand the unquestionable heinousness of the crime of the Suitors! And can we ever hope to understand exactly the role of the gods in the *Iliad* and the *Odyssey*? We can catch a glimpse of a small part of the ideas which Homer held in common with his contemporaries concerning the gods of legend; but most of these ideas, if we as much as suspect their existence, remain incomprehensible, because for us they are unmotivated. A true understanding of the nature of scholarship, therefore, will show us that there are problems in Homer so difficult that no given method will lead us to a sure conclusion; and that others are perhaps altogether insoluble; none the less, philological criticism of Homer is only of value to the extent that it succeeds in reconstructing that community of thought through which the poet made himself understood to those who heard him sing.

There is a natural sense of an author's style which only he and his contemporaries can share. Here we are not considering the linguistic problem of distinguishing between poetic style—*ἡ τοῖς ξενικοῖς κεχρημένη λέξις*—and the style of everyday speech—*ἡ ἐκ τῶν κυρίων ὀνομάτων λέξις*. It is rather a question of the relation which those who read or hear the work of a certain author establish between it and other works which are known to them, in particular with works treating a similar subject in more or less the same fashion. It is clear, for example, that someone today who judges an author's style to be good or bad | can only do so by making a comparison, perhaps an unconscious comparison, with styles that he knows, and in particular with styles of works which some point of resemblance leads him to associate with the work in question. We can recognize the beauty, the propriety, or the originality of a style only by comparing it with other styles which are like it or which make a contrast with it. Of this the author is aware, knowing that the success of his work depends on how well it stands up to this comparison; keeping in mind the literary education of those whom he hopes to have for an audience, he strives to make this comparison favourable to him. Consequently, when we judge the style of Homer,[2] we must not overlook those styles which were familiar to him, and which he knew were familiar to his contemporaries. More particularly, we must come to

[1] Cf. Bérard, *Introduction à l'Odyssée* (Paris 1924), i. 199 ff.

[2] Is there any need to state that the use of the term 'Homer' in these pages does not necessarily imply that the *Iliad* and the *Odyssey* are the work of the same author? This term will sometimes denote *the poet (or the poets) of the* Iliad *and the* Odyssey, sometimes *the text of the* Iliad *and the* Odyssey.

know the style of the heroic poems with which the *Iliad* and the *Odyssey* were competing, whether these poems were the work of poets of earlier generations, or whether they were the work of those who, in Homer's own day, were the rivals of his renown. Only then will the modern reader have that sense of style which Homer knew, at the moment when he composed them, would be the criterion by which his own poems would be judged.

To see that we cannot acquire by direct means this sense of the style of heroic poetry in general, we have only to consider that, outside the *Iliad* and the *Odyssey*, we have no poem or fragment of a poem which we know with certainty to be of equal antiquity. Nor can we base our reasoning on a comparison between the *Iliad* and the *Odyssey* or between different parts of these poems: not only would the element of imitation then enter into the problem, but in addition any conclusion which we might thus formulate would be as fragile as the hypothesis on which it was based. To obtain any information about the style of the other heroic poems which were known to the literary public in Homer's day, we must have recourse to indirect modes of investigation. Use has been made hitherto of three sources of information, all of which point to the same solution: that the style of Homer is traditional and similar to the style universally adopted by poets of his time in composing heroic | song. The first source from which this conclusion can be drawn is the example of other heroic poetries.[1] They give us valuable hints, but hints of too general a character. To know that Homeric style is traditional is not enough: we must know further which words, which expressions, which parts of the diction, give it this character, so that we can distinguish between what is traditional and what is Homer's own creation. The second source from which these conclusions can be drawn is a comparison between the style of Homer and the style that we see in the fragments of the *Cycle*, in the *Shield of Heracles*, and even in Hesiod and the *Homeric Hymns*.[2] Such a comparison gives us many indications of the character of epic style, but we cannot hope to obtain from it a truly satisfactory conclusion. The problem is complicated by the meagreness of the remains of the *Cycle* and by the brevity of the *Shield*, as well as by the fact that these poems and hymns belong to different periods and clearly do not all follow the tradition with equal fidelity. Moreover, it is probable that their diction is in large part inspired by the poems of Homer. The surest source and the one that tells us most about the style of the heroic poems which have been lost, is the text of the *Iliad* and the *Odyssey* themselves. We must study these poems if we are to reconstitute the notions that Homer's audience held of heroic style before they heard his verse.

[1] Cf. E. Drerup, *Homerische Poetik* (Würzburg 1921), 27 ff.

[2] Cf. the work of P.-F. Kretschmer, *De iteratis Hesiodeis* (Vratislav 1913).

§ 2. THE STUDY OF HOMERIC LANGUAGE

This reconstitution has already been significantly advanced by critical study of elements of style common to the *Iliad* and the *Odyssey* and to other epic poems, although it would appear at first sight that such study has concentrated on the separate problem of the linguistic phenomena of our text of Homer. Philology has sought to show that certain dialectal forms have been conserved and certain artificial forms created under the influence of the hexameter. The scholars of antiquity, as we learn from some of their remarks preserved in Eustathius and in *scholia*, invoked the influence of metre, ἀνάγκη | τοῦ μέτρου, specifically of dactylic metre, to explain anomalous forms and irrational uses. In this way they explain ῥερυπωμένα (ζ 59), Κικόνεσσι (ι 39), εὐρυχόρωι (ζ 4). They give the same reason for the use of the singular ἐσθῆτα in ε 38. That they went so far as to give this explanation of the repetition of οἶσε in χ 481 is very significant.[1] Modern scholars have in their turn concerned themselves with this problem, particularly since Ellendt and Düntzer, who worked at the same time, but independently of each other, and arrived at similar conclusions. These two scholars sought in the dactylic form of the metre the reason for lengthened and shortened syllables, for apocope, for the use of the plural for the singular, for the use of the epithet according to its metrical value, etc.[2] A few years later, in 1875, G. Hinrichs advanced the theory that the words of Aeolic form in Homer were preserved from the time when the Ionians learned the *style* of epic poetry from the Aeolians.[3] In this way the foundations were established of that considerable work[4] which finally demonstrated that 'the language of the Homeric poems is the creation of epic verse':[5] epic bards, or *aoidoi*, preserved obsolete forms, introduced newer forms, and even created artificial forms under the constant pressure of their desire to have a language adapted to the needs of hexameter versification. K. Witte, in particular, has provided us with a definition of this complex and varied problem, and with a treatment of it which is both precise and systematic.[6] To his work there has been recently added | K. Meister's *Die homerische Kunstsprache*.[7]

[1] These examples are cited by V. Bérard, *Introd.*, i. 174–6.

[2] H. Düntzer, *Homerische Abhandlungen*, Leipzig 1872, 507–92. J.-E. Ellendt, *Ueber den Einfluss des Metrums auf Wortbildung und Wortverbindung*, Königsberg 1861 (*Drei homerische Abhandlungen*, Leipzig 1864).

[3] G. Hinrichs, *De Homericae elocutionis vestigiis Aeolicis*, Diss. Berol. 1875.

[4] Mention should be made of P. Thouvenin, *Metrische Rücksichten in der Auswahl der Verbalformen bei Homer*, Phil., 1905, 321–40, and of F. Sommer, 'Zur griechischen Prosodie, die Positionsbildung bei Homer', *Glotta* 1909, 145. Cf. E. Drerup, *Hom. Poetik*, i. 120–7, and especially V. Bérard, *Introd.*, i. 167–78. The latter has a bibliography of the subject.

[5] Kurt Witte, Pauly–Wissowa, viii. 2214.

[6] K. Witte, *Singular und Plural*, Leipzig 1907; 'Zur homerischen Sprache', *Glotta* 1909–13; 'Wortrhythmus bei Homer', *Rhein. Mus.*, 1913, 217–38; 'Ueber die Kasusausgänge οιο und ου, οισι und οις, ηισι und ηις im griechischen Epos; der Dativ des Plurals der dritten Deklination', *Glotta* 1914, 8 ff., 48 ff.; 'Homeros, B) Sprache', Pauly–Wissowa, Stuttgart 1913, viii. 2213–2247.

[7] Leipzig 1921.

The close relation between this study of what we may call a *hexametric* language, and the question of Homer's and his audience's literary education, is obvious. To establish in the *Iliad* and the *Odyssey* the existence of an artificial language is to prove that Homeric style, in so far as it makes use of elements of this language, is traditional. For the character of this language reveals that it is a work beyond the powers of a single man, or even of a single generation of poets; consequently we know that we are in the presence of a stylistic element which is the product of a tradition and which every bard of Homer's time must have used.

It is important for the present investigation that we know exactly what constitutes this proof that Homeric language is wholly traditional; the method of analysis by which this conclusion has been reached is essentially the same as the method we shall employ in these pages to demonstrate the traditional character of the *diction* of the *Iliad* and the *Odyssey*. Before we define this method, however, let us clarify this distinction between the language and the diction of Homer. By *language* we mean all the elements of phonetics, morphology, and vocabulary which characterize the speech of a given group of men at a given place and a given time. In the case of Homer, the problem of language consists in distinguishing, and in explaining the presence of forms, words, and constructions of archaic, Aeolic, Ionic, artificial, and possibly even 'Achaean' origin, which appear in the text of the *Iliad* and the *Odyssey*. By *diction* we mean the same elements of phonetics, morphology, and vocabulary considered under another aspect: as the means by which an author expresses his thought. It is this problem and this problem alone, to discover why Homer chose certain words, certain forms, certain constructions to express his thought, that we shall deal with in this volume. But in our attempt to learn | which part of Homer's diction is traditional and which part original, we shall make use of the same method which has been used to prove that Homer's language is a traditional language.

This proof of the traditional character of the language does not lie in the fact that numerous forms are found in Homer which can be classed as Aeolic or archaic: the presence of a Doric form in Aeschylus does not prove that he had borrowed the form from an earlier poet. The proof is rather that the dialectal and artificial elements of the language of Homer constitute a system characterized at once by great extension and by great simplicity. Put, for example, Ionic endings next to corresponding non-Ionic endings (-*ης*, -*εω*, -*ου*, -*εων*, -*σι*, etc., ncxt to -*α*, -*αο*, -*οιο*, -*άων*, -*εσσι*, etc.), put Ionic words next to non-Ionic words (*ἡμεῖς*, (*ἐρί*)*γδουπος*, *ἄν*, *πόλις*, *πολυκτήμων*, etc., next to *ἄμμες* (*ἐρί*)*δουπος*, *κε*, *πτόλις*, *πολυπάμων*, etc.), and you will find in both cases that the corresponding forms or words are almost always of different metrical value. With very few exceptions—and these exceptions can themselves be explained by the tradition, cf. TE, p. 181, n. 1 below—there is no example of what we find so abundantly in the language of a Greek poet who uses an individual style: I mean elements borrowed by him from another dialect which are of like metrical value with the corresponding elements of his own dialect. Such an example is the Doric ᾱ, which the Athenian dramatists use in choral passages to replace the Attic η̄: in *Oedipus at Colonus* (ll. 525–6) we read

> Κακᾶι μ' εὐνᾶι πόλις οὐδὲν ἴδριν
> γάμων ἐνέδησεν ἄται.

and again (1239–40)

> Ἐν ὧι τλάμων ὅδ', οὐκ ἐγὼ μόνος,
> πάντοθεν βόρειος ὥς τις ἀκτά . . .

etc. Thus the *simplicity of the system* of epic language consists in the fact that corresponding dialectal or artificial elements are of unique metrical value; and the *extension of the system* lies in the great number of cases in which, to a given element of one dialect, one can oppose the corresponding element of | another. It is evident that such a system can only be traditional: a poet who borrowed forms and words of a dialect other than his own, according to his personal taste, would inevitably, even if he made such borrowings infrequently, choose a certain number of equivalent metrical value.

To this proof provided by the system of the traditional character of Homeric language, there can be added explanations of factors which determine the creation and the preservation of this language; but these explanations, though they are essential to our understanding of the problem, are none the less not themselves proofs. We must know that this language was the creation of generations of bards who regularly kept those elements of the language of their predecessors which facilitated the composition of verse and could not be replaced by other, more recent, elements. We must know that on the analogy of existing forms the bards fashioned some which never existed in ordinary speech, for example ὁρόω, ὁρόωσα, etc. We must understand that the *-οιο* ending of the masculine genitive singular is of special value in composing hexameter lines, because it can end a word before the feminine caesura or in the middle of the dactyl of the fifth foot, which the *-ου* ending cannot do; or at the end of the line, which the *-ου* ending can do only in the case of certain words.[1] The knowledge of all these facts is indispensable; for they alone show us conclusively that we are dealing with a traditional *style*, and not, as Fick supposed, with a translation from Aeolic into Ionic.

[1] The figures are given by Boldt (*Programm Tauberbischofsheim*, 1880–1, 5). *-οιο* occurs 7 times in the first foot, 26 times in the second, 520 times in the third, 17 times in the fourth, 352 times in the fifth, 716 times in the sixth.

Nevertheless, only the system can provide us with the proof that the language of Homer is itself traditional.

§ 3. GENERAL CHARACTER OF FORMULARY DICTION

Scholarship has always admitted, although in rough and imprecise terms, that Homer's diction is made up to a greater or lesser extent of formulae; but no careful study was ever made of this matter until it | became necessary to refute theories which found in these formulae a proof of imitation. As we know, every repeated expression, indeed every echo of another expression, was considered a sure sign of imitation; and we know too what harsh treatment the lines and passages containing such expressions received at the hands of Sittl, and of Gemoll, and many another scholar.[1] This was the origin of the works of Rothe, of Scott, and of Shewan, who set out to demonstrate that formulae are found everywhere in Homer, and that there must have been a common stock from which every epic poet could draw.[2] The method followed by these scholars consists simply in showing that one can, whenever one wants to, find reasons for considering the formulae in any one part of the *Iliad* and *Odyssey* as imitated from those of any other part. In other words, the assumption that repetition is a proof of imitation will always allow us to analyse the poem according to any preconceived idea. But no one has gone beyond this purely negative conclusion; no one has done more than to show with certainty (a general certainty, however, and which does not extend to details) that Homeric formulae must derive from a traditional style. Consequently, Homeric scholarship has been forced to recognize a certain element of the formulary in the *Iliad* and the *Odyssey*, but it remains divided on the question of capital interest: what portion of Homeric diction is to be attributed to the tradition and what portion to the poet? Schmidt's *Parallel-Homer* has not answered this question, since on the one hand it is perfectly possible that the poet has repeated an expression of his own making, while on the other hand he may well have had occasion to use a given formula only once in the two epic poems which we know. The situation can be measured by | the opposition aroused by M. Meillet when he expressed the opinion that Homeric style is completely formulary. He wrote (*Les Origines indo-européennes des mètres*

[1] K. Sittl, *Die Wiederholungen in der Odyssee*, München 1882; A. Gemoll, 'Die Beziehungen zwischen Ilias und Odyssee', *Hermes* 1883, 34.

[2] C. Rothe, *Die Bedeutungen der Wiederholungen für die homerische Frage*. Berlin 1890; this author gives a bibliography of the subject. J. A. Scott, 'Repeated Verses in Homer', *AJPh* 1911, 321. A. Shewan, 'Does the Odyssey Imitate the Iliad?' *CQ* 1913, 234. Cf. Bérard, *Introd.*, ii. 389 ff. Drerup, *Hom. Poetik*, i. 368 ff. The number of verses entirely repeated, or made up of repeated expressions, is given by C. E. Schmidt, *Parallel-Homer*, Göttingen 1885, p. viii, as 5,605 for the *Iliad*, 3,648 for the *Odyssey*.

grecs, Paris 1923, 61): 'Homeric epic is entirely composed of formulae handed down from poet to poet. An examination of any passage will quickly reveal that it is made up of lines and fragments of lines which are reproduced word for word in one or several other passages. And even lines, parts of which are not found in another passage, have the character of formulae, and it is doubtless pure chance that they are not attested elsewhere. It is true, for example that *A* 554:

ἀλλὰ μάλ' εὔκηλος τὰ φράζεαι ἅσσ' ἐθέλῃσθα

does not appear again in the *Iliad* or anywhere in the *Odyssey*; but that is because there was no other occasion to use it.' Commenting on these sentences, A. Platt (*Classical Review* 38, 1924, 22) wrote: 'things are said about the epic on p. 61 [of Meillet's work] which make one stare.'

There is only one way by which we can determine with some degree of precision which part of Homer's diction must be formulary: namely, a thorough understanding of the fact that this diction, in so far as it is made up of formulae, is entirely due to the influence of the metre. We know that the non-Ionic element in Homer can be explained only by the influence of the hexameter; in just the same way, formulary diction, of which the non-Ionic element is one part, was created by the desire of bards to have ready to hand words and expressions which could be easily put into heroic verse. The epic poets fashioned and preserved in the course of generations a complex technique of formulae, a technique designed in its smallest details for the twofold purpose of expressing ideas appropriate to epic in a suitable manner, and of attenuating the difficulties of versification.

While this diction by formulae is in itself so complicated, as we shall soon have occasion to see, that its analysis requires immense labour, its principle is none the less essentially a simple one, and can be expressed in a few words. To create a diction adapted to the needs of versification, the | bards found and kept expressions which could be used in a variety of sentences, either as they stood or with slight modifications, and which occupied fixed places in the hexameter line. These expressions are of different metrical length according to the ideas they are made to express; that is, according to the nature of the words necessary for the expression of these ideas. Of these formulae, the most common fill the space between the bucolic diaeresis and the end of the line, between the penthemimeral caesura, the caesura κατὰ τρίτον τροχαῖον, or the hephthemimeral caesura and the end of the line, or between the beginning of the line and these caesurae; or else they fill an entire line. The ways in which these expressions are joined to each other so as both to make a sentence and to fill out the hexameter, are many and vary in accordance with each type of expression.

One example will serve to illustrate the complex mode of operation of this basically simple principle. Let us choose a relatively uncomplicated case, a sentence made up of a simple subject and simple predicate. If one can fill the first half of the line with the predicate, and if one further disposes of a series of grammatical subjects each of which separately can fill the second half of the line, then with these materials one can form as many different lines as one has subjects. This is exactly the idea which Homer uses to express the idea 'and X replied'. With the help of a pronoun, a conjunction, and an adverb, the verb becomes an expression which fills the line as far as the feminine caesura:

τὸν δ' ἠμείβετ' ἔπειτα

To match this, we have a series of proper names expanded by epithetic words which are able to fill the space between the feminine caesura and the end of the line. There are 27 different lines in the *Iliad* and the *Odyssey* which the poet forms in this way:[1]

τὸν / τὴν } δ' ἠμείβετ' ἔπειτα {

πολύτλας δῖος Ὀδυσσεύς (thrice)
ποδάρκης δῖος Ἀχιλλεύς (twice)
βοῶπις πότνια Ἥρη (4 times)
Γερήνιος ἱππότα Νέστωρ (8 times)
θεὰ γλαυκῶπις Ἀθήνη (7 times) |
βοὴν ἀγαθὸς Διομήδης
βοὴν ἀγαθὸς Μενέλαος (twice)
Δόλων, Εὐμήδεος υἱός
Ποσειδάων ἐνοσίχθων (twice)
Διὸς θυγάτηρ Ἀφροδίτη
ποδήνεμος ὠκέα Ἶρις
μέγας κορυθαίολος Ἕκτωρ (twice)
φιλομμειδὴς Ἀφροδίτη
Διώνη, δῖα θεάων
θεὰ λευκώλενος Ἥρη
θεὰ Θέτις ἀργυρόπεζα
μέγας Τελαμώνιος Αἴας (twice)
γέρων Πρίαμος θεοειδής (5 times)
Μέδων πεπνυμένα εἰδώς
περίφρων Πηνελόπεια (4 times)
διάκτορος Ἀργειφόντης
συβώτης, ὄρχαμος ἀνδρῶν
περικλυτὸς Ἀμφιγυήεις (4 times)
πολύτλας δῖος Ὀδυσσεύς
φίλη τροφὸς Εὐρύκλεια
ἄναξ ἀνδρῶν Ἀγαμέμνων (thrice)
πατὴρ ἀνδρῶν τε θεῶν τε

[1] Here and elsewhere we indicate the number of times an expression is used, except in cases where it is used only once.

Or again, the epic poet could make a line by joining any one of these subject hemistichs to any predicate hemistich which completes the sentence and which fills the space between the beginning of the line and the feminine caesura and ends in a short vowel. For the hemistich, πολύτλας δῖος Ὀδυσσεύς, for example, we find:

αὐτὰρ ὁ μερμήριξε
δή τοτε μερμήριξε
αὐτὰρ ὁ βῆ διὰ δῶμα
αὐτὰρ ὁ πῖνε καὶ ἦσθε
αὐτὰρ ἐπεὶ τό γ' ἄκουσε
αὐτὰρ ὁ δέξατο χειρὶ
ἦ τοι ὁ πῖνε καὶ ἦσθε
(twice) ὣς ὁ μὲν ἔνθα καθεῦδε
ὣς ὁ μὲν ἔνθ' ἠρᾶτο
ὣς φάτο, ῥίγησεν δὲ |
(4 times) ὣς φάτο, γήθησεν δὲ
ὣς φάτο, μείδησεν δὲ
ὣς ἔφατ', οὐδ' ἐσάκουσε
(twice) τὴν μὲν ἰδὼν γήθησε
(8 times) τὸν δ' αὖτε προσέειπε
τὸν δ' ἠμείβετ' ἔπειτα
τὸν δ' ὡς οὖν ἐνόησε
δεύτερος αὖτ' ἀνάειρε
κρητῆρ' αὖτ' ἀνάειρε
ἔνθα στὰς θηεῖτο
ἔνθα καθέζετ' ἔπειτα
(twice) τοῖς ἄρα μύθων ἄρχε
σμερδαλέον δ' ἐβόησε
(twice) γήθησέν τ' ἄρ' ἔπειτα

} πολύτλας δῖος Ὀδυσσεύς

The number of lines in Homer made up in this way of two hemistichs is enormous. We find for example:

ὣς φάτο, μείδησεν δὲ {
πολύτλας δῖος Ὀδυσσεύς
θεὰ λευκώλενος Ἥρη (twice)
βοῶπις πότνια Ἥρη
πατὴρ ἀνδρῶν τε θεῶν τε (twice)
Καλυψὼ δῖα θεάων
βοὴν ἀγαθὸς Μενέλαος
θεὰ γλαυκῶπις Ἀθήνη
ποδάρκης δῖος Ἀχιλλεύς

{ Γερήνιος ἱππότα Νέστωρ (5 times)
θεὰ γλαυκῶπις Ἀθήνη (thrice)
Ποσειδάων ἐνοσίχθων (twice)
μέγας Τελαμώνιος Αἴας

τοῖς ἄρα μύθων ἦρχε (ἄρχε) {
πατὴρ ἀνδρῶν τε θεῶν τε (thrice)
Καλυψὼ δῖα θεάων
Πολίτης, ὄρχαμος ἀνδρῶν
περίφρων Πηνελόπεια (thrice)
συβώτης, ὄρχαμος ἀνδρῶν
πολύτλας δῖος Ὀδυσσεύς (twice)

ὣς φάτο, γήθησεν δὲ {
βοὴν ἀγαθὸς Διομήδης
πολύτλας δῖος Ὀδυσσεύς |

ὣς φάτο, ῥίγησεν δὲ {
θεὰ γλαυκῶπις Ἀθήνη
Καλυψὼ δῖα θεάων
πολύτλας δῖος Ὀδυσσεύς

αὐτὰρ ὁ πῖνε καὶ ἦσθε {
διάκτορος Ἀργειφόντης
πολύτλας δῖος Ὀδυσσεύς

The practical character of these expressions from the point of view of verse composition is obvious. A consideration of the number of expressions which form the complete predicate of a sentence and whose metrical value is – ⏖ – ⏖ – ⏑ ending in a short vowel, and of the number of other expressions which can stand as subject and whose metrical value is ⏑ – ⏖ – ⏖ – ⏔ beginning with a single consonant, will give a notion of the enormous resources at the disposal of the epic poet. When the context required it, and when the sense allowed it, he could make any combination of these expressions, having thus at the same time a correct line and a complete sentence. To show how many times Homer does make use of this device, we shall complete the list already begun of line. containing a predicate hemistich which appears both with πολύτλας δῖος Ὀδυσσεύς and with other subject expressions of the same metrical value.

τὸν / τὴν } δ' αὖτε προσέειπε {
πολύτλας δῖος Ὀδυσσεύς (8 times)
θεὰ γλαυκῶπις Ἀθήνη (14 times)
μέγας κορυθαίολος Ἕκτωρ (thrice)
ἄναξ ἀνδρῶν Ἀγαμέμνων (5 times)
Γερήνιος ἱππότα Νέστωρ
Δόλων, Εὐμήδεος υἱός
βοῶπις πότνια Ἥρη
ἄναξ ἀνδρῶν Ἀπόλλων (thrice)
ποδήνεμος ὠκέα Ἶρις (thrice)
διάκτορος Ἀργειφόντης (5 times)
ποδάρκης δῖος Ἀχιλλεύς
περικλυτὸς Ἀμφιγυήεις
Ποσειδάων ἐνοσίχθων (twice)
Θεοκλύμενος θεοειδής (thrice)
συβώτης, ὄρχαμος ἀνδρῶν (4 times)
περίφρων Πηνελόπεια (19 times)

		Μελάνθιος αἰπόλος αἰγῶν (twice) |
		φίλη τροφὸς Εὐρύκλεια (7 times)
		ἄναξ Διὸς υἱὸς Ἀπόλλων
		φιλομμειδὴς Ἀφροδίτη
		βοὴν ἀγαθὸς Μενέλαος
		γέρων Πρίαμος θεοειδής
		Μέδων πεπνυμένα εἰδώς
		βοῶν ἐπιβουκόλος ἀνήρ (twice)
		Λυκάονος ἀγλαὸς υἱός (twice)
		Μενοιτίου ἄλκιμος υἱός
Cf.	*τὸν δ' αὖτε προσέειπεν*	*Ἀλέξανδρος θεοειδής* (thrice)
		ἐυστέφανος Κελαδεινή
	τὸν / *τὴν* / *τούς* } *δ' ὡς οὖν ἐνόησε*	*πολύτλας δῖος Ὀδυσσεύς*
		Λυκάονος ἀγλαὸς υἱός
		θεὰ λευκώλενος Ἥρη (twice)
		θεὰ γλαυκῶπις Ἀθήνη
		Κόων ἀριδείκετος ἀνδρῶν
		ποδάρκης δῖος Ἀχιλλεύς
Cf.	*τὸν δ' ὡς οὖν ἐνόησεν*	*Ἀλέξανδρος θεοειδής*
	τοὺς / *τὸν* } *δὲ ἰδὼν γήθησε*	*πολύτλας δῖος Ὀδυσσεύς*
		ἄναξ ἀνδρῶν Ἀγαμέμνων (twice)
	ἔνθα στὰς θηεῖτο	*πολύτλας δῖος Ὀδυσσεύς*
		διάκτορος Ἀργειφόντης
	ἔνθα καθέζετ' ἔπειτα	*πολύτλας δῖος Ὀδυσσεύς*
		Ὀδυσσῆος φίλος υἱός
		περίφρων Πηνελόπεια

To sum up, with the 25 predicate expressions which are joined to *πολύτλας δῖος Ὀδυσσεύς* to form a complete line, we find 39 other subject expressions of the same metrical value, all of them made up of a noun and of one or two epithetic words.

We have limited ourselves hitherto to the use of the general term *expression.* Before we decide how far we are justified in referring to the tradition such expressions as those above, before, that is, we determine the method | of research proper to the study of the traditional element in Homeric diction, we must first agree on the sense of the word *formula.* In the diction of bardic poetry, the formula can be defined as an expression regularly used, under the same metrical conditions, to express an essential idea. What is essential in an idea is what remains after all stylistic superfluity has been taken from it. Thus the essential idea of the words *ἦμος δ' ἠριγένεια φάνη ῥοδοδάκτυλος Ἠώς* is 'when day broke'; that of *βῆ δ'* ἴμεν is 'he went'; that of τὸν δ' αὖτε προσέειπε is 'said to him'; and, as we shall have occasion to see in detail further on, that of πολύτλας δῖος Ὀδυσσεύς is 'Odysseus'. We can say that an expression is used regularly when the poet avails himself of it habitually, and without fear of being reproached for doing so too often. If, for example, Homer invariably uses τὸν δ' ἠμείβετ' ἔπειτα whenever he wants to express, in words that fill the line up to the feminine caesura and end in a short vowel, the idea of the predicate of a sentence whose essential meaning is 'X answered him', then these words can be considered a formula; for the frequency of the expression and the fact that it is never replaced by another prove that the poet never hesitated to use it, wherever he could, to express his thought. And again, if it turns out that Homer constantly uses a certain group of words, πολύτλας δῖος Ὀδυσσεύς for example, to express the subject of this sentence, then this group of words can be considered a formula. And if, finally, we find that the subject of τὸν δ' ἠμείβετ' ἔπειτα is generally provided by a series of expressions analogous to πολύτλας δῖος Ὀδυσσεύς, in that each of them is made up of a noun and of one or two epithetic words, we can then conclude that we are in the presence of a *formula type*. By definition and by necessity, therefore, the formula and the formula type are part of the technique which Homer used to express his ideas in his poems. But the definition in no way implies, and should in no way imply whether the formula belongs to the tradition or whether it is, on the contrary, the poet's creation. For the Homeric formula is being considered here as a means of versification, and not in terms of its traditional or original character. It is an expression which, whatever may have been its history, made the process of versification easier for the poet or poets of | the *Iliad* and the *Odyssey* at the moment when these poems were composed.

We can thus say without hesitation that the lines and the half-lines quoted above are formulae; but we cannot say that they are traditional. The idea of τὸν δ' ἠμείβετ' ἔπειτα, for example, is never expressed otherwise in the Homeric poems in the same portion of the line; when we consider this, and at the same time the fact that Homer makes use of this expression in every part of his work, 39 times in the *Iliad* and 19 times in the *Odyssey*, we get some notion of the regularity with which the poet makes use of a formula to the exclusion of any other way of expressing the same idea in that portion of the line. This fidelity to the formula is even more evident in the case of πολύτλας δῖος Ὀδυσσεύς, which the poet uses 5 times in the *Iliad* and 33 times in the *Odyssey*, without ever thinking of using other words to express the same idea, without ever so much as considering the possibility of utilizing the portion of the line taken up by the epithetic words for the expression of some original idea. Similarly, we find that with very few exceptions the poet makes use of one type of formula to complete a sentence of which the predicate extends only to the feminine caesura: of the 254 lines which begin with one of the predicate expressions which we found used with πολύτλας δῖος Ὀδυσσεύς, all end in an expression made up of a noun and one or two epithetic words, with three exceptions:

Α 413 = *Σ* 428	τὸν δ' ἠμείβετ' ἔπειτα Θέτις κατὰ δάκρυ χέουσα		
ο 430	τὸν	δ' αὖτε προσέειπε(ν)	ἀνήρ, ὅς ἐμίσγετο λάθρηι
ο 434	τὴν		γυνὴ καὶ ἀμείβετο μύθωι.

Θέτις κατὰ δάκρυ χέουσα may well be a formula, made to be used whenever the poet had to describe the traditional role of Thetis, the mother lamenting the destiny of her son. In the two other cases, which concern the child-stealing Phoenician and the treacherous maidservant, we can be sure that the poet was in the unusual position of talking about persons for whom he knew no names, and did not want to invent any.

This research could be continued in various directions to determine the extent to which Homeric expressions can be classified as formulae. We could, for example, take the series of expressions| whose essential idea is 'X spoke to him in a certain tone or with a certain gesture', and we should find series of predicate formulae of a type consisting of pronoun–conjunction–participle–verb:

(50 times)	τὸν δ' ἀπαμειβόμενος προσέφη	πολύμητις Ὀδυσσεύς
(8 times)	τὸν δ' ἄρ' ὑπόδρα ἰδὼν προσέφη	
(3 times)	τὸν δ' ἐπιμειδήσας προσέφη	
(2 times)	τοῖς δὲ δολοφρονέων μετέφη	
	καί μιν φωνήσας προσέφη	
	τὸν δ' ἀναχωρήσας προσέφη	

And again we should find that lines of this type are almost invariably completed by a subject expression made up of a noun and one or two epithetic words:

τὸν / τὴν / τοὺς	δ' ἀπαμειβόμενος προσέφη	πόδας ὠκὺς Ἀχιλλεύς (11 times)
		νεφεληγερέτα Ζεύς (15 times)
		κρείων Ἀγαμέμνων (5 times)
		Τελαμώνιος Αἴας (2 times)
		Πρίαμος θεοειδής
		ξανθὸς Μενέλαος (4 times)
		κρατερὸς Διομήδης
		ἑκάεργος Ἀπόλλων
		κορυθαίολος Ἕκτωρ

τὸν / τὴν	δ' ἐπιμειδήσας προσέφη	νεφεληγερέτα Ζεύς
		κρείων Ἀγαμέμνων

τὸν / τὴν	δὲ μέγ' ὀχθήσας προσέφη	νεφεληγερέτα Ζεύς (3 times)
		πόδας ὠκὺς Ἀχιλλεύς (4 times)
		ξανθὸς Μενέλαος (3 times)
		κρείων Ἐνοσίχθων
		κλυτὸς Ἐννοσίγαιος

τὸν / τὴν / τοὺς	δ' ἄρ' ὑπόδρα ἰδὼν προσέφη	πόδας ὠκὺς Ἀχιλλεύς
		κρατερὸς Διομήδης
		νεφεληγερέτα Ζεύς
		κορυθαίολος Ἕκτωρ

And finally, we could also establish in the case of these predicate expressions a formula type composed of a pronoun, a conjunction, a participle, and of προσέφη or προσέφης |:

ι 446	τὸν δ' ἐπιμασσάμενος	προσέφη	κρατερὸς Πολύφημος
ω 516	τὸν δὲ παρισταμένη		γλαυκῶπις Ἀθήνη
Ω 55	τὸν δὲ χολωσαμένη		λευκώλενος Ἥρη
Δ 183	τὸν δ' ἐπιθαρσύνων		ξανθὸς Μενέλαος
Ξ 41	τὸν καὶ φωνήσας		κρείων Ἀγαμέμνων
Ι 196	τὼ καὶ δεικνύμενος		πόδας ὠκὺς Ἀχιλλεύς
Χ 355	τόν δὲ καταθνήισκων		κορυθαίολος Ἕκτωρ
Ψ 438	τὸν καὶ νεικείων		ξανθὸς Μενέλαος
χ 194	τὸν δ' ἐπικερτομέων	προσέφης,	Εὔμαιε συβῶτα
Π 843	τὸν δ' ὀλιγοδρανέων		Πατρόκλεες ἱππεῦ

All the lines of Homer could be explored in this fashion for the formulae and the formula types which he uses. If the work were done with care, and if we limited ourselves to expressions which reappear with a significant degree of frequency, we should end with a considerable collection of Homeric formulae, and we should be able to explain the artifices of versification which they subserve. But we should really have no more than a catalogue of evidence more or less comparable to Schmidt's *Parallel-Homer*. It would not tell us the origin of these formulae, nor how they go together to form an organized set, nor—the question of supreme importance—what portion of them must derive from the tradition and what portion from the originality of a particular poet. Showing the regularity with which Homer makes use of certain formulae would in no way constitute a proof that these formulae are traditional. As in the case of non-Ionic words and forms in Homeric language, metrical convenience can only explain the origin and survival of traditional elements which have already been identified by other means. The proof that we are looking for of the traditional character of Homeric formulae lies in the fact that they constitute a system distinguished at once by great extension and by great simplicity.

§ 4. THE METHOD OF ANALYSIS OF TRADITIONAL DICTION

In what way ought we to go about finding, in the multitude of formulae, this system which is the solution of the problem? It must be shown that there exist in Homer series of formulae | containing the same parts of speech, of the same metrical value, and only exceptionally presenting elements which are superfluous from the point of view of versification. In order to avoid any *petitio principii*, we must show to what extent nouns, pronouns, verbs, adjectives, adverbs, prepositions, conjunctions, and particles of every variety of meaning and metrical value appear in series of formulae of like character. Only after we have established along these lines systems of formulae of differing metrical value and containing different parts of speech, shall we know with certainty what portion of Homeric diction can be referred to tradition.

The lines and parts of lines quoted above will illustrate what has just been said. We have seen that in a whole series of lines, a proper noun, with the help of some epithetic word, creates a formula which exactly fills that portion of the line which extends from the feminine caesura to the end. A formula constructed in this fashion can be called a noun–epithet formula; and when we say that it belongs to a distinct formula type, we mean that it is of a given metrical value and is made up of particular parts of speech. Now if a complete study of names of persons, names which must themselves always appear in lines of the type in question, reveals on the one hand that there exists in the case of a considerable number of them a noun–epithet formula in a particular grammatical case and of a given type, and on the other hand that none of these persons, or almost none, is designated by more than one noun–epithet formula in this case and of this type, then we shall have established an extended system of great simplicity, and with it the proof that this system, in so far as it deals with unique elements, is traditional. The whole series of subject hemistichs occurring after the feminine caesura which we had occasion to quote above (TE, pp. 10–13), constitutes such a system. First, there is a series of forty different noun–epithet formulae, all of the same measure and all but three beginning with a single consonant; secondly, of these forty different noun–epithet formulae, only six are not unique in Homer from the point of view of sense and of metre: Βοῶπις πότνια Ἥρη ∼ θεὰ λευκώλενος Ἥρη and ἄναξ Διὸς υἱὸς Ἀπόλλων ∼ ἄναξ ἑκάεργος Ἀπόλλων, Διὸς θυγάτηρ Ἀφροδίτη| ∼ φιλομμειδὴς Ἀφροδίτη. If we subtract these six equivalent formulae from the series, we have left a series of 34 noun–epithet formulae in a particular case and of a particular type designating 34 different persons. That gives us a widely extended system entirely free from any element superfluous from the point of view of versification.

It is obvious that one poet could never have created this entire series of formulae. He may be credited with a few of them; but even in making these few formulae, how came he never to make more than one of a particular metrical value for a given person? A study of the noun–epithet formula in Apollonius and in Virgil will show us in the most conclusive manner that it is impossible for a poet by himself to create more than an insignificant number of noun–epithet formulae; and that if he does succeed in creating as many as two or three, there will already be equivalent formulae among them. This study of the noun–epithet formula in a non-traditional style will be the subject of the next chapter. Here we mention only in passing this corroboration of the proof which the system gives us of the traditional character of the formula.

The three pairs of formulae to which we have drawn attention clearly lie outside this proof. One of the formulae in each pair must certainly be traditional, being a unique element which could be added to the system; but we have no way of knowing which one of the two should be regarded in this way. Let us remark here that it is not necessarily the case that any of these formulae, because they are elements unaffected by the influences which determine the simplicity of the system, are therefore original creations of the poet. Towards the end of this volume we shall see sure indications that the majority of equivalent noun–epithet formulae used for the same person are as traditional as are unique formulae.[1] If we speak | of the former here, where we are concerned with method of analysis of diction, it is only to point out that these are elements which resist our method of analysis. Moreover, such equivalent noun–epithet formulae are generally not greater in number in comparison with unique formulae than we found in the case of this particular series: 6 equivalent noun–epithet formulae alongside of 34 unique formulae; or 40 noun–epithet formulae of the same length to designate 37 different persons.

We concluded that the 34 unique noun–epithet formulae which serve to designate persons, and which fall between the feminine caesura and the end of the line, constitute of themselves a system whose extension and simplicity are proof of its traditional character as a whole. But these noun–epithet formulae in the nominative form only a part of a much more widely extended system: there is another series of noun–epithet formulae of persons in the nominative which fall between the hephthe-

[1] We shall frequently have cause to use the terms *equivalent formulae* and *unique formulae*; in each case one must understand *from the point of view of sense and metrical value*. In the same way we shall speak of *equivalent epithets* (ταλασίφρονος ∼ μεγαλήτορος for Odysseus; ἱπποδάμοιο ∼ ἀνδροφόνοιο for Hector), and of *unique epithets* (δῖος of Odysseus; φαίδιμος of Hector). It is evident that the distinction is of the greatest importance for the study of the formulary element in epic diction, since under the same metrical conditions, the bard will in one case have a choice between two formulae or two epithets, whereas in the other case he has no choice. We shall also assume the right to use these terms in the singular: *equivalent formula*, *unique epithet*, etc.

mimeral caesura and the end of the line—*πολύμητις Ὀδυσσεύς*, *πόδας ὠκὺς Ἀχιλλεύς*, etc. (cf. TE, pp. 15–16); another series of noun–epithet formulae of persons in the nominative which fall between the bucolic diaeresis and the end of the line—*δῖος Ὀδυσσεύς*, *δῖος Ἀχιλλεύς*, etc. (cf. TE, p. 16); and another analogous series falling between the beginning of the line and the penthemimeral caesura—*διογενὴς Ὀδυσσεύς*, *Ἕκτωρ Πριαμίδης*, etc. Each of these series reveals both a large number of formulae and the almost complete absence of any element superfluous from the point of view of versification. Thus we are in the presence of a system of formulae which is a set of subsystems; and its character is such as to exclude any possibility of its being the work of an individual poet.

We can establish these systems not only for noun–epithet formulae of persons in the nominative. These same formulae provide like series in the genitive, although, owing to exigencies of versification which we shall examine in their place, these series are | less rich. Nor are systems of noun–epithet formulae confined to series of formulae in the same case. If we take all the noun–epithet formulae for Achilles, in all five grammatical cases, we shall have 45 different formulae of which not a single one is of the same metrical value in the same case as any other. If we take all those which are used for Odysseus, we shall find 46 different ones, and of these only 2 are of equivalent metrical value, and hence lie outside the demonstration in the same way as the equivalent formulae mentioned above. Like systems can be established for *horses*, for *the human race*, for *the Achaeans*, for *ship*, etc. Let us finally cite a third way of proving the traditional character of some epithets by means of the system. A large number of epithets in Homer apply without distinction to all nouns of a certain category; *δῖος*, for example, applies to any hero, and Homer in fact uses it with the names of 32 different heroes. If we gather together all epithets of this kind which apply to heroes, in all their grammatical cases, we find that they constitute a system of 164 forms representing 127 different metrical values.

Let us remark here that we are indicating as briefly as possible the different ways in which the proof provided by the system can be used; for the subject under discussion at this point is the method of analysis, not the analysis itself. That will be carried out in the third chapter. We do no more here than note a few of its conclusions.

The investigation thus outlined of Homer's use of the epithet could be made for any part of speech, as long as the poems provide us with a sufficient quantity of evidence. One would find, for example, that the personal pronoun is used regularly in certain types of formulae, although these are by their nature far more complex than noun–epithet formulae.

The *Iliad* and the *Odyssey* exhibit, for example, 139 cases of the use of αὔταρ ὁ, and from these one could set up a number of distinct series to prove the traditional character both of the expression | itself and of its use at the beginning of the line:

αὐτὰρ ὁ { γ' ἀσθμαίνων / λὰξ προσβάς / θυμὸν ἔχων / αὖτις ἰών / πεζὸς ἐών

etc.

αὐτὰρ ὁ { μακρὸν ἄυσεν / ἄψ ἐπόρουσε / βῆ πρὸς δῶμα / βῆ Λυκίηνδε / βῆ ῥ' ἰέναι / μερμήριξε

etc. Or one could compose a series of formulae containing ὣς ὁ μέν, νῦν δ' ὁ μέν, ἀλλ' ὁ μέν, etc., to prove the traditional character of ὁ μέν where it occurs in the first foot of the line. If the investigation were pushed far enough, one would be in the possession of considerable data on the technique of the use of the pronoun; one would know with certainty that it is traditionally used in certain positions, in certain formulae, in certain formula types.

These few examples can give some notion of the immense complexity of the problem of traditional style. We are faced with the analysis of a technique which, because the bard knew it without being aware that he knew it, because it was dependent on his memory of an infinite number of details, was able to attain a degree of development which we shall never be in a position perfectly to understand. But this analysis is the only way we have of finding out how far the style of the *Iliad* and the *Odyssey* is due to tradition. It is our only way of giving some precision to our general impression of Homeric style, the impression formulated by M. Meillet in the passage quoted above (TE, p. 9).

In the present study we propose to analyse this technique as it applies to the epithet.[1] This is the part | of speech which lends itself most easily to the sort of investigation which we have described. In most cases, the epithet combines with the substantive which must accompany it, or with its substantive and a preposition, to make complete formulae which fill the entire space between a caesura and either the beginning or the end

[1] *Epithet* can be defined as a qualifying word added to a substantive without the intermediary of the copula. Thus it is not necessarily an adjective: it can also be a substantive ἄναξ, βασιλεύς) or even a composite expression (εὐρὺ κρείων, βοὴν ἀγαθός).

of the line. Other types of formula in which this part of speech occurs are comparatively few. The analysis of formulae containing, say, nouns would on the other hand be very much more complicated. Besides the two categories of formula which have just been named, one would have to deal with noun–noun formulae, conjunction–noun formulae, preposition–noun formulae, etc. And the analysis of other parts of speech would be yet more complex. It is doubtless largely by analogy with the results obtained for the epithet that we should form our judgement of the use of other parts of speech; and it may be that the epithet is the one case in which we can hope to bring our investigation reasonably close to what we want, an analysis sufficiently complete to allow us to determine with some degree of certainty whether Homer's diction is in fact entirely made up of formulae.

§ 5. TRADITION AND THE POET'S FREEDOM OF CHOICE

But the greatest advantage in selecting the epithet as the object of our researches into traditional style is the semantic distinction which we are thereby enabled, or better, which we are thereby forced to make between two kinds of epithets—the particularized epithet, which concerns the immediate action, and the ornamental epithet, which has no relation to the ideas expressed by the words of either the sentence or the whole passage in which it occurs. And this semantic distinction leads us to a surer judgement of the traditional character of Homeric style as a whole than we can derive from the proof provided by the system. The reason for this is, that as we are forced to recognize the character of the fixed epithet in Homer, a character that distinguishes it from any epithet occurring in the work of a poet who uses an individual style, we find ourselves at grips with a conception of style entirely new | to us. We are compelled to create an aesthetics of traditional style.

The matter at stake is the poet's freedom of choice. Was Homer, or was he not, obliged to use traditional formulae? And is he a greater poet for having used them, or for having rejected them and sought instead words appropriate to the particular nuance of his thought?

The conclusions of those who have demonstrated that the variety of forms observed in epic language could be explained by necessities of versification have already given rise to the objection that this would deprive the poet of all power of choice. A complicating factor is that words and forms borrowed from alien dialects are among the principal means of ennobling the style of Greek poetry. Thus E. Drerup protests that to make the exigency of verse alone responsible for the non-Ionic elements in Homeric language is to exclude from the problem 'that subjective element which in all poetry, without exception, determines the formation of language and verse: I mean, the art of the poet . . .' He goes on to add that if the poet uses such forms as τάων, πάντεσσι, ἄμμες, it is not because he had to: he could perfectly well have used the Ionic form of these words, if in a different part of the line. According to Drerup, he chose Aeolic forms because he judged their tone more suitable for his poetry as well as because they were more manageable in versification.[1]

But here Drerup is wrong and K. Witte is right: the former's reasoning is based on a fundamental error: one cannot speak of the poet's freedom to choose his words and forms, if the desire to make this choice does not exist. Homer had inherited from his predecessors a language whose several elements were used solely in accordance with the needs of composition in hexameters. If it had been otherwise, if this or that archaic or Aeolic word or form had survived chiefly because it was able to give the style the nobility of a λέξις ξενική, then the system of epic language would have included a multitude of metrically equivalent elements. But this is not the case. Generally speaking, | whenever Homer has to express the same idea under the same metrical conditions, he has recourse to the same words or the same groups of words. Where Witte is at fault is in not having confined himself to showing that the non-Ionic elements in epic language, at the moment when they became alien to the spoken language of the bards and of their audience, received an artistic consecration, and that this was what *maintained* them in heroic language. It does indeed give a false impression of the character of this language to imply that its creation was, so to speak, a mechanical process. This is a mistake which we shall be at pains to avoid in these pages, when we come to deal with the origin and development of formulary diction. None the less, Witte expressed no more than the truth when he said that in Homer, convenience of versification alone determines the choice of a dialectal or artificial element in the traditional language. Homer's use of this or that archaic or dialectal form is a matter of habit and convenience, not of poetic sentiment.

Our study of the use of the epithet in Homer will lead us to a similar conclusion: that the use of the fixed epithet, that is, of the ornamental as opposed to the particularized epithet, is entirely dependent on its convenience in versification. Now it happens that the epithet has caught the attention and aroused the admiration of modern readers more than any other element in Homeric style; whereas Homer's own audience, it should be said, must have been just as impressed with his λέξις ξενική as with his epithets. We cannot fully appreciate the 'foreign' element in Homeric language, first, because we do not know enough of the Ionic dialect in Homer's time, and second, because our modern poetry is

[1] *Homerische Poetik*, 121 ff.

unfamiliar with any analogous device to create a noble style. But in the epithet we have an element which is extremely familiar to us, one by which, perhaps more than by any other aspect of style, we judge an author's genius, his originality, the fineness of his thought. Consequently, when we find that the majority of epithets in Homer—in fact, all ornamental epithets—are traditional and are used | in so far as they make versification easier for the poet, we are confronted with two alternatives: either we must conclude that the style of Homer does not deserve the honour in which it has been held, or else we must entirely change our conception of an ideal style. We shall adopt the latter point of view. But this is not the place to give the reasons for doing so; nor is it the place to explain how the ideal of traditional style differs from that of individual style, the only one which the unforewarned modern reader recognizes as existing, because it is the only one with which he is familiar. It behoves us first to give the proof that the use of the ornamental epithet in Homer is entirely dependent on its power to facilitate versification.

II

THE USE OF THE EPITHET IN EPIC POEMS OF NON-TRADITIONAL STYLE

1. *The use of the epithet in the* Argonautica. 2. *The use of the epithet in the* Aeneid.

IT might be believed that the systems of noun–epithet formulae which we have shown to exist in Homer are a common property of all hexametric poetry, being due not to the influence of metre over successive generations, but to the influence of metre on the style of poets of any period whatever. A study of the heroic poems of Apollonius and Virgil will provide us with sure evidence on this point.

§ 1. THE USE OF THE EPITHET IN THE *ARGONAUTICA*

Before we begin this investigation, we must state one of its conditions: only an epithet which can be ornamental has a place in a system of noun–epithet formulae; the formula must be usable in any situation where it would help the poet in his versification. Thus the epithet ἀεικελίης, by which Apollonius characterizes a ship which fell apart in a storm (ii. 1128), could obviously not be used in the description of a stouter ship; for this purpose, we need epithets like θοή, γλαφυρή, κοίλη, etc., which denote the qualities of any good ship. In making this distinction between epithets which can be ornamental and those which cannot, we are not anticipating the conclusions of later chapters, where we shall find that only the fixed epithet, the epithet which is a part of formulary diction, can be really ornamental. For | to remove any possible doubt, we shall try to establish systems for Apollonius and Virgil, not by means of epithets which are certainly ornamental, but by means of those which can be ornamental. Thus in the penultimate chapter of this essay we shall have occasion to show that Apollonius uses the epithet ἀρήιος in view of the immediate context. But the word *could* be used as an ornamental epithet of Jason in any passage of the *Argonautica* where it would facilitate versification, since this hero never plays the coward. Hence we must find out whether the noun–epithet formula in which this epithet occurs is or is not part of a system of noun–epithet formulae.

In the *Argonautica*, we find that the name Ἰήσων is used with and without epithet in the following proportions:[1]

	with epithet	without epithet
Ἰήσων	3	26
Ἰήσονος	—	—
Ἰήσονι	—	4
Ἰήσονα	—	8
	3	38

The word γηθόσυνος (iv. 171), in one of the three cases in which an epithet occurs, is really a predicative adjective which by a poetic artifice has usurped the place of an attributive. The other two cases are:

i. 349 Ἡρακλέης, ἀνὰ δ' αὐτὸς ἀρήιος ὤρνυτ' Ἰήσων
ii. 122 Αἰακίδαι, σὺν δέ σφιν ἀρήιος ὤρνυτ' Ἰήσων

Apollonius also uses the name Αἰσονίδης to designate the hero of his poem: |

	with epithet	without epithet
Αἰσονίδης	4	27
Αἰσονίδαο	—	16
Αἰσονίδεω	—	3
Αἰσονίδηι	—	5
Αἰσονίδη	1	8
	5	59

In *I* 460 ἀμήχανος, like γηθόσυνος above, is strictly speaking a predicate adjective. The other cases all contain the epithetic word ἥρως:

iv. 477 ἥρως δ' Αἰσονίδης ἐξάργματα τάμνε θανόντος
iv. 1160 ἥρως Αἰσονίδης, μεγάροις δ' ἐνὶ πατρὸς ἑοῖο
iv. 1526 ἥρως τ' Αἰσονίδης, ἀδινῆι περιθαμβέες ἄτηι
iii. 509 ἥρως Αἰσονίδη, φρονέεις, μέμονάς τε πόνοιο

[1] These figures are based on the index of A. Wellauer at the end of his edition of the *Argonautica*, Leipzig 1828. The quotations are from the edition of R. Merkel, Leipzig 1913.

For the common noun νηῦς in the *Argonautica* we find:

	with epithet	without epithet
νηῦς	1	4
νεώς	—	1
νηός	7	47
νηί	1	19
νηῦν	1	—
νῆα	9	55
νῆες	1	1
νηῶν	—	7
νηυσί	—	3
νήεσσι	—	1
νῆας	—	4
	20	142 |

In 20 cases, epithets accompany this noun. Of these, ἀεικελίης (ii. 1128) is clearly too particularized to be used as an ornamental epithet, and so are Κολχίδος (iv. 484), Κολχίδα (ii. 1097), and ἐπαρτέες (i. 235); while μεταχρονίην (iv. 1383, 1566) and πανημερίην (i. 1358) replace adverbs. The remaining lines in which νηῦς is accompanied by an epithet are these:

iv. 1268	νηῦς ἱερὴ χέρσου πολλὸν πρόσω· ἀλλά μιν αὐτή
i. 401	Τῖφυν ἐυστείρης οἰήια νηὸς ἔρυσθαι
i. 319	δειδέχατ' Ἀργῴηι ἄμυδις παρὰ νηὶ μένοντες
ii. 211	Ἀργῴης ἐπὶ νηὸς ἄγει μετὰ κῶας Ἰήσων
iii. 316	ἀνέρες, ὅππηι τε γλαφυρῆς ἐκ νηὸς ἔβητε
iv. 580	αὐδῆεν γλαφυρῆς νηὸς δόρυ, τό ῥ' ἀνὰ μέσσην
i. 111	αὐτὴ γὰρ καὶ νῆα θοὴν κάμε· σὺν δέ οἱ Ἄργος
i. 1328	πορφύρεον, κοίλην δὲ διὲξ ἁλὸς ἔκλυσε νῆα
ii. 71	τρηχὺ θοὴν ἐπὶ νῆα κορύσσεται, ἣ δ' ὑπὸ τυτθόν
ii. 897	νῆα θοὴν ἄξειν· δὴ γὰρ θεοῦ ἐτράπεθ' ὁρμῆι
iv. 101	νῆα θοὴν ἐλάαν αὐτόσχεδον, ὄφρ' ἔτι νύκτωρ
ii. 575	νῆα θοὴν εἴσβαινον ἐρέσσεμεν, οὐ δὲ πελείης
iv. 855	ἠῶθεν δὲ θοῆς πρυμνήσια λύετε νηός

A comparison of the way Ἰήσων and Αἰσονίδης are used in the *Argonautica* and the way Homer uses Ὀδυσσεύς shows a relative frequency that leaves no doubt of the abundance with which the latter poet avails himself of the epithet:[1] |

[1] The most complete word-index of the *Iliad* and the *Odyssey* is that of Gehring, *Index*

	with epithet	without epithet
Ὀδυσεύς	16	72
Ὀδυσσεύς	186	111
Ὀδυσῆος	30	36
Ὀδυσσεῦς	—	1
Ὀδυσσῆος	41	34
Ὀδυσσέος	—	1
Ὀδυσῆι	8	24
Ὀδυσσῆι	5	5
Ὀδυσῆα	20	37
Ὀδυσσέα	—	1
Ὀδυσσῆα	7	9
Ὀδυσεῦ	3	9
Ὀδυσσεῦ	28	3
	344	343

No importance should be attached to the mere number of times these different names are used, since that obviously depends on the length and the subject of the poems: the significant thing is the relative use, in each author, of the name with and without epithet. This tells us that Homer uses an epithet with the name of Odysseus approximately seven times as often as does Apollonius with the name of Jason.

A similar comparison of the use of the word νηῦς in the works of these two poets gives us another striking ratio. The cases listed as without epithet in the following table comprise a number of particularized adjectives: νηῦς ἑκατόζυγος (*Υ* 247), νηὸς ἐεικοσόροιο (*ι* 322), νηὸς ἐπ' ἀλλοτρίης (3 times), νῆες . . . νέαι ἠδὲ παλαιαί (*β* 293); two improperly formed adjectives: νῆ' Ἀγαμεμνονέην (*K* 326), Νεστορέῃ παρὰ νηὶ (*B* 54); and 18 cases where we see a change of grammatical case: νηὶ παρὰ πρυμνῇ, etc. Also included in this category are 25 cases in which the poet has used this word with the genitives Ἀργείων, Ἀχαιῶν, or Δαναῶν, even though these

Homericus, Leipzig 1891. Ebeling's *Lexicon Homericum*, 2 vols., Leipzig 1885–8, is both less complete in quoting the line in which each word appears and also somewhat less accurate than Gehring's *Index*; and the fact that the lines in which words occur are quoted according to the different meanings of the word makes this work harder to use in a study like this one, where we need to collect all the lines containing a form identical with, or similar to, another form. However, the *Lexicon* is particularly explicit in giving the epithets that occur with each noun, and hence has been of great value for the purposes of this essay. Prendergast's *Concordance to the Iliad*, London 1875, and Dunbar's *Concordance to the Odyssey*, Oxford 1880, are of special utility for the study of the effects of analogy on epic style, a study in which one must be able to examine at once all the lines that contain certain words or certain expressions.

The text of the *Iliad* is quoted after the edition of Monro and Allen, Oxford 1908; that of the *Odyssey*, after the edition of Allen, Oxford 1907.

genitives are really epithetic in meaning, since the audience know perfectly well who are the owners of the ships so described. The table tells us that Homer uses an epithet with νηῦς almost four times as often as Apollonius: |

	with epithet	without epithet
νηῦς	11	13
νηύς	48	55
νεός	7	3
νηί	53	35
νῆα	70	52
νῆες	36	16
νέες	7	4
νηῶν	22	39
νεῶν	3	37
νήεσσι	10	26
νέεσσι	4	2
νηυσί	80	95
νῆας	76	109
νέας	8	9
	435	495

We may also point out, keeping well in mind, however, the difference in length between the two works in question, that Homer has 23 different epithets for νηῦς, Apollonius, only 5.

These proportions, already so striking by their difference, become yet more significant in light of the observation that almost all the noun–epithet expressions for this word in Apollonius are borrowed from Homer. ἀρήιος is used 32 times in the *Iliad* and *Odyssey*, and always in the same position as on the two occasions when Apollonius makes use of it. There is, moreover, a definite likeness between those two lines and *Π* 166:

ῥώοντ'· ἐν δ' ἄρα τοῖσιν ἀρήιος ἵστατ' Ἀχιλλεύς

With ἥρως Αἰσονίδης we may compare the Homeric formulae ἥρως Ἀτρείδης (5 times), ἥρως 'Ιδομενεύς (twice), ἥρως Μηριόνης (once), ἥρως Αὐτομέδων (twice), etc., which likewise occur regularly at the | beginning of the line. γλαφυρῆς ἐκ νηός followed by a verb-form of three syllables ending the line is found 4 times in the *Odyssey*:

ι 548 μῆλα δὲ Κύκλωπος γλαφυρῆς ἐκ νηὸς ἑλόντες
μ 310 οὓς ἔφαγε Σκύλλη γλαφυρῆς ἐκ νηὸς ἑλοῦσα

ν 117 πρῶτον Ὀδυσσῆα γλαφυρῆς ἐκ νηὸς ἄειραν
ν 283 οἱ δὲ χρήματ' ἐμὰ γλαφυρῆς ἐκ νηὸς ἑλόντες

The fact that νῆα θοήν is found several times in Homer, as in Apollonius, at the beginning of the line and before the hephthemimeral caesura, may be of little importance, since it may be the result of a coincidence. On the other hand, it should be pointed out that some of the lines in Apollonius containing this or another epithet of νηῦς have a complex word order in which the relative positions of noun and epithet are such as we should never find in Homer:

i. 1328 πορφύρεον, κοίλην δὲ διὲξ ἁλὸς ἔκλυσε νῆα
i. 855 ἠῶθεν δὲ θοῆς πρυμνήσια λύετε νηός

We should also observe the absence of the most common formula types of the *Iliad* and *Odyssey*, those which exactly fill the space between a caesura and either the beginning or the end of the line. But although we thus find no direct imitation of Homer in the case of some of these epithets, it is none the less quite evident that expressions containing κοίλη, γλαφυρή, and θοή in Apollonius are inspired by reminiscences of his predecessor. Only ἐυστείρης (once), ἱερή (once), and Ἀργώιης (twice), words which could stand as epithets of no ship other than the Argo, seem to be due to the originality of Apollonius. As far as epithets are concerned, the Rhodian poet created little or nothing that we can regard as a technique of diction.

§ 2. THE USE OF THE EPITHET IN THE *AENEID*

We could deal more easily with the point in question if we had some hexameters written by a Greek poet who did not know Homer; but there undoubtedly never was such a poet. The best way, therefore, of determining to what point the originality of a poet who did not have Homer as a model could have | created a technique of diction, is a study of the *Aeneid* or of another Latin poem in hexameters. To be sure, the Roman poets, and not least Virgil, were familiar with Homer; but his particular style and expressions do not easily admit of exact imitation in another language.

The name *Aeneas* is used by Virgil with and without epithet in the following proportions:[1]

[1] The figures for the names *Aeneas, Achates,* and *Turnus* are based on the index of names in O. Ribbeck's edition of Virgil, Leipzig 1867; those for *navis* are based on the *Lexicon zu Vergilius* by Merguet, Leipzig 1907.

	with epithetic word	with no epithetic word
Aeneas	49	103
Aeneae (gen.)	3	18
Aeneae (dat.)	3	10
Aenean	5	30
Aenea (abl.)	—	3
Aenea (voc.)	2	8
	62	172

Inscius (vi. 711), *ignarus* (x. 25, x. 85), *hospitis* (vii. 463), *ferus* (iv. 466), *laetum* (vii. 288), and *fatalem* (xi. 232), are all too particularized to count as ornamental epithets. Virgil is closer to Homer than Apollonius in the frequency with which he uses the epithet here. *Aeneas* is accompanied by an epithet one half as often as Ὀδυσσεύς.

The cases listed in the following table as without epithet include occurrences of the word *navis* with *tarda* (v. 280), *solitae* (ii. 462), *fessas* (i. 168, v. 29), these being too particularized to be ornamental. With this word Virgil uses an epithet even less often than does Apollonius with νηῦς:[1] |

	with epithetic word	with no epithetic word
Navis	—	1
Navis	—	1
Navem	1	5
Naves	—	1
Navis	1	19
Navibus	1	9
	3	38

Without dwelling on the obvious fact that Roman poetry owes its entire conception of the epithet to Greek poetry, we can see the direct influence of Homer in the epithets used by Virgil with the words in question. *Aeneas Anchisiades* in the line

vii. 521 Aeneas Anchisiades et fidus Achates

shows memory of the Homeric lines

[1] To be exact, Homer has an epithet with νηῦς between 6 and 7 times as often as Virgil has with *navis*.

P 754 Αἰνείας τ' Ἀγχισιάδης καὶ φαίδιμος Ἕκτωρ
Υ 160 Αἰνείας τ' Ἀγχισιάδης καὶ δῖος Ἀχιλλεύς

Magnanimum (i. 260, ix. 204) may be derived from *μεγάθυμος*, but it is more likely an exact reminiscence of *μεγαλήτορος Αἰνείαο* which appears four times in Homer. *Magnus* (x. 159), *magni* (x. 830) seem to have been inspired by Homer's frequent use of *μέγας*. *Aeneas heros* (vi. 103) can be compared with *Λήϊτος ἥρως* (*Ζ* 35), *Τηλέμαχός θ' ἥρως* (δ 21, 303), *Πηνέλεών θ' ἥρωα* (*Ν* 92), etc.

Bonus (v. 770, xi. 106) could have been suggested by *ἀγαθός*; but if it was, we should have to suppose that the Roman poet badly misunderstood this epic word, attributing to it the moral sense which it bore in the Greek language of his own | time. When the poet uses *bonus* in these two cases, he is thinking of the kindness which his hero was wont to show. It may be better to consider this an original idea. Even if he owes a portion of his epithets to Homer, Virgil attained in the choice of some of these words that originality which makes of his poem much more than a mere Roman version of the *Iliad* and the *Odyssey*. The expressions *pius Aeneas* (17 times) and *pater Aeneas* (16 times) derive from the most profoundly original aspect of Virgil's thought.

Thus we find in the *Aeneid* a not infrequent use of non-traditional epithets; but this leaves us very far from finding in it what could be called a system. There is not, in Virgil, the necessary variety of expressions designed to serve in different parts of the line; and what is yet more conclusive, there is an abundance of expressions identical both in metre and in sense. *Pius Aeneas* and *pater Aeneas* are of like metrical value, and if we regard the Virgilian epithet as a true ornamental word, we must conclude that their sense is the same.

The expression *pius Aeneas* most often begins in the first foot. We find

At pius Aeneas	(4 times)
Tum pius Aeneas	(4 times)
quam pius Aeneas	(twice)
quem pius Aeneas	(once)
hoc pius Aeneas	(once)
quid pius Aeneas	(once)
sum pius Aeneas	(once)

It also occurs in two other positions:

praecipue pius Aeneas	(twice)
actutum pius Aeneas	(once)

vii. 5 At pius exsequiis Aeneas rite solutis

Pater Aeneas, being of the same metrical value and beginning in the same way with a single consonant, does nothing to facilitate versification: | it only makes possible a series of expressions similar to those listed just above:

At pater Aeneas	(4 times)
Tum pater Aeneas	(twice)
quos pater Aeneas	(once)
hinc pater Aeneas	(once)
iam pater Aeneas	(twice)
et pater Aeneas	(once)
huc pater Aeneas	(once)
cum pater Aeneas	(once)
sic pater Aeneas	(once)

Bonus occupies the same position, and has the same metrical value:

quos bonus Aeneas	(twice)

Note finally that *Tros* in *Tros Aeneas* (xii. 723) could be replaced by *pius* or *pater* or *bonus*.

The other expressions containing *Aeneas* in the nominative with an epithetic word of different metrical value from those listed above are:

i. 596	Troius Aeneas, Libycis ereptus ab undis
vi. 103	Incipit Aeneas heros: non ulla laborum
viii. 521	Aeneas Anchisiades et fidus Achates
x. 159	hic magnus sedet Aeneas secumque volutat
xii. 938–9	stetit acer in armis Aeneas, volvens oculos, dextramque repressit
ix. 40–1	namque ita discedens praeceperat optimus armis Aeneas

Thus out of 41 cases in which an epithetic word is used with *Aeneas* in the nominative, 35 exhibit an epithet of the measure ⏑ ⏑, and in 31 the whole expression has the measure ⏑ ⏑ – – –, and begins in the first foot. A comparison with the series of noun–epithet formulae on Table I (TE, p. 39) will show the difference between the style of Virgil, who | employs the epithet solely as an artifice of style, and Homer, whose use of the epithet is guided by his desire to make versification easier. In the case of certain names, which occur less frequently in the *Iliad* and *Odyssey* combined than does *Aeneas* in the *Aeneid*, it can be observed that the majority of noun–epithet expressions containing them are of the same metrical value with formula types which we can call principal, on the grounds that they are by far the most common. The metre of all these formula types is such as to fill the space between a caesura and the beginning or end of the line, so that they can be switched about in the manner described in the preceding chapter. Thus we find:

	formulae of	
	principal types	other measures
Aeneas (152 times in the *Aeneid*)	2	39
Ἄρης (43 times in Homer)	15	12
Διομήδης (42 times in Homer)	34	7
Ἀγαμέμνων (100 times in Homer)	63	15
Ἀπόλλων (111 times in Homer)	51	15
Νέστωρ (55 times in Homer)	32	7

In two cases Virgil uses for *Aeneas* a noun–epithet expression extending exactly from a caesura to one of the extremities of the line. One of these is the expression *Aeneas Anchisiades*, borrowed from Homer, which leaves only the expression *Troius Aeneas* as more or less the product of the poet's originality. Without these principal formula types, it is hardly possible to set up a system of formulae. Undoubtedly the formula-series *at pius Aeneas*, *tum pius Aeneas*, etc., and *at pater Aeneas*, *tum pater Aeneas*, etc., were helpful to Virgil in his versification; we can be certain that their frequent use was in part determined by their convenience. But if these formulae, all of the same metrical value, attest the influence of verse on style, they still do not constitute of themselves a system. |

Another indication of the absence in Virgil of anything that might constitute a system of noun–epithet formulae is the presence of formulae alike both in metre and in sense. For a single noun in Homer, there are sometimes noun–epithet formulae which are metrically the same; e.g. *θεὰ λευκώλενος Ἥρη* along with *βοῶπις πότνια Ἥρη*, etc., cases which themselves can be explained by the influence of metre (cf. Chap. V). But these cases are exceedingly few in comparison with the number of unique noun–epithet formulae, and they almost invariably show either an epithet borrowed from another formula in which its metre makes it indispensable, or an epithet that can be applied to any noun of a given category. Many heroes, as we know, make their appearance in Homer; and yet there is but one case in which two noun–epithet formulae of a single hero which have the same metrical value both contain an epithet peculiar to that hero: *ποδάρκης . . . Ἀχιλλεύς* ∼ *ποδώκης . . . Ἀχιλλεύς* (cf. TE, p. 178). Whereas in Virgil we find that four epithets peculiar to Aeneas have the same metrical value: *pater*, *pius*, *Tros*, and *bonus*. The influence of metre in epic style on the one hand determined the abundance of noun–epithet formulae, as we have had occasion to point out; but on the other hand, it determined a rigorous simplicity for the whole set of these formulae, excluding with very few exceptions any formula which might match another in both sense and metre. Thus of the 723 formulae indicated on Table I (TE, p. 39), only 81 show the same metrical value as another noun–epithet formula used for the same person. When we compare with these figures the proportion of equivalent formulae for *Aeneas*—of 41 noun–epithet formulae in the nominative case, 39 repeat the metrical value of others—we find a proportion so different as to make plain that it would be impossible to establish, in terms of the noun–epithet formulae of Aeneas, a system characterized at once by great extension and great simplicity.

A comparison of a different sort between the works of Virgil and of Homer will demonstrate with equal certainty that the former poet uses the epithet for reasons entirely apart from convenience of versification. It makes little difference to Homer | if he uses a greater or smaller number of epithets with the names of his several heroes. Epithets being for him no more than a device to facilitate the handling of nouns, the frequency with which he uses them with a particular noun will be a function of the metrical value of the latter. Epithets can be of service to the poet in the disposition of some names. They may be less useful to him, and even an encumbrance, in the case of others. For example, epithets are used in Homer with the nominatives of a number of names whose measure is ⏑ – – in fairly constant proportion:

	with epithet	without epithet	proportion
Ὀδυσσεύς	202	183	1:0·8
Ἀθήνη	139	105	1:0·8
Ἀπόλλων	66	45	1:0·7
Ἀχιλλεύς	102	83	1:0·8

Similarly, the proportions are generally the same for the use of epithets with names whose metrical value is – –.[1]

[1] The name *Νέστωρ*, which appears with epithet in a proportion quite different from that of other names of heroes of the same metrical value, is a good example of why we must not lose sight of the action of the poem when we make numerical comparisons; and at the same time it shows us how rough these comparisons are. This name is used 39 times with epithet and 13 times without, a proportion of 1 : 3. The explanation for this unusual proportion is not far to seek. Nestor is most likely to be mentioned under circumstances requiring him to address an assembly or in some way or other to give advice. Thus of the 52 times that the name *Νέστωρ* appears, it is found 21 times at the end of a line announcing the beginning of a speech; and the subject expression of such lines, as we have shown, regularly consists of a noun–epithet formula. Had the lord of the Pylians been less of an orator, he would doubtless have received fewer epithets.

	with epithet	without epithet	proportion
Ἥρη	47	38	1:0·8
Ἕκτωρ	87	83	1:0·9
Αἴας	43	43	1:1

For names whose measure is ⏑ ⏑ – –, the proportion changes radically, because these words do not need epithets:

	with epithet	without epithet	proportion
Ἀγαμέμνων	78	22	1:0·3
Διομήδης	41	1	1:0·03
Μενέλαος	86	19	1:0·2

Names of metrical value – ⏑⏑ – show a different proportion:

	with epithet	without epithet	proportion
Ἰδομενεύς	14	24	1:1·7
Μηριόνης	13	24	1:1·6

Finally, the proportions of the use of epithets with names of the same metrical value with *Aeneas* are consistent among themselves, but at variance with the proportions found for names of different metrical value:

	with epithet	without epithet	proportion
Αἰνείας	5	26	1:5·2
Πάτροκλος	5	39	1:7·8
Σαρπηδών	5	11	1:2·2
Ἥφαιστος	4	20	1:1·5

The proportion of the use of epithets with *Aeneas* in Virgil is 41 : 111, or 1:2·7. If we remember what has already been explained, that a small discrepancy in proportions is not an important factor, we may be led to conclude that this proportion is virtually the same with that of names of like measure in Homer. But the fact that this proportion holds only | for the protagonist of the *Aeneid* shows us how Virgil made a point of using epithets in the very situation where Homer, whose guide was facility of versification, used them least. The case of the name *Turnus*, for example, gives us an indication of the normal use of the epithet in Virgilian style. The Rutulian warrior's name is found 58 times in the nominative, and on two occasions only is it accompanied by a word which could be classed as an ornamental epithet.[1] The conclusion is only too obvious. Where Virgil did not use the epithet by way of exception, as in the case of *Aeneas* and *Achates*, he hardly made use of it at all. Inspired by his reading of the *Iliad* and the *Odyssey*, the Roman poet wished to endow Aeneas with ornamental words analogous to those possessed by the heroes of Homer. He did not appreciate, or even suspect, that the use of these words depended on the help they provide in the handling of names; and so he did without them in the case of *Turnus*, where they would have been of great service, and used them abundantly with *Aeneas*, where they were less advantageous for the making of verse.

[1] *Dux* (ix. 28), *princeps* (ix. 535); *ingens* (xii. 927), Turnus' third epithet, cannot be ornamental.

III

THE EPITHET AND THE FORMULA I: THE USAGE OF THE FIXED EPITHET

1. Noun–epithet formulae of gods and heroes; principal types. 2. Noun–epithet formulae of gods and heroes; less frequent types. 3. Is the diction of the Iliad *and the* Odyssey *entirely formulary? 4. The choice of epithets. 5. Epithets and noun–epithet formulae of heroines. 6. Epithets and noun–epithet formulae of peoples. 7. Limits of the method of investigation. 8. Preposition–noun–epithet formulae and noun–epithet–verb formulae for certain names of countries. 9. Noun–epithet formulae and noun–epithet–preposition formulae of ships. 10. Noun–epithet formulae of horses. 11. Noun–epithet formulae of the human race. 12. Noun–epithet formulae and noun–epithet–preposition formulae of shields.*

§ 1. NOUN–EPITHET FORMULAE OF GODS AND HEROES; PRINCIPAL TYPES.[1]

WE can now begin the study of Homeric formulae containing epithets. Principal-type formulae, | those that exactly fill the space between the beginning or end of a line and a metrical break (caesura or diaeresis), will be examined first, because they occur with by far the greatest frequency and because they are most obviously

[1] Must we give reasons for making numerical comparisons in this study of Homeric style? To those who object that a study of style ought not to be a problem in statistics we can reply that the use of figures is our only means of verifying with precision what would otherwise remain a vague impression. The purpose of these pages is to show in its full extent a quality of Homeric style which everyone can observe, but of which no one is in a position to appreciate the supreme importance without a numerical study. And furthermore, each detail of this numerical investigation is of distinct value in helping us to understand Homer; they compensate, in some degree, for the restrictions imposed on our sensibility by a foreign language and a poetry different from our own. The mere reading of Homer, for example, will never tell us that the word πολυφλοίσβοιο is never found outside the expression πολυφλοίσβοιο θαλάσσης, that after προσέφη Odysseus is invariably designated by the epithet πολύμητις and never any other, that in more than half of the cases in which the name occurs Ὀδυσσεύς is accompanied by some epithet, that this same hero is never qualified by πολυμήχανος except in the vocative case, etc., etc. To know all these things is to have so many distinct data on what constitutes Homeric style. It is true that even the most sensitive member of Homer's original audience | would not have noticed if the poet had changed this or that detail of this customary style; but this style, which he knew to be the poet's, and which he expected, was the aggregate of these details.

Numbers have been used in the study of Homeric style in such a way as to win them a bad reputation; viz. in comparisons based on minute or hypothetical differences. We shall studiously avoid such comparisons, knowing that in a matter of style, numerical differences, being largely dependent on the action of the poem, can be no more than approximate. To say 'six times more often', or 'eight times more often', is no more than an alternative way of saying 'much more often'.

the product of a technique of diction. Then, after we have noted the forces which act in this first class of formulae—the influence of metre, the arrangement of words in the line, the relation between the essential idea and the formula, the factor of analogy—we shall be in a better position to make a judgement concerning the rarer types of formula which, it would seem, may be the independent creations of Homer.

In order to draw conclusions which are general and not exceptional, it is necessary to examine a large number of formulae. At the same time, we must keep in mind that the character of any series of formulae (noun–epithet formulae, noun–epithet–preposition formulae, etc.) will inevitably depend on the character of the noun about which the formulae are constructed. The greatest danger in a study of Homeric formulae is that one may be led to assume that they follow rules which have nothing to do with the ideas denoted by the single words. We must never forget that formulary technique is designed to express the thought of epic poetry, hence varies constantly in conformity with the idea which is to be expressed. To choose an example: the name of a hero will more often be the subject of a sentence than will the name of a city or the majority of common nouns. Odysseus does many things; a ship or Troy are less frequently conceived as the authors of an action. In other words, for the name of a hero, the epic poet stands in need of a series of noun–epithet formulae in the nominative case more often than for other nouns. In the same way, the poet will seldom have occasion to use a preposition with the name of Odysseus, whereas the occasions of saying | *next to the ship, in the ship, to the ship* will be frequent in any poem in which a ship plays a part; and therefore the poet needs a series of noun–epithet–preposition formulae for *ship* which he does not need for *Odysseus*. Hence it is clearly correct procedure to give separate treatment to nouns which by their nature present distinct problems of versification, and to keep together only those which are alike in the circumstances of their use.

a. Noun–epithet formulae of gods and heroes in the nominative case; principal types

Table I (TE, p. 39) shows all the examples in which certain names in the nominative case, in combination with one or two epithets, form an expression which exactly fills the space between a metrical break and the beginning or end of a line. We have chosen eleven names among those most frequently met with in the poems. This Table shows: (1) the metrical value of the principal-type formulae, all the formulae of these types that appear in the nominative with the eleven names selected, and the number of times that these formulae occur in the *Iliad* and the *Odyssey*. The expressions given in square brackets are those which do not actually contain the name of the god or hero, but can take its place; for example, πατὴρ ἀνδρῶν τε θεῶν τε for Zeus and Τυδέος υἱός for Diomedes. For the

TABLE I—NOUN–EPITHET FORMULAE OF GODS AND HEROES IN THE NOMINATIVE CASE; PRINCIPAL TYPES

(An asterisk * indicates that the metre of a name makes a noun–epithet formula impossible in the metre in question)

	Between the bucolic diaeresis and the end of the line – ⏑ ⏑ – –		Between the hepthemimeral caesura and the end of the line ⏑ ⏑ – ⏑ ⏑ – –		Between the feminine caesura and the end of the line ⏑ – ⏑ ⏑ – ⏑ ⏑ – ⏑		Between the beginning of the line and the penthemimeral caesura – ⏑ ⏑ – ⏑ ⏑ –		Noun–epithet formulae of different types	Different types of formulae
Ὀδυσσεύς	δῖος Ὀδυσσεύς ἐσθλὸς Ὀδυσσεύς	60 3	πολύμητις Ὀδυσσεύς πτολίπορθος Ὀδυσσεύς	81 4	πολύτλας δῖος Ὀδυσσεύς	38	διογενὴς Ὀδυσσεύς	4	12	8
Ἀθήνη	Παλλὰς Ἀθήνη [ὀβριμοπάτρη]	39 2	γλαυκῶπις Ἀθήνη	26	θεὰ γλαυκῶπις Ἀθήνη Ἀλαλκομενηὶς Ἀθήνη	51 2	Παλλὰς Ἀθηναίη	8	11	6
Ἀπόλλων	Φοῖβος Ἀπόλλων	33	Διὸς υἱὸς Ἀπόλλων ἑκάεργος Ἀπόλλων κλυτότοξος Ἀπόλλων	2 6 1	ἄναξ Διὸς υἱὸς Ἀπόλλων ἄναξ ἑκάεργος Ἀπόλλων	5 3	[Φοῖβος ἀκερσεκόμης]	1	15	5
Ἀχιλλεύς	δῖος Ἀχιλλεύς ὠκὺς Ἀχιλλεύς	34 5	πόδας ὠκὺς Ἀχιλλεύς μεγάθυμος Ἀχιλλεύς	31 1	ποδάρκης δῖος Ἀχιλλεύς	21			10	7
Ζεύς	μητίετα Ζεύς εὐρύοπα Ζεύς	18 14	νεφεληγερέτα Ζεύς Ζεὺς τερπικέραυνος στεροπηγερέτα Ζεύς	30 4 1	[πατὴρ ἀνδρῶν τε θεῶν τε] Ὀλύμπιος εὐρύοπα Ζεύς	15 1	Ζεὺς ὑψιβρεμέτης	5	39	24
Ἥρη	πότνια Ἥρη	11	λευκώλενος Ἥρη	3	βοῶπις πότνια Ἥρη θεὰ λευκώλενος Ἥρη	11 19			3	3
Ἕκτωρ	Φαίδιμος Ἕκτωρ ὄβριμος Ἕκτωρ	29 4	κορυθαίολος Ἕκτωρ	25	μέγας κορυθαίολος Ἕκτωρ	12	Ἕκτωρ Πριαμίδης	6	11	7
Νέστωρ	ἱππότα Νέστωρ	1			Γερήνιος ἱππότα Νέστωρ	31			7	4
Ἄρης	χάλκεος Ἄρης ὄβριμος Ἄρης	5 5	χρυσήνιος Ἄρης	1	βριήπυος ὄβριμος Ἄρης Ἄρης ἆτος πολέμοιο	1 3			12	10
Διομήδης	[Τυδέος υἱός]	8	κρατερὸς Διομήδης ἀγαθὸς Διομήδης	12 1	βοὴν ἀγαθὸς Διομήδης	21			7	5
Ἀγαμέμνων	*		κρείων Ἀγαμέμνων	26	ἄναξ ἀνδρῶν Ἀγαμέμνων	37	[ἥρως Ἀτρείδης]	3	15	6

sake of simplicity the figures for the *Iliad* and the *Odyssey* are not given separately. The different proportions in the use of these formulae in the two poems are for the most part dependent on the individual circumstances of each poem, and the few differences which would seem to derive from purely stylistic considerations will be treated in their place in Chap. V. Table I shows also: (2) how many times these same nouns, in combination with one or two epithets, make up formulae differing in metrical value from the principal types; and the number or types of formula of this kind which are represented. This will serve to show the much greater frequency of principal-type formulae.[1] |

The most important fact this table helps us to see is that the formulae in it constitute a system distinguished at once by great extension and by great simplicity. Of the 55 different formulae which there appear, only 9 are not unique in both sense and metre: *Διὸς υἱὸς Ἀπόλλων, ἑκάεργος Ἀπόλλων, ἄναξ Διὸς υἱὸς Ἀπόλλων, ἄναξ ἑκάεργος Ἀπόλλων, νεφεληγερέτα Ζεύς, Ζεὺς τερπικέραυνος, στεροπηγερέτα Ζεύς, βοῶπις πότνια Ἥρη, θεὰ λευκώλενος Ἥρη*. These equivalent formulae will be examined in their place. Outside of these 9 formulae there are 46 that cannot be replaced by any others, and these 46 do not reveal an unlimited number of metrical values. They in fact represent 7 different metrical values, those of the formulae *δῖος Ὀδυσσεύς, ἐσθλὸς Ὀδυσσεύς, πολύμητις Ὀδυσσεύς, πτολίπορθος Ὀδυσσεύς, πολύτλας δῖος Ὀδυσσεύς, Ἀλαλκομενηὶς Ἀθήνη, διογενὴς Ὀδυσσεύς*. And these 46 different unique formulae represent 723 occurrences in the poems. It is obvious that a system of formulae of this kind could not be the creation of one man: it must be wholly traditional. But there is no need to insist on this. Let us turn to that relation between hexameter and diction which explains the creation and the preservation of the system, and the way in which it is used.

A. *Noun–epithet formulae of gods and heroes in the nominative case after the bucolic diaeresis.* This formula, as Table I shows, is one of the three (the others are those that occur after the feminine and after the hephthe-

[1] As we have noted above (TE, p. 24), only the ornamental epithet can belong to a system of noun-epithet formulae. This has made necessary the exclusion from this chapter of certain particularized epithets. The way in which these particularized epithets are distinguished from fixed epithets will be explained in its place (TE, pp. 153 ff.). Here we wish to note their exclusion from this chapter merely because, as in one or two other places, we are seeking to give all the noun–epithet formulae or all the epithets of certain categories. It is proper, therefore, to list the epithets thus excluded so that the reader can recognize that their exclusion from this chapter can affect only in the slightest degree the simplicity of the several systems of noun–epithet formulae and of epithets which we shall have occasion to establish. The number of epithets in question is 14. We have excluded from Table I the formulae *Ὀδυσσεὺς πολύτροπος, Ὀδυσσεὺς Ἰθακήσιος*; from Table III the epithets *ὑπέρθυμος, πελώριος*; from the list of special epithets of heroes (TE, p. 83), *μάχης ἀκόρητον, ἀνάλκιδος, πολυμήλου, ἀγήνορι, ἔκπαγλος*; from the list of epithets of ships (TE, p. 112), *κυανοπρωιρείους, εὔπρυμνοι*; from the list of special epithets of heroines (TE, p. 97), *στυγερῆς, δολόμητις*; from the list of special epithets of peoples (TE, p. 99), *ὑπερκύδαντας*.

mimeral caesurae) | which are most likely to exist for any hero and which we encounter most frequently in reading the poems. To understand its importance, we must consider the relation between its position and the rest of the hexameter line. Between the caesura of the third foot and the bucolic diaeresis extends a portion of the line of which the metre is either ⏑ ⏑ – ⏑ ⏑ or ⏑ – ⏑ ⏑, according to whether the caesura is masculine or feminine. Both by its metre and by its position, this part of the line is particularly suitable to the verb. Its metre ends in a foot which can be either a dactyl or a spondee, usually the former, and is thus adapted to the many verb-forms ending in -*ατο*, -*ετο*, -*υτο*, -*εε*, and to imperfects and second aorists such as *ἤλυθε*, *ἤγαγε*, *κτάνε*, *ἔκλυε*, *πόρε*, *προσέστιχε*, etc., which are so abundant in Homeric Greek. On the other hand, the position of this part of the line is convenient for the verb precisely because the fourth foot is followed by the bucolic diaeresis, which allows the poet to continue the sentence or to end it as he chooses and as the sense requires. If he wishes to end it, he has to begin another a wide array of series of conjunction–noun formulae, verb–conjunction–noun formulae, etc., which we cannot discuss here, such as *αὐτὰρ* '*Ὀδυσσεύς*, *οὐ γὰρ* '*Ὀδυσσεύς*, *χαῖρε δ'* '*Ὀδυσσεύς*, *καί που* '*Ὀδυσσεύς*, *ἦρχε δ'* '*Ὀδυσσεύς*, *ὦρτο δ'* '*Ὀδυσσεύς*, etc. Or if he wishes to continue the sentence, he has at his disposal series of noun–epithet formulae which can serve either as the subject, or, in the oblique cases, as the object of the verb.

A phenomenon of the greatest importance, because it shows us how far this diction of formulae was developed, is that in the entire series of formulae following the diaeresis given in Table I, each hero and each god (except in the one case of *ἱππότα Νέστωρ* has a subject formula of appropriate metrical value beginning with a single consonant. This allows the poet to precede these formulae by a verb with one of the endings listed above. With formulae of this kind he can avoid the hiatus of a short syllable and still keep the dactylic movement desired for the fourth foot just before the bucolic diaeresis. Or in the less frequent cases when he must see a verb ending in a spondee, that is, a form like *ἁμάρτηι*, | *προσηύδα* or *ἐνίκα*, this series of noun–epithet formulae beginning with a single consonant will prevent both the hiatus of a long vowel and overlengthening, maintaining the quick movement which is especially sought for in the latter half of the line.[1] As for the portion of the line preceding

[1] The term *overlengthening* means the metrical phenomenon of a long closed syllable, i.e. a syllable which is long by nature and is also long by position. An example is the syllable -*ων* in *περίφρων Πηνελόπεια*. Such a syllable takes a perceptibly longer time to pronounce than a syllable which is long either by nature or by position, and for this reason Homer avoids it towards the end of the line where the rapidity of movement is essential to the rhythm. Thus among the many noun–epithet formulae which we have had, and shall have, occasion to cite in this volume, only three show over-lengthening at the end of the fourth foot. One we have just mentioned; the other two are *Ἀχαιῶν χαλκοχιτώνων* and *ποδάρκης δῖος Ἀχιλλεύς* (cf. TE, p. 188). See, on this subject, A. Platt, 'On Homeric Technique', *Classical Review* 1921, 143.

the caesura of the third foot, it will contain participial expressions or objects of the verb, or any part of the sentence other than the subject and the verb.

I. Among the 60 times δῖος Ὀδυσσεύς is used, there are 13 examples in which a verb fills the space between the caesura of the third foot and the bucolic diaeresis:

α 398	καὶ δμώων, οὓς μοι ληΐσσατο δῖος Ὀδυσσεύς
γ 121	ἤθελ', ἐπεὶ μάλα πολλὸν ἐνίκα δῖος Ὀδυσσεύς
ζ 217	δή ῥα τότ' ἀμφιπόλοισι μετηύδα δῖος Ὀδυσσεύς
η 230, τ 1, τ 51	αὐτὰρ ὁ ἐν μεγάρωι ὑπελείπετο δῖος Ὀδυσσεύς
θ 381	δὴ τότ' ἄρ' Ἀλκίνοον προσεφώνεε δῖος Ὀδυσσεύς
ν 63	ὣς εἰπὼν ὑπὲρ οὐδὸν ἐβήσετο δῖος Ὀδυσσεύς
υ 1	αὐτὰρ ὁ ἐν προδόμωι εὐνάζετο δῖος Ὀδυσσεύς
ω 424	Ἀντινόου, τὸν πρῶτον ἐνήρατο δῖος Ὀδυσσεύς
ω 482	ἐπεὶ δὴ μνηστῆρας ἐτίσατο δῖος Ὀδυσσεύς
Β 244	Θερσίτης· τῶι δ' ὦκα παρίστατο δῖος Ὀδυσσεύς
Τ 141	χθιζὸς ἐνὶ κλισίῃσιν ὑπέσχετο δῖος Ὀδυσσεύς

Analogous series can be found for the names of other heroes and for the names of the gods. |

	ὀρέξατο, ἐξέσσυτο, κατέκτανε, ποιήσατο, ἐκόσμει, ἀκόντισε, προσηύδα, ἠλεύατο	φαίδιμος Ἕκτωρ
(thrice)	ἐπετείλατο, ἡγήσατο, παρίστατο, μετώιχετο	Παλλὰς Ἀθήνη
	ἐχώσατο, ἐρύσατο, προσηύδα, μετηύδα, παρίστατο, ἀγάσσατο, κοτέσσατο, μυθήσατο	Φοῖβος Ἀπόλλων
	παρελέξατο	μητίετα Ζεύς

ἠμείβετο πωλέσκετο ἀνέστη ἐκέκλετο ἐπεύξατο κορύσσετο ἀνέσχετο προσηύδα τετάρπετο	δῖος Ἀχιλλεύς
προσηύδα διέπτατο καθέζετο	πότνια Ἥρη
ἀκόντισε ἐπῴχετο κιχήσατο φερέσθω |	Τυδέος υἱὸς

Just as we detected a series of subject formulae used with the predicate formula τὸν δ' ἠμείβετ' ἔπειτα (TE, p. 10), so we find series of subject formulae used with some of the verbs mentioned above. These series will not necessarily be as extensive as the series of subjects found with τὸν δ' ἠμείβετ' ἔπειτα. In many cases we find that a particular verse-form will always be used with one noun–epithet formula, as for example εὐνάζετο δῖος Ὀδυσσεύς, ἐτίσατο δῖος Ὀδυσσεύς, ἠλεύατο φαίδιμος Ἕκτωρ, etc. It is important in this matter to bear in mind the relation which must always subsist between the thought and the diction of epic poetry. The commonness of a series of verb–subject formulae such as we are seeking to establish here depends entirely on how often the poet needs to express a particular set of ideas which can, up to a point, be represented by the same words. For example, neither ἀκόντισε nor ἠλεύατο will be used to describe an act of a god, because the gods never take so active a part in the quarrels of men. Only a hero can be the subject of these two verbs. Furthermore, a hero will only be the subject when he must be actually named in order to prevent ambiguity; for the poet is not so much the prisoner of the technique as to have to use a formula where it is not appropriate. Thus we find ἀκόντισε Τυδέος υἱός (once) and ἀκόντισε φαίδιμος Ἕκτωρ (once), but ἀκόντισε δουρὶ φαεινῷ (6 times). We find ἠλεύατο φαίδιμος Ἕκτωρ (once), but ἠλεύατο χάλκεον ἔγχος (6 times). The cause of the frequency or the rarity of these formulae is clear. In the entire length of his two poems, Homer twice only had occasion to express between the penthemimeral caesura and the end of the line the idea 'X hurled his spear', and only once the idea 'X dodged the spear'. In contrast, he six times found it necessary to express in the same portion of the line the simpler idea 'he hurled his spear',[1] and six times the idea 'he dodged the | spear'. Let us take another example of the same sort. The expression *τοῦ* (*τῆς, τῶν*) *δ' ἔκλυε* is used only when a god listens to a prayer that is addressed to him. We find:

τοῦ / *τῆς* / *τῶν*	*δ' ἔκλυε*	*Παλλὰς Ἀθήνη* (4 times) *Κυανοχαίτης* *μητίετα Ζεύς* (thrice) *Φοῖβος Ἀπόλλων* (thrice) *πότνια μήτηρ.*

It is evident that this series of expressions is met with in the Homeric poems only because the poet happened on these twelve occasions to mention a prayer addressed to a god. The frequency or the rarity of a formula thus depends solely on the poet's need to express some one idea more or less often; and whereas the frequency of one expression proves it to be a formula, the rarity of another does not necessarily mean that it is original and not traditional. The significance of the following series of formulae must therefore be sought not in their extension, but in the way they form a set; this shows us the poetic device which consists in joining certain types of verbs with certain types of noun–epithet formulae. When we find, for example, that a given verb is used sometimes with one subject formula, sometimes with another, we learn that the poet could have used any subject formula beginning with a dactyl and single consonant after any verb ending with a vowel before the bucolic diaeresis. That the series are not richer and easier to find than they are is a consequence of the limited number of combinations of verb and subject expression which the poet had occasion to make with the help of this device.

The nature of Homeric diction, then, is such that anyone who wanted to point out all the circumstances without exception in which Homer made use of a given type of formula would find himself engaged in a task which would either be impossible because of its length or would at best become a valueless | enumeration of lines. Let us consider some examples from the use of the formula types in question. Among the lines in which these formulae occur, some are sufficiently alike to prove that we are dealing with a poetic device for combining the words of the sentence. For example, we find that Homer very often fills the portion of the line that extends from the caesura of the third foot to the end of the line by beginning with a verb cxtending to the end of the fourth foot, and

[1] This stylistic need to eschew the repetition of a name where it would be awkward is the cause of another artifice, a series of formulae which do no more than elaborate the idea of the verb. Examples of such formulae are *χάλκεον ἔγχος* and *δουρὶ φαεινῶι*. In the same way, alongside of *κορύσσετο δῖος Ἀχιλλεύς* we have *κορύσσετο νώροπι χαλκῶι* (twice); alongside of *ἐκέκλετο δῖος ὑφορβός, δῖα γυναικῶν, δῖος Ἀχιλλεύς* we have *ἐκέκλετο μακρὸν ἀύσας* (10 times), *ἐκέκλετο φώνησέν τε* (twice); alongside of *κόρυθ' εἵλετο φαίδιμος Ἕκτωρ* (twice) we have *λίθον εἵλετο χειρὶ παχείηι* (twice), *δορὺ δ' εἵλετο χειρὶ παχείηι, ξίφος εἵλετο χειρὶ παχείηι*, etc.

finishing the line by a subject formula. He follows προσεφώνεε by eleven different subject formulae, προσηύδα by six different subject formulae, etc., and consequently we have an abundance of examples tending to show that the poet was aware that any verb placed between the caesura of the third foot and the end of the fourth foot and ending in a vowel could be followed by any subject formula of the δῖος Ὀδυσσεύς type, and hence made use of these elements of diction whenever they could represent his thought. But what artifice of composition ought we to see in lines such as

> *A* 182 ὥς ἔμ' ἀφαιρεῖται Χρυσηΐδα Φοῖβος Ἀπόλλων

or

> σ 117 / υ 120 ὣς ἄρ' {ἔφαν / ἔφη}, χαῖρεν δὲ κλεηδόνι δῖος Ὀδυσσεύς,

lines to which we cannot find any others directly analogous? To know with certainty whether in these lines Homer was making new combinations of words, one would have to begin by examining other categories of formulae from those with which we are occupied here. In the case of the first line one would be obliged to study the verb–direct object formulae occurring between the beginning of the line and the bucolic diaeresis. In the case of the two others one would have to make a study of verb–oblique case formulae occurring between the trithemimeral caesura and the bucolic diaeresis. One would have to abandon, for no little while, the domain of what we know to be formulary, to deal with expressions less evidently related to the tradition. The present study will discuss in their place formulae of this kind containing epithets. We shall consider in detail the formulae of less frequent | type, whose presence in the poems is indicated in the last two columns of Table I. But this study of formulae of less frequent type can be carried out only after the study of principal-type formulae has provided us with indications of their character and of the way they are used. An attempt to show all the ways formulae of a given category are used would thus be to lose oneself in an endless labyrinth of investigation. We must be content with being able to show with precision, first, that each hero who plays an important role in the poems has a subject formula of a given metrical value, and second, that the poet makes use of this formula in combination with certain other words every time it is possible for him to express in this way his essential thought. We have a right to demand conclusive proof that a given formula or formula type is part of the technique of diction, but this technique itself we cannot hope to learn in its finest details.

We find in Homer:

> δῖος Ὀδυσσεύς
> δῖος ὑφορβός
> φαίδιμος υἱός (twice)

προσεφώνεε	θεῖος Ὄνειρος δῖ' Ἀφροδίτη (twice) Τεῦκρος ἀμύμων νήδυμος Ὕπνος
μετηύδα	δῖος Ὀδυσσεύς Πηνελόπεια δῖα θεάων
cf. προσηύδα	φαίδιμος Ἕκτωρ Παλλὰς Ἀθήνη Πηνελόπεια (twice) δῖα θεάων (twice) μάντις ἀμύμων δῖος Ἀχιλλεύς δῖος Ὀδυσσεύς πότνια Ἥρη (4 times) πότνια Κίρκη Φοῖβος Ἀπόλλων (twice) φαίδιμος υἱός |
παρίστατο	δῖος Ὀδυσσεύς Παλλὰς Ἀθήνη δῖα θεάων δῖος ὑφορβός Φοῖβος Ἀπόλλων πότνια μήτηρ
ἡγήσατο	Παλλὰς Ἀθήνη (thrice) δῖος Ὀδυσσεύς δῖα θεάων δῖα ὑφορβός Κυανοχαίτης
ἀνέσχετο	δῖα γυναικῶν δῖος Ἀχιλλεύς
cf. ὑπέσχετο	δῖος Ὀδυσσεύς μάντις ἀμύμων
ποιήσατο	φαίδιμος Ἕκτωρ τερπικέραυνος Κυλλοποδίων
ἐξέσσυτο	φαίδιμος Ἕκτωρ νήδυμος Ὕπνος
ἐκέκλετο	δῖος ὑφορβός δῖα γυναικῶν δῖος Ἀχιλλεύς,

and so on.

II. Another device much favoured by the poet and involving this type of noun–epithet formula consists in placing before the bucolic diaeresis a verb preceded by ὁ δ', ἡ δ', or even, if necessary, a verb preceded by ὁ δ' ἄρ', the only purpose of ἄρα (ἄρ', ἄρ, ῥ, ῥα) here, as often elsewhere, being to provide the syllable or syllables necessary to fill a metrical gap. The poet adopts this device when he needs to begin a new sentence with a new subject in the third foot. | We find:

ὁ δ' ἔγρετο
ὁ δ' ἀνείρατο
ὁ δ' ἐδείπνεε
ὁ δ' ἐπεύξατο } δῖος Ὀδυσσεύς

ὁ δ' ἄρ' ἔσθορε
ὁ δ' ἀμείβετο } φαίδιμος Ἕκτωρ

ἡ δ' ἕσπετο Παλλὰς Ἀθήνη

ὁ δ' ἐπεύξατο
ὁ δ' ἀνέσχετο } δῖος Ἀχιλλεύς

ὁ δ' ἔβραχε χάλκεος Ἄρης

Compare:

ὁ δ' ἀμείβετο { φαίδιμος Ἕκτωρ
δῖα γυναικῶν (7 times)
πότνια μήτηρ (twice)

ὁ δ' ἅμ' ἕσπετο ἰσόθεος φώς (thrice)

III. A third device is the use between the caesura of the third foot and the bucolic diaeresis of an expression made up of a verb and a direct object. Very often this direct object is a relative pronoun beginning a subordinate clause. We find:

χρόα νίζετο
δόλον ἤγαγε
ὅπα σύνθετο
οὓς κτήσατο } δῖος Ὀδυσσεύς

τὸν ἔκτανε
τήν οἱ πόρε } δῖος Ἀχιλλεύς

(thrice) τοῦ
τῶν } δ' ἔκλυε
μιν ἐφίλατο
φρένας εἵλετο| } Παλλὰς Ἀθήνη

τά οἱ πόρε χάλκεος Ἄρης

(twice) κόρυθ' εἵλετο φαίδιμος Ἕκτωρ

	τήν οἱ πόρε	
	ὅ τοι πόρε	
	στόματ' ἔτραπε	Φοῖβος Ἀπόλλων
	κυνέην βάλε	
	φόβον ἔμβαλε	
	νέφος ἤγαγε	
(twice)	κακὰ μήδετο	
	φρένας εἵλετο	μητίετα Ζεύς
	τὸ γὰρ μένε	
(thrice)	τοῦ δ' ἔκλυε	

Compare:

τά			δῖα Καλυψώ (twice)
ἅ	οἱ		παρθένος ἀδμής
τήν	σφιν	πόρε	πότνια Κίρκη
τόν	τοι		Φοῖβος Ἀπόλλων (thrice)
			χάλκεος Ἄρης
			δῖος Ἀχιλλεύς
			πότνια μήτηρ

τὸν ἔκτανε		δῖος Ἀχιλλεύς Δάρδανος ἀνήρ
δόλον νέφος	ἤγαγε	δῖος 'Οδυσσεύς Φοῖβος Ἀπόλλων
κόρυθ' εἵλετο		φαίδιμος Ἕκτωρ
φρένας εἵλετο		Παλλὰς Ἀθήνη μητίετα Ζεύς

Note also

ὁ δ' εἵλετο θεῖος ἀοιδός

IV. Formulae of this type frequently occur after a verb followed by δέ. This enables the poet to begin a sentence in the third foot and specify its subject afterwards when | the form of the verb rules out the device, considered above, of preceding the verb by ὁ δ', ἡ δ'. We find, for example:

(4 times)	νόησε δὲ	
	γήθησε δὲ	δῖος 'Οδυσσεύς
	ἡγεῖτο δὲ	
	νόησε δὲ	φαίδιμος Ἕκτωρ
	σάωσε δὲ	πότνια Ἥρη
	ἐπέρεισε δὲ	Παλλὰς Ἀθήνη
	ἀνῆκε δὲ	Φοῖβος Ἀπόλλων

Compare:

νόησε δὲ {δῖος ὑφορβός / δῖος 'Οδυσσεύς / φαίδιμος Ἕκτωρ.

V. The poet has at his disposal yet another device with which to begin in the third foot a sentence whose subject is to be specified subsequently: tmesis, with δ' inserted between the adverbial prefix and the verb. We find, for example:

ἀνὰ δ' ἵστατο / ἐπὶ δ' ὤρνυτο } δῖος 'Οδυσσεύς

ἀνὰ δ' ἥρπασε Παλλὰς Ἀθήνη

and also

ἐπὶ δ' ἴαχε λαὸς Ἀχαιῶν.

VI. In all these cases, the δῖος 'Οδυσσεύς type formula is preceded by an expression beginning at the penthemimeral caesura and containing a verb. The other most common way of using this type of formula is by putting καί or ἤ in front of it, thereby creating expressions which, as regards their function in composing the line, must be considered as conjunction–noun–epithet formulae occurring after the hephthemimeral caesura. They must be so considered because in recitation it is not possible to pause between a conjunction and a following | subject expression, so that the caesura must fall in the middle of the fourth foot. We find:

καὶ δῖος Ἀχιλλεύς (twice)
καὶ δῖος 'Οδυσσεύς (7 times)
ἢ δῖος 'Οδυσσεύς
καὶ Παλλὰς Ἀθήνη (9 times)
καὶ φαίδιμος Ἕκτωρ (7 times)
καὶ χάλκεος Ἄρης
καὶ Φοῖβος Ἀπόλλων (twice)
ἢ Φοῖβος Ἀπόλλων
καὶ μητίετα Ζεύς

etc. This formula type is preceded by expressions of various length. We find noun–epithet expressions which begin with the line:

Αἰνείας τ' Ἀγχισιάδης {καὶ φαίδιμος Ἕκτωρ / καὶ δῖος Ἀχιλλεύς
Ἀτρείδης τε ἄναξ ἀνδρῶν καὶ δῖος Ἀχιλλεύς
Γλαῦκος δ' Ἱππολόχοιο πάις καὶ Τυδέος υἱός
Ἕκτωρ τε Πριάμοιο πάις καὶ χάλκεος Ἄρης
κυανοχαῖτα Ποσειδάων καὶ φαίδιμος Ἕκτωρ
Τυδείδης τε μενεπτόλεμος καὶ δῖος 'Οδυσσεύς.

Often the preceding expression begins in the third foot:

Στρατίος καὶ δῖος Ὀδυσσεύς
Πάρις καὶ Φοῖβος Ἀπόλλων
πρόμαχοι καὶ φαίδιμος Ἕκτωρ (thrice)
Τρῶες { *καὶ φαίδιμος Ἕκτωρ* / *καὶ Παλλὰς Ἀθήνη* }
Ἄρης καὶ Παλλὰς Ἀθήνη
ἐγὼ { *καὶ δῖος Ὀδυσσεύς* / *καὶ Φοῖβος Ἀπόλλων* / *καὶ Παλλὰς Ἀθήνη* (twice). }

VII. As in the case of some other principal-type formulae, so after the bucolic diaeresis we find a secondary series of noun–epithet formulae in the nominative case. These formulae, instead of beginning with a single consonant, begin with a vowel. This makes it possible to | use them where a consonant would have made the preceding syllable long. These formulae are especially useful after verb-forms ending in *-αι*. We find, for example:

ἔμμεναι	*ὄβριμος Ἄρης*
ἀποπαύσεται *κυλίνδεται*	*ὄβριμος Ἕκτωρ*
ἀποαίνυται *κεχολώσεται*	*εὐρύοπα Ζεύς*
βιάζεται	*ὠκὺς Ἀχιλλεύς*
κοτέσσεται	*ὀβριμοπάτρη* (twice).

The infrequent use of formulae of this type is explained by the fact that verb-forms in *-εται* are much less common than verb-forms in *-ετο*, *-ατο*, *-υτο*, *-εε*, etc. Homer generally uses the aorist or imperfect tense in narration. The present tense or the future he needs only in speeches or in passages describing permanent features of the world like the gods, the use of the narrative present, so widespread in later writers, being to him quite unknown. Moreover, forms in *-εται* are by their nature not easy to handle in versification.

Other uses of this formula type are various. We note a few cases where it is preceded by a verb–object expression:

ἀφίει μένος	*ὄβριμος Ἄρης*
τελέσῃ ἔπος	*ὄβριμος Ἕκτωρ*
τιθεῖ νόον *βλάπτε φρένας*	*εὐρύοπα Ζεύς*
κτάνε Παίονας	*ὠκὺς Ἀχιλλεύς*.

B. *Noun–epithet formulae of gods and heroes in the nominative case after the hephthemimeral caesura.* This series of formulae owes its abundant usage chiefly to lines introducing speeches and containing the words προσέφη or μετέφη; some examples of these have already been quoted (TE, pp. 15–16). Before we look for their general utility in versification, we should consider to what extent this type of noun–epithet formula occurs apart from such lines. We find: |

	times employed with προσέφη or μετέφη	times employed otherwise
πολύμητις 'Οδυσσεύς	72	9
γλαυκῶπις Ἀθήνη	7	19
ἑκάεργος Ἀπόλλων	3	3
Διὸς υἱὸς Ἀπόλλων	2	—
πόδας ὠκὺς Ἀχιλλεύς	27	4
νεφεληγερέτα Ζεύς	22	8
λευκώλενος Ἥρη	2	1
κρείων Ἀγαμέμνων	10	16
κρατερὸς Διομήδης	10	2
κορυθαίολος Ἕκτωρ	10	15

Apart from the lines which introduce speeches, we find two series of formulae of this type; as in the case of the formula type previously studied, here too we have a set of expressions beginning with a single consonant, and a set of expressions beginning with a double consonant:

Beginning with a single consonant		Beginning with a double consonant	
πολύμητις 'Οδυσσεύς	9	*πτολίπορθος 'Οδυσσεύς*	4
		γλαυκῶπις Ἀθήνη	19
ἑκάεργος Ἀπόλλων	3	*κλυτότοξος Ἀπόλλων*	1
πόδας ὠκὺς Ἀχιλλεύς	4	*μεγάθυμος Ἀχιλλεύς* [cf. θ 520]	1
		νεφεληγερέτα Ζεύς	8
		Ζεὺς τερπικέραυνος	4
		στεροπηγερέτα Ζεύς	1
λευκώλενος Ἥρη	1		
κορυθαίολος Ἕκτωρ	15		
		χρυσήνιος Ἄρης	1
		κρατερὸς Διομήδης	2
		κρείων Ἀγαμέμνων	16

| In the case of formulae of this category it is clear that the bards did not feel the same need as in the case of those occurring after the fourth foot

to have a complete set of formulae beginning in the same way. One cannot make as many combinations as one would like with these noun–epithet formulae found after the hephthemimeral caesura. We have

μετὰ δὲ } γλαυκῶπις Ἀθήνη
παρὰ δὲ }

μετὰ δὲ κρείων Ἀγαμέμνων.

But you cannot make analogous expressions with the formula κορυθαίολος Ἕκτωρ. Hence it must be concluded that the influence of metre is less strongly felt here than in the case of the other formula type. Because noun–epithet formulae in this position were comparatively rare apart from lines introducing speeches, the influence of metre was less exigent, and poets were satisfied with expressions made to be used after μετέφη or προσέφη and capable of being used in the majority of other cases.

II. This type of formula also furnishes a means of beginning a new sentence in the middle of the line. Here the verb is most likely to be found in one of the lines following. We have:

φ 404 ἀτὰρ πολύμητις Ὀδυσσεύς,
. . . .
409 . . . τάνυσεν μέγα τόξον . . .

K 488 ἀτὰρ πολύμητις Ὀδυσσεύς,
. . . .
490 . . . ἐξερύσασκε,

Λ 153 ἀτὰρ κρείων Ἀγαμέμνων
αἰὲν ἀποκτείνων ἕπετ' Ἀργείοισι κελεύων.

Ψ 110 ἀτὰρ κρείων Ἀγαμέμνων
οὐρῆάς τ' ὤτρυνε καὶ ἀνέρας ἀξέμεν ὕλην

E 29 ἀτὰρ γλαυκῶπις Ἀθήνη
χειρὸς ἑλοῦσ' ἐπέεσσι προσηύδα θοῦρον Ἄρηα.

| III. Another device of the same sort is found in the use of ἀνὰ δέ, μετὰ δέ, παρὰ δέ, etc.

B 279 παρὰ δὲ γλαυκῶπις Ἀθήνη
εἰδομένη κήρυκι σιωπᾶν λαὸν ἀνώγει

B 446 μετὰ δὲ γλαυκῶπις Ἀθήνη
. . . .
450 . . . διέσσυτο

B 476 ὣς τοὺς ἡγεμόνες διεκόσμεον ἔνθα καὶ ἔνθα
ὑσμίνηνδ' ἰέναι, μετὰ δὲ κρείων Ἀγαμέμνων

ξ 268–9 = *ρ* 437–8 ἐν δὲ Ζεὺς τερπικέραυνος
φύζαν ἐμοῖς ἑτάροισι κακὴν βάλεν.

IV. Formulae of this type are sometimes preceded by a verb-form ending in a short vowel and of the metre ◡◡ – or ◡ –.

(4 times)	ἴδε δῶκε βάλε	γλαυκῶπις Ἀθήνη
cf.	ἴδεν	πολύμητις Ὀδυσσεύς
(thrice)	βάλε λάβε ἦρχε ἕλετο	κρείων Ἀγαμέμνων
	εἶχε	χρυσήνιος Ἄρης
	βάλε	πτολίπορθος Ὀδυσσεύς.

Compare:

ἕλετο ῥοδοδάκτυλος Ἠώς

Verbs ending in a long syllable can also be used before these formulae; here in the middle of the line overlengthening need not be so carefully avoided.

	ἀπέβη ἐρέειν ἕλῃι ἔχει|	κορυθαίολος Ἕκτωρ.
	ἔβη ἄγων κιὼν	πολύμητις Ὀδυσσεύς
	ἵει φιλεῖ πάθοι	ἑκάεργος Ἀπόλλων
(twice)	φιλεῖ	νεφεληγερέτα Ζεύς
	δώηι	Ζεὺς τερπικέραυνος
	προΐει καλέει ἰδὼν	κρείων Ἀγαμέμνων
	μίγη	κρατερὸς Διομήδης
	ἵει φιλέειν ἀπέβη	γλαυκῶπις Ἀθήνη
cf.	ἄγαγεν πέφνεν	πόδας ὠκὺς Ἀχιλλεύς.

Compare:

ἀπέβη	γλαυκῶπις Ἀθήνη κρατὺς Ἀργειφόντης κορυθαίολος Ἕκτωρ πόδας ὠκέα Ἶρις Τελαμώνιος Αἴας ξανθὸς Μενέλαος
οὖρον ἵει	γλαυκῶπις Ἀθήνη ἑκάεργος Ἀπόλλων
cf. προΐει	μένος Ἀλκινόοιο.

c. *Noun–epithet formulae of gods and heroes in the nominative case after the feminine caesura.* Formulae of this type have already been studied in the first chapter as an example of the usefulness of a series of noun–epithet formulae in versification. Here we can make a few remarks on the character of the part of the line preceding this type of formula. It, like the two types already studied, is usually preceded by a verb, and this verb is always | in the third person. It never happens that a character in either of the poems says, for example, 'I, much-enduring Odysseus, did such and such a thing'.[1] Hence the verb preceding an expression of the type πολύτλας δῖος Ὀδυσσεύς will almost always have the ending -ε (or more rarely -εῖτο, -ᾶτο, -ῶτο). The endings -ετο, -ατο, which we have seen to be so common before the bucolic diaeresis, do not fit here. Or if it is not a verb-form, the word preceding this type of formula is most likely to be ἔπειτα or δέ. Consequently, the next word, the first word of the formula, will in most cases have to begin with a single consonant in order that there be no hiatus and that the final syllable of the preceding word be kept short. We have already established (TE, p. 10) series of noun–epithet formulae which begin in this way. One can adduce as evidence of the controlling influence of metre the fact that of the 271 formulae of the metre in question, used of the 11 persons whose names figure in Table I, only 6 begin otherwise than with a single consonant.

Δ 8 = *E* 908	Ἥρη τ' Ἀργείη καὶ Ἀλαλκομενηὶς Ἀθήνη	
δ 173	νηυσὶ θοῇσι γενέσθαι Ὀλύμπιος εὐρύοπα Ζεύς	
E 388	καί νύ κεν ἔνθ' ἀπόλοιτο	Ἄρης ἆτος πολέμοιο.
E 863	δείσαντας· τόσον ἔβραχ'	Ἄρης ἆτος πολέμοιο.
Z 203	Ἴσανδρον δέ οἱ υἱὸν	Ἄρης ἆτος πολέμοιο.

[1] The second person is not used repeatedly except in a few lines introducing speeches:

. . . προσέφης Πατρόκλεες ἱππεῦ (thrice)
. . . προσέφης Εὔμαιε συβῶτα (15 times).

Because the metrical form of the nominatives Πάτροκλος and Εὔμαιος makes their use difficult the poet has had recourse to the artificial form Πατρόκλεες and to the second person singular of the verb.

The subject expressions contained in the lines just given should not, however, be considered part of a subordinate series as were, for example, *ὠκὺς Ἀχιλλεύς, εὐρύοπα Ζεύς*, etc. The first line is clearly traditional in its entirety, and bears a resemblance to a number of other lines in which the names of two or more gods are combined. δ 173 is in all probability the result of a comparatively unusual way of using traditional words and expressions; this is an aspect of the problem of formulae which is discussed later in this same chapter (TE, pp. 79 f.). As for the expressions for Ares, here we certainly | have an example of a case where the poet had no entirely satisfactory formulae. Thus in *E* 388 there is hiatus of a short syllable, while in *N* 521, *οὐδ' ἄρα πώ τι πέπυστο βριήπυος ὄβριμος Ἄρης*, the poet avoided hiatus, but was forced to use *βριήπυος* after a short vowel in a short syllable (for these metrical irregularities, see below, TE, pp. 70–1).

D. *Noun–epithet formulae of gods and heroes in the nominative case between the beginning of the line and the penthemimeral caesura.* These formulae, as Table I shows, are far less frequent than those of the three types just examined. They are without exception used as subject of a verb in the preceding line. For example:

β 351 εἴ ποθεν ἔλθοι
διογενὴς Ὀδυσεὺς θάνατον καὶ κῆρας ἀλύξας

ε 386 ἧος ὁ Φαιήκεσσι φιληρέτμοισι μιγείη
διογενὴς Ὀδυσεὺς θάνατον καὶ κῆρας ἀλύξας

β 365 ὁ δ' ὤλετο τηλόθι πάτρης
διογενὴς Ὀδυσεὺς ἀλλογνώτωι ἐνὶ δήμωι

K 274 τοῖσι δὲ δεξιὸν ἧκεν ἐρωδιὸν ἐγγὺς ὁδοῖο
Παλλὰς Ἀθηναίη

M 67 κακὰ φρονέων ἀλαπάζει
Ζεὺς ὑψιβρεμέτης,

etc. Compare:

Λ 299 τίνα δ' ὕστατον ἐξενάριξεν
Ἕκτωρ Πριαμίδης

Δ 488 τοῖον ἄρ' Ἀνθεμίδην Σιμοείσιον ἐξενάριξεν
Αἴας διογενής.

β. *Noun–epithet formulae of gods and heroes in the oblique cases; principal types*

One must not expect to establish for noun–epithet formulae of gods and heroes in the oblique cases any system so complete | as the one given on Table I. The names of persons in the poems are used less often in the other cases than they are in the nominative, and we are correspondingly less likely to find examples here of each of the formula types we have designated as principal. Now this is in large part due to the fact that the arrangement of words in the sentence less frequently required a formula in an oblique case that could fill the space between a metrical break and the beginning or end of a line; but it is even more due to the evident and important fact that the very existence of a formula depends entirely on its potential usefulness to the individual poet and to the whole line of epic bards. The bards had frequent need of noun–epithet formulae in the nominative case that could be used, say, after the hephthemimeral caesura; therefore it was to their interest to find an expression of that length for every hero and every god that played a role of importance in epic story. And such an expression once found, it was to the interest of other bards to borrow it without change, thereby making it an integral part of epic diction. But if a bard had found a formula of this basic length for a hero who rarely makes an appearance in the heroic world, or even if for a comparatively important hero he had found an expression in some oblique case which could be used only on rare occasions, it was much less likely that other bards would borrow these expressions, and therefore much less likely that they would pass into the tradition. In the study of traditional epic style, we should always keep before us the conception of the apprentice poet: he is essential for our understanding of the formation and preservation of the epic technique of diction. We must remember that the young poet, as he learned how to compose heroic verse by hearing other bards recite, would, when it became his turn to compose, have stored in his memory those expressions which he could frequently turn to account. This test of the usefulness of each expression would be made anew as each poet became master of his art, and it was this test that finally produced the complex technique which we find in the style of Homer. And because the poet's need thus varied from one expression or series of expressions to another, we find that the series of noun–epithet formulae in the oblique cases, unlike those in the nominative case, are often incomplete. |

There is a second reason, of an entirely different sort from the one just given, for the comparative rarity of principal-type formulae in the oblique cases: that is, the metrical impossibility of using some names with an epithet or epithets in a certain part of the line. For example, it is obvious that no noun–epithet formula containing the form *Ἀγαμέμνων* could fit after the bucolic diaeresis. In the same way, there could be no noun–epithet formulae after the feminine or the hephthemimeral caesura with the forms *Ἀγαμέμνονος*, *Ἕκτορος*, *Νέστορος*, *Ἀγαμέμνονι*, etc. The metrical values of the syllables beginning and ending these words make any such formulae impossible. When to this limitation imposed by the metre of a name we add the fact that heroic style does not admit the

Table II. NOUN–EPITHET FORMULAE OF GODS AND HEROES IN THE GENITIVE CASE; PRINCIPAL TYPES

(An asterisk * indicates that the metre of a name makes a noun–epithet formula impossible)

	Between the feminine caesura and the end of the verse ⏑ – ⏖ – ⏖ – ⊼	No.	Between the penthemimeral caesura and the end of the verse ⏖ – ⏖ – ⏖ – ⊼	No.	Between the beginning of the line and the penthemimeral caesura – ⏖ – ⏖ –	No.	Formulae found in other places	Different metres of those other formulae
Ὀδυσσῆος	Ὀδυσσῆος θείοιο	27	Λαερτιάδεω Ὀδυσῆος	12	*		32	9
Ἀθήνης	Ἀθηναίης ἀγελείης	4					4	2
Ἀπόλλωνος	ἑκηβόλου Ἀπόλλωνος Ἀπόλλωνος ἑκάτοιο	2 2	ἑκατηβόλου Ἀπόλλωνος	4	Φοίβου Ἀπόλλωνος	4	2	2
Ἀχιλλῆος	Ἀχιλλῆος θείοιο	2	Πηληιάδεω Ἀχιλῆος	8			10	8
Διός	[ἐρισθενέος Κρονίωνος] Διὸς νεφεληγερέταο	2 6	πατρὸς Διὸς αἰγιόχοιο	3	Ζηνὸς ἐριβρεμέτεω Ζηνὸς ἐριγδούπου	1 1	31	12
Ἕκτορος	*		*				16	3
Νέστορος	*		*				10	6
Ἄρηος	*						1	1
Διομήδεος	*		Διομήδεος ἱπποδάμοιο	6	*		2	2
Ἥρης							2	1
Ἀγαμέμνονος	*		Ἀγαμέμνονος Ἀτρείδαο	13	*		2	1

placing of a name between two epithetic adjectives in one line, it can be seen how the technique of noun–epithet formulae, which was created by the hexameter verse and by the high style, is at the same time severely limited by them. If, however, we find here fewer complete series of formulae of the same length, we none the less continue to find a predominance of those which fall between the caesurae and the beginning and end of the line; and we can note here too the interchange of formulae which occurs so often in the nominative case.

The noun–epithet formula between the bucolic diaeresis and the end of the line, which is so often met with and is useful in so many ways in the nominative case, does not exist in the genitive. Such formulae are obviously ruled out by the metrical value of the nouns when they are in this grammatical case. The noun–epithet formula in the genitive after the hephthemimeral caesura is hardly more common. With the names of the eleven persons listed on Tables I and II, we find only two formulae of this kind:

θείου Ὀδυσῆος (twice)
Διὸς αἰγιόχοιο (19 times).

The use of θείου Ὀδυσῆος in β 259 is without doubt traditional, as is shown by comparison with another line:

β 259 μνηστῆρες δ' ἐς δώματ' ἴσαν θείου Ὀδυσῆος
δ 621 δαιτυμόνες δ' ἐς δώματ' ἴσαν θείου βασιλῆος. |

The essential idea, 'the guests went into the house of X', must have had some currency in epic verse. In the other case,

φ 244 ἐς δ' ἄρα καὶ τὼ δμῶε ἴτην θείου Ὀδυσῆος,

we see the simple substitution of ἴτην for ἴσαν. The substitution of one verb-form for another of the same measure is an important device of formulary diction; we shall deal with this device later apropos of the inflexion of ἵκω. Διὸς αἰγιόχοιο, which might appear at first sight sufficiently frequent to be of more general usage, is even more certainly a formula designed to be used in the expression of a specific essential idea: it occurs where the poet wants to indicate kinship with Zeus. We find:

(7 times)	κούρη	Διὸς αἰγιόχοιο.
(twice)	κούρῃ	
	κούρην	
(4 times)	κοῦραι	
	υἱὸς	
	θύγατερ	

These expressions should therefore be considered as belonging to a more complex formula type which fills out the line after the penthemimeral caesura. There are only three other cases in which *Διὸς αἰγιόχοιο* is used:

> *B* 491 εἰ μὴ Ὀλυμπιάδες Μοῦσαι, Διὸς αἰγιόχοιο
> θυγατέρες
> *B* 348 πρὶν Ἄργοσδ' ἰέναι, πρὶν καὶ Διὸς αἰγιόχοιο
> *O* 175 ἦλθον δεῦρο φέρουσα παραὶ Διὸς αἰγιόχοιο.

B 491 clearly recalls the kinship formulae just quoted, and the two other lines reveal some memory of them. This question of the formula reserved for the expression of a particular idea will be dealt with further on in less summary fashion. It was necessary to insist on the point here in order to show that there are no noun–epithet formulae in the genitive case after the hephthemimeral caesura which can be used freely in different combinations, like the many which appear in the nominative. |

The all but complete absence in the genitive case of formulae of this length can be explained by the arrangement of the sentence in the hexameter line. In the first place, the abundance of these formulae in the nominative depends in large measure on the frequent occurrence of lines announcing the beginning of a speech and containing the verbs *προσέφη* or *μετέφη*. Apart from these, we have observed how the part of the line after one of the caesurae of the third foot or the hephthemimeral caesura is adapted to the verb: a subject expression can then complete both line and sentence. It is another matter altogether when a name in the genitive is to be fitted into the line, as we can see by examining the cases in which the name of Odysseus appears in the genitive. *Ὀδυσσῆος* (*Ὀδυσῆος*, *Ὀδυσσέος*, *Ὀδυσσεῦς*) appears 71 times in the poems with epithet and 72 times without. Now it is obvious that a noun appears in the genitive case under one of the four following conditions: either it depends on a verb which takes the genitive, or on another substantive, or on a preposition, or it is part of a genitive absolute construction. We find:

Governed by a verb	17 times
Depending on another substantive	120 times
In a genitive absolute	once
Governed by a preposition	5 times.

The substantive on which the genitive of the name of Odysseus depends on 120 occasions appears in various parts of the line, at the beginning, at the end, before one of the caesurae of the third foot (where it is most frequent), etc. Sometimes it is even found in the preceding or following line. But with the exception of two cases, it is not found in the part of the line following one of the caesurae of the third foot. This arrangement of the words of the sentence is almost wholly excluded because it would have resulted in an awkward line in which both the caesura of the third foot and the hephthemimeral caesura or the bucolic diaeresis would have claimed the listener's attention. A sentence containing two substantives, one a genitive depending on the other, must necessarily have a verb. If we place these elements in the order which we see, for example, in

π 104 ἐλθὼν ἐς μέγαρον Λαερτιάδεω Ὀδυσῆος

the line will be correctly articulated. There is a strong pause in the | third foot, along with other much weaker pauses elsewhere in the line. But if one were to place a substantive after the caesura, followed by another in the genitive depending on it, there would be the same strong pause after the first substantive that one feels in π 104 between μέγαρον and Λαερτιάδεω Ὀδυσῆος. If the two substantives can be separated from each other, this difficulty will of course be eliminated, and this is what the poet has in fact done in the two exceptional cases of which we spoke. In one of these, the verb is in the next line:

ρ 264 Εὔμαι', ἦ μάλα δὴ τάδε δώματα κάλ' Ὀδυσῆος,
ῥεῖα δ' ἀρίγνωτ' ἐστί.

In the other, the verb is contained in the fifth foot:

α 207 εἰ δὴ ἐξ αὐτοῖο τόσος πάις εἰς Ὀδυσῆος.

But arrangements of the words of the sentence such as these are seldom possible. Another correct arrangement would be to put the substantive on which the genitive depends in the part of the line preceding the caesura of the third foot and then to have the verb follow the caesura. But there are very few verbs of the measure ⏑ – or ⏑ ⏑ –, as was pointed out in the discussion of formulae of the type πολύμητις Ὀδυσσεύς. The only examples are the very two lines already quoted, where the feminine caesura is followed by ἴσαν or ἴτην. For like reasons, verbs governing the genitive case could not be used with noun–epithet expressions in the genitive after the hephthemimeral caesura. Hence a formula of this length, of the utmost importance in the nominative case, hardly exists at all in the genitive, because it would be of little use. It will be seen from what has been said how inexact it is to speak of the declension of noun–epithet formulae. It is wrong to assume that the bards wanted noun–epithet formulae of a particular length in all possible cases. In whatever case these formulae exist, they have metrical values dependent on their usefulness, and it is a matter of pure chance that one can sometimes arrange them in such a way as to make a paradigm in which all the cases are of the same length.

Noun–epithet formulae of gods and heroes in the genitive case after the feminine and masculine caesurae of the third foot. For the reasons discussed above, the | most common noun–epithet formulae in the genitive case are those that follow one of the caesurae of the third foot. We have already seen that in the nominative case the noun–epithet formula after the trochaic caesura of the third foot is of frequent occurrence, whereas after the penthemimeral caesura it is much more rare. This is because of the tendency of the preceding part of the line to end in a verb-form in the third person and in the past tense. It is otherwise when the genitive case follows. When this happens, the word preceding the caesura is most often the substantive on which the genitive depends. For formulae following the feminine caesura we have:

	Preceded by the substantive on which genitive depends	Preceded by the verb	Preceded by another part of speech
Ὀδυσσῆος θείοιο	21	6	—
Ἀθηναίης ἀγελείης	3	—	1
Ἀπόλλωνος ἑκάτοιο	2	—	—
ἑκηβόλου Ἀπόλλωνος	—	—	2
Ἀχιλλῆος θείοιο	—	2	—
Διὸς νεφεληγερέταο	2	3	1
ἐρισθενέος Κρονίωνος	1	—	1

For noun–epithet formulae in the genitive case following the penthemimeral caesura we have:

	Preceded by the substantive on which genitive depends	Preceded by the verb	Preceded by another part speech
Λαερτιάδεω Ὀδυσῆος	11	1	—
ἑκατηβόλου Ἀπόλλωνος	2	2	—
Πηληιάδεω Ἀχιλῆος	7	—	1
πατρὸς Διὸς αἰγιόχοιο	2	1	—
Διομήδεος ἱπποδάμοιο	3	2	1

| We can see the prevalence of the substantive before formulae of both measures in the genitive case. But the endings of substantives do not show the same regularity of metrical value as the endings of verbs in the third person past indicative. Consequently a series of formulae was needed for this purpose which could be used after forms such as στεροπή,

θεράπων, ψυχή, βίης, βίη, ἄλοχος, ἑτάρους, etc. Here we note a tendency we have already had occasion to point out: with very few exceptions, the formulae of these two series begin in the way that will provide the greatest facility of versification. All those that follow the trochaic caesura, except *Διὸς νεφεληγερέταο* and *ἑκηβόλου Ἀπόλλωνος*, begin with a vowel. In the nominative case, on the other hand, the noun–epithet formulae of this length almost all begin with a single consonant. The initial vowel in the genitive formulae is required by the *-ος, -ον, -ατ', -σιν, -ας*, etc. endings of the preceding substantives. For like reasons, noun–epithet formulae in the genitive after the penthemimeral caesura all begin with a single consonant which can make a long syllable by position when it is preceded by one of these endings.

When a verb is joined to two substantives of which one is in the genitive case and depends on the other, the result is an idea which is fairly complex and therefore likely to occur only once. This sort of concatenation of words will have fewer parallels than one consisting of subject and verb only. But when the idea is often repeated, we can clearly perceive the device of making new verses by the substitution of one formula for another. We can compare:

Β 666	*υἱέες υἱωνοί τε βίης Ἡρακληείης*	
Ε 631	*υἱός θ' υἱωνός τε Διὸς νεφεληγερέταο*	
Υ 10	*ἐλθόντες δ' ἐς δῶμα Διὸς νεφεληγερέταο*	
Δ 386	*δαινυμένους κατὰ δῶμα βίης Ἐτεοκληείης*	
θ 452	*ἐπεὶ δὴ λίπε δῶμα Καλυψοῦς ἠυκόμοιο*	
Ξ 311	*οἴχωμαι πρὸς δῶμα βαθυρρόου Ὠκεανοῖο*	
θ 287	*βῆ δ' ἴμεναι πρὸς δῶμα περικλυτοῦ Ἡφαίστοιο*	
υ 248	*ἐλθόντες δ' ἐς* }	*δώματ' Ὀδυσσῆος θείοιο* |
(4 times)	*δμώων οἳ κατὰ* }	
ρ 230	*αἴ κ' ἔλθῃι πρὸς* }	
ο 313	*καί κ' ἐλθὼν πρὸς* }	*δώματ' Ὀδυσσῆος θείοιο*
β 394	*βῆ δ' ἴμεναι πρὸς* }	
Ζ 269 }	*ἀλλὰ σὺ μὲν πρὸς νηὸν Ἀθηναίης ἀγελείης*	
Ζ 279 }		
Η 83	*καὶ κρεμόω προτὶ νηὸν Ἀπόλλωνος ἑκάτοιο*	
(thrice)	*Τηλέμαχος φίλος υἱὸς* }	
γ 398	*Τηλέμαχον φίλον υἱὸν* }	*Ὀδυσσῆος θείοιο*
ω 151	*ἔνθ' ἦλθεν φίλος υἱὸς* }	
π 395 }	*Νίσου φαίδιμος υἱὸς Ἀρητιάδαο ἄνακτος*	
σ 413 }		
α 29	*μνήσατο γὰρ κατὰ θυμὸν*	{ *ἀμύμονος Αἰγίσθοιο*
δ 187		{ *ἀμύμονος Ἀντιλόχοιο*

For noun–epithet formulae in the genitive case occurring between the penthemimeral caesura and the end of the line, we can compare:

δ 23 } δ 217 }	ὀτρηρὸς θεράπων Μενελάου κυδαλίμοιο	
Ψ 113 } Ψ 124 }	Μηριόνης θεράπων ἀγαπήνορος Ἰδομενῆος	
λ 90 } λ 387 }	ἦλθε δ' ἐπὶ ψυχὴ	Θηβαίου Τειρεσίαο Ἀγαμέμνονος Ἀτρείδαο
Ε 781	ἔστασαν ἀμφὶ βίην Διομήδεος ἱπποδάμοιο	
Ρ 24	οὐδὲ μὲν οὐδὲ βίη Ὑπερήνορος ἱπποδάμοιο.	

Noun–epithet formulae in the genitive case which extend from the beginning of the line to one of the caesurae of the third foot are usually dependent on a substantive in the preceding line. They frequently serve to end a sentence in the middle of the line.

The poet has even less often occasion to use the dative and accusative cases of the names of his characters than he does the genitive. Of the 687 times he mentions the name of Odysseus, the | name is only 42 times in the dative case, and of these 42 times, an epithet is used in only 13. The accusative is used only 74 times, 27 with an epithet. If the same were true of the names of other characters, it would very likely be possible, even with a usage as infrequent as this, to perceive with some clarity series of formulae of the same length. But even a hero of the importance of Achilles is mentioned with an epithet only 11 times in the dative case, and only 17 times in the accusative. The name of Apollo appears in conjunction with an epithet but 7 times in the dative case and 4 times in the accusative. Hence it is hardly possible, in these two cases, to determine the existence of series of formulae. The traditional character of the principal-type formulae in these cases will be easier to understand later when we discuss the question of analogy and choice of epithet.

In the vocative case one fairly common type of noun–epithet formula may be noted: the formula that fills a whole line. We find, for example:

θ 382	Ἀλκίνοε κρεῖον, πάντων ἀριδείκετε λαῶν (6 times)
Η 47	Ἕκτορ, υἱὲ Πριάμοιο, Διὶ μῆτιν ἀτάλαντε (twice)
α 45	ὦ πάτερ ἡμέτερε Κρονίδη, ὕπατε κρειόντων (thrice)
Β 434	Ἀτρείδη κύδιστε, ἄναξ ἀνδρῶν Ἀγάμεμνον (8 times)
Ρ 12	Ἀτρείδη Μενέλαε διοτρεφές, ὄρχαμε λαῶν (7 times)
Π 21	ὦ Ἀχιλεῦ, Πηλῆος υἱέ, μέγα φέρτατ' Ἀχαιῶν (thrice)
ε 203	διογενὲς Λαερτιάδη, πολυμήχαν' Ὀδυσσεῦ (22 times)
Κ 87	ὦ Νέστορ Νηληιάδη, μέγα κῦδος Ἀχαιῶν (6 times).

§ 2. NOUN–EPITHET FORMULAE OF GODS AND HEROES; LESS FREQUENT TYPES

In the study of noun–epithet formulae we have hitherto confined our attention to the clearly defined elements of a system. We have considered only those types of formula which, because they exactly fill an articulated part of the hexameter line, can be of general usage in the composition of heroic poetry. It being once established, as we have said, that certain formulae of the same length occur regularly under similar circumstances, and that of these none are equivalent in both sense and metre, we have a right to assume that these formulae are part of a traditional system. This was demonstrated | by a comparison with hexametric poems by authors whose diction was individual. By using this criterion, we were able to relate to a single system most of the noun–epithet formulae of certain major characters in the nominative case, as can be seen by comparing the figures in the last two columns of Table I with the figures in the other columns. But there still remains a considerable number of formula types that cannot be classified in this way, the examples in which similar formulae of a given length appear being too few to enable us to see in them formula types of general usage. These less frequent formula types fall into two categories. The first category includes noun–epithet formulae in which the epithet does not combine with the substantive to make a formula of a particular length, but rather by itself fills a distinct portion of the line, especially the portions extending from the caesurae of the third foot to the bucolic diaeresis and from this to the end of the line. The second category contains noun–epithet formulae designed to express more or less specific ideas, ideas unlike others in the poems and therefore needing more or less special words and arrangements of words.

a. Epithets used independently of a noun–epithet formula of a fixed metrical value

Formulae of the first category clearly belong to the tradition, since they are used with the same abundance which helped us to distinguish principal-type noun–epithet formulae. The poet often finds it necessary to fill the space between one of the caesurae of the third foot and the bucolic diaeresis or the end of the line, or between the bucolic diaeresis and the end of the line, either so that other words can occupy their usual positions, or so that he can prolong his sentence and end it at the point at which he wants to begin another. This device is available only because certain epithets can be used to describe any god or any hero. There is an important distinction to be made between these epithets, which can be called *generic*, and the others, which can | be used for only one god or one hero, and should be called *distinctive*. Distinctive epithets are Φοῖβος, γλαυκῶπις, νεφεληγερέτα, πολύμητις, ποδάρκης, πολύτλας, etc. Among generic epithets are: λαοσσόος, which is said of Athena (*N* 128), Ares (*P* 398), Eris (*Υ* 48), Apollo (*Υ* 79), and Amphiaraus (*ο* 244); θεοειδής, which is said of 14 heroes; δαΐφρονος, which is said of 15 heroes; ἀμύμονος, which is said of 12 heroes, etc. The generic epithets which can fill the portions of the line indicated have rigorously fixed positions, so much so that they clearly must have had, for the poets who used them, an existence independent of any particular type of noun–epithet formula. So *δουρικλυτός* (18 times), *δαΐφρονος* (26 times), *ἀμύμονος* (37 times) always come before the bucolic diaeresis; and *ἰσόθεος φώς* (14 times), *κυδαλίμοιο* (20 times), etc., only come at the end of the line.

I. It is easy to see that if the poet can put the name of a hero in the part of the line preceding the penthemimeral caesura, he can, if the other elements of the sentence allow it, follow this part of the line with *δουρικλυτός* and then finish the line with the help of one of the numerous expressions of different sorts which come after the diaeresis, especially verb-formulae. There are three lines in which Odysseus is called *δουρικλυτός*:

Λ 396	*ὣς φάτο, τοῦ δ' Ὀδυσεὺς δουρικλυτὸς ἐγγύθεν ἐλθών*
Λ 401	*οἰώθη δ' Ὀδυσεὺς δουρικλυτός, οὐδέ τις αὐτῶι*
Λ 661 = *Π* 26	*οὔτασται δ' Ὀδυσεὺς δουρικλυτὸς ἠδ' Ἀγαμέμνων.*

The first of these lines can be compared with others resembling it:

Ξ 446	*τὸν μὲν Ὀιλιάδης δουρικλυτὸς ἐγγύθεν ἐλθών*
Ε 72	*τὸν μὲν Φυλείδης δουρικλυτὸς ἐγγύθεν ἐλθών*
ρ 71	*τοῖσι δὲ Πείραιος δουρικλυτὸς ἐγγύθεν ἦλθε.*

In *Λ* 401 the poet stops the sentence at the diaeresis. He does the same in:

N 476 *ὣς μένεν Ἰδομενεὺς δουρικλυτός, οὐδ' ὑπεχώρει.*

We can find no other line which, like *Λ* 661, ends with a conjunction and a name; but it must be | only by chance that more such lines do not appear in the *Iliad* and the *Odyssey*. The use of this epithet is so various that we can be quite sure that the poet composed the line after the pattern of many others in which *δουρικλυτός* appeared in the same position. Consider the other ways in which he used the word. Most often he finished the line with a form of a verb:

Β 645	*Κρητῶν δ' Ἰδομενεὺς δουρικλυτὸς ἡγεμόνευεν*
Β 650	*τῶν μὲν ἄρ' Ἰδομενεὺς δουρικλυτὸς ἡγεμόνευε*
Β 657	*τῶν μὲν Τληπόλεμος δουρικλυτὸς ἡγεμόνευεν*
N 210	*Ἰδομενεὺς δ' ἄρα οἱ δουρικλυτὸς ἀντεβόλησεν*
N 467	*τὸν δέ τοι Ἰδομενεὺς δουρικλυτὸς ἐξενάριξεν*
Ψ 681	*τὸν μὲν Τυδείδης δουρικλυτὸς ἀμφεπονεῖτο.*

Other lines in which we come across this epithet are:

Ε 45	*τὸν μὲν ἄρ' Ἰδομενεὺς δουρικλυτὸς ἔγχει μακρῶι*
ο 544	*τὸν δ' αὖ Πείραιος δουρικλυτὸς ἀντίον ηὔδα*
Π 472	*τοῖο μὲν Αὐτομέδων δουρικλυτὸς εὕρετο τέκμωρ*
Π 619	*τὸν δ' αὖ Μηριόνης δουρικλυτὸς ἀντίον ηὔδα*
Φ 233	*ἦ, καὶ Ἀχιλλεὺς μὲν δουρικλυτὸς ἔνθορε μέσσωι.*

II. διίφιλος fulfils the same function after the feminine caesura as does δουρικλυτός after the masculine. It is used for Odysseus:

K 527	ἔνθ' Ὀδυσεὺς μὲν ἔρυξε διίφιλος ὠκέας ἵππους,

for Achilles:

Σ 203	αὐτὰρ Ἀχιλλεὺς ὦρτο διίφιλος· ἀμφὶ δ' Ἀθήνη,

and for Hector:

N 674	Ἕκτωρ δ' οὐκ ἐπέπυστο διίφιλος, οὐδέ τι ᾔδη
Z 318	ἔνθ' Ἕκτωρ εἰσῆλθε διίφιλος, ἐν δ' ἄρα χειρί
Θ 493	τόν ῥ' Ἕκτωρ ἀγόρευε διίφιλος· ἐν δ' ἄρα χειρί
K 49	ὅσσ' Ἕκτωρ ἔρρεξε διίφιλος υἷας Ἀχαιῶν.

III. ἱπποδάμοιο has the same function after the bucolic diaeresis. With δαΐφρονος it forms a half-line. It is instructive to observe how the poet used the one formula or the other, or both at once, according to the demands of versification.

B 23 = 60	εὕδεις, Ἀτρέος	υἱὲ δαΐφρονος ἱπποδάμοιο
Δ 370	ὤ μοι, Τυδέος,	
Λ 450	ὦ Σῶχ', Ἱππάσου	
Θ 152	ὤ μοι, Τυδέος υἱὲ δαΐφρονος, οἷον ἔειπες	
Σ 18	ὤ μοι, Πηλέος υἱὲ δαΐφρονος, ἦ μάλα λυγρῆς	
H 38	Ἕκτορος ὄρσωμεν κρατερὸν μένος ἱπποδάμοιο.	

IV. This way of using epithets is not confined to those which exactly fill the line between a caesura and the bucolic diaeresis or between one of these and the line-end. They are the most common, because it is greatly to the poet's advantage to have words ending at the bucolic diaeresis or at the end of the line. βοὴν ἀγαθός, which extends past the bucolic diaeresis, serves a like purpose, although its use in this way is only twice attested in the poems:

	N 123	Ἕκτωρ δὴ παρὰ νηυσὶ βοὴν ἀγαθὸς πολεμίζει
	O 249	οὓς ἑτάρους ὀλέκοντα βοὴν ἀγαθὸς βάλεν Αἴας
Cf.	*P* 102	εἰ δέ που Αἴαντός γε βοὴν ἀγαθοῖο πυθοίμην.

V. μεγάθυμος serves in the same way before the feminine caesura:

O 440	τὸν δ' Ἕκτωρ μεγάθυμος ἀπέκτανε. ποῦ νύ τοι ἰοί
Λ 459	Τρῶες δὲ μεγάθυμοι ὅπως ἴδον αἷμ' Ὀδυσῆος
Z 145	Τυδεΐδη μεγάθυμε, τίη γενεὴν ἐρεείνεις;

There is no point in accumulating more examples. We note the use of δαΐφρων for Achilles in *B* 875; of ἀρήιος for the same hero in *Π* 166; of βροτολοιγῶι ἶσος Ἄρηι for Hector in *Λ* 295 and *N* 802. λαοσσόος is possibly the only epithet of this kind which we find used for the gods. Other epithets of heroes used in this fashion are the following:

Between the penthemimeral caesura and the bucolic diaeresis: *πεπνυμένος, θεοείκελος, μεγαλήτορος, δουρικλυτόν, θεοείκελον, μεγαθύμου, μεγαλήτορι, μεγαθύμωι, μεγαλήτορα*; between the feminine caesura and the bucolic diaeresis: *ἀρήιον, ἀγακλυτόν, ἀμύμονος, ἀμύμονα, δαΐφρονι, δαΐφρονα, διίφιλε*; between the bucolic diaeresis and the end of the line: *ἰσόθεος φώς, κυδαλίμοιο, ποιμένι λαῶν, ποιμένα λαῶν, ὄρχαμος ἀνδρῶν, ἀντιθέοιο, ὄρχαμε λαῶν.* |

VI. The device of using an epithet alone to fill a distinct part of the line would in all likelihood never have come into being without the generic epithet. But once it had become current, once poets had grown familiar with the several possibilities of its use, they began to treat specific epithets in the same way, choosing those which, like the majority of generic epithets, extend between a caesura and the bucolic diaeresis, or between the latter and the line-end. Such a use in Homer is that of *Νηλήιος*, which can apply to Nestor and to his sons:

Ψ 349 ὣς εἰπὼν Νέστωρ Νηλήιος ἂψ ἐνὶ χώρηι
Ψ 514 τῶι δ' ἄρ' ἐπ' Ἀντίλοχος Νηλήιος ἴλασεν ἵππους.

We can compare the latter line with another in which the poet preferred to fill the same space with an epithet qualifying the horses instead of using *διίφιλος*, as he often does in similar situations:

P 614 εἰ μὴ Κοίρανος ὦκα ποδώκεας ἤλασεν ἵππους.

VII. The poet makes use of essentially the same device when he comes upon a hero's name itself able to fill the space between the penthemimeral caesura and the bucolic diaeresis, and inverts the usual word-order, putting the epithet in the first half of the line:

E 151 ἀλλά σφεας κρατερὸς Διομήδης ἐξενάριξε
Λ 246 δή τότε γ' Ἀτρείδης Ἀγαμέμνων ἐξενάριξε.

These lines may be compared with:

N 467 τὸν δέ τοι Ἰδομενεὺς δουρικλυτὸς ἐξενάριξεν.

We now arrive at that area of formulary diction in which it becomes more difficult to distinguish between what is certainly traditional and what could be a single poet's original creation. Noun–epithet formulae designed for the expression of some more or less particular idea do not by definition make up sets of analogous cases, and may even not conform to standard measures. One might be tempted to conclude from this that they are due to Homer's | originality. But a closer examination of the circumstances under which epic diction developed will show that the singularity of a formula is no proof that it is not traditional.

β. Formulary diction and the operation of analogy

We must once more return, as we have done so many times already, to the relation between the ideas of epic poetry and the words which express them. It was the constant tendency of epic diction to make the expression of the ideas of heroic poetry as simple and as easy as possible, and to this end it employed the means of analogy, only abandoning it when the complexity of the ideas to be expressed made its use no longer feasible. In more definite terms: the bards, always trying to find for the expression of each idea in their poetry a formula at once noble and easy to handle, created new expressions—in so far as the result was compatible with their sense of heroic style—in the simplest way possible: they modified expressions already in existence. To this process are due all the series of formulae which we have so far examined. In each of these series it would be pointless to look for the original or the oldest formula. But in every case there must have been an original expression from which the series was produced by the system of imitation we call analogy. Analogy is perhaps the single most important factor for us to grasp if we are to arrive at a real understanding of Homeric diction. To understand the role of analogy in the formation of epic language is to understand the interdependence of words, ideas, and metre in heroic poetry. It is to see to what extent the hexameter and the genius of the bards influenced epic style. And finally, it is to recognize that there are limits beyond which analogy could no longer advance the simplification of the technique, so that some formulae remained more or less unexampled.

Philologists have long recognized that formal associations | bring about changes in the spoken language and thus constitute one of the most important causes of the continual modification of language. They were more reluctant to recognize that this linguistic process found in the literary language of epic poets a realm in which it could operate in a fashion unknown to any spoken language; that the desire of bards to possess 'alien' forms for the embellishment of their style and also to have forms adapted to the mould of the hexameter was in large part realized by the means of analogy. Ellendt, who with Düntzer was the first to explain the influence of metre on Homeric forms in a methodical fashion, does not stress the role of analogy, the importance of which was not yet fully perceived by the philologists of his time; but most of the examples which he cites are cases of analogy. To say, for example, that the influence of metre determined the masculine ending of an adjective where we should expect the feminine, or that, for the same reason, an adjective has sometimes two endings and sometimes three, is to say that the poet created new forms on the model of old forms. Linguistic science did not come early to this explanation of certain Homeric forms, although it did recognize that certain forms and constructions could never have belonged to a spoken dialect of Greek. Only with K. Witte did scholars begin to have recourse to analogy in order to explain the use of the singular for the plural and vice versa, overlengthened forms, *εἴσω* with the genitive, etc. His demonstration, as our knowledge now stands, leaves no doubt of the general truth of his conclusions: animated by the desire to find forms that would fit the hexameter, the bards created new forms on the model of those already in existence.

It is quite obvious, so much so that there is no need to insist on it, that analogy, operating in the same way as with artificial forms, is responsible for the creation of the whole formulary element which has been pointed out in these pages. The simple perception of a resemblance between two expressions too close to be the work of chance is equivalent to an admission that one of these expressions is imitating the other or that both of them are, in the last analysis, imitating a single model. But we are not fully aware of the influence which the factor of | analogy must have exerted on the minds of epic poets until we observe that it is the cause of a great number of the anomalies of versification found in the *Iliad* and the *Odyssey*. The poet often allowed himself to be guided by his sense of the likeness of one expression to another, even though this forced him to leave final vowels in hiatus or to make position for short vowels *ἐν θέσει*.

K. Witte brought attention to the case in which Homer, on the model of *μερόπων ἀνθρώπων*, which we find 9 times in the text, created *μέροπες ἄνθρωποι*, which we find in *Σ* 288. The habit of bringing together two words in a certain place in the line led the poet to be careless of the fault in quantity incident to their use in the nominative. In the same way Homer, or another bard, made *οὖλε Ὄνειρε* after *οὖλον Ὄνειρον*; *ἄφθιτα αἰεί* after *ἄφθιτος αἰεί*; *τετελεσμένα ἦεν* after *τετελεσμένον ἔσται*, etc., just as he also, still deferring to habit, put certain formulae in certain places in the line, even when the following formula produced hiatus or did not make position. Examples of this kind are plentiful; we can here cite only some of the most striking of those that involve noun–epithet formulae.

I. We discovered, in Chap. I (TE, pp. 10–13), substantial series of lines in which a predicate formula, ending at the feminine caesura with a vowel, is followed by a subject formula beginning with a consonant which completes the line. The habit of using this kind of line had such a hold over the poet's thought that he sometimes began with a predicate hemistich of the type described when he did not have the requisite, subject hemistich beginning with a single consonant. The only subject formula for Telemachus which can stand after the feminine caesura is Ὀδυσσῆος φίλος υἱός, correctly used in lines like

β 2 ὄρνυτ' ἄρ' ἐξ εὐνῆφιν Ὀδυσσῆος φίλος υἱός
γ 352 οὔ θην δὴ τοῦδ' ἀνδρὸς Ὀδυσσῆος φίλος υἱός.

But the poet was obliged to leave hiatus when, on the model of such lines as

τ 102 } ἔνθα καθέζετ' ἔπειτα { πολύτλας δῖος Ὀδυσσεύς
τ 59 } { περίφρων Πηνελόπεια,

he wanted to make an analogous line for the son of Odysseus:

π 48 ἔνθα καθέζετ' ἔπειτα Ὀδυσσῆος φίλος υἱός.

Again, on the model of

η 1 ὣς ὁ μὲν ἔνθ' ἠρᾶτο πολύτλας δῖος Ὀδυσσεύς,

the poet made

γ 64 ὣς δ' αὔτως ἠρᾶτο Ὀδυσσῆος φίλος υἱός.

In composing

B 571 Ὀρνειάς τ' ἐνέμοντο Ἀραιθυρέην τ' ἐρατεινήν

the poet was remembering lines such as

B 496 οἵ θ' Ὑρίην ἐνέμοντο καὶ Αὐλίδα πετρήεσσαν
B 519 οἳ Κυπάρισσον ἔχον Πυθῶνά τε πετρήεσσαν,

and so on.

II. We have already observed the tendency of verb-forms in -ετο, -ατο, -εε, etc. to occur before the bucolic diaeresis. διέπτατο (thrice), ἐπέπτατο (thrice), and ὑπέρπτατο (4 times) occur always in this position. Now a very common way of completing a line after such verb-forms is to follow them by a subject formula beginning with a single consonant. Thus the line *O* 83 is metrically correct:

ὣς κραιπνῶς μεμαυῖα διέπτατο πότνια Ἥρη.

The existence of lines like this one and of this one in particular suggested to the poet further on, when he is speaking of Iris, an analogous line, even though he disposed of no formula beginning in the requisite way to designate this goddess:

O 172 ὣς κραιπνῶς μεμαυῖα διέπτατο ὠκέα Ἶρις.

The expression ἱερὰ καλά is found with hiatus in *Ψ* 195; 4 times correctly elsewhere in the poems. We find before a caesura of the third foot

δ 473 ῥέξας ἱερὰ κάλ'
λ 130 ῥέξας ἱερὰ καλά

and at the line-end

Ψ 209 ἐλθεῖν ἀρᾶται, καὶ ὑπίσχεται ἱερὰ καλά
Λ 727 ἔνθα Διὶ ῥέξαντες ὑπερμενεῖ ἱερὰ καλά. |

At the same time the form ὑπέσχετο (10 times) occurs always before the bucolic diaeresis. His sense of the expression ἱερὰ καλά at the end of the line, of ὑπέσχετο before the diaeresis, and in addition of the whole line Ψ 209 led the poet to make

Ψ 195 Βορέῃ καὶ Ζεφύρωι, καὶ ὑπίσχετο ἱερὰ καλά.

III. A great many cases where the poet uses a short syllable ἐν θέσει without making position are to be similarly explained. One of the clearest examples is

ω 494 αἶψα δ' Ὀδυσσῆα ἔπεα πτερόεντα προσηύδα,

made on the model of

Θ 351 = Τ 341 αἶψα δ' Ἀθηναίην } ἔπεα πτερόεντα προσηύδα.
π 7 = ρ 543 αἶψα δ' ἄρ' Εὔμαιον }

A more complex but equally certain case is

λ 322 κούρην Μίνωος ὀλοόφρονος, ἥν ποτε Θησεύς.

ὀλοόφρονος is found in this position in two other lines:

α 52 Ἄτλαντος θυγάτηρ ὀλοόφρονος, ὅς τε θαλάσσης
κ 137 αὐτοκασιγνήτη ὀλοόφρονος Αἰήταο.

At the same time the poet commonly refers to a woman by κούρη followed by the name of her father. At the beginning of the line we find κούρη Ἰκαρίοιο (5 times), κούρην Βρισῆος, κούρην δὲ Πριάμοιο. It is the combined example of this expression at the beginning of the line, of ὀλοόφρονος before the diaeresis, and of lines like the two quoted that determined the arrangement of words which we see in λ 322.

These cases of hiatus and of short syllables ἐν θέσει are of interest in the study of metrics, but they can only furnish hints of the influence exerted by analogy in epic versification. But the examination of cases in which the operation of analogy produced, not metrical irregularities, but the very ideas of heroic poetry will throw light on one of the most fundamental problems of formulary diction, a problem which no study of formulae can leave in darkness: | that of the relation between the influence of metre and the thought of epic poets. Possibly the greatest risk one runs in the study of traditional diction is that one may give the impression that the action of metre on diction is something mechanical.

Many critics, from the days of Ellendt and Düntzer to our own, have wanted to deny the sovereign influence of the hexameter because they thought that to admit it would be to attaint the personal genius of Homer.

The cause of this misunderstanding, on the part of those who have studied the influence of metre as well as on the part of those who would deny it, is an insufficiently clear conception of the actual circumstances under which this diction of formulae developed. If we do not take account of the processes by which the bards were led to create a formulary diction, we shall fail to see, or shall see only imperfectly, that its creation was both natural and aesthetically unexceptionable. Analogy is a case in point. If we do not fully recognize the psychological value which it had for the poets of epic verse, we shall not know to what extent it operated together with their taste to contribute to the formation of the style of the *Iliad* and the *Odyssey*.

One discovers in Homer not a few cases in which the sounds of one expression have suggested another quite different in meaning. One of the most striking examples of this is the resemblance between the two expressions ἀμφήλυθεν ἡδὺς ἀυτμή (μ 369) and ἀμφήλυθε θῆλυς ἀυτή (ζ 122), a resemblance too close to be the work of chance. It is impossible to know which of these two expressions is the older. But it is not necessary to know this in order to draw the following conclusions: whichever of the two formulae one chooses as the model of the other, these conclusions will be the same. Let us imagine a poet familiar with the formula ἀμφήλυθεν ἡδὺς ἀυτμή who wishes to describe a scene in which one of his characters hears the shouting of women. It is a most likely assumption that the word ἀυτή immediately occurred to him to describe this shouting. At the thought of this word, the poet, with that sense of metre which all poets working in a rigorously fixed form must possess, as he looked for words to express himself, will at once have thought of ἀυτμή, and this | word will have evoked for him the expression used in the description of a sacrifice: ἀμφήλυθεν ἡδὺς ἀυτμή. ἀμφήλυθε, used to describe the odour of sacrifice as it spreads through the air, is also suitable for the description of a sound that seems to fill the air. And ἡδύς suggested θῆλυς because of the identity of the vowels and the final consonant in the two words; the latter word itself could not have been far from the poet's mind, since 'the shouting of women' was the idea to be expressed. That the point of departure for this association of words and ideas was ἀυτή and ἀυτμή is of course not entirely certain. It is equally possible that ἀμφήλυθε first reminded the poet of the original expression. But in any case the mental process of the bard who created the expression is plain. The words for which he was looking in order to express his thought in the hexameter were suggested to him by the resemblance of the sound of words. ἀμφήλυθεν ἡδὺς ἀυτμή was the model for ἀμφήλυθε θῆλυς ἀυτή, but before he imitated the model, the poet must have had the desire to express a particular idea. And even after the new expression had presented itself to him, he still had the right to reject it and look for other words. There must be a fairly large number of different ways to express in hexameter verse the essential idea 'he heard the shouting of women'. But the bard did not seek out those different ways, or else, after considering some of them, he came back to the expression which a pun had suggested to him and with which he was satisfied. The same is true in all cases where the influence of the hexameter can be discerned. It must on the one hand be recognized that this influence was entirely subordinate to the taste of the poets; but it is on the other hand just as certain that without this influence, the diction of epic poetry, that is its style, would have been something very different from what we know.

In the case we have just been examining, and in all cases like it, we must be on our guard against a common error. It is highly improbable, even if it be assumed that the two poems we have are entirely the work of a single author, that one of the expressions in question was inspired by Homer's memory of another expression in the *Iliad* or *Odyssey*. The point is not so much that Homer must have composed a great deal of verse which we do not have, as that we can assign to the work of one poet only a fraction of the lines in which | this influence of sound in the formation of ideas can be discerned. In most of the following examples the two formulae will have been handed down in their present form by the tradition.

We cannot ascertain which expression in each of the pairs cited below is the older. What is important is only the certain fact that either one or the other of them was inspired by a pun.[1]

Λ	306	λαίλαπι τύπτων	μ	400	λαίλαπι θύων
Λ	466	ἵκετ' ἀυτή	*Ξ*	174	ἵκετ' ἀυτμή
A	48	ἕζετ' ἔπειτ' ἀπάνευθε νεῶν	ζ	236	ἕζετ' ἔπειτ' ἀπάνευθε κιών
A	464	αὐτὰρ ἐπεὶ κατὰ μῆρ' ἐκάη	*I*	212	αὐτὰρ ἐπεὶ κατὰ πῦρ ἐκάη
φ	411	χελιδόνι εἰκέλη αὐδήν	χ	240	χελιδόνι εἰκέλη ἄντην
α	242	οἴχετ' ἄιστος ἄπυστος	δ	788	κεῖτ' ἄρ' ἄσιτος ἄπαστος
K	306	θοῇς ἐπὶ νηυσὶν Ἀχαιῶν	*Σ*	259	θοῇς ἐπὶ νηυσὶν ἰαύων
α	29	κατὰ θυμὸν ἀμύμονος	κ	50	κατὰ θυμὸν ἀμύμονα
Υ	61	ἄναξ ἐνέρων Ἀιδωνεύς	*A*	172	ἄναξ ἀνδρῶν Ἀγαμέμνων, etc.
I	402	Ἴλιον ἐκτῆσθαι, εὖ ναιόμενον πτολίεθρον	*B*	133	Ἴλιον ἐκπέρσαι εὖ ναιόμενον πτολίεθρον

[1] The first five examples are cited by Ellendt (*Drei homerische Abhandlungen*, Leipzig 1864, 50–2). In citing various lines to show the influence of metre, he confuses expressions of the kind we are discussing with others which are only examples of the device of interchanging formulae which we examined in the first part of this chapter. It must be observed that some of his examples are based on puns which are doubtful to say the least. It takes an adventurous mind to see a proof of analogy in such comparisons as ὃς πᾶσι ∼ ἱππεῦσι or ἐπεὶ ∼ ἐπ' ἡ- .

Σ	358	*ἀνστήσασ' Ἀχιλῆα πόδας ταχύν· ἦ ῥά νυ σεῖο*	*Σ*	2	*Ἀντίλοχος δ' Ἀχιλῆι πόδας ταχὺς ἄγγελος ἦλθε*
P	9	*Πάνθου υἱὸς ἐυμμελίης ἀμέλησε*	*P*	59	*Πάνθου υἱὸν ἐυμμελίην Εὔφορβον*
Ψ	744	*ἐπ' ἠεροειδέα πόντον*	*μ*	233	*πρὸς ἠεροειδέα πέτρην*
P	73	*ἀνέρι εἰσάμενος, Κικόνων ἡγήτορι Μέντηι*	*α*	105	*εἰδομένη ξείνωι, Ταφίων ἡγήτορι Μέντηι*[1]
ξ	329	*πίονα δῆμον*	*Ψ*	750	*πίονα δημῶι.* |

Analogy, which was a factor of such importance in the formation of diction, tended always to lead it in the direction of a greater simplification in the expression of essential ideas. By excluding the new or original expression which could be rendered by a traditional formula, it inclined the poets to express every new idea, wherever possible, by words resembling the words used to express some similar idea. The series of noun–epithet formulae cited in the first part of this chapter show how analogy was able to establish a fixed manner of expressing certain actions of gods and heroes. The reasons why it was not possible to establish similar series for every type of noun–epithet formula will become clear once it has been shown that there were limits beyond which analogy could no longer introduce simplification. There were two obstacles: the variety of the metrical value of words, and the complexity of the essential ideas which the bards had to express in their verse. It is a consequence of these two factors that, although we sometimes find series of formulae which are amenable to detailed analysis, Homeric diction, even in the matter of noun–epithet formulae, remains something so complex as to put a complete analysis of its technique beyond our powers.

It was said earlier that some names in the nominative or the oblique cases cannot be used in noun–epithet formulae of certain lengths. It is true that in cases of this kind the poet can try to paraphrase the name of the hero. For *Διομήδης*, Homeric diction offers *Τυδέος υἱός*, which appears in the *Iliad* eight times after the bucolic diaeresis and is thus adapted to the many occasions which require a subject formula of a hero in this position. But the name of the father of Agamemnon and Menelaus does not begin with a single consonant, and the bards found no other expression which might replace *Ἀτρέος υἱός*. But this formula, because it begins with a vowel, is far less useful. Hence despite the great convenience in general of noun–epithet | formulae in the nominative case filling this

[1] By an association of sounds such as this the bards at times introduced forms of one verb into the inflexion of another in which they could never have existed. Thus *ἐείσατο*, which properly belongs to the inflexion of *εἴδεται*, is in *χ* 89 and *O* 415 made part of the inflexion of *εἶμι*. Cf. K. Meister, *Die homerische Kunstsprache*, 19–21.

position, Ἀτρέος υἱός is found, in the nominative, only once in all Homer after the bucolic diaeresis:

P 79 τόφρα δέ τοι Μενέλαος ἀρήιος Ἀτρέος υἱός.[1]

When it came time to relate an action of one of the sons of Atreus, Homer had to do without the devices which had served so well with δῖος Ὀδυσσεύς, δῖος Ἀχιλλεύς, and other subject formulae of like metrical value.

The names of the fathers of certain heroes likewise furnished expressions in the vocative case filling the space between the beginning of the second foot and the feminine caesura. One of the poet's habitual devices is to use one of these expressions to summon a hero after putting an exclamation or an imperative, or the like, in the first foot. We find:

Δ 370	ὤ μοι, Τυδέος υἱὲ δαΐφρονος ἱπποδάμοιο
Θ 152	ὤ μοι, Τυδέος υἱὲ δαΐφρονος, οἷον ἔειπες
K 159	ἔγρεο, Τυδέος υἱέ· τί πάννυχον ὕπνον ἀωτεῖς;
B 23 = 60	εὕδεις, Ἀτρέος υἱὲ δαΐφρονος ἱπποδάμοιο
Z 46, *Λ* 131	ζώγρει, Ἀτρέος υἱέ, σὺ δ' ἄξια δέξαι ἄποινα[2]
Σ 18	ὤ μοι, Πηλέος υἱὲ δαΐφρονος, ἦ μάλα λυγρῆς.

Neither for Odysseus nor for Ajax does Homer seem to know formulae that might be used in lines such as these, and so in their case he had to do without this device. Table II shows other cases of this kind in which names of heroes in the genitive case cannot be used in certain types of formula. Examples of this sort can in fact be found for names of any length. An absolute simplification in the use of noun–epithet formulae of gods and heroes | would only be possible if all names were of identical metrical value.

γ. *Noun–epithet formulae reserved for the expression of specific ideas*

The complexity of the ideas to be expressed in heroic poetry checked the operation of analogy in exactly the same way. To express certain ideas the bards had to choose words of different lengths, with different endings, words which had to be arranged in different ways in the hexameter line. It is evident that the more specific an idea is, the fewer

[1] The accusative case of Ἀτρέος υἱός appears twice:

Δ 98	αἴ κεν ἴδηι	Μενέλαον ἀρήιον Ἀτρέος υἱόν.
Δ 205	ὄφρα ἴδηις	

The resemblance after the trithemimeral caesura between these two lines and the one quoted above reveals that we have here a formula more extended than Ἀτρέος υἱός; this rules out, in Homer at least, any general usage of the latter formula at the end of the line.

[2] It is worth noticing that the person addressed in *Z* 46 is Menelaus, whereas in *Λ* 131 it is Agamemnon: a curious example of the bards' inclination to frugality in the use of formulae.

will be the analogous cases of its appearance out of which a traditional formula type and a traditional way of using formulae of the type might be established. Apart from the noun–epithet formulae which, owing to their frequency, have been designated as belonging to the principal types, we find only short series of expressions, ranging from a group of several analogous expressions to expressions which are wholly isolated, and seem to have nothing in common with other formulae because they are reserved for wholly isolated ideas.

That aspect of formulary diction in heroic poetry which is sure to be the first to strike the attention of the reader of Homer is the common use of the whole lines to express certain specific ideas. The more or less frequent occasions for describing certain actions of gods and men led the poets to create and to preserve these formulae even though each of them could describe only one particular action. So, to cite a few of the most common examples, the author says 'day broke' (*Iliad*, thrice; *Odyssey*, 19 times) by

ἦμος δ' ἠριγένεια φάνη ῥοδοδάκτυλος Ἠώς.

'Would that' (*Iliad*, 4 times; *Odyssey*, 5 times) is said

αἲ γὰρ Ζεῦ τε πάτερ καὶ Ἀθηναίη καὶ Ἄπολλον.

'After they had eaten' (*Iliad*, 7 times; *Odyssey*, 13 times) is

αὐτὰρ ἐπεὶ πόσιος καὶ ἐδητύος ἐξ ἔρον ἕντο.

Other whole-line formulae of the same kind are less obvious, the | poet having less often had occasion to express the ideas which they contain, but they are used as regularly as those of more frequent occurrence. Thus, 'he stayed [or stays] on an island suffering pain' is said of Philoctetes in the *Iliad* and of Odysseus in the *Odyssey*:

B 721 } ἀλλ' ὁ μὲν ἐν νήσωι { κεῖτο } κρατέρ' ἄλγεα πάσχων.
ε 13 } { κεῖται }

In four places in the poems a character weeps and cannot speak: Antilochus (*P* 695), Eumelus (*Ψ* 396), Penelope (δ 704), and Eurycleia (τ 471):

τὼ δέ οἱ ὄσσε
δακρυόφι πλῆσθεν, θαλερὴ δέ οἱ ἔσχετο φωνή.[1]

There are some noun–epithet formulae, too, which are part of formulae reserved for the expression of a particular idea and occur with the utmost rarity apart from a particular group of words. In such cases the substantive and its epithet are parts of formulae more complex than the simple

[1] For other cases of the same kind, and for a notion of the frequency of these whole-line formulae, see the list of lines common to the *Iliad* and *Odyssey* at the end of Dunbar's *Concordance to the Odyssey*.

noun–epithet formula, and one must not try to separate the substantive and epithet from the other words of the formula. We have already noticed (TE, p. 58) a noun–epithet expression of this kind, *Διὸς αἰγιόχοιο*, which owes its frequent use to the poet's need to express after the hephthemimeral caesura the idea 'son' (or 'daughter' or 'daughters') of Zeus, and appears elsewhere in three lines only, themselves apparently patterned after this special usage. Most of the less frequent types of formulae are of this sort, and an attempt to list them all would be bound to fail by the length of the task, and would anyway lose its interest as it turned into a mere catalogue. It will be enough to present a few examples.

I. The noun–epithet formula for Odysseus

– ⏑⏑ διογενὴς ⏑⏑ – πτολίπορθος Ὀδυσσεύς

appears only once in the poems:

θ 3 ἂν δ' ἄρα διογενὴς ὦρτο πτολίπορθος Ὀδυσσεύς. |

Now as chance would have it, the poet (or poets) had in four passages of the *Iliad* and the *Odyssey* occasion to express, and to fill a whole line in doing so, the idea 'X got up'. This makes it certain that θ 3 was suggested to the poet by the memory of a formula-type reserved for the expression of this particular idea:

Ψ 293	τῶι δ' ἄρ' ἐπ' Ἀτρείδης ὦρτο ξανθὸς Μενέλαος
Η 163 = Ψ 290	τῶι δ' ἐπὶ Τυδείδης ὦρτο κρατερὸς Διομήδης
Ψ 812	ἂν δ' ἄρα Τυδείδης ὦρτο κρατερὸς Διομήδης.

II. Most of the noun–epithet formulae of Zeus belong to the category of those reserved for the expression of a specific idea. It is the greatest of all the gods whom one invokes in making a wish, or whom one calls to witness in making a vow, or who is envisaged as the arbiter of human destiny; and, as we have already seen, he is also frequently mentioned as the father of a god or of a mortal. This explains why the figures for Zeus are proportionally much higher than those of the other characters in the last two columns of Table I, which give the number of formulae and formula types other than the principal types for each character on the Table.

The disposition of the name and of the epithets of Zeus which we see in *H* 411,

ὅρκια δὲ Ζεὺς ἴστω, ἐρίγδουπος πόσις Ἥρης,

is the same as in

θ 465 } ο 180 } οὕτω νῦν Ζεὺς θείη, } ἐρίγδουπος πόσις Ἥρης
Κ 329 ἴστω νῦν Ζεὺς αὐτός, }

and almost the same as in

ὥς τοι Ζεὺς τελέσειεν, ἐρίγδουπος πόσις Ἥρης.

Ebeling correctly remarks that this expression is used 'quando quis jurat aut optat'. It is a formula created for that use and for no other (on this formula see also TE, pp. 181–2). |

III. Similarly *Κρονίδης Ζεύς* appears before the bucolic diaeresis only when the poet is speaking of the glory or the grief which fate has assigned to men:

Θ 141	*νῦν μὲν γὰρ τούτωι Κρονίδης Ζεὺς κῦδος ὀπάζει*
Φ 570	*ἔμμεναι· αὐτάρ οἱ Κρονίδης Ζεὺς κῦδος ὀπάζει*
Σ 431	*ὅσσ' ἐμοὶ ἐκ πασέων Κρονίδης Ζεὺς ἄλγε' ἔδωκεν*
Ω 241	*ἦ ὀνόσασθ' ὅτι μοι Κρονίδης Ζεὺς ἄλγε' ἔδωκε.*

IV. Zeus only thrice receives the title *ἀθάνατος* in the *Iliad* and the *Odyssey*:

Β 741	*υἱὸς Πειριθόοιο, τὸν ἀθάνατος τέκετο Ζεύς*
Ξ 434 *Φ* 2	*Ξάνθου δινήεντος, ὃν ἀθάνατος τέκετο Ζεύς.*

The whole expression, which ends the line after the feminine caesura, is a way of stating in a different measure the idea of kinship with Zeus in *υἱὸς Διὸς αἰγιόχοιο* (cf. TE, p. 58).

V. The bards so often found themselves wanting to express this same idea that they created a special formula for daughters of Zeus which could stand after the feminine caesura and began with a consonant:

Διὸς κούρηι μεγάλοιο (8 times)
Διὸς θύγατερ μεγάλοιο
Διὸς κοῦραι μεγάλοιο.

VI. The expression *Ζεῦ τε πάτερ* appears only in the line

αἲ γὰρ Ζεῦ τε πάτερ καὶ Ἀθηναίη καὶ Ἄπολλον

which is found 4 times in the *Iliad* and 5 times in the *Odyssey*.

VII. Elsewhere Zeus receives the title of *πάτερ* in the vocative case only in the first foot, where it serves regularly to begin a prayer or a cry of reproach. We find:

(5 times)	*Ζεῦ πάτερ, Ἴδηθεν μεδέων, κύδιστε μέγιστε*
Γ 365 = *υ* 201	*Ζεῦ πάτερ, οὔ τις σεῖο θεῶν ὀλοώτερος ἄλλος*
η 331	*Ζεῦ πάτερ, αἴθ' ὅσα εἶπε τελευτήσειεν ἅπαντα.*

The expression occurs 32 times in this position. |

VIII. In lines so constructed the second foot usually begins with a vowel. When it begins with a consonant the poet uses Ζεῦ ἄνα, which we find in the poems thrice, always at the beginning of the line:

Γ 351 Ζεῦ ἄνα, δὸς τείσασθαι ὅ με πρότερος κάκ' ἔοργε,

and so on.

IX. The case of two formulae is of especial interest: ἀργυρότοξος Ἀπόλλων and Ἄρτεμις ἰοχέαιρα, which are of a metrical value not usual in noun–epithet formulae in the nominative case. These formulae were called into existence because Apollo and Artemis are the gods who cause mortals to die a death without violence, from sickness or old age. Hence the bards found it to their advantage to have an expression which could regularly serve to express the notion of this manner of death. We find:

η 64 τὸν μὲν ἄκουρον ἐόντα βάλ' ἀργυρότοξος Ἀπόλλων
ρ 251 αἲ γὰρ Τηλέμαχον βάλοι ἀργυρότοξος Ἀπόλλων
ο 478 τὴν μὲν ἔπειτα γυναῖκα βάλ' Ἄρτεμις ἰοχέαιρα
Ζ 428 πατρὸς δ' ἐν μεγάροισι βάλ' Ἄρτεμις ἰοχέαιρα.

The same idea is found in Ω 758–9:

κεῖσαι, τῶι ἴκελος ὅν τ' ἀργυρότοξος Ἀπόλλων
οἷς ἀγανοῖς βελέεσσιν ἐποιχόμενος κατέπεφνεν,

and in λ 172–3:

ἢ δολιχὴ νοῦσος, ἣ Ἄρτεμις ἰοχέαιρα
οἷς ἀγανοῖς βελέεσσιν ἐποιχομένη κατέπεφνεν.

§ 3. THE PREDOMINANCE OF TRADITIONAL FORMULAE

We have said that the purpose in any study of the formulary element in Homeric diction must be to learn to distinguish in the *Iliad* and the *Odyssey* what belongs to the tradition and what is due to the originality of the poet or poets who composed the poems. In order to make a quantitative analysis that would fulfil this purpose, we have consistently chosen our examples, wherever it was possible to do so, from the noun–epithet formulae used in the nominative case for the six heroes | whose names appear on Table I. The greater part of these formulae we have been able to assign to the tradition:

	Principal-type formulae	Formulae in which the epithet fills a specific part of the line	Special-type formulae	Unclassified formulae	Types of unclassified formulae
Ὀδυσσεύς	190	5	1	6	5
Ἀχιλλεύς	92	8	—	2	2
Ἕκτωρ	76	7	—	4	2
Νέστωρ	32	1	—	6	3
Διομήδης	34	—	3	4	2
Ἀγαμέμνων	63	3	—	12	5

An examination of the formulae counted in the last two columns of the above table, the formulae which resist the method of analysis we have been following, will show that without being over-bold we can assign the majority of them to the system of diction, and that in any case the epithets they contain are with but two exceptions the same as those already noted in some of the principal-type formulae. It will, however, be seen at the same time that if we want to keep our conclusions within the limits of moderation, we must allow that some at least of these cases reveal more or less independent ways of using traditional words.

I. We should perhaps assign to the tradition the noun–epithet formulae in the lines following, if we consider that these epithets, which fill the space between a caesura of the third foot and the bucolic diaeresis, behave exactly as do certain generic epithets which we have observed in this position. Two of these lines have a certain likeness:

Σ 234	*μυρόμενοι· μετὰ δέ σφι ποδώκης εἶπετ' Ἀχιλλεύς*
X 471	*ἤματι τῶι ὅτε μιν κορυθαίολος ἠγάγεθ' Ἕκτωρ,*

The line

δ 763 *εἴ ποτέ τοι πολύμητις ἐνὶ μεγάροισιν Ὀδυσσεύς* |

recalls lines such as

H 148 *αὐτὰρ ἐπεὶ Λυκόοργος ἐνὶ μεγάροισιν ἐγήρα.*

II. *εὐρὺ κρείων*, which appears only in *Λ* 238, owes its existence to its presence in two formulae of greater length:

(thrice)	*ἥρως Ἀτρείδης εὐρὺ κρείων Ἀγαμέμνων*
(7 times)	. . . *Ἀτρείδης εὐρὺ κρείων Ἀγαμέμνων.*

The frequent usage of these last formulae is hard to explain. If they are traditional, we must grant that the poet (or poets) liked to use them in spite of their metrical value, which is unusual among noun–epithet formulae in the nominative case. The same must be true of the noun–epithet formula which we see in these lines:

Θ 532	*εἴσομαι εἴ κέ μ' ὁ Τυδείδης κρατερὸς Διομήδης*
Λ 660 = *Π* 25	*βέβληται μὲν ὁ Τυδείδης κρατερὸς Διομήδης,*

and of this expression used for Nestor:

Θ 80	*Νέστωρ οἶος ἔμιμνε Γερήνιος, οὖρος Ἀχαιῶν*
O 370 = 659	*Νέστωρ αὖτε μάλιστα Γερήνιος, οὖρος Ἀχαιῶν*
γ 411	*Νέστωρ αὖ τότ' ἐφῖζε Γερήνιος, οὖρος Ἀχαιῶν.*

But we must not forget that the predilection for these formulae was probably shared by all bards.

III. The memory of such lines as

Γ 275 τοῖσιν δ' Ἀτρείδης μεγάλ' εὔχετο, χεῖρας ἀνασχών,

together with the memory of lines like

I 368 αὖτις ἐφυβρίζων ἕλετο κρείων Ἀγαμέμνων,

explains the creation of

Λ 177 ὣς τοὺς Ἀτρείδης ἔφεπε κρείων Ἀγαμέμνων.

The creation of *Λ* 333 can be explained in the same way. The noun–epithet expression which we see in

Δ 512 οὐ μὰν οὐδ' } Ἀχιλεύς, Θέτιδος πάις ἠυκόμοιο
Π 860 τίς δ' οἶδ' εἴ κ' }

owes its creation to the memory of expressions such as Ἑλένης πόσις ἠυκόμοιο and Κρόνου πάις ἀγκυλομήτεω. But there is no way of knowing whether the lines formed in this way are the work of Homer or whether, | on the contrary, he had heard in the recitation of another bard lines in which these names and epithets were already put into this position in the hexameter line.

IV. The line

ο 485 τὸν δ' αὖ διογενὴς Ὀδυσεὺς ἠμείβετο μύθωι

is quite exceptional, seeing that the poet could have adopted the line which he regularly uses to express the same idea:

τὸν δ' ἀπαμειβόμενος προσέφη πολύμητις Ὀδυσσεύς (50 times).

ο 485 was suggested on the one hand by lines like

Ω 200 ὣς φάτο, κώκυσεν δὲ γυνὴ καὶ ἀμείβετο μύθωι
ι 506 } ὣς ἐφάμην, ὁ δέ μ' οἰμώξας ἠμείβετο μύθωι,
λ 59 }

and on the other by lines like

τὸν δ' αὖ Τηλέμαχος πεπνυμένος ἄντιον ηὔδα (43 times).

But here too there is no way of knowing whether Homer was the first to make this new combination of old formulae.

V. The two formulae which we have yet to consider are shorter, and their use would seem to be due to the fact that the poet was using in the line other elements of the sentence with well-established positions, and consequently found himself unable to use his ordinary formulae. Thus in

β 27 ἐξ οὗ Ὀδυσσεὺς δῖος ἔβη κοίλῃς ἐνὶ νηυσί.

The expression ἐξ οὗ occurs 12 out of 18 times at the beginning of the line. The last half of the line can be compared with

H 381 ἠῶθεν δ' Ἰδαῖος ἔβη κοίλας ἐπὶ νῆας.

The expression κοίλῃς ἐνὶ νηυσί, as we shall see further on, belongs to a system of noun–epithet–preposition formulae for νηῦς. In addition we find twice (τ 596 and ψ 18):

ἐξ οὗ Ὀδυσσεύς
ᾤχετ'

And in σ 181 we have a line like the one under discussion:

ὤλεσαν, ἐξ οὗ κεῖνος ἔβη κοίλῃς ἐνὶ νηυσίν. |

VI. The epithet τλήμων, found twice in the *Iliad*, presents a particular interest because it never occurs in the *Odyssey*, despite the greater importance of the role played by Odysseus in the latter poem. One might be tempted to see in it a word original with the poet of the *Iliad* or of the *Doloneia*, only the meaning of the epithet rules out such a conclusion. Like πολύτλας, τλήμων could never have been invented for the *Iliad*. It is an epithet whose origin is in some poem describing the wanderings of Odysseus, and which eventually came, like πολύτλας, to be applied to him under all circumstances. For in the *Iliad* Odysseus has not yet suffered more than other heroes. So we have here a formula indubitably deriving from the tradition and yet never used by the poet (or poets) of the *Odyssey*. Ought we to infer that the author of the *Odyssey* knew this formula but never had occasion to make use of it? It could be pointed out in support of this conclusion that the other words of these two lines are elsewhere often found in the same positions:

K 231 ἤθελε δ' ὁ τλήμων Ὀδυσεὺς καταδῦναι ὅμιλον
K 498 τόφρα δ' ἄρ' ὁ τλήμων Ὀδυσεὺς λύε μώνυχας ἵππους.

It is also true that in the *Odyssey* Odysseus never has occasion to manage horses or to enter the throng of battle. But all this remains uncertain.

It would be wrong to see in the preceding pages nothing more than a list of uncertainties. The very fact that we cannot arrive at certain conclusions concerning the origin of the formulae means that the mind of the poet (or poets) of the *Iliad* and the *Odyssey* was so thoroughly steeped in traditional formulae that he never once, for the nominative case of the six names in question, created of his own accord an epithet revealing the personal stamp of his thought. Traces of originality remain, perhaps; but of an originality that does no more than rearrange the words and expressions of the tradition without important modifications. The poet's greatest originality in the handling of epithets would have been to use some noun–epithet | formulae a little more or a little less frequently than other poets. All the epithets of the *Iliad* and the *Odyssey* we call 'Homeric'. But the entire investigation which we have just carried out has not turned up a single epithet which can be called 'Homeric' as the epithets of Pindar have the right to be called 'Pindaric'.

§ 4. THE CHOICE OF EPITHETS

This conclusion is bound to be displeasing to some, who will think it too absolute. On the one hand, scholars who set great store by the unity of the Homeric poems, and stress the subtleties of thought and style which they feel they have discovered in the *Iliad* and *Odyssey*, will find it in contradiction with their notion of the genius of Homer. It may be that, arguing from what they will consider to be the improbability of the results of this investigation, they will conclude that our method is false or, at the best, inexact. On the other hand, those scholars who see in the *Iliad* and the *Odyssey* poems of different periods of time, and works of several or many poets, may be unwilling to believe that the tradition could have been followed by all these poets with such fidelity that a precise investigation could fail to uncover any significant differences in the use of the epithet between the two poems and even between different parts of the same poem. These objections represent too well the reactions which many will have to the conclusions of this study, for us to pass them by in silence. The following chapters will give positive indications proving that Homer was not concerned with finding original epithets, and they will at the same time show how much importance should be attributed to certain differences in the way epithets are used in the two poems. But before the discussion of these problems is begun, there should remain no doubts of the validity of the method of analysis which we have followed in the preceding pages. There does exist a means of controlling the fundamental accuracy of the conclusions just drawn. There is another aspect of the problem of the traditional use of the epithet which requires an investigation altogether independent of the one just completed; | the results of this investigation will show whether too much importance has been given to the influence of metre and the operation of analogy, and whether, in the foregoing pages, too many epithets have been assigned to the tradition.

What we have in mind is the choice of epithets. Hitherto we have only examined noun–epithet formulae of certain metrical values which conform to the shape of the hexameter and make up part of a technique of diction. This examination has established that there exists only a small number of noun–epithet formulae which have the same metrical value with another noun–epithet formula used in the same grammatical case for the same character. It should follow that with a few exceptions the poet uses the same epithet every time he uses a formula of a given length. If all epithets in Homer were distinctive, an investigation into the choice of epithets would have to stop there, and we should have to declare ourselves satisfied with this first proof of the traditional character of the epithet. For most of the epithets applied to the gods, this is true. Fortunately, this is the least likely place where one would be tempted to look for the original epithets of Homer. It is otherwise with the epithets used for the heroes. Here the distinctive epithet, as we shall shortly be able to see with precision, is comparatively rare, and epithets employed indifferently for two or more heroes are far more numerous and occur with far greater frequency.

In every noun–epithet formula there are two elements, of which one is fixed and the other variable. The fixed element is the substantive. Apart from its variation in the genitive and dative plural, it has always the same metrical value, and this predetermined value is what the poet must reckon with. The variable element is the epithet. It can be assigned whatever metrical value the poet chooses, and it can begin or end pretty much as he wants. So the poet creates the noun–epithet formula of the desired measure by adding the *x* syllables of the epithet to the predetermined syllables of the substantive. Here is where the generic epithet can be especially | useful. Suppose the poet wants a noun–epithet formula of a given metrical value: he can make one with the same generic epithet in the case of all heroes whose names are of the same measure. We have already seen that a single epithet serves to combine with the names of both Achilles and Odysseus to form those extremely serviceable noun–epithet formulae which follow the diaeresis and begin with a single consonant. We find, after the diaeresis:

δῖος Ὀδυσσεύς (98 times)
δῖος Ἀχιλλεύς (55 times)

This epither δῖος is used in like fashion for other heroes whose only point of resemblance to Achilles and Odysseus is that they too are heroes and that their names are of the same measure and begin with a short vowel:

δῖος {
Ἀγήνωρ (thrice)
Ἀλάστωρ (twice)
Ἐπειγεύς
Ἐπειός (thrice)
Ἐχέφρων
Ὀρέστης (thrice)
ὑφορβός (4 times)
}

The use of δῖος in the nominative case and in this position and with names of heroes of this metrical value is almost exclusive. Elsewhere we find it in only five places and with three names of different metrical value (for these five cases, see TE, p. 149).

Cases of this sort are not hard to find. We can quote some of the most striking.

I. After the bucolic diaeresis:

ἱππότα
- *Νέστωρ* (30 times)
- *Φυλεύς*
- *Τυδεύς*
- *Οἰνεύς*
- *Πηλεύς* (twice)

φαίδιμος
- *Αἴας* (6 times)
- *Ἕκτωρ* (30 times)

Cf. *φαίδιμος υἱός* (11 times).

II. After the hephthemimeral caesura:

κρείων
- *Ἀγαμέμνων* (30 times)
- *Ἐλεφήνωρ*
- *Ἐνοσίχθων* (7 times)
- *Ἐτεωνεύς*
- *Εὔμηλος*
- *Ἑλικάων*
- *Ἀγαπήνωρ*

κρατερὸς
- *Διομήδης* (18 times)
- *Λυκομήδης* |
- *Λυκόοργος*
- *Μεγαπένθης* (twice)
- *Πολυποίτης*
- *Διώρης* (twice)

Cf. *κρατερός τ' Ἐφιάλτης*.

III. After the feminine caesura:

βοὴν ἀγαθὸς
- *Μενέλαος* (20 times)
- *Διομήδης* (21 times)

βοὴν ἀγαθὸν
- *Μενέλαον* (5 times)

ἄναξ ἀνδρῶν
- *Ἀγαμέμνων* (37 times)
- *Ἀγχίσης*
- *Αὐγείας*
- *Αἰνείας*
- *Εὐφήτης*
- *Εὔμηλος*

γέρων ἱππηλάτα
- *Πηλεύς* (4 times)
- *Οἰνεύς*
- *Φοῖνιξ*

Cf. *γέρων δ' ἱππηλάτα Νέστωρ* (twice)

ἀμύμονος
- *Αἰακίδαο* (twice)
- *Ἀντιλόχοιο* (4 times)
- *Ἀλκινόοιο* (twice)
- *Αἰγίσθοιο*
- *Ἀγχίσαο*

ἀμύμονι
- *Βουκολίωνι* (twice)
- *Πουλυδάμαντι*

ἀμύμονα	Πηλείωνα (10 times) Πουλυδάμαντα (twice) Βελλεροφόντην (twice) Λαομέδοντα (twice) Γοργυθίωνα Δηιοπίτην Δευκαλίωνα.

IV. We have already explained (TE, pp. 60–2) why the poet needed a noun–epithet | formula in the genitive case, although he did not need one in the nominative case, after the penthemimeral caesura. We find:

μεγαλήτορος	Ἀλκινόοιο (7 times) Αἰνείαο (4 times) Ἀγχίσαο (twice) Ἠετίωνος (twice) Ἀμφιμάχοιο Ἰκαρίοιο Ἱπποτάδαο Εὐρυλόχοιο Εὐρυμέδοντος

When the initial sound of the name forbids the use of μεγαλήτορος, the poet uses μεγαθύμου:

μεγαθύμου	Τυδέος υἱός (thrice) Πρωτεσίλαο (twice) Πηλείωνος (twice) Πανθοΐδαο Ναυβολίδαο Τηλεμάχοιο Πειριθόοιο Δευκαλίωνος

V. In the examples given so far, the epithet precedes the name. The bards also created a large number of formulae for the end of the line by using a single epithet to follow a name. These formulae are not all of the same length, but in all of them the metrical value of the hero's name determines the choice of the epithet:

(twice)	Γλαῦκος	ἀμύμων
(twice)	Τεῦκρος	
	Κλυτόνηος	
	Μενέλαος	
(7 times)	Πριάμοιο	
(thrice)	Ἑλένοιο	
(twice)	Ἀρηιθόοιο	
(twice)	Ταλαιονίδαο	|

	Πηνελέωο	ἄνακτος
	Τεύκροιο	
	Τειρεσίαο	
	Ἡφαίστοιο	
	Φιλοκτήταο	
	Αὐγηιάδαο	
	Σεληπιάδαο	
	Ἡρακλείδαο	

(27 times)	Ὀδυσσῆος	θείοιο
(twice)	Ἀχιλλῆος	
	Ἡρακλῆος	
(twice)	Οἰκλῆος	

(8 times)	Πρίαμος	θεοειδής
(10 times)	Ἀλέξανδρος	
(5 times)	Θεοκλύμενος	
(twice)	Εὐρύμαχος	
	Ναυσίθοος	
	Ἀλκίνοος	
	Εὐρύλοχος	
	Ἀσκάνιος	
	Πολύξεινος	
	Δηίφοβος	
	Ἄρητος	
	Χρομίος	
	Νεοπτόλεμος	

(19 times)	Ἕκτορα	δῖον
(thrice)	Ἀγήνορα	
(thrice)	Διομήδεα	
(4 times)	Νέστορα	
(twice)	Ἀγαμέμνονα	
(twice)	Σαρπηδόνα	
	Ὑψήνορα	
	Ἀρετάονα	
	Λυκομήδεα	
	Μέντορα	
	Μέμνονα	

It is clear that each of these series of formulae owes its existence to the influence of the verse operating through analogy. To try to discover in which formula the use of a given epithet is oldest would be pointless. The significant fact is that the bards had no hesitation in applying to any hero an epithet which at some point in time had first been ascribed to one particular hero. It was used a first time for this one person; then it was used again for the same person, when the rhythm allowed it and made its use easy. Then the bards applied it to other persons whose names were of the same metrical value with that of the original owner. This process had a twofold effect on heroic style. If at some time other epithets of like metrical value had been used | to describe certain heroes, the bards were led to abandon and forget them, save in those quite rare cases when an epithet referred to some characteristic of one of the greatest heroes or contained some detail of historical interest. On the other hand the same process kept new equivalent epithets from being introduced. Of course the bards' fondness for the ancient and traditional epithet must not be forgotten; but this fondness never stopped them from seeking and finding new generic epithets with other metrical values. If the poets loved the generic epithet, and made liberal use of it, it was chiefly because they found it very convenient.

To what extent did the influence of metre succeed in expanding the use of the generic epithet while restraining the use of the distinctive epithet? To what extent was it able to exclude from the diction of epic poetry any epithet of a hero, generic or distinctive, which was of the same metrical value with another epithet of a hero already in the tradition? A precise solution of these two problems requires an examination of all the epithets of heroes in Homer. We can begin by comparing the number of distinctive and the number of generic epithets among them. Afterwards, by determining the variety in metrical form of generic epithets, we can discover whether we are dealing with a system which, by reason of its extension and its simplicity, could never have come into being in the verse of a poet whose diction was individual. This is an investigation completely independent of the one made of the noun–epithet formulae of heroes. When a little while ago we listed series of formulae containing generic epithets, we chose from among the most common, that is, from those that combine with their substantives to form principal-type formulae. But the investigation which we are proposing to make of the variety of the metrical values of generic epithets has no connection with formulae, and its only purpose is to show under what circumstances Homer was able to replace one generic epithet of a hero by another, at whatever point in the line these epithets occurred. |

The following list gives all the epithets of the *Iliad* and the *Odyssey* reserved for a single hero. This list and Table III together contain all the epithets in Homer which refer to the character of a hero.[1] Patronymics and expressions of a hero's family relationship are not given: these sometimes replace the epithet when the metrical value of the father's (or grandfather's) name makes their use possible. Thus these patronymics and patronymic expressions constitute of themselves a system of epithets, a system, however, less extended than the system of generic epithets and unconnected with it, since it cannot be used for every hero.

The epithets which are used for only one hero are 40 in number. They fall into two distinct categories: those which are used for heroes whose role in epic poetry is or must have been of the first importance, and those

[1] *πόδας ὠκύς* is given as a distinctive epithet of Achilles even though it is used in *ν* 260 of another hero:

Ὀρσίλοχον πόδας ὠκὺν ὃς ἐν Κρήτῃ εὐρείῃ.

The presence of the epithet in this line is to be explained as an exceptional consequence of the operation of analogy, similar to the metrical anomalies discussed above. The epithets applied to men in Homer which are not given either in the list or in Table III are the following: A. *γέρων*, which can be applied to any aged hero: *γέρων ἱππηλάτα Νέστωρ*, *γέρων Πρίαμος θεοειδής*, *γέρων ἀγαθὸς Πολύϊδος*, etc. B. Epithets of profession or trade: *κῆρυξ*, *ἡνιοχῆα*, *ἱερεύς*, *μάντιος*, *οἰωνιστήν*, *χρυσόχοον*, *συβῶτα*, *αἰπόλος*, *ὑφορβός*, *ἀλήτης*. C. *ὀλοόφρονος*, used only of wizards: *ὀλόφρονος Αἰήταο*, *Μίνωος ὀλοόφρονος*. D. Epithetic expressions designating two or more heroes at once: *μάχης εὖ εἰδότε πάσης*, *πεπνυμένω ἄμφω*, *πολέμου ἀκορήτω*, *μεμαότε θούριδος ἀλκῆς*, *θεράποντες Ἄρηος*, *ἐγχεσιμώρους*, *μήστωρας ἀυτῆς*, etc. E. *λαοῖσι τετιμένον*, said of the bard Demodocus. F. *πεπνυμένα μήδεα εἰδώς*, said of heralds.

TABLE III. GIVING ALL THE FIXED EPITHETS USED IN THE *ILIAD* AND THE *ODYSSEY* WITH THE NAMES OF TWO OR MORE HEROES

Metre		Nominative		Genitive		Dative		Accusative		Vocative	
I. ⏑ ⏑	A.	μέγας	3					μέγαν	2		
	B.	κλυτός	1					κλυτόν	4		
		θρασύς	1					θρασύν	2		
	C.	ἐύς	1								
II. ⏑ –	A.	μέγας	2					μέγαν	3		
	B.	ἐύς	1					ἐύν	1		
III. – ⏑	A.	δῖος	12	δίου	2	δίωι	4	δῖον	17	φαίδιμ'	2
	B.									δῖε	3
IV. –́ –		ἥρως	10			ἥρωι	2	ἥρω'	3	ἥρως	1
V. ⏖ –	A.	ἀγαθός	3					ἀγαθόν	2		
	B.	ξανθός	2			ξανθῶι	1	ξανθόν	1		
		κρατερός	8			κρατερῶι	1	κρατερόν	2		
	C.	ἥρως	4								
	D.	κρείων	7					κρείοντ'	1		
VI. – ⏑ ⏑	A.	φαίδιμος	6								
	B.	ἄλκιμος	3					ἄλκιμον	3		
	C.	ἱππότα	5								
VII. ⏑ – –	A.	ἀμύμων	6	ἀγανοῦ	11			ἀγανόν	1		
	B.	δαίφρων	4								
VIII. ⏑ – ⏑ ⏑	A.	ἀρήιος	8	ἀμύμονος	12			ἀρήιον	3	ἀγακλεές	1
								ἀγακλυτόν	4		
	B.	διίφιλος	4	δαίφρονος	15			διίφιλον	1	διοτρεφές	5
	C.					ἀμύμονι	2	ἀμύμονα	9		
	D.					δαίφρονι	7	δαίφρονα	5	διίφιλε	2

Table III (*cont.*)

Metre		Nominative		Genitive		Dative		Accusative		Vocative	
IX. ⏖ – ⏑	A.			θείοιο	3	βασιλῆι	1	βασιλῆα	1	μεγάθυμε	2
	B.	μεγάθυμος	3					μεγάθυμον	2		
		πτολίπορθος	1					πλήξιππον	1		
	C.							κρείοντα	1		
	D.					ἥρωϊ	4	ἥρωα	5		
X. ⏖ – ⊼	A.	θεοειδής	14	βασιλῆος	4	βασιλῆι	3	μενεχάρμην	2		
		μενεχάρμης	1	θείοιο	5			βασιλῆα	4		
								θεοειδέα	3		
	B.			κρατεροῖο	1	πληξίππωι	1	μεγάθυμον	5		
						πτολιπόρθωι	3	πλήξιππον	2		
								πτολίπορθον	1		
	C.	ἀγαπήνωρ	1								
XI. ⏑ ⏑ – ⏖	A.	πεπνυμένος	7	μεγαλήτορος	13			δουρικλυτόν	2		
		θεοείκελος	2					θεοείκελον	1		
		δουρικλυτός	8								
	B.	ἱππηλάτα	5					ἀγαπήνορα	1		
	C.			ἀγαπήνορος	2						
	D.			μεγαθύμου	14	μεγαλήτορι	4	θεοειδέα	1		
						μεγαθύμωι	1	μεγαλήτορα	3		
	E.							πτολιπόρθιον	1		
XII. ⏑ – ⏑				ἄνακτος	3			ἄνακτα	2		
XIII. ⏑ – ⊼				ἄνακτος	15	ἄνακτι	2	ἄνακτα	2		
XIV. ⏑ – ⏖ –	A.	ὑπέρθυμος	2	ἀγακλειτοῦ	1	ἀρηιφίλωι	1	ἀγακλειτόν	1		
		ἀρηίφιλος	2	ὑπερθύμου	1			ὑπέρθυμον	3		
				ἀρηιφίλου	1			ἀρηίφιλον	1		
				ἐυμμελίω	1						
				ἀγακλῆος	2						
	B.	ἄναξ ἀνδρῶν	6	ἐυμμελίης	1			ἐυμμελίην	1		
	C.	μενεπτόλεμος	5	διοτρεφέος	4			βοὴν ἀγαθόν	3		
		βοὴν ἀγαθός	4								

XV. – ⏔ –	A.	αἰχμητής	1					αἰχμητήν	3		
	B.	ἴφθιμος	2	ἀντιθέου	1	ἀντιθέῳ	5	ἀντίθεον	2		
		ἀντίθεος	5					ἴφθιμον	2		
								ἱππόδαμον	1		
	C.	διογενής	4							διογενές	3
XVI. – – – –	A.	δουρικλειτός	2					δουρικλειτόν	1		
								τηλεκλειτόν	1		
XVII. – ⏑ ⏑ – ⊼	A.	ἰσόθεος φώς	5	κυδαλίμοιο	6	ποιμένι λαῶν	6	ποιμένα λαῶν	12	κοίρανε λαῶν	2
						χαλκοκορυστῇ	1	θυμολέοντα	2		
								χαλκοκορυστήν	2		
	B.	ὄρχαμος ἀνδρῶν	5	ἀντιθέοιο	7			ὄρχαμον ἀνδρῶν	1	ὄρχαμε λαῶν	4
		ὄζος Ἄρηος	5	ἀνδροφόνοιο	2			ὄζον Ἄρηος	2		
				ἱπποδάμοιο	7			ἱππιοχάρμην	2		
				ἰφθίμοιο	1						
XVIII. ⏑ – ⏔ – ⏑	A.			ὑπερθύμοιο	4						
	B.			βοὴν ἀγαθοῖο	1						
XIX. ⏔ – ⏔ – ∧	A.	πεπνυμένα εἰδώς	2	τηλεκλειτοῖο	1						
	B.	ἠΰς τε μέγας τε	2			ἠΰν τε μέγαν τε	2				
		ἀτάλαντος Ἄρηι	1			ἀτάλαντον Ἄρηι	2				
XX. ⏔ – ⏔ – ⏔ – ⊼	A.	θεόφιν μήστωρ ἀτάλαντος	3			θεόφιν μήστωρ' ἀτάλαντον	1				
	B.	ἐπιείκελος ἀθανάτοισι	3			ἐπιείκελον ἀθανάτοισι	2				
	C.	βροτολοιγῷ ἶσος Ἄρηι	2			βροτολοιγῷ ἶσον Ἄρηι	1				
XXI. ⏑ – ⏔ – ⏔ – ⊼	A.	Διὶ μῆτιν ἀτάλαντος	1					Διὶ μῆτιν ἀτάλαντον	1	Διὶ μῆτιν ἀτάλαντε	5
		θοῷ ἀτάλαντος Ἄρηι	2					θοῷ ἀτάλαντον Ἄρηι	5		
	B.							ἀμύμονά τε κρατερόν τε	2		

which describe heroes who are mentioned only once or twice and seem to have played only minor parts in heroic story.

The epithets of the first category are: |

Hero	Epithet	Frequency of epithet
1. Odysseus	πολύμητις	82
2. —	πολύτλας	38
3. —	πολύφρονα	5
4. —	ταλασίφρονος	13
5. —	ποικιλόμητιν	6
6. —	τλήμων	2
7. —	ἐσθλός	3
8. Achilles	πόδας ὠκύς	31
9. —	ποδάρκης	21
10. —	ῥηξήνορος	3
11. —	ποδώκεος	11
12. —	θυμολέοντα	1
13. —	θεοῖς ἐπιείκελ'	6
14. Hector	ὄβριμος	4
15. —	κορυθαίολος	38
16. Agamemnon	εὐρὺ κρείων	11
17. —	κύδιστε	10
18. Heracles	κρατερόφρονα	1
19. —	μεγάλων ἐπιίστορα ἔργων	1
20. Ajax	ταχύς	9
21. Patroclus	ἱππεῦ	4
22. Nestor	Γερήνιος	35
23. Amphiaraus	λαοσσόον	1
24. Orestes	τηλεκλυτός	1
25. Aegisthus	δολόμητις	2
26. Polydeuces	πὺξ ἀγαθός	2

In the second category are 14 epithets of 14 heroes:

27. Ilus	παλαιοῦ δημογέροντος
28. Deiphobus	λευκάσπιδα
29. Polydamas	ἀμωμήτοιο
30. Mentor	πολυίππου

31. Pelegon	κλυτὸν ἔγχει |
32. Lycaon	γέρων αἰχμητά
33. Amphius	λινοθώρηξ
34. Scamandrius	αἵμονα θήρης
35. Acamas	ἠίθεον
36. Oresbius	αἰολομίτρην
37. Thyestes	πολύαρνι
38. Menesthius	αἰολοθώρηξ
39. Arybas	ῥυδὸν ἀφνειοῖο
40. Dymas	ναυσικλειτοῖο

So there are fewer epithets reserved for single heroes in the *Iliad* and the *Odyssey* than there are books in the two poems. It is a number small in itself, and it looks even smaller when it is compared with the number of generic epithets—61.

Table III shows the metrical value of all epithets applied to more than one hero in Homer. The number placed after each form does not indicate the number of heroes for whom the epithet is used in all its grammatical cases, but only the number of heroes described by that particular form.

The development of this system of generic epithets cannot be fully appreciated unless we realize that it is designed to prevent not only hiatus but also overlengthening. To maintain rapidity of rhythm, the bards tried to avoid, especially at the end of the line, as Platt observed, syllables long both by nature and by position. Matching

ἄναξ ἀνδρῶν {
Ἀγαμέμνων (37 times)
Ἀγχίσης
Αὐγείας
Αἰνείας
Εὐφήτης
Εὔμηλος

we find

βοὴν ἀγαθὸς {
Μενέλαος (20 times)
Διομήδης (21 times).

Matching

κρείων {
Ἀγαμέμνων (30 times)
Ἐλεφήνωρ
Ἐνοσίχθων (7 times)
Ἐτεωνεύς
Εὔμηλος
Ἑλικάων
Ἀγαπήνωρ |

we find

ξανθὸς {
Μενέλαος (18 times)
Ῥαδάμανθυς
Μελέαγρος

κρατερὸς { Διομήδης (18 times)
Λυκομήδης
Λυκόοργος
Μεγαπένθης (twice)
Πολυποίτης
Διώρης (twice).

Of the 164 forms of generic epithets listed in Table III, 91 cannot be replaced by any other form, while 73 are metrically congruent with another generic epithet. In the case of the first group—which in general includes the most common epithets—we are in the presence of a rigorously fixed system showing both great extension and complete absence of any superfluous element, indications that the whole system should be considered traditional. It follows that the system made up of these forms is observed with equal rigour in all the lines of the *Iliad* and the *Odyssey*, whether these poems are the work of one poet or of several poets working at different periods of time. But for the 73 forms which are not metrically unique this certain proof is lacking. It is clear that at least one form of each measure must be part of the system, but we shall not be in a position to know whether they should be referred to the tradition in their entirety or only in part until we have considered the three possible explanations of their presence in epic diction. (1) A greater or smaller portion of these forms could be the original creation of the author or the authors of the *Iliad* and the *Odyssey*. (2) They could represent elements introduced into the poem by bards of different periods. If so, the use of one form rather than of its metrical equivalent would provide a means of distinguishing earlier and later parts of the poems. (3) They could be simply elements of traditional diction in which the selective process of composition did not operate | with sufficient rigour to leave only one form of a given metrical value.

These equivalent generic epithets, together with some equivalent noun-epithet formulae noticed in Table I, provide material for discussion in subsequent chapters. But we should not because of them fail to appreciate the extension and the simplicity of the system. Of 9 epithets which Virgil uses in the nominative case for Aeneas—*Tros* ∼ *pius* ∼ *bonus* ∼ *pater*, *magnus* ∼ *heros*, *optimus armis* ∼ *acer in armis*, *Anchisiades*, *Troius*—7 have metrical equivalents. In the entire breadth of the *Iliad* and the *Odyssey* there is not one epithet of a hero, generic or distinctive, that can replace δῖος, which qualifies 32 heroes, in any of its five grammatical cases. That the poet was satisfied with this one epithet which has the metrical value – ⏑ and begins and ends with a single consonant would be remarkable even if it were an isolated phenomenon. But the same is true, although in a less striking fashion, of the 90 other forms of unique epithets. The influence of metre, operating through analogy, took hold of the device of the generic epithet and developed it to an extent which the modern reader finds it hard fully to comprehend, because he is familiar with no other poetry in which a device of this kind can be even faintly discerned.

It is evident that the existence in Homeric diction of this system of generic epithets capable of being applied to any hero must inevitably involve a choice of epithets not according to the character of the hero, but according to the metrical value of his name. An investigation showing exactly to what extent the same epithets are applied to two heroes whose names are metrically equivalent will give us precise information on this point, and it will at the same time enable us to compare the conclusions of the two investigations which we have carried out, the one on the use of noun–epithet formulae and the one on the choice of epithets. If on the one hand there is a need for noun–epithet formulae of certain metrical values, and if on the other hand, except when the poet uses a | distinctive epithet or a patronymic, there is only one epithet for each metrical value, it should follow that if the two heroes in question are mentioned frequently they will be in large measure described by the same epithets.

The names of the two principal heroes of the *Iliad* and the *Odyssey* happen to be of the same metrical value. The names of Achilles and Odysseus are declined in like fashion and both have two variant pronunciations—*'Οδυσεύς* or *'Οδυσσεύς*, *Ἀχιλεύς* or *Ἀχιλλεύς*. A comparison between two other names would be more complicated: *Αἴας* and *Ἕκτωρ*, for example, are of like metrical value in the nominative case, but genitive case *Ἕκτορος* would have to be compared with *Ἀτρέος* rather than with *Αἴαντος*.

Homer uses for the five grammatical cases of Achilles, 46 different noun–epithet formulae representing the same number of different metrical values, and for Odysseus, 45 different noun–epithet formulae representing 44 different metrical values. For there is but one case of equivalent formulae, in which a generic epithet parallels a distinctive epithet: *'Οδυσσῆος ταλασίφρονος* ∼ *'Οδυσσῆος μεγαλήτορος*.

Among the different metrical values of these formulae, 17 are common to the two series. These formulae of like metrical value are the following:

I. Four cases in which the poet uses a distinctive epithet for both heroes.

Metre	Formulae	Frequency
5 6 1. — ⏖ — ⊼	*ἐσθλὸς 'Οδυσσεύς*	3
	ὠκὺς Ἀχιλλεύς	5
4 5 6 2. ⏖ — ⏖ — ⊼	*πολύμητις 'Οδυσσεύς*	83
	πόδας ὠκὺς Ἀχιλλεύς	31
3 4 5 6 3. ⏑ — ⏖ — ⏖ — ⊼	*πολύτλας* } *δῖος* { *'Οδυσσεύς*	38
	ποδάρκης } *δῖος* { *Ἀχιλλεύς*	21
4. The entire line	*διογενὲς Λαερτιάδη, πολυμήχαν' 'Οδυσσεῦ*	22
	ὦ Ἀχιλεῦ, Πηλῆος υἱέ, μέγα φέρτατ' Ἀχαιῶν	3

II. One case in which the poet uses a patronymic for both heroes.

Metre	Formulae	Frequency
3 4 5 6 5. ⏖ – ⏖ – ⏖ – ⏓	Λαερτιάδεω Ὀδυσῆος	12
	Πηληιάδεω Ἀχιλῆος	8

III. Four cases in which he uses a distinctive epithet or a patronymic for one hero and a generic epithet for the other.

Metre	Formulae	Frequency
1 2 3 4 6. ⏑ – ⏖ – ⏖ – ⏖	Ὀδυσσῆι μεγαλήτορι	1
	Ἀχιλλῆι ῥηξήνορι	1
7. The same	Ὀδυσσῆα μεγαλήτορα	3
	Ἀχιλλῆα ῥηξήνορα	1
2 3 4 8. ⏖ – ⏖ – ⏖	Ὀδυσῆα πολύφρονα	5
	Ἀχιλῆα δαΐφρονα	1
2 3 4 5 6 9. ⏖ – ⏖ – ⏖ – ⏖ – ⏓	Ὀδυσῆος } ἀμύμονος { ἀντιθέοιο	1
	Ἀχιλῆος } ἀμύμονος { Αἰακίδαο	1

IV. Eight cases in which he uses the same generic epithet for both heroes.

Metre	Formulae	Frequency
5 6 10. – ⏖ – ⏓	δῖος { Ὀδυσσεύς	60
	δῖος { Ἀχιλλεύς	34
11. The same	φαίδιμ' { Ὀδυσσεῦ	5
	φαίδιμ' { Ἀχιλλεῦ	4
3 4 5 6 12. ⏑ – ⏖ – ⏖ – ⏓	Ὀδυσσῆος } θείοιο	26
	Ἀχιλλῆος } θείοιο	2
13. The same	Ὀδυσσῆι } πτολιπόρθωι	2
	Ἀχιλλῆι } πτολιπόρθωι	1
14. The same	Ὀδυσσῆα } πτολίπορθον	2
	Ἀχιλλῆα } πτολίπορθον	3
2 3 4 15. ⏖ – ⏖ – ⏖	Ἀχιλῆος } ἀμύμονος	8
	Ὀδυσσῆος } ἀμύμονος	2
16. The same	Ἀχιλῆι } δαΐφρονι	3
	Ὀδυσῆι } δαΐφρονι	3
1 2 3 4 17. ⏖ – (⏖ – ⏑) ⏑ – ⏖	Ὀδυσεὺς } ⏖ – ⏑ διίφιλος	1
	Ἀχιλεὺς } ⏖ – ⏑ διίφιλος	1

§ 5. EPITHETS AND NOUN–EPITHET FORMULAE OF HEROINES

In the epithets applied to women appear the same two tendencies which we have just examined in the epithets of heroes. There is, first, the development of the generic at the expense of the distinctive epithet, and second, the almost complete absence of equivalent generic epithets. This system of generic epithets is naturally of much smaller extension than the one observed for heroes, since the role of women in Homer is far more restricted.

Helen is the only woman in Homer who clearly has | distinctive epithets of her own.[1] We find:

Ἑλένη Διὸς ἐκγεγαυῖα
Ἀργείη Ἑλένη
Ἑλένηι . . . εὐπατερείηι.

A few other epithets occur with one woman only; but their character suggests that this is the result of chance. If we had a larger amount of epic poetry, we should probably find these epithets occurring with the names of other women. There is evidence for this in the metrical values of the epithets, which with two exceptions, ἐΰζωνος and ἐυστέφανος, show no duplication. We may conclude that they in all probability belong to the epithetic system.

In the nominative:

κλυτός
ἐΰζωνος
ἐυστέφανος
θεῶν ἄπο κάλλος ἔχουσα
περικαλλής

In the dative:

καλλιπλοκάμωι

In the accusative:

ἐΰπεπλον
ξανθήν
ἰφθίμην
θαῦμα βροτοῖσι
περικαλλέα
γυναικῶν εἶδος ἀρίστη

The epithets applied to two or more women are the following (the figures indicate the number of women qualified by each form): |

In the nominative:

δῖ'	1	ἠΰκομος	1
δῖα	3	θυγατρῶν εἶδος ἀρίστη	2
καλή	4	ἰκέλη χρυσέηι Ἀφροδίτηι	2
καλλιπάρηιος	5	τανύπεπλος	2
λευκώλενος	3	δῖα γυναικῶν	3
περίφρων	3	ἐυπλόκαμος	2
βοῶπις	3		

[1] The only epithets applied to women which do not figure in the following lists are terms for servants:

θαλαμηπόλος Εὐρυμέδουσα
Εὐρυνόμη θαλαμηπόλος
φίλη τροφὸς Εὐρύκλεια.

In the genitive:

καλλισφύρου	2
ἠυκόμοιο	2
καλλικόμοιο	2

In the dative:

λευκωλένωι	1
τανυπέπλωι	1
δίηι	1

In the accusative:

λευκώλενον	2
καλήν	2
καλλιπάρηιον	3
θυγατρῶν εἶδος ἀρίστην	3

Of the 37 different forms of generic epithets of heroines, all but five are of unique metrical value and irreplaceable by any other generic epithet.

As with heroes, we discover series of noun–epithet formulae in which one epithet is found with several names of like measure:

περίφρων { Ἀδρηστίνη, Πηνελόπεια, Εὐρύκλεια }

καλή { Πολυδώρη, Πολυκάστη, Πολυμήλη }

καλλισφύρου { Ἀκρισιώνης, Εὐηνίνης }

We can discern in λευκώλενος the same independent use of the epithet as in δουρικλυτός: λευκώλενος serves in the same way to fill the space between the penthemimeral caesura and the bucolic diaeresis when versification is thereby made easier for the poet.

Ζ 377 πῆι ἔβη Ἀνδρομάχη λευκώλενος ἐκ μεγάροιο;

can be compared with

σ 198 ἦλθον δ' ἀμφίπολοι λευκώλενοι ἐκ μεγάροιο
τ 60 ἦλθον δὲ δμωιαὶ λευκώλενοι ἐκ μεγάροιο,

and similarly

Γ 121 Ἶρις δ' αὖθ' Ἑλένηι λευκωλένωι ἄγγελος ἦλθεν |

can be compared with

Ω 194 δαιμονίη, Διόθεν μοι Ὀλύμπιος ἄγγελος ἦλθε
μ 374 ὠκέα δ' Ἠελίωι Ὑπερίονι ἄγγελος ἦλθε,

etc.

ἠυκόμοιο and καλλικόμοιο answer to the same purpose after the bucolic diaeresis and are used in a fashion analogous to ἱπποδάμοιο and κυδαλίμοιο (cf. TE, p. 66).

§ 6. EPITHETS AND NOUN–EPITHET FORMULAE OF PEOPLES

Epithets reserved for the description of single peoples are the following:

Ἄβαντες . . . θοοί, ὄπιθεν κομόωντες
Ἀβίων . . . δικαιοτάτων ἀνθρώπων
Ἀμαζόνας ἀντιανείρας
ἱπποπόλων Θρῃκῶν
Ἰάονες ἑλκεχίτωνες
Μυσῶν . . . καρτεροθύμων
Παίονες ἀγκυλότοξοι
Παίονας . . . δολιχεγχέας
Σιδόνες πολυδαίδαλοι
Φρύγας . . . αἰολοπώλους
Καρῶν . . . βαρβαροφώνων
Τρῶας ἀγήνορας
χαλκοκνήμιδες Ἀχαιοί
κάρη κομόωντες Ἀχαιοί
Φοίνικες πολυδαίδαλοι
Φοίνικες ναυσικλυτοί
Φαίηκες ναυσικλυτοί[1]
Φαίηκες δολιχήρετμοι
Φαιήκεσσι φιληρέτμοισι

Other epithets used for only | one people none the less cannot be considered distinctive. If they designate but one people, it is because peoples other than the Trojans and Achaeans play no important role in the poems. These epithets describe no particular quality of the peoples whom they qualify, and the fact that their metrical values are not repeated by other generic epithets of peoples may be taken as evidence that they too are generic.

In the nominative:

ἑλίκωπες
ἀγχιμαχηταί
φαιδιμόεντες
ἐυκνήμιδες
**μήστωρες ἀυτῆς*
**θεράποντες Ἄρηος*
**μενεπτόλεμοι*

In the genitive:

ἀγχεμάχων

In the dative:

**κυδαλίμοισιν*
θωρηκτῇσιν

In the accusative:

ἑλίκωπας
ἐυκνήμιδας
**θεράποντας Ἄρηος*

[1] *ναυσικλυτοί* is reckoned a distinctive epithet even though it describes the Phaeacians as well as the Phoenicians: it obviously cannot be generic. Note that the resemblance in sound and metre between *Φοίνικες ναυσικλυτοί* and *Φαίηκες ναυσικλυτοί* is so close that one of them must have suggested the other.

The 11 epithets which in the preceding and in the following lists are marked with an asterisk are used also of individual heroes. We have here a characteristic example of the bards' tendency to use their epithets economically. In the same way some epithets used for gods and goddesses are also applied to mortals.

The epithets used by Homer to describe two or more peoples are as follows:

In the nominative:

μένεα πνείοντες	2
*ἐγχεσίμωροι	1
χαλκοχίτωνες	1
*μεγάθυμοι	3
*αἰχμηταί	1
*ἱπποκορυσταί	1
*μεγαλήτορες	3
*δῖοι	2
*ἱππόδαμοι	2
*κέντορες ἵππων	2
*ἀγανοί	2

In the genitive:

*μεγαθύμων	5
*αἰχμητάων	5
ἀσπιστάων	4
χαλκοχιτώνων	4
*ἀγερώχων	2
πύκα θωρηκτάων	2
μεγαθύμων ἀσπιστάων	2
*ἐγχεσιμώρων	1
*ἱπποδάμων	1
φιλοπτολέμων	1
*ἀγανῶν	1

In the dative:

φιλοπτολέμοισι	3
φιλοπτολέμοισιν	2
*ἱπποδάμοις	1
*ἱπποδάμοισι	1
*ἱπποδάμοισιν	1
*ἀντιθέοισιν	2

In the accusative:

*μεγαθύμους	2
μένεα πνείοντας	1
χαλκοχίτωνας	1
*μεγαλήτορας	1
ἱπποκορυστάς	1

Of the 46 different forms of generic epithets of peoples we see 4 which are not unique in metrical value: ἱπποδάμοισιν ∾ ἀντιθέοισιν recalling ἱπποδάμοιο ∾ ἀντιθέοιο, which we have already met among the generic epithets of heroes; and αἰχμητάων ∾ ἀσπιστάων.

We have already noticed more than once that when the bards were unable to fit a name into a formula of a particular length, they would often make use of a synonym. One of the most striking | examples of their use of this device is their treatment of the three names of the Achaeans: Ἀχαιοί, Δαναοί, and Ἀργεῖοι.[1]

The use of λαόν and of υἷας with Ἀχαιῶν makes possible the use of object formulae after the bucolic diaeresis. κοῦροι Ἀχαιῶν is of course an equivalent formula of δῖοι Ἀχαιῶν. But the expression λαὸς Ἀχαιῶν, although of like metrical value with these two, is not their equivalent, because it permits the bards the use of singular verb-forms, especially of

[1] Cf. Düntzer, *Homerische Abhandlungen*, 538.

forms in -*ετο* and -*ατο* in places where the corresponding plural forms would not have served.

A noun–epithet formula in the genitive case after the bucolic diaeresis cannot be formed with any of these three names. The noun–epithet formula in the genitive after the hephthemimeral caesura exists only thanks to *Δαναῶν*. But that the bards used these three names to make noun–epithet formulae is not the significant point. What is noteworthy is

TABLE IV. NOUN–EPITHET FORMULAE FOR THE ACHAEANS; PRINCIPAL TYPES

5 6 — ⏑⏑ — ⏑̄		4 5 6 ⏑⏑ — ⏑⏑ — ⏑̄		3 4 5 6 ⏑ — ⏑⏑ — ⏑⏑ — ⏑̄	
υἷες Ἀχαιῶν	62	*μεγάθυμοι Ἀχαιοί*	3	*ἐυκνήμιδες Ἀχαιοί*	18
κοῦροι Ἀχαιῶν	9	*κούρητες Ἀχαιῶν*	1	*κάρη κομόωντες Ἀχαιοί*	17
δῖοι Ἀχαιῶν	8	*Δαναοὶ ταχύπωλοι*	1		
λαὸς Ἀχαιῶν	4	*ἥρωες Ἀχαιοί*	2		
		ἑλίκωπες Ἀχαιοί	3		
		Δαναῶν ταχυπώλων	9	*Ἀχαιῶν χαλκοχιτώνων*	24
Ἀργείοισιν	6				
υἷας Ἀχαιῶν	24	*ἥρωας Ἀχαιῶν*	7	*ἐυκνήμιδας Ἀχαιούς*	10
λαὸν Ἀχαιῶν	18	*ἑλίκωπας Ἀχαιούς*	3	*κάρη κομόωντας Ἀχαιούς*	20

rather that *Ἀχαιοί* is very frequently accompanied by an epithet, whereas *Ἀργεῖοι* and *Δαναοί* are, apart from the two formulae quoted, almost never so accompanied. Outside of *Δαναῶν ταχυπώλων* the poet made use of *Ἀργεῖοι* and *Δαναοί* in but one noun–epithet formula occurring more than twice in the poems. | This is the whole-line formula used to summon the Achaean army in the vocative case:

ὦ φίλοι ἥρωες Δαναοί, θεράποντες Ἄρηος (4 times).

The three names are used in all their cases as follows:

	with epithet	without epithet
Ἀχαιοί	197	415
Δαναοί	22	114
Ἀργεῖοι	7	148

It is obvious that the poet uses or omits the epithet according to its usefulness in versification, this in turn depending on the metrical value of the substantive.

§ 7. LIMITS OF THE METHOD OF INVESTIGATION

When we leave behind epithets of persons and peoples and turn our attention to those used with other substantives, we straightway find ourselves facing difficulties that prevent our drawing equally sure conclusions from the method of investigation hitherto followed. The reason for this lies in the circumstance that outside of formulae referring to persons and peoples—both these groups may from one point of view be considered as persons—we can no longer distinguish any system either of noun–epithet formulae or of epithets sufficiently extended to prove the system traditional as a whole. We can, to be sure, discover in names of countries and in common nouns many systems of noun–epithet formulae and of epithets which in their entirety are too extended to have their origin in the verse of a poet of individual diction. But this extension is not so great that we can conclude from it with certainty that the possession of a unique metrical value is proof of the traditional character of this or that particular noun–epithet formula. For example: if we take a generic epithet of a hero, *δαΐφρονος*, which is said of 15 heroes, or *μεγαλήτορος*, which is said of 13 heroes, that each of these epithets, and each alone, presents one of the | 21 different metrical values attested for generic epithets of heroes in the genitive case, may be regarded as certain proof that both epithets are integral parts of a traditional system. Or again, we have a certain proof of the traditional character of *πολύτλας δῖος Ὀδυσσεύς* in that this formula is, first, unique in metre among the 14 noun–epithet formulae used in the nominative case for this hero, and second, is of the same metrical value with a great many other noun–epithet formulae of heroes—we pointed out 40 of them (TE, pp. 10–13). But when we try to determine whether the epithets *εὐρυάγυια* and *τειχιόεσσαν*, to choose two examples, are traditional or original, whether they are generic or distinctive, we no longer have this certainty. The different epithets of cities which are beyond doubt generic amount to only seven, in all the five cases.[1] Thus the uniqueness in metre of *εὐρυάγυια* and *τειχιόεσσαν* among these seven epithets is no more than a probable indication of their character. The same is true of the noun–epithet formulae in which these two epithets occur:

Δ 52	*Ἄργος τε Σπάρτη τε καὶ εὐρυάγυια Μυκήνη*
B 141 = *I* 28	*οὐ γὰρ ἔτι Τροίην αἱρήσομεν εὐρυάγυιαν*
η 80	*ἵκετο δ' ἐς Μαραθῶνα καὶ εὐρυάγυιαν Ἀθήνην*
B 559	*οἳ δ' Ἄργος τ' εἶχον Τίρυνθά τε τειχιόεσσαν*
B 646	*οἳ Κνωσόν τ' εἶχον Γόρτυνά τε τειχιόεσσαν.*

[1] The epithets of cities which can with certainty be considered generic are the following. The figures indicate the number of different cities described by each form. In the genitive case: *ἐυκτιμένης* (2), *ἐρατεινῆς* (1), *ἱεράων* (1). In the dative: *ἐυκτιμένηι* (3), *ἠγαθέηι* (3), *ἱερῆι* (2), *εὖ ναιομένωι* (1). In the accusative: *ἐυκτίμενον πτολίεθρον* (4), *ἐρατεινήν* (7), *ἐρατεινάς* (1), *ἐυκτιμένην* (2), *ζαθέην* (4), *ἱερόν*, *ἱερήν* (3), *ἠγαθέην* (1), *εὖ ναιομένον* (2).

If it could be shown that in the case of cities there exist frequent types of noun–epithet formula serving to adapt the sentence to the hexameter, we should very likely find that εὐρυάγυια Μυκήνη and εὐρυάγυιαν Ἀθήνην, which have the measure of one of the principal types, could be regarded as traditional formulae. And again if τειχιόεσσαν and εὐρυάγυιαν were used a little more frequently after the bucolic diaeresis, as they are in four of the lines quoted, it could perhaps be shown | that their function is analogous to that of ποιμένα λαῶν and ὄρχαμον ἀνδρῶν (cf. TE, p. 67). But these proofs are lacking in Homer, and in consequence we can be almost sure that the formulae and epithets in question are part of the traditional technique of diction, but this conclusion must remain to some extent conjectural.

We see that what keeps us from establishing clear systems of noun–epithet formulae and generic epithets in the case of names of countries is the small quantity of Homer's work that we possess. It is important to keep in mind this fact that the size of the poems imposes strict limits on the study of formulary technique. It is clear, for example, that only because the *Iliad* and the *Odyssey* are as long as they are can we describe at some length and in some detail the usefulness of noun–epithet formulae of heroes in versification, and discover the system, which appears to be virtually complete, of generic epithets of heroes. For if, of what we have, only a fourth remained, we should not have been able to point out in such number the different ways in which principal-type noun–epithet formulae of heroes are used, and the formulae which we could have pointed out would not have presented the great variety of metrical values which is an essential part of the proof. In the same way, we should not have found in the first part of the *Odyssey*, for example—where the number of heroes that appear is small in comparison with the *Iliad*—more than a fraction of the epithets which we were able to list in Table III; and moreover it would have been impossible to know with certainty in a great many cases whether a particular epithet, used with only one hero, should be considered distinctive or generic. It is only because the *Iliad* and the *Odyssey* are of a certain length, and because they are mostly about heroes, that we have a number of noun–epithet formulae for heroes large enough to allow us to demonstrate absolutely that certain formulae and epithets are integral parts of epic diction. And because the poems are not still longer, and the cities mentioned are so few, we cannot establish for names of cities any systems of sufficient complexity to be surely considered traditional in their entirety. |

In addition to these restrictions which the limited extent of the Homeric poems imposes on our method of investigation, there is another restriction when we deal with common nouns. Common nouns, unlike names, do not fall into a small number of categories. As we have said, the richness of a series of formulae of a particular type depends solely on the frequency of the poet's need to express a particular category of ideas. There is, for example, a very large number of names all falling into the category *hero*; we find for them series of noun–epithet formulae, some of great length, which show the same metrical value in a given grammatical case and thus allow us to recognize with certainty a traditional formula type. Similarly, the system of generic epithets of heroes given in Table III clearly owes its existence to the large number of names which fall into this category of *hero*. But this is no longer true for common nouns. With few exceptions, the idea expressed by each common noun has nothing to do with the ideas expressed by other nouns or names. It is not easy to imagine, for example, how one would put other nouns into the same category with *horse*, or *sea*, or *shield*, and how one would go about finding expressions analogous to those that describe what a horse, or the sea, or a shield do or have done to them. The actions of heroes and the actions of horses are not the same. One does not do with a shield what one does with a ship, nor what one does with a sword, nor in fine what one does with any object other than a shield. And the characteristics of the sea are such that epithets applied to it cannot be ascribed to any other thing. True, there does sometimes exist a certain common stock of ideas between some expressions and even between some nouns. The poet says 'he went to the ships', just as he says 'he went to Ilium', and we in fact discover ἔβη κοίλας ἐπὶ νῆας and ἔβη προτὶ Ἴλιον ἱρήν. The epithet ἀτρυγέτοιο can be used of the air as well as of the sea; κλυτά is said of arms, of houses, of tribes, of gifts. But this sort of resemblance of ideas | between expressions in which different nouns appear and between different nouns themselves is rather the exception than the rule.

The result is that when we come to common nouns we are limited to the study of epithets and noun–epithet formulae of a single noun. It is just as if our only evidence to determine which noun–epithet formulae of Odysseus should be referred to the tradition were the fact that out of his 46 noun–epithet formulae, 44, in all five grammatical cases, are of unique metrical value. In the case of the name of Odysseus we are certainly dealing with a system much too simple and much too extended to have any place in the work of a poet whose diction is original. The evidence for this provided by the almost complete absence in Virgil and Apollonius of anything which might be regarded as even the most fragmentary system of noun–epithet formulae is conclusive. But the systems of noun–epithet formulae which can be discovered for common nouns do not always show an extension and simplicity capable of proving them traditional in their entirety. Often we have the proof for a set of formulae without having it for each element. For these systems are seldom so extended that we can conclude with absolute certainty that this or that particular formula, which in a given grammatical case is the only one to be of a certain metrical value, is traditional. For the word for ship, *νηῦς*, we have a system of formulae of sufficient extension to prove it traditional in its entirety; and often, as in the case of formulae such as *μερόπων ἀνθρώπων* (10 times), *θνητῶν ἀνθρώπων* (7 times), *μώνυχες ἵπποι* (8 times), *ὠκέες ἵπποι* (11 times), etc., the frequency of the formula gives us another indication of its traditional character. But when we come to such formulae as *ἵπποι ἀερσίποδες* (twice), or *ἵππους ὠκύποδας* (once), the measures of which are not duplicated among the noun–epithet formulae of the horse, this proof is lacking, and the only conclusion we can safely draw is that these two formulae very probably belong to the tradition.

It is thus evident that outside of noun–epithet formulae and epithets of heroes we are compelled to forgo quantitative analysis. This is the only case in which the length of the poems and the | frequency of a single category of ideas give us an abundance and a variety of material sufficient to allow us to carry out such an analysis without leaning too much on hypothesis. We cannot exactly fix the line between epithets of names of countries and of common nouns that derive from the tradition and those that do not; but whenever we come to nouns of this sort which occur with some frequency, we can recognize the importance of formulae containing them and occupying one of the principal positions in the hexameter line; and we can observe the artifices of composition which the more often attested of these formulae subserve. We are of necessity limited to describing some of the outstanding poetic devices which the epithets make possible; but the description has a value of its own, because it enables us to see the great variety of ideas which the formulary technique is designed to express. We shall find in some cases that the need to use a particular noun with a preposition has given rise to series of noun–epithet–preposition formulae. For the expression of other categories of ideas there exist systems of noun–epithet–verb formulae. The circumstances attendant on the use of certain substantives have brought about a complete lack of formulae of certain metrical values in certain grammatical cases. We shall see, in fine, the ways in which the technique adjusts itself to the boundless complexity of ideas which the bards in their heroic verse wanted to express.

The course we have followed in this study appears to be the only one possible in the study of formulary technique. We selected for our subject the formulae of a given category, viz. those that contain fixed epithets, and as the point of departure of the study we took those formulae which occur with the greatest frequency and are used in the simplest manner: those noun–epithet formulae which complete both sentence and hexameter line and provide the grammatical subject for the expression of what is undoubtedly the most common idea in epic poetry—'X did Y'. Then we followed the technique of the use of the fixed epithet in formulae that serve to express more and more particular and more and more | complex ideas until we came to a point at which the rarity of formulae, which is to say the particularity of ideas, makes a judgement of their origin no longer possible. Any study of other categories of formulae will have to follow the same way. Starting out from the common usage of certain formulae for which systems can easily be established, one will always arrive at a point where further investigation is inhibited by the complexity of ideas. There is no doubt, moreover, that the study of another category of formulae could not be pursued so far as can noun–epithet formulae of heroes, at once the simplest and the most frequently occurring of all formulae. Should we, then, extend to the whole of Homeric diction the conclusion which we were able to draw from the study of the noun–epithet formulae in the nominative case of the seven principal heroes—that not one of them appears to be original? Obviously it is not possible to give a certain answer to this question, since these noun–epithet formulae of heroes, because they express the most common idea in all epic poetry, that of 'X hero', could therefore be more precisely determined than other groups of words expressing ideas more rare. It is clearly more prudent to be content with what can be certainly known than to seek further with the help of an unverifiable hypothesis. We shall have carried this study far enough if we show that for the expression of a certain portion of the various ideas of heroic poetry, the bards made use of a formulary technique adapted to the expression of these ideas in hexameters. In the following pages which form the conclusion of this chapter, we shall accordingly confine ourselves to showing that there do exist formulae to express various categories of ideas which have nothing in common with the actions or experiences of human characters.

§ 8. PREPOSITION–NOUN–EPITHET AND NOUN–EPITHET–VERB FORMULAE FOR CERTAIN NAMES OF COUNTRIES

In dealing with epithets of persons and peoples, it was enough to consider formulae made up of a name and of one or several epithetic words. Now and then the poet does have occasion to use a preposition with the name of | a hero, but this does not happen so often that the bards have any great need of series of noun–epithet–preposition formulae. And we find, in fact, that the epithets of heroes used in formulae of this kind are almost always generic epithets which, filling by themselves the space between two caesurae or between a caesura (or diaeresis) and the beginning or end of the line, have an existence independent of any formulae of given metrical value (cf. TE, pp. 67 ff.). This holds true for all the cases, except two, in which the poet uses a preposition–noun–epithet expression for Odysseus.

γ 163	ἀμφ' Ὀδυσῆα ἄνακτα	δαίφρονα ποικιλομήτην
χ 115	ἔσταν δ' ἀμφ' Ὀδυσῆα	
χ 202	βήτην εἰς Ὀδυσῆα	
χ 281	τοὶ δ' αὖτ' ἀμφ' Ὀδυσῆα	
Λ 482	ὥς ῥα τότ' ἀμφ' Ὀδυσῆα	
φ 223	κλαῖον ἄρ' ἀμφ' Ὀδυσῆι δαίφρονι χεῖρε βαλόντε	
α 48	ἀλλά μοι ἀμφ' Ὀδυσῆι δαίφρονι δαίεται ἦτορ	
π 100	ἢ πάις ἐξ Ὀδυσῆος ἀμύμονος ἠὲ καὶ αὐτὸς	
ε 149	ἡ δ' ἐπ' Ὀδυσσῆα μεγαλήτορα πότνια νύμφη	
Λ 419	ὥς ῥα τότ' ἀμφ' Ὀδυσῆα διίφιλον ἐσσεύοντο	
θ 502	Ἀργεῖοι, τοὶ δ' ἤδη ἀγακλυτὸν ἀμφ' Ὀδυσῆα.	

One of the two cases in which the poet uses for Odysseus a preposition–noun–epithet expression containing an epithet that does not fall between one of the caesurae of the third foot and the bucolic diaeresis or the end of the line, shows a reminiscence of ἀγακλυτὸν ἀμφ' Ὀδυσῆα.

ω 409 ὣς δ' αὔτως παῖδες Δολίου κλυτὸν ἀμφ' Ὀδυσῆα.

In the other case we have a noun–epithet expression usually preceded by καί (cf. *A* 264, *Θ* 275, *K* 112, etc.), which amounts to a fixed type of conjunction–noun–epithet formula. The metre of most prepositions being such that they can replace καί, the poet comes to have a formula type which can be classed as conjunction– or preposition–noun–epithet.

β 17 καὶ γὰρ τοῦ φίλος υἱὸς ἅμ' ἀντιθέωι Ὀδυσῆι

can be compared with

θ 518 βήμεναι ἠύτ' Ἄρηα σὺν ἀντιθέωι Μενελάωι
Υ 407 αὐτὰρ ὁ βῆ σὺν δουρὶ μετ' ἀντίθεον Πολύδωρον,

etc. |

With names of countries, the case is different. With these names, as with many common nouns, it is often necessary to use prepositions, and for this reason we find, along with series of noun–epithet formulae, other series, equally or more important, of preposition–noun–epithet formulae. The most common formulae of this kind for names of countries are those that occur after the caesurae of the third foot or between the beginning of the line and the penthemimeral caesura (cf. Table V, p. 108).

The constantly recurring need to express the idea of someone's arriving at some place gave rise to a series of formulae involving forms of ἱκάνω,

TABLE V. PREPOSITION–NOUN–EPITHET FORMULAE USED FOR NAMES OF COUNTRIES; PRINCIPAL TYPES

προτὶ Ἴλιον ἠνεμόεσσαν	5	ἐνὶ Τροίηι εὐρείηι	4	Ἴλιον εἰς ἱερήν	1
ποτὶ Ἴλιον ἠνεμόεσσαν	1	κατὰ Τροίην ἐρίβωλον	1	Τροίηι ἐν εὐρείηι	4
ὑπὸ Ἴλιον ἠνεμόεσσαν	1			δήμου ἀπὸ Τρώων	7
				δήμωι ἔνι Τρώων	8
Ἰθάκης ἐς πίονα δῆμον	2			ἐν δήμωι Ἰθάκης	
μυχῶι Ἄργεος ἱπποβότοιο	2	ἐν Ἄργεϊ περ πολυπύρωι	1	Ἄργος ἐς ἱππόβοτον	4
ἑκὰς Ἄργεος ἱπποβότοιο	2	ἀπ' Ἄργεος ἱπποβότοιο	2	Ἄργος ἀν' ἱππόβοτον	1
Πυθοῖ ἔνι πετρηέσσηι	1			Πυθοῖ ἐν ἠγαθέηι	1
Λακεδαίμονος ἐξ ἐρατεινῆς	2	ἐνὶ Σπάρτηι εὐρείηι	1		
Σπάρτην ἐς καλλιγύναικα	1				
		ἀπ' αἰγλήεντος Ὀλύμπου	2		
		κατ' Οὐλύμπου νιφόεντος	1		
		κατὰ πτύχας Οὐλύμποιο	1		
ἐκ Πύλου ἠμαθόεντος	1	Πύλωι ἔνι μητέρι μήλων	1	ἐν Πύλωι ἠγαθέηι	1
				ἐς Πύλον ἠγαθέην	4

ἱκνεύμεναι, and *ἵκω*. The most common are forms with the metrical value ⏓ – ⏓, which can stand at the end of the line or before the caesurae of the third foot. Of this metrical value we find:

I. from *ἱκάνω*: *ἱκάνεις, ἱκάνει, ἵκανον, ἵκανε(ν).*
II. from *ἵκω*: *ἵκωμι.*
III. from *ἱκνεύμεναι*: *ἵκεσθον, ἱκέσθην, ἵκοντο, ἵκωμαι, ἵκηαι, ἵκηται, ἵκησθε, ἵκωνται, ἱκοίμην, ἵκοιο, ἵκοιτο, ἵκοισθε, ἱκέσθω, ἵκεσθαι, ἀφῖχθαι.*

This device has all the more flexibility because the prepositions *εἰς* and *ἐπί* can replace each other or be omitted altogether. At the end of the line we find:

	Τροίην δ' ἐρίβωλον	ἱκέσθην / ἵκοντο
	Σχερίην ἐρίβωλον	ἵκοιτο
	Ἰθάκης ἐς δῆμον	ἵκηται
	πολυδίψιον Ἄργος	ἱκοίμην
	Φθίην ἐρίβωλον	ἱκοίμην
	κλυτὸν Ἄργος	ἱκοίμην
cf.	κλισίην εὔτυκτον	ἵκανε
	δόμον περικαλλέ'	ἵκανε
	εἰς οὐρανὸν εὐρὺν	ἵκανε
	τὰ νείατα πείραθ'	ἵκηαι
	θοὰς ἐπὶ νῆας	ἵκοιτο.

But if the poet places these verb-forms before one of the caesurae of the third foot, he needs formulae to complete the line. We find: |

Θ 47 *O* 151 *Ξ* 283	Ἴδην δ' { ἵκανεν / ἵκανον / ἱκέσθην } πολυπίδακα, μητέρα θηρῶν
Θ 456 *E* 360	{ ἂψ / ὄφρ' } ἐς Ὄλυμπον { ἵκεσθον / ἵκωμαι } ἵν' ἀθανάτων ἕδος ἐστίν
E 367 *E* 868	{ αἶψα δ' ἔπειθ' ἵκοντο / καρπαλίμως δ' ἵκανε } θεῶν ἕδος, αἰπὺν Ὄλυμπον
ο 193	αἶψα δ' ἔπειθ' ἵκοντο Πύλου αἰπὺ πτολίεθρον
cf. *I* 414	εἰ δέ κεν οἴκαδ' ἵκωμι φίλην ἐς πατρίδα γαῖαν
B 17 = 168	καρπαλίμως δ' ἵκανε θοὰς ἐπὶ νῆας Ἀχαιῶν
Z 370 = 497 *ρ* 85 = 178 *ω* 362 *Λ* 769	{ αἶψα δ' ἔπειθ' ἵκανε / αὐτὰρ ἐπεί ῥ' ἵκοντο / οἱ δ' ὅτε δή ῥ' ἵκοντο / Πηλῆος δ' ἱκόμεσθα } δόμους εὖ ναιετάοντας

§ 9. NOUN–EPITHET AND NOUN–EPITHET–PREPOSITION FORMULAE OF SHIPS

The importance of ships in epic poetry is responsible for the formation of what is without doubt the most complex of all formulary systems created for common nouns; and the *Iliad* and *Odyssey* seem to give us examples of most of the formulae of which the system is made. Table VI shows that the bards had two distinct series of formulae for ships which could fill the space between a caesura (or the bucolic diaeresis) and the beginning or end of the line: a series to be used with a preposition and a series to be used without. In some cases the simple noun–epithet formula made a formula of different metrical value when a preposition was added to it. Thus from νῆας ἐίσας and νῆα μέλαιναν, which occur after the bucolic diaeresis, are formed κατὰ νῆας ἐίσας and ἐπὶ νῆα μέλαιναν, which come after the hephthemimeral caesura. But in most cases the noun–epithet–preposition formula was especially created to contain the preposition, and without it would have been of little utility or none at all.

This table brings out clearly the two chief characteristics of a formulary system: we see, first, that there are series of formulae of particular metrical values for the different cases, singular and plural; and second, that most of these formulae | are unique in sense and metre. Note that the formulae containing the genitives Ἀχαιῶν and Ἀργείων are not equivalent formulae. Their function in Homer is to denote the fleet before Troy, as it must have been in any poem in which this fleet played a part; but if the story was about any other set of ships, they would be of no use. It is easy to pick out from the formulae we have, or even to reconstitute, those

Table VI. Noun–epithet and noun–epithet–preposition formulae for ships; principal types

5 6 – ⏑⏑ – ⋀̄		4 5 6 ⏑⏑ – ⏑⏑ – ⋀̄		3 4 5 6 ⏑ – ⏑⏑ – ⏑⏑ – ⋀̄		1 2 3 – ⏑⏑ – ⏑⏑ – ⏑		3 4 5 6 – – ⏑⏑ – ⏑⏑ – ⋀̄	
ὠκύαλος νηῦς	2								
ποντόπορος νηῦς	4								
νηῦς εὐεργής	3								
νηὸς ἐΐσης	5	νεὸς ἀμφιελίσσης	5	νεὸς κυανοπρῴροιο	8			νηὸς κυανοπρῴροιο	3
νηὶ μελαίνῃ	8	μεγακήτεϊ νηί	1			νηὶ πολυκλήϊδι	3		
νῆα μέλαιναν	9	εὐεργέα νῆα	8						
		περικαλλέα νῆα	1						
[νῆες Ἀχαιῶν]	4								
νῆες ἐΐσαι	1								
*									
νηυσὶ θοῇσι	1	νήεσσι θοῇσιν	2						
νηυσὶν ἐΐσῃς	1								
[νηυσὶν Ἀχαιῶν]	2								
[νῆας Ἀχαιῶν]	3	νέας ἀμφιελίσσας	4	νέας κυανοπρῳρείους	1	νῆας ἐϋσσέλμους	7		
νῆας ἐΐσας	11			[νέας Δαναῶν ταχυπώλων]	1				

	κοίλης ἐπὶ νηός	2	νεὸς προπάροιθε μελαίνης ἐυσσέλμου ἐπὶ νηός θοῆς παρὰ νηὸς ἐίσης	I 3 I	νηὸς {ὑπὲρ / ἐπὶ} γλαφυρῆς	I I	κοίλης ἐπὶ νηὸς ἐίσης	I
	{ἐν / παρὰ / σὺν} νηὶ μελαίνῃ κοίλῃ παρὰ νηί	3 I I I	θοῇ {παρὰ / ἐνὶ / σὺν} νηὶ μελαίνῃ ἐυσσέλμῳ {ἐπὶ / ἐνὶ} νηί	2 I I I I	ἐν νηὶ γλαφυρῇ [νηυσὶν ἐπ' Ἀργείων]	I I	κοίλῃ παρὰ νηὶ μελαίνῃ	2
	{ἐπὶ / περὶ} νῆα μέλαιναν	3 2	θοὴν {ἀνὰ / ἐπὶ} νῆα μέλαιναν	I I	νῆα παρὰ γλαφυρήν	I		
			ἐυσσέλμων {ἀπὸ / ἐπὶ} νηῶν μελαινάων {ἀπὸ / ἐπὶ} νηῶν	I 2 3 4				
	κοίλῃς ἐνὶ νηυσίν παρὰ νηυσὶ θοῇσιν [{παρὰ / ἐπὶ} νηυσὶν Ἀχαιῶν]	5 3 I 4	νέεσσ' ἐν ποντοπόροισιν [θοῇς ἐπὶ νηυσὶν Ἀχαιῶν]	I I	νηυσὶν ἐπὶ γλαφυρῇς	I	ἐν ποντοπόροισι νέεσσι	2
	κοίλας ἐπὶ νῆας κατὰ νῆας ἐίσας [{παρὰ / ἐπὶ} νῆας Ἀχαιῶν]	II I I 6	[θοὰς ἐπὶ νῆας Ἀχαιῶν]	10	νῆας {ἀνὰ / ἐπὶ} γλαφυράς [νῆας ἐπ' Ἀργείων]	15 3 I	[κοίλας ἐπὶ νῆας Ἀχαιῶν]	3

which must have been more generally usable. In fact we find νῆες εἶσαι along with νῆες Ἀχαιῶν, κατὰ νῆας ἐίσας along with κατὰ νῆας Ἀχαιῶν, etc.; whence we can infer that in poems in which some other fleet was mentioned, we should find, not κοίλας ἐπὶ νῆας Ἀχαιῶν but κοίλας ἐπὶ νῆας ἐίσας, not θοῇς ἐπὶ νηυσὶν Ἀχαιῶν but θοῇς ἐπὶ νηυσίν ἐίσῃς, etc. Of the 69 formulae given on Table VI, those which are not unique amount to only six: ποντόπορος νηῦς ∼ νηῦς εὐεργής, νηυσὶ θοῇσι ∼ νηυσὶν ἐίσῃς, παρὰ νηὶ μελαίνῃ ∼ κοίλῃ παρὰ νηί.

The 23 epithets of ships in Homer present 70 different forms, of which two only, δολιχηρέτμοιο (twice) and κυανοπρῴροιο (12 times), can be interchanged:

Nominative: γλαφυρή (1)
εὐεργής (3)
ποντόπορος (4)
ὠκύαλος (2)
κοίλη (1)
θοή (3)

Genitive: ἀμφιελίσσης (5)
γλαφυρῆς (11)
{ δολιχηρέτμοιο (2)
{ κυανοπρῴροιο (12)
ἐίσης (5)
ἐυζύγου (1)
ἐυσσέλμου (-οιο) (6)
θοῆς (3) |
κοίλης (5)
ποντοπόροιο (4)
ὠκυάλου (1)
μελαίνης (5)

Dative: γλαφυρῇ (4)
ἐυσσέλμῳ (2)
θοῇ (18)
κοίλῃ (4)
μεγακήτεϊ (3)
μελαίνῃ (29)
πολυζύγῳ (1)
πολυκλήιδι (5)

Accusative: γλαφυρήν (2)
θοήν (30)
κοίλην (3)
μέλαιναν (21)
περικαλλέα (2)
εὐργέα (8)

Nominative: γλαφυραί (4)
εἶσαι (1)
ἐύζυγοι (1)
ὠκύποροι (1)
ἐύσσελμοι (4)
θοαί (5)
μέλαιναι (12)
μιλτοπάρῃοι (2)
ἀμφιέλισσαι (5)

Genitive: ἐυσσέλμων (3)
θοάων (5)
μελαινάων (9)
ὀρθοκραιράων (2)
ὠκειάων (2)
ὠκυπόρων (5)

Dative: κοίλῃς (12)
ἐίσῃς (1)
γλαφυρῇς (-σι, -σιν) (17)
δολιχηρέτμοισι (1)
θοῇς (-σι, -σιν) (11)
κορωνίσι(ν) (17)
μελαίνῃσι(ν) (5)
πολυκλήισι (6)
ποντοπόροισι(ν) (11)
ὠκυπόροισι(ν) (5)

Accusative: ἀμφιελίσσας (9)
γλαφυράς (18)
ἐίσας (11)
ἐυσσέλμους (12)
θοάς (16)
κοίλας (14)
κυανοπρῳρείους (1).

We may at first have the impression that this system of epithets of ships demonstrates in a neater and more cogent fashion than does the system of generic epithets of heroes (Table III) how the influence of verse was able to create, for the handling of a name in hexameter, an extended system of epithetic forms in which no form superfluous for versification has any place. The almost complete absence in this system of equivalent forms comes about precisely because the epithets of ships are not applicable to other objects. *περικαλλέα* is the only exception worth mentioning among the 23 epithets of ships. Consequently the selection of a single epithet to provide one or several forms of certain metrical values was made here much more easily than in a case where epithets could be used with a large number of different names (see TE, pp. 184 ff.). |

§ 10. NOUN–EPITHET FORMULAE OF HORSES

With the exception of *ἵππων ὠκυπόδων* (once), noun–epithet formulae of horses of the three principal types are all in the nominative or accusative case. The reason for the predominance of these two grammatical cases is clearly that horses are almost always described as either accomplishing some action or obeying someone's orders.

TABLE VII. NOUN–EPITHET FORMULAE OF HORSES, PRINCIPAL TYPES[1]

5 6 — ◡◡ — ⊼		4 5 6 ◡◡ — ◡◡ — ⊼		1 2 3 — ◡◡ — ◡◡ —	
μώνυχες ἵπποι	8	*καλλίτριχες ἵπποι*	3	*ἵπποι ἀερσίποδες*	2
ὠκέες ἵπποι	11	*ἐριαύχενες ἵπποι*	1		
		ὑψηχέες ἵπποι	1		
μώνυχας ἵππους	28	*καλλίτριχας ἵππους*	11	*ἵππους ὠκύποδας*	1
ὠκέας ἵππους	20	*ἐριαύχενας ἵππους*	4		
[*χαλκόποδ' ἵππω*]	2	*κρατερώνυχας ἵππους*	3		
		ὑψηχέας ἵππους	1		

χαλκόποδ' ἵππω occurs twice in Homer, in both cases in connection with the harnessing of horses:

Θ 41	*ὣς εἰπὼν*	*ὑπ' ὄχεσφι τιτύσκετο χαλκόποδ' ἵππω.*
N 23	*ἔνθ' ἐλθὼν*	

[1] The expressions *χρυσάμπυκας ἵππους* (4 times) and *ἐρυσάρματες* (-*ας*) *ἵπποι* (-*ους*) (twice) have been omitted. The first is used only for horses of the gods, and the second is not an ornamental epithet: it establishes a distinction between chariot horses and draught horses.

Therefore this formula is not the equivalent of *μώνυχας ἵππους*, since ordinarily horses are mentioned in groups of three, the two that draw the chariot and the *παρήορος*. It is to be observed that the survival of the dual in these two lines is not to be explained by metrical necessity; it survived because the formula *ὑπ' ὄχεσφι τιτύσκετο χαλκόποδ' ἵππω*, created at a time when the dual was a part of living speech, was preserved in its entirety to express the idea 'he put to the chariot the two horses which were to draw it'. The equivalent formulae which appear in the Table | are therefore 4 in number: *ἐριαύχενες ἵπποι* ~ *ὑψηχέες ἵπποι* and *ἐριαύχενας ἵππους* ~ *ὑψηχέας ἵππους*.

§ II. NOUN–EPITHET FORMULAE OF THE HUMAN RACE

To designate *men*, Homer uses *βροτοί*, *ἄνθρωποι*, *ἄνδρες* (*ἀνέρες*) or *θνητοί*[1] without any distinction; but notwithstanding the great variety of

TABLE VIII. NOUN–EPITHET FORMULAE OF THE HUMAN RACE; PRINCIPAL TYPES

4 5 6 ⏑⏑ – ⏑⏑ – ⏓		3 4 5 6 ⏑ – ⏑⏑ – ⏑⏑ – ⏓	
μέροπες ἄνθρωποι	1		
μερόπων ἀνθρώπων	10	*ἐπιχθονίων ἀνθρώπων*	5
θνητῶν ἀνθρώπων	7	*καταθνητῶν ἀνθρώπων*	6
μερόπεσσι βροτοῖσιν	1		
θνητοὺς ἀνθρώπους	1		

measures which these four synonyms provide, none of them is of such metrical value that it could become part of a noun–epithet formula following the bucolic diaeresis. Except for *καὶ θνητοῖσι βροτοῖσι* (twice) and *ἀνδράσι γε θνητοῖσι* (thrice), which occur at the beginning of the line, all noun–epithet formulae of the human race which occur more than once in the poems are designed to be used either after the feminine caesura or after the hephthemimeral caesura.

Strictly speaking, *θνητῶν ἀνθρώπων* could serve in every place where we find *μερόπων ἀνθρώπων*; but on each occasion one or the other of these formulae is chosen according to whether a syllable needs to be made long by position, or whether the poet wants to avoid over-lengthening.

Formulae in the genitive case are here much more common than in the nominative. We found the contrary to be true for formulae of men and

[1] Cf. H. Düntzer, op. cit., 538.

gods. The frequency is chiefly due to the need for expressing two different categories of ideas. The human race is most often spoken of in relation to one of the things which belong to it. Thus we find: |

γενεαὶ
ἀλόχους
τέρας } μερόπων ἀνθρώπων
(twice) πόλεις
πόλις
λόγοι
ἔπεα θνητῶν ἀνθρώπων.

These formulae in the genitive case are also used very often with τις to express the idea 'some mortal'. We find:

Σ 403 οὐδέ τις ἄλλος
ἤιδεεν οὔτε θεῶν οὔτε θνητῶν ἀνθρώπων
cf. η 247.
ι 502 Κύκλωψ, αἴ κέν τίς σε καταθνητῶν ἀνθρώπων
cf. ρ 587, γ 114, Ζ 123.
α 167 θαλπωρή, εἴ πέρ τις ἐπιχθονίων ἀνθρώπων
cf. χ 414, ψ 65.

§ 12. NOUN–EPITHET FORMULAE AND NOUN–EPITHET–PREPOSITION FORMULAE OF SHIELDS

The circumstances under which it behoves the poet to speak of shields, as compared with other nouns which we have studied, are very few, and noun–epithet and noun–epithet–preposition formulae descriptive of shields are almost never of general usage, but usually serve rather to narrate a particular phase of battle or of single combat. Hence the greater part of these formulae are of the kind which we termed specific, when we had occasion to study them above in the case of persons (TE, pp. 75 ff.), and, as we have seen, it is fruitless to try to establish any system of such formulae by isolating the noun–epithet formula: being by definition reserved for the expression of a particular idea, or of a particular set of related ideas, the specific formula cannot be separated from the other words which together with it fulfil this function. When we deal with formulae of shields containing an epithet, therefore, the most we can do is to recognize the regular use of the most frequent of them, as they appear in the expression of a particular idea. |

I. The most common formula in which we encounter an epithet of a shield is κατ' ἀσπίδα πάντοσ' ἐΐσην (9 times), used to describe the incident so frequently recurrent in Homeric battle, when a warrior receives a blow of a spear on his shield. We find:

Γ 356 = Η 250	καὶ βάλε(ν) Πριαμίδαο	κατ᾽ ἀσπίδα πάντοσ᾽ ἐίσην
Ρ 517	καὶ βάλε(ν) Ἀρήτοιο	κατ᾽ ἀσπίδα πάντοσ᾽ ἐίσην
Υ 274	καὶ βάλε(ν) Αἰνείαο	κατ᾽ ἀσπίδα πάντοσ᾽ ἐίσην
Γ 347	καὶ βάλε(ν) Ἀτρείδαο	κατ᾽ ἀσπίδα πάντοσ᾽ ἐίσην
Ν 160	καὶ βάλεν, οὐδ᾽ ἀφάμαρτε,	κατ᾽ ἀσπίδα πάντοσ᾽ ἐίσην
Λ 434 = Ρ 43	ὣς εἰπὼν οὔτησε	κατ᾽ ἀσπίδα πάντοσ᾽ ἐίσην
Ψ 818	ἔνθ᾽ Αἴας μὲν ἔπειτα κατ᾽ ἀσπίδα πάντοσ᾽ ἐίσην νύξ᾽.	

II. The same formula appears in four places without preposition; in all four, a hero lifts up his shield to ward off a spear thrust:

Μ 294	αὐτίκα δ᾽	ἀσπίδα μὲν πρόσθ᾽ ἔσχετο πάντοσ᾽ ἐίσην
Φ 581	ἀλλ᾽ ὅ γ᾽ ἄρ᾽	ἀσπίδα μὲν πρόσθ᾽ ἔσχετο πάντοσ᾽ ἐίσην
Ν 157 = 803	Πριαμίδης, πρόσθεν δ᾽ ἔχεν ἀσπίδα πάντοσ᾽ ἐίσην.	

III. The expression ἀσπίδες ὀμφαλόεσσαι appears six times in the *Iliad*, and always at the end of a line. Twice it is introduced by ἀτάρ: the two occasions Δ 446–451 = Θ 60–5 are identical descriptions of the collision of two armies in battle. In the four other cases it is introduced by καί; at first sight one is tempted to see in them four different ways of using the expression; but a deeper examination reveals that the poet was each time making use of the same device. In καὶ ἀσπίδες ὀμφαλόεσσαι we have a formula whose use is well worth studying with some care; for it is the type of a large number of noun–epithet formulae designed to facilitate the making of verse in quite particular circumstances which the poet would only rarely find himself having to confront. In this way, the use of καὶ ἀσπίδες ὀμφαλόεσσαι is appropriate here as the last detail which we shall consider in this chapter on the technique of the use of the epithet. We have now arrived at a point at which the method of investigation which we have used serves no longer, the complexity of the ideas and of the expressions which they translate | no longer allowing us to establish systems of sufficient extension either of epithets or of noun–epithet formulae, nor at last even to pick out specific noun–epithet formulae by the frequency of their occurrence. But here, at the limit of our investigation, this last example gives us a glimpse of how the bards created formulae which they could use, even when the idea to be expressed was no longer such as to be often met with in a heroic poem. Now the conclusion which we can draw from this is of course of an exceedingly general nature; but considering the quantity of formulae of heroes which we were able to refer to the tradition, and the variety which we were able to observe in the use to which these formulae were put in hexameter composition, we may perhaps conclude without exaggeration from this last example that among the noun–epithet formulae of the *Iliad* and the *Odyssey*, there are very few whose creation can be attributed to the author, or the authors, of these poems.

The poet tells of the clangour of arms in *M* 161, of the great store of arms in the possession of a certain hero in *N* 264, of the lapped appearance of the arms of the Achaeans as they march into battle in *Π* 214, of the density and the shine of their arms as they prepare for battle in *T* 360. He wants to make the image of his thought more vivid to his audience, and to this end, in each of these four passages, he names some of the arms that figure in his image. The question of how he shall express his thought thus becomes in each case the question, how shall he introduce into his hexameter lines a series of subjects and a single predicate shared by these subjects. His answer to the question offers him both variation of style and convenience of versification: he names one subject, places the predicate after it (or vice versa), and then adds as many subjects as he wishes. This arrangement in the line of the several elements of the sentence would not be any easier for the poet than another, if, to designate the different arms, he did not dispose of conjunction–noun–epithet formulae falling between the beginning and the internal breaks and the end of the line. That part of the sentence formed by the initial subject and the predicate must end at the end of the line or at one of the principal breaks, because by itself it already constitutes a grammatically complete sentence, and the poet will have to make a distinct pause after it, as he sings: then the supplementary subject or subjects will follow, | filling the spaces between the beginning or end of the line and the internal breaks.

In *Π* 212 ff. and in *M* 159 ff. we have only 'helmets' as initial subject and 'shields' as supplementary subject:

Π 212 ὡς δ' ὅτε τοῖχον ἀνὴρ ἀράρῃ πυκινοῖσι λίθοισι
δώματος ὑψηλοῖο, βίας ἀνέμων ἀλεείνων,
ὣς ἄραρον κόρυθές τε καὶ ἀσπίδες ὀμφαλόεσσαι.

M 159 ὣς τῶν ἐκ χειρῶν βέλεα ῥέον, ἠμὲν Ἀχαιῶν
ἠδὲ καὶ ἐκ Τρώων· κόρυθες δ' ἀμφ' αὖον ἀύτευν
βαλλομένων μυλάκεσσι καὶ ἀσπίδες ὀμφαλόεσσαι.

In *N* 264 ff. we have 'spears' as initial subject, and 'shields', 'helmets', and 'breastplates' as three supplementary subjects. The same subjects appear in *T* 357 ff., only in a different order, made necessary by the metrical value of the other parts of the sentence:

N 264 τῶ μοι δούρατά τ' ἔστι καὶ ἀσπίδες ὀμφαλόεσσαι,
καὶ κόρυθες καὶ θώρηκες λαμπρὸν γανόωντες.

T 357 ὡς δ' ὅτε ταρφειαὶ νιφάδες Διὸς ἐκποτέονται
ψυχραί, ὑπὸ ῥιπῆς αἰθρηγενέος Βορέαο,
ὣς τότε ταρφειαὶ κόρυθες λαμπρὸν γανόωσαι
νηῶν ἐκφορέοντο καὶ ἀσπίδες ὀμφαλόεσσαι
θώρηκές τε κραταιγύαλοι καὶ μείλινα δοῦρα.

IV

THE MEANING OF THE EPITHET IN EPIC POETRY

1. *Can the fixed epithet have a particularized meaning?* 2. *The generic epithet.* 3. *The particularized epithet.* 4. *The epithet outside epic poetry.* 5. *Can the fixed epithet be translated?*

THE investigation carried out in the preceding chapter was made with the assumption that to ascertain the reasons for the use of a fixed epithet in a given case there is no need to consider what it denotes. In our study of the various devices which fixed epithets make possible, the facility of versification which they afford the poet appeared the only factor determining their use. Some of those who know Homer well will be dissatisfied with this procedure. To them it will seem inconceivable that the poet was not guided to some extent in his choice of a fixed epithet by the effect that it might produce in its particular context. Nor will they be willing to admit that the poet did not choose the set of epithets applicable to a given hero for reasons that have to do with his character or his role in the poem. Some will believe that by entirely passing over the signification of the fixed epithet we have arrived at false conclusions, others that our conclusions are incomplete. The purpose of this chapter is to show that these objections are based on an inexact understanding of the meaning of the fixed epithet, and that they lose their point once one understands the fundamental difference between an epithet forming part of a traditional diction and one which is used in an individual style; between an epithet in epic poetry and one appearing anywhere else in Greek | poetry or in our own. In other words, it must be shown, first, that the fixed epithet in Homer is invariably used without relevance to the immediate action whatever it may be, and second, that the generic epithet does not define any characteristic that distinguishes one hero from another, but only the characteristic that makes him a hero. Once it is understood how the meaning of a fixed epithet is modified by being used over and over again with a certain name or a certain category of names, it will become clear, not only that we omitted nothing essential in considering the use of fixed epithets in terms of their metrical value, but also that in attempting to explain the use of the fixed epithet by its signification, readers have arbitrarily supposed that the literary education of the Homeric audience was the same as that of the modern reader, and that the ideal of style which Homer followed was the ideal that inspires an author of our own days.

§ 1. CAN THE FIXED EPITHET HAVE A PARTICULARIZED MEANING?

In order to see the character of the problem more clearly and fully to grasp its importance, let us consider the many cases in which, if we are to follow Homer's thought exactly, we must choose between the ornamental and the particularized meaning of an epithet. In the first line of the *Iliad* the poet puts the name of Achilles' father next to his own. Does he do this in order to give us genealogical information? Or does he do it rather to remind us of the glory of Achilles' father? δῖος in the seventh line: is Achilles so qualified that he may be introduced into the poem in all his glory, alongside of Agamemnon who is entitled ἄναξ ἀνδρῶν? What reason led the poet in line 9 to say 'son of Leto and of Zeus' instead of merely giving the god his own name? Is this some nuance of style which, by naming him indirectly, enhances the grandeur of the god? ἑκηβόλου in line 14: does the poet deliberately confer this title upon Apollo in order to anticipate for us the part the god will play with his bow? Are the Atreidae in line 16 called 'marshals of the host' in order that we may know that it is as supreme commanders of the Achaean army that the priest makes supplication to them? In line 34, is the sea πολυφλοίσβοιο because a storm is raging? And then in line 37 we have again the question of Apollo as archer. |

It would be wrong to believe that this passage at the beginning of the poem, where we most expect to find them, is alone in containing so many epithets which could be understood as particularized. Let us move on to the *Odyssey*, to the episode of the slaughter of the suitors. πολύμητις in χ 1: an allusion to Odysseus' wiliness in ensnaring the suitors? πικρὸν ὀιστόν in line 8: does that mean that the arrow is well honed for Antinous? κακόν and μέλαιναν in line 14: should these epithets bring to our minds the particularly dreadful deaths of the suitors? ἁπαλοῖο δι' αὐχένος in the sixteenth line: do we learn from this that Antinous was delicate in body? Or does the epithet rather evoke the contrast between the softness of his neck and the hardness of the arrow's point? In line 24 the suitors try to find arms along the 'well builded' walls: did Homer choose this word ἐυδμήτους in order to tell us that once they are overwhelmed by panic fear, the solid appearance of the walls will offer them no hope of escape? Then in line 34 we find πολύμητις once more: is the epithet put here to remind us again that wily Odysseus has become master of his enemies by a ruse?

The length of this enumeration may seem tedious to a reader well versed in the *Iliad* and *Odyssey*; he may object that we are insisting on a distinction known to many. But Düntzer grasps the character of the problem well when he says (*Hom. Ab.*, 511) that if the distinction is generally known, yet it is not properly taken into account in the interpretation of Homer. And in fact, what has been, and still is uncertain, is just how far we should admit the ornamental, at the expense of the particularized, interpretation of these and similar words.

This problem was already dealt with by Aristarchus, as we know from the scholiasts and Eustathius. We have sufficient evidence from them to be able to gauge the true importance as well as the limitations of the solution he offered.[1]

The ancients designated what we call the particularized | meaning of an epithet by the expression *οὐ κόσμου χάριν ἀλλὰ πρός τι*. Thus at *β* 94, where Penelope's deceipt of the suitors is being described,

στησαμένη μέγαν ἱστὸν ἐνὶ μεγάροισιν ὕφαινε,

the scholiasts tell us, '*μέγαν* is not added poetically as an ornament, but refers to the long time required by the work'.[2] Similar is the remark of the scholiast at *Σ* 416 where Hephaestus leaves his forge to go to Thetis:

δῦ δὲ χιτῶν', ἕλε δὲ σκῆπτρον παχύ, βῆ δὲ θύραζε.

'*παχύ* is essential to the sentence; it is used because Hephaestus, of whom the poet says (*Σ* 410) *πέλωρ αἴητον ἀνέστη*, is lame, and leans upon his sceptre.'[3] It is clear that the authors of these remarks were above all guided by their desire to discover fine points of Homeric style. We gain some conception of the exaggeration to which they were led by what they say of *Φ* 218, where the poet has the river Scamander speak:

πλήθει γὰρ δή μοι νεκύων ἐρατεινὰ ῥέεθρα.

Aristarchus, perceiving only the patent contradiction between the idea of the epithet and that of the sentence, concludes in his usual fashion that the epithet must be ornamental (see below). But others found this ingenious explanation for the epithet: 'The epithet is well chosen to indicate the kind of river that is being thus polluted.'[4] Finally, we cite the scholiast of BLV at *B* 467, where the Achaeans are marching into battle:

ἔσταν δ' ἐν λειμῶνι Σκαμανδρίωι ἀνθεμόεντι.

[1] A. Roemer, *Aristarchs Athetesen in der Homerkritik*, Leipzig 1912, 336 ff.; Lehrs, *Aristarchi Studia Homerica*, Leipzig 1865, 199.

[2] Schol. HMQS, *οὐ ποιητικῶς κόσμου χάριν προσέρριπται τὸ μέγαν ἀλλὰ πρὸς τὸ πολυχρόνιον τῆς τοῦ ἔργου κατασκευῆς.*

[3] Schol. A, *ὅτι οὐ παρέλκει τὸ παχύ, ἀλλὰ πρὸς τὸ ἐπερείδειν χωλὸν ὄντα τὸν Ἥφαιστον*, etc.

[4] Schol. B, *καλῶς τὸ ἐπίθετον, εἰς ἔνδειξιν τοῦ ὅτι τὰ τοιαῦτα ῥεύματα μεμίανται.*

'The plain was formerly in flower.[1] The epithet is thus used in the same way as ἐϋμμελίω Πριάμοιο (Δ 47), ἥρως Αἰγύπτιος (β 15), and ἠΰκομος Νιόβη (Ω 602).' |

To the interpretation οὐ κόσμου χάριν ἀλλὰ πρός τι the ancients opposed the interpretation οὐ τότε ἀλλὰ φύσει. Aristarchus, in accordance with his principle of finding ἡ ἐκ τῆς λέξεως λύσις, was the first to put forward the explanation in a methodical way. The character of his interpretation is not in doubt. He took those cases in which no particularized meaning of the epithet is possible, and offered the ornamental meaning as their only conceivable explanation. Thus apropos of Θ 555:

> ὡς δ' ὅτ' ἐν οὐρανῶι ἄστρα φαεινὴν ἀμφὶ σελήνην
> φαίνετ' ἀριπρεπέα

'the moon is brilliant,' Aristarchus tells us, 'not at that moment, but in general'.[2] Porphyry describes the reasoning of the great critic in more detail: 'How can the stars shine around the radiant moon? The solution of the passage is found in its context. The moon is brilliant not at this moment, but by its nature.'[3] And from the scholiast of L we know that Aristarchus believed that Homer's image was of the new moon: 'Aristarchus says that *brilliant* means by its nature, even though the moon is not full; for if there was a full moon, the stars would actually have been invisible.'[4] Aristarchus compares this use of φαεινήν to that of the same epithet in ζ 74, where Nausicaa sends for her linen to take it to be washed:

> κούρη δ' ἐκ θαλάμοιο φέρεν ἐσθῆτα φαεινήν.

'Not that her linen is radiant at this moment: it is dirty; but it is clean by nature.'[5] For κλυτά (ζ 58), which is said of these same garments, the scholiasts simply compare Θ 555, which, together with the term ἐζήτησαν in a remark of Apollonius (*Lex.* 161, 20), informs us that this last line was the example *par excellence* of the | ornamental interpretation advanced by Aristarchus.[6] We know other cases in which he offered the same solution: Σκαμανδρίωι ἀνθεμόεντι (Β 467), ἐρατεινὰ ῥέεθρα (Φ 218) and ἐϋμμελίω Πριάμοιο (Δ 47), which we have already mentioned as cases deemed

[1] τῶι ἄνθη πρώην ἔχοντι.

[2] οὐ τὴν τότε οὖσαν φαεινήν, ἀλλὰ τὴν καθόλου φαεινήν (cf. Roemer, op. cit., 338).

[3] ἐκ τῶν ἀδυνάτων καὶ τοῦτο· πῶς γὰρ δυνατὸν περὶ τὴν φαεινὴν σελήνην ἀριπρεπῆ εἶναι τὰ ἄστρα; λύεται δ' ἐκ τῆς λέξεως· τὸ φαεινὴν οὐκ ἐπὶ τῆς τότε ἀλλ' ἐπὶ τῆς φύσει, ὡς ἐπὶ τοῦ ἐσθῆτα φαεινήν, καὶ τοῦ ἐρατεινὰ ῥέεθρα.

[4] Schol. L, Ἀρίσταρχος τὴν κατὰ φύσιν λαμπρὰν λέγει, κἂν μὴ πλήθουσα ᾖι· εἰ γὰρ πλησιοσέληνος ἦν, ἐκέκρυπτο ἂν μᾶλλον τὰ ἄστρα.

[5] Schol. EHPV, οὐ τὴν τότε οὖσαν φαεινήν· ῥερύπωται γάρ· ἀλλὰ τὴν φύσει καθαράν.

[6] Apoll. *Lex.* 161, 20. λαμπρά· ἐν δὲ τῆι Θ τῆς 'Ιλιάδος φαεινὴν ἀμφὶ σελήνην. ἐζήτησαν πῶς τότε ἡ σελήνη δύναται φαεινὴ εἶναι ὅτε τὰ ἄστρα λαμπρὰ φαίνεται. ὅθεν ὁ Ἀρίσταρχος λύων φησὶ φαεινὴν οὐ τὴν τότε λαμπρὰν ἀλλὰ τὴν φύσει λαμπράν, ὥσπερ καὶ ἐπὶ τῆς ἐσθῆτος τῆς Ναυσικάας . . . ἀλλὰ δῆλον, φησίν, ὅτι ἔνταυθα ἀκουστέον τὴν φύσει λαμπράν.

particularized by other ancient writers—οὐ τότε ἀλλὰ πρώην; and finally ἤνοπι χαλκῶι which appears in the whole-line formula

Σ 349 = κ 360 αὐτὰρ ἐπεὶ δὴ ζέσσεν ὕδωρ ἐνὶ ἤνοπι χαλκῶι.[1]

Some penetrating minds had apparently observed that the tripod would in reality be filled with vapours and covered by smoke.

Aristarchus applied the same explanation to cases where an ennobling epithet qualifies a wicked or an unworthy man. Thus Herodian tells us in connection with Ζ 160, where the wife of Bellerophon's host attempts to seduce the hero,

τῶι δὲ γυνὴ Προίτου ἐπεμήνατο, δῖ' Ἄντεια,

'the epithet is added as an ornament, as in the case of δῖα Κλυταιμνήστρη (γ 266).'[2] Eustathius gives us more fully what was apparently Aristarchus' explanation of cases of this kind. He says of α 29, where Zeus speaks to the other gods.

μνήσατο γὰρ κατὰ θυμὸν ἀμύμονος Αἰγίσθοιο,

'the Homeric Zeus here speaks of the wicked Aegisthus as 'blameless', not referring to his crimes [evidently some found irony in this], but to his natural virtues: he had high birth, beauty, intelligence, and other things of the same sort.'[3] Elsewhere he repeats this explanation: 'ἀμύμων is said of Aegisthus and others who, though unworthy in other respects, are yet | blameless in their valour, or blood, or in other like characteristics.'[4] Notice especially the expressions at the end of these explanations: καὶ εἴ τί που ἄλλο and ἤ τι τοιοῦτον.

Certain ancient writers found in these illogical usages reason to condemn or to correct the lines in which they appear. From the scholiast of A at Λ 123 we know that these condemnations and corrections stem in part from no less renowned a critic than Zenodotus. Homer speaks of the sons of Ἀντιμάχοιο δαΐφρονος, who took gold from Paris in return for opposing the restoration of Helen, and eleven lines further on he repeats the expression. Zenodotus wanted to correct the epithet to κακόφρονος. Thus we learn that Aristarchus was here the champion of the traditional text of the poems.[5]

Eustathius gives for the use of ἀντίθεοι μνηστῆρες (ξ 18), who nine lines below are termed μνηστῆρσιν ὑπερφιάλοισιν, the same explanation we have

[1] Schol. A at ἔστιν οὖν ὡς τὸ φαεινὴν ἀμφὶ σελήνην.

[2] κατὰ κόσμον ποιητικὸν προσέρριπται ὡς καὶ ἐπὶ τοῦ δῖα Κλυταιμνήστρη.

[3] 1387, 20. ἀμύμονα γοῦν ὀνομάζει νῦν τὸν ἀτάσθαλον Αἴγισθον ὁ Ὁμηρικὸς Ζεύς, οὐκ ἐκ τῶν ἐκείνου κακῶν λαβὼν τὸ ἐπίθετον ἀλλ' ἀφ' ὡς εἰκὸς εἶχε καλῶν. εἶχε δὲ τὸ εὐγενές, τὸ εὐειδές, τὸ συνετὸν καὶ εἴ τί που ἄλλο.

[4] 1857, 44. ἀμύμων καὶ Αἴγισθος καὶ ἕτεροι, φαῦλοι μὲν ἄλλως. ἄμωμοι δὲ κατ' ἀνδρίαν ἢ γένος ἤ τι τοιοῦτον.

[5] Ζηνόδοτος ἀντὶ τοῦ δαΐφρονος γράφει κακόφρονος.

just observed: 'They are perhaps like to the gods by their birth and their beauty and their wealth and their courage; the epithet is peculiarly Homeric, like calling Paris *θεοειδῆ*.'[1] Another way of describing an ornamental meaning was therefore to say that the epithet was 'Homeric' or 'of the poet'. These are expressions we find most often used to explain the special cases in which a character in speaking of an enemy or adversary makes use of ennobling epithets. Although the scholiasts are somewhat confused in their explanation of these usages, there can be no doubt that this interpretation, *Ὁμηρικὸν τὸ ἐπίθετον, τοῦ ποιητοῦ τὸ ἐπίθετον*, was part of the teaching of Aristarchus on the illogical use of the epithet.[2] When Aristonicus writes of *Ψ* 581, where Menelaus chides the victorious Antilochus for his conduct in the chariot race, but at the same time calls him *διοτρεφές*: *ἀθετεῖται, ὅτι ἀκαίρως λέγει διοτρεφές, ὀργιζόμενος αὐτῶι*, we can be sure | that this condemnation derives from some other critic who was opposed by Aristarchus. For Aristarchus *ἀκαίρως*, 'inappropriate', is not cause for condemnation, but for an ornamental interpretation, as we learn from this same Aristonicus at *Φ* 218 (*ἐρατεινὰ ῥέεθρα*): *ἄκαιρον τὸ ἐπίθετον . . . ὅμοιον οὖν τῶι ἐσθῆτα φαεινήν*. The other cases which the scholiast of V compares with *διοτρεφές* in *Ψ* 581 therefore also belong to those cited in Aristarchus' complete exposition of the illogical uses of the epithet. Let us consider them. In *Γ* 352 Menelaus begs Zeus to allow him to revenge himself on *δῖον Ἀλέξανδρον*.[3] In *Z* 377 Hector asks of a servant where *Ἀνδρομάχη λευκώλενος* has gone.[4] And in *Φ* 331 Hera, asking a favour of her son Hephaestus, calls him *κυλλοπόδιον*.[5]

There is no need to insist on the excellence of Aristarchus' criticism, and on the incontestable rightness of his method of reasoning from the context. But it must be obvious that this criticism is incomplete by the very fact that makes it certain. On the one hand, Aristarchus' method frees him of all necessity of explaining exactly why Homer used an epithet in a way no Alexandrian poet would ever have dreamed of, or why these usages did not puzzle Homer's audience as they did the contemporaries of Aristarchus. And on the other hand, this explanation can only apply in cases when a particularized sense would be too out of place to be admissible. It is not only that there are lines in which the epithet, which at first appears to have been illogically used, can be more or less justified by such

[1] *εἰ δὲ τοὺς ἰσοθέους λέγει, διά τε τὸ γένος τυχὸν καὶ κάλλος καὶ πλοῦτον καὶ ἀνδρίαν, Ὁμηρικώτερόν ἐστι, καθὰ καὶ τὸ θεοειδῆ που εἰπεῖν τὸν Πάριν* (*Γ* 27, 450).

[2] Cf. Roemer, op. cit., 339 ff. and Eustathius' *ὁ Ὁμηρικὸς Ζεύς* (1387, 20; quoted above, TE, p. 122, n. 3).

[3] Ariston. *δῖον ἀκαίρως ὁ Μενέλαος τὸν ἐχθρὸν λέγει.*

[4] Schol. BLV, *τοῦ ποιητοῦ τὸ ἐπίθετον, οὐ τοῦ προσώπου.*

[5] Cf. also the scholiast of T at *K* 220: (*θυμὸς ἀγήνωρ*): *παρέλκει τὸ ἐπίθετον. καί ἐστιν Ὁμηρικόν, ὡς τὸ Ἀνδρομάχη λευκώλενος.*

explanations as ἐν εἰρωνείαι, οὐ νῦν ἀλλὰ πρώην, εὐλογητικὸς ὁ ποιητής; the fact is that chance alone has brought it about that the circumstances are at variance with the idea of the epithet. The poet simply used certain epithets as ornaments without ever thinking that his audience would try to relate them to the circumstances of the moment. In some of the cases it so fell out that the idea of the epithet and the meaning of the sentence could not be reconciled. In these cases Aristarchus' explanation is applicable. But on other | occasions when the poet uses an epithet as ornament it must happen that the circumstances are such that the epithet can be given a highly plausible sense. Aristarchus' method provides no means of recognizing these latter cases.

Modern scholars, with the exception of a few short remarks, paid no attention to this problem which exercised so many of the ancients, until Düntzer wrote his essay *On the Interpretation of Fixed Epithets in Homer.*[1] Düntzer saw how the questions of the meaning of the epithet and of its use according to its metrical value were interrelated, and in this essay he prepared the way for his study of the influence of metre on Homeric style. The relation which he thus established between these two problems was undoubtedly the most important step since Aristarchus towards the understanding of the fixed epithet in Homer. 'What I wish above all to show', he wrote (510), 'is the capital fact that in the epithet the poet makes no reference whatever to the matter of the sentence, that he in no way represents the changing aspect of things by means of epithets relevant to the immediate situation.' Düntzer understood that the problem of the meaning of the epithet is far more complex than the ancients suspected. The proofs which he put forward in favour of his categoric conclusion were two: the illogical use of the epithet, and its use to facilitate versification. He judged it impossible that the poet could choose an epithet with a view both to its signification and to its metrical value.

How were Düntzer's views received? At the time when he wrote, the conviction that the ideal of poetry is the same for all periods of history was far more widespread than it is now, and as a result most of Düntzer's contemporaries were shocked by the notion that Homer might have chosen his words for any reason other than their signification. For them each word in a poem must be the product of the long and careful | selection of its author; and consequently some scholars, notably Ameis and La Roche, attacked Düntzer's conclusions. They attacked the weak points of his argument by calling attention to the equivalent forms in Homeric diction which Düntzer himself believed to be incompatible with his theory. Having made only a cursory examination of the matter, he

[1] Düntzer, *Hom. Abh.*, 507–16. For criticism before Düntzer, see Ebeling, s.v. ἀμύμων.

had no notion of the extent to which the influence of metre was able to create systems of epithets, nor had he proofs in sufficient abundance to allow him to discount these equivalent elements.[1] Yet we can now see that the objections made by Düntzer's adversaries have little weight next to his own proof. Other scholars accepted his views and came to the melancholy conclusion that Homer was not what he had been thought to be. Thus the author of the article *épithète*, in the 1870 Larousse, describes with considerable accuracy the use of the epithet according to its metrical value—a hero has but one epithet in a given grammatical case, an entire group of heroes different in character but whose names are of like metrical value receive the same epithet, etc.—and concludes, 'Thus Homer has within his reach a large store of words which come of themselves to complete the verse when they are needed . . . Let it be said: his method is childish, his poetics exceedingly simple.' But most of all, Düntzer's theory suffered from indifference. His work was not forgotten, but no one carried it on, and the problem of the meaning of epithets remained in the uncertain state in which it had been before his contribution to Homeric studies. This indifference would be understandable if it involved only his categoric opinion that all fixed epithets in Homer are ornamental. But the argument that the use of the epithets according to its metrical value is incompatible with its use according to signification deserved either acceptance or refutation. Yet Cauer, when, in the latest edition of his *Grundfragen* (p. 449), he lists cases in which he believes the fixed epithet to be indubitably used in a particularized sense, passes over this consideration in silence. |

The consequence of this scholarly indifference to Düntzer's theory is that everyone has continued to be guided by his personal inclination in the interpretation of epithets. Some can use this approach with intelligence; others use it so as to bring us back to the days when indications of the weather were found in the epithets of the sea, and when Ruskin explained φυσίζοος αἶα (*Γ* 243) by saying: 'The poet has to speak of the earth in sadness; but he will not let that sadness affect or change his thought of it. No; though Castor and Pollux be dead, yet the earth is our mother still—fruitful, life-giving.'[2]

[1] To uphold his theory, Düntzer was obliged to amend ποδώκης in *Σ* 234 to ποδάρκης and νύκτα διὰ δνοφερήν in *ο* 50 to νύκτα δι' ὀρφναίην. For the same reasons, he insisted that the epithets in the expressions κλυτὸς Ἐννοσίγαιος and κρείων Ἐνοσίχθων were not both fixed epithets.

[2] This interpretation of Ruskin is no more extravagant than many another put forward by modern criticism. The reader will find examples to his heart's content in two essays of A. Schuster, *Ueber die kritische Benützung homerischer Adjective*, Programm des Gymnasiums in Clausthal, 1859, and *Untersuchungen über die homerischen stabilen* Beiwörter I, Progr. Stade, 1866. Schuster (following Nitsch) proposes to explain πολύτλας in the *Iliad* by 'firm in the face of danger'; χειρὶ παχείῃ of Penelope's arm in *φ* 6 describes 'the rounded and well-fleshed arm of a delicate woman'; Menelaus is called ἀρηίφιλος in *Γ* because in this book, where he shows his

For example, in J. T. Sheppard's recent book, *The Pattern of the Iliad* (London 1922), we read on the subject of *A* 36, in which Chryses addresses his prayer to Apollo as Ἀπόλλωνι ἄνακτι, 'Apollo here is King because he is strong to punish Agamemnon' (p. 15). And the same author says, commenting on the opening lines of the *Iliad*, 'Having once noticed this series Διὸς βουλή, δῖος Ἀχιλλεύς, Λητοῦς καὶ Διὸς υἱός, you will feel the effect of line 74, where Calchas addresses Achilles as διίφιλε. Achilles (line 86) modestly transfers the epithet to Apollo' (p. 16, n. 1).

The weak point in Düntzer's work is that, like Aristarchus, he did not look for the positive explanation of the | ornamental meaning of epithets. The illogical usages of the epithet and its use according to its metrical value are only proofs that the fixed epithet cannot be particularized. But the reasons that determine its ornamental nature must be sought elsewhere: *the fixed epithet is ornamental because it is traditional.* The way in which someone who reads Homer for the first time gradually modifies his understanding of certain of these epithets will show us the truth of this essential fact.

Knowing little or nothing of the style of Homer, the student begins by giving, as far as he can, a particularized sense to all the epithets he encounters. In doing so, he unconsciously follows the habit of thought impressed on him by his familiarity with modern literature, in which every qualifying adjective stands in relation to the sentence or the passage in which it appears. Only where it is not possible to establish any relation between the epithet and the immediate situation will he of necessity regard the epithet as ornamental. But this necessity of falling back on the ornamental meaning derives only in small measure from those cases in which the particularized meaning of the epithet stands in outright contradiction to the idea of the sentence. Its cause is rather that the idea of most epithets has nothing to do with the idea of the sentence, and hence can neither complement nor contradict it. The student's experience, it must be noted, will differ slightly according to whether the epithet refers to a concrete physical characteristic or to a moral quality; but in either case the result is the same. He will, for example, soon give up seeking the particular reason that led the poet to call Hector κορυθαίολος or Menalaus ξανθός or a ship μελαίνῃ in a given line: the quest would carry him too far. In epithets expressive of a moral quality, which naturally are almost all of persons, we frequently find no precise idea, but an idea so vague as to make some relation with the meaning of the sentence

valour in the combat with Paris, he is particularly favoured by the god of war. It must be understood that the inspiration of notions such as these was above all the desire to defend the traditional text: Geppert, *Ueber den Ursprung der homerischen Gesänge*, Leipzig 1840 (ii. 203) went so far as to question the authenticity of *E* 565, *Ψ* 302, 541, 596, because Nestor therein receives the epithets ὑπέρθυμος and μεγάθυμος, epithets befitting young and active men.

possible by virtue of this very want of precision. δῖος, διογενής, or μεγαλήτορος, unlike κορυθαίολος, ξανθός, or μελαίνης, do at a pinch allow one to assign a particular reason for their use: the poet must have chosen them deliberately to lay stress, at the right moment, on the noble character of one of his heroes. But it is not possible to think of this particular reason for their use every time | δῖος, διογενής, or μεγαλήτορος appears in Homer. The unremitting vigilance that this would require would soon flag, and would in any case offer little real satisfaction. Consequently, the student quickly gives up seeking the particular reason for the presence of these epithets too, and comes to accept them without further ado as ornamental.

The student does not go through this process once and for all for a given epithet. He must repeat the process for each new combination of epithet and substantive. An epithet is not ornamental in itself, whatever may be its signification: it is only by dint of being used over and again with a certain substantive or group of substantives that it acquires this quality. It becomes ornamental when its meaning loses any value of its own and becomes so involved with the idea of its substantive that the two can no longer be separated. The fixed epithet then adds to the combination of substantive and epithet an element of nobility and grandeur, but no more than that. Its sole effect is to form, with its substantive, a heroic expression of the idea of that substantive. As he grows aware of this, the reader acquires an insensibility to any possible particularized meaning of the epithet, and this insensibility becomes an integral part of his understanding of Homeric style.

It is not, then, only in cases where no relation between the idea of the epithet and that of the sentence is possible that the reader acquires this insensibility. He soon comes to acquire it just as much in passages where special reasons, sometimes very good reasons, could be adduced for the choice of the epithet. Let us pick an example. The novice in the study of Homer, whether he begins with the *Iliad* or the *Odyssey*, rapidly becomes familiar with certain set ways of speaking of ships, and one of the most frequent of these is the expression 'swift ship', θοή. He comes across this expression so often when the ship is at anchor, or drawn up on the beach, or wrecked, that he soon learns not to expect any particularized meaning from it. Hence when he comes to ν 168, where the Phaeacians speak of the ship which Poseidon has turned to stone, and reads the expression *swift ship*, it does not occur to him to look for the particular reason why this epithet was used. He will find in the phrase no statement of pity for the fate of this ship, | so swift when it bore Odysseus to his home.[1] He has invested the epithet θοή, wherever it modifies the substantive νηῦς, with a purely ornamental quality. He no longer reads 'swift ship'; he reads

[1] This conceit is due to the poet William Morris.

'fast-sailing-ship'. Having encountered so many times this single combination of words, this unity of diction, he at last attributes to it a unity of thought. The expression awakens in him a single idea, that of a hero's ship which possesses the speed characteristic of the finest ships; but in the world of epic poetry he knows only the finest ships—there are no others. So he thinks simply of ship, in the genre of epic poetry, the only kind, as it seems, that there was in the heroic age. He understands the noun–epithet formula in its totality and it never occurs to him to analyse it, and attribute to epithet and substantive their distinct ideas.

There is no need to adduce further cases where the reader is unconcerned to find Homer's special reasons for choosing this or that epithet. Nor does the validity of the experience we have just described require that all readers without exception read the line in question without referring the epithet to the immediate circumstances. One reader will find a particularized sense where another does not; in another case it will be the other way round, always depending on such circumstances as the reader's knowledge of Homeric language, the speed with which he is reading, the intensity of his desire to catch the subtleties of Homer's thought. The only point of importance is that this indifference does exist; and that in so far as it exists, it is due to the reader's having already become familiar with a certain combination of substantives and epithets.

When he confronts a generic epithet, the student's understanding is qualified by considerations of a slightly more complex order. He finds the epithet modifying not one object, but a set of similar objects, and he eventually comes to feel the epithet as ornamental with any member of the set. He finds, for example, *δαίφρονος* used ornamentally with Tydeus, Priam, Achilles, Atreus, Odysseus, | and others of the twenty-three heroes whom it describes: it does not take him long to sense that to look for a particularized meaning in the case of each of these heroes would be lost labour. So when in *Z* 162 the poet tells him of Antea's attempt to seduce her husband's guest Bellerophon, the word *δαίφρονα* will not cause him to refer the notion of intelligence contained in the epithet to the hero's discreet behaviour on this occasion.[1] This is the first and last time that he will find this epithet joined to the name of Bellerophon, but that name belongs to the category of *hero*, and his familiarity with the ornamental sense of the epithet now extends to all words in that category.

It is important to keep clearly in mind that it is our familiarity with the noun–epithet combination, and this alone, that makes us neglect the possibility of relating the idea of the epithet to that of the sentence in which it occurs. We can easily see that in the case of *δαίφρονα Βελλερο-*

[1] Such was the interpretation of Alexander Pope:

> In vain she tempted the relentless youth,
> Endued with wisdom, sacred fear, and truth.

φόντην the imprecise signification of the epithet itself has a good deal to do with the way in which the student understands it. What is true of a large portion of generic epithets of persons is true here: the signification of the word, even when it is known, is so vague that the reader has little initial impulse to seek a particularized meaning for it. Its want of precision makes it harder in any case to find such a meaning, or, we might say, even less possible than it might otherwise be. So with *φυσίζοος αἶα* in *Γ* 243. Few students will read this epithet thinking of the meaning Ruskin contrived to give it—even in death, the earth is always our mother—and this is so even if they come across the expression for the first time. (It in fact occurs in our text of Homer only twice.) The truth of the matter is that it is next to impossible to attribute such a meaning to it. To discover it, Ruskin needed all his well-known fondness for the poignant in poetry, along with a false conception of the history of ideas which led him to attribute to the poet a way of thinking that must have been foreign to him. A particularized sense is scarcely more possible for *φυσίζοος* than for Hector's epithet | *κορυθαίολος*, and it is for this reason, not because of familiarity, that most readers take *φυσίζοος* as ornamental: to do otherwise would involve too much research into the poet's thought. Naturally, not everyone will agree on the amount of probability or possibility of a particularized sense in any given case: differences of conception may be very great. But we are here interested only in the individual experience: if an alert reader can overlook a possible relation between the idea of an epithet and the idea of the sentence in which it occurs, a relation which he may afterwards recognize as possible, the only explanation of his negligence must be his habit, born of familiarity, of understanding a certain combination of substantive and epithet as the expression of a unified idea.

The experience of a member of Homer's audience must have been fundamentally the same as that of a modern student, only much wider and deeper. From their earliest childhood, his audience must have heard again and again long recitations of epic poetry, poetry composed always in the same style. The diction of this poetry, accessible to the modern reader only by way of long study, was familiar to them in its smallest details. The experience we have described of the beginner, who learns how to understand *θοήν* in *νῆα θοήν*, or *δαίφρονος* with the name of a hero, must have come quickly to a member of Homer's audience, and long before he heard a line sung by Homer. And so with other noun–epithet combinations which a modern student learns to associate in thought after years of reading: Homer's audience would have made these associations easily. If we today, using dictionary and grammar to go slowly through the text of only two poems, can acquire a complete indifference to the particular meaning of an epithet in certain combinations, the original audience of those poems, who had become familiar with their style by no conscious effort but by having heard a quantity of epic verse countless times greater, must have already acquired this indifference even for expressions | which appear but twice or thrice in the *Iliad* and *Odyssey*, too rarely for us to regard in this way. This problem of the assimilation of the noun–epithet combination cannot be reduced to a definite equation; for our desire to find a particularized meaning varies according to the idea of the epithet and the meaning of the sentence. But the question, whether, in a given case, Homer's audience had become thoroughly indifferent to any particular meaning of an epithet, is ultimately one of numbers. It is a question of knowing whether or not that audience had heard the expression a *sufficient number of times* to acquire this indifference. The fact that a reader attributes a particularized meaning to an epithet indicates simply that the reader has not encountered this combination of noun and epithet often enough to have fused into one the two ideas represented by the two words. But if we could know that Homer's audience had heard the expression often enough, there could be no doubt that the function of the epithet was ornamental.

For us there is but one way of finding the terms of this hypothetical equation. We must be in a position to suppose that Homer's audience had heard a given expression not twice, and not thrice, but twenty and thirty times, as many times as the most ardent champion of the particularized meaning could demand. To be able to make such a supposition, we must go back to the evidence of noun–epithet formula systems: they alone can give us unambiguous information concerning the frequency of such expressions. We are not mistaken in believing that Homer's audience had previously heard many another epic poem. Therefore, once it is established that a given noun–epithet expression forms part of a traditional system designed for the use of a given noun, or in other words that it is a *fixed* epithet, we can be certain that this audience, long before they ever heard the *Iliad* and the *Odyssey*, were too familiar with the expression to think of finding in it any particularized meaning.

We are thus led to conclude that no noun–epithet formula which *certainly* forms part of a traditional | system of noun–epithet formulae can contain an epithet whose meaning is particularized. And this conclusion should be categoric, should admit of no exception. To know that a noun–epithet formula includes a traditional epithet which is also a fixed epithet, is to know that those who first heard the songs of Homer had already had the experience at which the modern reader so easily arrives in the case of *νῆα θοήν*.

The trouble which Alexandrian scholars gave themselves to explain cases where an epithet seems to be used illogically shows us how much they felt such usages to be unusual and even strange.[1] But like the scholars of modern times, they never asked themselves why Homer did not regard these usages as they did. The answer is that the kind of interpretation which, in the course of reading, occurs to a man accustomed to a literature in which every adjective is used for a particular reason simply never occurred to Homer at all. A total indifference is the only possible explanation, and so every case of what seems an illogical use of an epithet proves how much the poet and his listeners had become familiar with the noun–epithet formulae of a traditional style. These usages are so many independent confirmations of the conclusion we reached by examining the reaction of the novice reader to νῆα θοήν.

It would be appropriate here to cite a passage of Hesiod, which illustrates for us how this indifference to the particularized meaning of the epithet existed only when the tradition was in its prime. The Berlin papyri 9739 and 10560 give us a fragment which we know by a reference in Pausanias to have been attributed in antiquity to Hesiod.[2] The fragment tells of the suit for Helen | by the princes of Greece. Line 21 reads

ἐκ δ' Ἰθάκης ἐμνᾶτο Ὀδυσσῆος ἱερὴ ἴς.

In Homer the expression πολύτλας δῖος Ὀδυσσεύς appears 38 times, 5 times in the *Iliad*, and in neither poem is it ever replaced, although it is obvious that in the *Iliad* Odysseus has been tried by suffering no more than any other Achaean chief.[3] But the author of the fragment felt that it would be awkward to give this title to Odysseus as a young man, and so put in another expression, even though the new expression involved two metrical errors. Here is proof that indifference to the ornamental meaning of an epithet had already begun to lessen at a relatively early period; and in the light of this evidence we can go so far as to conclude that a use of the epithet in an illogical sense, if it is not proof that the line containing it derives from the original poem, at least shows it to be a line composed early and when the traditional diction still maintained its vigour and a rigorous fixity. It is known that some critics of antiquity, and some of modern times as well, have claimed these uses as evidence of interpolation. The assumption is that the interpolator was not only wicked, but also exceedingly stupid. In fact we should draw exactly the opposite conclusion. Only a small portion at most of these uses can be removed

[1] On these apparently illogical uses of epithets, see Cauer, *Grundfragen*³, 450–1; and E. Drerup, *Homerische Poetik*, 460 ff., who gives examples of similar phenomena in other epic poetries.

[2] Pausanias iii. 24. 10, lines 100 ff.

[3] Note also ω 176 where one of the suitors in the Underworld speaks of the man who killed him as πολύτλας δῖος Ὀδυσσεύς.

from the text,[1] hence | we should have to conclude that the interpolator, instead of looking for a particularized meaning of the epithet, as was his wont, was imitating in erudite fashion the oddities of Homeric style.

The above demonstration of the ornamental meaning of the fixed epithet in Homer has the advantage, as we have said, of being positive. It shows the actual development in the mind of the reader of an indifference to the meaning. Now let us consider the other proof of the ornamental meaning, that put forward by Düntzer; viz. the incompatibility of the use of the epithet for metrical reasons with its use for its own signification. It may be thought that, in doing so, we are returning to a point already thoroughly established. It is in fact evident that the technique of noun–epithet formulae and generic epithets such as we have described it could play little part in composition of poetry if the poet had to concern himself with the signification of the epithet. If there can be any relation between the idea expressed by the fixed epithet and the idea expressed by the sentence, a given noun–epithet formula can only be used when the poet chooses it to complete the meaning of the sentence. If the epithet did possess a particularized meaning, we could not suppose that the poet would have allowed himself to be guided by considerations of metrical convenience. The result would have been an intolerable ambiguity. The complementary idea added to the sentence by the particularized epithet would be due to pure chance rather than to the free choice of the poet, and there would be no way of distinguishing the case where the particularized meaning was deliberately selected from the case in which, on the contrary, the meaning was produced by a fortuitous juxtaposition of words. A different explanation capable of resolving the two kinds of usage would be to suppose that the poet makes use of the epithet only where he actually wishes to give it a particularized meaning. But to counter this argument, there is no need to bring up examples of illogical usage or to cite a series of formulary lines; it is clear that if this argument were true, the technique of the use of the epithet would be | due to the desire of

[1] Cases of this sort abound. Here are some other striking examples. In *Θ* 46 Zeus chariots in broad daylight 'between earth and starry heaven'; the interpretation admits of no doubt, the gods having been assembled since dawn. Likewise in *ι* 527, though it has long since been day, Polyphemus 'stretches forth his hands to starry heaven', just as Nestor does in *O* 371. But *μ* 380 shows us the poet at his most careless of the relation between the idea of the epithet and the meaning of the sentence: Helios tells Zeus how he used to take joy in his oxen 'while he climbed up starry heaven'. There can be no question of the sun's scattering the stars from the sky. The expression means, as the context shows, 'from dawn to noon', and no more. The fact is that in all nine cases without exception where the heaven is described by the epithet 'starry', it is broad day. In *O* 440 Ajax laments the death of his comrade Mastorides, slain by 'great-hearted' Hector. Priam chides Hector's brothers for their want of valour, yet calls them *Ἀγάθωνα . . . δῖον* (*Ω* 249) and *ἀγαθόν . . . Πολίτην* (*Ω* 250). In *σ* 5 the poet speaks of the *πότνια μήτηρ* of the beggar Iros. *ἀντίθεον Πολύφημον* (*α* 70) and *Κύκλωπος μεγαλήτορος* (*κ* 200) are also among the more interesting cases.

singers to introduce the epithet into the lines of their song. One could no longer explain this technique by pointing out that it makes it possible to use nouns which are essential parts of speech. In short, the only way of justifying the particularized meaning of the fixed epithet would be categorically to deny its use for its metrical value and to maintain that all the epithetic systems which we have observed are the creation of pure chance, that they are curious phenomena of Homeric diction, but have no real importance at all.

However, if the several devices pointed out in the preceding chapters are in fact so many proofs of the ornamental meaning of the fixed epithet, it is none the less valuable to point out a few of the serious offences against taste with which Homer would have to be charged if we persist in reading him as we read a modern author. Once we have understood that certain ideas concerning modern literature cannot be attributed to Homer, we shall have a more solid foundation for the study of Homeric style.

If a poet is to use only the *mot juste*, the word carefully selected as the best one, he must have a mind free from all cares of versification, since the *mot juste*, as criticism has defined it, is chosen purely for its sense. From this point of view, any concession to metre impairs the precision of the poet's thought. So modern poetry has been criticized on the grounds that the poet's need to find rhyming words may hinder him from expressing his thought in the most accurate and the most economical way possible, a reproach expressed in the well-known lines of Boileau:

> Maudit soit le premier dont la verve insensée
> Dans les bornes d'un vers renferma sa pensée,
> Et donnant à ses mots une étroite prison,
> Voulut avec la rime enchaîner la raison.[1]

Just as a postclassical poet must find his rhymes, so a classical Greek or Latin poet had to fit into a strict framework of alternating long and short syllables words whose metrical value was for the most part fixed. And as a modern poet can make the writing of verse easier by letting his ideas be guided by rhyme, so a Greek or Roman poet could yield himself to the use of the epithet. In that way he could either fill an empty portion of the

[1] Sat. II. Cf. His *Art Poétique*, II:

> Quelque sujet qu'on traite, ou plaisant ou sublime,
> Que toujours le bon sens s'accorde avec la rime.
> L'un l'autre vainement ils semblent se haïr;
> La rime est une esclave et ne doit qu'obéir,

and Voltaire, *Œdipe*, *Cinquième lettre*: 'Les vers ne sont beaux que si l'on peut en ôter les *rimes* et les mettre en prose sans qu'ils perdent rien de leur sens et de leur énergie.' This attitude to rhyme had already deeply influenced Elizabethan poetry. Spenser in particular made a strong effort to dispense with rhyme.

line, or else arrange his words differently. The desire to make the composition of verse easier has given rise on the one hand to dictionaries of rhymes, and on the other to *Gradus ad Parnassum*, collections where the writer of Latin verse will find listed under each noun a set of epithets which can be used with it, 'filler pieces of every length', as they have been contemptuously described. The invention of these *Gradus* appears to be modern, but the lack of them did not keep the Greek poets, later poets with individual styles as well as Homer, from incurring reproaches for their dependence on the epithet.

Lucian's *Timon* begins: '*Ὦ Ζεῦ φίλιε καὶ ξένιε καὶ ἑταιρεῖε καὶ ἐφέστιε καὶ ἀστεροπητὰ καὶ ὅρκιε καὶ νεφεληγερέτα καὶ ἐρίγδουπε*, and whatever else the crazy poets call you, especially when they're in trouble with the metre; that's when you put on a multitude of names in order to prop up their staggering numbers and to fill in the holes in their scansion.'[1] The three epithets *ἀστεροπητά*, *νεφεληγερέτα*, and *ἐρίγδουπε* show that Lucian is above all thinking of Homer; at the same time it is clear that he made no distinction on these grounds between Homer and poets with an individual style. Certainly Lucian was no closer than his contemporaries to guessing how far the technique of the epithet had developed in Homeric poetry. He did understand what a temptation the use of this part of speech was for a poet; | he thought that in giving way to it, the poet must impair the quality of his thought; and so he felt that Homer had thereby committed a stylistic fault. We have here an attitude valid just as long as it can be held that the meaning of the fixed epithet can be even vaguely particularized. Homer, by adopting an epithetic technique in comparison with which the *Gradus ad Parnassum* are at once cumbersome and pathetically inadequate, is far more culpable, accordingly, than Théodore de Banville, who asserted that a poet must let his thoughts be guided by rhyme. Banville, after all, had at his disposal a fair selection of words to make a given rhyme, whereas most of the time Homer had but one epithet for each metrical need. Let us consider a few of the cases in which Homer can be charged with a blind faith in its diction and a failure to recognize that the epithet in Boileau's words, 'est un esclave et ne doit qu'obéir'.

I. We have seen, on the one hand, that in a great many cases it is impossible to find a particularized meaning in an epithet. On the other hand, almost all substantives in Homer are used, in varying proportions, both with and without epithets. These two points are perfectly obvious, but putting them together raises a question of capital importance: why does the poet omit the epithet in one place and put it in in another? Why, for

[1] *καὶ εἴ τί σε ἄλλο οἱ ἐμβρόντητοι ποιηταὶ καλοῦσι, καὶ μάλιστα ὅταν ἀπορῶσι πρὸς τὰ μέτρα· τότε γὰρ αὐτοῖς πολυώνυμος γιγνόμενος ὑπερείδεις τὸ πῖπτον τοῦ μέτρου καὶ ἀναπληροῖς τὸ κεχηνὸς τοῦ ῥυθμοῦ.*

example, does Odysseus have an epithet in 344 cases and not have one in 343 cases? Let us leave in abeyance the question of metrical convenience and concern ourselves instead with the bard's aesthetic sense. Obviously the poetry would be too weighed down if the poet provided each and every noun with an epithet. But while this may, up to a point, explain the quantity of epithets in a given number of lines, it is not always easy to explain a specific case. We are still in the dark, for example, as to why Sparta does not deserve an epithet quite as much as Pylos in α 93,

πέμψω δ' ἐς Σπάρτην τε καὶ ἐς Πύλον ἠμαθόεντα,

considering that the two lands are equally favoured in δ 702,

ἐς Πύλον ἠγαθέην ἠδ' ἐς Λακεδαίμονα δῖαν.

There are hundreds of other examples where there are two or more nouns and only one has an epithet. Usually, as in the case just cited, the reader will pay no attention; but there are cases where an attentive reader will find some explanation almost indispensable. When there are several heroes, as in *Ξ* 425,

Πουλυδάμας τε καὶ Αἰνείας καὶ δῖος Ἀγήνωρ.

Why does Agenor get the epithet rather than Aeneas, who is certainly the stoutest warrior of the three, or even rather than Polydamas? Likewise *M* 88–9,

οἱ μὲν ἅμ' Ἕκτορ' ἴσαν καὶ ἀμύμονι Πουλυδάμαντι,
οἳ πλεῖστοι καὶ ἄριστοι ἔσαν.

Hector has certainly as much right as Polydamas to an ennobling epithet. This fashion of favouring one hero over another is yet more inexplicable in *P* 534,

Ἕκτωρ Αἰνείας τ' ἠδὲ Χρομίος θεοειδής.

Chromius, a Mysian chieftain, is in fact mentioned only in this book, and in it, thrice: encouraged by Hector he enters the fray along with Aretus, hoping to capture the body of Patroclus; beaten back by the valour of the two Ajaxes, he withdraws, leaving on the field of battle the body of his comrade, slain by Automedon. The record of his deeds hardly requires that the poet show him greater honour than the bravest warriors of Troy. Finally consider *Ω* 249–51, where Priam accuses his sons of cowardice,

νεικείων Ἕλενόν τε Πάριν τ' Ἀγάθωνά τε δῖον
Πάμμονά τ' Ἀντίφονόν τε βοὴν ἀγαθόν τε Πολίτην
Δηίφοβόν τε καί Ἱππόθοον καὶ Δῖον ἀγαυόν.

Agathon is mentioned nowhere else by Homer; nor is Dios. Polites, who the poet has told us (*B* 792) was noted for his swiftness of foot, appears elsewhere in the poem only in *N* 533, when he leads his wounded brother Deiphobus from the battle. What makes the heroic epithets used here stranger still is that a few lines later Priam qualifies the most valiant of his sons | with epithets which seem in no way more honorific:

> Ω 257–8 Μήστορά τ' ἀντίθεον καὶ Τρωΐλον ἱππιοχάρμην
> Ἕκτορά θ', ὃς θεὸς ἔσκε μετ' ἀνδράσιν.

It is clear that we have here examples of usage in some ways akin to the illogical usages that drew the attention of ancient scholars. There, it was a matter of the meaning of the epithet. In the cases we have just been considering, there is no question of meaning, but we still want to know why the poet chose to use an epithet at all. There is but one explanation, the indifference of the audience, not only to the meaning of the epithet, but also to its connotations of nobility.

A more general proof of this indifference is the frequency with which certain names of heroes are variously accompanied by epithets. Why is the name of Agamemnon used in the nominative case as often as the name of Patroclus, but seven times more often with an epithet? Because he is the commander-in-chief of the Achaean army? Why then does Diomedes in the nominative case appear without an epithet only once out of 42 times, whereas out of an equal number of occurrences Agamemnon in the nominative appears without epithet twelve times? Again why does Menelaus, fine warrior that he was, but clearly no Achilles or Odysseus, deserve the epithet four times as often as they? So with the gods: possibly reasons could be given to explain why Apollo, Athena, Hera, and Ares have approximately the same proportion of epithets when their names appear in the nominative case. But why then should not Zeus, the greatest of all the gods, not have still more of them? For in actuality, the epithet is found with his name in this grammatical case less than with the names of the other gods. We might also have to explain why Iris enjoys the epithet more than any other deity (24 times out of 27).[1]

Metrical convenience alone can explain these differing proportions; and therefore we must abandon the idea which offers itself so naturally to us that the courage or the majesty of a hero or a god led the poet to attribute the epithet to him more often. Anyone | inclined to believe that Homer chose an epithet in a given passage in order to honour a particular character, will have to concede that, far from indicating the virtues and the deserts of his heroes and gods, the poet has actually falsified our conception of their character. Surely Homer did not believe, as the use of the epithets would suggest, that Menelaus was a braver warrior than

[1] For these proportions, see above TE, pp. 34–5. The name of Zeus appears in the nominative 112 times with epithet, 122 times without, a proportion of 1 : 1·1 ; that of Ares, 27 times with epithet, 23 times without, or 1 : 0·8.

Achilles or even Ajax, or that Diomedes surpassed Ajax, or that Patroclus merited fewer titles of honour than any other hero.

Let us return to the Homeric audience's indifference to the fixed epithet. It is to be sure a relative indifference, as becomes evident if we imagine a Homeric hero who has some importance in the story, but is never described by an epithet at all: the hearers would not notice the absence at first, but eventually it would ring strange to them. But these same hearers, as we have just seen, were undisturbed by even considerable variations in the frequency of the use of epithets, and never looked for the specific motivation of an honorific epithet in a given case. This must have been so. How, for example, could a member of Homer's audience hear the epithet *divine* (δῖος) an average of about once every 68 lines,[1] and find in it any particularly ennobling significance? Or, in the case of a less usual epithet, say ἀρηΐφιλος or μενεχάρμης, how could he distinguish between this epithet and so many others which equally evoked a general heroic quality? If we look at the question in a different light, that of the totality of epithets, consider what a grave impediment to the fine rapidity of Homeric style would be created by the requirement that we find in every fixed epithet a specific motivation for its use. Let us note by the way that most of such specific motivations as have been pointed out were found not in a continuous reading of Homer, but rather in the process of annotation or criticism, or in the course of translation, by applying to the text that search for subtleties of thought which is so essential for our authors and even | for Pindar, but inappropriate to an author who has no individual style.

It is easy to understand why Homer was able to dispose his epithets so unevenly. For him and for his audience alike, the fixed epithet did not so much adorn a single line or even a single poem, as it did the entirety of heroic song. These epithets constituted for him one of the familiar elements of poetry, elements which we of a later age find it so difficult to appreciate, but the importance of which, for both poet and audience, is shown by everything in Homer: by the story, by the characters, by the style. In this respect, fixed epithets were just like the other familiar elements of poetry. The audience would have been infinitely surprised if a bard had left them out; his always putting them in hardly drew their attention. Epic lines without epithets would have seemed to them like a heroic character without his traditional attributes. But even now, who among those of us who have any knowledge of the legend has asked why Odysseus should be *crafty* in this or that particular episode? Just so, Homer's listeners demanded epithets and paid them no attention, showing thereby the same lack of exact observation that becomes a habit with the modern reader. And it is this lack of exact observation that explains

[1] 408 times in 27,803 lines.

uses of the epithet which appear to us unmotivated, because we look for their motivation in the lines where they occur, rather than in all the poetry Homer's audience had already heard before they ever heard him sing.

II. We have considered the epithet as a word chosen to emphasize the heroic quality of a person or thing. If we take as point of departure another way of using the epithet, which again shows how Homer sacrificed precision of thought to ease of versification, we shall see that it is impossible to understand how the audience felt about the meaning of the epithet as long as we are unaware of the principle that the epithet adorns all epic poetry rather than a single line. There is a large group of epithets which Homer uses for a character in only one grammatical case. Why, we may ask, does Homer, with but one exception, call Odysseus δῖος only in the nominative case? Here is an epithet which describes Odysseus 99 times in the *Iliad* and *Odyssey*; had the poet selected it, even occasionally, with a view | to the momentary circumstances of his narrative, it would inevitably have to appear in the oblique cases more often than it does since Homer mentions Odysseus 302 times in the oblique cases and 385 times in the nominative. Here we cannot adduce the exigency of metre, as we can elsewhere, as for πολύτλας, for example, which would have a genitive form πολύτλαντος. The poet is able to put δῖος in the oblique cases in a great many positions in the hexameter. This limitation of the epithet to a single case is too widespread to be the work of chance. Achilles is qualified by the same epithet, δῖος, 55 times in the nominative and twice only in an oblique case. Odysseus is πολύμητις 81 times, but only in the nominative, although the genitive πολυμήτιος, used of Hephaestus (*Φ* 355), demonstrates that this case was a metrical possibility. Similarly, we find in the nominative case only ὠκύς (5 times) or πόδας ὠκύς (32 times) for Achilles; κορυθαίολος (37 times) or φαίδιμος (29 times) for Hector; κρείων (30 times) for Agamemnon; πεπνυμένος (35 times) for Telemachus; ἱππότα (32 times) for Nestor. Going on to the genitive, θείοιο is said of Odysseus solely in this grammatical case (31 times), likewise ταλασίφρονος (11 times). With one exception the Achaeans are χαλκοχίτωνες only in the genitive (24 times). Hector is ἀνδροφόνοιο only in this form (11 times). Ships are described as κορωνίσι only in the dative plural (17 times). Odysseus is πολυμήχανε (22 times) and φαίδιμε (5 times) only in the vocative. These are some of the most striking examples; others could be cited, and if we added all the cases where an epithet is used for a particular person or thing only in either the nominative or the vocative, or in either the nominative or the accusative, or only in the oblique cases—for many nouns and epithets have identical metrical quantities in these sets of grammatical cases—we have a list comprising almost every fixed epithet.

Perhaps it will be thought that this restriction is one in appearance only, and that in reality a single idea is expressed by several epithets. Thus the idea of πολύτλας, which appears only in the nominative, would be expressed by ταλασίφρονος in the genitive; δῖος in the nominative would correspond to θείου in the genitive, to ἀντιθέωι in the dative; πολύμητις in the nominative would correspond to πολυμήχανε in the vocative; πόδας ὠκύς to ποδώκεος; etc. But this hypothesis is too little in accordance with what we find in Homer. What other epithet has Hector to correspond to | κορυθαίολος, or to φαίδιμος, or to ἀνδροφόνοιο? What epithet of Telemachus can we find to compare with πεπνυμένος? Which among all the epithets of Zeus answers to μητίετα and πατὴρ ἀνδρῶν τε θεῶν τε? Among the epithets of the Achaeans, χαλκοχιτώνων expresses a unique idea, and likewise κορωνίσι among the epithets of ships. What nominative epithet of Odysseus can be compared with ἀμύμονος or μεγαλήτορος, which are given to the hero only in the oblique cases? It is evident that the similarities of meaning which we can find among different epithets are not the result of a plan. They depend solely on the bards' desire to designate, in one way or another, either a salient characteristic of a single hero, or else one of the characteristics of the hero in general. These characteristics are in fact very few. A close examination of the 61 generic epithets of heroes which appear on Table III reveals that they all refer to five qualities: courage, strength, fame, royalty, and that heroic but vague concept, 'divinity'.

There is therefore but one way to account for the frequent limitation of an epithet to one or more grammatical cases: by the ornamental meaning of the fixed epithet. Otherwise only a fantastic coincidence would explain why, every time the poet wanted to complete the thought of his sentence by means of an epithet, the substantive described by this epithet was in the one grammatical case in which this epithet appears. Hence we see that the circumstances of the moment, even if they are perfectly consonant with the meaning of the epithet, never suggest that epithet to the poet. And so we are led once more to the same conclusion which we reached both by the study of illogical uses of the epithet, and by considering the reader's actual experience of the constantly recurring noun–epithet formula.

Still, the question can always be asked whether, even granted the particularized meaning of the epithet, this limitation of its use to one or a few grammatical cases is not a fault. For the poet, it would seem, was quite unaware of the need to vary his epithets or to use a proper number of them in a given stretch of verse. To answer that question we must again have recourse to the audience's indifference to | the fixed epithet. They quickly learned not to look for any particularized meaning. They were so familiar with the fact that the noun–epithet combination is no more than a heroic mode of expressing a noun that all they expected to find in the epithet was an element ennobling the style; from this point of view our explanation of the similarity of meaning shown by several epithets is valid, since the epithet expresses above all the heroic character of a person or thing. And so the audience became indifferent to which fixed epithet the poet used in a given line. This indifference is the complement of the indifference he felt for the use or the omission of the fixed epithet. Though Homer's listener had no concern for that variety of expression which we require in our modern styles, he did expect a character or object frequently mentioned to have a certain number of epithets. But after a while, when he had heard a certain number of them he paid them no more attention. It was inevitable that he would hear a certain number of them, since a noun occurring with any frequency will appear in different grammatical cases and in combination with different expressions, thereby giving rise to the use of epithets of different metrical values, which is to say, to different fixed epithets. The necessities of versification themselves provoke that variety of epithets which is required, it could be said, by the inattention of the audience.

The attitude, as described above, of Homer's audience both to the use or the omission of the fixed epithet and to its meaning shows us how we should go about interpreting one of the most controversial elements of traditional diction. For most of the principal Homeric heroes, there exists a line consisting entirely of their names in the vocative case and certain of their titles:

διογενὲς Λαερτιάδη, πολυμήχαν' Ὀδυσσεῦ (22 times)

ὦ Νέστορ Νηληιάδη, μέγα κῦδος Ἀχαιῶν (6 times)

etc. (For other lines of this sort, see TE, p. 63.) These lines have received | two opposed interpretations. On the one hand, the character and the length of such expressions have suggested that they would forcibly strike the minds of the audience, and that we should see in them the poet's intention to give the speeches which they introduce an exceptional tone of grandeur or ceremony or respect. But on the other hand, it has not been possible to define the reasons why speeches beginning in this way require lines producing such a tone any more than other speeches; no trait can be found in them to distinguish them from speeches beginning otherwise. Some critics have concluded that we should not find in such lines any special tone. The truth is that both sides are right, and both wrong: these lines do confer a tone of grandeur and ceremony and respect καί τινος τοιούτου; but they confer it not so much to the speeches in which they occur as to the whole of epic poetry. Homer's audience had heard such lines too often to give any great attention to the epithets in them and to the reasons behind their use. But they were familiar and pleasant to an audience for which they made up an important part of that ornamentation without which heroic poetry would have ceased to be itself.

This common limitation of the fixed epithet to one or more grammatical cases provides us, perhaps more than the other proofs of its ornamental meaning, with the certain conviction that it is never used, even by way of exception, in a particularized sense. We may indeed be tempted to find in illogical usage, in the indifference the reader develops to frequently recurring noun–epithet formulae, and in the obvious incompatibility between the use of the epithet for its convenience and its use for its meaning, no more than proofs of a general character, proofs which may apply to the majority of cases, but do not for all that rule out the possibility that sometimes the particular circumstances of the narrative suggested the epithet to the poet, who then arranged for its inclusion in the line. According to this explanation, the audience would have understood the epithet as Paul Cauer maintains.[1] Cauer recognizes that the fixed | epithet is usually ornamental and capable of being used in a context which it contradicts, and goes on to say: 'Often the contrast between the signification and the application of a word is so great that there results therefrom a powerful new meaning.' He would even like to see in such usages the peculiar genius of the poet, who did not allow his own thinking to be crushed by the traditional material of his diction: 'In cases of this kind (i.e., where the fixed epithet has a particularized meaning) faded colours are restored to their brightness, and what had no life is made once more animate.' Some scholars may welcome this explanation, which at once admits that the fixed epithet is traditional and flatters the individual genius of Homer; even though the price it demands is the admission that the poet's work is largely made up of what is 'faded' and 'lifeless'. For with the best will in the world, one will find only occasional examples of the use of the fixed epithet in a particularized sense. As so often happens, those who try to find in Homer the profundity and the *finesse* which they admire in contemporary art end by denigrating the habitual in order to praise the exceptional.

The truth is that the proofs already given do not allow of any exceptions. They all bear witness to so strong, and so habitual, an indifference in Homer's audience to any possible particularized meaning that it could not be overcome, no matter how perfectly matched the idea of the epithet and the meaning of the sentence. But to these proofs let us add one provided by the phenomenon we have just examined, the limitation of some epithets to one or to several grammatical cases. We shall find in

[1] *Grundfragen*³, ii. 450.

this way a demonstration more specific, if less penetrating, than those based on the indifference of the audience. The proof in question is fairly simple, and has already been indicated. An epithet used in a particularized sense should be so used regardless of the grammatical case of the noun it qualifies. Consequently, the epithet of a hero, for example, should be used in a particularized sense almost as often in the oblique cases as in the nominative, since usually a hero is mentioned only slightly more often in the nominative than in the other cases. Thus the total or almost total absence of a given epithet in the oblique cases would indicate the total or almost total absence of the particularized meaning of the epithet in the nominative. The relation | can be expressed in the form of a proportion A:B::C:X, where A is the number of occurrences of the noun in the oblique cases, B is the number of times the noun is accompanied by an epithet in these cases, C is the number of occurrences in the nominative case, and X is the number of times the epithet could be employed with a particularized meaning in the nominative case.

Be it noted that this equation is proposed as a means of calculating not the actual number of occurrences of the nominative case of the epithet with a particularized meaning, but rather the maximum possible number of times the epithet could be so employed, factor B representing not the number of times the epithet has a particularized meaning in the oblique cases, but simply the number of times it appears in those cases. In order

		A : B : : C : X
Ulysses	δῖος (99 times)	302:1::385:1·3
	πολύμητις (81 times)	302:0::385:0
	πολύτλας (38 times)	
Achilles	δῖος (55 times)	175:2::185:2·1
Agamemnon	ἄναξ ἀνδρῶν (37 times)	84:0::100:0
	κρείων (26 times)	
Hector	φαίδιμος (29 times)	248:0::170:0
	κορυθαίολος (37 times)	
	μέγας (12 times)	
	Πριαμίδης (7 times)	
	ὄβριμος (4 times)	
Diomedes	βοὴν ἀγαθός (21 times)	37:0::42:0
	κρατερός (12 times)	
Zeus	πατὴρ ἀνδρῶν τε θεῶν τε (15 times)	448:0::234:0
	ὑψιβρεμέτης (5 times)	
	μητίετα (18 times)	448:1::234:0·5

to remove any element of doubt, we are supposing the meaning of the epithet in the oblique cases to be always particularized. Thus for the epithets in the above list, one could count on one or two particularized uses of δῖος with the name of Odysseus, and two or three with the name of Achilles, | and perhaps a single particularized use of μητίετα. If the use of these epithets in the oblique cases is ornamental, as is probable, we could not even count on so many. And could anyone claim to discover the two lines of the *Iliad* and *Odyssey* in which the form δῖος, referring to Odysseus, is relevant to the immediate action?

The equation can be reversed if our initial supposition is that if the fixed epithet had a particularized sense in the oblique cases, it would likewise have had it in the nominative. The equation would then be C:D::A:X, where C is the number of occurrences of the noun in the nominative, D is the number of times the epithet describes the noun in the nominative case, A is the number of occurrences of the noun in the oblique cases, and X is the number of times the epithet could be used with a particularized meaning in the oblique cases.

The form of the epithet given in the list below is the first encountered with the noun in question; thus δαίφρονος (7 times) represents δαίφρονος (4 times), δαίφρονι (once), and δαίφρονα (twice).

		C : D : : A : X
Ulysses	δαίφρονος (7 times) ἀμύμονος (9 times) μεγαλήτορος (8 times) πολυμήχανε (23 times) Διὶ μῆτιν ἀτάλαντον (8 times) θείου (31 times) πολύφρονα (5 times) ταλασίφρονος (12 times)	385:0::302:0
Achilles	Πηληιάδεω (16 times)	185:0::175:0
Hector	ἱπποδάμοιο (5 times) ἀνδροφόνοιο (11 times)	170:0::248:0
Diomedes	ἱπποδάμοιο (8 times)	42:0::37:0
Nestor	μεγαθύμου (5 times)	52:0::58:0

It is evident that the success of the above demonstration depends on the limitation of the epithet to either the nominative or the | oblique cases. But is there any reason to believe that the group of epithets we have been considering is at all different from any other group of fixed epithets?

Always to take refuge in the argument that every last case has not been proved is an inferior mode of reasoning.[1]

III. Let us now look at one last feature of the fixed epithet, a feature which, if it were to be judged by the attitudes of the modern reader, would betray a truly lamentable want of creative freedom. We refer to the simple phenomenon which has been the basis of all the investigations of the previous chapters, the uniqueness from the point of view of versification of the great majority of fixed epithets. Perhaps the very abundance of the phenomenon has hindered the full appreciation of its importance. It is here that we must come to grips with a conception of style entirely different from our own and which demands an entirely different kind of understanding. What the unique epithet implies is an absolute indifference to any other epithet which could accompany the same noun and be of the same metre. There is no need to conjecture what other epithet Homer might have put in the place of πολύτλας or δῖος or γλαυκῶπις or Παλλάς; we know without asking that there is an infinite number of possible epithets which could be applied to Athena and to Odysseus and would reproduce any given metre. At no period could the poets of Greece have exhausted the possibilities of new words to be created and of new combinations of old words to be made, had they been impelled by a desire to express their personal thoughts in a personal idiom. Homer's innocence of any such desire is demonstrated anew by each example after the first of the use of a unique epithet or noun–epithet formula. Starting with the second, each one of the 38 occurrences of πολύτλας, of the 188 occurrences of δῖος, of the 51 occurrences of γλαυκῶπις, of the 47 occurrences of Παλλάς attests Homer's renunciation—his unconscious renunciation, of course—of any expression of the quality of his own thought by means of the epithet. |

In the light of so many compelling proofs, what do we do with the aesthetic principles which Lucian put forth, and which critics like Boileau and Voltaire analysed and taught, the guiding principles still of our own literature? We must eschew them entirely when we study Homer. When we read the *Iliad* and the *Odyssey* we should not have them in our minds at all; we should rather conceive that here is a poet who marked his works with genius not because he was able to model the words on his own thoughts, but because he was able to make use of traditional words and expressions. For us to recognize a renunciation of this sort demands a tremendous effort of the imagination. Even those who have accepted the influence of metre on diction have not all been able to do it.[2] It is not easy to put aside the literary conventions of

[1] Let us mention here a fact analogous to this limitation of the epithet to a single grammatical case; viz., the frequency with which the epithet accompanies certain synonymous nouns. Thus Ἀχαιοί has an epithet in 32 per cent of its occurrences, Δαναοί in 16 per cent, and Ἀργεῖοι in 4 per cent only. Cf. TE p. 101.

[2] e.g. J. Meylan-Faure when he writes (*Les Épithètes dans Homère*, Lausanne 1899, 9): 'Si

one's own era in favour of those of another. But this step is for all of us the first condition of a true understanding of the style of Homer.

§ 2. THE GENERIC EPITHET

The division made in the preceding chapter between the generic and the distinctive epithet is not an arbitrary one, made simply for its usefulness in analysing epithetic technique. It is a clear semantic division, every bit as essential to our understanding of the meaning the bard gave to the epithet as is the division between the ornamental and the particularized epithet. *δῖος*, for example, confined to a single hero will not have the same meaning as *δῖος* applied to many heroes. The former will refer to an individual character; the latter will refer only to a quality of the hero, to one of the several traits which distinguish ordinary men from those of the mythic and marvellous world of the bards. In other words, we must learn to choose between 'divine, and therefore a hero' and 'divine, as other heroes are not'. If, in Homer, *δῖος* were said only of Odysseus or Achilles, we should have to | take it more or less in the sense of *θεῖος* in the Alexandrian epigram (*A.P.* 9. 188. 3–4, anonymous):

> *πρῶτος δ' εἴς τε θεὸν καὶ ἐς οὐρανὸν ὄμμα τανύσσας,*
> *θεῖε Πλάτων, ἤθη καὶ βιὸν ηὐγάσαο.*

The author of this epigram calls Plato *divine* because he wants us to understand that here was a philosopher whose works and whose life revealed a kind of divinity which did not belong to other philosophers. This is how we must understand *πολύμητις* and *πολύτλας* of Odysseus, and *πόδας ὠκύς* and *ποδάρκης* of Achilles. The two epithets of Odysseus, used only of him, tell us that he was a man of extraordinary ingenuity and that in the course of his life he experienced extraordinary suffering. The two epithets of Achilles, though they would seem to refer to a part of the legend not dramatized in the *Iliad* and possibly not known to Homer, ascribe to his hero a swiftness of foot unmatched by other heroes. But if we find that Homer applied the epithet *δῖος* to heroes who differ too much among themselves in rank, prowess, and character for us to conceive of some 'divinity' common to all of them but not shared by other heroes, we shall have to reject for this word the distinctive meaning which comes so naturally to the mind of the modern reader, and is so appropriate to the Alexandrian epigram.

The same is true of *μεγαλήτορος*, *ἀμύμων*, *θεοειδής*, *δαΐφρων*, and of all other Homeric epithets denoting an abstract quality. If they are used of

c'était uniquement la forme métrique qui déterminait le choix de l'épithète, pourquoi ne trouve-t-on pas par example, l'adjectif *ταχύς* avec *νηῦς*? On a bien su former plus tard *ταχυναυτεῖν*.'

one hero only, we must see in them the designation of a particular feature; if they are used indifferently for all heroes, we can see in them no more than the designation of a characteristic feature of the generic hero. When the epithet refers to something definite, the difference between the generic and the distinctive meaning becomes more striking still. The epithet πτολίπορθος used for one hero will mean 'the man who more than anyone else sacks cities', or else, if it is used only of Odysseus, e.g., it will mean 'the sacker of Troy'. But if the poet uses πτολίπορθος for any hero, then we can understand only: 'a man who, being a hero, was capable of | sacking cities'. The epithet κρείων, said of one hero, will mean 'a man whose power deserves particular mention'; said of only Agamemnon, it will mean 'commander-in-chief'; but used for any hero, it will mean, 'a man who reigns, like other heroes'. In just the same way, if ἄναξ ἀνδρῶν is reserved for Agamemnon, it will suggest the great number of those subject to him; but when it is said indifferently of a number of heroes, we find ourselves led once more to the meaning indicated above for κρείων. The expression βοὴν ἀγαθός will, if used only of one hero, say Diomedes, assign to that hero an unusual power of voice, just as ποδάρκης assigns to Achilles a singular swiftness; said of any hero whatever, the expression will mean no more than 'good at the war-cry as ordinary men are not'.

The modern reader begins to recognize the ornamental and the generic meanings of the epithet at the same time; generally speaking, he is likely to grasp the generic meaning first. The reason is mainly that the sundry uses of the epithet show the generic meaning too clearly for anyone not to notice it; and the reader's growing indifference to the ornamental meaning confirms his sense of the generic epithet. The student finds δῖος, e.g., used first for Achilles (*A* 7), and as long as only Achilles is characterized by Homer in this way, he will consider it a distinctive adjective of this hero. Even later on, perhaps, when he finds the word used of Odysseus (*A* 145), he will imagine that those two heroes share the distinction of being 'divine'. But after he hears the word used of Nestor (*B* 57), Agamemnon (*B* 221), and Alexander (*Γ* 329), he will give up looking for a distinctive meaning in the epithet, and will even forget the names of those who were graced with it earlier. And if he arrives at this stage after having heard the word used with only five heroes, how sure will be his sense of the impossibility of any special meaning after he has read both Homeric poems and has found it used therein for 32 heroes who have in common only the fact that they are heroes! There is no better way of describing the formation of the reader's sense | of the generic epithet than to enumerate these 32 names.

1. Achilles.
2. Odysseus.
3. Agamemnon.

4. Diomedes.
5. Nestor.
6. Patroclus.
7. Menestheus the Athenian.
8. Thrasymedes, Nestor's son.
9. Machaon, son of Asclepius.
10. Hector.
11. Alexander.
12. Agenor, a Trojan warrior.
13. Priam.
14. Sarpedon, King of the Lycians.
15. Memnon.
16. Tydeus, father of Diomedes.
17. Oeneus, father of Tydeus.
18. Areithous, father of Menesthius.
19. Alastor, a Pylian warrior; mentioned thrice: the first time merely as a Pylian, the other two times when he carries the wounded Teucer and Hypsenor from the battle.
20. Epeigeus, a Myrmidon, named once when he is killed by Hector in the fighting over the body of Sarpedon.
21. Epeius, who built the Wooden Horse. He appears in the *Iliad* only in *Ψ* when he outboxes Euryalus, but is defeated in the discus-throw.
22. Lycomedes, an Achaean, named five times; he performs a few feats of little note.
23. Ereuthalion, mentioned only as a warrior killed by Nestor in his youth.
24. Hypsenor, a Trojan, mentioned once when he is killed by Eurypylus.
25. Aretaon, a Trojan, mentioned once when he is killed by Teucer.
26. Agathon, son of Priam, mentioned only once, when Priam is about to go to Achilles and orders his sons to make ready his chariot. |
27. Mentor, the aged friend of Telemachus.
28. Amarynceus, King of the Epeians; at whose funeral games Nestor once distinguished himself.
29. Echephron, named twice in the *Odyssey* as a son of Nestor.
30. Eumaeus, Odysseus' swineherd.
31. Philoetius, Odysseus' cowherd.
32. Orestes.

The generic meaning of δῖος, when it is used of a hero, is evident; the question remains whether the same is true of all the epithets on Table III. Often a closer look at the use of an epithet which one had taken to be distinctive will show that it cannot have such a meaning. *ἄναξ ἀνδρῶν* generally coincides with the name of Agamemnon, and since Agamemnon is *par excellence* king of men, one comes to consider the phrase a title reserved for him. But in reality Homer uses the same expression for five other persons: Anchises, Aeneas, Augeias, Euphetes, Eumelus. It could conceivably be argued that Anchises and his son have exceptional power as kings of the Dardanians; Augeias, however, was only a king of Elis, Eumelus is a minor prince of Thessaly commanding a force of eleven ships, and Euphetes is named once only as a prince of Elis who gave his sword to Phyleus. The same meaning has been sought for *κρείων* with the name of Agamemnon, although the word is said six times of Alcinous and once each of Agapenor, Eumelus, Helicaon, Haemon, and Elephenor. Ebeling, clearly influenced by the idea that these epithets ought to signify the possession of extraordinary power, adds the following remark to his listing of these names: 'Hi omnes erant nobili genere orti et principes illustres.' But all the heroes are noble and illustrious. If only Agamemnon and Alcinous were so described, one might think of the extent of their sovereignty. But the others hardly stand out in the crowd of epic kings. Agapenor is a king of Arcadia. Of Eumelus we have already spoken. Helicaon is named only as a son of Antenor, the sage Trojan counsellor who seems not even to have been an independent ruler. | Haemon is named only once and then only as one of the Pylian warriors under the command of Nestor. Elephenor is the king of the Abantes. He appears only once outside the Catalogue: when he is killed by Agenor (*Δ* 463). *ἱππότα* might be taken as a distinctive epithet of Nestor. But it is said also of Tydeus, of Peleus, of Oeneus, of Phyleus. The meaning 'Sacker of Troy' was already ascribed to *πτολίπορθος* in ancient times,[1] since in the *Odyssey* this epithet is given exclusively to Odysseus. In the *Iliad*, however, it is not only given to Odysseus (who has not yet sacked Troy), but also to Achilles (*Θ* 372, *O* 77, *Φ* 550, *Ω* 108), to Oileus (*B* 728) and to Otrynteus (*Υ* 384). The last of these comes up only as the father of one Iphition, slain by Achilles. It would seem natural that a reader who sees Menelaus being called *ξανθός* should conclude that this hero is distinguished by the colour of his hair; but leaving aside Achilles and Odysseus, whom Homer also describes as blond-haired, we find the same epithet used for Meleager and for Rhadamanthys.

Clearly we have no grounds for trying to establish a distinctive meaning of these epithets by means of an adjustment of the text. They are found all through the Homeric poems; and there is no reason to single out any one of them. *πτολίπορθος*, for example, is intrinsically no better and no worse adapted to a distinctive use than is *βασιλεύς* or *βοὴν ἀγαθός* or any other epithet referring to some specific matter.

It might be thought that certain epithets such as *ἄναξ ἀνδρῶν*, *κρείων*, *ἱππότα*, *ξανθός*, which are used in Homer for several persons, none the less keep their distinctive meaning, since we find them most often used with a single name. Their use with other names is so rare, the argument goes, as not to affect the issue. The same reasoning can be adduced to justify the meaning 'Sacker of Troy' for *πτολίπορθος* in the *Odyssey*, whatever its

[1] Aristonicus on *B* 278.

meaning in the *Iliad.* To answer this question, we must turn to the evidence of the metre. As we have seen, the fact that an epithet has a unique metrical value in an extensive system proves it to be traditional. But the fact that an epithet of a hero has a unique metrical value proves it to be not only traditional, | but also generic. When the bard needed an ornamental epithet applicable to a hero and had no distinctive epithet, he had to use a generic epithet of a particular metrical value; if he knew only one of these, he had no choice but to use that one. Hence when a bard sang stories other than those of the siege of Troy and the return of Odysseus, and recounted the deeds of the protagonists of those other stories, he would join the epithets we find in Homer to other names. The legend of Meleager must have been popular with the Homeric audience: in the narrative of that legend it was he who received the epithet *ξανθός*. In the stories of the Seven against Thebes, Tydeus was *ἱππότα*, and Polynices, *ξανθός*.[1] It is not easy to find outside the Trojan cycle a name of the same metrical value as that of Odysseus so that we can imagine the epithet *πτολίπορθος* being often used with it, but we can be sure that in the narrative of the deeds of Achilles, Homer's audience had come across the epithet in a far greater number of lines than those of our *Odyssey*, and that for them these epithets belonged every bit as much to Achilles as to Odysseus. Moreover, it is quite unnecessary to limit our consideration to the use of epithets with the names of principal characters. Given the immense number of heroes who figure in the stories of the heroic age, it is certain that Homer's audience had heard the majority of generic epithets used many times with a wide variety of names. If *ἄναξ ἀνδρῶν* is used of ten persons in the *Iliad* and *Odyssey* alone, with how many other names would it have been found in the wide realm of epic poetry?

In the matter of the generic meaning of the epithet as in that of its ornamental meaning, we can conclude that the poet was guided in his choice by considerations of versification and in no way by the sense. We now have the alternatives of believing either that Homer sacrificed his thought to the convenience | of versification or that he felt an epithet used for more than one hero to be applicable to any hero. The use of the generic epithet in accordance with its measure is quickly demonstrated. *δῖος* appears in the nominative with the names of twelve heroes of which nine are of the same metrical value: *Ἀχιλλεύς*, *Ὀδυσσεύς*, *Ἀλάστωρ*, *ὑφορβός*, *Ἀγήνωρ*, *Ἐπειγεύς*, *Ἐπειός*, *Ἐχέφρων*, *Ὀρέστης*. The other names are *Ἀλέξανδρος* (thrice), *Μενεσθεύς* (once), and *Οἰνεύς* (once). Against these five usages, we find 183 for the nine names with the metre ⏑ – –, beginning with a vowel. *ἱππότα* is yet more rigorously limited to names of the same

[1] Cf. *Thebaid*, fr. II (Allen), l. 1:

αὐτὰρ ὁ διογενὴς ἥρως ξανθὸς Πολυνείκης.

metrical value, being said only of *Νέστωρ*, *Φυλεύς*, *Τυδεύς*, *Οἰνεύς*, *Πηλεύς*. *κρείων* appears in the nominative only with *Ἀγαμέμων*, *Ἀγαπήνωρ*, *Ἑλικάων*, *Ἐλεφήνωρ*, *Εὔμηλος*. *ξανθὸς* is used only for *Μελέαγρος*, *Ῥαδάμανθυς*, *Μενέλαος*. But there is no need to cite other examples of this kind; we should have to cite almost every epithet that appears on Table III. One can compare the lists of noun–epithet formulae given above (TE, pp. 85–6), when it was a question of demonstrating the utility of the generic epithet in the nature of verse. Clearly coincidence cannot be the explanation of this limitation of the epithet to names of a given measure. Homer therefore assigned to his characters divinity, horsemanship, power, and even blond hair, according to the metrical value of their names, with no regard to their birth, their character, their rank, or their legend: except in so far as these things were common to all heroes.

Except, that is to say, in so far as these things are interchangeable. If being 'divine', for example, has about the same value as being 'king' or 'horseman' or 'blameless' or 'strong' or any of the other qualities indicated by the generic epithet, then the poet was led by considerations of metre to stress one of these qualities for a given hero more than for another. To understand fully that generic epithets do in fact have the same value, we must refer to the relation between the generic meaning and the ornamental | meaning of the epithet. The problem of the epithet has often been complicated by the failure to grasp this relation clearly; but it is actually simple enough: before an epithet can have a generic meaning, it must have an ornamental meaning. The reason is that a particularized epithet cannot be generic. Used for the purposes of completing the thought of the sentence in which it appears, it must inevitably imply that the quality which it attributes to the hero is peculiar to him. If the poet, for example, wished us to understand that a given hero was exhibiting his 'divinity' (*δῖος*), or his strength (*κρατερός*), or his royalty (*βασιλεύς*), etc., the epithet would distinguish him as possessing to a peculiar degree the quality in question. This is the semantic explanation of the ornamental meaning of the generic epithet. The metrical explanation is equally neat: the generic epithet, if it is to assist in the making of verse, must be applicable to any hero without regard to momentary circumstances. Granted, then, that the generic epithet is ornamental, we must recognize the indifference, as we have studied it above, of poet and audience alike to its signification, an indifference which led them to consider the fixed epithet as a word adorning all epic poetry rather than a single line. Just as they took no notice of the limitation of the epithet of a hero to a particular grammatical case, so they took no notice of its limitation to a particular group of heroes. For them a generic epithet was simply one of the ennobling words of the language of poetry, essential to the traditional style, but embodying an idea which their indifference put on the same level of importance as the ideas of other generic epithets.

This feeling of the audience for the meaning of the generic epithet is attested by some of the illogical uses of the epithet. These uses fall into two categories: those in which the epithet is used with a noun which in most cases it can logically accompany, and those in which the epithet seems always to be in contradiction with the noun. In the first category fall, for example, χειρὶ παχείῃ, an expression which is usually perfectly acceptable, but is odd when used for the hand of Penelope (φ 6); and πότνια μήτηρ, an expression applicable to most mothers, but surprising when it is used of the mother of the beggar Irus (σ 5). The examples of the second category come from | the transfer of a generic epithet to a person to whom it seems ill-adapted. In the first category the contradiction is between the idea of the epithet and the meaning of the sentence, whereas in the second it is more between the epithet and the noun it accompanies. Thus δῖα is a generic epithet of heroines applicable to most women in epic; but when it describes Clytemnestra or Anteia, it seems out of place. ἀμύμων, which is used in Homer for 24 heroes, seems to fit 23 of them perfectly well, but raises a question in the case of the twenty-fourth, Aegisthus. The same is true of the epithets in the expressions ἀντίθεοι μνηστῆρες and Ἀντιμάχοιο δαΐφρονος. This latter category of illogical usage is of interest here, because it attests not only the ornamental meaning of the epithet, but also the poet's inattention to which name the epithet was to accompany. If the poet paid so little attention to the signification of δῖα when he used it for Clytemnestra, it is obvious that he was paying no more attention when he used it for Odysseus or for Priam or for Alexander, or even for that Aretaon who appears in the *Iliad* only to be killed by Teucer. If he used the epithet ἀμύμονος for Aegisthus with so little thought for the character of that villain, there is no reason to suppose he took any more thought for the character of Odysseus, of Alcinous, or of that Gorgythion who likewise enters the poem only to lose his life at the hands of Teucer. One usage of this kind which has given rise to much controversy is δῖος for the swineherd Eumaeus. Monro saw in it Homer's desire to amuse his audience, although the epithet is used 14 times of Eumaeus in the course of five books and at moments when the swineherd exhibits the greatest valour. If Monro had been consistent, he ought to have seen in it the poet's deliberate intention to show us that a swineherd can have as much worth as a man of high degree, and can by his courage be equally entitled to the epithet 'divine'. But such an interpretation of the epithet fails to take into account how little concerned the audience was over which noun accompanied this generic epithet. Homer used δῖος for the swineherd, first because Eumaeus lived in the age of heroes, and second because it was the only epithet he could find, which, together with ὑφορβός (Εὔμαιος would not work), made up a noun–epithet formula | coming after the bucolic diaeresis and beginning with a single consonant. His audience found nothing out-of-the-way or ludicrous in a swineherd's being called 'divine' because it never occurred to them for an instant to analyse the noun–epithet formula. It is the same with ἥρωι Δημοδόκωι in θ 483 and Φιλοίτιος, ὄρχαμος ἀνδρῶν (υ 185, 254).

To finish this investigation into the meaning of the generic epithet, let us consider a last reproach which could be made to Homer; that he sacrificed the distinctive epithet to the generic epithet. We have established, for example, that there are in Homer only 40 distinctive epithets of heroes as compared with 61 generic epithets. Hence it could be said that in order to make easier the composition of verse, the bards did not trouble to characterize their heroes, and that owing to the use of generic epithets most of the heroes of the *Iliad* and *Odyssey* are alike. The fallacy of this argument is in looking to a hero's epithets for a résumé of his character. Even among the 40 distinctive epithets of heroes, few refer specifically to their persons. We learn the characters of men and women in the *Iliad* and *Odyssey* not from epithets but from what they do and from what they say. To make this point clear we can leave aside the audience's indifference to the signification of the fixed epithet and concern ourselves with a proof of a different kind, viz., the paucity of distinctive epithets of heroes and peoples in the *Catalogue of Ships*.

Ten of the heroes who have distinctive epithets in Homer figure in the *Catalogue*. They are Odysseus, Achilles, Hector, Ajax, Diomedes, Nestor, Lycaon, Amphius, and Acamas; the number of their distinctive epithets to be found in the whole of the *Iliad* and *Odyssey* comes to 22. Of these 22, only 5 appear in the *Catalogue*: ποδάρκης . . . Ἀχιλλεύς (*B* 688), κορυθαιόλος Ἕκτωρ (*B* 816), ταχὺς Αἴας (*B* 527), Γερήνιος ἱππότα Νέστωρ (*B* 601), Ἄμφιος λινοθώρηξ (*B* 830). Thus neither Odysseus nor Agamemnon receives distinctive epithets, and it is furthermore clear that the | epithets just quoted, with the one exception of λινοθώρηξ, occur only because the poet needed formulae of a certain length to complete his lines. λινοθώρηξ, exceptional in that it describes a hero mentioned elsewhere only in *E* 612 when he is killed by Ajax, is a vestige of an old tradition. What created and preserved this epithet of an unimportant hero cannot have been convenience of verse-making: it must have been the value of the detail it gives us. Its meaning therefore is particularized and not ornamental, and it is the only epithet in the whole *Catalogue* which was put in to describe one of the heroes who fought before Troy.

The treatment of peoples is the same. Of the peoples who are provided with distinctive epithets, eight are named in the *Catalogue* (cf. TE,

p. 99): Abantes, Thracians, Mysians, Paeonians, Phrygians, Carians, Trojans, Achaeans. Homer gives them altogether eleven distinctive epithets of which only three occur in the *Catalogue*: *Παίονας ἀγκυλοτόξους* (*B* 848), *Καρῶν . . . βαρβαροφώνων* (*B* 867), *Ἄβαντες . . . θοοί, ὄπιθεν κομόωντες* (*B* 542). But neither the Trojans nor the Achaeans receive their epithets. Those we have quoted clearly belong with *λινοθώρηξ*. It is inconceivable that these three peoples played any role in the legend important enough for the bards to create and preserve for them distinctive epithets of a definite metrical value. The presence in the poem of these epithets must be due to the interest of the details they give us. From them, as from *λινοθώρηξ*, we catch a glimpse of the ancient origin, almost the historical origin, of the *Catalogue*.

But even in these four exceptional cases, Homer is far from using the epithet for the sake of description, as would seem natural and inevitable to us. He is only including some traditional data. The descriptions of his heroes, the information he gives us of their characters, are conveyed by means other than the epithet.

§ 3. THE PARTICULARIZED EPITHET

Our investigation has led us to conclude as categorically as did Düntzer that the meaning of the fixed epithet in Homer is | ornamental. But it is important not to fall into the error, or rather into the misunderstanding, which was certainly the principal cause of the opposition which the ideas of that scholar aroused in his contemporaries. Düntzer did not sufficiently understand the difficulty of knowing whether the epithet is really fixed. Indeed, he omitted the term *fixed* in the formal statement of his conclusions (cf. TE, p. 124), not taking into account that the term *epithet* by itself has been used in so many ways in the criticism of ancient and modern literature that it has come to mean no more than a qualifying adjective with a poetic ring, i.e. a qualifying adjective which by its signification or its use differs from adjectives of the spoken language.[1]

[1] Brunot's definition (*La Langue et la pensée*, Paris 1922, 633) can be quoted here: 'Les charactérisations sont fort souvent appliquées à des noms à l'aide d'épithètes, c'est-à-dire de mots ou d'expressions rapportées sans l'intermédiaire d'aucun verbe copule.' For the epithet in Greek or Latin poetry, there is no need to look for a more restricted meaning of the term. Quintilian's definition, which directly or indirectly inspired those of Hatzfeld and Darmesteter and that of Marmontel (quoted by Littré) is more quaint than exact: 'Ornat enim *ἐπίθετον* quod recte dicimus appositum; a nonnullis sequens dicitur. Eo poetae et frequentius et liberius utuntur; namque illis satis est convenire id verbo, cui apponitur; itaque et *dentes albos* et *humida vina* in iis non reprehendemus' (8. 6. 40). Quintilian, as not only his words but also his two examples show, confounded in a single vague notion Homer's ornamental epithet and the particularized epithet of later Greek poetry. If we make exception for the truly ornamental epithet of Homer (which can be more precisely termed the *fixed epithet*), we shall find that Brunot's definition is both precise and extensive enough to contain and to define the various uses of those words in Greek and Latin poetry which have been called epithets.

But, as we have seen, the indispensable condition of any interpretation of the epithet in Homer is to know whether it was always used in an ornamental sense with a given epithet to the point of becoming merged with it in an expression of a single idea. If it was not so merged, we must recognize that the audience would have had an impression of it quite different from the one we have just set forth.

It is precisely because of this habit of being content with an approximate sense of what the epithet is that the reader can make a similar mistake in his understanding of the epithet with a particularized meaning. In both cases he sees only a word which can be applied in greater or lesser degree to the action of the moment. One might think that the reader's commerce with modern | literature, by instilling in him the habit of looking for a particular motivation of the use of every qualifying adjective, would guarantee his recognition of the occasions when Homer does deliberately choose an epithet to complete the thought of his sentence. But the truth is that his experience of so many epithets which do not clearly reveal the intention of the author ultimately engenders (as does any other obscure or misunderstood element in the works of an author) an uncertainty which soon spreads to matters which he would otherwise have understood correctly. The reader of Homer will sometimes fail to recognize the epithet used for a particular purpose because he has not been able to distinguish it from an epithet whose use he could not explain. Let us take as an example the epithet πολύτροπος, which describes Odysseus in κ 330. In itself there is nothing in this epithet to distinguish it from πολύμητις or πολυμήχανε. The reader has probably discovered some sort of particular motivation for these two epithets; but his sense of these motivations will be incomplete or faulty. Consequently he will assimilate πολύτροπος to these other two epithets in his mind, and he will look for its meaning in the same hesitant and inadequate fashion that he was forced to adopt in their case. But for Homer's audience, if πολύτροπος is not a fixed epithet, and we shall shortly see that it is not, it must have been quite otherwise. They were in no uncertainty about fixed epithets; they knew by long habit which epithets are ornamental; and so they must have understood πολύτροπος as a word having no connection with ornamental epithets, a word to which they had not learned to be indifferent, and thus realized straightway that the poet had special reasons for putting it into his song.

Where, then, shall we look for the particularized epithet? The intrinsic limitations of our investigation of the fixed epithet compelled us to withhold judgement on a number of noun–epithet formulae and generic epithets, because we were unable to establish their traditional character by means of the system. It is among their number that we should begin looking for the particularized epithet, keeping in mind that we do not yet know whether they are fixed epithets which have eluded our demonstration, or whether they are particularized epithets, used for their signification rather than for their metre, and hence lie outside the range of this demonstration. What we | need therefore to discover them is a proof that they cannot be ornamental epithets.

We have seen that the cases in which the ornamental character of an epithet cannot be determined with certainty fall into two categories: cases where the noun–epithet formula is not unique, and thus escapes the system, and cases in which we lack sufficient examples to establish a system so complex as to be certainly traditional in its entirety. Let us first examine the cases of the first category.

When we find two or even more epithets or noun–epithet formulae of the same metre used with the same substantive, we can sometimes see that the poet is deliberately choosing a particular word in view of the immediate context. It was when the poet wanted to include an adjective for its sense rather than for its convenience that the influence of metre ceased to dictate the use of an epithet of a given measure, and the poet chose another, even though it duplicated that measure. Consequently, we can regard the repetition of metrical quantities as a sign that the epithet has been used to complete the meaning of the sentence; but a sign only, not a proof. Here many scholars have erred, failing to see that there may be other factors determining the use of equivalent noun–epithet formulae; e.g. the epithet may have been an element in a more complex formula, and so exempt from the influence of metre; or the noun–epithet formula may have been made by analogy with other noun–epithet formulae, which appear regularly in other grammatical cases, or with other nouns. These factors in traditional diction will be studied in the following chapter; here we must simply be aware that they exist, and that consequently the particularized meaning of the equivalent epithet is by no means a necessary conclusion.[1] |

Since metrical value does not offer a starting-point, how shall we discover the particularized epithet? We have two ways only of doing so. They may at first sight appear incomplete, but they are in practice adequate. They are the context and the other uses of the epithet. First we must consider singly the lines containing the epithets in question in order to establish the possibility of giving a particularized meaning to the epithet, remembering that the relation between the meaning of the epithet and that of the sentence must be such as to pertain directly to the

[1] A point missed by C. Francke in his study *De nominum propriorum epithetis Homericis*. Gryphiswaldiae 1887, 16 ff. He likewise did not grasp the poet's desire to avoid long closed syllables in the latter part of the line.

action of the moment. It will be objected that opinions here will differ, and the objection has some force. But in practice, if we keep in mind the directness which is from every point of view the mark of Homeric style, and firmly exclude any interpretation which does not instantly and easily come to mind, we shall find that there is hardly a case where variety of opinion is possible. The second method, which involves the other uses of the epithet, will then serve to control the choice which our tact has made. After what we have learned of the ornamental meaning of the Homeric epithet, we must recognize the principle that an epithet used in a given noun–epithet formula cannot sometimes be ornamental, sometimes particularized: *it must always be either the one or the other.* The ornamental meaning of the epithet, as we have studied it in the case of the fixed epithet, is such that we cannot imagine in the audience a partial indifference to the signification of any ornamental epithet. We have no reason whatever to attribute to the Homeric audience the hesitation of understanding felt by the modern reader, as he tries to find empirically the motivation for the use of an epithet, without any certainty of succeeding in his search. True, it is conceivable that an epithet in Homer was in the process of becoming fixed; for obviously every epithet was particularized to begin with. But that is the only kind of epithet which would allow of more than one interpretation, and it is unlikely in the extreme that any such exist in the lines of Homer. This state of transition through which an ornamental epithet must pass would have been short. If a figure is required, one could say that after an epithet had been used about a hundred times with an ornamental meaning | by the bards who first adopted it, it could no longer retain its particularized meaning. The chances of our observing any epithet in the course of this metamorphosis in the small fragment of epic poetry which we possess are almost negligible. Moreover, the principle thus formulated is confirmed in practice. We shall find that certain epithets which in several cases seem to have a particularized meaning, have such a meaning in all cases, which sometimes amount to as many as ten or fourteen.

Let us note the cases which we have found in our investigation of an epithet whose metrical value is repeated and which is used with a particularized meaning.

I. Circe, who has not succeeded in her attempt to change Odysseus into a pig, begs him to spare her, and in her terror she recalls the words of Hermes:

κ 330 ἦ σύ γ' Ὀδυσσεύς ἐσσι πολύτροπος, ὅν τέ μοι αἰεί
φάσκεν ἐλεύσεσθαι χρυσόρραπις Ἀργειφόντης.

The metrical values and the positions of noun and epithet are the same as in *K* 527.

ἔνθ' Ὀδυσεὺς μὲν ἔρυξε διίφιλος ὠκέας ἵππους.

These are the only lines in which the poet has used a noun–epithet formula of this type for Odysseus, but we have already observed a formula of this metrical value for the name of Achilles (*Σ* 203, cf. *Ω* 472) and we have seen that διίφιλος is regularly used when the poet needs an epithet to fill the line between the feminine caesura and the bucolic diaeresis (TE, p. 66). διίφιλος therefore is the only generic epithet of a hero of this metrical value (cf. Table III). It is thus evident that in the passage in question Homer did not make use of the epithet which would have come immediately to his mind had he not been thinking of the action of the moment. Finally, let us note that this epithet appears elsewhere in Homer only in the first line of the *Odyssey*, where it is used with ἄνδρα and cannot have an ornamental meaning.

II. The epithet διίφιλος, whose function in the technique of the use of the epithet we have just recalled, is used 5 times for Achilles, and we also find for the same hero πελώριος (twice), which in every case is found to have the same metrical value as the other | epithet. Similarly, we find διίφιλος used 4 times for Hector, but in *Λ* 820 πελώριος. As has already been said, we need more here than the mere demonstration of a particularized meaning in these three cases: either the epithet πελώριος is a generic epithet of a hero and always ornamental, or it is always particularized in each of the 10 cases of its use. (1) It is given to Achilles in *Φ* 527 where the poet is telling us how Priam watched him from the walls as he drove the Trojan army before him. (2) In *X* 92 Hector will not yield to the pleas of his father and mother,

ἀλλ' ὅ γε μίμν' Ἀχιλῆα πελώριον ἆσσον ἰόντα

(3) In *Λ* 820 when the Achaeans are suffering great reverses, Patroclus asks Eurypylus in desperation if he has any hope of stopping πελώριον Ἕκτορα. (4) Helen identifies the Achaean heroes for Priam as he observes them from the Scaean gate. When he asks (*Γ* 226)

τίς τ' ἄρ' ὅδ' ἄλλος Ἀχαιὸς ἀνὴρ ἠΰς τε μέγας τε,
ἔξοχος Ἀργείων κεφαλήν τε καὶ εὐρέας ὤμους;

she answers him:

Γ 229 οὗτος δ' Αἴας ἐστὶ πελώριος, ἕρκος Ἀχαιῶν.

(5–6) Line *H* 211, where Ajax again receives this epithet, occurs in a passage where this hero, who is arming himself for his duel with Hector, is compared with Ares, who, four lines above, has himself received the same epithet. (7) Ajax receives the epithet a third time in *P* 360 at a moment when, in the thick of battle, he bestrides the body of Patroclus. (8) And finally, in *P* 174, he receives the epithet from the lips of Hector, who is trying to explain to Glaucus why he fled from Ajax and abandoned the body of Sarpedon. (9–10) In the other two cases the epithet is applied to one Periphas (*E* 842, 847), an Aetolian hero slain by Ares. Although this Periphas is mentioned nowhere else in Homer, we can be certain that he figured in the legend as a warrior conspicuous for his size.

There is one important fact to observe in the use of this particularized epithet πελώριος. In all ten cases it falls before the bucolic diaeresis, and there can be no doubt that it was in great | part metrical convenience that occasioned its use. However, that in no way invalidates the conclusion we have drawn. It is true that the poet needed an epithet to fill the portion of the line between the feminine caesura and the bucolic diaeresis; but he would certainly have employed διίφιλος in these cases if the situation of the moment had not suggested to him the other adjective. Although we can see in these passages the influence of the metre, we can see at the same time the conscious choice of a word. Moreover, the variety of the metrical values of the names of the heroes described by this epithet is an indication that metrical convenience was not the only operative factor. An equivalent epithet such as μενεχάρμης, -ην, for example, is used only with the names Ἀντίλοχος, Ἱππόνοον, Ἱππόλοχον, which suggests a purely metrical reason for their use and an ornamental meaning—a suggestion which is rapidly confirmed by a consideration of the occasions of its use, for example in *Λ* 303 or *Ψ* 419.

III. The epithet Ἰθακήσιος is used twice of Odysseus. Elsewhere, when the poet wishes to fill the portion of the line between the masculine caesura and the bucolic diaeresis, he uses δουρικλυτός. The fact that δουρικλυτός makes the final syllable of Ὀδυσεύς long both by nature and by position is not relevant here; a long closed syllable is not avoided after this caesura as it is in the last three feet of the hexameter, as we can discover by a consideration of the lines containing δουρικλυτός (see TE, pp. 65–6), πεπνυμένος, and θεοείκελος. The contexts indicate a clearly particularized meaning for Ἰθακήσιος. In the assembly in *β*, Leocritus asserts that the suitors have nothing to fear from a single man, and that, if 'Odysseus of Ithaca' were to return, he would soon meet his death at their hands:

β 246 εἴ περ γάρ κ' Ὀδυσεὺς Ἰθακήσιος αὐτὸς ἐπελθών.

In this line there is a strong resemblance to the other in which this epithet occurs:

χ 45 εἰ μὲν δὴ Ὀδυσεὺς Ἰθακήσιος εἰλήλουθας.

Here Eurymachus says that if Odysseus is truly the man he claims to be, he is justified in his desire to take revenge on the suitors. It cannot be denied that these two lines are both inspired by a common model; but that is no reason for us to refuse to see the relation between the epithet and | the verb. We should, however, refrain from finding in the epithet the meaning 'the true Odysseus'; the meaning is simply 'Odysseus returning to his homeland'. We see here a traditional mode of using the epithet in a particularized sense.

IV. *ὑπέρθυμος* has often been translated by 'proud' or 'arrogant', a signification which is not confirmed by its use (cf. *Δ* 365, *E* 77, *Ψ* 302, etc.). But *ὑπερφίαλος*, which has the same metrical value, clearly shows the particularized meaning given by the translation 'arrogant'. This epithet is used thrice for the Trojans (cf. *Τρῶες ὑπέρθυμοι*, 5 times; *Τρῶας ὑπερθύμους*, twice). In each of these three cases the poet puts the word in the mouth of one of the enemies of Troy. (1) In *Φ* 224 it is Achilles who, after he has overcome the river Scamander, boasts that he will not give over killing the 'arrogant Trojans' until he has made an end of Hector. (2) in *Φ* 414 Athena, who has crushed Ares beneath a tremendous rock, tells him that he has got what he deserved for having defended the 'arrogant Trojans' against the wishes of his mother Hera. (3) In *Φ* 459 Poseidon, to induce Apollo to quit the field of battle, recounts to him the indignities which Laomedon once inflicted upon them both, and expresses his surprise that Apollo did not join the other gods in punishing the 'arrogant Trojans'. (4) The epithet is used in *E* 881 for Diomedes (cf. *ὑπέρθυμον Διομήδεα Δ* 365) in a line spoken by Ares: who complains before Zeus that Athena is rousing the 'arrogant Diomedes' to do battle with the gods. Ares himself has just been wounded by Diomedes. (5) In *ι* 106 Odysseus tells how he came to the land of the Cyclops:

Κυκλώπων δ' ἐς γαῖαν ὑπερφιάλων ἀθεμίστων.

(6–14) In the nine other cases of the use of the epithet, it is applied to the suitors, four times by Odysseus, once by Penelope, and four times by the poet himself, and in each case there is more than the inherent wickedness of the suitors to explain the use of the word. In each passage there is either a definite crime on the part of the suitors—the wasting of Odysseus' flocks (*ψ* 356, *ξ* 27), the plot against the life of Telemachus (*δ* 790), the corruption of the servant girls (*υ* 12), the indignities suffered by Odysseus disguised as a beggar (*υ* 291); or else there figures the hatred which they inspire in Odysseus (*ο* 315, *π* 271,) and in Penelope (*σ* 167), or finally, the idea of revenge (*ν* 373).|

V. In *γ* 81 we find *'Ιθάκης ὑπονηίου*, which in metre matches the expression *'Ιθάκης εὐδειέλου*, which likewise appears only once. But the frequency with which we find *'Ιθάκην εὐδείελον* in the accusative (5 times) shows us that *'Ιθάκης εὐδειέλου* was the form regularly used in the genitive. Thus we know that the poet has Telemachus use the word *ὑπονηίου* not to indicate from what Ithaca he has come, but to describe the island of Ithaca, for the benefit of the audience, of course, rather than of Nestor.

The meaning of the epithet can be closely compared with that of ἀργηστής, which Aeschylus uses as an epithet of ἀφρός, 'white foam' (*Septem* 60): since ὑπονηίου is not regularly used in a noun–epithet formula, it would have drawn the attention of the audience and awakened in their minds a particular image.

VI. The epithet κυανοπρωιρείους is used but once in the accusative (γ 299), but we know by its common appearance in the genitive (12 times) that it was the epithet which served regularly in the accusative. Now we find on two occasions another epithet of ships with the same metrical value: φοινικοπαρήιους, which appears in the repeated line λ 124 = ψ 271:

> οὐδ' ἄρα τοὶ ἴσασι νέας φοινικοπαρήιους.

In both lines we are dealing with the prophecy of Tiresias: in order to assuage the anger of Poseidon, Odysseus must make a long voyage after his return to Ithaca. He must go in search of a people who know neither the sea nor the ships that sail upon it. The epithet does not necessarily have an occult significance, as we seem to find in ἀθηρηλοιγόν; but it was certainly one of the words which, in the tradition of epic song, belonged to the prophecy spoken to Odysseus by the old blind seer of Thebes.

VII. We find in α 29 ἀμύμονος Αἰγίσθοιο, where ἀμύμονος is the only generic epithet of a hero with this metrical value (cf. Table III); but in γ 309–10 we read:

> ἦ τοι ὁ τὸν κτείνας δαίνυ τάφον Ἀργείοισι
> μητρός τε στυγερῆς καὶ ἀνάλκιδος Αἰγίσθοιο.

VIII. 18 times we find ἐυκνήμιδες Ἀχαιοί, and 10 times ἐυκνήμιδας Ἀχαιούς, but Δ 66–7 = 71–2 ὑπερκύδαντας Ἀχαιούς. These lines occur in a dialogue between Athena and Hera, who are devising a plan | to break the armistice. The epithet is unquestionably chosen to mark the warm feelings of both goddesses toward the Achaeans.

IX. We find νῆες ἐύσσελμοι 4 times in the *Odyssey*, twice at the beginning of a line; with it we can compare νῆας ἐυσσέλμους (12 times) which occurs seven times in this position. But in Δ 247–9, where the poet could have used ἐύσσελμοι, we read:

> ἦ μένετε Τρῶας σχεδὸν ἐλθέμεν, ἔνθα τε νῆες
> εἰρύατ' εὔπρυμνοι, πολιῆς ἐπὶ θινὶ θαλάσσης,
> ὄφρα ἴδητ' αἴ κ' ὔμμιν ὑπέρσχῃ χεῖρα Κρονίων;

Evidence for the particularized meaning of εὔπρυμνοι is in fact plentiful: we shall see further on that an epithet placed in a line following that of its substantive is virtually never ornamental.

X. We have pointed out that certain heroes, and certain peoples in the *Catalogue*, who play no more than a minor role in the legend, none the less receive distinctive epithets; and we observed that the reasons for their use must be sought elsewhere than in the influence of metre. In the case of the epithets in question we found that their survival was determined by the historical interest of the details they embody; but there are other distinctive epithets which cannot be explained in this way; all we can do in their case is to recognize that they are particularized epithets, a fact which accords both with their signification and with the way in which the poet used them. These epithets are three: *Φόρβαντος πολυμήλου* (*Ξ* 490), *πολυμήλου Φυλακίδαο* (*Β* 705), *ἀγήνορι Λαομέδοντι* (*Φ* 443), *Λαομέδων ἔκπαγλος* (*Φ* 452).

XI. Let us finally note two noun–epithet expressions for which equivalent formulae cannot be found, but which none the less clearly exhibit a particularized meaning: *μάχης ἀκόρητον* (*Υ* 2) and *Πατροκλῆος δειλοῖο* (4 times). Here, as in the four cases which we have been considering in the preceding paragraph, the ornamental meaning is excluded by the fact that we cannot explain by the influence of metre the existence in the tradition of distinctive epithets with the metrical values and in the grammatical cases of these. It is true of course that there is no hero more important than Achilles in the epic story, but even for him we cannot suppose that a formula of this | metre, containing a distinctive epithet, was of sufficient use to become part of the technique of the use of formulae, in which case the distinctive epithet would have become ornamental. And so with the epithet of Patroclus *Πατροκλῆος δειλοῖο*; it could never have been so helpful to the bards in their composition as to have been given a permanent place in their traditional language.

What has just been said of the formulae of Achilles and Patroclus applies with still greater force to the epithets in the expressions *ἀνάλκιδος Αἰγίσθοιο* (*γ* 310, already quoted TE, p. 160), *Κλυταιμνήστρη δολόμητις* (*λ* 422), and *στυγερήν . . . Ἐριφύλην* (*λ* 326). For the less importance these characters had in the legend, the more difficult it is to explain the survival of a distinctive epithet by the influence of metre.

Let us now turn our attention to noun–epithet expressions whose fixed character cannot be established by means of the system. Fortunately, we discover that cases in which it is impossible to decide the meaning of the epithet are fewer than one might expect. Most of the time the epithet does not lend itself by its signification to any particularized meaning, and in cases where it does, we can recognize the ornamental meaning by comparing its use there with its use in other lines of the two poems. On the other hand, the particularized epithet reveals itself sometimes by its signification and at other times by its position in the line and in the sentence. It is often easy to determine that, from the point of view of versification, the poet could not derive any use from the epithet, and that consequently we must not attempt to find the motivation for its use in the influence of metre.

I. We saw above that the same epithet for the same man cannot have at one time a particularized meaning and at another time an ornamental meaning. It would obviously be of little value to cite all the cases in which this principle applies; let us rather confine ourselves to indicating by a few examples the possible extent of its application. If, in reading line χ 43, where the trapped suitors attempt to flee,

πάπτηνεν δὲ ἕκαστος ὅπηι φύγοι αἰπὺν ὄλεθρον,

we feel a desire to see in the epithet *αἰπύν* the poet's intention to | stress the complete and absolute destruction of the suitors, we shall soon be disappointed when we look for an analogous meaning in the 23 other lines where this epithet accompanies *ὄλεθρος*. The same method will show us the ornamental meaning in the expressions *Κίλλαν τε ζαθέην* (*A* 38, cf. *I* 151, *B* 508, 520); *ἱερὴν ἑκατόμβην* (*A* 99, cf. *Ψ* 146, γ 144, δ 478); *πολυάικος πολέμοιο* (*A* 165, cf. *Υ* 328); *διοτρεφέων βασιλήων* (*A* 176, cf. *B* 98 and especially δ 63); *πικρὸν ὀιστόν* (χ 8, cf. *Δ* 134, 217, *N* 592, etc.); *ἐυδμήτους . . . τοίχους* (χ 24, cf. υ 302, χ 126); etc.

II. Let us point out first of all those numerous particularized epithets whose very signification rules out an ornamental meaning, since it is applicable only to certain members of the group. These epithets, which Düntzer designates by the term 'determinative' (*bestimmende*), offer no difficulty from the point of view of meaning, being easily recognizable: it will suffice to mention a few of them: *ἰφθίμους ψυχάς, ἀπερείσι' ἄποινα, χρυσέωι . . . σκήπτρωι, ἀγλαὰ . . . ἄποινα, κρατερὸν . . . μῦθον, χαρίεντα . . . νηόν, μέγαν οὐδόν, αἵματος ἀνδρομέοιο, χολωτοῖσιν ἐπέεσσι*, etc.

III. The mere fact that an epithet is separated from its noun by other words in the sentence does not necessarily prove that its use has not been occasioned by concerns of versification. On the contrary, we have already met in the case of epithets whose use is partially independent of the formula (TE, p. 66) lines in which we see the fixed epithet separated from its noun; thus the lines

K 527 ἔνθ' Ὀδυσεὺς μὲν ἔρυξε διίφιλος ὠκέας ἵππους

H 38 Ἕκτορος ὄρσωμεν κρατερὸν μένος ἱπποδάμοιο.

We have also seen that the epithet of Zeus, for example, in the expression *ὃν (τὸν) ἀθάνατος τέκετο Ζεύς* (thrice, TE, cf. p. 78) should be considered ornamental. But the fixed epithet, apart from the two types of formula which we have just indicated, is never separated from its noun. There are only two possibilities: either the epithet must be part of a system of formulae designed to express in the hexameter a noun or a category of nouns of the first importance, nouns frequently met with in epic poetry and thus requiring a system of great complexity; or else it must be contained in a formula designed to express a | particular idea. Otherwise we should have to suppose for a noun which appears only rarely in the poetry a system so complex that it would contain not only formulae of the principal types, those which fall between a caesura and one of the ends of the line, but also types of formulae which are used rarely even with the names of heroes; and these are by far the most frequent of nouns. Thus, for line *A* 10,

> νοῦσον ἀνὰ στρατὸν ὦρσε κακήν, ὀλέκοντο δὲ λαοί,

νοῦσον could not appear so often in poetry and in such a variety of circumstances that we could imagine a traditional device by which it and the epithet modifying it could be placed in the line in the position in which we see them here; nor can we suppose that the essential idea 'he sent a plague throughout the camp' would be so common that the bards would have created a traditional formula to express it in the space contained between the beginning of the line and the hephthemimeral caesura. The only possible reason for the presence of κακήν in this line is the particular desire of the poet to introduce this word into his sentence; and therefore we must recognize that he wanted to say, not to be sure that the plague in question was worse than other plagues, but that at this time it was bad for the Achaeans.

We have no reason to believe that Chryses played so important a role in the legend of Troy that the bards would have invented for his name the device of a fixed epithet which could have been used with it and would at the same time complete the line after the bucolic diaeresis; therefore we must translate the expression in *A* 11:

> οὕνεκα τὸν Χρύσην ἠτίμασεν ἀρητῆρα
> Ἀτρείδης.

not by 'Chryses the priest', but by 'Chryses, who was a priest'.

The frequency (38 times) with which the expressions φίλος υἱός, φίλον υἱόν appear, and the positions in the lines and the contexts in which they appear, leave no doubt that they are simply metrical variants of υἱός, and that the epithet in this expression has the same ornamental sense which it has in φίλον ἦτορ. But there is no reason to believe that φίλην was regularly used with παῖδα whenever it was convenient—which must have been very rarely—to | fill the line between the feminine and the hephthemimeral caesurae. Therefore we must try to find the motivation for its use in *A* 20 in the poet's own thought,

> παῖδα δ' ἐμοὶ λύσαιτε φίλην, τὰ δ' ἄποινα δέχεσθαι.

Similarly we know that the epithet in χ 18,

βλημένου, αὐτίκα δ' αὐλὸς ἀνὰ ῥῖνας παχὺς ἦλθεν,

was designed to suggest a particular image.

We have already one proof of the particularized meaning of the epithets we have been considering; where the epithet was not constantly used with a given noun, it could never have become indifferent to the audience. But we must take into consideration another sign of the particularized meaning of the epithets which we have been examining, a sign of psychological nature and one we should regard as among the many various factors which determined the character of the technique of noun–epithet formulae. This is the fact that if between the noun and its epithet there intervenes another word more important than a mere conjunction or particle, the attention of the audience will momentarily abandon the substantive, and when it is recalled, the close union between the epithet and the idea of the noun will have been broken. The audience will no longer be solely concerned with the idea of the noun, as they were from the one end to the other of a formula of which the epithet immediately precedes or follows the noun, and consequently they will inevitably give more attention to the epithet, as to a word whose idea is important in its own right. We see then that a fixed epithet is never separated from its noun except in the case of those nouns which appear so frequently in poetry that it is certain that the indifference of the audience to any possible particularized meaning would be quickly formed. And so, in considering the mental processes of the Homeric audience, we end with the same conclusion to which we were led by the consideration of metre and convenience of versification. Here, as when we considered the role of analogy in the development of traditional diction (TE, pp. 71–3), we can see what a marvellous thing the bards | succeeded in creating. In allowing themselves to be guided by the material elements of the hexameter and by the metrical values of the words they used, and in constantly looking for facility in the making of verse, they created a style which conformed in the highest degree to the rules of thought. The clarity of the sentences of epic poetry is born from the very difficulty of rendering them in the rhythm of the hexameter line.

IV. These cases of the separation of noun and epithet lead us to those in which the epithet is found in the line following the one containing the noun, and what we learned of the first group applies even more to the second. The epithet in the following line is always particularized, with the exception of the exceedingly rare cases of an epithet of which the use is almost independent: possibly διίφιλος in *Π* 169 is the only epithet so used in Homer. In the first place, the close bond in the mind of the audience between noun and epithet, which, as we have just seen, is necessary to the ornamental sense, is severed by the interruption which comes naturally at the end of an Homeric line—an interruption which does not necessarily come from a pause, although this will be the case with most lines, but from the rhythm, as the poet finishes one movement of six feet and begins another. Moreover, the presence of an epithet in a following line is of even less advantage in the making of verse than a separation of noun and epithet in the same line. The technique of epithets, as we have studied it, is solely designed to help the poet to fit a noun into a line of six feet; once the noun has been fitted in and the line is complete, the epithet has no further function. To expect a metrical utility of the epithet in a following line, with the one exception we noted of the epithet used independently, we should have to assume that the Homeric line had not six feet, but twelve.

Cases when the epithet appears in the line following that of its noun are few. We can list those to be found in the two books *A* and *χ*. *A* 1 *μῆνιν . . . οὐλομένην*. *A* 37 *Ἀργυρότοξ' . . . Σμινθεῦ*. *A* 247 *Νέστωρ | ἡδυεπὴς . . . λιγὺς Πυλίων ἀγορητής*. *A* 481 *κῦμα . . . πορφύρεον*. *χ* 79 *φάσγανον . . . χάλκεον, ἀμφοτέρωθεν ἀκαχμένον*. *χ* 123 *κυνέην . . . ἵππουριν*. The last of these examples deserves some attention. We find the following lines | 4 times ((*Γ* 336, *O* 480, *Π* 137, *χ* 123) when Homer is describing a warrior arming himself:

> κρατὶ δ' ἐπ' ἰφθίμωι κυνέην εὔτυκτον ἔθηκεν
> ἵππουριν· δεινὸν δὲ λόφος καθύπερθεν ἔνευεν.

Used in this way, the epithet *ἵππουριν* is typical of a fairly large number of epithets which occur in traditional descriptions. These epithets can be used like *ἵππουριν* with some degree of frequency, but it would be impossible for them ever to lose their particularized meaning. What we have here is an image which Homer's audience liked to have evoked for them, and since Homer, on each of these occasions, was concerned with the image, *ἵππουριν* must have maintained its particularized meaning.

§ 4. THE EPITHET OUTSIDE EPIC POETRY

Let us leave the particularized epithet, and turn back to the fixed epithet in order to summarize its characteristics and to compare them with those of the epithet as it was used in later Greek poetry. These characteristics are essential to our understanding of Homeric thought, and they are few; to be exact, four: (1) Fixed epithets are used in accordance with their metrical value and not in accord with their signification; (2) they are traditional; (3) they are always ornamental; (4) they are often generic. And these four characteristics—a point which cannot be too much insisted on—are interdependent. The traditional epithet would not be possible if the bards had not wanted them in a great variety of metrical values. The ornamental meaning is not possible in an epithet which is not traditional. And the generic meaning is not possible in an epithet which is not ornamental. It follows then that in any poetry in which the first of these conditions, use according to metrical value, is not met, the epithet can have neither an ornamental nor a generic meaning. This is as much as to say that, outside epic poetry, all epithets of Greek, Latin, and modern poetry are particularized and are related to the action of the context in which they occur. For we find that apart from the Greek hexameter no metrical form has had such influence on style as to create a traditional diction; the technique of epithets in epic poetry, being a product of the hexameter, could not | be adapted to any other rhythmical structure; and outside epic poetry, we find no other poetry in hexameters which shows such influence of the verse-form to even a slight degree. Since this influence could not become operative without the collaboration of many poets in the course of many generations, the hexametric style of another age could never be traditional except in so far as it imitated a style other than its own, i.e. that of Homer. And as we have seen in the case of Apollonius and Virgil, this imitation did not go far.

To appreciate this capital and categoric fact that the ornamental epithet does not exist outside epic poetry, let us consider the epithets of several poets who used them in a notable way.

To understand Pindar's epithets, the reader does not have to familiarize himself with the noun–epithet expression, as he does to understand the epithet in Homer; from this point of view we are a much more satisfactory audience for the Theban poet than we are for the author of the *Iliad* and the *Odyssey*. For those who heard a Pindaric ode being performed for the first time expected, just as we do, an individual style in which each word subserved the immediate purposes of the author. Let us look at the epithets which adorn the beginning of the fourth *Pythian*. ἀνδρὶ φίλωι (l. 1) means 'a man who is dear to me'; the expression means as much as if the poet had said παρ' ἀνδρὶ ὅς φίλος μοί ἐστιν, because Pindar is not recognizing a fact: he is asserting one. εὐίππου . . . Κυράνας (l. 2): the ode is celebrating the victory of Arcesilas in the chariot race. χρυσέων . . . αἰετῶν (l. 6): since not all eagles are made of solid gold, this epithet is one of those we have called 'determinative'. ἱερὰν νᾶσον (l. 11): the island of Thera was famous for the number of its cults, which rules out the generic meaning of the epithet ἱερός in Homer: in the *Iliad* and *Odyssey* it is applied to Troy, to the Echinades Islands, to Thebes in the Troad, to Euboea, to Zeleia, to Onchestus, to Pylos, and to the city of the Cicones. As for the ornamental meaning, it cannot apply here in Pindar, because the epithet has clearly been chosen to underline the dominant idea of the sentence and the poem: the circumstances of the colonization of Cyrene were sanctified from the beginning to the end. καρποφόρου Λιβύας (l. 11): the poet's thought is 'colonizer of Libya, which is | a fertile land and therefore what a colonizer would wish for'. εὐάρματον πόλιν (l. 13): another word pertaining to Arcesilas' victory. Into our understanding of this epithet, if, as we have every right to suppose, it is an invention of Pindar, there enters another factor alien to the Homeric epithet, viz., the striking character of a new word. This would have directed the attention of the audience to the epithet alone, while it made him at the same time aware of Pindar's originality. All this is very far from πολύτλας δῖος 'Οδυσσεύς, which is found 38 times in the short space of the *Iliad* and *Odyssey*, and which had been used countless times in epic poetry which Homer's audience had already heard. Of course we cannot be entirely sure that in this line of Pindar we are seeing the first use of εὐάρματον; what is certain is that there is a large number of novel epithets in the works of Pindar. For anyone who wants undeniable evidence of this, we can point to ἀναξιφόρμιγγες (*Ol.* 2. 1), ἰοπλοκάμων (*Pyth.* 1. 1), μεγιστόπολι (*Pyth.* 8. 2), etc.[1] But our investigation in the preceding chapters has not yielded a single epithet, even particularized, which one could venture to say is probably the creation of Homer. ἀργινόεντι μαστῶι (l. 14): the figurative meaning of the noun at once excludes any notion of an ornamental meaning for the epithet: Cyrene was built on a white hill.

In the opening lines of *The Persians*, we find possibly a greater profusion of epithets than in any other passage of extant Greek drama. In these lines, the chorus of Persian old men describes Xerxes' army and gives the names of its leaders. We have here a catalogue which clearly reveals its author's memory of Homer; but Aeschylus' use of the epithet in it could not be more different from Homer's in the *Catalogue*, in the second book of the *Iliad*. The latter, as we have seen (TE, pp. 152–3), is a mere list of names and facts, and the epithets which appear in it are not chosen for the sake of description. In setting forth the constituents of the Achaean and Trojan armies, Homer had no notion of expressing | any judgement; it never occurred to him to draw any conclusion from his list. What he was doing, rather like an impartial historian, was to keep his promise to give the names of the captains of the ships and the numbers of the ships themselves (*B* 493), and with the Trojan and allied army he acted likewise. In Aeschylus we find something else altogether. Already in the third line, the words τῶν ἀφνεῶν καὶ πολυχρύσων ἑδράνων manifest the poet's intention to describe not so much the Persian army itself, as the huge size of the army and the fabulous wealth of the empire that is sending it forth

[1] Cf. Gildersleeve, *Pindar*, London 1885, p. xi, and Jebb, *Bacchylides*, London 1905, 62–8.

against Greece. And in these opening lines, the Athenian audience can already sense the moral idea which will dominate the play: the contrast between the power of the empire and its defeat. With the proper skill of a great dramatic poet, Aeschylus has turned all his epithets with a view to the realization of this idea: *ἄναξ Ξέρξης βασιλεὺς Δαρειογενὴς* (l. 5), *πολυχρύσου στρατιᾶς* (l. 9), *τὸ παλαιὸν Κίσσιον ἕρκος* (l. 17),

> *οἷος Ἀμίστρης ἠδ' Ἀρταφρένης*
> *καὶ Μεγαβάτης ἠδ' Ἀστάσπης,*
> *ταγοὶ Περσῶν, βασιλῆς βασιλέως*
> *ὕποχοι μεγάλου, σοῦνται στρατιᾶς*
> *πολλῆς ἔφοροι, τοξοδάμαντές τ'*
> *ἠδ' ἱπποβάται, φοβεροὶ μὲν ἰδεῖν,*
> *δεινοὶ δὲ μάχην*
> *ψυχῆς εὐτλήμονι δόξηι·*

(ll. 21–8), etc. But there is no need to insist on the point, since the particular purpose of each epithet is unmistakable. Let us notice instead, how in borrowing some epithets from Homer, Aeschylus has given them a particularized meaning they never had in the *Iliad* or *Odyssey*, a meaning which we could even call Aeschylean; for in them we can perceive the personal thought of the poet. *πολυχρύσοιο* is in Homer a distinctive epithet of Mycenae. It appears only in the genitive case in a formula which ends the line, *πολυχρύσοιο Μυκήνης* (*H* 180, *Λ* 46, *γ* 304), and its ornamental function is merely to mention the possibly unique wealth of that city. But in the catalogue of *The Persians*, Aeschylus, who has already said *πολυχρύσου στρατιᾶς* (l. 9), uses the epithet again for Sardis and then for Babylon (ll. 45, 53). Now in Aeschylus' mind these cities | were indeed conspicuous for their wealth; but the audience and even the poet himself were too much preoccupied with the moral implication of the word to give the material implication any real thought. *ἱππιοχάρμης* occurs only twice in Homer, in *Ω* 257 for Troilus and in *λ* 259 for one Amythaon, a son of Tyro and Cretheus, characters who were certainly no better horsemen than other heroes. But when Aeschylus uses the epithet (l. 29), we see vividly the fiery charge of the captain going to his defeat. So Mazon translated: 'Artembarès, sur son destrier'.

In Apollonius too, Homer's fixed epithet is particularized. We saw that the only epithet used with the name *'Ιήσων* is *ἀρήιος* borrowed from Homer (cf. TE, p. 24): so if this epithet were ornamental, we should have a case where the Rhodian poet, like a true bard, was continuing the epic tradition. But it is impossible to overlook, in the two occasions of its use, the effect on the poet's choice of the immediate action. In i. 349, the epithet is used at the point where Heracles has declined the captaincy of the expedition and is proposing Jason in his stead. The Demigods approve, and 'warlike Jason rose up right pleased' to accept the honour. In ii. 122 the epithet occurs as the Demigods are putting the Bebryces to flight: 'and the sons of Aeacus rushed on them, and warlike Jason joined the attack'.

Apollonius was a poet of great originality, and his work, far from being an imitation of Homer, is an individual interpretation of the ancient story. We may learn more from Virgil, who deliberately set out to model his work on the *Iliad* and the *Odyssey*, how difficult, or even impossible, it is for a poet, with the best will in the world, to give a truly ornamental meaning to an epithet. The epithets of Aeneas are: *Anchisiades* (once), *magnanimum* (twice), *magnus* (twice), | *heros* (once), *bonus* (twice)—epithets imitated from Homer (cf. TE, p. 30–1); and *pius* (17 times) and *pater* (16 times)—which are original in Virgil. The epithets borrowed from Homer have undergone the same change as ἀρήιος in Apollonius: *bonus* (v. 770, xi. 106) refers to the kindness of Aeneas, first when he speaks words of comfort to the Trojans who have chosen to stay in Sicily, and second when he grants the Latins an armistice for the burial of their dead: *magnanimum* is put into the mouth of Jupiter when in i. 260 he reassures Venus of the celestial destiny of her son; and again into the mouth of Euryalus, who says that he could never show fear when 'great-hearted' Aeneas is his leader (ix. 204): *magnus* is said of the hero when the poet describes him (x. 159) seated on the prow of his ship, leading the fleet to battle. The meaning of the epithet resembles that of ἱππιοχάρμης in Aeschylus. In x. 829–30 Aeneas speaks to young Lausus, whom he has just slain:

> Hoc tamen infelix miseram solabere mortem:
> Aeneae magni dextra cadis.

The poet calls Aeneas *heros* when he answers the Sibyl's terrifying predictions with what we can call heroic intrepidity (vi. 103). Nor is even the patronymic *Anchisiades* without its particular motivation in viii. 521: it comes at the solemn moment when Aeneas has received Evander's promise of help and is about to hear thunder break the silence of the heavens and see revealed above him the arms his mother had promised him.

In his frequent use of *pius* and *pater*, Virgil comes closer to Homer without ever succeeding fully in his imitation. When he uses these epithets, he never wholly loses sight of the idea of 'piety' in the one, and 'paternity' in the other; and his choice varies as he thinks in some places of Aeneas and the gods, in other places of Aeneas and men. This was inevitable. The epithets have no justification apart from the two ideas which guided the author from the beginning to the end of his work:

Aeneas as one who, by the will of the gods, overcame superhuman difficulties to found the Roman | race in Italy, and Aeneas as the father of that race—ancestral father, father who upheld the Trojans who followed him, and father as god and protector of his people. As one or other of these aspects of his hero comes to the fore, he chooses the appropriate epithet. For example, in the passage where Aeneas announces himself to Dido (i. 378),

> Sum pius Aeneas, raptos qui ex hoste Penatis
> Classe veho mecum, fama super aethera notus,

it is inconceivable that *pius* should be replaced by *pater*, because the idea of the sentence is Aeneas' divine mission. When he sacrifices to Juno, Aeneas calls himself *pius* in his prayer (viii. 84), and not *pater*. Evander, speaking to the body of his son Pallas, says (xi. 170): 'What greater funeral honours could I bestow on you, Pallas, than those of pious Aeneas?' And again, Aeneas is *pius* when he prays to the Sun (xii. 175); when he addresses the body of Lausus (x. 826):

> Quid tibi nunc, miserande puer, pro laudibus istis,
> Quid pius Aeneas tanta dabit indole dignum?

when reluctant but obedient to the will of the gods he leaves Dido (iv. 393); when he sees his ships burning and begs Jupiter to extinguish the flames (v. 685), etc. Conversely, he is *pater*, and not *pius*, when he is the father of Ascanius: the epithet has this definite particularized sense on two occasions (iii. 343 and xii. 440), and perhaps no example shows with equal clarity how far the expression *pater Aeneas* is from a noun–epithet formula such as πατὴρ ἀνδρῶν τε θεῶν τε. Again, Aeneas is *pater* when he enters Dido's hall in company with the young men of Troy and takes his seat on a purple couch (i. 699): *pius* would have seemed strange to Virgil under these circumstances. He is *pater* when he does not allow the boxer Entellus's ardour to lead him to cruelty (v. 461). Here Goelzer, who ordinarily translates *pater* by 'divin', finds himself compelled to translate it 'paternel'. Aeneas is also *pater* in v. 545 when he speaks of the cavalry manœuvres to be executed by the young Ascanius. The meaning here seems to be not 'father of Ascanius', but father of his people, and especially of the younger generation whose destiny depends on his. The same meaning is found in v. 348, viii. 606, and ix. 172.

On rare occasions, it seems that the poet could have used the epithet | without any thought of the circumstances of the moment, as in v. 700, where *pater Aeneas*, after the burning of his fleet, wonders if he should abandon his plan of going to Italy; or in v. 26, when *pius Aeneas* orders Palinurus to change course for the shores of Sicily. But even in these cases the epithet is far from being truly ornamental. Even if we deny any relation in them between the epithet and the circumstances of the moment—since such a relation cannot be clearly established—there is still a relation between the epithet and the circumstances of the poem, and the reader must think of this. There is no question of the meaning we see in δῖος Ὀδυσσεύς or πολύμητις Ὀδυσσεύς; for Odysseus with his 'divinity' and his craftiness belongs to the legend; whereas Aeneas, with his 'piety' and his 'paternity', belongs to Virgil. δῖος and πολύμητις, for the audience, describe the Odysseus of all the epic poems which sang his deeds; *pius* and *pater*, for the lettered audience of Rome as for us, describe the Aeneas of the *Aeneid.*

§ 5. CAN THE FIXED EPITHET BE TRANSLATED?

As we come to the end of our investigation into the meaning of the fixed epithet in Homer, a question arises: how should it be translated? It goes without saying that translators in general, as we all know, tend to take their style and their thought from their own age rather than from Homer's, and for the epithet they are especially concerned to find some non-existent particularized meaning which recalls their own personality. Let us, however, consider whether it is possible to reproduce in translation the true meaning of the fixed epithet.

In fact we must recognize that it is hardly possible, because a modern writer cannot expect his audience to become familiar with the noun–epithet formula, and that is the essential condition for a real understanding of the epithet. Of course we can avoid far-fetched attempts to invent particularized meanings such as many translators have made, above all translators who were themselves poets. But we thereby solve only a small part of the problem. For nothing can keep the modern reader from following his own literary | habits and looking for the specific motivation for the use of each epithet, and for some specific meaning to assign to it.[1] Moreover, how could we in a translation make clear the crucial difference between the ornamental and the fixed epithet? Take lines ι 502–5, in which Odysseus is boating to Polyphemus:

Κύκλωψ, αἴ κέν τίς σε καταθνητῶν ἀνθρώπων
ὀφθαλμοῦ εἴρηται ἀεικελίην ἀλαωτύν,
φάσθαι Ὀδυσσῆα πτολιπόρθιον ἐξαλαῶσαι,
υἱὸν Λαέρτεω, Ἰθάκῃ ἔνι οἰκί' ἔχοντα.

How can we render the ornamental meaning of πτολιπόρθιον without

[1] Let us quote here the remark of M. Bréal (*Pour mieux connaître Homère*, Paris 1906): 'Ces accompagnements traditionnels n'étaient pas seulement une ressource pour le rhapsode: ils étaient un repos pour l'auditeur.' The rest provided by the fixed epithet depends, of course, on its being truly ornamental, and on its not requiring us to ask why it was used, as we must for a particularized epithet.

losing at the same time the particularized meaning of the words of the following line? We have the same problem in the scene of the quarrel in the first book of the *Iliad*: how can *κύδιστε* in line 122 be translated, so that a reader sees no irony even though the genuinely insulting phrase *φιλοκτεανώτατε πάντων* comes immediately after it? How can *θεοείκελε* be translated as purely ornamental in line 131,

> *μὴ δὴ οὕτως, ἀγαθός περ ἐών, θεοείκελ᾽ Ἀχιλλεῦ,*
> *κλέπτε νόωι,*

without omitting any of the contempt of the expression *πάντων ἐκπαγλότατ᾽ ἀνδρῶν*, which Agamemnon uses 15 lines later?

> *A* 146 *ἠὲ σύ, Πηλείδη, πάντων ἐκπαγλότατ᾽ ἀνδρῶν.*

The mind gives up before so impossible a task.

And furthermore what can be gained by an effort to find an exact equivalent for the ornamental epithet, and so to translate Homer's thought with the least addition of foreign ideas? Perhaps if we did so we should have committed a worse error than those who draw on their own ideas to translate the epithet. For if the particular reason for the use of an epithet is not clearly indicated, the reader will be confused; | he will search and find some meaning or other, and the necessary delay will break the rapid movement of Homer's clear sentences. The problem we are facing here goes far beyond the mere translation of epithets. It is the problem of translation in general, of the choice to be made between what is obscure, but literally faithful, and what is clear, but inexact. The choice between these extremes will always depend on the relative obscurity and inexactitude in each case; and still more on the translator.

V

THE EPITHET AND THE FORMULA II: EQUIVALENT NOUN–EPITHET FORMULAE

1. *The equivalent noun–epithet formula and the operation of analogy.* 2. *The equivalent noun–epithet formula contained in a more complex formula.* 3. *Equivalent generic epithets.* 4. *Three equivalent noun–epithet formulae.* 5. *The unity of style in the* Iliad *and the* Odyssey.

WITTE observes the lack of success of those who have looked to various cultural, religious, or dialectal differences in Homer for a solution of the problem of the composition of the Homeric poems, and expresses the opinion that the solution to this problem must be sought elsewhere: 'The way to the Homer analysis of the future will be through a history of the language of Greek epic whose author will adopt the fundamental principle which makes an understanding of the literary language of the epic possible: viz., that the language of the Homeric poems is the creation of the epic line.'[1] In the application of this principle the author has not been particularly successful, because he has not sufficiently understood the complexity of traditional diction and the special conditions of its analysis.[2] But the conclusions of his essay, like the

[1] *Sprachliche Kriterien im Dienste der höheren Homerkritik*, Pauly–Wissowa, 8² (1913), 2238 ff.

[2] In the statement of his proposed method, Witte shows (op. cit.) that by 'influence of the metre' he understands conservative influence only, whereas creative influence is for him a sign that a line is late. However, he himself has had to recognize this creative influence by the presence in Homer of Ionic elements: ἄν, the endings -σι, -οις, -ῃς of the dative, -ου for the genitive, etc. In fact it is clear that everything which cannot be Aeolic is due to the creative influence of the hexameter, just as everything which cannot be Ionic is due to its conservative influence, and therefore no single element resulting from this creative influence can be condemned unless all such elements are condemned. Witte's arbitrary hypothesis deprives his examples of their value. For example, he believes δυναμένοιο (with the long υ), which appears in α 276 πατρὸς μέγα δυναμένοιο and λ 414 ἀνδρὸς μέγα δυναμένοιο, to be late because the same verb is found in other forms with a short root vowel 117 times. But the metre requires that the vowel be lengthened or that the form in question be avoided altogether. The bards did lengthen it, and their doing so added flexibility to their diction. The forms δύναμαι, δύνανται, δυνήσατο, etc., which provide the 117 examples of the verb with a short υ, have nothing to do with δυναμένοιο, because their natural metrical value is not an obstacle to their inclusion in the line. As for the rarity of this form, it is clearly due to chance and to the fact that the need to use the genitive case of the present participle of δύναμαι does not often arise. The same is true of πτολιπόρθιος (ι 504, 530). As Table III shows, it is the only epithet of a hero with this metrical value; given the complexity of the system of generic epithets as we see it on this table, the unique measure of this epithet can be regarded as a proof that it is traditional. The only way in which Witte could have demonstrated the lateness of the two forms δυναμένοιο and πτολιπόρθιος would have been first to quote the genitive case of the present participle of a verb expressing the idea of 'power' and having the same metrical shape as δυναμένοιο, and

| conclusions of those scholars who have explained the dialectal and artificial forms of epic language by the influence of metre, amply attest the soundness of the principle he lays down. We have found in the *Iliad* and the *Odyssey* systems of epithets and of noun–epithet formulae so extensive as to be explicable only by the conception of a poet faithful in its smallest details to a traditional diction created by bards under the persistent influence of the heroic line. Consequently, if we were to find that in some parts of the poems, or in some lines, this traditional diction is wholly or partly neglected in favour of other words or expressions, we should know forthwith that the lines in question are the work of a poet or interpolator of a date later than that of the author of the original poem. The style of a later author would be easily detectable by our not being able to observe the influence in it of the hexameter: our examination of Apollonius and Virgil has shown us that a poet whose style does not follow an established tradition is capable only to an infinitesimal degree of creating a style designed to facilitate the composition of verse.

Such is our principle of analysis. Now let us consider the | conditions required for its application; they prove to be as complex as the principle itself is simple. To know that a form, or a word, or an expression is not traditional, we must know what form, word, or expression *with the same metrical value* the poet could have used in its place. For as long as the word or words are not duplicated in metrical value, they can be explained by the influence of the hexameter. Except in the case of an expression which by its very nature could not be of use in the making of verse—and it is doubtful that any such could be found in Homer—we cannot claim to be so familiar with bardic diction that we could with confidence refuse to recognize as traditional any element which would add flexibility in composition. In other words, the only material to be found in bardic poetry which would admit the application of our principle is equivalent elements. When we find in Homer two or more ways of expressing the same essential idea in a given part of the line, by the same word or words, then and only then can we go ahead and see if these expressions are to be found in different parts of the *Iliad* and *Odyssey*, and whether there are parts of these poems in which these elements are especially common.

In the course of the preceding chapters we found a fairly large number of elements of this kind in the form of equivalent generic epithets and noun–epithet formulae.[1] In all probability, these are the only elements

second, to find some other epithet in Homer which the poet could have used in the place of *πτολιπόρθιος*; which is not possible. The same holds of the other examples offered by Witte.

[1] We should mention here the cases noted by Franke in which a single noun has two distinct meanings and a separate epithet for each one. Thus *ὀξὺν Ἄρηα* (5 times) and *οὖλον Ἄρηα* (once) are not equivalent epithets, nor are *βροτολοιγὸν Ἄρηα* (once) and *πολύδακρυν Ἄρηα* (thrice). In the first of each of these pairs, the name refers to the god, in the second it is used in the figurative sense of 'war'.

of the language of the *Iliad* and *Odyssey* to which the principle formulated can be applied with advantage, being the only elements of which the essential idea can be unambiguously grasped in a sufficiently large number of instances. Formulae of categories other than that of the noun–epithet formula express such a variety of ideas that it would be much too difficult to find among them a large enough number of cases in which we could definitely say that the poet was expressing the | same idea in different words of the same metrical value. The noun–epithet formula, however, being, as we have seen, no more than the heroic way of expressing a noun, and being solely designed to fit the noun into the hexameter, perfectly fills the conditions required for the analysis of the poems which we propose to make. The noun–epithet formula further lends itself to this sort of examination in that the technique of the use of the epithet is itself in large part capable of analysis, so that in one way or another we are bound to obtain valuable results. The technique of the use of the epithet as we have studied it is so complex that if we find nothing in Homer which runs counter to it, that is, if we find no noun–epithet formulae which do not show the influence of the hexameter, we shall have very strong proof that the *Iliad* and *Odyssey*, as they have come down to us, are, with the possible exception of a few lines or one or two short passages, the product of a time when the bardic tradition was in its full vigour. A technique of this sort could only have been learned by a bard taught by other bards and obeying implicitly, if unconsciously, the imperative of the verse-form; and for whom a new epithet or an epithet used in an original way was a thing which had never entered his mind.

§ 1. THE EQUIVALENT NOUN–EPITHET FORMULA AND THE OPERATION OF ANALOGY

The equivalent epithets and noun–epithet formulae which we have come across in the course of our investigation do not exhibit in its extreme form the influence of metre, as do those epithets and formulae which are metrically unique. One expression is useful in composition; equivalent expressions add no further advantage. From this point of view it might at first seem as if the presence of equivalent elements in epic diction were contrary to the very principle of the influence of metre. Düntzer, here at one with his adversaries, was so convinced of this that he found it necessary to resort to emendation in the defence of his theories (cf. TE, pp. 154–5). At the end of this chapter we shall see that there are | noun–epithet formulae which appear to exclude this influence; but on the other side, a large portion of the equivalent noun–epithet formulae which disturbed Düntzer actually attest it, and so lose their value as indices of date in Homeric analysis.

A great many equivalent noun–epithet formulae derive naturally from that operation of analogy which, as we saw (TE, pp. 68–74), is the dominant factor in the development of hexametric diction from its beginning to its end. It was by the association in thought of different groups of words that the bards elaborated their whole technique of diction, creating a word, a form, or an expression on the model of an already existing word, form, or expression, composing a clause or a sentence on the model of another clause or sentence. This operation of analogy, the power of which is attested by each artifice of epic diction, is too powerful to stop once it has created a metrically unique formula. In the bard's mind there will always be an association between the words of one unique expression and those of another, and thus, by analogy, he will draw from two unique formulae one which will repeat the metre of an already existing formula. So, for example, the bards, by the effect of analogy, had chosen an epithet with which to compose the noun–epithet formula for 'ship' in the accusative case following the hephthemimeral caesura and beginning with a vowel: *εὐεργέα νῆα* (0 : 7 times).[1] In the same way they chose the epithet *ποντοπόροιο* (2 : 2 times), *ποντοπόροισι(ν)* (10 : 0 times) to the exclusion of any other epithet of ship with | the same metrical value. The purpose of this epithet was to serve, in the genitive singular and the dative plural, to extend a clause or a sentence from the bucolic diaeresis to the end of the line:

> *Ο* 704 *Ἕκτωρ δὲ πρύμνης νεὸς ἥψατο ποντοπόροιο*
>
> *ξ* 295 *ἐς Λιβύην μ' ἐπὶ νηὸς ἐέσσατο ποντοπόροιο,*

etc. We have already noted epithets of heroes and heroines used for a like purpose (TE, p. 66). *ποντοπόροισι* serves also in another, noun–epithet–preposition formula *ἐν ποντοπόροισι νέεσσι* (*Γ* 46, 444), equally unique in metrical value. Now here are two epithets *ποντοπόροιο* and *εὐεργέα* which in certain oblique cases are the only ones of a certain metrical value and which, in these cases, do not encroach upon each other. But the nominative of either one or the other can equally well serve with *νηῦς* to make a subject noun–epithet formula beginning with a consonant and extending from the bucolic diaeresis to the end of the line: *νηῦς εὐεργής* or *ποντόπορος νηῦς*. Analogy could equally well lead the bards to choose

[1] In this chapter it will be useful to indicate whether the expression is found in the *Iliad* or the *Odyssey* or in both. For this purpose, we shall use a colon; the number before it will refer to the *Iliad*, the number after it to the *Odyssey*. Thus *μεγάθυμοι Ἀχαιοί* (2 : 1 times) means that this expression occurs twice in the *Iliad* and once in the *Odyssey*. In this chapter, where we are dealing with the unity of style of the two poems, this distinction will show us how the style of one resembles that of the other. However, the fact that an expression appears in only one poem should not be taken to indicate a difference in diction, because we must not see a difference of style where there is only a difference of subject (cf. A. Shewan, *The Lay of Dolon*, London 1912, 37 ff.).

ποντοπόρος νηῦς on the model of ποντοπόροισι νέεσσι, νηὸς . . . ποντοπόροιο as νηῦς εὐεργής on the model of εὐεργέα νῆα. And even after one of these expressions had been chosen, the other epithet, closely bound up with νηῦς, remained, ready to spring to mind at any time. So we find in Homer ποντοπόρος νηῦς, μ 69, ν 95, 161, ξ 339, νηῦς εὐεργής, Ω 396, μ 166, π 322.

One might suppose that an association of words producing the one or the other of these two expressions would be due to some single, especially original, poet of the *Iliad* or the *Odyssey*. That is no more than barely possible; much more probably, both formulae were in the common stock of epic diction, both kept there by the ever-present model of the formulae in the oblique cases, so that Homer learned them both from his predecessors. The frequency of noun–epithet formulae of this type, and the fact that they are found throughout the poems, seems to show that they cannot be considered the work of some one author of the *Iliad* or *Odyssey*. Or possibly one could see in these equivalent noun–epithet formulae, not evidence of the time of composition, but unconscious traits of some one poet, who expressed himself by his | choice of one or the other. If we had very many noun–epithet formulae of this kind we might have the material for an analysis of the poems. But almost always the frequent use of a formula puts an end to the operation of analogy. Moreover, we shall shortly have the opportunity to examine the cause which led the poet sometimes to choose one equivalent formula and sometimes another.

Let us cite the other cases we have observed in which the equivalent noun–epithet formula is the natural result of the operation of analogy.

I. *A* 86 Ἀπόλλωνα διίφιλον; the poet could just as well have used the epithet ἑκήβολον which we find in ἑκήβολον Ἀπόλλωνα (1 : 0 time). But he composed his line on the model of Ὀδυσῆα διίφιλον (*Λ* 419, 473), Ἕκτωρ . . . διίφιλος (*Z* 318, *Θ* 493), etc., διίφιλος, -ον, -ε, functioning here before the bucolic diaeresis as an independently used generic epithet of a hero (cf. TE, p. 66).

II. *A* 502 Δία Κρονίωνα ἄνακτα ∼ κελαινεφέα Κρονίωνα (*Λ* 78). The latter of these two expressions was doubtless the one regularly used by the bards, as we can judge by κελαινεφέι Κρονίωνι (3 : 0 times). The former comes partly from Δία Κρονίωνα, a unique expression which occurs mostly in the formula Δία Κρονίωνα προσηύδα (*A* 539, *T* 120), and partly from such expressions as Ἰδομενῆα ἄνακτα (*B* 405, *K* 112, τ 181), Ποσειδάωνα ἄνακτα (*O* 8), etc.

III. *E* 509 Ἀπόλλωνος χρυσαόρου; one might have expected ἑκατηβόλου which we find in ἑκατηβόλου Ἀπόλλωνος (3 : 0 times). The expression is formed from Ἀπόλλωνα χρυσάορον (*O* 256), where ἑκατηβόλον would not have fitted.

IV. *Ζ* 205 χρυσήνιος Ἄρτεμις ∼ χρυσόθρονος Ἄρτεμις (*Ι* 533, ε 123). The former expression could have had χρυσήνιος Ἄρης (θ 285) as a model; the latter, χρυσόθρονος Ἥρη (*Α* 611), χρυσόθρονος Ἠώς (0:7 times).

V. *Η* 41 χαλκοκνήμιδες Ἀχαιοί ∼ μένεα πνείοντες Ἀχαιοί (*Γ* 8, *Λ* 508). The second expression must have been the regular one: it occurs in the accusative at *Ω* 364. The first expression comes from a mixture of ἐυκνήμιδες (-ας) Ἀχαιοί (-ούς) (31:5 times) and Ἀχαιῶν χαλκοχιτώνων (27:2 times).

VI. *Θ* 161 Δαναοὶ ταχύπωλοι ∼ μεγάθυμοι Ἀχαιοί (2:1 times); from Δαναῶν ταχυπώλων (9:0 times) and μεγάθυμοι Ἐπειοί (2:0 times), | μεγάθυμος Ἀγήνωρ (*Ν* 598), Αἰτωλῶν μεγαθύμων (2:0 times), etc.

VII. κλυτὸς Ἐννοσίγαιος (*Θ* 440, *Ι* 362, *Ξ* 135, 510, *Ο* 184, ε 423, ζ 326) ∼ κρείων Ἐνοσίχθων (*Θ* 208, *Ν* 10, 215, *Ξ* 150, *Φ* 435, ε 282, 375). The former expression is from κλυτὸς Ἀμφιγυήεις (*Σ* 614), κλυτὸς Ἱπποδάμεια (*Β* 742), etc. + γαιήοχος Ἐννοσίγαιος (3:1 times); the latter is from κρείων Ἀγαμέμνων (26:1 times), κρείων Ἀγαπήνωρ (*Β* 609), etc. + Ποσειδάων ἐνοσίχθων (13:10 times).

VIII. Ζεὺς τερπικέραυνος (*Μ* 252, *Ω* 529, ξ 268, ρ 437) ∼ νεφεληγερέτα Ζεύς (22:8 times). Obviously it was the second expression that was regularly used. The epithet in this expression provides the metrically unique Διὸς νεφεληγερέταο (6:0 times). The first expression was suggested by the dative Διὶ τερπικεραύνωι (4:8 times), in which case the epithet is also unique in metre.

IX. *Ν* 128 Ἀθηναίη λαοσσόος ∼ Ἀθηναίη κούρη Διός (β 296, ν 190). The first of these is modelled on Ἄρης λαοσσόος (*Ρ* 398), Ἔρις . . . λαοσσόος (*Υ* 48), λαοσσόον Ἀμφιάραον (ο 244), etc.; the second on κούρη Διὸς αἰγιόχοιο (3:5 times).

X. *Η* 23, 37, *Π* 804, *Υ* 103, θ 334, ἄναξ Διὸς υἱὸς Ἀπόλλων ∼ ἄναξ ἑκάεργος Ἀπόλλων (*Ο* 253, *Φ* 461, θ 323). The latter expression, containing the distinctive epithet of the god, is undoubtedly the older; the former derives from Λητοῦς καὶ Διὸς υἱός (*Α* 9), Διὸς υἱὸν ἑκηβόλον Ἀπόλλωνα (*Α* 21), etc.

XI. *Σ* 234 ποδώκης (εἴπετ') Ἀχιλλεύς, where the poet could have used ποδάρκης. ποδάρκης is only found in the nominative, in the expression ποδάρκης δῖος Ἀχιλλεύς (21:0 times); in the oblique cases we always find ποδώκεος Αἰακίδαο (8:2 times), ποδώκεα Πηλείωνα (10:0 times), and (of particular relevance here) ποδώκεος ἀντ' Ἀχιλῆος (*Υ* 89). It is clear that with a model such as this last expression it would be more than natural for a poet to think of ποδώκης rather than ποδάρκης.

XII. *Σ* 616 (κατ') Οὐλύμπου νιφόεντος ∼ αἰγλήεντος Ὀλύμπου (2:1 times). The second expression was regularly used. The first was created from ὄρεα νιφόεντα (*Ξ* 227, τ 338) + κατ' Οὐλύμπου τόδ' ἱκάνω (-εις) (2·0 times).

XIII. *Υ* 79 λαοσσόος . . . Ἀπόλλων, where ἑκατηβόλος might have been expected (we find ἑκατηβόλου 3:1 times). Here is the same association of words as with Ἀθηναίη λαοσσόος | (*N* 128). λαοσσόος, said of four gods, can be considered a generic epithet of the gods.

XIV. *X* 216 διίφιλε φαίδιμ' Ἀχιλλεῦ ~ θεοῖς ἐπιείκελ' Ἀχιλλεῦ (5:1 times). The latter expression is regularly used; the first derives from φαίδιμ' Ἀχιλλεῦ (4:1 times)+διίφιλος, an independently used generic epithet of heroes (cf. the first of these examples, Ἀπόλλωνα διίφιλον).

XV. *Ψ* 168 μεγάθυμος Ἀχιλλεύς ~ πόδας ὠκὺς Ἀχιλλεύς (29:0 times). The latter expression is used ordinarily; the former recalls μεγάθυμος Ἀγήνωρ (2:0 times), μεγάθυμοι Ἀχαιοί (2:1 times), etc.

XVI. *Γ* 8, *Λ* 508 μένεα πνείοντες Ἀχαιοί ~ Δαναοὶ θεράποντες Ἄρηος (4:0 times); the former expression is built from a generic epithet, cf. μένεα πνείοντες Ἄβαντες (*B* 536); the latter comes from θεράποντες Ἄρηος, an epithet of the two Ajaxes, and doubtless of any group of heroes (*Θ* 79, *K* 228),+Δαναοί, often used alone here before the hephthemimeral caesura (5:1 times).

XVII. *β* 433 Διὸς γλαυκώπιδι κούρῃ ~ Διὸς κούρῃ μεγάλοιο (4:3 times). We can infer from its frequency that the second of these was the one regularly used; the first is a blend of it and of γλαυκώπιδι κούρῃ.

XVIII. *δ* 143 Ὀδυσσῆος μεγαλήτορος ~ Ὀδυσσῆος ταλασίφρονος (1:12 times). The frequency of the latter expression indicates that the distinctive epithet was ordinarily used; the former expression recalls formulae in which μεγαλήτορος appears as a metrically unique generic epithet of a hero (cf. Table III); Οἰνῆος μεγαλήτορος (1:0 time), Αἴαντος μεγαλήτορος (1:0 time), μεγαλήτορος Ἀλκινόοιο (0:7 times), etc., and especially the formula used in the dative, Ὀδυσσῆι μεγαλήτορι (1:3 times).

XIX. *δ* 173 Ὀλύμπιος εὐρύοπα Ζεύς ~ Ὀλύμπιος ἀστεροπητής (3:0 times). The first expression comes from εὐρύοπα Ζεύς (9:7 times)+ Ὀλύμπιος, which is used alone as the name of Zeus before the bucolic diaeresis (13:2 times); the second is formed after the dative Ζηνὶ . . . ἀστεροπητῇ (*H* 443).

XX. *δ* 578 νηυσὶν ἐίσῃς ~ νηυσὶ θοῇσι (3:1 times). The first expression is modelled on νῆας ἐίσας (8:3 times), νηὸς ἐίσης (1:4 times), etc.; the second on θοὰς ἐπὶ νῆας (15:0 times), νῆα θοήν (2:23 times), etc.

XXI. *θ* 520, *ν* 121 μεγάθυμον Ἀθήνην ~ γλαυκῶπιν Ἀθήνην *α* 156. | The latter expression is formed from γλαυκῶπις Ἀθήνη (28:51 times); the former, like μεγάθυμος Ἀχιλλεύς, is from μεγάθυμοι Ἀχαιοί (2:1 times), μεγάθυμος Ἀγήνωρ (2:0 times), etc.

XXII. *ο* 133 κάρη ξανθὸς Μενέλαος ~ βοὴν ἀγαθὸς Μενέλαος (13:8 times). The latter expression is formed in the ordinary way with the generic epithet; the former comes from ξανθὸς Μενέλαος (13:5 times)+ κάρη κομόωντες Ἀχαιοί (2:1 times). The formation of this expression thus matches that of χαλκοκνήμιδες Ἀχαιοί (*H* 41), quoted above.

XXIII. ο 420 κοίλῃ παρὰ νηί (at the end of a line) ∼ παρὰ νηὶ μελαίνῃ (1 : 4 times). The latter expression is modelled on νηὶ μελαίνῃ (8 : 16 times), νῆα μέλαιναν (1 : 14 times), etc.; the first is modelled on κοίλας ἐπὶ νῆας (13 : 1 times), κοίλῃ παρὰ νηὶ μελαίνῃ (0 : 2 times), etc.

§ 2. THE EQUIVALENT NOUN–EPITHET FORMULA CONTAINED IN A MORE COMPLEX FORMULA

Three successive stages can be distinguished in the development of the technique of noun–epithet formulae: in the first, the influence of metre has not yet brought about the adoption of the unique noun–epithet formula; in the second it has done so; and in the third, the association of unique formulae has created a superabundance. The noun–epithet formulae which we have been examining above belong to the third stage; other traditional equivalent formulae, those which cannot be explained by the operation of analogy, belong to the first. For example, the expressions ἐριαύχενες ἵπποι ∼ ὑψηχέες ἵπποι, ἐριαύχενας ἵππους ∼ ὑψηχέας ἵππους, if they are traditional, must fall into the first category, because, since they have the same metrical value in all grammatical cases, and resemble neither each other nor any epithet of horses, their existence implies two original and independent creative acts. We do not yet know whether the equivalent noun–epithet formulae which we have still to consider should be attributed to this first stage in the formation of epic diction; it may be that they are the personal creations of the poet or poets of the *Iliad* and the *Odyssey*. But we must assume this first explanation in order | to discover whether traditional formulae of this sort will reveal any features by which we can recognize them for what they are.

We find such features immediately, and they show us how it is that a certain portion at least of the formulae we have been studying have escaped the tendency of the bards to preserve only one unique formula for each need. The answer lies in a psychological fact: the habit of using a definite group of words containing a noun–epithet formula has often been so strong with the bards that the epithet contained in this group of words has been exempted from the constant simplification of the technique of the use of the epithet. We shall take one of the most obvious examples. We find in Homer the expression Ὀδυσῆα πολύφρονα (0 : 5 times) which is metrically equivalent to Ὀδυσῆα δαΐφρονα (1 : 4 times). δαΐφρονα being a metrically unique generic epithet of a hero (Table III), it is evident that from the point of view of versification, the bards could have used it quite as well as πολύφρονα. And the epithet would in all likelihood have disappeared if it had not been part of the whole-line formula

α 83 = ξ 424 = υ 239 = φ 204 νοστῆσαι } Ὀδυσῆα πολύφρονα ὅνδε δόμονδε.
υ 329 νοστήσειν }

The existence of the formula Ὀδυσῆα πολύφρονα in Homer is then by no means a negation of the influence of metre; on the contrary, it bears witness to the severe conditions imposed by this influence on any equivalent formula which was to keep its place in the system; and it shows us how the language of heroic poetry, created by the heroic hexameter, was handed down from one generation of bards who heard and remembered it to the next.[1]

Nowhere else in Homer do we find an example as clear as this one, in which the expression is preserved in a more complex | formula and can easily be used in isolation by analogy. We can even suppose the existence of equivalent formulae preserved in a traditional expression which are impossible to distinguish because the expression appeared only once, or even not at all, in our texts. But before we go on to cases of that kind, let us point out the other examples of equivalent formulae, clearly preserved because of their presence in more complex formulae, which our investigation has yielded.

I. We find Δαναοὺς θεράποντας Ἄρηος in *Η* 382 (∼ μένεα πνείοντας Ἀχαιούς; cf. μένεα πνείοντες Ἀχαιοί, *Γ* 8, *Λ* 508). But it is in the nominative case that we find the more complex formulae which enabled this formula to remain in use. With the exception indicated, in fact, the noun–epithet formula in question appears only in *Β* 110 = *Ζ* 67 = *Ο* 733 = *Τ* 78:

ὦ φίλοι ἥρωες Δαναοί, θεράποντες Ἄρηος.

We have already seen that this equivalent formula was created by analogy with other unique noun–epithet formulae. Thus we can trace its history from its first appearance to the moment when it was used by Homer, and we see that the traditional diction which brought it into being was also responsible for its preservation.

II. ἐρίγδουπος πόσις Ἥρης (4:3 times), Ὀλύμπιος ἀστεροπητής (3:0 times). This formula is found five times out of seven in a line expressing a wish:

θ 465 = ο 180	οὕτω νῦν Ζεὺς θείη, ἐρίγδουπος πόσις Ἥρης
ο 112	ὥς τοι Ζεὺς τελέσειεν, ἐρίγδουπος πόσις Ἥρης,

or calling Zeus to witness:

Η 411	ὅρκια δὲ Ζεὺς ἴστω,	ἐρίγδουπος πόσις Ἥρης.
Κ 329	ἴστω νῦν Ζεὺς αὐτός,	

[1] This was how the Aeolic prefix ἐρι- survived along with Ionic ἀρι-. Not only the bards' habit of using epithets with the Aeolic prefix, but also their sense of the formula which contained such epithets, protected the prefix here from their tendency to keep only those elements of the λέξις ξενική which differed metrically from the corresponding Ionic forms. Thus ἐρίηρος generally occurs in the line-end formulae ἐρίηρος ἑταῖρος (1:0 time), ἐρίηρες ἑταῖροι (4:6 times), ἐρίηρας ἑταίρους (1:8 times). The other uses are ἑτάρους ἐρίηρας (*Γ* 47), ἐρίηρον ἀοιδόν (0:3 times). ἐριαύχενες appears only in the formulae ἐοιαύχενες ἵπποι (1:0 time), ἐριαύχενας ἵππους (4:0 times); etc.

The other two lines give us a striking insight into the close relation between the noun–epithet formula and the idea of prayer. In both of them the idea of a wish, even though it is not made explicit, was still very much in the mind of the poet. In *N* 153 Hector speaks of the Achaeans:

ἀλλ', οἴω, χάσσονται ὑπ' ἔγχεος, εἰ ἐτεόν με
ὦρσε θεῶν ὥριστος, ἐρίγδουπος πόσις Ἥρης. |

And in *Π* 88, Achilles gives Patroclus permission to enter the battle:

εἰ δέ κεν αὖ τοι
δώῃ κῦδος ἀρέσθαι ἐρίγδουπος πόσις Ἥρης,
μὴ σύ γ' ἄνευθεν ἐμεῖο λιλαίεσθαι πολεμίζειν.

III. νηὸς . . . δολιχηρέτμοιο ∼ νηὸς κυανοπρῴροιο (3:9 times). The first of these occurs twice:

τ 339	νοσφισάμην	ἐπὶ νηὸς ἰὼν δολιχηρέτμοιο.
ψ 176	ἐξ Ἰθάκης	

IV. In the two cases where Athena is called μεγάθυμον (∼ γλαυκῶπιν, cf. above TE, p. 179), we find the formula in the expression διὰ μεγάθυμον Ἀθήνην (θ 520, ν 121).

V. Ζεὺς τερπικέραυνος (∼ νεφεληγερέτα Ζεύς, 22:8 times, cf. TE, p. 178) appears three times out of four in a preposition–conjunction–noun–epithet formula:

M 252	ἐπὶ δὲ	Ζεὺς τερπικέραυνος.
ξ 268 = ρ 437	ἐν δὲ	

VI. The poet's choice between the two formulae βοῶπις πότνια Ἥρη (11:0 times) and θέα λευκώλενος Ἥρη (19:0 times) seems to have been determined by a whole series of associations. Thus we find

A 595 = *Φ* 434	ὣς φάτο, μείδησεν δὲ θεὰ λευκώλενος Ἥρη
E 767 = *Θ* 381 = *Ξ* 277 = *O* 78	ὣς ἔφατ', οὐδ' ἀπίθησε θεὰ λευκώλενος Ἥρη
A 551 = *Δ* 50 = *Π* 439 = *Σ* 360 = *Υ* 309	τὸν δ' ἠμείβετ' ἔπειτα βοῶπις πότνια Ἥρη.

VII. The same is true of ἀρήιοι υἷες Ἀχαιῶν (7:0 times), ἐυκνήμιδες Ἀχαιοί (17:1 times). On the one hand we have

Λ 800 = *Π* 42 = *Σ* 200	Τρῶες, ἀναπνεύσωσι δ' ἀρήιοι υἷες Ἀχαιῶν
Υ 317 = *Φ* 376	καιομένη, καίωσι δ' ἀρήιοι υἷες Ἀχαιῶν

and on the other

Γ 86 = 304 = *H* 67	κέκλυτέ μευ, Τρῶες καὶ ἐυκνήμιδες Ἀχαιοί
A 17, *Λ* 149, *Ξ* 49, *Ψ* 272, 658	. . . ἄλλοι ἐυκνήμιδες Ἀχαιοί.

In the case of other equivalent formulae we cannot | distinguish with certainty the group or groups of words which may have determined their survival. It may be that chance alone has deprived us of the evidence, or, more likely, that the formulae are associated with a great many expressions. But since positive proof is impossible here, we can try negative proof: we can ascertain whether these metrically equivalent expressions are proportionately more common in one of the two poems, or some one part of either of them. If this attempt fails, we shall know with certainty that associations of words alone have determined the choice in the mind or minds of the one or several poets of the *Iliad* and *Odyssey*.

I. πολυφλοίσβοιο θαλάσσης *Α* 34 *Β* 209 *Ζ* 347 *Ι* 182 *Ν* 798 *Ψ* 59
θαλάσσης εὐρυπόροιο *Ο* 381

πολυφλοίσβοιο θαλάσσης ν 85, 220
θαλάσσης εὐρυπόροιο δ 432 μ 2.

II. ὀξέι δουρί *Δ* 490 *Ε* 73, 238 *Λ* 95, 421 *Ν* 542
ἔγχει μακρῶι *Ε* 45, 660 *Ν* 177

ὀξέι δουρί *Π* 317, 806 *Υ* 488 *Φ* 91
ἔγχει μακρῶι *Ο* 745 *Φ* 402 χ 279, 293.

III. δόρυ χάλκεον *Ν* 247 *Π* 346, 608 *Π* 862
δόρυ μείλινον *Ε* 694 *Π* 114, 814

δόρυ χάλκεον κ 162, 164
δόρυ μειλινον *Φ* 178.

IV. In order to be as precise as possible in our investigation, we shall omit for the expressions μείλινον ἔγχος ∼ χάλκεον ἔγχος those lines in which the equivalent formula is clearly the product of an association of words:

N 184 = 404 = 503 = *Π* 610 = *Ρ* 305 = 526	ἀλλ' ὁ μὲν ἄντα ἰδὼν ἠλεύατο χάλκεον ἔγχος
ο 282 = π 40	ὣς ἄρα φωνήσας οἱ ἐδέξατο χάλκεον ἔγχος.

The alternation of the two expressions will then be:

μείλινον ἔγχος *Ε* 655 *Ζ* 65
χάλκεον ἔγχος *Γ* 317 *Δ* 481 *Ε* 620 *Ν* 296 *Π* 318 *Υ* 163

μείλινον ἔγχος *Υ* 272 *Φ* 172 *Χ* 293
χάλκεον ἔγχος *Φ* 200 *Χ* 367 α 104, 121 β 10.

V. περικλυτοῦ Ἡφαίστοιο θ 287 ω 75
πολύφρονος Ἡφαίστοιο θ 297, 327.

VI. ἑλίκωπες (-ας) Ἀχαιοί (-ούς) *Α* 389 *Γ* 234

ἥρωες (-ας) Ἀχαιοί (-ούς) *Μ* 165 *Ν* 629, *Ο* 219, 230

ἑλίκωπες (-ας) Ἀχαιοί (-ούς) *Π* 569 *Ρ* 274

ἥρωες (-ας) Ἀχαιοί (-ούς) *Ο* 261, 702 *Τ* 34, 41

ἑλίκωπες (-ας) Ἀχαιοί (-ούς) *Ω* 402

ἥρωες (-ας) Ἀχαιοί (-ούς) *α* 272 *ω* 68.

VII. ἐριαύχενες (-ας) ἵπποι (-ους) *Κ* 305 *Λ* 159 *Ρ* 496 *Σ* 280

ὑψηχέες (-ας) ἵπποι (-ους) *Ε* 772

ἐριαύχενες (-ας) ἵπποι (-ους) *Ψ* 171

ὑψηχέες -ας ἵπποι (-ους) *Ψ* 27 . |

Little need be said of the distribution of these formulae in the different parts of the two poems. It is only too obvious not only that does it not corroborate any theory of analysis hitherto advanced, but also that it could not support any analysis whatever.

§ 3. EQUIVALENT GENERIC EPITHETS

Equivalent generic epithets, too, have been preserved in epic poetry by the association of words: in their case, it is the nouns they accompany which have assured their preservation. Afterwards these epithets could in their turn be used by analogy with other nouns, and even with nouns which themselves were the cause of the preservation of some other epithet.

To ascertain the circumstances which have determined the choice of the equivalent generic epithet, we shall take under investigation the most common and at the same time the most important of the groups of equivalent epithets exhibited in Table III. This is the group ἀντίθεος ∼ ἀνδροφόνοιο ∼ ἱπποδάμοιο ∼ ἴφθιμος, when these epithets are applied to persons. This group is particularly worthy of study in that all four epithets have the same metrical values in every grammatical case.

We observed that every epithet must originally have been particularized. By the same token, it must at some time in its existence have been distinctive. In order to become ornamental, it must at some point have been constantly used with one noun. Later, when it had become purely ornamental and the poet hardly gave thought to its signification, it could be applied to another noun by a process of analogy in which its signification played little part. We can see this transformation of the generic epithet in the use of ἀνδροφόνοιο. This epithet, which occurs only in the genitive singular, is used with three names: Ἄρεος (3:0 times), Ἕκτορος (10:0 times), Λυκούργου (*Ζ* 134). We have no way of knowing for sure whether the epithet began as a qualifier of the god or of the Trojan hero. But in any case, Hector must have been | the first hero to receive it, and in the thought of the poet or poets of the *Iliad* he was the hero with whose name it was almost exclusively associated; so that we are almost tempted to classify it as a distinctive epithet and to consider its occurrence with the name of Lycurgus an exceptional effect of the operation of analogy. But it makes little difference: for this one usage with the name of another hero to have been made, the epithet must have reached a point where its use as an epithet of Hector can be described more as an unconscious habit of the poet than as a tie between the signification of the epithet and the role of the hero.[1]

We do not know the origins of *ἱπποδάμοιο* and *ἀντιθέοιο*, but we find that Homer's choice of the one or the other is ordinarily decided by which hero he is speaking of, or by whether he is using a more complex formula containing the noun–epithet expression. Thus we always find *ἀντίθεος* for Odysseus:

Ὀδυσσῆος . . . ἀντιθέοιο	δ 741, τ 456
ἀντιθέου Ὀδυσῆος	υ 369, φ 254
ἀντιθέωι Ὀδυσῆι	*Λ* 140, α 21, β 17, ζ 331, ν 126, χ 291.

for Sarpedon:

ἀντιθέωι Σαρπηδόνι	*E* 629, *Π* 649
ἀντίθεον Σαρπηδόνα	*E* 663, 692, *Z* 199, *M* 307

for the Polyphemi, both the Lapith and the Cyclops:

ἀντίθεον Πολύφημον	*A* 264, α 70

for Menelaus:

ἀντιθέωι Μενελάωι	θ 518, ω 116

and for the Lycians:

ἀντιθέοισι . . . Λυκίοισιν	*Π* 421, *M* 408 |

ἱπποδάμοιο is always chosen for Diomedes:

Διομήδεος ἱπποδάμοιο	*E* 415, 781, 849, *H* 404 = *I* 51 = 711, *Θ* 194, γ 181

for Castor:

Κάστορα (θ') ἱππόδαμον	*Γ* 237 = λ 300

and for the Trojans:

Τρώεσσι (μεθ') ἱπποδάμοις	*H* 361, *Θ* 525
Τρωσὶν (ἐφ') ἱπποδάμοις	*Θ* 110

Δ 352 = *T* 237 / *Θ* 516 = *T* 318 *Τρωσὶν ἐφ' ἱπποδάμοισι(ν)* { *ἐγείρομεν ὀξὺν Ἄρηα* / *φέρειν πολύδακρυν Ἄρηα.*

[1] The same can be said of *Διὶ μῆτιν ἀτάλαντος*. This epithet four times qualifies Odysseus, and seems to mark his ingenuity: cf. *πολύμητις*. But it is also found twice with the name of Hector in a formula of address (*H* 47 = *Λ* 200).

And it is the only epithet for the formula:

Β 23, 60	Ἀτρέος	υἱὲ δαΐφρονος ἱπποδάμοιο.
Δ 370	Τυδέος	
Λ 450	Ἱππάσου	

In two cases only does Homer use either ἀντιθέοιο or ἱπποδάμοιο with a name elsewhere qualified by the other of these two epithets or by ἀνδροφόνοιο or ἰφθίμοιο; but given the number of unimportant heroes who receive these epithets, that must be partly chance. The two exceptions are Ἕκτορος ἀνδροφόνοιο (10:0 times) ~ Ἕκτορος ἱπποδάμοιο (5:0 times), and ἀντίθεος Θρασυμήδης (*Π* 321), Θρασυμήδεος ἱπποδάμοιο (10:0 times). What led the poet to abandon the almost distinctive epithet of Hector, as well as the epithet he had already used for Thrasymedes, was the proximity in his mind of formulae like

(8:0 times)	Διομήδεος	ἱπποδάμοιο.
(2:0 times)	Ἀντήνορος	
(*P* 24)	Ὑπερήνορος	
(*γ* 17)	Νέστορος	

One might think it possible to find in some one part of the *Iliad* a marked preference for one or the other of the two expressions for Hector. A study of their distribution will show that this is not possible.

Ἕκτορος ἀνδροφόνοιο	*Α* 242		*Ι* 351	*Π* 77, 840		*P* 428, 616, 638
Ἕκτορος ἱπποδάμοιο		*Η* 38			*Π* 717	

Ἕκτορος ἀνδροφόνοιο	*Σ* 149		*Ω* 509	
Ἕκτορος ἱπποδάμοιο		*Χ* 161, 211		*Ω* 804.

The epithet ἴφθιμος (-οιο, -ου) appears only five times with the names of five heroes, hence we cannot know for sure whether associations of other words were responsible for its use. It is also very likely that the spondaic measure of this epithet, which distinguishes it from its three equivalents, enabled it to survive: five of the six times it is used to describe a hero, it occurs at the beginning of a line. For this epithet, and also for the several occurrences of ἀντιθέοιο and ἱπποδάμοιο, in which the association with the name of a definite hero is not clearly indicated, it will be advantageous to look at the distribution throughout the poems, in case some sections show a marked preference for one of them. We have accordingly omitted from the following chart the several occurrences of the four epithets which clearly derive from an association with a particular name.

ἀντίθεος, -οιο, -ῳ, -ον, -οισι	*Γ* 186	*Δ* 377	*Ε* 705		*Θ* 275
ἱπποδάμοιο				*Ζ* 299	
ἴφθιμος, -οιο, -ον, -ων			*Ε* 695		

ἀντίθεος, -οιο, -ωι, -ον, -οισι	*I* 623 *K* 112		*N* 791	
ἱπποδάμοιο				*Ξ* 10, 473
ἴφθιμος, -οιο, -ον, -ων		*Λ* 290, 373		
ἀντίθεος, -οιο, -ωι, -ον, -οισι	*Ξ* 322		*Π* 321	
ἱπποδάμοιο				*P* 24
ἴφθιμος, -οιο, -ον, -ων		*O* 547		*P* 554
ἀντίθεος, -οιο, -ωι, -ον, -οισι	*Υ* 232, 407 *Φ* 91, 595 *Ψ* 360			
ἱπποδάμοιο				
ἴφθιμος, -οιο, -ον, -ων				*Ψ* 511
ἀντίθεος, -οιο, -ωι, -ον, -οισι	*Ω* 257		ζ 241 η 146 λ 308 ξ 182 ο 237	
ἱπποδάμοιο		γ 17		
ἴφθιμος, -οιο, -ον, -ων				

As we have done on the preceding pages, when we examined the distribution of alternate equivalent formulae, so here we need do no more than point out the obvious impossibility of inferring from it any theory of analysis whatever.

§ 4. THREE EQUIVALENT NOUN–EPITHET FORMULAE

Of all the equivalent noun–epithet formulae which have appeared in the course of our investigation, there remain three only in which the epithet cannot be at once explained by the operation of analogy or by the association of words, or is not sufficiently frequent to allow the negative test of distribution. This means that we have found in Homer three cases only which do not reveal themselves | as the natural products of the conditions governing the creation and the conservation of epic diction.

I. *Π* 298 στεροπηγερέτα Ζεύς ∼ νεφεληγερέτα Ζεύς (22:8 times). The poet's reason for rejecting νεφεληγερέτα becomes clear directly we read the line in question:

Π 297–8 ὡς δ' ὅτ' ἀφ' ὑψηλῆς κορυφῆς ὄρεος μεγάλοιο
κινήσηι πυκινὴν νεφέλην στεροπηγερέτα Ζεύς.

It is to avoid the repetition of the sound νεφελη-. There is no real possibility that στεροπηγερέτα is a particularized epithet. The context hardly encourages such an interpretation,[1] and to accept it, we should have to suppose that this epithet with its entirely traditional appearance and its non-Ionic ending is the creation of Homer or of his period: for an adjective with so special a meaning could hardly have maintained itself for long, had it been usable only as a particularized epithet in the exceedingly

[1] This is also C. Franke's opinion (*De epithetis homericis*, 21, n. 5), and he is a scholar who does not ordinarily hesitate to ascribe a particularized meaning to an equivalent epithet.

rare situations where it suited the poet's thought. A much more acceptable explanation, and one that accords with all we have learned of the history of the technique of the use of the epithet, is that the whole line

κινήσῃ πυκινὴν νεφέλην στεροπηγερέτα Ζεύς

is traditional. In that case the use of the epithet would give us an unusually valuable insight into the history of the heroic style before Homer. The survival of the epithet would depend on the fact that the portion of the simile in which the line occurs dates from the pre-Ionian origins of epic poetry. The words Homer uses to express the essential idea of the line, 'Zeus scatters the clouds', would be as old as the epithet itself.

II. *N* 624 *Ζηνὸς ἐριβρεμέτεω* ∼ *O* 293 *Ζηνὸς ἐριγδούπου*. The latter of these expressions can be explained as an analogical formation from *ἐρίγδουπος πόσις Ἥρης* (4 : 3 times), *Διὸς . . . ἐριγδούποιο* (*E* 672), etc.; but the epithet in the first expression appears only here. Since it seems to occur in a genuine passage, and since it is almost certainly of | Aeolic origin,[1] its survival must be explained by a beginning-line formula, *Ζηνὸς ἐριβρεμέταο*, which by chance does not turn up elsewhere in our poems; or else by the existence of some formula reserved for the expression of a special idea which is also missing from our texts.

III. *λ* 604 *Ἥρης χρυσοπεδίλου* ∼ *Ἥρης ἠυκόμοιο* (*K* 5). The latter expression is the one we should expect to find, being formed from the generic epithet of heroines and goddesses seen in *Βρισηίδος ἠυκόμοιο* (*B* 689), *Ἑλένης . . . ἠυκόμοιο* (7 : 0 times), *Ἀθηναίης . . . ἠυκόμοιο* (3 : 0 times), etc. *χρυσοπεδίλου* is not so easily explained. It represents what may be the only case in Homer of a distinctive epithet in a formula which by its nature can be used but rarely: for Hera's role in the epic cannot be compared with that of Zeus. A formula of this kind would offer no difficulty if it were found with the name of Zeus; but it seems actually to negate the influence of metre with the name of Hera. It cannot be coincidence that it occurs in one of the lines modern scholarship has most placed in doubt, as we can see from the evidence collected by G. M. Bolling.[2] There is, however, an indication of the lateness of the line which may be more compelling than those Bolling cites. This is the presence in the expression of a long closed syllable, closed by two consonants. Among the many common noun–epithet formulae we have had occasion to cite in this volume, both in the tables and in the text, there are three only besides *Ἥρης χρυσοπεδίλου* which have a long closed syllable before the bucolic diaeresis, and in them the syllable is closed by only one consonant: *ποδάρκης δῖος Ἀχιλλεύς*, *Ἀχαιῶν χαλκοχιτώνων*, and | *περίφρων Πηνελόπεια*.

[1] It is possible that an Ionian poet borrowed the prefix *ἐρι-* from *ἐρίηρες*, *ἐριαύχενες*, *ἐριούνης*, etc.; but *ἀριδείκετος*, *ἀρίζηλος*, *ἀρίγνωτος*, *ἀριπρεπές*, etc. imply that Ionian bards were more likely to choose the other form of the prefix.

[2] Cf. G. M. Bolling, *The External Evidence for Interpolation in Homer*, Oxford 1925 (reissue 1968), 26.

In the cases of the first and second of these three formulae, it seems likely that their fixity was what exempted them from the tendency to avoid overlengthening in the latter part of the line. In the case of the third, it was undoubtedly the difficulty, if not the impossibility, of finding an epithet with the metre ⏑ – – ⏑ ending with -*ος* or -*ις* which made necessary the use of an epithet which we find correctly used with the names *Εὐρύκλεια* and *Ἀδρηστίνη*. But in the case of *Ἥρης χρυσοπεδίλου* there is no factor of habitual use, nor of necessity, as we can see from the existence of the alternative *Ἥρης ἠυκόμοιο*. Therefore we have here a certain proof that the line is the work of a poet who had lost the sense of the ancient heroic rhythm.

§ 5. THE UNITY OF STYLE OF THE *ILIAD* AND *ODYSSEY*

All the fixed epithets, then, which we have come across in our investigation, except one—and we have certainly considered most of those in Homer—alike reveal the influence of the heroic line. If the appearance of *πολύτλας δῖος Ὀδυσσεύς* 5 times in the *Iliad* and 33 times in the *Odyssey* is to be regarded as significant, what value should we assign to the unity of that diction which we have been able to observe in its smallest details in both Homeric poems alike? We cannot exaggerate the importance of a conclusion which does not derive from a general comparison and is not based on exceptional phenomena of style, but is the consequence of an accumulation of identical details of diction, whereby we see the poet or poets of the two poems making use of the same epithets and the same noun–epithet formulae, and reacting in the same way to the influence of the metre. What gives the conclusions of this investigation their value is the sheer quantity of points of resemblance between the styles of the different parts of the poems.

Having said this, we can now consider some special indications of the identity of style in the *Iliad* and *Odyssey*, indications which have come to light in the course of this chapter. They appear in some of the equivalent noun–epithet formulae common to the two poems. |

I. The poet (or the poets) of the *Odyssey* calls Odysseus *ταλασίφρονος* only in the genitive (12 times), and uses *μεγαλήτορι* (thrice) and *μεγαλήτορα* (thrice) always in the dative and the accusative. In one case only does he depart from this practice, and this very natural exception (cf. TE, p. 179) need not concern us here. The significant point is that the author or authors of the *Odyssey* did not generally say *Ὀδυσσῆος μεγαλήτορος*. Here is a stylistic habit at once firmly established and very delicate, since it would after all have been such an easy matter for the poet to break his own rule. It shows us how unconscious the use of the epithet must have been in Homer; a conscious approach to style would never have been so consistently governed by habit. But we find exactly the same distinction in the *Iliad*: Ὀδυσσῆος ταλασίφρονος (*Λ* 466), Ὀδυσσῆι μεγαλήτορι (*E* 674).

II. In the *Iliad* Diomedes is always qualified by the epithet ἱπποδάμοιο (7 times), although the poet could just as well have used ἀντιθέοιο, both of these epithets being equally applicable to Diomedes or any other hero. But we find Διομήδεος ἱπποδάμοιο in γ 181.

III. πολυφλοίσβοιο θαλάσσης occurs 6 times in the *Iliad* and twice in the *Odyssey*, and likewise θαλάσσης εὐρυπόροιο in *O* 381 and δ 432, μ 2.

IV. We have κλυτὸς Ἐννοσίγαιος (5:1 times) and κρείων Ἐνοσίχθων (5:2 times).

V. The choice of Ζεὺς τερπικέραυνος rather than νεφεληγερέτα Ζεύς is determined by the same delicate association of words in both poems:

ξ 268 = ρ 437 ἐν δὲ Ζεὺς τερπικέραυνος
M 252 ἐπὶ δὲ Ζεὺς τερπικέραυνος

Thus we find a remarkable similarity between the diction of the *Iliad* and that of the *Odyssey*, but we must be careful not to see in this any proof of what is usually meant by the unity of the Homeric poems. All we know is that the author or authors of these two poems faithfully maintain the tradition of bardic diction, and that this is why their styles, to judge | from their use of epithets, match each other in the smallest details. We do have a guarantee that both poems—excepting of course a few short passages—are entirely ancient. But if we are ever to learn the number of bards who contributed to the *Iliad* and the *Odyssey*, we must look elsewhere than in their style.[1]

[1] There remains in particular the problem of *insertions*—'les vers et groupes de vers *superflus* qui sont authentiquement homériques en leur teneur, mais qui sont illégitimement répétésen des endroits où ils n'ont que faire' (V. Bérard, *Introduction à l'Odyssée* ii. 391).

2

Homeric Formulae and Homeric Metre*

I

THE TRADITIONAL STYLE

MUCH has been written on the problem of hiatus[1] in Homer,[2] and it is a genuinely complex problem, demanding the consideration of a large number of details; but the answers given so far can none the less be briefly stated. One argument has been that the rarity of certain kinds of hiatus in particular,[3] and of all kinds in general, shows the efforts made by the poet (or poets) of the *Iliad* and *Odyssey* to avoid them, and that this is corroborated by the practice of writers of poetry and even of prose in the historical period. The reason for this desire to avoid hiatus is that the Greek poets considered it cacophonous. Those on the other hand who argue for the authenticity of some or of all kinds of hiatus base their judgement on the failure of every attempt that has been made to expel them from the traditional text. Their argument is: hiatus is allowed in Homer because we find it there.

It is quite true that no one has yet succeeded | in removing all examples of hiatus from the text of Homer. It can even be said without fear of contradiction that no scholar has been able to eliminate from those lines of the *Iliad* and *Odyssey* which he considers genuine all examples of what is regarded as the most undesirable of all kinds of hiatus: that of a short vowel which occurs neither before the trochaic caesura, nor before the bucolic diaeresis,[4] nor before the last foot, nor (some maintain the

* *Les Formules et la métrique d'Homère* (Société des Belles Lettres, Paris 1928).

[1] We define hiatus as the juxtaposition without elision of two vocalic sounds, one at the end of one word, the other at the beginning of the next.

[2] The word 'Homer' in this treatise will sometimes mean 'the poet' or 'the poets of the *Iliad* and *Odyssey*', and sometimes 'the traditional text of the *Iliad* and *Odyssey*'.

[3] We are using the expression 'kind of hiatus' with the precise meaning of a class of final vocalic sounds, either short vowels, or else long vowels or diphthongs, which occur before hiatus in a definite part of the line.

[4] Since this expression has been used in different senses, we should state that we are using it here to mean a pause, however slight, in the sentence at the end of the fourth foot. To

legitimacy of this kind of hiatus) at the end of the first trochee. Consequently, those who venture to emend the text in order to remove hiatus are not justified in doing so, because any correction of a hiatus, on the sole grounds that it is one, is arbitrary as long as it cannot be demonstrated that all examples of hiatus of the same kind with the one emended do not belong to the original *Iliad* and *Odyssey*.

But whatever their errors of method, those who contest the authenticity of hiatus in Homer have accomplished more than their adversaries, because the premiss of their argument is the positive one of avoidance of cacophony. It has been pointed out, to be sure, that in a majority of cases hiatus coincides with a pause in the line and in the sentence, and that in addition its harshness is relieved by certain phonetic considerations, such as that the 'long' diphthongs *ωι* and *ηι* are found in hiatus more often than diphthongs which could be pronounced more rapidly.[1] But these factors, essential though they are to the understanding of the problem, should not be regarded as proofs. They *attenuate* the cacophony of certain cases of hiatus, but they do not eliminate it. Despite all that can be done in this direction, the argument of those who do not wish to accept hiatus remains valid: Homer in general | sought to avoid hiatus as something harmful to the rhythm of his verse.

A method of research is incomplete if it limits itself to giving as a rule what is no more than a result; but that is exactly what has so far been done in the study of hiatus in Homer, even when the term 'rule' has not been used: the conception of *legitimate* and *illegitimate* hiatus implies the establishment of rules without knowledge of the causes that would justify their existence.

A principal source of this error has been an insufficiently precise notion of the meaning of 'rule'. Among the various senses of the word, two especially have been confused. According to the first, a rule is a clearly articulated *principle* of composition, which the poet must learn to follow if he does not wish to incur the censure of his contemporaries. This is the only sense in which a rule can be said to be a cause, although even then, it should be observed, it is likely not to be a direct cause. If Horace, for example, avoids hiatus, it is not so much because Greek poetry taught him to keep hiatus out of his verse, as because the clearly formulated rule trained him to find hiatus ugly. It is obvious, however, that this sense of the word 'rule' cannot apply to hiatus in Homer: a rule can only act as

indicate the *strong* pause which occurs when a sentence or a clause ends with the fourth foot, there is the convenient term of Havet, 'bucolic punctuation' (*Cours élémentaire de métrique grecque et latine*, 4th edition, Paris 1896, 8).

[1] Monro says that -*ωι* stays long in hiatus 23 per cent of the time, -*ηι* 19 per cent, -*ευ* 6·7 per cent, -*ου* 6 per cent, -*η* 5·7 per cent, -*ω* 4 per cent, -*ει* 1·8 per cent, -*οι* 1·6 per cent, -*αι* 1·3 per cent (*Hom. Gram.*², 356).

a cause in the process of composition. It can teach one to make a line of six dactylic feet, or to make lines without hiatus; or it could teach one to make hiatus, though only on condition that this would enhance the beauty of the line, which is, of course, not possible. If Homer, as an apprentice bard, had learned from his master that it is permitted to leave short syllables in hiatus before the trochaic caesura, etc., he would thereby have learned a rule which, being of a negative character, could not be a cause. But if some cause inclined him to make hiatus, then this rule gave him the licence to keep it. If, therefore, we give to the word 'rule' the meaning of an articulated principle of composition, the only meaning which would enable it to be a cause, it will be inapplicable to hiatus in Homer. |

The other meaning for the word 'rule' under discussion is that of *usage* pure and simple. In this case, far from being a cause, the rule is merely a way of describing a series of conditions and results. An example is Seymour's statement: 'Hiatus is allowed . . . when the final vowel of the first word is long and stands in the accented part of the foot.'[1] What this scholar has done is to describe what the true causes, under certain phonetic conditions, led the poet or poets of the *Iliad* and *Odyssey* to do. If one wants to do more than merely describe what appears in the text, one must search out the causes, which alone are capable of showing us a rule of any real value. From this point of view, it can be said that those who base their arguments on the cacophony produced by hiatus have gone further into the problem than those who believe in the legitimacy of different kinds of hiatus: the first group have at least pointed out the reasons which in general made the poet avoid hiatus of all kinds. As long as it is not known for what causes the poet made hiatus where he did, theories based on the notion of metrical licence can do no more than summon the purely negative argument that it is impossible to remove examples of hiatus from the text. To investigate the problem properly, one should not try to establish a rule, but to formulate the answer to a question which brings us from the realm of the abstract to the real circumstances of the composition of epic poetry: what causes led a poet composing in hexameter verse to depart from his habitual metrical practice?

We find the general nature of these causes directly we begin to reflect on the difficulties which a poet would inevitably encounter in the process of versification; and we see at the same time that the identical causes must have been responsible for the lengthening of final short syllables: the poet found it easier to express himself in words involving metrical irregularities than | to look for other words. If it had been otherwise, we

[1] *Introduction to the Language and Verse of Homer*, Boston 1885, 40–1.

should have to assert that these irregularities were means of adding beauty to the line; and this is obviously untrue. The facts we are speaking of here are entirely evident, and any study of hiatus must take them for granted. But so far a knowledge of the general character of causes has not led to any investigation into the particular causes of individual cases of hiatus from which we might understand why it was that Homer tolerated metrical irregularities which poets of the historical period avoided at all costs. For here we see that Homer had special reasons which led him to choose words involving metrical irregularities rather than look for other words to replace them.

One fact should guide us in our choice of the kind of metrical irregularity to use as the basis of our investigation: the more the irregularity disturbs the euphony of the line, the more clearly will emerge the causes that provoked it. For the more reprehensible the metrical fault, the more powerful must have been the poet's motivation for committing it. Therefore we shall ask under what circumstances the poet found it preferable to leave a short syllable in hiatus and to lengthen a final short syllable.

The poet also avoids in general the hiatus of long syllables and the use of long closed syllables in the latter part of the line.[1] But these faults are less shocking to the ear than the ones we have just named. The fact that Homer tolerates them in a fairly large number of cases shows us that he did not much hesitate to lay aside his habitual metrical practice for them, and that therefore the causes that occasioned them are relatively minor and harder for us to recognize in analysing the structure of the line. They are then of less value to our investigation than those aberrations whose rarity,| as well as considerations of euphony, clearly show us how much, and why, the poet sought to avoid them. Hiatus of short syllables must have been a common occurrence in the spoken language, and the final short syllable in the place of a long is in direct contradiction with the rhythm of the hexameter.

A parallel study of these two metrical irregularities will offer considerable advantage. If, as we have the right to suppose, there are factors of versification determining not hiatus alone but all metrical irregularities at the end of a word, we shall find the problem of hiatus in Homer put in an entirely new way. What was a narrow and particular problem will be extended to the whole question of the connection of words in the hexameter line.

Under what circumstances, then, did Homer find it preferable to

[1] In accordance with our definition in *L'Épithète traditionelle dans Homère*, Paris 1928 (TE, p. 41 above), we mean by 'long closed syllable' a syllable containing a long vowel or diphthong followed by one or more consonants.

express his thoughts in words involving metrical irregularities rather than to look for other words which would have avoided them? To answer this question, we must take into account the conditions in which he was composing his verse.

For him, as for all bards, composition was a process of memory. He had to remember the words, the expressions, the sentences he had heard from other bards who had taught him the traditional style of heroic poetry. He had to remember the place or the places which traditional words and expressions occupied in the complex mould of the hexameter. And he had to remember the innumerable devices which enabled him to combine these words and expressions into complete sentences and lines of six dactylic feet embodying the ideas proper to the narration of the deeds of heroes. From generation to generation bards had preserved words and phrases which, once happily discovered, could be drawn on for the making of poetry. In pursuing the twofold purpose of easy versification and heroic style, they had created a formulary diction and a technique for its use, and this formulary technique,[1] | preserved in its smallest details because it provided the bard with materials of versification which he could never have found for himself, took on the shape of traditional things. The apprentice bard, as he became familiar with it, allowed it to gain such an ascendancy over his mind, that when he set forth in hexameter verse his own version of the deeds of heroes, he used few words or phrases of his own, or none at all. And this suited his audience perfectly, who expected him faithfully to follow the style which they knew and enjoyed.

It is not our intention here to describe the technique of epic diction. A proof of its traditional character is a complex separate problem, incapable of brief summary. We recognize, however, that while some scholars have accepted the fully or almost fully formulary character of Homeric diction, others reject it, seeing in the 'style of Homer' a personal creation of the poet. For the benefit of the latter, we must point out that this essay is not an independent work, examining the hypothesis of the formulary style of the *Iliad* and *Odyssey*. It was rather suggested by the conclusions of our earlier work *The Traditional Epithet in Homer*. In that volume we described the essential conditions of an analysis of the technique of formulae used by Homer, and we then undertook the analysis of one category of formulae. Those who believe Homeric style to be more or less the creation of a single man should therefore consider these pages as a sequel to the earlier book, which should be read first. Or else they should provisionally accept the hypothesis, and wait for the formulary character of Homeric diction to be demonstrated to them by some of the

[1] Cf. the definition of the formula in TE, p. 13 above.

traditional devices of versification which we shall have occasion to examine on the following pages.

Now when we take into account that bardic diction is in great part, or even entirely, made up of | traditional formulae, we see that by its very nature it often compels the poet who is using it to depart from his normal metrical practice. The causes of this are of two different kinds.

(1) The first is related to the bard's use of formulary diction. The technique of the use of formulae consists on the one hand in the modification of formulae so as to adapt them to the expression of ideas more or less like those of the original formulae; and on the other hand in making different combinations of them. Each of these two aspects of the use of formulae can occasion metrical irregularities. (*a*) To express a thought, the poet will modify a formula in itself correct. But the modification, involving the exchange of one ending for another, or of one prefix or word for another prefix or word, or the omission of a conjunction, cannot be carried out without harm to the metre. (*b*) In the case of two consecutive formulae, the technique, which consists principally in combining formulae each having a fixed place or fixed places in the line, can only operate if the ending of the first formula is in metrical accord with the beginning of the second. Hence the rigorous fixity of the hexameter is a block to the free exploitation of formulary technique. The bard, accustomed to expressing his thought through the medium of traditional expressions, will often have to choose between using two formulae which perfectly express his thought but whose junction entails a metrical fault, and renouncing formulae to make up expressions of his own. Given this fundamental contradiction between the rhythm and formulary technique, we can see what a temptation it was for the bard—a temptation unknown to a poet with an individual style—to join together two formulae even when he had to commit a metrical fault to do so. From this point of view, it is not surprising that we find a limited number of cases where the poet did violence to the metre for the sake of his formulae: what is surprising is that we do not find more.

(2) The second category of causes obliging the poet to allow irregularities of metre has to do with the history of traditional diction. It happened in some cases that the loss of an | initial or medial consonant in a word belonging first to the spoken language, and then to poetry, created a flaw in the formulae containing it. But the bards nevertheless could not bring themselves to abandon these formulae, which had now become undesirable from the point of view of rhythm and harmony, because they played too important a role in the expression of the ideas of heroic poetry.|

II

THE MODIFICATION OF FORMULAE

IF we are to know how the bard was led by formulary technique to produce metrical irregularities, we must understand the role of analogy in the formation and use of epic diction. Here we shall merely summarize what we have already written on this subject in *The Traditional Epithet in Homer*.

The moment we notice a resemblance between two expressions too exact to be the result of chance, we have observed the effect of analogy: for either the one expression is imitating the other, or both are imitating a single model, directly or indirectly. In these two circumstances of imitation and resemblance lies the explanation of the development and the survival of epic diction. At first, to go back to the origins, a bard found to express some idea an expression at once noble and adapted to hexameter composition. These qualities preserved it until the day when the same bard, or another, wanted to express an idea more or less close to that of the expression in question, and found he could do so by modifying it. Thus in the course of time there came into being series of formulae from the most simple to the most complex types.[1] These series were what the apprentice bard heard in the verse of his masters, and he learned them and remembered them easily because of their resemblance to each other. Later, when he himself began to compose in heroic metre, he was guided by this resemblance between | one expression and another, just as had been his predecessors from whom he had learned the style in which he sang. On the model of one word he chose another; he drew a new expression from an already existing expression; and he formed whole clauses and sentences from clauses and sentences like them. It is therefore on this sense of resemblances that the creation and the survival of formulae, as well as the technique of their use, depends. And to this same sense of resemblances we can trace the majority of metrical irregularities at the end of a word to be found in the *Iliad* and *Odyssey*.

Kurt Witte notes that *μέροπες ἄνθρωποι* was composed by a poet guided by the memory of *μερόπων ἀνθρώπων* (9 times).[2] Similarly, Monro saw that *ἄφθιτα αἰεί* (*N* 22) derives from *ἄφθιτον αἰεί* (*B* 46, 186, *Ξ* 238).[3] But neither scholar was able to show that these analogical

[1] We use the words 'type of formula' in the precise sense of a group of words made up of definite parts of speech and having a definite metrical value.

[2] Pauly–Wissowa, viii[2] (1913), col. 2223.

[3] *Hom. Gram.*[2], 357.

formations depend on more than a simple resemblance between two groups of words. In both cases there is also a resemblance of use, and this generally supposes the same position in the line and often the presence of other words common both to the metrically correct and to the metrically incorrect expression.

Thus *μέροπες ἄνθρωποι* appears in the line

Σ 288 πρὶν μὲν γὰρ Πριάμοιο πόλιν μέροπες ἄνθρωποι,

which should be compared with

Σ 342	πιείρας πέρθοντε πόλεις	} μερόπων ἀνθρώπων.
Σ 490	ἐν δὲ δύω ποίησε πόλεις	
Υ 217	ἐν πεδίωι πεπόλιστο, πόλις	

And to follow aright the mental processes of the poet who made the expression *μέροπες ἄνθρωποι* we should also keep in mind such lines as

A 19	ἐκπέρσαι	} Πριάμοιο πόλις(ν)	{ εὖ δ' οἴκαδ' ἱκέσθαι
N 14	φαίνετο δὲ		καὶ νῆες Ἀχαιῶν
X 165	ὣς τὼ τρὶς		πέρι δινηθήτην.

The poet has two formulae: the first says 'Priam's city' and extends from the trithemimeral to the hephthemimeral caesura; the other says 'city | (*or* cities) of mortal men', and extends from the trochaic caesura[1] to the end of the line. Then when he wanted to express the idea 'Priam–city–mortal men', the formula *Πριάμοιο πόλιν* took its accustomed place in the line, and his habit of saying 'city–of mortal men', beginning with *πόλις* in the same position, led him by the easy exchange of two endings to make 'city–mortal men'. If one does not know the existence of these two formulae having in common *πόλις* after the trochaic caesura, one cannot understand exactly how the expression *μέροπες ἄνθρωποι* was created. The habit of making lines out of formulae, and following the resemblances between certain ideas and between the words which express them, became imperious to the point of dictating aberrations of metre.

Let us consider in the same light the composition of *ἄφθιτα αἰεί*. We find *ἄφθιτον αἰεί* in

B 46	εἵλετο δὲ	} σκῆπτρον πατρώιον	} ἄφθιτον αἰεί.
B 186	δέξατό οἱ		
Ξ 238	δῶρα δέ τοι δώσω καλὸν θρόνον		

In *ἄφθιτον αἰεί* the poet had a formula to express the idea 'imperishable forever' which was of use to him whenever he wanted to describe a treasure of the gods (*Ξ* 238) or a treasure which the gods had given to men (*B* 46, 186, cf. *B* 101 ff.). Since the greater number of these formulae

[1] Using Havet's terminology (*Cours élémentaire de métrique*, 6), we give the name 'trochaic caesura' to what the ancients called ἡ κατὰ τρίτον τροχαῖον τομή.

fell between two caesurae or between a caesura and one of the ends of the line, he could often complete his line and at the same time express a poetic idea by joining the formula directly to the noun (*Ξ* 238) or to another epithet or to another expression describing the noun (*B* 46, 186). The memory of this device was in Homer's mind when he wanted to describe Poseidon's palace, and habit was stronger than the desire to make a line free of metrical fault:

> *N* 21–2 Αἰγάς, ἔνθα τέ οἱ κλυτὰ δώματα βένθεσι λίμνης
> χρύσεα μαρμαίροντα τετεύχαται, ἄφθιτα αἰεί. |

In the first of the two cases we have just examined—μέροπες ἄνθρωποι, there is a final short syllable in the place of a long, and in the second—ἄφθιτα αἰεί, there is a short vowel in hiatus. These first two examples were deliberately chosen. In the first place, they are cases in which scholars other than ourselves have recognized the causes of metrical irregularity. In the second place, the mental processes which led to the modification of each of them are extremely clear, the reason being that both the original formulae and the devices of versification of which they are a part appear in Homer with enough frequency to leave us in no doubt of the bard's habit of using them. And finally, we wanted to show by the juxtaposition of these two examples that similar factors of versification are operative in both of them: the lengthening of the final short syllable is produced by the modification of a traditional formula, and so is a short vowel in hiatus. As we have occasion to cite other examples of metrical aberration in the course of this study, we shall group these two kinds separately; but we shall do so only for convenience of classification. In no case does a short vowel in hiatus result from causes which, in other conditions, could not produce the lengthening of a final short syllable.

Other Examples of Metrical Irregularities Resulting from the Modification of Formulae

A. *Short vowels in hiatus*

I. E 568 τὼ μὲν δὴ χεῖράς τε καὶ ἔγχεα ὀξυόεντα.

The expression at the end of the line was suggested by ἔγχει ὀξυόεντι which appears seven times in the *Iliad* and once in the *Odyssev.*

II. κ 403 νῆα μὲν ἂρ πάμπρωτον ἐρύσσατε ἤπειρόνδε. |

This line should be compared with κ 423

νῆα μὲν ἂρ πάμπρωτον ἐρύσσομεν ἤπειρόνδε.

It is worth noting that, since the line with hiatus precedes the line without it, there can be no question of the memory of a line already composed in this text: the poet must have been guided only by his memory of formulary diction, both here and 20 lines later on, when he was able to draw from it a line metrically correct.

III. In the line following the last example we see the same substitution of a second person for a first person ending. *κ* 404

κτήματα δ' ἐν σπήεσσι πελάσσατε ὅπλα τε πάντα

was inspired by the memory of a line which we find in *κ* 424

κτήματα δ' ἐν σπήεσσι πελάσσομεν ὅπλα τε πάντα.

IV. *Ψ* 195 *Βορέῃ καὶ Ζεφύρῳ, καὶ ὑπίσχετο ἱερὰ καλά.*

This time the fault was occasioned by the substitution of a past for a present ending: cf. *Ψ* 209

ἐλθεῖν ἀρᾶται, καὶ ὑπίσχεται ἱερὰ καλά.

ὑπέσχετο is found 11 times, always before the bucolic diaeresis.

V. We have a similar case in *Ψ* 224

ὣς Ἀχιλεὺς ἑτάροιο ὀδύρετο ὀστέα καίων.

The latter part of this line was modelled on a formula used two lines above:

ὡς δὲ πατὴρ οὗ παιδὸς ὀδύρεται ὀστέα καίων.

VI. On the one hand we find *βάσκ' ἴθι* 5 times at the beginning of the line, 4 times in the formula *βάσκ' ἴθι, Ἶρι ταχεῖα.* On the other hand *θοὰς ἐπὶ νῆας Ἀχαιῶν* appears 9 times at the end of the | line. It was natural for a bard accustomed to using these formulae to think of them when he wanted (*B* 8) to express in hexameters the idea 'go, baleful dream, to the ships of the Achaeans': the beginning and the end of his line were already made, and to complete it he had only to find, on the model of *βάσκ' ἴθι, Ἶρι ταχεῖα*, a noun–epithet formula in the vocative case with the same measure as *Ἶρι ταχεῖα*. Such a formula would not be far from his thoughts, since three lines before he had said *οὖλος ὄνειρος*, which requires only a simple modification of the ending to yield *οὖλε ὄνειρε.*

VII. We have a slightly different case in *X* 206

οὐδ' ἔα ἱέμεναι ἐπὶ Ἕκτορι πικρὰ βέλεμνα.

The short vowel at the end of the third foot is in hiatus. We find the expression which suggested this line in *Π* 382:

πρόσσω ἱέμενοι, ἐπὶ δ' Ἕκτορι κέκλετο θυμός.

Instead of the modification of an ending, we have here the simple omission of the conjunction *δ'*.

VIII. τετελεσμένα ἦεν in *Σ* 4 has its origin in the use of a device more complicated than the last few we have been looking at. To express the idea 'what is (or will be) accomplished', etc., after the caesura of the third foot, the bards created a series of formulae comparable, in terms of the close resemblance of one formula to another in each series, to that of θεὸν ὣς τιμήσουσι, etc. (cf. below, FM, pp. 224ff.). Thus we find in the *Iliad* and *Odyssey*:

τὸ δὲ καὶ	τετελεσμένον ἔσται	(10 times)
ὡς καὶ		(twice)
καὶ ὡς		
καὶ μὴν		(twice)
καὶ εἰ	τετελεσμένον ἐστί	(thrice).

By the modification of an ending, the impersonal expression becomes attached to a masculine antecedent (*A* 388):

ἠπείλησεν μῦθον, ὁ δὴ τετελεσμένος ἐστί. |

The memory of all the formulae in this series, but especially of the line just quoted, was what directed the poet when he wanted to express the idea 'those things which had been accomplished' (*Σ* 4):

τὰ φρονέοντ' ἀνὰ θυμὸν ἃ δὴ τετελεσμένα ἦεν.

B. *Short final syllables in the place of long*

I. λ 402 βοῦς περιταμνόμενον ἠδ' οἰῶν πώεα καλά.

Only one ending distinguishes the line from ω 112

βοῦς περιταμνομένους ἠδ' οἰῶν πώεα καλά.

II. *Δ* 440 Δεῖμός τ' ἠδὲ Φόβος καὶ Ἔρις ἄμοτον μεμαυῖα.

The metrical irregularity in this line came about when the poet, to make the latter part of his line, modified a correct formula which we find in *E* 518

Ἄρης τε βροτολοιγὸς Ἔρις τ' ἄμοτον μεμαυῖα.

The omission of τ' here can be compared with that of δ' in *X* 206, noted above (FM, p. 200).

III. λ 365 βόσκει γαῖα μέλαινα πολυσπερέας ἀνθρώπους.

Cf. *B* 804 ἄλλη δ' ἄλλων γλῶσσα πολυσπερέων ἀνθρώπων.

IV. The expression δμῶες ἐνὶ οἴκῳ which comes at the end of line λ 190 should be compared with the expression at the end of π 140: δμώων τ' ἐνὶ οἴκῳ. |

III

THE JUXTAPOSITION OF FORMULAE

THE metrical irregularities of which we examined a few examples in the preceding chapter result from a modification in the body of the formula. In the cases which we shall now consider, the fault is caused by the way in which a formula is used. It is the result of the juxtaposition of two formulae, where the end of the first is not in metrical accord with the beginning of the second. We cannot better explain this difference than by making an analysis of one of the most striking examples of this latter variety.

We find in Homer extended series of predicate formulae standing between the beginning of the line and the trochaic caesura and ending with the past tense of a third person singular verb, or with ἔπειτα. The usefulness of these hemistichs lies in the fact that for the majority of his characters, the bard disposes of subject formulae consisting in a name and one or two fixed epithets, which stand between the trochaic caesura and the end of the line and begin with a single consonant, and of which any one can be joined to any one of the predicate formulae to produce at the same time a complete sentence and a metrically correct hexameter line. It is one of the most common devices in Homer. We see it, for example, in lines like

ε 354 αὐτὰρ ὁ μερμήριξε }
ζ 1 ὣς ὁ μὲν ἔνθα καθεῦδε } πολύτλας δῖος 'Οδυσσεύς.
Θ 97 ὣς ἔφατ', οὐδ' ἐσάκουσε }

(For other examples of this kind, see below, FM, p. 226 and above, |TE, pp. 10–13|.) Now the habit of using this device had such a hold on the mind of the poet of the *Odyssey* that he sometimes made use of these hemistichs even in cases where he had not the necessary subject formula beginning with a single consonant. Whenever the name or a synonym of the name allowed it, the bards created a subject formula of the metrical value we specified; but neither the name *Τηλέμαχος* nor its synonym *'Οδυσσῆος υἱός* allowed the creation of such a formula. All that they could do was to form the expression *'Οδυσσῆος φίλος υἱός*, which has the right combination of short and long syllables, but begins with a vowel. This formula serves perfectly well to make lines like

β 2 ὄρνυτ' ἄρ' ἐξ εὐνῆφιν }
ο 59 τὸν δ' ὡς οὖν ἐνόησεν } 'Οδυσσῆος φίλος υἱός,

etc. But when, remembering the device of combining predicate hemistich and subject hemistich, and in particular such formulary lines as

> *E* 114 δὴ τότ' ἔπειτ' ἠρᾶτο βοὴν ἀγαθὸς Διομήδης
> η 1 ὣς ὁ μὲν ἔνθ' ἠρᾶτο πολύτλας δῖος Ὀδυσσεύς,

the bard was led by his sense of resemblances into using the formula for Telemachus, the result was a line with a metrical fault:

> γ 64 ὣς δ' αὔτως ἠρᾶτο Ὀδυσσῆος φίλος υἱός.

The same causes led the bard to make hiatus when, after the model of lines like

> τ 59 ἔνθα καθέζετ' ἔπειτα { περίφρων Πηνελόπεια
> τ 102 { πολύτλας δῖος Ὀδυσσεύς,

he made

> π 48 ἔνθα καθέζετ' ἔπειτα Ὀδυσσῆος φίλος υἱός.

We have been speaking of the character of the device which led the poet to compose the two lines containing short vowels in hiatus, but to understand the power which such devices exerted over his mind, we must also take into account the | direct relation between the formulae used in a device and the ideas they are designed to express. We shall have occasion below to see that Homer knew but one formula to express, in words extending from the trochaic caesura to the end of the line and beginning with a single consonant, the idea 'they will honour (or they honour, or they honoured) him like a god'. Similarly, there were no formulae other than the ones we quoted to express, in the same portion of the line, the ideas 'in the same way Telemachus prayed' and 'Telemachus sat there'. Now those who will not admit that, to express his ideas, Homer was virtually compelled to compose lines containing metrical faults, can make either of two objections, both of which we must take into consideration: Homer could have expressed his idea by arranging his words otherwise, either by disposing them differently in the line, or by distributing them in two or more lines; or else he could have produced a line free from metrical fault if he had been willing to use other words to express his idea.

In order to answer the first of these objections, taking line π 48 (quoted just above) as example, we must first have before our eyes the passages which contain the other two lines which serve especially as the model for this one. Penelope comes down from the women's quarters:

> τ 55 τῇ παρὰ μὲν κλισίην πυρὶ κάτθεσαν, ἔνθ' ἄρ' ἐφῖζε,
> δινωτὴν ἐλέφαντι καὶ ἀργύρωι· ἥν ποτε τέκτων
> ποίησ' Ἰκμάλιος, καὶ ὑπὸ θρῆνυν ποσὶν ἧκε
> προσφυέ' ἐξ αὐτῆς, ὅθ' ἐπὶ μέγα βάλλετο κῶας.
> ἔνθα καθέζετ' ἔπειτα περίφρων Πηνελόπεια.
> ἦλθον δὲ δμωιαὶ λευκώλενοι ἐκ μεγάροιο.

Penelope orders Eurycleia to bring a chair for their guest:

τ 100 ὣς ἔφατ', ἡ δὲ μάλ' ὀτραλέως κατέθηκε φέρουσα
δίφρον ἐύξεστον καὶ ἐπ' αὐτῶι κῶας ἔβαλλεν·
ἔνθα καθέζετ' ἔπειτα πολύτλας δῖος Ὀδυσσεύς.
τοῖσι δὲ μύθων ἦρχε περίφρων Πηνελόπεια.

It can be seen that in both passages the line preceding the one in question ends with the mention of a | fleece thrown over a chair which has just been brought up. We find no lines closely matching τ 58, but with τ 101 we can compare:

τ 97 Εὐρυνόμη, φέρε δὴ δίφρον καὶ κῶας ἐπ' αὐτοῦ
φ 177 πὰρ δὲ τίθει δίφρον τε μέγαν καὶ κῶας ἐπ' αὐτοῦ
φ 182 πὰρ δὲ φέρων δίφρον θῆκεν καὶ κῶας ἐπ' αὐτοῦ.

We can see how strong was the poet's habit of putting the word for fleece at the end of the line as we recognize the existence of a series of formulary lines expressing the idea 'to bring up a chair and throw a fleece upon it', where κῶας always occurs in the same position.

Now let us concern ourselves with the lines following those in question. τ 60 can be compared with

σ 198 ἦλθον δ' ἀμφίπολοι λευκώλενοι ἐκ μεγάροιο.

And with τ 103 can be compared

E 420 τοῖσι δὲ μύθων ἦρχε {θεὰ γλαυκῶπις Ἀθήνη
H 445 τοῖσι δὲ μύθων ἦρχε Ποσειδάων ἐνοσίχθων
α 28 τοῖσι δὲ μύθων ἦρχε πατὴρ ἀνδρῶν τε θεῶν τε,

etc. (cf. TE, p. 12, above). In both cases we are clearly dealing with formulary lines, and so we learn that the formulae following τ 59 and 102, like those preceding them, have fixed positions in the line.

This disposition of formula reveals to us one of the most important aspects of epic diction: the interconnection of formulae. If each formula has its fixed place or places in the line, not only will it have to join other formulae without producing metrical faults, but it will also have to join the preceding and the following formulae without leaving any lacuna in the line. Consequently a formula placed between one formula which ends a line and another formula which begins a line, must have exactly the measure of one line. In other words, an idea placed between one idea whose expression ends a line and another idea whose expression begins a line, will have to be expressed by words which exactly fill one hexameter. That is what we find in the | two passages quoted. In the first, between the idea 'a fleece thrown over it' and the idea 'the servant-girls came out', of which the first is regularly expressed at the end and the other at the beginning of a line, comes the third idea 'Penelope sat down on it.' Likewise, in the second passage, between the idea 'she threw a fleece over it' and the idea 'Penelope was the first to speak', there fits exactly the idea 'Odysseus sat down on it'.

Now let us see whether, in the passage where the use of the formula Ὀδυσσῆος φίλος υἱός made necessary the hiatus of a short vowel, the poet was acting under the influence of this same need to carry out the interconnection of formulae. Telemachus has come into Eumaeus' cabin, where he refuses to accept the chair offered him by the beggar whom he does not recognize as his father:

π 46 ὣς φάθ', ὁ δ' αὖτις ἰὼν κατ' ἄρ' ἕζετο· τῶι δὲ συβώτης
χεῦεν ὕπο χλωρὰς ῥῶπας καὶ κῶας ὕπερθεν·
ἔνθα καθέζετ' ἔπειτα Ὀδυσσῆος φίλος υἱός.
τοῖσιν δ' αὖ κρειῶν πίνακας παρέθηκε συβώτης
ὀπταλέων.

In the line preceding the one containing the hiatus, there is a mention of a fleece, as in the two other passages. As for the line which follows, it can be compared with α 141 = δ 57,

δαιτρὸς δὲ κρειῶν πίνακας παρέθηκεν ἀείρας,

which belongs to the same series of formulary lines. τοῖσιν δ' αὖ which replaces δαιτρὸς δέ is only a device to fill the first foot of the line, the idea 'before them' being adequately expressed by the prefix in παρέθηκεν as the two previously quoted lines show.[1] Thus we can see that to insert between the ideas 'a fleece on top' and '[the swineherd] put trenchers of meat before them' the third idea 'Telemachus sat down there', the poet was obliged to express this idea by words occupying a single line. And we saw that, far from having difficulty in finding the right words, they were immediately suggested to him by a device which would have given him a metrically perfect line for almost any other character in heroic legend. We must therefore recognize that | what led Homer to make the hiatus was not merely the desire for easy versification, but even more the desire not to break the interconnection of ideas and undo the structure of the whole passage. The inadequacy was in the formulary technique, which did not provide Telemachus with a subject formula of the required measure beginning with a single consonant; the poet had little to do with it.

We spoke of another objection which could be made to our use of the term 'necessity': that the poet might have expressed the idea 'Telemachus sat down there' in the same portion of the line using other words altogether. To answer this objection with certainty, one would need a solution to the fundamental problem of Homeric diction: is there anything other than formulae in the *Iliad* and *Odyssey*? Did the poet ever try

[1] We note in passing that ἀείρας in α 141 = δ 57 is also a device to fill out the line, as we see from its absence in π 49.

to express his thought by words and expressions of his own? For the question is not whether the poet could have found such words, but whether it ever occurred to him to look for them. In TE (pp. 79 f. above) we were at one point only in a position to undertake the quantitative analysis needed to settle this matter. There we were able to demonstrate that almost all the noun–epithet formulae used for some of the principal characters in the *Iliad* and *Odyssey* are traditional, and we found that those few which did not lend themselves to our method of analysis reveal no special feature indicating that they are the original creation of the poet (or poets) of our poems. Thus we discovered that the only category of noun–epithet formulae which seemed to offer material for the search for original expressions, viz., the category of noun–epithet formulae in which two or more express the same essential idea in words of the same metrical value (TE, pp. 173 ff. above), shows no trace of original workmanship. It is true that these conclusions apply to only a portion of formulae, and to those in particular which might be expected to be most traditional. But the categoric nature of these conclusions concerning the traditional character of noun–epithet formulae suggests that they should be extended to most other formulae; and more important, these conclusions give us firm ground for the construction of an aesthetic of style which | distinguishes the poet of a traditional style from one who uses an individual style to express personal ideas. Once the central fact has been understood that the genius of Homer manifested itself in the expression of traditional ideas by means of equally traditional words and groups of words, it will be seen that there is hardly any reason to suppose that to repair the hiatus of a short vowel, he would have abandoned the bardic style. Only by unconsciously following the sense of style formed in us by our familiarity with modern literature, can we imagine that Homer could have discarded an established artifice in order to invent a line which would have been hard to find in the first place, and once found, would have contrasted violently, by its originality, with the traditional expressions surrounding it.

Other Examples of Metrical Irregularities Resulting from the Juxtaposition of Formulae

A.—*Short Syllables in Hiatus*

a. Before the trochaic caesura

1. *B* 571 Ὀρνειάς τ' ἐνέμοντο Ἀραιθυρέην τ' ἐρατεινήν.

The part of the line between the beginning and the trochaic caesura can be compared with

B 496 οἵ θ' Ὑρίην ἐνέμοντο καὶ Αὐλίδα πετρήεσσαν

B 583 Βρυσειάς τ' ἐνέμοντο καὶ Αὐγειὰς ἐρατεινάς
B 591 οἳ δὲ Πύλον τ' ἐνέμοντο καὶ Ἀρήνην ἐρατεινήν.

Cf. also *B* 499, 605, 633, 639, where we likewise find ἐνέμοντο before the trochaic caesura and preceded by the name of a town, then followed in the latter part of the line either (1) by the name of another town governed by the same verb and accompanied by an epithet which fills the part of the line not filled by the name; or (2) by two names of towns governed by the same verb. To enumerate the towns which sent troops to the war, the bards created, among other devices, one consisting in saying in the first half of the line 'who inhabited such and such a town', and in the second half, 'and such and such a town (*or* towns)'—a device which could be expanded by the addition in the following lines of other names of towns, accompanied by other epithets where | necessary: cf. *B* 496–8, 591–4, 605–6, 639–40. But to make lines of this shape without metrical fault, the second half-line, expressing in the accusative case the idea 'and such and such a town', had to begin with a single consonant, as it does in *B* 496, 583, 591 (already quoted), and in *B* 605 καὶ Ὀρχομενὸν πολύμηλον and in *B* 633 καὶ Αἰγίλιπα τρηχεῖαν. But Ἀραιθυρέην does not lend itself to this device; because of its metrical value it must come directly after the trochaic caesura, which has the advantage that the line can then end with the generic epithet of towns ἐρατεινήν. Cf.

Ἀρήνην
Μαντινέην
Ἠμαθίην
Μηιονίην
} ἐρατεινήν.

The conjunction 'and', καί not being possible, can be expressed by τε (τ') as in a great many other formulae expressing the idea of 'such and such a town' in the latter part of the line: Πυθῶνά τε πετρήεσσαν (*B* 519), Τίρυνθά τε τειχιόεσσαν (*B* 559), Ἕλος τ', ἔφαλον πτολίεθρον (*B* 584), etc. Thus to express the idea 'and Araethyrea' (in the accusative) between the trochaic caesura and the end of the line, the poet had to hand all the words he needed; but if he wanted to avoid the hiatus of a short syllable, he would have to renounce the type of line formula in which ἐνέμοντο stands before the trochaic caesura. He preferred the hiatus.

II. *Γ* 376 κεινὴ δὲ τρυφάλεια ἅμ' ἕσπετο χειρὶ παχείῃ.

τρυφάλεια occurs thrice in the first half of the line, before the trochaic caesura. ἅμ' ἕσπετο occurs 6 times in the position it occupies in the line quoted, and χειρὶ παχείῃ occurs 17 times at the end of the line. The last two formulae join without metrical fault to express the idea 'came away in his hand'. But τρυφάλεια ends with a vowel. Here, as in the other cases we examined, the poet was faced with the choice of making easily out of traditional formulae a line | with a metrical fault, or having to make a new line in an unaccustomed fashion, or possibly a whole new group of lines.

III. *Δ* 91 *λαῶν, οἵ οἱ ἕποντο ἀπ' Αἰσήποιο ῥοάων*

which can be compared with

Δ 202 *λαῶν, οἵ οἱ ἕποντο Τρίκης ἐξ ἱπποβότοιο*
I 44 *ἑστᾶσ', αἵ τοι ἕποντο Μυκήνηθεν μάλα πολλαί.*

Cf. also *Τρώων· οἱ δ' ἅμ' ἕποντο* (*P* 753). The latter part of the line recalls the hemistichs of the series *ἀπ' Ὠκεανοῖο ῥοάων* (*T* 1), *παρ' Ὠκεανοῖο ῥοάων* (*χ* 197), *ἰδὲ Ξάνθοιο ῥοάων* (*Z* 4).

IV. *Σ* 48 *Μαῖρα καὶ Ὠρείθυια ἐυπλόκαμός τ' Ἀμάθεια.*

This line occurs in the roll-call of the Nereids. The poet found the same answer to the difficulties in this list of names as he did to those of the names of cities in the *Catalogue of Ships*: when the names and conjunctions did not fill out the divisions of the line, he supplemented them with ornamental epithets, as in *Σ* 40

Νησαίη Σπειώ τε Θόη θ' Ἁλίη τε βοῶπις.

But for heroines and goddesses there existed no ornamental epithet with the measure ⏑ – ⏕ – beginning with a single consonant—or at least we find no such epithet in Homer (cf. TE, p. 97 above). Consequently, to fill the space between the trochaic caesura and *τ' Ἀμάθεια* at the end of the line, the poet had to use *ἐυπλόκαμος*, being guided by his memory of such formulae as *ἐυπλόκαμος Ἑκαμήδη* (twice) and *ἐυπλόκαμος Δημήτηρ* (*ε* 125). The use of the same epithet again caused the hiatus of a short syllable in *Ξ* 6:

εἰς ὅ κε θερμὰ λοετρὰ ἐυπλόκαμος Ἑκαμήδη.

V. *Φ* 426 *τὼ μὲν ἄρ' ἄμφω κεῖντο ἐπὶ χθονὶ πουλυβοτείρῃ.*

The form *κεῖντο* appears nowhere else in Homer, but *κεῖτο* | occurs 5 times before the trochaic caesura. *χ* 186 in particular demands comparison with the line just quoted, because we find in it the same accumulation of particles at the beginning:

δὴ τότε γ' ἤδη κεῖτο, ῥαφαὶ δ' ἐλέλυντο ἱμάντων.

Six other Homeric lines end with *ἐπὶ χθονὶ πουλυβοτείρῃ.*

VI. *δ* 407 *ἔνθα σ' ἐγὼν ἀγαγοῦσα ἅμ' ἠοῖ φαινομένηφιν.*

To this line let us compare ψ 295

ἐς θάλαμον δ' ἀγαγοῦσα πάλιν κίεν. οἱ μὲν ἔπειτα.

ἅμ' ἠοῖ φαινομένηφιν occurs 8 times in Homer, always at the end of the line; cf. *ἅμα δ' ἠοῖ φαινομένηφιν* (thrice).

VII. κ 314 = 366

εἷσε δέ μ' εἰσαγαγοῦσα ἐπὶ θρόνου ἀργυροήλου.

To this line let us compare on the one hand κ 233

εἷσεν δ' εἰσαγαγοῦσα κατὰ κλισμούς τε θρόνους τε,

and on the other hand

η 162 ἀλλ' ἄγε δὴ ξεῖνον μὲν ἐπὶ θρόνου ἀργυροήλου
Σ 389 τὴν μὲν ἔπειτα καθεῖσεν ἐπὶ θρόνου ἀργυροήλου.

VIII. μ 199 αἶψ' ἀπὸ κηρὸν ἕλοντο ἐμοὶ ἐρίηρες ἑταῖροι.

To the first part of this line we can compare *αἶψα δὲ δεῖπνον ἕλοντο* (twice), *οἱ δ' ἄρα δεῖπνον ἕλοντο*, etc. As for the second part, we find *ἐμοὶ ἐρίηρες ἑταῖροι* in five other lines. The construction of lines μ 397 = ξ 249 is similar:

ἐξῆμαρ μὲν ἔπειτα ἐμοὶ ἐρίηρες ἑταῖροι.

IX. τ 542 ἀμφὶ δ' ἔμ' ἠγερέθοντο ἐυπλοκαμῖδες Ἀχαιαί.

The causes of hiatus in this line resemble | those we noted above for lines Σ 48 and Ξ 6 (p. 208). We find on the one hand

β 392 ἀθρόοι ἠγερέθοντο· θεὰ δ' ὄτρυνεν ἕκαστον

(cf. ω 468); and on the other hand

β 119 τάων αἳ πάρος ἦσαν ἐυπλοκαμῖδες Ἀχαιαί.

X. ψ 345 ὁππότε δή ῥ' Ὀδυσῆα ἐέλπετο ὃν κατὰ θυμόν.

The form *Ὀδυσῆα* is found 16 times in this position. The first part of the line is like the first part of

α 74 ἐκ τοῦ δὴ Ὀδυσῆα Ποσειδάων ἐνοσίχθων
ω 149 καὶ τότε δή ῥ' Ὀδυσῆα κακός ποθεν ἤγαγε δαίμων.

We see the latter part of the line again in

N 8 οὐ γὰρ ὅ γ' ἀθανάτων τιν' ἐέλπετο ὃν κατὰ θυμόν.

To ascertain that a metrical irregularity has arisen from the habit of combining formulae, it is not always necessary to discover in other parts of the Homeric texts the two half-lines whose juxtaposition occasioned the fault. Sometimes it is clear that the fault has come about from the habitual use of short expressions made up, in sundry ways, of adverbs, conjunctions, particles, and prepositions, expressions serving to allow the poet to graft on to a sentence an additional clause, or to tie two sentences together. Thus in three places a short syllable before the trochaic caesura is followed by ὁ δέ (ὁ δ'):

Λ 378 ἐν γαίῃι κατέπηκτο· ὁ δὲ μάλα ἡδὺ γελάσσας
N 38 νοστήσαντα ἄνακτα· ὁ δ' ἐς στρατὸν ᾤχετ' Ἀχαιῶν
φ 393 εἰσορόων 'Οδυσῆα· ὁ δ' ἤδη τόξον ἐνώμα.

Homer makes frequent use of this expression to join sentences or clauses together. Leaving aside cases where ὁ δέ (ὁ δ') occurs elsewhere in the line, we find it after the trochaic caesura in *A* 47, 191, 474, *Δ* 108, 498, 522, etc., and in α 20, 322, β 365, δ 226, etc. It is not hard to see | how the poet came to use it even after a short vowel.

Likewise, the hiatus in the two lines

X 125 αὔτως ὥς τε γυναῖκα, ἐπεί κ' ἀπὸ τεύχεα δύω
λ 249 τέξεις ἀγλαὰ τέκνα, ἐπεὶ οὐκ ἀποφώλιοι εὐναί

is the clear consequence of the poet's habit of joining two parts of a sentence by ἐπεί; Homer uses this conjunction after the trochaic caesura in *A* 112, 274, 281, 299, 381, 576, *B* 16, 115, *Γ* 99, *Δ* 269, *E* 27, 510, etc., and in α 37, 205, 220, 238, 396, β 96, 155, 297, γ 70, 250, 322, 358, 368, δ 490, 647, etc.

β. Before the bucolic diaeresis

I. *B* 3 ἀλλ' ὅ γε μερμήριζε κατὰ φρένα ὡς Ἀχιλῆα.

To this line compare

Θ 169 τρὶς μὲν μερμήριξε κατὰ φρένα καὶ κατὰ θυμόν,
υ 10 πολλὰ δὲ μερμήριζε κατὰ φρένα καὶ κατὰ θυμόν,

and

A 558 τῆι σ' ὀίω κατανεῦσαι ἐτήτυμον ὡς Ἀχιλῆα.

II. *O* 172 ὣς κραιπνῶς μεμαυῖα διέπτατο ὠκέα Ἶρις.

To this line compare *O* 83

ὣς κραιπνῶς μεμαυῖα διέπτατο πότνια Ἥρη.

ὠκέα Ἶρις appears 19 times in Homer, always at the end of the line; there is no formula for this goddess which falls between the bucolic diaeresis and the end of the line and begins with a single consonant.

III. *Λ* 461 αὐτὰρ ὅ γ' ἐξοπίσω ἀνεχάζετο, αὖε δ' ἑταίρους.

We find on the one hand *P* 108

αὐτὰρ ὅ γ' ἐξοπίσω ἀνεχάζετο, λεῖπε δὲ νεκρόν |

(cf. *E* 443, 600, *Π* 710); and on the other hand *N* 477

Αἰνείαν ἐπιόντα βοηθόον· αὖε δ' ἑταίρους.

IV. α 60 ἐντρέπεται φίλον ἦτορ, Ὀλύμπιε, οὔ νύ τ' Ὀδυσσεύς.

The form Ὀλύμπιε appears 4 times, and always before the bucolic diaeresis, where it fills the space between the trochaic caesura and this diaeresis. So in the present case it is inserted between the formula occupying the first half of the line—cf. *O* 554

ἐντρέπεται φίλον ἦτορ, ἀνεψιοῦ κταμένοιο—

and the formula at the end of the line—cf.

β 163 τοῖσιν γὰρ μέγα πῆμα κυλίνδεται· οὐ γὰρ Ὀδυσσεύς
ω 443 κέκλυτε δὴ νῦν μευ, Ἰθακήσιοι· οὐ γὰρ Ὀδυσσεύς.[1]

V. β 417 νηὶ δ' ἐνὶ πρύμνηι κατ' ἄρ' ἕζετο· ἄγχι δ' ἄρ' αὐτῆς.

To this line compare:

ἦ τοι ὅ γ' ὣς εἰπὼν κατ' ἄρ' ἕζετο, τοῖσι δ' ἀνέστη (6 times)

and

P 10 Πατρόκλοιο πεσόντος ἀμύμονος· ἄγχι δ' ἄρ' αὐτοῦ
φ 433 ἀμφὶ δὲ χεῖρα φίλην βάλεν ἔγχει, ἄγχι δ' ἄρ' αὐτοῦ.

VI. κ 458 ἠμὲν ὅσ' ἐν πόντωι πάθεν ἄλγεα ἰχθυόεντι.

This line recalls

α 4 πολλὰ δ' ὅ γ' ἐν πόντωι πάθεν ἄλγεα ὃν κατὰ θυμόν.

and

δ 381 = 470 νόστον θ', ὡς ἐπὶ πόντον ἐλεύσομαι ἰχθυόεντα.

and so on. |

VII. ρ 301 δὴ τότε γ', ὡς ἐνόησεν Ὀδυσσέα ἐγγὺς ἐόντα.

To this line compare

ο 59 τὸν δ' ὡς οὖν ἐνόησεν Ὀδυσσῆος φίλος υἱός.

ἐγγὺς ἐόντα appears in Homer 11 times, always at the end of the line.

[1] On this use of the epithet, cf. TE, pp. 64 ff. above.

γ. At the end of the first foot

I. *B* 8 βάσκ' ἴθι, οὖλε ὄνειρε, θοὰς ἐπὶ νῆας Ἀχαιῶν.

Earlier we investigated the causes of the hiatus of the final vowel in οὖλε: the poet was guided by his memory of lines composed with the device βάσκ' ἴθι, Ἶρι ταχεῖα (4 times). The hiatus of the final vowel of ἴθι is to be explained in the same way. In the first case, there is a modification of endings; in the line above, two formulae which do not go well together happen to be juxtaposed.

δ. Short vowels in hiatus which do not occur before a break in the line

We cannot with certainty detect juxtaposition of formulae in all such cases of hiatus. This is to be expected: by far the most common formula types are those to be found between two breaks in the line or between one break and the beginning or end of the line. When we have expressions designed to be joined to other expressions in order to make a variety of sentences, there is almost always a pause in the sentence at the point of junction, and consequently they will be joined at one of the regular breaks in the line. None the less, in some examples of so-called illegitimate hiatus, the metrical fault can be attributed to the juxtaposition of formulae, although the modification of formulae, a more common cause of these phenomena, may also play some part.

I. *A* 533 Ζεὺς δὲ ἑὸν πρὸς δῶμα· θεοὶ δ' ἅμα πάντες ἀνέσταν.

Ζεὺς δέ occurs 8 times in Homer at the beginning of the line; we find as well Ζεύς τε (twice). πρὸς δῶμα occurs 16 times before the | trochaic caesura. The expression ἑὸν πρὸς δῶμα is not found elsewhere, but in ζ 256 we read πατρὸς ἐμοῦ πρὸς δῶμα and in υ 192 ἡμέτερον πρὸς δῶμα; the modification of ἐμοῦ to ἑόν would have been easy, especially when a word of this measure was needed to fill the space between formulae whose positions were fixed.

II. *Λ* 678 πεντήκοντα βοῶν ἀγέλας, τόσα πώεα οἰῶν
ξ 100 δώδεκ' ἐν ἠπείρωι ἀγέλαι· τόσα πώεα οἰῶν.

πώεα οἰῶν was inspired by πώεα καλά which occurs 4 times at the end of the line. The *Iliad* and the *Odyssey* show us, moreover, a type of line which the poet could not use and at the same time indicate that the flocks were of sheep without changing καλά to οἰῶν:

Σ 528 τάμνοντ' ἀμφὶ βοῶν ἀγέλας καὶ πώεα καλά
μ 129 ἑπτὰ βοῶν ἀγέλαι, τόσα δ' οἰῶν πώεα καλά.

Outside the formula in question, οἰῶν occurs thrice at the end of the line in the formula πῶυ μέγ' οἰῶν, and once in the expression κώεσιν οἰῶν.

III. *Ψ* 263 θῆκε γυναῖκα ἄγεσθαι ἀμύμονα ἔργα ἰδυῖαν.

The beginning of the line derives from formulae like the one which begins *Π* 223:

θῆκ' ἐπὶ νηὸς ἄγεσθαι, ἐὺ πλήσασα χιτώνων.

Furthermore, the poet could not otherwise arrange the words which precede the trochaic caesura in *Ψ* 263 if he wished to make use of the formula which follows the caesura: cf.

ω 278 χωρὶς δ' αὖτε γυναῖκας ἀμύμονα ἔργα ἰδυίας.

IV. φ 216 Τηλεμάχου ἑτάρω τε κασιγνήτω τε ἔσεσθον.

Τηλεμάχου ἕταροι is attested twice at the beginning of the line. τε κασιγνήτω (-οι, -ους) is found in the same position in

ο 16 ἤδη γάρ ῥα πατήρ τε κασίγνητοί τε κέλονται
Z 239 εἰρόμεναι παῖδάς τε κασιγνήτους τε ἔτας τε. |

The form ἔσεσθον also occurs at the end of the line in its only other use in Homer (π 267); and with but two exceptions, ἔσεσθαι (11 times) and ἔσεσθε (twice) appear in the same place. In addition, the poet had the sense of a formula where κασίγνητοί τε was followed by a verb of which it was the subject, such as ο 16, quoted above.

B. *Breves in longo*

α. Before the penthemimeral caesura

I. In the *Catalogue of Ships*, the need to insert the names of towns between the breaks and the extremities of the line brought about cases of *breves in hiatu* (see above FM, pp. 206 ff.). The same need occasioned *breves in longo*:

B 734 οἳ δ' ἔχον Ὀρμένιον, οἵ τε κρήνην Ὑπέρειαν,

with which we may compare on the one hand

B 603 οἳ δ' ἔχον Ἀρκαδίην, ὑπὸ Κυλλήνης ὄρος αἰπύ
B 735 οἵ τ' ἔχον Ἀστέριον Τιτάνοιό τε λευκὰ κάρηνα

and on the other hand

B 682 οἵ τ' Ἄλον οἵ τ' Ἀλόπην οἵ τε Τρηχῖν' ἐνέμοντο.

II. *B* 500 οἵ τ' Ἐλεῶν' εἶχον ἠδ' Ὕλην καὶ Πετεῶνα.

Cf.

B 559 οἵ δ' Ἄργος τ' εἶχον Τίρυνθά τε τειχιόεσσαν·
B 607 καὶ Τεγέην εἶχον καὶ Μαντινέην ἐρατεινήν

and

B 683 οἵ τ' εἶχον Φθίην ἠδ' Ἑλλάδα καλλιγύναικα.

III. *Z* 299 Κισσηίς, ἄλοχος Ἀντήνορος ἱπποδάμοιο

was modelled on lines such as

E 415 ἰφθίμη ἄλοχος Διομήδεος ἱπποδάμοιο. |

IV. By the same process in μ 294 = 352 the substitution of one name for another resulted in a *brevis in longo*:

ὣς ἔφατ' Εὐρύλοχος, ἐπὶ δ' ᾔνεον ἄλλοι ἑταῖροι.

This line was patterned after lines like

Γ 461 ὣς ἔφατ' Ἀτρεΐδης, ἐπὶ δ' ᾔνεον ἄλλοι Ἀχαιοί.

V. *N* 587 θώρηκος γύαλον, ἀπὸ δ' ἔπτατο πικρὸς ὀιστός.

We need compare this line with only one other:

E 99 θώρηκος γύαλον, διὰ δ' ἔπτατο πικρὸς ὀιστός.

VI. *P* 109 ἐντροπαλιζόμενος ὥς τε λὶς ἠυγένειος.

We have on the one hand

Z 496 ἐντροπαλιζομένη, θαλερὸν κατὰ δάκρυ χέουσα
Φ 492 ἐντροπαλιζομένην· ταχέες δ' ἔκπιπτον ὀιστοί

and on the other hand

Σ 318 πυκνὰ μάλα στενάχων ὥς τε λὶς ἠυγένειος.

VII. *Υ* 368 ἔγχει δ' ἀργαλέον, ἐπεὶ ἦ πολὺ φέρτεροί εἰσιν.

We find ἔγχει at the beginning of the line in the expressions ἔγχει χαλκείῳ (7 times), ἔγχει μάρνασθαι (*Π* 195), etc., and ἀργαλέον before the penthemimeral caesura in the expressions δεινόν τ' ἀργαλέον (4 times), πρῆξαι δ' ἀργαλέον (π 88), etc. For the last half of the line cf.

K 557 ἵππου δωρήσαιτ', ἐπεὶ ἦ πολὺ φέρτεροί εἰσιν
Υ 135 ἡμέας τοὺς ἄλλους, ἐπεὶ ἦ πολὺ φέρτεροί εἰμεν
ι 276 οὐδὲ θεῶν μακάρων, ἐπεὶ ἦ πολὺ φέρτεροί εἰμεν.

From like causes derives the *brevis in longo* of π 89:

ἄνδρα καὶ ἴφθιμον, ἐπεὶ ἦ πολὺ φέρτεροί εἰσι. |

VIII. ζ 294 τόσσον ἀπὸ πτόλιος ὅσσον τε γέγωνε βοήσας.

To this let us compare

Δ 514 ὣς φάτ' ἀπὸ πτόλιος δεινὸς θεός· αὐτὰρ Ἀχαιούς

and

ε 400 = ι 473 ἀλλ' ὅτε τόσσον ἀπῆν ὅσσον τε γέγωνε βοήσας.

IX. λ 322 κούρην Μίνωος ὀλοόφρονος, ἥν ποτε Θησεύς.

The first part of this line follows expressions like κούρην Βρισῆος (thrice), κούρηι Μαρπήσσης (Ι 557), κούρηι 'Ικαρίου (ω 195), etc. ὀλοόφρονος, an epithet of magicians, like the generic epithet[1] of heroes δουρικλυτός, serves to fill the space between the penthemimeral caesura and the bucolic diaeresis (cf. TE, p. 65 above). Such is its use in α 52,

Ἄτλαντος θυγάτηρ ὀλοόφρονος, ὅς τε θαλάσσης,

and in κ 137

αὐτοκασιγνήτη ὀλοόφρονος Αἰήταο.

But it necessitated a short syllable before the penthemimeral caesura when the poet used it to fill the space between κούρην Μίνωος and ἥν ποτε Θησεύς (cf. ὧ ποτ' Ἀχιλλεύς, ἣν ἄρ' Ἀχιλλεύς, εἴ ποτ' 'Οδυσσεύς, etc.).

X. μ 336 χεῖρας νιψάμενος, ὅθ' ἐπὶ σκέπας ἦν ἀνέμοιο.

Compare

β 261 χεῖρας νιψάμενος πολιῆς ἁλός, εὔχετ' Ἀθήνηι
κ 182 χεῖρας νιψάμενοι τεύχοντ' ἐρικυδέα δαῖτα

and

ζ 210 λούσατέ τ' ἐν ποταμῶι, ὅθ' ἐπὶ σκέπας ἔστ' ἀνέμοιο. |

It is in the case of final short syllables before the hephthemimeral caesura that we most often meet metrical irregularities deriving from the habitual use of a fixed expression to join two clauses or sentences. We have already considered (FM, p. 210) one such case: ὁ δέ (ὁ δ') before the trochaic caesura. Knös lists 175 cases of a short syllable before the hephthemimeral caesura. After these final short syllables the expressions of the kind mentioned most frequently to be found are ὁ δέ (ὁ δ') (21 times), and ἐπεί (4 times). We have pointed out the frequency with which these same expressions occur after the trochaic caesura. We find ὁ δέ (ὁ δ') used after the penthemimeral caesura in Α 239, Β 268, 515, 621, 707, Γ 349, Δ 524, 535, 537, etc., and in α 326, β 387, γ 252, 490, δ 251,

[1] We apply the word 'generic' to an ornamental epithet which indicates a quality common to all the members of a class and can be used of any of them indifferently (cf. TE, p. 64 above).

701, etc. By its frequency we can judge how often the poet must have been tempted to use this expression even when a short syllable preceded it.

Let us observe in passing how ἄρα is added to this expression in order to make it easier to use: to join two sentences the poet says, without difference of meaning, ὁ δ', ὁ δέ, ὁ δ' ἄρ', or ὁ δ' ἄρα.

ἐπεί is found after the penthemimeral caesura in *A* 114, 153, 231, *E* 252, 441, 686, etc., and in α 297, 299, β 199, δ 523, etc.

β. Before the hephthemimeral caesura

I. ι 62 = 105 = κ 77 = 133

ἔνθεν δὲ προτέρω πλέομεν ἀκαχήμενοι ἦτορ.

The form πλέομεν appears ten times in Homer, always before the hephthemimeral caesura. The formula ἀκαχήμενος ἦτορ ends a line 4 times. To the line in question may be compared especially

κ 80 = ο 476 ἑξῆμαρ μὲν ὁμῶς πλέομεν νύκτας τε καὶ ἦμαρ.

II. π 358 ὣς ἔφαθ', οἱ δ' ἀνστάντες ἔβαν ἐπὶ θῖνα θαλάσσης.

To this line we can on the one hand compare

δ 674 αὐτίκ' ἔπειτ' ἀνστάντες ἔβαν δόμον εἰς 'Οδυσῆος
ρ 177 ὣς ἔφαθ', οἱ δ' ἀνστάντες ἔβαν πείθοντό τε μύθωι,|

etc., and on the other

Δ 248 εἰρύατ' εὔπρυμνοι, πολιῆς ἐπὶ θῖνα θαλάσσης
ζ 236 ἕζετ' ἔπειτ' ἀπάνευθε κιὼν ἐπὶ θῖνα θαλάσσης,

and so on.

III. υ 303 Κτήσιππον δ' ἄρα Τηλέμαχος ἠνίπαπε μύθωι.

We can compare

χ 284 Ἀμφιμέδοντα δὲ Τηλέμαχος, Πόλυβον δὲ συβώτης.

ἠνίπαπε μύθωι occurs 16 times, always at the end of the line.

IV. Memory of a line of the same type as the line just quoted was the cause of another *brevis in longo*:

χ 267 Εὐρυάδην δ' ἄρα Τηλέμαχος, Ἔλατον δὲ συβώτης.

It is significant that this line precedes χ 284. The poet allowed the metrical fault not because he remembered having used this type of line shortly before, but because he had preserved the form of this type in his memory.

γ. Before the trithemimeral caesura

I. *B* 780 οἱ δ' ἄρ' ἴσαν ὡς εἴ τε πυρὶ χθὼν πᾶσα νέμοιτο.

We find on the one hand

Γ 8 οἱ δ' ἄρ' ἴσαν σιγῆι μένεα πνείοντες Ἀχαιοί

and on the other hand

T 366 λαμπέσθην ὡς εἴ τε πυρὸς σέλας, ἐν δέ οἱ ἦτορ.

Out of 8 occurrences in Homer, ὡς εἴ τε comes 7 times in the position where we see it here.

II. *H* 206 ὣς ἄρ' ἔφαν, Αἴας δὲ κορύσσετο νώροπι χαλκῶι. |

This line was made on the model of lines like

Π 130 ὣς φάτο· Πάτροκλος δὲ κορύσσετο νώροπι χαλκῶι.

Compare with the first part of this line

Γ 161 ὣς ἄρ' ἔφαν, Πρίαμος δ' . . .
σ 75 ὣς ἄρ' ἔφαν, Ἴρωι δὲ . . .

ὣς ἄρ' ἔφαν occurs 9 times at the beginning of the line.

III. δ 845 μεσσηγὺς Ἰθάκης τε Σάμοιό τε παιπαλοέσσης.

To this compare on the one hand

N 33 μεσσηγὺς Τενέδοιο καὶ Ἴμβρου παιπαλοέσσης
Ω 78 μεσσηγὺς δὲ Σάμου τε καὶ Ἴμβρου παιπαλοέσσης

etc., and on the other hand

δ 671 = ο 29 ἐν πορθμῶι Ἰθάκης τε Σάμοιό τε παιπαλοέσσης.

Like the examples presented earlier to illustrate how the modification of formulae can be the cause of metrical irregularities, the examples presented immediately above have been chosen from among the most striking. We cannot hope to demonstrate categorically that all the metrical irregularities in word-endings in Homer, or a definite proportion of them, are caused by the technique of the use of formulae: the means to do so are lacking. A formula appears in Homer just as many times as the poet had occasion to express some one idea in the two poems. Hence certain formulae and formula types, designed to express ideas that recur at close intervals in heroic poetry, occur 10, 20, or 50 times, or more; and hence also there are many formulae which occur but once. A formula declares itself by its frequency. When we observe that, to express a certain essential idea, the poet never hesitates to use a certain group of words, we know that that group of words, by definition, constitutes a formula. | But an expression occurring once, unless it happens closely to resemble another expression, or evidently to belong to a definite series of formulae, will offer no such indication of its nature. That does not prove that it is not a formula. To argue that it does, we should have to suppose that in the limited space of our two poems, Homer had occasion to use more than once each and every idea for which he possessed a formula.

Keeping this fact in mind, we could add to the examples already given many others in which the part of the line preceding the metrical fault is certainly traditional, although the part following the fault is not, and vice versa. For example, the first part of *E* 857

νείατον ἐς κενεῶνα ὅθι ζωννύσκετο μίτρῃ

recurs unchanged in *Λ* 381 and *Π* 821; but ζωννύσκετο is found nowhere else in Homer. The last part of *I* 426

ἥν νῦν ἐφράσσαντο ἐμεῦ ἀπομηνίσαντος

appears again in *T* 62; but the nearest thing to the first part of the line is Ἕκτορα δὲ φράσσαντο in *O* 671. Further study in this direction would make it certain that the great majority of irregularities which we can detect are the result of the interplay of formulae. But in any given case, the possibility would remain that the cause was other than formulary.

It would be more useful to turn our steps in another direction, towards the investigation of formula types, and of the operation of analogy which determined their existence. It can be shown, for example, that of the 175 cases of a short final syllable before the penthemimeral caesura listed by Knös, the caesura is 24 times preceded by a participle in -όμενος, -όμενον or -άμενος, -άμενον, in either the nominative or accusative: μαχησόμενος (*A* 153), ἐπερχόμενον (*A* 535), ἀποπτάμενος (*B* 71), etc., ἐπιμασσάμενος (ι 302), ὀισάμενος (ι 339), αἰνύμενος (ι 429), ἐρειδόμενος (κ 170), etc. A study of these 24 cases shows that with a single exception (*Ψ* 89), they all involve one of the | two following devices of versification: (1) The poet develops his sentence, which is already grammatically complete at the end of the line, by adding to the beginning of the following line a participle or expression containing a participle in apposition with the subject or object of the sentence. Thus:

οὐ γὰρ ἐγὼ Τρώων ἕνεκ' ἤλυθον αἰχμητάων
A 153 δεῦρο μαχησόμενος, ἐπεὶ οὔ τί μοι αἴτιοί εἰσιν.

τὸν μὲν ἐγὼ βούλευσα κατὰ μεγαλήτορα θυμόν
ἄσσον ἰών, ξίφος ὀξὺ ἐρυσσάμενος παρὰ μηροῦ,
οὐτάμεναι πρὸς στῆθος, ὅθι φρένες ἧπαρ ἔχουσι,
ι 302 χείρ' ἐπιμασσάμενος.

In 15 of the 24 cases when a participle in -όμενος, -άμενος is used before the penthemimeral caesura and is followed by a word beginning with a vowel, we find this device. The other is close to it. (2) The poet begins his line with a finite form of the verb, and the participle preceding the penthemimeral caesura agrees with the subject of the verb (unexpressed) or with its object which has been given in the line before. So

> *Π* 736 ἧκε δ' ἐρεισάμενος, οὐδὲ δὴν χάζετο φωτός.
>
> αὔριον ἣν ἀρετὴν διαείσεται, εἴ κ' ἐμὸν ἔγχος
> *Θ* 536 μείνῃ ἐπερχόμενον· ἀλλ' ἐν πρώτοισιν, ὀίω.

The usefulness of these two devices is evident. With the first the poet can continue a sentence already sung as far as the penthemimeral caesura of the next line. In addition to the many other formulae with which he can go on after the caesura, he disposes of a large number of expressions which can make a transition to the next sentence: ὁ δέ, ὁ γάρ, ὁ μέν, ἐπεί, ἀτάρ, ἠδέ, ἀλλά, ὑπὸ δέ, ἐπὶ δέ, ἀπὸ δέ, etc. By means of the second device he can put the finite verb and the participle in the first half of the line, ending his sentence at the penthemimeral caesura or else continuing it by adding the object of the verb. The complex pattern of the hexameter, moreover, does not offer many places in which participles in -όμενος, -άμενος can be put, especially | if there are other words to dispose in the line. Hence the frequent use of these two devices. Homer uses the first of them without metrical fault in *Α* 31, 43, 134, 159, 198, 457, *Β* 15, 32, 69, 689, etc., in α 94, 281, 317, β 3, 136, 215, 261, 264, 268, 300, 351, 360, 400, 401, etc.; and the second in *Β* 151, etc., in β 80, 97, etc. Clearly, not only the memory of particular formulae, but also the sense of the device which embodies them itself, helped determine those lines in which the final syllables of participles in -όμενος, etc., is short before the penthemimeral caesura. The expression θυμοῦ δευόμενον· ὁ δέ . . . in *Υ* 472 was inspired by such particular formulae as θυμοῦ δευομένους· ἀπὸ γάρ . . . in *Γ* 294; but it was also inspired by the general sense of the device which we observe in them both. Hence we can be certain that χείρ' ἐπιμασσάμενος· ἕτερος δέ . . . in ι 302 was as much determined by the existence of this device as by the memory of a line like τ 480 where this device has no part: χείρ' ἐπιμασσάμενος φάρυγος λάβε; and that ᾤχετ' ἀποπτάμενος, ἐμὲ δέ . . . (*Β* 71) is a result of this device, even though ἀποπτάμενος appears nowhere else in Homer before the penthemimeral caesura.

There can be found in Homer many other devices which we may regard as the cause of metrical irregularities in cases where the particular formulary model is missing. Of the 104 cases cited by Knös of the hiatus of a short vowel before the trochaic caesura, the caesura is 7 times preceded by ἔπειτα, 10 times by the accusative case of the proper name of a hero (*Πελάγοντα*, Ἀχιλῆα, Ὀδυσῆα, etc.), and 21 times by the middle form of a verb in the third person singular of a past tense (καθῆστο, ἕποντο, ἔφαντο, σεύαιτο, etc.); a complete investigation would reveal that the occurrence of these forms in this part of the line results from the sense of a number of fixed devices used in the composition of the hexameter. Again, of the 61 cases listed by Knös of the hiatus of a short vowel before the bucolic diaeresis, 21 show the diaeresis preceded by a verb in -ετο, -ατο, -υτο, -ιτο. The cause of this phenomenon is not only the poet's memory of a number of particular formulae, but also the existence in epic diction of traditional ways of composing heroic lines by putting verb-forms with these endings before the bucolic diaeresis (cf. TE, pp. 40 ff. above).| A similar phenomenon is that of the 13 cases of a short vowel in hiatus at the end of the first foot, we twice find ἔπλετο (*O* 227, *ο* 327) and once ἕσπετο (*N* 300) ending a sentence or a clause begun in the preceding line.

We shall not here attempt to describe these various devices. The time required would be immense, and it would always remain true that we could at best find a proof of general character of the cause of the hiatus of short vowels and the irrational lengthening of short syllables; and that even if in this way we approached the conclusion that all such metrical irregularities are the product of the operation of analogy, we could never hope finally to reach this conclusion. There would always be cases like κυνάμυια ἄγει (*Φ* 421), ἰσχία ἀμφοτέρωθεν (*Υ* 170), ἡνία ἠίχθησαν (*Π* 404), ἕρκεα ἴσχει (*E* 90), δόλον κατὰ εἴδατα βάλλων (*μ* 252), etc., cases in which the degree of uncertainty attaching to the formulary nature of the expressions forbids us to draw conclusions about the cause of the hiatus. There are examples of lengthened short syllables of which the same must be said: πλεῖον ἐλέλειπτο (*θ* 475), θαμέες ἔχον (*K* 264), γαμβρὸς ἢ πενθερός (*θ* 582), ἐυπλεκέες, ἑκατόμβοιος (*B* 449), etc.

In our earlier book (TE, pp. 103 ff. above), we were more than once led to make the observation which we must now make again concerning the formulary element in the Homeric poems: as one proceeds from the sure ground of expressions whose frequency is a demonstration of their formulary character, and often of their traditional character as well, one inevitably arrives at a point where all the expressions appear to be formulae, but no one of them is incontrovertibly a formula. This is a consequence of the shortness of the *Iliad* and *Odyssey*. What we know of the formulary diction of heroic poetry we know because of the number of lines in the two Homeric poems which provide us with sufficiently numerous repetitions of formulae and formula types; what we do not know is hidden from us by the fact that such lines are not more numerous than they are. The essential ideas of Homer are very likely not, because they are traditional (let us suppose for the moment that they are all without exception traditional), less varied in themselves | than those of an author whose style is individual; and the expressions and combinations of expressions by which he states these ideas are of a like order of complexity. Consequently we must renounce the thought of a complete analysis of Homeric diction. We can say that a large portion of this diction is traditional and formulary, and that all of it may well be. In the present state of our knowledge a more categoric conclusion is denied us.

[43–4]

IV

THE STRUCTURE OF THE FORMULA

STILL other reasons beyond the limitations imposed on the analysis of formulary diction prevent us from explaining in terms of the functioning of that diction all the examples we find of the two irregularities which are the object of this study. In a number of cases, it is certain that the irregularity—if it is one—forms an integral part of traditional diction, since it exists within a group of words whose fixed pattern and constant use shows it to be a formula, so that an explanation from the modification of a formula correct in itself, or from the juxtaposition of two formulae, is thereby excluded. These cases are with certainty to be explained as the results of the survival of older forms of speech: rather than give up formulae which had become incorrect by reason of changes in the spoken language, changes which were reflected in the language of epic poetry, the bards preferred to keep them even though they did violence to the rhythm.

We said 'irregularity—if it is one'. The cases in question consist for the most part of formulae containing an initial or medial digamma, and we cannot affirm categorically that the sound represented by this letter was or was not pronounced by the poet or poets of the *Iliad* and the *Odyssey.* If it was pronounced, there was no metrical irregularity and therefore we need not discuss these cases here. But if this consonant was not pronounced by Homer, we must ask which causes, within the history of formulary diction, led the singers to tolerate metrical faults which would otherwise not have existed. Hence in this chapter we leave the solid terrain of | the use of formulae to enter on a problem in which hypothesis will necessarily play a large part.

The cases in Homer in which the loss of an original digamma is most clearly indicated are those involving a postpositive ὥς in the sense of 'as'.

In our texts of the *Iliad* and the *Odyssey*, this word is preceded by a *brevis in longo* in the following examples:[1] *κακὸς ὥς* (*Z* 443), *κακὸν ὥς* (*B* 190, *O* 196), *θεὸς ὥς* (*Γ* 230, *Λ* 58, *ξ* 205), *θεὸν ὥς* (*I* 155, 297, 302, *M* 176, *X* 434, *ε* 36, *η* 71, *θ* 173, *τ* 280, *ψ* 339), *μόλιβος ὥς* (*Λ* 237), *φυτὸν ὥς* (*Σ* 57, 438), *κύνες ὥς* (*E* 476), *σύες ὥς* (*λ* 413), *συὸς ὥς* (*σ* 29), *πάις ὥς* (*δ* 32), *πέλεκυς ὥς* (*Γ* 60), *ἀθάνατος ὥς* (*ζ* 309), *αἴγειρος ὥς* (*Δ* 482), *αἰγυπιὸς ὥς* (*N* 531), *ἠέλιος ὥς* (*Ξ* 185, *τ* 234), *ἠέλιον ὥς* (*σ* 296), *νηπύτιον ὥς* (*Y* 200,

[1] The following list is from Knös, *De digammo homerico*, 167.

431), τηλύγετον ὥς (*N* 470), βόες ὥς (*Λ* 172), ὄρνιθες ὥς (*Γ* 2), ὄρνιθας ὥς (*B* 764).

In a single case, there is a short syllable in hiatus before this word: παῖδα δὲ ὥς (σ 323). And in six cases there are long vowels in hiatus: Διὶ ὥς (*B* 781), μελίῃ ὥς (*N* 178), λύκοι ὥς (*Δ* 471, *Λ* 72, *Π* 156), νηπύτιοι ὥς (*N* 292, *Y* 244).

On the other hand, postpositive ὥς does not make position in *Γ* 196, *Θ* 94, *N* 137, χ 299. And it permits the elision of a preceding word in the following cases: θεὸς δ' ὥς (*E* 78, *K* 33, *N* 218, *Π* 605), ἀστὴρ δ' ὥς (*Z* 295, ο 108), ὄλμον δ' ὥς (*Λ* 147), λέονθ' ὥς (*Λ* 383, *M* 293, *Π* 756), νιφάδες δ' ὥς (*M* 156), λέων δ' ὥς (*Ω* 41), ὄρνις δ' ὥς (α 320), πατὴρ δ' ὥς (β 47, 234, ε 12), θεοῦ δ' ὥς (η 11), ἰχθῦς δ' ὥς (κ 124), βοῶν δ' ὥς (μ 396).

According to the generally accepted etymology, postpositive ὥς derives from an Indo-European *s̯u̯ō attested by the Old High German *sō* 'thus', the Gothic *swē* 'as', and the Oscan *svaí* 'so' (cf. Boisacq, *Dictionnaire étymologique*, 1084); it then became *'ϝως before becoming ὥς. The form *'ϝως gives us the initial consonant necessary to make the final short syllables in the cases listed long by position. Let us note here that the distribution of cases falling into the two categories | rules out any possibility of assigning the earlier or the later form of the word to definite portions of the poems which thereby might be considered relatively early or late:

1. 'ϝως	2. ὥς
B 190, 764, 781 *Γ* 2, 60 *Γ* 230 *Δ* 471, 482 *E* 476	*Γ* 196 *E* 78
Z 443 *I* 155, 297, 302 *Λ* 58, 72 *Λ* 172, 237	*Z* 295 *Θ* 94 *K* 33 *Λ* 147
M 176 *N* 178 *N* 292, 470, 531	*Λ* 383 *M* 156 *M* 293 *N* 137 *N* 218
Ξ 185 *O* 196 *Π* 156 *Σ* 57, 438 *Y* 200, 244, 431	*Π* 605, 756
X 434 δ 32 ε 36 ζ 309 η 71 θ 173	*Ω* 41 α 320 β 47, 234 ε 12 η 11
λ 413 ξ 205 σ 29, 234, 296, 323 τ 280 ψ 339	κ 124 μ 396 ο 108 χ 299

Of what advantage can it be to us in our investigation to know that at a certain period the word ὥς had an initial consonant, seeing that there is in Homer a large number of cases in which it clearly cannot have one? There are two explanations to cover these two ways of using the word. The first supposes that the cases of *brevis in longo* and of hiatus, such as we observe them, were the work of the poet (or poets) of the *Iliad* and the *Odyssey*. According to the other explanation, these irregularities are such only in appearance, being due not to Homer but to those who transmitted the text of the poems. But in reality, as we shall see, both explanations bear witness to the same set of facts in the history of epic diction. Let us examine them in turn.

When the spoken language changed and the initial consonant of *ὥς* was lost, the bards were faced with the choice of either abandoning a number of traditional expressions which had now become metrically incorrect, or continuing to use them despite their faultiness. In several cases they took the second | alternative, partly out of mere habit, but mostly out of the desire to keep a convenient and traditional way of expressing certain essential ideas in certain portions of the hexameter line. The nature and the force of this desire will appear by a consideration of the lines containing the expressions *θεὸς ὥς*, *θεὸν ὥς* which we find 7 times in the *Iliad* and 6 times in the *Odyssey*, always with the measure ⏑ – –.

These expressions come 7 times before the bucolic diaeresis, where they are followed by a form of the verb *τιμάω* or of its synonym *τίω*:

1. *I* 155		κέ	ἑ	δωτίνῃσι		
2. *I* 297	οἵ		σε			τιμήσουσι
3. ε 36		κέν			θεὸν ὣς	
4. τ 280	οἳ δή			μιν περὶ κῆρι		
5. ψ 339						τιμήσαντο
6. *Λ* 58	Αἰνείαν θ', ὃς Τρωσὶ			θεὸς ὣς τίετο δήμωι.		
7. ξ 205	ὃς τότ' ἐνὶ Κρήτεσσι					

The portions of these 7 lines which follow the trochaic caesura bear a striking resemblance to each other. There is no more than a difference of ending between the final hemistichs of 1, 2, and 3 and those of 4 and 5, while the resemblance of 6 and 7 to the others becomes clearer as soon as we realize that the word *δήμωι*, in them both, adds nothing to the sense, since *Τρωσί* and *Κρήτεσσι* have already shown by whom it is that the heroes in question are honoured, and there can be no thought of a distinction between nobles and people. The adjunction of *δήμωι* serves only to amplify the nobility of the style, and is occasioned only by the need to complete the rhythm of the line. The use of this word is comparable to that of *δουρὶ φαεινῶι*, the adoption or omission of which after *ἀκόντισε* depends on whether the poet wants to end his sentence at the bucolic diaeresis or at the end of the line.[1] Because *θεὸν ὥς* can fit in before the bucolic diaeresis, the bards disposed of a device which, by a simple variation of ending, allowed them to express the ideas 'they will honour

[1] On this device, cf. TE, p. 43 above.

him as a god' and 'they honoured him as a god', and which, by the substitution of the nominative -ς for the accusative -ν and the adjunction of δήμωι, allowed them to express the idea 'he was honoured as a god'. We have here a typical device of formulary diction: | a single essential idea is expressed with differences of tense, voice, mood, and person by a set of expressions which differ among themselves only by variations of ending and the presence or lack of one or two inessential words. It is all the product of analogy: one expression suggested another, and the whole series created in this way, being easily learned by each new generation of bards because of the clear resemblance of the members of the series to each other, was kept.

But that θεὸς ὥς and θεὸν ὥς are thus able to fit into the line before the bucolic diaeresis is not the only advantage of this group of similar expressions. Formulary diction can be likened to a net of which each mesh is a single formulary expression: the form of each mesh will be adapted to that of the meshes surrounding it. Thus with but one exception, the forms τιμήσουσι (4 times), τιμήσαντο (twice), τιμήσασθαι, τιμήεντα, τιμήεντος, occur after the bucolic diaeresis, as do likewise, without exception, εἰσορόωντα (7 times), εἰσορόωντας (thrice), εἰσορόωντι (twice), εἰσορόωντο, εἰσορόωσαι (twice), εἰσορόωσα (twice), εἰσορόωσι(ν) (5 times), εἰσοράασθαι (6 times), εἰσοράασθε, εἰσορόωσαν, εἰσοροώσηι. There can be no question here of investigating the various usages in versification of a verb occurring after the bucolic diaeresis. Such an investigation would be very long, and would demand as well a preliminary knowledge of the methods of analysis of formulary diction and an understanding of the limitations of such analysis. Let us merely set forth instead the frequency with which the two verbs in question occur after the bucolic diaeresis, since it is this phenomenon which makes θεὸν ὥς so useful before the bucolic diaeresis. The latter expression can be followed by any of the forms of εἰσοράω already listed to express the essential idea 'honour as a god' in moods and tenses which the verbs τιμάω and τίω alone would not allow. Thus we find:

η 71 καὶ λαῶν οἵ μίν ῥα θεὸν ὣς εἰσορόωντες
θ 173 ἐρχόμενον δ' ἀνὰ ἄστυ θεὸν ὣς εἰσορόωσιν
Cf. *M* 312 ἐν Λυκίηι, πάντες δὲ θεοὺς ὣς εἰσορόωσι.

The present forms of τιμάω and τίω (τιμῶσι, τιμῶντες, τίουσι, τίοντες) do not allow the use in the present tense of the device which they make possible in the past and future. |

Let us now leave aside the composition of these formulae and consider what help they give in their complete form to the versifying poet. In the nine lines quoted, the idea 'honour (or honoured) as a god' is expressed by groups of words which extend from the trochaic caesura to the end of the line and begin with a single consonant. We had occasion to show in

TE (pp. 10 ff.) above that because of their relation to the trochaic caesura, formulae of this metrical value have an exceedingly important role in versification. In a great many cases the bard has at his disposal two sentences which can express a third idea by the joining of the first part of one to the second part of the other. Thus the sentence AB and the sentence XY can furnish the materials for the sentences AY and XB. But this exchange can only take place on condition that A is metrically equivalent to X, and B to Y. Moreover it will be advantageous, or even necessary, that A and X end, and B and Y begin, at one of the breaks in the line. For most of the time there will be a pause, more or less marked, between the two parts of a sentence which can thus be separated and rejoined. In the work just referred to we set forth many cases of this device (TE, pp. 10 ff. above). For example:

AB	*ο* 340	τὸν δ' ἠμείβετ' ἔπειτα πολύτλας δῖος Ὀδυσσεύς
XY	*ε* 94	αὐτὰρ ὁ πῖνε καὶ ἦσθε διάκτορος Ἀργειφόντης
AY	*θ* 338	τὸν δ' ἠμείβετ' ἔπειτα διάκτορος Ἀργειφόντης
XB	*ζ* 249	ἦ τοι ὁ πῖνε καὶ ἦσθε πολύτλας δῖος Ὀδυσσεύς
AB	*E* 426 = *O* 47	ὣς φάτο, μείδησεν δὲ πατὴρ ἀνδρῶν τε θεῶν τε
XY	*E* 420	τοῖσι δὲ μύθων ἦρχε θεὰ γλαυκῶπις Ἀθήνη
AY	*ν* 287	ὣς φάτο, μείδησεν δὲ θεὰ γλαυκῶπις Ἀθήνη
XB	*X* 167 = *α* 28	τοῖσι δὲ μύθων ἦρχε πατὴρ ἀνδρῶν τε θεῶν τε.

One should not expect to find the device of interchange as clearly demonstrated in the case of the hemistichs θεὸν ὣς τιμήσουσι etc. as in the case of the hemistichs of the lines quoted above. In the latter case, the device is as evident as it is because the sentences thus formed are of the simplest kind, expressing ideas which recur with great frequency in heroic poetry. | None the less, we do have enough evidence to show us how useful the expressions θεὸν ὣς τιμήσουσι etc. are to the poet. We find, for example, more than a slight resemblance between the first parts of the following lines:

N 206 καὶ τότε δὴ περὶ κῆρι Ποσειδάων ἐχολώθη
Ω 61 Πηλέι, ὃς περὶ κῆρι φίλος γένετ' ἀθανάτοισι
ζ 158 κεῖνος δ' αὖ περὶ κῆρι μακάρτατος ἔξοχον ἄλλων
η 69 ὣς κείνη περὶ κῆρι τετίμηταί τε καὶ ἔστιν.

The poet was able to make three of the lines quoted earlier by joining a hemistich modelled on the type of those which begin these lines to a hemistich of the series we have been discussing:

τ 280 = *ψ* 339 οἵ δή } μιν περὶ κῆρι θεὸν ὣς { τιμήσαντο
ε 36 οἵ κέν } μιν περὶ κῆρι θεὸν ὣς { τιμήσουσι.

To understand fully how great a resource of versification this device of interchangeable hemistichs is for the poet, one has only to continue on one's own the process of interchange with τιμήσαντο, and τιμήσουσι, and to see how easy this device is to carry out. And in composing lines in this way, one can be sure that one is faithfully reproducing Homer's own process of versification. There is nothing in the *Iliad* and *Odyssey* to indicate that the poet ever refrained from this interchange of formulae, nothing to indicate that he ever replaced them by words of his own finding, as long as he was able to use the old words to express his thought. Thus we could, for example, make the following:

καὶ {τότε / νῦν} δὴ περὶ κῆρι θεὸν ὣς {τιμήσαντο / τιμήσουσιν / εἰσορόωσιν / εἰσορόωντες}

Πηλέι, ὃν περὶ κῆρι θεὸν ὣς {τιμήσαντο / τιμήσουσιν / εἰσορόωσιν / εἰσορόωντες.}

The game is too easy to need to be continued here. But it is precisely its ease for us which shows how convenient for the poet was the metrical value of the formula series θεὸν ὣς τιμήσαντο etc. | And be it noted that this convenience is not limited to the series of hemistichs falling before the trochaic caesura which we have just discussed. The demonstration could be continued by means of hemistichs of other lines in which θεὸν ὣς falls before the bucolic diaeresis. Thus the first part of the line θ 173

ἐρχόμενον δ' ἀνὰ ἄστυ θεὸν ὣς εἰσορόωσιν

belongs to the formula series contained in the following lines:

η 40 ἐρχόμενον κατὰ ἄστυ διὰ σφέας· οὐ γὰρ Ἀθήνη
π 170 ἔρχησθον προτὶ ἄστυ περικλυτόν· οὐδ' ἐγὼ αὐτή

and so on.

Now that we have seen, first, how θεὸν ὣς before the bucolic diaeresis combines with certain verb-forms which extend from that caesura to the end of the line, and second, how formulae composed in this manner are joined to other hemistichs falling before the trochaic caesura, we know how much the traditional diction would have been disturbed if the poets had had to give up θεὸν ὣς scanned ⏑ – – after the initial consonant of ὣς had been lost. There is no way of arranging otherwise, in the same portion of the line, words expressing the idea 'they honoured him as a god' so as to avoid any metrical fault. The poets would have had to renounce the whole idea so nobly conceived, and conceived in words so intimately and so naturally tied to other words and other expressions in formulary diction. It was by necessity, therefore, that they accepted here the presence of a short syllable where the rhythm demanded a long. Nor can it be claimed that we are misusing the word 'necessity', in that it is after all just possible to arrange in some other fashion, in the hexameter line, the idea 'they honoured him as a god'. He who would urge such an objection must make an expression of the same brevity, adapting itself with the same ease, by interior modifications, to differences of tense, mood, voice, and person, and showing the same natural ability to join with other words in the hexameter with which it would be associated. It can be stated without hesitation that there is no one of this time capable of creating such an expression. | The modern reader must here fully recognize his own powerlessness. And by our own utter inability to replace a single device of epic diction, we can form some estimate of the quality of a diction which is nothing more than the complete set of such devices.

The necessity confronting the bards either to allow a metrical fault or else to renounce a device entirely can be just as clearly observed in the use of *θεὸν ὥς* at the end of the line. Odysseus, in the embassy scene, says to Achilles:

I 301 *σὺ δ' ἄλλους περ Παναχαιούς*
τειρομένους ἐλέαιρε κατὰ στρατόν, οἵ σε θεὸν ὥς
τείσουσ'· ἦ γάρ κέ σφι μάλα μέγα κῦδος ἄροιο.

Hecuba speaks to her dead son from the walls of Troy:

X 432 *ὅ μοι νύκτας τε καὶ ἦμαρ*
εὐχωλὴ κατὰ ἄστυ πελέσκεο, πᾶσί τ' ὄνειαρ
Τρωσί τε καὶ Τρωιῇσι κατὰ πτόλιν, οἵ σε θεὸν ὥς
δειδέχατ'· ἦ γάρ κέ σφι μάλα μέγα κῦδος ἔησθα
ζωὸς ἐών.

As soon as one understands that *δειδέχατ'* is from the point of view of meaning only the equivalent of *τιμήσαντο*, exactly like *εἰσορόωσιν*—since *τιμήσαντο* cannot be used here—one realizes that in both cases the poet is making use of an identical device: he has a fixed way of expressing, between the bucolic diaeresis and the end of the following line, the idea 'who will honour (*or* honoured) you because you would give them (*or* gave them) great glory'.

In the first passage, the modification of the idea by the substitution of *κε* for *καί* and of *ἄροιο* for *ἔησθα* is typical of the way in which the bards modify a formula in order to adapt it to the nuances of the idea. There is no need to stress the fact that this device too would have had to be abandoned if the bards had wished to avoid the final *brevis in longo*: no other disposition of the words falling after the bucolic diaeresis is possible. Thus there was a twofold reason for keeping *θεὸν ὥς*.

Equally clear, in the three lines in which it appears, is the device containing the expression ἠέλιος ὥς, ἠέλιον ὥς. In *Ξ* 185 it is used of the veil behind which Hera hides her countenance,

καλῶι νηγατέωι· λευκὸν δ' ἦν ἠέλιος ὥς, |

in *σ* 296 it is used of a necklace,

χρύσεον, ἠλέκτροισιν ἐερμένον, ἠέλιον ὥς,

and in *τ* 234 of a chiton,

τὼς μὲν ἔην μαλακός, λαμπρὸς δ' ἦν ἠέλιος ὥς.

The bard, knowing that he could express the idea 'like the sun' between the bucolic diaeresis and the end of the line, ends his description with the fourth foot and completes the line with the formula in question. In the expressions λευκὸν δ' ἦν, λαμπρὸς δ' ἦν, of the first and the third of the lines cited, we find another fixed device: the technique of formulary diction, which we have described as the union of formulae of which each has its fixed place or places in the line, can be described from another point of view as a technique of making at the same time a sentence and a line. It goes without saying that the device to which we have just called attention would also have to be abandoned if the loss of the initial consonant of ὥς were to be taken into account.

There is no profit in studying at any greater length the various devices which make use of expressions wherein ὥς follows a *brevis in longo*. In the first place, both the methods of investigation and the conclusions would be the same as in the previous cases, and in the second place, where there are expressions appearing once only in our texts, the device is much harder to establish: the success of such analysis of diction depends necessarily on a certain abundance of analogous usages. But let us note that, for the validity of our conclusions, it is not necessary to know that every formula implying the existence, at some point, of ‛ϝως is traditional. A bard may well have created, on the model of θεὸς ὥς or of some other formula, a new expression containing this metrical fault now consecrated by custom. But the irregularity must have had its origin in the survival of the formula as we have described it.

The other possible explanation of the use of postpositive would be to suppose that the initial ϝ had survived in the pronunciation of the poets in the same way as the | initial consonant of σῦς; so that they said sometimes ‛ϝώς and sometimes ὥς, just as they sometimes said σῦς and sometimes ὗς. It is obvious that this explanation is by nature susceptible neither of proof nor of refutation; for that, we should need epigraphic evidence which does not exist. But the truth of this theory would in no way change our conclusions on the survival of the formula. In one case this survival would have caused a metrical fault, in the other it would have ensured the preservation, in the language of the poets, of a form which had disappeared in common speech.

This hypothesis of the presence in Homer of a form ʽϝώς brings us naturally to other cases in which hiatus or *breves in longo* are explained by the presence or by the loss of an initial digamma or an initial consonant group δϝ-, as in δήν, δεινός, δέος, δείσας, etc.[1] The problem is not quite the same for ὥς as for other words with initial or postinitial digamma, because in the case of the latter the omission of the consonant is not frequent enough to make it certain that Homer knew a form of the word without the initial consonant.[2] There are three different ways of explaining the use of words which bear the trace of an initial or postinitial digamma: (1) The digamma was pronounced by the poet and the nature of its sound was such that he could lengthen a naturally short syllable where a long was needed, | or could leave short a syllable short by nature where a short syllable was needed (so Hartel, *Homerische Studien*, iii. 70 ff.; Solmsen, *Untersuchungen zur griechischen Laut- und Verslehre*, 129 ff.). (2) In the language of the poets, the digamma survived, and was pronounced or omitted from pronunciation like the initial σ of σῦς or the τ of πτόλις, as the needs of verse-making required. (3) The digamma had entirely disappeared from the poetic language at the time when the *Iliad* and the *Odyssey* were composed, and its seeming survival is due to the fact that the poets, if they were to repair the metrical faults resulting from this disappearance, would have had to revise drastically their whole formulary diction, or even give it up altogether. This necessity which forced the bards either to give up the formula θεὸν ὣς τιμήσουσι or to tolerate a metrical irregularity arose, according to this mode of explanation, whenever a formula contained a word which had once begun with a digamma. Now the problem of the digamma in fact demands an investigation which will begin from a full knowledge of formulary technique, and will follow the method which we have here used for the formula in question. The investigation should also be carried out for the

[1] There is no need to treat words beginning with δϝ separately from words beginning with ϝ, because from the point of view of metre we have the same problem in μάλα δήν (thrice) as in πυκινὸν ἔπος (4 times): the position of the consonant has no effect on the lengthening of the syllable. The spellings περιδδείσασα (*Φ* 328), περίδδεισαν (*Λ* 508), etc. in ASMΩ do not put an end to our indecision since they may well be the invention of a scribe who corrected περιδείσασα to make it metrically right but did not dare to write τε δδείσῃ in *Ω* 116. Equally possible, Homer may have pronounced περιδδείσασα, the bards of his time having devised this artificial pronunciation to repair the metrical fault occasioned by the loss of ϝ. They may have hesitated to pronounce μάλα δδήν for the same reason that the scribe would have hesitated to write it. If the δ were pronounced double, the case would be analogous to the double pronunciation of the liquids μ, ν, λ, ρ (see below, p. 232).

[2] Phonetic reasons as well suggest that the aspirate digamma was lost before other initial digammas.

Homeric Hymns, all of which show traces of the digamma even though some of them can be assigned to a fairly late date,[1] and it should lead to some affirmative conclusions, to judge by the results of this essay as well as those of *The Traditional Epithet in Homer*. But these conclusions, however clear they may be, will always be limited in their scope. We shall at best be able to demonstrate a possibility. We shall be able to prove that the suppression of the digamma does not justify the condemnation of an expression, and we shall have demolished the solid basis on which those editors relied who wished to reintroduce the digamma into | the text of the *Iliad* and the *Odyssey*. But we shall not have proved that Homer did not pronounce this consonant, because the two alternative explanations will be as available as they were before. As we said above, only epigraphical evidence could give us a certain solution to the problem. Meanwhile, anyone who chooses one of three hypotheses as the ground of his conclusions, will inevitably have to concede the uncertainty of his hypothesis.

It is, then, impossible to know whether those words which at one time had an initial digamma are true examples of hiatus and of *breves in longis* which in turn, as it has been suggested, served as models for other cases in which the digamma played no part. It is an hypothesis incapable of either proof or refutation, based on another hypothesis of the same order. But since we are working here in a domain where we can only match one hypothesis against another, we can reasonably suppose that the bards would have more easily tolerated those irregularities which were consecrated by their traditional usage (FM, p. 234). It is conceivable that the bards developed for those words which had lost an initial digamma a feeling analogous to that of the French for the 'aspirate' *h*, a feeling maintained by the Ionians of Archilochus' time for the original initial consonant of *οἱ* (Arch. 29. 2 δέ οἱ, Simonides 7. 79, cf. Bechtel, *Griechische Dialekte*, iii. 39). Such a feeling may have led the bards to make a sharp distinction between irregularities involving a lost digamma and those in which this sound played no part; an irregularity of the first kind may have seemed to them entirely acceptable from the point of view of rhythm.

[1] Hartel, in his *Homerische Studien*, finds in Homer 3,354 observances of the digamma against 617 negligences, a proportion of 5·4 : 1. For the *Hymns*, Allen, Halliday, and Sikes, *The Homeric Hymns* (Oxford 1936), give (p. cii) the following figures:

	Observances	Neglects
Demeter	47	35 = 1·342 : 1
Apollo	69	34 = 2 : 1 approx.
Hermes	27	49 = 0·55 : 1
Aphrod.	46	24 = 1·9 : 1
Dion. vii	9	4 = 2·25 : 1
Pan xix	2	5 = 0·4 : 1
Minor Hymns	20	17 = 1·175 : 1

[corrected reference.—Ed.]

Moreover, to return to the methodology outlined at the beginning of this study, the existence of such models cannot be considered a cause: it could only be one of the factors which allowed the poet to maintain in the lines he sang the irregularity which the true causes led him to commit in the first place.

The lengthening of final short syllables before the liquid consonants ῥ, λ, μ, ν, does not properly enter into the frame of this essay, since it is clear, both from their nature and from the way in which the poet makes use of words beginning with them, | that we are dealing here with a device used generally to make syllables long by position. None the less, there will be some profit in touching briefly on the origin of this lengthening, since it involves the survival of formulae, and especially since scholarship is agreed in recognizing this survival.

It has been possible to establish with certainty that in a large number of cases words beginning with one of the consonants ῥ, λ, μ, ν, once began with two consonants. Thus ῥήξειν (*M* 198 τεῖχός τε ῥήξειν) derives from a root *ϝρηγ-; ῥέω (*Σ* 402 περὶ δὲ ῥόος) from σρεϝ ; ῥινῶν (*T* 39 στάξε κατὰ ῥινῶν) from σριν-; νιφόεντι (*N* 754 ὄρει νιφόεντι) from σνιφ-; νυοί (*Ω* 166 ἰδὲ νυοί) from σνυ-; μοῖραν (*Π* 367 οὐδὲ κατὰ μοῖραν) from σμοιρ-; νευρῇι (*Δ* 118 αἶψα δ' ἐπὶ νευρῇι) from σνευρ-; etc.[1] 'It is not indeed necessary to maintain that in these cases the lost consonant was pronounced at the time when the Homeric poems were composed. We have only to suppose that the *particular combination* in question had established itself in the usage of the language before the two consonants were reduced by phonetic decay to one . . . the habit of lengthening before initial liquids was extended by analogy, from the stems in which it was originally due to a double consonant to others in which it had no such etymological ground.'[2] Such are: εἶδε νέφος (*Δ* 275), ἴδε δὲ νεφεληγερέτα Ζεύς (*Ξ* 293), ἡ δὲ μέγαν (*Γ* 125), ἐνὶ μεγάροισι (*Ω* 497), etc.

This study would not be complete without a few words on the formula πότνια Ἥρη which appears 24 times in Homer. Both Hoffman and Knös, embarrassed by the frequency of this formula, were unwilling to include it in their lists of *hiatus illiciti qui vocantur*, where in fact it would have stood out in contrast with expressions which appear but once or twice in the poems. And yet there was no ground for making such an exception. Hoffman (*Quaest. Hom.* i. 93) observes that the expression always comes at the end of the line, and adds, with the approval of Knös (*De Dig.* | *Hom.* 180) that the expression 'came to Homer from older poetry'. The correctness of the first of these observations is beyond dispute, and we have every reason to believe the second; but to see them as causes would

[1] Meillet et Vendryes, *Traité de grammaire comparé*, Paris 1924, 50 ff.

[2] Monro, *Homeric Grammar*², 345.

be wrong. To do so, one would have to argue that an expression with a fixed position in the line produces hiatus by this very fact, and that earlier poetry (Hoffman must mean the earlier form of the Homeric line) allowed this irregularity more freely. But these two hypotheses are groundless.

There are two ways only of explaining the hiatus in the expression *πότνια Ἥρη*. The first is that the formula was created when the name of the goddess began with a consonant, the former existence of which is indicated by the aspiration.

The other explanation is that the poets were compelled by their technique of versification to find a noun–epithet formula for Hera in the nominative case, capable of being used after the bucolic diaeresis, and beginning with a single consonant; and that they were unable to find an epithet metrically more satisfactory than *πότνια*. It is clear that *Ἥρη* must come at the end of this portion of the line. The task then is to find an epithet suitable in meaning, able to be used ornamentally, with the measure – ⏑ ⏑, beginning with a single consonant, and ending with *-ος* or *-ις*. These conditions are not easily met, and it would not be surprising if the bards found themselves unable to do so.[1] Given the actual state of our knowledge of the etymology of *Ἥρη*, one of these explanations is as good as the other. What they both together imply, however—and for the purposes of this study this is the important point—is that the formula *πότνια Ἥρη* was traditional and not the creation of Homer, and that therefore this poet is not responsible for the hiatus within the formula. And in fact we have indubitable proofs of the traditional character of the formula *πότνια Ἥρη*. One of the principal problems discussed in *The Traditional Epithet in Homer* is precisely that of proving the traditional character of noun–epithet formulae; and we demonstrated that in order to do this, one must establish systems of formulae of a given type which are of wide extension and which entirely exclude any element superfluous from the point of view of versification: i.e. any element equivalent to another in both sense and metre. We established a system of this kind for noun–epithet | formulae of gods and heroes which exactly fill the space between a caesura and the beginning or end of the line, and in the Table in which this system is presented (TE, p. 39 above) occurs the formula *πότνια Ἥρη*. It has on the one hand the same metrical value as eight other noun–epithet formulae which we find used for the ten other gods and heroes whose names appear in the Table: *δῖος Ὀδυσσεύς, Παλλὰς Ἀθήνη, Φοῖβος Ἀπόλλων, δῖος Ἀχιλλεύς, μητίετα Ζεύς, φαίδιμος Ἕκτωρ, χάλκεος Ἄρης, Τυδέος υἱός*; on the other hand it is never replaced in the Homeric

[1] Cf. in TE, (pp. 188–9 above) a similar case where the poets were obliged to use the formula *περίφρων Πηνελόπεια* although this expression involved the use of a long closed syllable before the bucolic diaeresis.

poems by another noun–epithet formula of the same metrical value. Thus it is an integral part of a system of formulae of too wide an extension and too rigorous an economy to be the work of a single poet.

Finally, let us observe that by a happy coincidence, the expression *πότνια Ἥρη* gives us a perfect example of how, once a metrical irregularity becomes a part of the poetic diction, and once the poets become accustomed to hearing it, it ceases to be observed by them altogether. One of the rare cases of formulae equivalent in both sense and metre which appear more than once or twice is that of *βοῶπις πότνια Ἥρη* (11 times) ∼ *θεὰ λευκώλενος Ἥρη* (19 times).[1] The use of the second of these formulae would have avoided the hiatus contained in the first. But we find the two formulae used with an alternation which rules out the preference of a single poet, and which shows that the poet (or poets) of the *Iliad* and the *Odyssey* found each of these expressions as correct as the other. This is for us a precious indication, proving that we must consider those metrical irregularities in Homer which were consecrated by the tradition in an entirely different way from those which we might encounter in the work of a later poet whose style is free from the traditional.

[1] Cf. TE, (p. 182 above).

V

CONCLUSIONS

THE study which we have made of the relation between the formulary character of bardic diction and the presence of short syllables in hiatus and of lengthened final short syllables in Homer, has revealed three facts which dissuade us from correcting the received text of the *Iliad* and the *Odyssey* in order to remove these metrical irregularities. (1) The so-called illegitimate cases of hiatus of short syllables, those that do not occur before one of the breaks in the hexameter line, result from the same causes as those which have been termed legitimate. (2) The hiatus of short syllables and also—we can say it without having recourse to another demonstration—that of long syllables, results from the same causes as do lengthened final short syllables. (3) The conditions of versification having been different for a bard in a traditional style from what they were or are for a poet with an individual style, we have no right to apply the same canons of criticism to them both.

I. We found a number of cases in which an 'illegitimate' hiatus of a short syllable results from a modification in the body of a formula: *ἄφθιτα αἰεί, τετελεσμένα ἦεν, ἐπὶ Ἕκτορι*, etc., and again we found 'legitimate' cases of short syllables in hiatus resulting from the same cause: *ἔγχεα ὀξυόεντα, πελάσσατε ὅπλα τε πάντα, ἐρύσσατε ἤπειρόνδε*, etc. We found cases in which the juxtaposition of two formulae brought about 'legitimate' hiatus: *ἐνέμοντο Ἀραιθυρέην, κατὰ φρένα ὡς Ἀχιλῆα, βάσκ' ἴθι, οὖλε ὄνειρε*, etc.; and likewise we found cases where juxtaposition caused 'illegitimate' hiatus: *Ζεὺς δὲ ἑὸν πρὸς δῶμα, γυναῖκα ἄγεσθαι, πώεα οἰῶν*, etc. And with this recognition of common causes disappears any reason to make a distinction between different kinds of hiatus: either all cases of short syllables in hiatus | should be expunged from the text, or else the fact that a short syllable is in hiatus elsewhere than before a metrical break is no indication that the expression in which it occurs is not Homeric.

But more important, perhaps, than the discovery that the causes are the same for both kinds of metrical irregularity is that we learn why the 'illegitimate' cases of a short syllable in hiatus are less frequent than others; it is precisely this relative infrequency which has aroused scholarly suspicion. We have been able to point out the reasons of this infrequency, viz., that the temptation to join two formulae arose most often with those formulae which fall between two breaks in the line, or between one break and the beginning or end of the line. For formulae of these kinds can most often be interchanged, and the device of interchange can always be found wherever the juxtaposition of two formulae occasions a metrical fault. Once we know this, we can abandon the old explanation of 'legitimate' hiatus as justified by the pause in utterance at one of the metrical breaks in the line. Those hiatus which do not occur before one of the breaks in the line do not have this *raison d'être*; but if pause in utterance had played any part in the creation of hiatus, we should have expected the disparity in number of the two kinds of irregularity—which can now be explained by the workings of formulary diction—to be larger than it is. We ought to find more 'legitimate' hiatus, and almost no 'illegitimate' hiatus at all. But since we have cases of the latter, and their genuineness has been proved, their existence casts doubt on the whole theory of a pause, and in any case, the theory is no longer needed.

II. The two problems which have been shown to be one, of 'legitimate' and 'illegitimate' short syllables, are now joined by a third, that of the lengthened final short syllable. Anyone who now wishes to maintain the principle that a short syllable in hiatus is by its nature an intrusion into the genuine text of Homer will have to remove all examples of both kinds of hiatus. It is a peculiarity of Homeric scholarship that so much effort has been made to rid the text of hiatus, while so little attention has been paid to the lengthening of final short syllables, seeing that such lengthening is hardly more desirable from the point of view of metre than hiatus. |

III. If all Greek poetry other than Homer had been lost, no one of course would ever have objected to the hiatus of short syllables. It was solely because he had in mind poetry of the Classical period, when such hiatus was forbidden, that van Leeuwen came to object so strenuously to this metrical fault: 'Neque criticus, cui sint aures, aequo animo tulerit hiatus quales sunt ἐπὶ ἄλλωι, τὸ ἐμόν'[1] But this connection between Homeric poetry and poetry of a later period dissolves once we recognize the fundamental difference between the formulary style of Homer and the individual style of poets who worked independently of a traditional diction. They were in the habit of looking for words and groups of words which would exactly express the particular nuances of their thought, and so they never found themselves, like the Homeric bard, at a loss for words to express their ideas in metre without metrical fault. Their thought, moreover, was as little fixed as their diction, always remaining sufficiently flexible to allow modification according to the demands of metre, just as the thought of a modern poet can be modified in favour of rhyme. When the bard composed his lines, he had had no experience of searching for original expression; his versification was not

[1] Enchiridium dictionis epicae[2] (Lugduni Batavorum 1908) 81.

a pursuit of new words or new groups of words. When he first learned the art of poetry, he accepted a traditional diction, created for the expression of ideas appropriate to the recitation of heroic deeds. This diction already contained a number of metrical irregularities sanctioned by age; and the nature of the diction was such that in using it the poet was led to make other faults which he could have avoided only by resorting to words of his own invention. Leaving aside the impossibility of finding words which would really sort metrically with traditional formulary expressions, the poet simply was not in the habit of looking for words of his own. He was a poet of a traditional style: he would have had to become a poet of an individual style. The poets of the Classical period never found themselves in the same metrical difficulty. Since they had no formulae to begin with, their habits of versification did not compel them to make metrical faults; and if by some chance they | did happen to fashion a faulty verse, the flexibility of their thought, their habitual resources for expressing their thought, always sufficed to overcome the difficulty without trouble. The two styles differed, and the problems of metrics were different for each of them.

We have now in general demonstrated the authenticity in the text of Homer of the hiatus of short syllables and the lengthening of final short syllables. To the negative proof of the impossibility of removing these irregularities from the text, we have added the positive proof of their causes. None the less, we must take care not to exaggerate the import of these conclusions: we have shown that the hiatus of short syllables is not in itself a sign that an example of it is not the work of Homer, and likewise for the lengthened final short syllable. But we have not proved that any single irregularity of this kind is necessarily an authentic part of the original poem. The possibility remains that a particular irregularity derives from a bard of more recent times, who would have made it for the same reasons as Homer, under the influence of formulary diction; or that it derives from an interpolator or copyist.

Papyri have revealed to us fragments of a hexameter poem which we know from a remark of Pausanias to belong to the Hesiodic *Catalogue of Women*.[1] The author of these lines is telling how Helen was sought in marriage by various Achaean lords, and at line 21 we read

ἐκ δ' Ἰθάκης δ' ἐμνᾶτο Ὀδυσσῆος ἱερὴ ἴς.

The structure of this line resembles that of other lines of the same fragment:

17 *ἐξ Ἄργεος ἐμνῶντο μά[λ' ἐγ]γύθεν· ἀλλ' ἄρα καὶ τούς*
67 *ἐκ Κρήτης δ' ἐμνᾶτο μέγα σθένος Ἰδομενῆος*
42 *ἐκ δ' ἄρ' Ἀθηνέων μνᾶθ' υἱὸς Π[*

[1] Berlin Papyri 9739, 10560. Paus. 3. 24. 10.

In composing line 21, the poet was mainly guided by his memory of lines like 67. But in place of the | subject formula πολύτλας δῖος Ὀδυσσεύς, which would have given him a line free from metrical error, he chose Ὀδυσσῆος ἱερὴ ἴς, an expression involving both the hiatus of a short syllable and the lengthening of a final short syllable. It is by this very choice that we know that this poet lived toward the end of the age of heroic verse. For Homer would not have hesitated to use πολύτλας δῖος Ὀδυσσεύς. When he composed, at a time when the technique of the formulary and traditional epithet was in its full vigour, the fixed epithet was purely ornamental and had no pertinence to the action of the immediate context. Odysseus is πολύτλας δῖος Ὀδυσσεύς 25 times in Homer, including 5 times in the *Iliad*, although at that point in his life he had not yet made the travels which earned him more than any other hero the right to the title of 'much-suffering'; Homer never once replaces this formula by another of the same measure. Similarly, Aegisthus is for Homer 'irreproachable', Clytemnestra is 'divine', Polyphemus is 'godlike', etc.[1] It was only when heroic poetry began to make way for individual styles of poetry that the bards became aware of the frequent contradictions between the idea of the epithet and the idea of the passage containing the epithet; and that must have been the time when the lines attributed to the *Catalogue of Women* were composed. The author of this fragment did not want to speak of the young Odysseus as 'much-suffering', and the best he could do by way of replacing that formula was Ὀδυσσῆος ἱερὴ ἴς, mediocre in thought, faulty in metre. The line is late; but the age to which it belongs proclaims itself not by the metrical errors, but by the presence of the non-Homeric formula.

It may well be that some lines of the *Iliad* and the *Odyssey* which contain word-endings of irregular metre are likewise the work of late poets. But if they should be excised from the text, it is for reasons other than these irregularities. If we can never be entirely sure that this or that line is part of the original Homeric poems, we can be sure that he (or those authors whom we comprise under his name) was master of a | formulary diction, and was led by that diction to make numerous faults of metre.

We must also recognize the possibility that among those cases of hiatus which are not clearly the result of the operation of formulae, some may be the work of a poet of individual style. It is just possible that such a poet composed lines with metrical faults, and felt himself justified in leaving them in their faulty state by the many similar cases in the poems. It is even possible, since we cannot assert categorically that the diction of the Homeric poems is wholly formulary, that Homer himself put together original combinations of words which involved metrical faults but were none the less allowed to remain in the poems. And finally, apart from the

[1] Cf. TE, pp. 119–45 above.

formulary technique as Homer knew it, let us name the third possible source of short syllables in hiatus and lengthened final short syllables: they could be what they have been so much desired to be, the work of an editor or copyist of historical times who changed the text through ignorance or negligence. But this last hypothesis is worth little consideration. If the original text was greatly changed in this fashion as it was handed down, it is unlikely that faults would have been introduced into it which from the very beginning of the historical period were regarded as offensive. That the editors and copyists, inspired, like van Leeuwen and Agar, by the example of poetry of individual style, should have energetically devoted themselves to the reconstitution of a text free from metrical error was most probable. But that they should have made changes which from their point of view detracted from the beauty of the text, is improbable, and could be explained only by oversight, not by intention.

We must then allow that this or that short syllable in hiatus or lengthened final short syllable may not have figured in the original poems; but this in no way invalidates the conclusions of our study, in which we have sought only to show that metrical irregularities do not of themselves reveal that they are not the work of Homer. It may be proper to condemn one or another passage in which a hiatus occurs | as the work of an interpolator: but it must be done because the passage contains some other sign of its age, or because its thought is alien to the poem as a whole. Or it may be proper to rewrite one or another line so as to make it metrically correct; but it must be done because the line contains forms or expressions unknown to Homer, or because it is impossible to understand it as it stands. For such corrections of the text, short syllables in hiatus and lengthened final short syllables can give us no hint, nor provide us with any guarantee.

3

The Homeric Gloss: a Study in Word-sense*

THERE are, in general, two distinct views held concerning those Homeric words whose meaning is, for us, unknown or conjectural. Some suppose that their original signification was known to Homer and his public, but was lost because of linguistic changes which took place between the epoch of Homer and the historical period of Greek literature. It is chiefly the hope of making good this loss which has inspired the many well-known attempts to explain these words by the methods of comparative philology. Others suppose that their meaning had already been more or less forgotten when the verses of the *Iliad* and *Odyssey* were composed.[1] This theory has been suggested often and variously, but always | more as an impression than as the conclusion of any constructive reasoning; and that for a quite natural cause: so long as it was believed that the processes of verse-making were the same for Homer as for any poet of ancient or modern times who wrote an individual style, it was impossible to explain reasonably how a poet could have used words which he did not understand. The purpose of this paper is to give an explanation of how this could really be, based on the conception that the Homeric style is a traditional style, a view which I have set forth in my study *L'Épithète traditionnelle dans Homère*. But the present

* First published in *Transactions of the American Philological Association* 59 (1928), 233–47.

[1] In this study a somewhat special distinction will be made in the use of the terms *signification, meaning, sense*. The *signification* of a word is that which it denotes, that is, the definition which would be given it as an entity isolated from all contexts. *Meaning* refers to the ideas, single or multiple, exact or vague, which a word arouses in the mind when used in connection with other words. The *sense* of a word is that particular delimitation of its meaning brought about by its *repeated* use in combination with certain other words, or in connection with the expression of certain categories of ideas, or in certain forms of literature. Thus to take an example in English: *Alexander the Great.* The signification of *great* is 'large in spatial dimension' (Webster); its meaning is 'eminent or distinguished by rank, power, or moral character' (Webster); its sense is—more or less exactly—'King of Macedon, 336–323. B.C.' For in this phrase, as it is ordinarily used and understood, the adjective does no more than specify that it is a certain Alexander who is mentioned. An example of the sense of a word determined by its repeat eduse in connection with the expression of certain categories of ideas is the word *idea* itself, in Greek or English, used as a term of Platonic philosophy. One example of the sense of a word resulting from its use in a certain form of literature is that possessed in old English ballads by 'merry,' or 'greenwood'.

The importance of these distinctions lies in the fact that, just as the meaning of a word replaces its signification, from the point of view of its thought content, just so does the sense replace the meaning.

pages will not take as the premises of their reasoning the conclusions of that essay. Rather I would point out, to begin with, one of the phenomena determining our own comprehension, or non-comprehension, of the glosses, and then show that this phenomenon, in turn, can be understood only in the light of a traditional technique of verse-making.

It must be granted that the definition of the gloss given by Aristotle (*Poetics*, 1457b3) is incomplete: 'By a *regular word* I mean one which is in common use, by a *gloss* one which is used abroad.'[1] For the third alternative is omitted: the word which is obsolete in all dialects. Indeed, to all purposes the glosses of Attic poetry were for the greater part archaisms. Only the smallest portion of an audience of Aeschylus could have known that ἄναξ was still employed in Cyprus, and κέλευθος in Arcadia;[2] they must have recognized them as words met with in Homer, or in more recent poetry, and felt simply that they were no more in common use. The definition of Liddell and Scott—'An *obsolete* or *foreign* word which needs explanation'—is unsatisfactory for the important reason, as we shall see, that by far the larger number of words which must be classed as glosses certainly needed no explanation. What is more, the essential characteristic of the gloss is its | form, and not its 'foreign' and so poetic quality, which is a consequence of its form. In the following pages I shall use the term *gloss* as signifying *an element of vocabulary which has either no correspondence, or at best a remote one, with any element of vocabulary in the current language of an author's public.*

The phenomenon which furnishes the point of departure of the present study is simply this: the words in Homer for whose meaning we are in the dark are limited almost entirely to the category of ornamental epithets, that is, of adjectives used attributively and without reference to the ideas of the sentences or the passages where they appear.

As a result of the direct and substantial nature of Homeric thought, finding its expression in a style which rigorously avoids abstraction, those words in the *Iliad* and *Odyssey* which have no correspondents in later Greek, with the exception of those which are ornamental epithets, are usually explained by the context. The explanation necessarily varies in exactness, according to the word and the circumstances of its use, but in only a very few instances does the meaning remain obscure. δαήρ, 'brother-in-law', which among early authors is found only in Homer, may be taken as an example of the way in which the signification of a word is thus revealed. In *Z* 344 Helen addresses Hector: δᾶερ ἐμεῖο; and then we have the verses spoken by Helen at the funeral of Hector:

[1] λέγω δὲ κύριον μὲν ᾧι χρῶνται ἕκαστοι, γλῶτταν δὲ ᾧι ἕτεροι, ὥστε φανερὸν ὅτι καὶ γλῶτταν καὶ κύριον εἶναι δυνατὸν τὸ αὐτό, μὴ τοῖς αὐτοῖς δέ.

[2] Buck, *Greek Dialects*[1] § 191.

Ω 768 *ἀλλ' εἴ τίς με καὶ ἄλλος ἐνὶ μεγάροισιν ἐνίπτοι*
δαέρων ἢ γαλόων ἢ εἰνατέρων ἐυπέπλων,
ἢ ἑκυρή.

Typical too is *ἕστωρ*, which appears in Greek only once, in Ω 272, where Homer relates the preparing of the wagon which is to carry Priam and the ransom to the camp of the Achaeans:

Ω 270 *ἐκ δ' ἔφερον ζυγόδεσμον ἅμα ζυγῶι ἐννεάπηχυ.*
καὶ τὸ μὲν εὖ κατέθηκαν ἐυξέστωι ἐπὶ ῥυμῶι,
πέζηι ἔπι πρώτηι, ἐπὶ δὲ κρίκον ἕστορι βάλλον,
τρὶς δ' ἑκάτερθεν ἔδησαν ἐπ' ὀμφαλόν, αὐτὰρ ἔπειτα
ἑξείης κατέδησαν, ὑπὸ γλωχῖνα δ' ἔκαμψαν. |

For *ἕστορι* there has been found no nearer correspondence than the doubtful one with Ionic–Attic *ἕρμα*, and *ὕσταξ*, glossed by Hesychius: *πάσσαλος κεράτινος*; but it is evident that it can signify only the *yoke-pin*.[1]

In some cases the context furnishes us with the meaning, though not the signification of a word. Certainly such a word has a certain quality of vagueness, and so of remoteness, which, if anything, must have made it all the more suitable to epic style; but nevertheless, in such instances, the meaning indicated is usually quite clear. The aorist *ἄεσα*, for instance, has no nearer correspondent in Homer than *ἰαῦσαι*, and in later Greek than *αὐλή*,[2] but a single use of the word gives its meaning:

π 366 *ἅμα δ' ἠελίωι καταδύντι*
οὔ ποτ' ἐπ' ἠπείρου νύκτ' ἄσαμεν, ἀλλ' ἐνὶ πόντωι
νηὶ θοῆι πλείοντες ἐμίμνομεν Ἠῶ δῖαν.

What is more, this word, used only in the aorist (6 times), is invariably joined with *νύκτα*. That it signify 'rest', 'pass', or, as its possible etymology would suggest, 'stay', can add little to our understanding of the verses where it appears. Similarly there is *ἐμμαπέως*, found only in *E* 836 and ξ 485, where the circumstances of its use easily and surely furnish some such meaning as 'rapidly':

E 835 *Ὣς φαμένη Σθένελον μὲν ἀφ' ἵππων ὦσε χαμᾶζε,*
χειρὶ πάλιν ἐρύσασ', ὁ δ' ἄρ' ἐμμαπέως ἀπόρουσεν·

ξ 484 *καὶ τότ' ἐγὼν Ὀδυσῆα προσηύδων ἐγγὺς ἐόντα*
ἀγκῶνι νύξας· ὁ δ' ἄρ' ἐμμαπέως ὑπάκουσε.

Even in such a case as that of *ἀμολγῶι* we do not really suffer anything from our inability to give a definition. The word is found always in the expression (*ἐν*) *νυκτὸς ἀμολγῶι* (5 times) which, taken as a whole, can

[1] See Leaf, *Iliad*² (London, 1902), II, pp. 623 ff.

[2] The etymological evidence adduced by the comparative method which will be cited in this paper is chiefly from Boisacq, *Dictionnaire étymologique de la langue grecque*, Heidelberg, 1923.

only mean 'in the dark of night'; it would | be difficult to devise a meaning which would be essentially different.

In a very rare number of cases we do find a word other than an ornamental epithet which must remain unexplained, for example ἐντυπάς, found only in Ω 163. In this passage the poet tells how Iris, arriving at the palace of Priam, found the household plunged in grief:

Ω 161 παῖδες μὲν πατέρ' ἀμφὶ καθήμενοι ἔνδοθεν αὐλῆς
δάκρυσιν εἵματ' ἔφυρον, ὁ δ' ἐν μέσσοισι γεραιὸς
ἐντυπὰς ἐν χλαίνῃ κεκαλυμμένος·

ἐντυπάς, evidently an adverb, has variously found the interpretations 'prostrate', 'bowed', 'closely-wrapped', and its meaning must remain doubtful. But it is almost sure that if we had even one other use of the word we could explain it: in no case do we find in Homer a word other than an ornamental epithet which, when used with any frequency, refuses to disclose its meaning.

The situation is only too different in the case of those glosses which are ornamental epithets. We are frankly ignorant, in spite of the fact that they are often frequently used, of the meaning of αἰγίλιπος (3 times, of cliffs); αἵμονα (once, in the phrase αἵμονα θήρης); ἀκάκητα (twice, of Hermes); ἀλαλκομενηΐς (twice, of Athene); ἁλοσύδνης (once of Thetis, once of Amphitrite); ἀλφηστάων (5 times, of mortals); ἀτρυγέτοιο (17 times of the sea, once of the air); ἀφήτορος (once, of Apollo); ἀμφιγυήεις (11 times, of Hephaestus), etc. There are as many other words of the same sort commencing likewise with the vowel alpha for which we may, or may not, know the meaning, for it is often as difficult in this connection to refute an explanation as it is to confirm one. These epithet glosses are used ornamentally, and the idea which each expresses has no bearing upon the ideas of the sentence or passage where they appear. They do not express an *essential*[1] idea and so they | are not, as are the other parts of speech, an integral part of the frame of thought.

We now know the relation, *for us*, between the context and the meaning of the glosses, and we have made the distinction between the glosses which we usually understand and those which can be explained only in the degree that they have some correspondence with other words in Homer or in later Greek; these latter will from now on be referred to as ornament glosses. But as yet no attempt has been made to decide whether, or to what extent, Homer was here in the same position as ourselves. Accordingly we shall first consider the possible conditions under which he might have understood the ornament glosses and then, if these are unacceptable, see how the explanation that he did not know their

[1] For the exact force of the term *essential* as used here cf. TE, p. 13 above.

signification, or their original meaning, accords with what we know from other sources concerning the traditional character of the epic language and diction.

If the poet (or the poets) of the *Iliad* and *Odyssey* knew the true signification of the ornament glosses, without having access to any traditional or recorded explanation, we shall be forced to make the date of composition of the poems go back to a time so ancient that it will find, certainly, no serious support. For we shall thus be obliged to suppose that the elements of vocabulary which make up the ornament glosses were then in current use in the spoken language, so that poet and public understood μερόπων, for instance, with the same facility as an audience of Pindar or Aeschylus understood any of the epithets of these poets. The thought may occur to some that we might be able to show linguistically that certain ornament glosses were formed in an earlier period of the language, but it is doubtful if we may hope to prove very much in this way. Such epithets as μώνυχες, νήγρετος, νηλής, or those containing an Aeolic element, as ζατρεφέων, ζαθέοισι, ἐρίηρος, ἐριαύχενες, etc., furnish no conclusive evidence, since their meaning is sufficiently indicated either by corresponding | elements in Homer, or by the meaning of the nouns with which they are joined. (This latter is the sole manner in which the context may help explain an ornamental epithet.) Such interpretations as διάκτορος, 'Giver' (διὰ + κτέρας), or ἀργειφόντης, 'of gleaming rays' (which M. Bérard seems to accept as originating with some Chaldean conception of Hermes as the planet),[1] and the like, are at the best doubtful. And even if the formation from ancient elements of vocabulary were proved in the case of certain ornament glosses, it would have only a proportionate bearing on the others. Without speaking of the limitations, in this connection, of the comparative method,[2] we lack almost altogether the two basic elements of the proof, by specific linguistic evidence, of the date when the ornament glosses were formed: the date of the poems and the sure signification of even a few of those ornament glosses which have no correspondences in Homeric or later Greek.

The answer to the question must be based upon our general estimation of the rapidity with which the Ionic dialect could have changed. Can we suppose that the time which elapsed between the period of Homer and that of Archilochus, of Theognis, even of Herodotus, to name periods for which we have a progressively increasing knowledge of Ionic vocabulary, is sufficient to justify the differences of phonology and vocabulary which make it impossible to explain so large a part of the Homeric vocabulary by corresponding elements in Greek of the historical period? The words in Archilochus and Theognis (with the exception of those imitated from

[1] *Introduction à l'Odyssée* (Paris, 1924), I, p. 202.

[2] Cf. Meillet, *Aperçu d'une histoire de la langue grecque*[1] (Paris, 1920), p. 40.

the epos) for which we are unable to find corresponding elements in Ionic or Attic prose are few or none. Unless, then, we wish to suppose, for the spoken Greek of Ionia between the period of Homer and historical times, an acceleration of linguistic change unparalleled elsewhere in the domain of Greek dialects, to what great antiquity must we assign Homer, if we would suppose | that he naturally understood the ornament glosses, explaining them by corresponding elements of current speech? This antiquity it is easy and necessary to accept for his language, but difficult to believe in for himself. And even if we were to grant this very great antiquity of the poet and to accept an explanation of very rapid linguistic change, we should have shown only how Homer might have understood those ornament glosses which were Ionic. He could not, under any circumstances, have understood without some written or traditional explanation the non-Ionic elements of vocabulary found in these words. Yet knowing as we now do, by the linguistic evidence, that the epos, with its language and style, was Aeolic before it became Ionic, and possibly Achaean before that, it would be rash to claim that the ornament glosses were exclusively Ionic.

It is important in this connection to make the following observation: with the exception of the ornament glosses there is no difficulty raised by supposing that the spoken language of Homer was substantially the same as that of Herodotus. Homer would have understood with a perfectly sufficient accuracy the meaning of the glosses which are not ornamental epithets, learning them, as we do, from the context, but better than we can, for he would have seen them used with far greater frequency and variety. This process of learning the meaning from the context is indeed the very thing we observe so abundantly at other periods in the case of those Homeric (or more exactly epic) glosses which we find in the verses of later poets. The list of epic-tragic and epic-poetic words which have no corresponding elements in styles more closely related to the spoken language is long: *ἦτορ* (Sim., Pind., Aesch.), *θύελλα* (Aesch., Soph.), *θυοσκόος* (Eur.), *μάρπτω* (Archil., Pind., Aesch., Soph., Eur., Ar., Anth. Pal.), *ματεύω* (Pind., Soph., Aesch., Ar., Theocr.), *ὄβριμος* (Pind., Aesch., Eur.), etc., etc. A striking example is furnished by the adoption by later poets of words containing the ancient glossic element *νη-*: *νημερτής* (Aesch., Soph., Ap. Rh.), *νήνεμος* (Aesch., Eur., Ar., | and once even in Aristotle and Plutarch), *νηλεής* (Pind., Aesch., Soph., Eur., Epigr. Gr.), etc.

There is a second way in which one might explain how Homer knew the true signification of the ornament glosses: it could have been handed down in writing, or as an oral tradition, by the corporation of Singers. But there is not the slightest evidence in the scholia or in any ancient writer which would confirm such an explanation, improbable enough in itself. Accordingly, if there had been such a tradition it was completely lost between the time of Homer and the beginnings of critical study of Homeric language, which we find already developed in the fifth century.[1] This is the sort of theory to which one would resort only when all other explanations had failed.

It is not yet definitely established to what extent the diction of Homer, taken as a whole, is formulaic and traditional. The complexity of the ideas of the epos, and the comparatively small amount of poetry which we possess, render impossible the complete analysis of a technique of composition which must be as varied as the thought it is designed to express. Only in the case of the ornamental epithets does an abundance of material render possible a quantitative analysis which indicates that they are probably all traditional.[2]

The ornamental epithet is always a fixed epithet, for its quality of ornament derives solely from the fact that it has been used repeatedly in conjunction with a certain noun and without reference to the thought of the sentence where it appears.[3] This repeated use is determined chiefly by the factor of metrical convenience; for the fixed epithet plays an important part in the traditional technique of epic composition | which Homer followed: it combines with the noun to form a noun–epithet formula of a certain metrical value.[4] The uses of noun–epithet formulae are varied and many, but their common utility lies in the fact that they fill exactly a certain portion of the verse where the noun, or its synonym, would not fit. The technique of the use of the fixed epithet as we find it in Homer reveals plainly an ancient and intense development. In those cases where the importance of a word, or of a category of words, has brought about its use frequently, and in different combinations of words, we find that the noun–epithet formulae constitute systems characterized by a great complexity and by a strict economy.[5] For example, in the case of the 37 most important characters of the *Iliad* and *Odyssey* we find that each has a noun–epithet formula which fills the hexameter exactly between the feminine caesura and the verse end (*πολύτλας δῖος Ὀδυσσεύς* (38 times), *διάκτορος Ἀργειφόντης*, etc.): in the number of such formulae lies the complexity of the system. On the other hand we find for these 37 characters only forty different formulae of the measure in question; that is to say, in the case of 33 of them, no matter how often they may be mentioned, the poet uses only one formula which fills the verse between

[1] As is indicated by the fragment of Aristophanes (222 Hall).

[2] TE, pp. 72 above.

[3] TE, pp. 126 above.

[4] TE, pp. 10 ff. and 39 above.

[5] 'by great extension and by great simplicity', TE, p. 6, cf. pp. 17–19 above.

the feminine caesura and the verse end: in this lack of formulae which could replace one another lies the economy of the system. It is this character of the system which is the proof of its integral antiquity. Such a system could not be the work of a single poet: it must represent the effort of generations of Singers, ever seeking and ever guarding the convenient expression, and using it when found, to the exclusion of all other formulae which could replace it. This system of noun–epithet formulae of the characters, in the nominative, falling between the feminine caesura and the verse end, is only one of the many which go to make up the technique of the use of the fixed epithet in the traditional | style: a complete description of this technique must necessarily be as long as the technique is complex.[1]

Now when one has seized the conception of a traditional and formulaic technique of verse-making, the presence of the ornament glosses in Homer has been explained. The epic poets over the generations guarded those words which, though they had passed from current usage, were yet metrically convenient, or, to be exact, were now metrically indispensable. Certainly the fact that these old words had a special poetic quality must not be neglected; it was one of the factors making their survival possible, but this semantic consideration is dominated by that of metrical convenience, as is proved by the economy of the formulaic systems. We can well see, in the case of the noun–epithet formulae, how deeply rooted was the tendency to preserve the gloss for its metrical convenience. *Εὐρύοπα* is an epithet of much-discussed meaning, of an Aeolic ending. It is always joined in Homer with *Ζεύς*, to make the formula *εὐρύοπα Ζεύς* which fills the hexameter between the bucolic diaeresis and the verse end (14 times), as does *μητίετα* (*μητίετα Ζεύς*, 18 times), a word somewhat clearer in meaning, but also Aeolic in form. The two formulae differ by the very important element of the initial sound; in no case could they replace each other; and we find in the *Iliad* and *Odyssey* no other noun–epithet formula which could replace either. The number of cases where one or the other of the formulae has helped the poet to complete his verse indicates their usefulness. Imagine, then, a poet who, dissatisfied with the ancient formula, wished to abandon it (this first supposition is difficult in itself). Not only would he have to renounce a traditional word consecrated by usage; he would, which is more tangible, be obliged to find an epithet of the same metrical value, that of a first paeon, and beginning and ending with the same metrical element. But in no case could he find in Ionic an epithet ending, in the masculine nominative, with a short vowel. Nor can *Ζεύς* be placed first, after the bucolic | diaeresis, since its initial consonant would necessarily make position, and might occasion the serious fault of over-lengthening.[2] It cannot be asserted that it would

[1] TE, pp. 19–20 above. [2] TE, p. 41 above.

be impossible to create in Ionic, for the king of the gods, other noun–epithet formulae of the metrical values of εὐρύοπα Ζεύς and μητίετα Ζεύς; but such formulae must be paraphrases.[1] And then too what immeasurable difficulty there would be in finding an expression which would equal εὐρύοπα or μητίετα in the quality of σεμνότης. Thus μητίετα, an Aeolic form, and εὐρύοπα, an ornament gloss, survived.[2]

Did Homer, then, accept blindly, as an unchangeable part of the traditional style which he inherited, a large number of words concerning whose meaning he was completely ignorant? We have seen that in the case of the other glosses he was instructed by the context, but that this source of knowledge is barren for the ornament glosses.

It may be considered as certain that Homer thought he understood the ornament glosses: it is not possible that as an ἀοιδός, as an *homme de métier*, he should not have had some explanation for each one of them. But his method of explaining them must have been radically different from that which has been followed in the etymological studies which in the last fifty years have been inspired by the perfection of the comparative method. For Homer, if we are to assign him to a point of time anywhere near the historical period of Greek literature, can only have explained the words in question by associations, however far-fetched, with words of which he knew the signification. His etymological science, for such it may be called, must have been dominated at every point by the principle of analogy; it is very doubtful if the conception | of phonetic alteration could have entered into it at all. The ancients explained μώνυχες as formed by haplology from μόνος and ὄνυξ; Homer must have understood the word similarly. The fact that the word probably had an earlier form * σμῶνυξ, * σμ—being the reduced form of I.E. * σεμ—'one', can have had no bearing on his comprehension of the epithet. For ἰόμωροι, an epithet of the Argives used in Δ 242 and Ξ 479, the scholiast gives the explanation 'famed for their arrows', a signification which certain moderns would deny because the initial vowel of ἰός, 'arrow,' is long. It is possible that this difference of quantity would prove the falsity of the scholiast's explanation as giving the *original* signification, but such must in all probability have been Homer's comprehension of the word, based on an association with the ideas found in ἐγχεσίμωρος and ὑλακόμωρος. In his discussion of the epithet ἰόεντα, a *hapax* joined in Ψ 850 with σίδηρον, Boisacq has done well to approve the derivation from ἴον, 'violet,' rather than to attempt, like Fick, to find a meaning 'subject to rust' (how inappropriately!) based on Sanskrit and Latin forms signifying 'poisonous'.

[1] TE, pp. 56 and 74–5 above.

[2] For the analysis of similar cases where the poet was, to all purposes, obliged to retain the ancient formula, see FM, pp. 224 ff. above.

Likewise διάκτορος must have been associated with ἄγω rather than with κτέρας. ἀργειφόντης was probably the 'slayer of Argos', though it might also have been given the other explanation which is furnished by the scholia: ἀργὸς καὶ καθαρὸς φόνου. It is evident that what we need here, in order to reconstruct the meaning which Homer gave to the ornament glosses, is not a rigid science of etymology, but a working out of the popular method.

And yet one would err seriously were he to consider that the epic poet gave to the ornament glosses a sense similar to that which he gave to words embodying a part of the essential thought. The characteristic sense of the ornamental epithet differs profoundly from that of the words which carry ahead the movement of the poem; for the ornamental epithet does not have an independent existence. It is one with its noun, | with which it has become fused by repeated use, and the resulting noun–epithet formula constitutes a thought unit differing from that of the simple noun only by an added quality of epic nobility.[1] The meaning of the fixed epithet has thus a reduced importance: it is used inattentively by the poet, and heard by the auditor in a like manner; it is a familiar word on which the mind need not dwell, since its idea has no bearing upon that of the sentence. It is this circumstance of the indifference of the auditor to the signification of the epithet which explains how the poet has often come to use it irrationally (φαεινὴν . . . σελήνην, Θ 555, ἀμύμονος Αἰγίσθοιο, α 29);[2] how he can allow himself to use it invariably under certain conditions (the type-hemistich τὸν δ' ἠμείβετ' ἔπειτα, in 251 cases out of 254, is completed by a noun–epithet formula filling the rest of the verse);[3] how he can use it disproportionately with certain nouns in certain grammatical cases (Odysseus is δῖος 99 times in the nominative, and only once in an oblique case); how the poet can repeatedly use epithets of vague connotation (δαίφρων, μεγάθυμος); and finally, in the case of the present problem, how he can use as epithets words which are comprehended only by more or less distant associations with other words, and to which he is often forced to attach a meaning very remote from the main current of his thought. The meaning 'abandoned even by goats,' which was probably given to αἰγίλιπος, 'ox-eyed' for βοῶπις, 'slayer of Argos' for ἀργειφόντης, when used in the *Iliad* or *Odyssey* led the mind far from the path where it was closely following the rapid movement of the story. It is not that this quality of remoteness is exclusive to the ornament glosses; many other epithets of certain meaning possess it equally—ποδάρκης of Achilles, λευκώλενος of Hera, νεφεληγερέτα of Zeus. But this inattentiveness of the auditor for the meaning of all ornamental epithets

[1] TE, pp. 124 ff. above. [2] TE, pp. 12 ff. above.
[3] TE, pp. 14 and 137 ff. above.

allows him to pass rapidly over the ornament glosses, feeling in them only an element which ennobles the | heroic style. They are words, it is true, for whose comprehension he must perform an etymological exercise of the mind; if he would realize their meaning as he hears them in a Singer's verses, he must turn his thought aside for them. But his familiarity with them, his habit of hearing them joined with certain nouns, absolves him from doing this: they are remote words, and he accepts them as such. He is fully alive to their sense, but scarcely heedful of their meaning. And so we come to Aristotle: 'Thus one's style should be unlike that of ordinary language, for if it has the quality of remoteness it will cause wonder, and wonder is pleasant.'[1]

[1] *Rhet.* 1404b10. *διὸ δεῖ ποιεῖν ξένην τὴν διάλεκτον· θαυμασταὶ γὰρ τῶν ἀπόντων εἰσὶν [ἄνθρωποι], ἡδὺ δὲ τὸ θαυμαστόν ἐστιν.*

4

The Distinctive Character of Enjambement in Homeric Verse*

'. . . *true musical delight . . . which consists only in apt numbers, fit quantity of syllables, and the sens evariously drawn out from one verse into another* . . .'
Milton in the introduction to *Paradise Lost*.

THE reader of the *Iliad* and *Odyssey* soon comes to mark in them, as a part of the larger movement of the thought, the way in which the sense passes from verse to verse. The impression is sharp, and yet it is very hard to place, for it comes partly from the joining of single verses, and partly from the sum of many verses. My wish, in these pages, is to bring into greater clearness this feature of Homeric style.

Seeking to clarify dim ideas one first thinks of the broader attempts made to set forth the order of thought in the Homeric sentence. There is Matthew Arnold's remark: '. . . he is eminently plain and direct, both in the evolution of his thought and in the expression of it, that is, both in his syntax and in his words.'[1] But there are ways and ways of being plain and direct. As so often in the course of the well-known essay, one regrets that Arnold did not keep the Greek more in view; and this regret deepens when, a few pages further on, he explains that rhyme is unsuited to a translation of Homer since it 'inevitably tends to pair lines which in the original are independent', for here he shows how exact a notion he had of the movement of the Greek. M. Maurice Croiset does go straight to Homer's language: 'Complicated groupings of ideas are absolutely unknown to Homeric poetry. . . . The ordinary | law of this naïve and clear style is juxtaposition. When, contrary to custom, the sentence happens to grow long, the successive ideas join on to one another in the order that they occur to the mind.'[2] Still I believe that one who wishes to know the exact artifice of words will be led even more surely by a brief sentence of Denis of Halicarnassus: '. . . the thought which follows is unperiodic, though it is expressed in clauses and phrases.'

* First published in *Transactions of the American Philological Association* 60 (1929), 200–20.

[1] *On translating Homer* (1861).

[2] *Histoire de la littérature grecque*[3] (Paris, 1910), I, p. 264.

This critic of the Augustan age, in the closing chapter of his essay *On the Ordering of Words*, wishes to show how by the use of enjambement and of word groups of varying lengths good poetry takes on a certain likeness to good prose, and as an example he cites a passage from the *Odyssey* which he divides thus:

ξ 1 αὐτὰρ ὅ γ' ἐκ λιμένος προσέβη τρηχεῖαν ἀταρπόν |
χῶρον ἀν' ὑλήεντα | δι' ἄκριας | ᾗι οἱ Ἀθήνη
πέφραδε δῖον ὑφορβόν, | ὅ οἱ βιότοιο μάλιστα
κήδετο οἰκήων οὓς κτήσατο δῖος Ὀδυσσεύς. |
τὸν δ' ἄρ' ἐνὶ προδόμωι εὗρ' ἥμενον | ἔνθα οἱ αὐλή
ὑψηλὴ δέδμητο | περισκέπτωι ἐνὶ χώρωι |
καλή τε μεγάλη τε | περίδρομος.

Denis, while quoting these verses, keeps pointing out that the word groups have different lengths, and that some of them run over from one line to another, and it is with the sources of the 'prosaic' movement of the style equally in mind that he says, after quoting the clause ἔνθα οἱ αὐλὴ ὑψηλὴ δέδμητο, 'Further, the thought which follows is unperiodic, though it is expressed in clauses and phrases. For having added περισκέπτωι ἐνὶ χώρωι he again adds καλή τε μεγάλη τε, an expression which is shorter than a clause, and after that περίδρομος, a word that in itself has a certain idea.'[1] Luckily we do not have to tell | apart here *clause*, *phrase*, and *expression*.[2] Since we shall have to do with them only as they are used unperiodically, we may take them, as well as *the word that in itself has a certain idea*, as longer and shorter word groups. The period, it may be well to remark, does not have to be a sentence which cannot be brought to a close before its end, although it very often is such; rather it is one in which there is a planned balance of the thought.[3] The unperiodic sentence is one which lacks this balance and in which, to cite Denis, 'the clauses are not made like one another in form or sound, and are not enslaved to a strict sequence, but are noble, brilliant, and free'.[4] That is, the ideas are added on to one another, in what Aristotle calls the *running* style.[5] This force of the term *unperiodic* is made clear by the sentence for which Denis uses it here: though the whole thought is formed by the sum of the word groups, yet it is not a thought whose parts are closely

[1] Chap. xxvi, p. 274 f. κἄπειτα ὁ ἑξῆς νοῦς ἀπερίοδος ἐν κώλοις τε καὶ κόμμασι λεγόμενος· ἐπιθεὶς γὰρ "περισκέπτωι ἐνὶ χώρωι", πάλιν ἐποίσει "καλή τε μεγάλη τε" βραχύτερον κώλου κομμάτιον, εἶτα "περίδρομος" ὄνομα καθ' ἑαυτὸ νοῦν τινα ἔχον. The text is cited after the edition of W. R. Roberts: *Dionysius of Halicarnassus on Literary Composition* (London, 1910).

[2] So I translate κῶλον, κόμμα, and κομμάτιον. On these terms see W. R. Roberts: *op. cit.*, pp. 307 f., 306, and L. Laurand: *Études sur le style des discours de Cicéron*[2] (Paris, 1926), pp. 135–40.

[3] Aristotle, *Rhet.* III, 9,

[4] Chap. xxii, p. 212, ll. 7 ff. οὔτε πάρισα βούλεται τὰ κῶλα ἀλλήλοις εἶναι οὔτε παρόμοια οὔτε ἀναγκαίᾳ δουλεύοντα ἀκολουθίᾳ, ἀλλ' εὐγενῆ καὶ λαμπρὰ καὶ ἐλεύθερα.

[5] *Rhet.* 1409a24: ἡ εἰρομένη λέξις; literally, 'the strung style,' as one strings beads or a garland.

bound together; it contains several ideas which have been added to one another, and which could not be foreseen, were not even looked for, until each one was told.

It is not the place here to say how well the words of Denis fit Homeric style as a whole. The passage is useful now since it gives us a means of grouping by a fixed and worthy plan the kinds of enjambement[1] in Homer, and also since it shows us | the aims of our search: to seize more surely the way in which the thought of the poet unfolds from verse to verse, and to feel more truly the rhythm which he has given to the hexameter in fitting to it the pattern of his thought.

Broadly there are three ways in which the sense at the end of one verse can stand to that at the beginning of another. First, the verse end can fall at the end of a sentence and the new verse begin a new sentence. In this case there is no enjambement. Second, the verse can end with a word group in such a way that the sentence, at the verse end, already gives a complete thought, although it goes on in the next verse, adding free ideas by new word groups. To this type of enjambement we may apply Denis' term *unperiodic*. Third, the verse end can fall at the end of a word group where there is not yet a whole thought, or it can fall in the middle of a word group; in both of these cases enjambement is *necessary*.

We must know how often the verses join in each of these ways, taking up enough examples to gain a clear notion of how they differ. We must also see how strongly the various forms of enjambement mark the end of the hexameter, and in doing this we shall have to see what force should be given the break in the rhythm at the end of certain verses. And we shall do well to see whether Homer's practice in this matter is like or unlike that of other poets using the same verse form. Apollonius and Virgil, since they have used the hexameter likewise for heroic tales, and since their worth is the greatest along with that of Homer in this field, are our best choice.

To know where there is no enjambement we must gauge the sentence. The varying punctuation of our texts, usually troublesome, will not do. I define the sentence as any independent clause or group of clauses introduced by a co-ordinate conjunction or by asyndeton; and by way of showing that this definition is fitting I would point out that the rhetoricians

[1] I use the term *enjambement* by itself in its largest sense, that of the running over of the sentence from one line to another. The word is often used by writers on prosody with the narrower force which it originally had, that of the running over of a group of closely joined words. In this sense enjambement is a thing of degree, so that the force of the word depends upon where it is used. I have thought it best to use special terms for these different ways in which the sentence can run over: *unperiodic enjambement*, *necessary enjambement*, and so on, terms which will be defined as they come up.

paid | little heed to the sentence as we understand it: for them the unit of style was the clause, and the only group of clauses of which Aristotle speaks is the period. Using this standard we can group together those verses which as a group are marked by the sharpest break at the end, and which thus bring out most cleanly the rhythm of the latter part of the hexameter.[1] This break, it should be noted, varies with the sense in each case, | being made up in varying portions of time and of intensity. It is rather one of time in *α* 10–11, where the voice pauses before passing from prologue to story. It is rather one of intensity in *A* 24–5, where one passes quickly to the contrast of the following sentence.

In Homer nearly one half of the verses finish where the sentence ends: this is the first of the cases where we shall find the ordering of Homer's thought throwing the rhythm into relief. In Apollonius and in Virgil the number is somewhat less. These poets, here closely alike, have about four such verses to Homer's five. But this is not in itself a striking difference: over a length of a hundred lines the practice in Homer can be almost the same as in Virgil, and such a passage as *N* 64–76, where ten out of thirteen verses end with the sentence, is nearly equalled by *Aeneid*, v, 70–9, where seven out of ten verses end in this way.

[1] The conclusions of this essay are based on the analysis of six passages of one hundred lines each from the *Iliad*, and the same number of lines from the *Odyssey*, the *Argonautica*, and the *Aeneid*. The verses chosen were the following: *A E I N P Φ*, 1–100; *α ε ι ν ρ φ*, 1–100; *Arg.* I, 1–100; I, 681–780; II, 1–100; III, 1–100; IV, 1–100; IV, 889–988 (ed. Merkel, Leipzig, 1913); *Aen.* I, III, V, VII, IX, XI, 1–100. The results of the analysis are as follows. (In column I are the verses which end with the sentence; in column II those verses which are followed by unperiodic enjambement; in column III those verses after which enjambement is necessary.)

Iliad	I	II	III
A 1–100	48	31	21
E 1–100	50	24	26
I 1–100	52	18	30
N 1–100	48	31	21
P 1–100	48	19	33
Φ 1–100	45	27	28
Average	48·5	24·8	26·6

Odyssey	I	II	III
α 1–100	35	33	32
ε 1–100	50	30	20
ι 1–100	46	21	33
ν 1–100	43	30	27
ρ 1–100	55	14	31
φ 1–100	40	32	28
Average	44·8	26·6	28·5

Argonautica	I	II	III
I 1–100	31	18	51
I 681–780	38	20	42
II 1–100	33	15	52
III 1–100	41	14	45
IV 1–100	35	13	52
IV 889–988	31	16	53
Average	34·8	16	49·1

Aeneid	I	II	III
I 1–100	36	11	53
III 1–100	40	16	44
V 1–100	37	12	50
VII 1–100	33	13	55
IX 1–100	45	11	44
XI 1–100	38	13	49
Average	38·3	12·5	49·2

There is more difference between Homer and the later poets in the use of verses which hold just a sentence, or in some cases two sentences, and which are notable since they best show the measure of the hexameter set off by itself. One meets such verses in the *Iliad* and *Odyssey* about every fifth or sixth line, which is about twice as often as in the *Argonautica* or the *Aeneid.*[1] Yet here too the practice of the three poets often meets. Even in the use of series of these verses, especially longer series of three, four, or five which are much more common in Homer, one does not have a difference which is striking; and the fact that some of these longer series do occur in Apollonius and Virgil would show that these poets had no special thought of avoiding them. A group of six sentence verses seems to be found only in Homer:

I 26 ἀλλ' ἄγεθ', ὡς ἂν ἐγὼ εἴπω πειθώμεθα πάντες·
φεύγωμεν σὺν νηυσὶ φίλην ἐς πατρίδα γαῖαν·
οὐ γὰρ ἔτι Τροίην αἱρήσομεν εὐρυάγυιαν. |
  Ὣς ἔφαθ', οἱ δ' ἄρα πάντες ἀκὴν ἐγένοντο σιωπῆι.
δὴν δ' ἄνεωι ἦσαν τετιηότες υἷες Ἀχαιῶν·
ὀψὲ δὲ δὴ μετέειπε βοὴν ἀγαθὸς Διομήδης.

But one finds groups of four or five such verses in both Apollonius and Virgil.[2] It is clear, in the matter of the verse which ends with the sentence, or which holds just a sentence, that the three poets all felt the need, or the fittingness, of bringing out the rhythm of the end of the hexameter, and of the hexameter as a whole.

One may group under four headings the various means by which Homer can continue beyond the end of a verse a sentence which, at that point, already gives a whole thought. First, he can add a free verbal idea, using a dependent clause, a participial phrase, or a genitive absolute:[3]

α 4 πολλὰ δ' ὅ γ' ἐν πόντωι πάθεν ἄλγεα ὃν κατὰ θυμόν
ἀρνύμενος ἥν τε ψυχὴν καὶ νόστον ἑταίρων.

The second means of unperiodic enjambement is the addition of an adjectival idea, that is, one describing a noun found in the foregoing verse.[4]

A 1 Μῆνιν ἄειδε, θεά, Πηληιάδεω Ἀχιλῆος
οὐλομένην, ἣ μυρί' Ἀχαιοῖς ἄλγε' ἔθηκε.

[1] In the verses examined the number of verses containing just a sentence or just two sentences, and the average number of lines between occurrences, is as follows: *Il.* 117 (19·5), *Od.* 91 (15·2), *Arg.* 44 (7·3), *Aen.* 59 (9·7).

[2] Groups of four verses, *A* 53–6, *E* 19–22, *φ* 82–5, *Arg.* III, 30–3; of five verses, *I* 52–6, *Φ* 71–5, *Aen.* IX, 11–15; of six verses, *I* 26–31.

[3] *A* 5, 10, 22, 27, 60, 63, 64, 69, 90, 95. α 29, 34, 38, 40, 65, 89, 93, 94, etc. *A* 12, 13, 20, 26, 30, 44. α 4, 24, 36, 37, 72, etc. *A* 46, *φ* 69, etc.

[4] *A* 1, 98. α 7, 48, 53, 96, 99, etc. α 22, 50, 51, 69, 71, 86, 100, etc. *A* 3, *E* 16, 93.

Third, the added idea may be adverbial, dwelling more fully on the action named in the foregoing verse. This idea is usually expressed by a phrase, sometimes by a simple adverb:[1]

A 14 στέμματ' ἔχων ἐν χερσὶν ἑκηβόλου Ἀπόλλωνος
χρυσέωι ἀνὰ σκήπτρωι. |

This type of unperiodic enjambement is less usual than the two given before, as is the next. This last means is that of adding by a co-ordinate conjunction a word or phrase or clause of the same grammatical structure as one in the foregoing verse:[2]

A 4 αὐτοὺς δὲ ἑλώρια τεῦχε κύνεσσιν
οἰωνοῖσί τε πᾶσι.

Such are the forms of unperiodic enjambement. I have described them at length since they, more than anything else, give the rhythm in Homer its special movement from verse to verse. This is so, first, because they occur twice as often in Homer as in Apollonius or Virgil, about once in four lines in the one, and once in eight lines in the others;[3] and this difference in number, added to that noted for verses which end with the sentence, leaves room for the equally different use of necessary enjambement to which we shall come in turn. But the forms of unperiodic enjambement color the Homeric rhythm even more because, when used with a formulaic diction, they give rise to a very special kind of break at the verse end. It is the place here to deal with this fact that the use of set phrases by Homer is closely bound up with the way in which his verses join. In doing so we shall not only see how in certain cases words distributed between two verses should be grouped, but we shall also learn why this and the other types of enjambement have been used in different measures by Homer and by the later poets.

The action of the formula upon the movement cannot be better shown than by setting side by side the prologues of the *Odyssey* and the *Aeneid*; and it may be said in passing that there are few passages which show more clearly than these two how thoroughly Virgil had filled himself with sense of his *exemplarium Graecum.* Virgil has modeled his movement upon Homer in the following way. His first verse begins with a principal clause (where *virum* and *cano* recall ἄνδρα and ἔννεπε), | and finishes with the first part of a relative clause which runs on into the next verse. *litora* in the third line is a run over word as πλάγχθη is in the second.[4] Virgil begins his second sentence quite as Homer does with *multum ille . . .*, and this is echoed by *multa quoque . . .*, in the same way that the sentence πολλῶν

[1] *A* 14, 29. α 14, 17, 18, 19, 23, 49, 61, 70, etc.

[2] *A* 4, 15, 37, 62, 94. ε 45, 63, 65, etc.

[3] See above, p. 254 n. 1.

[4] In the same way Apollonius runs his first sentence over into the second verse by μνήσομαι.

δ'. . . is echoed by πολλὰ δὲ . . . . The added participial phrase ἀρνύμενος ἥν τε ψυχὴν καὶ νόστον ἑταίρων is replaced in Virgil by a relative clause with the same temporal force: *dum conderet urbem inferretque deos Latio*, where the double predicate of the Greek has suggested that of the Latin. Finally, the enjambement after the fourth verse of the *Odyssey* has been the model of that after the third verse of the *Aeneid*:

πολλὰ δ' ὅ γ' ἐν πόντωι πάθεν ἄλγεα ὃν κατὰ θυμόν
ἀρνύμενος ἥν τε ψυχὴν καὶ νόστον ἑταίρων

multum ille et terris iactatus et alto
vi superum.

Yet there is a difference. Homer has spoken first of the wanderings, then of the sufferings of Ulysses, and finally he says that they took place while he was trying to save his life and bring his comrades home. In the *Aeneid*, in spite of the Homeric movement which has been given to *iactatus*, the reader joins it very closely with *vi*. Virgil does not say first that his hero was buffeted about land and sea, and then add as an altogether free thought that it was by the might of the gods; he says almost that the might of the gods buffeted him about land and sea. The end of the verse after *alto* marks almost no break, and the editors put no mark of punctuation there. I say 'almost' since *iactatus* gives a whole idea and the enjambement is unperiodic. The word is not one which takes the reader into the next verse for his understanding of it, as happens for example in the twentieth verse of the *Argonautica*, where the enjambement has been suggested by the prologue of the *Iliad*:|

νῦν δ' ἂν ἐγὼ γενεήν τε καὶ οὔνομα μυθησαίμην
ἡρώων.

Here γενεήν τε καὶ οὔνομα are without meaning until ἡρώων is reached, and the enjambement is necessary, not unperiodic as in its model:

A 3 πολλὰς δ' ἰφθίμους ψυχὰς Ἄιδι προίαψεν
ἡρώων

where ἡρώων has almost the same force as οὐλομένην two lines above. The case in Virgil is not like this: the sentence might be ended with the verse, and the verse end does mark a break in the rhythm. But it is much slighter than that after ὃν κατὰ θυμόν. It is even slighter than the break after *E* 16:

Τυδείδεω δ' ὑπὲρ ὦμον ἀριστερὸν ἤλυθ' ἀκωκή
ἔγχεος.

And yet here the thought in itself would seem much more close set.

We join ἔγχεος more loosely to what has gone before than we do *vi superum* only because we have formed the habit of reading Homer by a fixed pattern. The reader of the *Iliad* and *Odyssey*, passing more slowly and with less ease through the same stages as the man who listened to the tales of the Singers, gradually forms in himself what may be called a *sense of the formula*. Meeting over and over the same group of words expressing the same idea, he comes to look on this group of words as a whole which has a fixed end. And the more he becomes used to these formulas, the more he ceases to read Homer as he would a writer who uses his own words and seldom uses them over. He does not go ahead word by word until the sentence ends. He reads by formulas; that is, since the technique of formulas is basically one of making verses out of traditional groups of words, he reads by word groups. He usually comes to do this first for the verses which introduce speech. Verse formulas such as τὸν δ' ἠμείβετ' ἔπειτα ποδάρκης δῖος Ἀχιλλεύς, which | strangely had at first seemed one of the most bizarre features of Homer's style, soon become a simple *Achilles answered*, and so he reads on into the sentence knowing just what it will say and sure that it will end with the verse. As a rule he is not this sure that the sentence will end with the verse; then although he brings the thought to a close at the end of the verse he will not do it so finally, knowing that other word groups may be added to the sentence; yet he does finish the thought with the verse, and whatever comes after is joined to an already whole thought. This is the case with one of the verse formulas used to tell how a spear strikes. There are in Homer the following lines where ἤλυθ' ἀκωκή ends the sentence:

E 66 ἡ δὲ διαπρό
ἀντικρὺ κατὰ κύστιν ὑπ' ὀστέον ἤλυθ' ἀκωκή·

P 49 = *X* 327 = χ 16 ἀντικρὺ δ' ἁπαλοῖο δι' αὐχένος ἤλυθ' ἀκωκή.

It is the memory either of these verses, or of others telling a like act by a like movement, that leads the reader to close the thought in *E* 16 also at the verse end, so that ἔγχεος in the next verse becomes 'a word that in itself has a certain idea', like οὐλομένην and ἡρώων in *A* 2 and 4. It is not a word which has much weight; it is indeed almost colorless. I would describe its force by saying that its length marks a rest during which the mind lingers on the already finished thought of the foregoing verse. Nor does this at all mean that there should be a comma after ἀκωκή in *E* 16; there is no pause of time there. The break in the rhythm comes solely from the fact that the mind, going from formula to formula, has closed the circle of the idea with ἀκωκή, and has placed ἔγχεος next to, but outside of this circle. οὐλομένην and ἡρώων have of course more color: such run-over words have in common that they dwell upon an already finished idea, but their weight comes from their meaning.

At times the memory of the formula may be even more cut out word for word than in the case just cited. The enjambement after α 7 has its special unperiodic movement because we read the verse on the pattern we have from *κ* 437 or *Δ* 409: |

α 7 αὐτῶν γὰρ σφετέρῃσιν ἀτασθαλίῃσιν ὄλοντο
νήπιοι

κ 437 τούτου γὰρ καὶ κεῖνοι ἀτασθαλίῃσιν ὄλοντο.

But more often the memory is less one of certain words and more one of a certain ordering of ideas. The pattern of the latter part of the following verse may be given as verb—Ἴλιον εἴσω:

P 159 αἶψά κε Πάτροκλον ἐρυσαίμεθα Ἴλιον εἴσω

and it is this basic pattern which leads us to close the thought at the end of *A* 71:

καὶ νήεσσ' ἡγήσατ' Ἀχαιῶν Ἴλιον εἴσω
ἣν διὰ μαντοσύνην, τήν οἱ πόρε Φοῖβος Ἀπόλλων.

Likewise one breaks the sentence at the end of *α* 4 partly because one knows verses where the sentence ends with ὃν κατὰ θυμόν, partly because one has read other verses where the sentence ends with a shorter phrase for the idea 'to suffer woes', such as *N* 670:

νοῦσον τε στυγερήν, ἵνα μὴ πάθοι ἄλγεα θυμῶι.

In other cases of unperiodic enjambement neither the *Iliad* nor the *Odyssey*, nor any other verses we have of the epos, give us any example of the word group which ends the verse being used elsewhere to end the sentence. ἑλώρια τεῦχε κύνεσσιν has no special likeness with any other phrase in Homer, and yet one finishes the thought at its end in *A* 4:

αὐτοὺς δὲ ἑλώρια τεῦχε κύνεσσιν
οἰωνοῖσί τε πᾶσι.

We do not join these verses at all in the same way as we do verses 5 and 6 or 6 and 7 of the *Aeneid*:

Multa quoque et bello passus, dum conderet urbem
inferretque deos Latio, genus unde Latinum
Albanique patres atque altae moenia Romae. |

The form of the enjambement is the same in the three cases: by using a co-ordinate conjunction the poet adds on a group of words with the same grammatical structure as a phrase in the foregoing verse. Yet in reading Virgil we rightly do not look for the thought to end with the verse; we go on to find a planned balance of ideas. We read 'while he was founding a city and bringing gods to Latium', a sentence in which the two word groups set off each other. In Homer however we read 'and made them prey for dogs, and for the birds of heaven too', making the second word group simply repeat the idea of the first. The enjambement after *genus unde Latinum* is even more clearly of the kind which, though unperiodic in structure, yet really looks beyond the verse end. This first word group names the first of the three epochs of Rome's history, and far from closing the thought after *Latinum* we go on to the second step of a well planned sequence. The full difference can be felt if one puts beside these verses of Virgil a passage from the *Iliad*:

I 80 ἐκ δὲ φυλακτῆρες σὺν τεύχεσιν ἐσσεύοντο
ἀμφί τε Νεστορίδην Θρασυμήδεα ποιμένα λαῶν
ἠδ' ἀμφ' Ἀσκάλαφον καὶ Ἰάλμενον υἷας Ἄρηος
ἀμφί τε Μηριόνην Ἀφαρῆά τε Δηίπυρόν τε
ἠδ' ἀμφὶ Κρείοντος υἱὸν Λυκομήδεα δῖον.

The flavor of this sentence comes from its fulness, which makes of it a 'catalogue', yet this fulness is gained only by the addition of ideas. No one verse looks forward to any other; each one comes to give us a free idea, since we have each time closed the thought at the end of the foregoing verse. But in Virgil we do not do this: we read on, having no desire to end the sentence until a new one begins. Now to come back to our first example, it is true that we have the memory of no other sentences to make us limit the thought with ἑλώρια τεῦχε κύνεσσιν; but guided so often elsewhere by the pattern of the formulas we have formed the habit of closing the thought at the verse end when we can. And if we, reading a strange tongue, come | thus to read by a fixed scheme, how much deeper must this scheme have been pressed upon the mind of Homer's hearers, knowing as they did the epic style with its traditional diction; for they had heard it since their first years, in the tales of many Singers, and in verses far outnumbering those of our sole *Iliad* and *Odyssey*.

There is only a small number of cases in Virgil where the unperiodic enjambement marks a break at the verse end with the same force as in Homer, as in *Aeneid*, III, 6, where the structure of the sentence itself suggests an end for it at *Idae*:

III, 5 classemque sub ipsa
Antandro et Phrygiae molimur montibus Idae,
incerti quo fata ferant, ubi sistere detur.

Yet even here the sentence leaves us the thought of men building ships while their minds are weighed down by uncertainty. In Homer one would not thus have blended the two ideas. Though the break in the rhythm is marked, it is not as clean as one which comes from the habit of ending the thought with the formula.

Apollonius' use of unperiodic enjambement is usually no nearer Homer's than is that of Virgil: in those cases where it is not strictly necessary to run the sentence on into the next verse one still finds, as a rule, that the thought in some way looks beyond the verse end. The joining of verses 682–3 in book 1 of the *Argonautica* may be cited as typical:

1, 681 εἰ δὲ τὸ μὲν μακάρων τις ἀποτρέποι, ἀλλὰ δ' ὀπίσσω
μυρία δηιοτῆτος ὑπέρτερα πήματα μίμνει,
εὖτ' ἂν δὴ γεραραὶ μὲν ἀποφθινύθωσι γυναῖκες.

Yet at times the Alexandrian does join verses in a way which recalls the epos by a roundabout use of Homeric diction. He has gone to some pains to avoid copying formulas of any great length, so that his lines which recall the style of the older epic are found to be made up of words and shorter phrases from a number of verses. The enjambement after 1, 774 is not unhomeric: |

βῆ δ' ἴμεναι προτὶ ἄστυ φαεινῶι ἀστέρι ἶσος,
ὅν ῥά τε νηγατέῃσιν ἐεργόμεναι καλύβῃσιν.

This is because the verse is made up of fragments of as many as four different verses in Homer (*N* 242, *ω* 154, *Λ* 747, *Z* 401). Still this enjambement is Homeric in somewhat the same way as ὄρωρεν (1, 713), meaning 'to be', is Homeric. Apollonius comes nearer the *Iliad* and *Odyssey* when he is copying the epic ordering of thought, rather than the epic words. His catalogue of the heroes who came to the quest of the fleece, by repeating verses of which the idea is 'and there came . . .', gives to these verses much the unperiodic force that we find in the like verses of the Catalogue in *B*—'these were led by . . .', or in the catalogue of Helen's wooers in Hesiod[1]—'and there wooed . . . '.

But even at the best Apollonius only faintly wins to his unperiodic enjambement the Homeric movement. Indeed he needed not only more of the traditional diction of the epos, he needed even more to have been born in an age without letters. Both Apollonius and Virgil, bent each upon making his own kind of epic, wrote out their verses without haste, forming their styles carefully from their wide knowledge of many forms of literature, from their memory of the words of many centuries. But Homer put all his trust in a technique of formulas which he accepted without thought of change: it was the traditional style and by it he could put together rapidly and easily his spoken verses. It may be doubted if he ever dreamed that in doing so he was cutting off from his poetry any new shades of style which would be his very own: that is not an ideal to which the poet who composes long tales without paper has any reason to be drawn, for new words and phrases in any number would jar badly the working of his formulas. What Homer sought in his style was to reach a traditional idea of perfection, not one that he had shaped himself, and

[1] *Catalogue of Women*, frag. 68 (Evelyn-White).

it is only in this spirit | that a poet can fit his thought to a purely formulaic diction, just as it is only by the ear that such a diction can be learned and only by the voice that it can be used.

Moreover Homer was ever pushed on to use unperiodic enjambement. Oral versemaking by its speed must be chiefly carried on in an adding style. The Singer has not time for the nice balances and contrasts of unhurried thought: he must order his words in such a way that they leave him much freedom to end the sentence or draw it out as the story and the needs of the verse demand. Periods of a sort there are in Homer. Denis is not altogether wrong in classing the style of this poet as 'mixed', but they are not the periods which the later oratory brought into Greek prose and poetry. They are of fixed forms which a single example will typify:

ι 56 ὄφρα μὲν ἠὼς ἦν καὶ ἀέξετο ἱερὸν ἦμαρ
τόφρα δ' ἀλεξόμενοι μένομεν πλέονάς περ ἐόντας·
ἦμος δ' ἠέλιος μετενίσσετο βουλυτόνδε
καὶ τότε δὴ Κίκονες κλῖναν δαμάσαντες Ἀχαιούς.

Apart from this traditional periodic element it is clear that Denis' other remark about the thought being unperiodically expressed generally fits the Homeric sentence: just how well will only be known by a special study. But we have noted in the present essay to just what degree this need of the oral poet to order his thought unperiodically in word groups has affected the way in which the thought is drawn out from verse to verse: it has made unperiodic enjambement twice as frequent, necessary enjambement twice as infrequent, as in the writers of the literary epic.

I have remarked that, because it is formulaic, unperiodic enjambement marks the end of the verse more sharply in Homer than in Apollonius or in Virgil. There remains to consider the fact that Denis found this way of ordering word groups prosaic. Just what he had in mind is made clear by certain of the sentences in which he describes the 'austere' | style. This style, he says, wishes its clauses 'to be like nature rather than like art. . . . As a rule it does not at all wish to compose periods in which the thought would give a sense of completeness. If it ever does this by chance it seeks to make them seem unstudied and simple.'[1] From this we know that Denis found the unperiodic ordering of the Homeric sentence prosaic because it seems natural and not artificial. He has touched there upon no small matter, and indeed upon one which does not permit comment here since it involves every part of Homeric style and calls for something more than a simple like or dislike of the word nature. I would only point

[1] *De Comp. Verb.* XXII, p. 212 . . . φύσει τ' ἐοικέναι μᾶλλον αὐτὰ [*sc.* τὰ κῶλα] βούλεται ἢ τέχνῃι . . . περιόδους δὲ συντιθέναι συναπαρτιζούσας ἑαυταῖς τὸν νοῦν τὰ πολλὰ μὲν οὐδὲ βούλεται· εἰ δέ ποτ' αὐτομάτως ἐπὶ τοῦτο κατενεχθείη, τὸ ἀνεπιτήδευτον ἐμφαίνειν θέλει καὶ ἀφελές, . . .

out in passing that this way of making verse seem prosaic is of a very different sort than the other which Denis notes, which comes from running a word group over from one verse into another and thus dimming the rhythm of the end of the hexameter.

Those cases in which the reader must go to the following verse to complete the thought of the sentence are of two sorts. First are those in which the poet ends the verse at the end of a word group as in

> *A* 57 οἱ δ' ἐπεὶ οὖν ἤγερθεν ὁμηγερέες τ' ἐγένοντο
> τοῖσι δ' ἀνιστάμενος μετέφη πόδας ὠκὺς Ἀχιλλεύς.

This sort of enjambement is not one of the more frequent. It occurs only about every twenty verses in the *Iliad*, the *Odyssey*, the *Aeneid*, and somewhat less often in the *Argonautica*.[1] It has nevertheless its part in the Homeric movement, for it is almost always found in Homer after common formulaic verses, as in the case cited, or in the traditional periods which have been mentioned above. |

The second sort of necessary enjambement is that in which the word group is divided between two verses. It differs from all the types of enjambement which I have hitherto cited in that it does not mark a break in time or sense at the end of the hexameter. Since all other orderings of words fall in the other classes, the word group here will be made up in all cases of the unbroken complex formed by the basic parts of the clause—subject, verb, and object, and of the words directly modifying these basic parts. The reader is unable to form a whole picture of a single action until he has this whole complex of words and has set its parts in their proper place in regard to each other, and so it is that no break can be made in the thought until the word group is ended. To this type of enjambement we may give Denis' name of prosaic. Modern writers on metric have likewise pointed out that when the thought of two verses is joined thus closely the rhythm becomes less purely poetic.[2] In the case of the hexameter the unfixed syllable of the last foot, the dactyl of the fifth foot, and the unwillingness to divide certain pairs of words between two verses, keeps the prosaic movement of the enjambement in Virgil and Apollonius, as well as in Homer, far from that which Shakspere and Tennyson reach at times in their blank verse. It has been said of Shakspere that his verse often becomes prose; but the Greeks and Romans at no time lost a very clear-cut sense that the basis of hexametric poetry was a unit of six dactylic feet. Still the difference between ancient and modern poets has no bearing

[1] *A* 17, 39, 57, 81. *α* 11, 16, 45, 81, 82, 83, etc. In the verses examined (see p. 254 n. above) cases of enjambement of this sort occur as follows: *Il.* 27, *Od.* 33, *Arg.* 14, *Aen.* 36.

[2] Saintsbury: *History of English Prosody* (London, 1908), II, p. 298; P. Verrier: *Principes de la métrique anglaise* (Paris, 1909), I, p. 181 ff.

upon the differences between ancient poets. For one who knows the varying styles and rhythms of Greek and Latin verse the fact that prosaic enjambement occurs only in every fifth verse in Homer, while it is found in every second or third verse in Apollonius and Virgil, is among the first reasons why the style and rhythm of these poets are so far apart. It is a difference which in itself does not bring out so strikingly as does unperiodic enjambement the way in which Homer orders | his thought. But in it above all lies the marked beat and swing of the Homeric rhythm.

It remains only to point out a way of joining verses which barely exists in Homer but which, while not one of the more common in Virgil, yet sets this poet off from Homer somewhat in the way that the formulas of unperiodic enjambement set Homer apart. It was an example of this kind which caught the thought of Ronsard pondering whether enjambement was fitting for French poetry:[1]

Laviniaque venit
litora.

Here we have in one verse an adjective which can have no meaning until we can join it with its noun in the next verse.[2] Now there is in Homer very rarely, about once in every two hundred lines, a somewhat like division, but looking more closely one sees that the adjective is almost always *πᾶς*, *πολύς*, or *ἄλλος*. These words are often used as substantives in the very expressions in which we now find them as adjectives, or more truly as half adjectives, for as one reads one still gives them some of their usual value:

A 78 *ἦ γὰρ ὀίομαι ἄνδρα χολωσέμεν ὃς μέγα πάντων*
Ἀργείων κρατέει.

The one case I have found in which a descriptive adjective is put in the first verse by itself is in *I* 74:

πολλῶν δ' ἀγρομένων τῶι πείσεαι ὅς κεν ἀρίστην
βουλὴν βουλεύσηι.

The case is unusual and, like most of the other unusual features | of Homeric style, due to a chance interplay of formulas.[23] Homer, putting together his traditional phrases, remembered first such common expressions falling at the end of the verse as *ὅς μέγ' ἄριστος*, *ὅς τις ἄριστος*, and then such expressions used at the beginning of the verse as *βουλὰς βουλεύει*

[1] *Préface à la Franciade de 1587.*

[2] In the verses examined (see above, note 9) this type of enjambement appears as follows: *A* 78; *E* 2; *I* 74, 97. *α* 78; *ρ* 12, 33; *φ* 70. *Arg.* I, 13, 23, 65; I, 685, 728, 732, 760, 766; II, 6, 19, 38, 41, 68, 76, 81, 91; III, 42, 46, 69; IV, 12, 26, 27, 96; IV, 890, 891, 893, 980. *Aen.* I, 2, 13, 29, 76, 85, 99, 100; III, 2, 5, 20, 22, 39, 45, 62, 69, 86, 91, 94; V, 4, 8, 28, 80, 92; VII, 6, 8, 27, 32, 43, 54, 55, 82, 83, 94, 100; IX, 19, 30, 38, 40, 49, 56, 63, 67, 75; XI, 9, 12, 25, 32, 37, 42, 55, 56, 57, 60, 96, 98.

[23] Cf. FM, Chaps, II–III above.

(*K* 415), βουλὰς βουλεύειν (*K* 147, 327; ζ 61), βουλὰς βουλεύουσι (*Ω* 652), and their joining made the enjambement of *I* 74–75. But in Apollonius we find the adjective in the first verse being used regularly, about once in every twenty verses; moreover he often puts a number of words between the adjective and the noun:

Arg. I, 685 ᾗε βαθείαις
αὐτόματοι βόες ὔμμιν ἐνιζευχθέντες ἀρούραις
γειοτόμον νειοῖο διειρύσσουσιν ἄροτρον.

Virgil goes still farther than Apollonius, thus placing the adjective by itself in about every tenth verse. In one case at least we have enjambement of this sort in three successive verses:

Aen. XI, 55 at non, Euandre, pudendis
volneribus pulsum aspicies, nec sospite dirum
optabis nato funus pater. hei mihi, quantum
praesidium, Ausonia, et quantum tu perdis, Iule.

Of the different forms of prosaic enjambement this is, of course, that which most completely obscures the end of the verse: in the movement of his thought from verse to verse Virgil is here the least Homeric.

Thus we have found that Homer more often brings his thought to a close at the end of the verse than do later writers of the epic, and that he marks more strongly the rhythm of the hexameter. That is the larger difference and the many details which go to make it up cannot well be given briefly: a study in style like the present one fulfils its aims as it goes ahead, forming | for us bit by bit a clearer sense of the way in which a poet has fitted his thought to the pattern of his verses. Of course one would like to say that Homer's enjambement is better or worse than that of Apollonius and Virgil. But to do that, one must first be sure of the merits of the running and periodic styles as a whole, at least in as far as they suit certain lines of thought, and one will have to go into all the broader problem of the order of thought in the Homeric sentence, of which this paper has treated only a very small part. The subject is vast, for we shall have to know the word order in the Homeric sentence and within the verse, the use of the parts of speech, the length of sentences and clauses and the way in which they are grouped. Yet I think the search will repay itself. We may very well find that M. Marcel Jousse, from his study of various oral poetries,[1] is right in believing that the order of ideas in oral verse is more closely suited to the inborn workings of the mind than it is in written style. But even before that I would place the reward of knowing what we already know, in a way: that the style of Homer is that which best tells what he wished to tell.

[1] *Le Style oral rhythmique et mnémotechnique chez les Verbo-moteurs* (Paris, 1925).

5

Studies in the Epic Technique of Oral Verse-Making. I. Homer and Homeric Style*

In my study of the traditional epithet in Homer[1] I dealt with those formulas in the *Iliad* and in the *Odyssey* which are made up of a noun and one or more fixed epithets, and showed that they were created to help the poet set the heroic tale to hexameters. The noun has a metrical value which allows little change, but by adding to it an ornamental epithet one can make a phrase of the needed length which, since the epithet has no bearing on the idea of the sentence, can be used as freely as the simple noun. I also showed that the technique of the use of the noun–epithet formulas is worked out to so fine a point that it could be only for the smallest part due to any one man. Unless the language itself stands in the way, the poet[2]—or poets—of the Homeric poems has—or have—a noun–epithet formula to meet every regularly recurring need. And what is equally striking, there is usually only one such formula. An artifice of composition of this variety and of this thrift must have called for the long efforts of many poets who all sought the best and easiest way of telling the same kind of stories in the same verse-form. Now no reader of the study, so far as I know, has failed to grant its main thesis, which I have just given. When fault has been found, it has rather been with what has seemed to be the bearing of the limited conclusions on the larger problem | of Homeric style. It has been objected that formulas are to be found in all poetry, where they come either from one writer's copying another or from his using his own diction over once he has formed it.[3]

* First published in *Harvard Studies in Classical Philology* 41 (1930), 73–147.

[1] TE, above.

[2] I shall use the term Homer as signifying either *the poet* (*or the poets*) *of the Iliad and Odyssey*, or *the text of the Iliad and Odyssey*. This use of the term is possible in a study like the present one which has to do only with that body of repeated phrases which is common to the poems as a whole. Whether we suppose one or several poets, we have, so far as the formulas are concerned, only a single style. For a demonstration of the unity of the diction so far as it is made up of noun–epithet formulas see TE, pp. 189-90 above.

[3] Paul Shorey, *Classical Philology*, XXIII (1928), p. 305; S. E. Bassett, *Classical Journal*, XXV (1930), p. 642.

Then others have thought that the noun–epithet formulas in Homer's style are an unusual feature, and that they might well have become fixed while the poet was elsewhere left to choose for his ideas what words he would.[1] These remarks, I think, are not without reason. I must claim to have said myself that one could not hope to show by the method used in the study that Homer's style is altogether traditional,[2] and I believe that the chapter on the epithet in Apollonius and Virgil shows that true noun–epithet formulas are absent from later Greek and Latin verse, if not from all written European literature.[3] But the statement that a certain part of Homer's diction is almost entirely traditional is one which is sure to suggest larger conclusions; and formulas—or what looks something like them at any rate—would seem to be fairly common in Greek, Latin, and modern verse. The conclusion that Homer's style is more or less formulaic will not be complete until we know just how large a place formulas have in the style of Homer and in that of later poets. No number of formulas found in later authors would disprove the fact that the fixed epithet in Homer is traditional; but they might keep us from saying that Homeric style is so formulaic that it can be understood only as a traditional and an oral style.

So it is that the criticisms which I have just mentioned seem to me to point out the next step which would naturally be taken in the study of the traditional element in Homer. Moreover, we must know the nature of Homeric style as a whole before it will be possible to go on to other studies which seem to me necessary for the understanding of the *Iliad* and the *Odyssey*,—such as the use of noun–epithet formulas in the Greek epic after Homer, which should tell us much about the Singers—ἀοιδοί—and about the making of the Homeric | poems; or the relation between the formulas, the dialectic forms, and the hexameter, wherein lies much knowledge of the early history of the epic; or the stylistic likenesses between the Greek epic and the oral epics of other nations, which must form the basis of any attempt to judge Homer by what we know about these other poems.

Since these topics have all to do with the style, and more closely with the diction of Homer, I think it may be as well here at the outset to explain what seems to me to be just now the value of studies of this sort. There is first of all the sure promise of better knowing the poet's thought as we note in just what way he has chosen to express it. But there is also the hope that we may thus save the question of the making of the Homeric poems from the danger of scepticism. The scholars of our time have proved the weakness of the attempts made for more than a century to show how the *Iliad* and *Odyssey* were pieced together, and though one

[1] P. Chantraine, *Revue de philologie*, III (1929), p. 299.
[2] TE, p. 106.
[3] TE, Chap. II: pp. 24–37 ; cf. pp. 165–72 above.

would hesitate to say, as Lucian makes Homer say,[1] that all the condemned verses are his, one reads the poems in a way which amounts to just about that. Yet those who have thus well refuted the theories which broke up the poems have themselves given no very good explanation of just how they were made. When they have turned to the positive side of their argument, which is the art of Homer, they have often added much to our enjoyment of the poetry, but they have often been as willful in their judgment as ever were those whom they sought to refute. Moreover, they have refused to see the need of answering certain valid questions which had been raised by the 'higher criticism.' For example, what reasons have they had for passing over the fact pointed out by Wolf that a limited use of writing for literary purposes, which is the most one can suppose for Homer's age, must have made for a poetry very unlike ours?[2] What source have they given for the tradition that Homer was recorded only at a later time?[3] How have they explained the unique number of *good* variant readings | in our text of Homer, and the need for the laborious editions of Aristarchus and of the other grammarians, and the extra lines, which grow in number as new papyri are found?[4] Finally, have they shown why the poems should be of such a sort as to lend themselves to the many attempts to show the parts of which they were made, and have they told why these attempts were often made by men of the best taste and judgment? Like those whom they were refuting they have, I think, failed, because they would not see that in style and form Homeric verse is unlike that to which they are used.

If we are to learn the true nature of the poems, and if we are to solve the question of their authorship, or know that it cannot be solved, or, as may well prove to be the case, if we are to find that its sure solution does not count for so much as one thinks, we must take another course. We must go back to the principle of Aristarchus of getting 'the solution from the text', but we must enlarge it until it covers not only the meaning of a verse or passage but the poems entire, and lets us know why the poet, or poets, of the *Iliad* and *Odyssey* made them as they are, or as they were at first. Whatever feature of poetic art we may study, we must follow it throughout the traditional text,[5] and try to see it clearly and fully; but

[1] *A True Story*, 2, 20.

[2] Quid? quod, si forte his [sc. graphio et tabula] instructus, unus in saeculo suo, Iliada et Odysseam hoc tenore pertexuisset, in ceterarum opportunitatum penuria similes illae fuissent ingenti navigio, quod quis in prima ruditate navigationis fabricatus in loco mediterraneo, machinis et phalangis ad protrudendum, atque adeo mari careret, in quo experimentum suae artis caperet. — *Prolegomena* 26. For our present knowledge about writing in the Homeric age, see below, p. 271, n. 1.

[3] Pausanias 7, 26, 13; Josephus, *Against Apion* 1, 2, 6 (Reinach).

[4] For the papyri of Homer, see Victor Bérard, *Introduction à l'Odyssée* (Paris, 1924), I, pp. 51–70.

[5] 'Traditional text' is of course a relative term. (Cf. G. M. Bolling, *The External Evidence*

our hope will not be to find places out of harmony with one another, but instead, after finding all the elements of the poems which bear upon that feature, to draw from them when we can, but from them only, a new idea of poetic artistry. This is, of course, in my own terms, nothing more than one use of the historical method of criticism,[1] which has been used by all good critics. What I wish to point out is not the need of a new method, but of a stricter use, in the supreme problem of Homer's idea of style and poetic form, of the one good one. It is here, rather than in the study of religious, | or cultural, or social, or historical details that we must look for the answer to the question of how the poems were made, since the statement of a fact can only be rightly judged when we know how the statement came to be made. Yet it is precisely in the matter of literary form that we are most likely to apply without thinking the ideas which have been gradually formed in us by the writings of later times.

The first move in this attempt to rebuild the Homeric idea of epic poetry will be to show that the *Iliad* and the *Odyssey* are composed in a traditional style, and are composed orally, then to see just how such poetry differs from our own in style and form. When that is done, we shall have solid ground beneath us when we undertake the problem of unity in the poems, or judge a doubtful verse, or try to point out how one epic poem would differ from another, or how the greatness of a Singer would show itself. We shall find then, I think, that this failure to see the difference between written and oral verse was the greatest single obstacle to our understanding of Homer, we shall cease to be puzzled by much, we shall no longer look for much that Homer would never have thought of saying, and above all, we shall find that many, if not most of the questions we were asking, were not the right ones to ask.

I. THE PLAN OF THE STUDY

The poet who composes with only the spoken word a poem of any length must be able to fit his words into the mould of his verse after a fixed pattern. Unlike the poet who writes out his lines,—or even dictates them,—he cannot think without hurry about his next word, nor change what he has made, nor, before going on, read over what he has just written. Even if one wished to imagine him making his verses alone, one could not suppose the slow finding of the next word, the pondering of

for Interpolation in Homer, Oxford, 1925, pp. 1–15.) The doubtful lines and groups of lines are, however, too few, and with the rarest exceptions too regular in language to affect the subject of these pages; so that for my purposes the traditional text is that of A. Ludwich (Leipzig, 1889–1907).

[1] Cf. Roger Bacon, *De augmentis scientiarum* 2, 4; Ernest Renan, *L'Avenir de la science* (Paris, 1892), p. 292; Alfred Croiset, *Histoire de la littérature grecque*[3] (Paris, 1910), I, pp. ix–xliii; TE, pp. 2–4 above.

the verses just made, the memorizing of each verse. Even though the poet have an unusual memory, he cannot, without paper, make of his own words a poem of any length. He must have for his use word-groups all made to fit his verse and tell what he has to tell. In composing he will do no more than put together for his needs phrases which he has often heard or used himself, and which, grouping themselves in accordance with a fixed pattern of thought, come naturally to make the sentence and the verse; and he will recall his | poem easily, when he wishes to say it over, because he will be guided anew by the same play of words and phrases as before. The style of such poetry is in many ways very unlike that to which we are used. The oral poet expresses only ideas for which he has a fixed means of expression. He is by no means the servant of his diction: he can put his phrases together in an endless number of ways; but still they set bounds and forbid him the search of a style which would be altogether his own. For the style which he uses is not his at all: it is the creation of a long line of poets or even of an entire people. No one man could get together any but the smallest part of the diction which is needed for making verses orally, and which is made of a really vast number of word-groups each of which serves two ends: it expresses a given idea in fitting terms and fills just the space in the verse which allows it to be joined to the phrases which go before and after and which, with it, make the sentence. As one poet finds a phrase which is both pleasing and easily used, the group takes it up, and its survival is a further proving of these two prime qualities. It is the sum of single phrases thus found, tried, and kept which makes up the diction. Finally, the poem which is a thing of sound and not of writing is known apart from its author only because it is composed in the same style which others use and so can remember. Writing may be known, and the poem may be dictated and recorded, and the knowledge of writing may thus have some bearing on the text of the poem. But it will not have any upon its style, nor upon its form, nor upon its life in the group of poets and the social group of which its author was a part.

Such in its broadest lines is the composition of oral poetry as it is practiced in our own times in Serbia, among the Tuaregs, in Afghanistan, and in many other places;[1] and it is clear that the best way of knowing whether a style is oral and traditional is to hear it in use, or, lacking that, to compare the recorded work of several poets who have made their verses out of the same formulas. But we cannot do either | of these things for the Greek epic. There is too little known about the making of the early

[1] Cf. F. S. Krauss, *Vom wunderbaren Guslarengedächtnis*, in *Slavische Volkforschungen* (Leipzig, 1908), pp. 183–9; A. van Gennep, *La Question d'Homère* (Paris, 1909), pp. 50–5; M. Jousse, *Le Style oral rhythmique et mnémotechnique chez les Verbo-moteurs* (Paris, 1925). The last work is valuable as an attempt to set forth the psychological basis of oral poetic style; it gives a bibliography of the literature on oral verse (pp. 236–40).

poetry in hexameters for us to liken the Singers to the Serbian Guslars without more ado, or to make of Homer a Singer like any other. Moreover, we cannot date the works of this early time at all surely, and we have nothing to show us that any one of the poems we have was made by a Singer. Opinion generally grants a vague body of traditional epic formulas, and we have a certain amount of poetry composed in a style which is either entirely or nearly like that of the *Iliad* and *Odyssey*; but the notion is also current that Homeric phrases found outside these two poems are more or less due to the studied imitation of the style which one poet made. We should be well off if we knew for sure that Homer could not write, but writing may have been known in Ionia in his time, whatever were the uses it was put to.[1] If we are to draw any solid conclusions | about the style of Homer, we have only one course to follow. Seeking 'the solution from the text' we must see whether the diction of the *Iliad* and of the *Odyssey* is of a sort which can be understood only as a traditional and oral technique of making verses by means of formulas. The reasoning will be as follows. First, we shall define the formula. Then we shall look to see what means there are of telling whether a formula is traditional or not. The nature of the formula will show us that the more formulas we find in a poet's diction, the smaller is the portion of them which could be the

[1] Certain scholars in recent years have supposed that the Greeks wrote at a very early date. Thus, B. F. C. Atkinson (*Encyclopaedia Britannica*, 14th ed., s.v. *alphabet*) believes that the Achaeans, that is to say, the Greeks before the Dorian invasions, knew the Phoenician alphabet. A. J. B. Wace (*Cambridge Ancient History*, II, p. 463) and J. B. Bury express a view which does not accord with this: 'In the Achaean age writing was an old and well-known art. . . . But it was writing without an alphabet' (*ibid.* p. 508). The evidence for the latter theory is the antiquity of the Minoan script and some undeciphered 'signs', to use Bury's word (*loc. cit.*), on some vases of the Third Late Helladic Period from Thebes and Tiryns. The evidence for the early knowledge of the Phoenician alphabet is likewise circumstantial. I quote Victor Bérard (*Les Phéniciens et l'Odyssée*[2], Paris, 1927, I, pp. 14–15), who, after telling of the inscription in alphabetic characters discovered at Byblos in 1923 (cf. *Syria*, V (1924), pp. 135–57), which belongs surely to the thirteenth century, writes: 'Ces quelques lignes feront une révolution dans la critique d'Homère et de la Bible. . . . Dès lors, il faut en tête du problème homérique poser la question préliminaire: Corneille, ayant vécu un siècle et demi après l'invention de l'imprimerie, a fait imprimer *le Cid*; peut-on croire qu'ayant vécu quatre siècles au moins — vraisemblablement six ou sept, — après l'invention de l'alphabet, les poètes de l'*Iliade* et de l'*Odyssée* ne l'aient pas connu?' On the other hand our oldest Greek inscriptions, those discovered at Thera in 1896, have been put by some in the eighth and possibly the ninth centuries (so Atkinson, *loc. cit.*); but Bury (*loc. cit.*) refuses to place them earlier than the seventh, though he supposes the Greeks to have used the alphabet since the tenth century. The problem being of this sort, it is clear that the Homeric scholar, who at present bases his conclusions upon the assumption on external evidence either of Homer's use or ignorance of writing, risks the future of his work. And besides there remain the questions of the uses to which writing was put, and of the degree to which it was known and used. Finally, there are illiterate poets in countries in which writing is fairly common, as in Serbia. The problem indeed is not at all that of whether or not writing was known in the Homeric age, but of knowing whether the *Iliad* and *Odyssey* were written. It is hard to imagine what sort of external evidence could ever fix us on that point. All that we can hope to know, and all that we really need to know, is whether Homer's style is written or oral. Once this question is proposed, that of the existence or of the uses of writing in Homer's time loses its value.

work of that single poet. We shall then be led to a study of the verse of poets who we know wrote, that we may learn how often the formula can appear in written verse. Finally, having seen if the formulas in Homer's verse are so much more common that they suffer no comparison with those of any written poetry, and having thus learned how much of the formulaic element is surely traditional, we shall be able to consider what reasons there are to say that Homer's is an oral style.

2. THE FORMULA

The formula in the Homeric poems may be defined as *a group of words which is regularly employed under the same metrical conditions to express a given essential idea.* The essential part of the idea is that which remains after one has counted out everything in the expression which is purely for the sake of style. Thus, the essential idea in the word-group ἦμος δ' ἠριγένεια φάνη ῥοδοδάκτυλος Ἠώς is 'when it was morning', that in βῆ δ' ἴμεν is 'he went', that in τὸν δ' αὖτε προσέειπε is 'he said to him'. The word-group is employed regularly when the poet uses it without second thought as the natural means of getting his idea into verse. The definition thus implies the metrical usefulness of the formula. It is not necessary that a poet use one certain formula when he has a given idea to express and a given space | of the verse to fill, since there can be formulas of like metrical value and meaning which can take the place of one another, though they are rare in Homer. But if a formula is to be used regularly there must be a steady need for it. For example, Homer uses θεὰ γλαυκῶπις Ἀθήνη fifty times to express in the last half of the verse, after the trochaic caesura of the third foot, the idea 'Athena'. The simple number of times the phrase appears is the direct measure of its usefulness, though if one wishes further proof a study of its uses shows it to be part of a fixed device for making hundreds of verses.[1] Kurt Witte's remark[2] that the language of the Homeric poems is the work of the epic verse is by definition true also of the Homeric diction so far as it is made up of formulas. When one has added the factor of the story, since it is this which gives the poet his ideas, and that of the poetic merit of the expression, which also must have its share in the making and the keeping of it, one may state the principle as follows: *the formulas in any poetry are due, so far as their ideas go, to the theme, their rhythm is fixed by the verse-form, but their art is that of the poets who made them and of the poets who kept them.*

When the element of usefulness is lacking, one does not have a formula but a repeated phrase which has been knowingly brought into the verse

[1] Cf. TE, pp. 10–3 above.
[2] Pauly–Wissowa, XVI (1913), col. 2214.

for some special effect. Thus, the definition excludes the refrain, as found in Aeschylus or Theocritus:

αἴλινον αἴλινον εἰπέ, τὸ δ' εὖ νικάτω . . .[1]

ἶυγξ ἕλκε τὺ τῆνον ἐμὸν ποτὶ δῶμα τὸν ἄνδρα,[2]

or in Shakespere or Marlowe:

Double, double toil and trouble,
Fire burn and cauldron bubble . . .[3]

To entertain divine Zenocrate.[4] |

The definition likewise excludes the echoed phrase.[5] I give examples from Theocritus and Shakspere:

—*χρῄσδεις ὦν ἐσιδεῖν; χρῄσδεις καταθεῖναι ἄεθλον;*
—*χρῄσδω τοῦτ' ἐσιδεῖν, χρῄσδω καταθεῖναι ἄεθλον . . .*[6]

First Witch.—All hail, Macbeth! hail to thee, Thane of Glamis!
Second Witch.—All hail, Macbeth! hail to thee, Thane of Cawdor!
Third Witch.—All hail, Macbeth! that shalt be king hereafter![7]

Non-formulaic too is the verse which is borrowed because the poet's public knows it and will recall its former use, as that in which Sophocles gives to the dying Clytemnestra the words which Agamemnon had spoken in the play by Aeschylus. I quote the verses of the older poet, then those in which they are imitated:[8]

ΑΓ. *ὤμοι πέπληγμαι καιρίαν πληγὴν ἔσω.*
ΧΟ. *σῖγα· τίς πληγὴν ἀυτεῖ καιρίως οὐτασμένος;*
ΑΓ. *ὤμοι μάλ' αὖθις δευτέραν πεπληγμένος . . .*[9]

ΚΛ. *ὤμοι πέπληγμαι.* *ΗΛ.* *παῖσον εἰ σθένεις διπλῆν.*
ΚΛ. *ὤμοι μάλ' αὖθις.*[10] |

1 *Agamemnon* 121, 139, 159.
2 Theocritus 2, 17; 22; 27; 32; 37; 42; 47; 52; 57; 63.
3 *Macbeth* IV, 1, 10–11; 20–1; 35–6.
4 Marlowe, *Tamburlaine, Part Two*, II, 4, 17; 21; 25; 29; 32.
5 For this stylistic device see B. G. Kramer, *Ueber Stichomythie und Gleichklang in den Dramen Shakespeares* (Duisburg, 1889), who quotes examples from Greek, Latin, and modern literature. Walter Raleigh in his *Milton* (London, 1900, pp. 205–8) discusses a striking case in *Paradise Lost* (IV, 641–56). It is only because they have been brought altogether wrongly into the problem of the formulas that I mention here anaphora—the repetition of a word at the beginning of successive clauses, and polyptoton—the repetition in a short space of different forms of the same word; both these devices are rhetorical.
6 Theocritus 8, 11–12.
7 *Macbeth* I, 3, 48–50.
8 For other cases see F. Schroeder, *De iteratis apud tragicos Graecos*, in *Dissertationes philologicae Argentoratenses*, VI (1882), pp. 119–21, who mentions (p. 4) Virgil's use of verses from Ennius.
9 *Agamemnon* 1343 ff.
10 *Electra* 1415 f. A bizarre case of this kind is given by Aristotle. Euripides, evidently to show his skill, took a verse of Aeschylus and by changing a single word added, Aristotle says, to its beauty (*Poetics* 1458b22): *Αἰσχύλος μὲν γὰρ ἐν τῶι Φιλοκτήτηι ἐποίησε*

φαγέδαινα δ' ἥ μου σάρκας ἐσθίει ποδός,

ὁ δὲ ἀντὶ τοῦ ἐσθίει τὸ θοινᾶται μετέθηκεν.

Finally a poet will often repeat a phrase after an interval in order to obtain some special effect, as Sophocles does when Oedipus, fearing for the first time that he himself is the slayer of Laius, repeats in horror the words by which he had banished from the land the unknown murderer.[1]

But the repeated phrase, as distinct from the formula, is used more often in less outstanding ways than these. When Bacchylides, for instance, wrote λευκώλενος Ἥρα,[2] or ὑψιπύλου Τροίας,[3] he was not using the words because he had a certain space of verse to fill and a certain idea to express: he was working epic phrases into his poem. Similarly, Pope in his translation of the *Odyssey*[4] borrowed Milton's phrase 'thick as autumnal leaves' from the Vallombrosa simile in *Paradise Lost.* The fact that he had nothing like this in the verses he was translating shows clearly what is evident enough anyway, that he was using the phrase for its idea rather than for any help it gave him in expressing certain ideas which he was seeking to put into verse. We shall see later that no distinction counts more for us than this between the real formula and the phrase repeated for the sake of its poetic thought or wording. I have quoted these examples here because they bear on the definition of the formula.

There is one other thing to note before leaving this subject: the problem of the formula is not that of literary influence. This fact more than any other has been overlooked by those who have dealt with traditional style. When Pindar, for example, wrote:

πτερόεντα δ' ἵει γλυκύν
Πυθῶνάδ' οἰστόν[5]

he was without doubt recalling the Homeric phrase—πτερόεντες ὀιστοί[6] —and the Homeric influence is proved. But what was a formula to Homer was none to Pindar. The task of getting his words into his verse was quite the same as if he had been using an expression of his own making. The formula is useful only so far as it can be used without changing its metrical value. The change of endings is too easy to have | any measurable effect upon the usefulness of a phrase. One counts by the thousands in Homer such cases as the change of ἐυκνήμιδες Ἀχαιοί to ἐυκνήμιδας Ἀχαιούς, or of θνητῶν ἀνθρώπων to θνητοὺς ἀνθρώπους. And to these must be added the change of δέ to τε, as when φέρων τ' ἀπερείσι' ἄποινα[7] becomes φέρω δ' ἀπερείσι' ἄποινα,[8] or even the omission of these particles, or such a change as that of μου to σου. But any less simple

[1] *Oedipus the King* 236 ff., and 816 ff. Cf. Schroeder, *op. cit.*, pp. 121–5.
[2] 8, 7 (Jebb). [3] 8, 46.
[4] Pope's *Odyssey* II, 970; *Paradise Lost* I, 302.
[5] *Olympian Odes* (Puech) 9, 11.
[6] *E* 171. [7] *A* 13 = 372. [8] *Ω* 502.

alteration in the word-group supposes thought of some length on the part of the poet.[1]

3. THE TRADITIONAL FORMULA

The question of who made the formula does not enter into its definition, since it would be equally helpful to a poet whether it was his own work or that of another. What means then are there of knowing whether the formulas in Homer are borrowed or not, since we have no right to suppose, as the basis of our reasoning, that the *Iliad* and the *Odyssey* are necessarily due to more than one man? The solution lies in the schematization of the Homeric style, which does away altogether with the need of knowing how many poets worked at these poems.

Formulas are of two sorts. First, there are those which have no close likeness to any other, as, so far as we know, is the case for ὀνείαθ᾽ ἑτοῖμα προκείμενα in the following verse, which is found three times in the *Iliad* and eleven times in the *Odyssey*:

οἱ δ᾽ ἐπ᾽ ὀνείαθ᾽ ἑτοῖμα προκείμενα χεῖρας ἴαλλον. |

The other kind of formula is that which is like one or more which express a similar idea in more or less the same words, as, for example, ἱερὸν πτολίεθρον ἔπερσε[2] is like ἱερὸν πτολίεθρον ἑλόντες,[3] or as ὀλέκοντο δὲ λαοί[4] is like ἀρετῶσι δὲ λαοί[5] and δαινῦτό τε λαός.[6] We may say that any group of two or more such like formulas make up a system, and the system may be defined in turn as a group of phrases which have the same metrical value and which are enough alike in thought and words to leave no doubt that the poet who used them knew them not only as single formulas, but also as formulas of a certain type. For example, one finds in the *Iliad* and the *Odyssey* a group of phrases which all express between the beginning of the verse and the trochaic cæsura of the third foot, in words which are much alike, the idea 'but when he (we, they) had done so and so':

[1] *Note on Method.* Formulas, in the strictest sense of the term, may be of any length, but in studying them we are forced to exclude the shorter word-groups, for the following reasons. If we dealt with formulas of all sizes we should have an unwieldy mass of material of varying importance, and it would be impossible to compare the formulaic element in different poets by means of the number of formulas found in their verse. In the second place, we must set a limit which will shut out any groups of words which are repeated merely by chance, or as the result of their natural order in the sentence. Accordingly I have regarded as formulas, or possible formulas, only expressions made up of at least four words or five syllables, with the exception of noun–epithet phrases, which may be shorter, as φίλον ἦτορ (Pindar, *Olympian Odes*, 1, 4). I have drawn the distinction at this point because of the fact that while an expression of five syllables will command the hearer's attention by itself, one of four syllables is much less noticeable; and by insisting upon four words in a shorter phrase one puts aside almost all the chance groups of connective words.

[2] α 2. [3] ι 165. [4] *A* 10. [5] τ 114. [6] *Ω* 665.

αὐτὰρ ἐπεὶ		δείπνησε	(twice)
		κατέπαυσα	(δ 583)
		τάρπησαν	(3 times)
		τάρπημεν	(twice)
		παύσαντο	(3 times)
	ῥ'	ἕσσαντο	(3 times)
		εὔξαντο	(4 times)
		ἤγερθεν	(4 times)
		ἵκανε	(ρ 28)
		ἵκοντο	(3 times)
		ὤπτησε	(*I* 215)
		ἐτέλεσσε	(λ 246)
		ἐνέηκε	(δ 233)

αὐτὰρ ἐπειδὴ	ζέσσεν	(twice)
	σπεῦσε	(3 times)
	τεῦξε	(twice)
αὐτὰρ ἐπὴν	ἔλθητε	(*O* 147)
	ἔλθῃσιν	(3 times)
	ἀγάγῃσιν	(*Ω* 155)

This scheme shows not only that the poet or the poets of the *Iliad* and the *Odyssey* had a formula to express the idea 'but when they had prayed', for instance, between the beginning of the verse and the trochaic cæsura of the third foot.[1] It shows also that he, or they, knew | a type of formula in which to *αὐτὰρ ἐπεί* was added an indicative verb-form of the measure ⏕ – ⏑, beginning with a single consonant; and also another type in which to *αὐτὰρ ἐπεί* was joined first *ῥ'*, one form of that helpful and many-shaped particle, then an indicative verb-form beginning with a vowel or diphthong and measured ⏕ – ⏑. Thirdly, there was a type where *αὐτὰρ ἐπεί*, lengthened by the addition of the syllable -*δη*, allowed the use of verb-forms of the value – ⏑. And lastly, there was a type of formula in which *αὐτὰρ ἐπεί*, changed to *αὐτὰρ ἐπήν*, made way for subjunctive forms of the verb. Each of these four groups of formulas may be called a system, since it is clear that the poet, or poets, who used them, felt the exact device, as I have taken care to analyze it, for fitting into the verse verb-forms of certain moods and measures. Finally, the four groups taken together form a larger system in which the common likeness, while less close, is no less real.

It is the system of formulas, as we shall see, which is the only true means by which we can come to see just how the Singer made his verses; but we are interested in it now solely as a means of measuring the schematization of a poet's style. There are in such a measuring two factors, that of length and that of thrift. The length of a system consists very obviously in the number of formulas which make it up. The thrift of a system lies in the degree in which it is free of phrases which, having the same metrical value and expressing the same idea, could replace one another. What the length and thrift of a system of formulas are can be best explained by describing one of the most striking cases in Homer, that of a system of noun–epithet formulas for gods and heroes, in the nominative.

[1] *A* 458, *B* 421, γ 447, μ 359.

All the chief characters of the *Iliad* and the *Odyssey*, if their names can be fitted into the last half of the verse along with an epithet, have a noun–epithet formula in the nominative, beginning with a simple consonant, which fills the verse between the trochaic cæsura of the third foot and the verse-end: for instance, πολύτλας δῖος Ὀδυσσεύς. It is the number of different formulas of this type, well above fifty, which makes the length of this system. But besides that there are in only a very few cases more than one such formula for a single character, though many of them are used very often, as πολύτλας δῖος Ὀδυσσεύς which is found 38 times, θεὰ γλαυκῶπις Ἀθήνη 50 times, Ποσειδάων ἐνοσίχθων 23 times. To be exact, in a list of 37 characters who have formulas of this type, which includes | all those having any importance in the poems, there are only three names which have a second formula which could replace the first.[1]

In the case of this system, as in that of other formulas, such as those of the types πολύμητις Ὀδυσσεύς and δῖος Ὀδυσσεύς, the length and the thrift of the system are striking enough to be sure proof that only the very smallest part of it could be the work of one poet.[2] But for the greater

[1] Cf. TE, pp. 17–19 above.

[2] Because of their unique value for the problem of the formulaic diction I give here these three systems. The formulas joined by a bracket are those which can replace one another and which must be taken from the system to keep its economy perfect, though one in each such group of formulas must be traditional since it adds to the length of the system. For these equivalent formulas see TE, pp. 173–90, where it is shown that they result from the play of analogy which underlies all the traditional diction. Beside the formulas of the three types named, the following list gives those of other types which have the same measure but whose metrical value is changed by the initial sound — vowel, single consonant, or double consonant. An asterisk indicates that the measure of the name makes the formula impossible.

δῖος Ὀδυσσεύς	60	πολύμητις Ὀδυσσεύς	81	πολύτλας δῖος Ὀδυσσεύς	38
ἐσθλὸς Ὀδυσσεύς	3	πτολίπορθος Ὀδυσσεύς	4		
Παλλὰς Ἀθήνη	39	γλαυκῶπις Ἀθήνη	26	{ θεὰ γλαυκῶπις Ἀθήνη	50
Ὀβριμοπάτρη	2			{ Ἀλαλκομενηὶς Ἀθήνη	2
δῖος Ἀχιλλεύς	34	πόδας ὠκὺς Ἀχιλλεύς	31	ποδάρκης δῖος Ἀχιλλεύς	21
ὠκὺς Ἀχιλλεύς	5	μεγάθυμος Ἀχιλλεύς	1		
μητίετα Ζεύς	18	{ νεφεληγερέτα Ζεύς	30	πατὴρ ἀνδρῶν τε θεῶν τε	15
εὐρύοπα Ζεύς	14	{ Ζεὺς τερπικέραυνος	4	Ὀλύμπιος εὐρύοπα Ζεύς	1
		{ στεροπηγερέτα Ζεύς	1		
πότνια Ἥρη	11	λευκώλενος Ἥρη	3	βοῶπις πότνια Ἥρη	11
		χρυσόθρονος Ἥρη	1	θεὰ λευκώλενος Ἥρη	19
φαίδιμος Ἕκτωρ	29	κορυθαίολος Ἕκτωρ	25	μέγας κορυθαίολος Ἕκτωρ	12
ὄβριμος Ἕκτωρ	4				
χάλκεος Ἄρης	5	χρυσήνιος Ἄρης	1	βριήπυος ὄβριμος Ἄρης	1
ὄβριμος Ἄρης	5			Ἄρης ἆτος πολέμοιο	3
Τυδέος υἱός	8	κρατερὸς Διομήδης	12	βοὴν ἀγαθὸς Διομήδης	21
		ἀγαθὸς Διομήδης	1		
*		κρείων Ἀγαμέμνων	26	ἄναξ ἀνδρῶν Ἀγαμέμνων	37

[continued overleaf

number of systems which are found in the diction of the Homeric poems we cannot make such sure conclusions, since their length is rarely so great and their thrift never so striking. This does not mean that the proof by means of the length and thrift of the system is possible only in the case of the noun–epithet formulas. It is clear without need of further search that the greater part of the system quoted above must be traditional, and that the type of the formula and the words *αὐτὰρ ἐπεί* at the beginning of the verse are surely so. But one can see that an attempt made in this fashion to see just how much of Homer's diction had been handed down to him could give only very partial results, even if the task were not of an impossible length, as it is. What we must look for is, more simply, the degree to which the diction of poetry outside the epos can become schematized. If, having gauged the systematization of Homer's verse and of that which we know to have been written in the individual style of single poets, we find a difference which forbids any comparison, we shall know that Homer's poetry was not made in the same way as was that of later poets. We shall then see that we are faced with a problem which can be solved only by granting that Homer composed his verses entirely in a style that was traditional and adapted to oral verse-making.

In making this comparison of the systems in Homer with those in later poetry we shall not, as it happens, have much to do with the thrift |

continued from p. 77]

Κυανοχαίτης	1	*κρείων ἐνοσίχθων*	7	*Ποσειδάων ἐνοσίχθων*	23
Ἐννοσίγαιος	1	*κλυτὸς ἐννοσίγαιος*	7		
*		*Πρίαμος θεοειδής*	1	*γέρων Πρίαμος θεοειδής*	7
φαίδιμος Αἴας	6	*Τελαμώνιος Αἴας*	10	*μέγας Τελαμώνιος Αἴας*	12
ἄλκιμος Αἴας	2				
δῖ' Ἀφροδίτη	4	*χρυσέη Ἀφροδίτη*	1	*Διὸς θυγάτηρ Ἀφροδίτη*	7
				φιλομμειδὴς Ἀφροδίτη	4
Φοῖβος Ἀπόλλων	33	*Διὸς υἱὸς Ἀπόλλων*	2	*ἄναξ Διὸς υἱὸς Ἀπόλλων*	5
		ἑκάεργος Ἀπόλλων	6	*ἄναξ ἑκάεργος Ἀπόλλων*	9
		κλυτότοξος Ἀπόλλων	1		
*		*ξανθὸς Μενέλαος*	12	*βοὴν ἀγαθὸς Μενέλαος*	13
		Μενέλαος ἀμύμων	1	*ἀρηΐφιλος Μενέλαος*	6
ἱππότα Νέστωρ	1			*Γερήνιος ἱππότα Νέστωρ*	31
		πόδας ὠκέα Ἶρις	10	*ποδήνεμος ὠκέα Ἶρις*	10
*		*		*Ἀλέξανδρος θεοειδής*	10

There are also many other formulas of these types for less important characters. If any character who has a rôle of any prominence in the poems does not appear on this list, it is because the metrical value of the name is an absolute barrier to the creation of such formulas. Such are the names, *Ἀντίλοχος*, *Αὐτομέδων*, *Ἑλένη*, *Εὐρύπυλος*, *Ἰδομενεύς*, *Πουλυδάμας*, *Σαρπηδών*, *Ἀλκίνοος* (but *μένος Ἀλκινόοιο*), *Ἀντίνοος*, *Εὐρύμαχος*, *Τηλέμαχος* (but *Ὀδυσσῆος φίλος υἱός*). *Ἄναξ ἀνδρῶν Αἰνείας* is found once, when Homer was led by the force of analogy to create a formula of the type *ἄναξ ἀνδρῶν Ἀγαμέμνων*; but in no other case does he use this name, with its three long syllables, at the verse-end.

of the system, since we shall find it hard enough to get together outside of Homer any systems which show the first quality of length. We | shall seldom get any farther than the overwhelming difference in the number of repetitions. Since this is the case, it is well to point out beforehand that the number of repetitions in a style, and the frequency with which they are used, bear directly upon the thrift of the diction. One may ask why Homer uses the formula αὐτὰρ ἐπεί ῥ' ἵκοντο three times.[1] That is one face of the coin. The other face is the question of why Homer did not use other words, of whatever sort they might be, for the expression of the idea 'but when they came'. That is, the repeated use of a phrase means not only that the poet is following a fixed pattern of words, it means equally that he is denying himself all other ways of expressing the idea. This may seem a very trivial point to make, if one has in mind only a few scattered formulas, none of them used more than a few times. But when one has even a single phrase used, for instance as is τὸν (τὴν) δ' ἠμείβετ' ἔπειτα, 48 times in the *Iliad* and 24 times in the *Odyssey*, it is as if Homer wished to tell us how little use he has for all other ways of expressing the idea, which we must suppose to be very numerous. Then, when one multiplies the case of the single formula by all those which are to be found in the two poems, and which require the 250 pages of C. E. Schmidt's *Parallel-Homer*[2] for their listing, one has the statement of a thrift of expression which it is rather hard, perhaps, for us to understand. Yet we must remember, as in the following pages we seek for formulas in later verse, that the poet's indifference to the new way of saying a thing is to be measured in the exact terms of the number of repetitions he uses and of the times he uses them. |

4. THE FORMULA OUTSIDE HOMER

Hesiod, the Homeric Hymns, the Fragments of the Early Epic

P. F. Kretschmer, in his study of repetitions[3] within the work of Hesiod,[4] found within the 1022 verses of the *Theogony* 338 repetitions of which the larger part are phrases found in Homer. This proportion does not come near that of the twenty-five or six thousand repetitions[5] in Homer's 27853 or so verses, nor would one look for it in poems of such different lengths. Still it is far above anything we shall find for the poetry of times in which writing was beyond any doubt the usual means of composition.

[1] *A* 484, *ρ* 85, 178.

[2] Göttingen, 1885.

[3] It is important to note that the terms *repetition*, *repeated phrase* and *repeated expression*, etc., when used in this study always imply that the word-groups in question are alike not only in words but also in metrical value. When the word *phrase* or *expression* is used in connection with repetition, in the sense of a more general similarity, I have taken care to explain the use of the term.

[4] *De iteratis Hesiodeis* (Vratislaviae, 1913), p. 29.

[5] I compute this figure from Schmidt's *Parallel-Homer*.

We find in Hesiod even more repetitions from poetry which could not be his. A. Rzach[1] notes 67 cases in the first 100 lines of the *Theogony* where a phrase is identical with one found in the *Iliad* or the *Odyssey*. The number of repetitions within the *Works and Days* is smaller—84 in a poem of 828 verses.[2] For the first hundred lines Rzach notes 55 Homeric parallels, but in the gnomic portion of the poem this number falls to 31 in a hundred lines.[3] But even this figure is far from any which is ever found outside the early hexametric poetry. It is not the place here to explain the varying degrees of repetition within the Hesiodic poems, nor the use of Homeric phrases. That will be possible only in a longer study in which one will throw aside the idea of imitation, which has weighed so heavily on the early poetry outside Homer, and take up the repetitions as part of a traditional technique of verse-making. One will then learn, I believe, a great deal about the nature of the epic diction, of its use for different subjects, and by different poets or schools of poets, and of its decline. Here we can only point out that the formula is used in Hesiod far more often than it ever is outside of the early epic; and the same thing is to be said for the *Shield of Heracles*, which in its 480 verses repeats itself 63 times,[4] and has in its first hundred | lines 74 Homeric phrases,[5] as well as for certain of the *Hymns* and for the fragments of the other early heroic poems. T. W. Allen, for instance, states that 20 verses of the *Hymn to Aphrodite* 'are taken from Homer with little or no variation',[6] and I find seven Homeric phrases in a ten-line fragment of the *Thebais*.[7]

The Elegiac Poetry[8]

N. Riedy found in Solon 48 phrases repeated without change from the *Iliad* or the *Odyssey* or the *Hymns*;[9] of these all but one are found in the 221 elegiac verses of this poet. There are none in his iambics. This makes about 21 epic phrases to a hundred verses, a figure fairly near that found for the gnomic part of the *Works and Days*. In the 932 verses of Theognis which Bergk thought genuine R. Küllenberg found 144 phrases repeated from Homer, Hesiod, or the *Hymns*, which would be about fifteen epic

[1] *Hesiodi Carmina* (Leipzig, 1902), pp. 1–19.
[2] *Ibid.*, pp. 127–45.
[3] vv. 202 ff.
[4] Kretschmer, *op. cit.*, p. 29.
[5] Rzach, *op. cit.*, pp. 273–82.
[6] *Homeric Hymns* (London, 1904), p. 197.
[7] Fr. 2 (Kinkel). *αὐτὰρ ὁ διογενής* (*Φ* 17); *παρέθηκε τράπεζαν* (*ε* 92); *αὐτὰρ ἔπειτα* (*Γ* 273); *δέπας ἡδέος οἴνου* (*γ* 51); *αὐτὰρ ὅ γ' ὡς* (*M* 40); *πατρὸς ἑοῖο* (*B* 662); *ἔμπεσε θυμῶι* (*Ξ* 207).
[8] The figures which I give for unaltered Homeric phrases in the elegiac poets are based upon the lists which Riedy and Küllenberg made of verbal likenesses of any sort between Solon and Theognis on the one hand, and Homer on the other, without limiting themselves, as we must do, to those cases in which the word-groups are not only alike, but also have the same metrical value and are of at least a certain length. The figures given in the following pages for Pindar, Bacchylides, Aeschylus, Sophocles, Euripides, Theocritus and Kyd have all been gotten by a like method. I have been able to utilize more directly the lists of Kretschmer and Rzach for Hesiod, and of Albrecht for Virgil.
[9] *Solonis elocutio quatenus pendeat ab exemplo Homeri* (Munich, 1903).

phrases to a hundred verses.[1] No one has studied the shorter repetitions within the elegiac poetry, but Küllenberg remarks that in the hexameter the elegy follows the epic.[2] So here too the formulaic element must be studied as a part of the traditional diction of the early verse in hexameters. But Küllenberg also states that the elegy follows itself in the pentameter. He quotes in proof 18 phrases, all found in the last half of the pentameter, which appear in the work of the elegiac poets a total of 99 times.[3] Moreover, certain of the systems into which these phrases fall are | long enough to show the traditional character of the greater part of the expressions which make them up, as in the following example:

Solon 3, 6; Theognis 194	*χρήμασι*	*πειθόμενος* (-οι, -αιν)
Solon 1, 12; 3, 11; Theognis 380	*ἔργμασι*	
Theognis 948	*ἀνδράσι*	
Theognis 756	*σώφρονι*	
Theognis 1152; Simonides 92a, 2	*ῥήμασι*	
Simonides 107b, 2	*λήματι*	

Such a large number of formulas and systems of this sort are found outside the hexameter only in this one place, and, if we knew surely that writing was the regular means for the composition of verse in the sixth century, there would very likely be no need of carrying our search any farther. But we do not. The example of Serbian poetry shows that traditional dictions can exist side by side for different verse-forms and for different types of poetry, and the doubt which hangs over the sources of Theognis's poem would point to anything but an originally written text. A study of the elegy, which kept in view the possibility that its style was in a larger or smaller measure oral and traditional, might explain the very many verses and passages in Theognis which some editors have given to Tyrtaeus, Mimnermus and Solon, because they are found, in more or less the same form, in their work as well.[4] If this small amount of poetry we have is at all typical, the common element in the elegy was very large. The conclusions of such a study, however, could have only a limited value for our own problem: it is hard to see how it could prove that Solon and Theognis first wrote out their verses, and though it would doubtless confirm Küllenberg's idea that there was a formulaic element in elegiac style, common to all poets, there are other ways of showing this to be true for Homer.

The Choral Poetry

When Riedy[5] remarks that in Solon epic formulas are about twice as frequent in the hexameter as they are in the pentameter, and when

[1] *De imitatione Theognidea* (Argentorati, 1877).
[2] *Op. cit.*, p. 49.
[3] *Op. cit.*, pp. 50–3.
[4] See E. Harrison, *Studies in Theognis* (Cambridge, 1902), pp. 100–34.
[5] *Op. cit.*, pp. 51 f.

Küllenberg says that the last half of the pentameter has formulas | found only in elegy, they are dealing with a fact which has been strangely overlooked, namely, that the formula can be useful only in the smallest degree in any other sort of verse than that for which it was made: the nature of the hexameter is such that only a small part of the epic formulas are found in more than one place in the verse; likewise one will hardly hope to find many of them in a verse-form in which the sequence of longs and shorts and the length of the kola are only rarely those of the epic verse. The one case in Solon's work of an Homeric phrase which is not found in elegy occurs in a skolion which may or may not be his:[1]

πεφυλαγμένος ἄνδρα ἕκαστον ὅρα.

Here the strong dactylic movement of the verse gives to the participle, and to ἄνδρα ἕκαστον, something of the movement we find in the Homeric line:

λίσσεθ' ὑπὲρ τοκέων γουνούμενος ἄνδρα ἕκαστον.[2]

It is surely not a very striking phrase, and one would be tempted to say it was only due to chance, if it were not for the hiatus which makes it certain that it was taken from the epic, for like μέλανος οἴνοιο in the fragment of the epic poet Antimachus, it shows a sense for the lost digamma of the epic phrase similar to the feeling of the French for 'h-aspiré'.[3] But such likeness in rhythm between epic and lyric can only rarely happen. H. Schultz[4] gives 52 cases in which Pindar has copied a phrase of the *Iliad* or the *Odyssey*, of which, it is well to note, 48 are made up of two words, and the remaining four of three words: the rhythm barred all longer Homeric expressions. Yet of these 52 there are only 19 which Pindar could use as he found them.[5] In the | case of the others he had to change the order of his words, or use them in other forms which would give them a new rhythm. They even then show the influence of the epic upon Pindar, but they do not show that he was helped in any way, since these words were no easier to work into his verse than any others which he might find himself. The number of phrases which Bacchylides took from

[1] *Scolia anonyma* 32 (Diehl); cf. I. M. Linforth, *Solon the Athenian* (Berkeley, 1919), p. 226.

[2] *O* 660.

[3] Antimachus fr. 19, 1 (Kinkel); ε 265, ι 196, ι 346; cf. FM, p. 231 above. There is a list of the frequent cases of this sort in Apollonius in the edition of G. W. Mooney (Dublin, 1912), pp. 416–421.

[4] *De elocutionis Pindaricae colore epico* (Göttingen, 1905), pp. 13, 31–3.

[5] They are: *Olympian* 1, 71 (= *Pythian* 2, 68 = *Isthmian* 4, 56) πολιᾶς ἁλός (μ 180); 1, 1 αἰθόμενον πῦρ (*Π* 293); 1, 4 φίλον ἦτορ (*Γ* 31); 3, 33 γλυκὺς ἵμερος (*Γ* 446); 6, 20 μέγαν ὅρκον ὀμόσσαι (κ 299); 6, 25 ὁδὸν ἁγεμονεῦσαι (ζ 261); 10, 15 χάλκεος Ἄρης (*E* 704); 12, 5 ἀγοραὶ βουλαφόροι (ι 112); *Pythian* 2, 89 μέγα κῦδος (*Θ* 176); 4, 174 κλέος ἐσλόν (*E* 3); 10, 27 χάλκεος οὐρανός (*P* 425); *Nemean* 1, 37 χρυσόθρονον Ἥραν (*A* 611); 10, 9 πολέμοιο νέφος (*P* 243); 10, 56 ὑπὸ κεύθεσι γαίας (*X* 482); 10, 64 μέγα ἔργον (ω 426); 10, 71 ψολόεντα κεραυνόν (ψ 330); fr. ad. 38 (Puech) νήπια βάζεις (δ 32); fr. ad. 51 φίλα τέκνα (*B* 315); fr. ad. 96 ναὶ θοᾶι (*A* 389).

Homer without change is equally small: H. Buss found eleven, all of two words.[1]

There is no need of pointing out that so few formulas in the work of Pindar and Bacchylides could have had no measurable effect on the way in which they made their verses; but besides that it is only too clear that these repeated phrases are not formulas. They are all of them high-sounding expressions which the poet has been able to work into his verse, as for example φίλον ἦτορ in the first of the *Olympian Odes*:

> εἰ δ' ἄεθλα γαρύεν
> ἔλδεαι, φίλον ἦτορ,
> μηκέθ' ἁλίου σκόπει. . . .[2]

Both the meaning and the movement of φίλον ἦτορ are here very far from those which Homer has made familiar to us:

> ὣς φάτο, τοῦ δ' αὐτοῦ λύτο γούνατα καὶ φίλον ἦτορ . . .[3]
>
> ὣς ἔφατ', αὐτὰρ ἐμοί γε κατεκλάσθη φίλον ἦτορ.[4]

Even in what may be the most Homeric of all the Pindaric imitations, that of a phrase of three words in an ode in dactylo-epitritic metre, the words which go before and after rob the phrase of much of its Homeric sound: |

> οὔτε δύσηρις ἐὼν οὔτ'
> ὢν φιλόνικος ἄγαν
> καὶ μέγαν ὅρκον ὀμόσσαις
> τοῦτό γέ οἱ σαφέως
> μαρτυρήσω.[5]

In Homer we had:

> ἀλλ' ἔκ τοι ἐρέω καὶ ἐπὶ μέγαν ὅρκον ὀμοῦμαι . . .[6]
>
> εἰ μή μοι τλαίης γε θεὰ μέγαν ὅρκον ὀμόσσαι.[7]

Far from being formulas by which he would regularly express his idea under certain metrical conditions, these phrases were to him fine expressions which his mind had kept solely for their beauty, and which the chance of his verse now let him use. One would not deny all usefulness to them, since they did after all fit into his verse, but that is exactly the usefulness of any phrase which goes to make up any poem.

Since, then, it is not the epic at least which gave the choral poet what Wilamowitz calls 'ein ganzer Apparat von konventionellen Wendungen

[1] *De Bacchylide Homeri imitatore* (Giessen, 1913), pp. 20–2, 41–2. They are: 5, 139 βούλευσεν ὄλεθρον (Ξ 464); 8, 7 λευκώλενος Ἥρα (Θ 484); 8, 46 ὑψιπύλου Τροίας (Π 698); 9, 43 τόξον τιταίνει (Θ 266); 10, 87 φάσγανον ἄμφακες (Κ 256); 12, 64 κυάνεον νέφος (Ψ 188); 12, 128 φαεσιμβρότωι Ἀοῖ (Ω 785); 12, 195 μεγάθυμος Ἀθάνα (θ 520); 15, 7 φρένα τερπόμενος (Ι 186); fr. 3, 10 μελίφρων ὕπνος (Β 34); fr. 18, 1 λάινον οὐδόν (θ 80).

[2] v. 3 ff.

[3] Φ 114 = δ 703 = ψ 205.

[4] δ 481 = 538 = κ 496.

[5] *Olympian Odes* 6, 18 ff.

[6] Α 233.

[7] ε 178 = κ 343.

und Schmuckstücken zu Gebote, so dass er noch leichter als der Rhapsode den einfachsten Gedanken nach Bedarf variieren und dehnen kann',[1] this conventional element in the style must be the work of the choral poets themselves. But Wilamowitz is surely mistaken here, for how could there be such a body of phrases for a poetry in which the order of long and short syllables in the verse varies with every poem? In ten pages of the concordance to Pindar there is not one repeated phrase, whereas not a column of the Homeric concordances but teems with them.[2] A comparison of the diction of Bacchylides with that of Pindar gives the same results. W. K. Prentice[3] gives | 72 cases in which there is some sort of likeness between the words of the two poets, as in these verses of Pindar and of Bacchylides:

> σὺν βαθυζώνοισιν ἀγγέλλων
> Τελεσικράτῃ Χαρίτεσσι γεγωνεῖν . . .[4]

> ᾗι σὺν Χαρίτεσσι βαθυζώνοις ὑφάνας
> ὕμνον . . .[5]

Such an example as this well shows the influence of the one poet on the other, or the use of ideas common to the poetry; but only in one of the 72 cases, in which the phrase is used without change—ταῖς ἱεραῖς Ἀθάναις in Pindar[6] and τᾶν ἱερᾶν Ἀθανᾶν in Bacchylides[7]—did the older poet spare the younger the trouble of making the expression over for his own needs.

Indeed, it seems to me that one gives a very wrong idea of the style of choral poetry in likening its conventional side to that of the epic. Homer is telling the old tales in words which his hearers scarcely heeded as they followed the story, for those words were to them the only ones which could be used, and they knew them far too well to think about them. But Pindar is moving alone in his own thought, choosing in a way that is his alone from the grand words of poetry. There is of course much that is traditional in his verse: he uses the old words, and follows a more or less fixed order of thought, and uses the old tales, and points the moral. Nor did he scorn the common devices, such as that of passing from one part of his theme to another by means of a relative clause, nor fail to use an epithet to fill his verse when that would help him, as Lucian charged the lyric poets with doing.[8] Tradition gave him these artifices, but it did not give him his phrases. These he must choose, and if he would use an

[1] *Die griechische Literatur des Altertums* in *Die griechische und lateinische Literatur und Sprache*[3] (Leipzig, 1912), p. 48.

[2] H. E. Bindseil, *Concordantiae omnium vocum carminum integrorum et fragmentorum Pindari* (Berlin, 1875); G. L. Prendergast, *Concordance to the Iliad* (London, 1875); H. Dunbar, *Concordance to the Odyssey and Hymns of Homer* (Oxford, 1880).

[3] *De Bacchylide Pindari artis socio et imitatore* (Halis Saxonum, 1910), pp. 35 ff.

[4] *Pythian Odes* 9, 2.

[5] Bacchylides 5, 9.

[6] *Dithyrambs* fr. 4, 4.

[7] 17, 1.

[8] *Timon* 1.

epithet he must think and pick.[1] We shall find in later verse what may be, per|haps, a small number of formulas, but it will be in verse in which the order of shorts and longs is fixed and recurring. Pindar, ever faced with a new metrical need, however often he might use his ideas again, could make good or bad sentences, but they must be his own. If we admire the epic style as a thing beyond the forces of a single man, we must wonder at the use that Pindar alone could make of words.

Attic Tragedy[2]

Since the verse of drama is dactylic even less often than that of the choral lyric, it contains still fewer Homeric phrases. Of the 112 passages in Aeschylus given by Susan B. Franklin as showing epic phrasing, there are only three in which the words have been left unchanged.[3] All three cases occur in the lyrics. Max Lechner found five examples in Sophocles of the unchanged Homeric phrase, likewise in lyric metres,[4] and in Euripides eight,[5] to which I can add two that he has overlooked. Of these ten expressions seven occur in lyrics, the other | three are found within a space of twelve verses, for a reason. Andromache, just before the first entry of the chorus in the play which bears her name, ceases to speak in trimeters, which so far have made up the play, and breaks into a lament in elegiac verse. In this passage of fourteen lines, which is the only example we have of elegy in tragedy, Euripides was seeking an epic tone, and to this end he used an unusually large number of Homer's words, and

[1] The failure to see that the epithet gave very different degrees of help to Homer and to the later poets comes from not seeing that it is the ornamental epithet alone that has a permanent usefulness—that is to say, an epithet which can be used without any reference to the idea of the verse or the passage. The ornamental epithet, in turn, is possible only in a style in which its constant recurrence in company with a certain noun has dulled the attention of the public to its meaning (see HG, above), and accordingly, it can exist only as a fixed part of a formulaic diction. The epithet which can have a bearing upon the thought of the sentence where it appears presents the problem of choice and thus loses by far the greater part of its usefulness. Cf. TE, pp. 118–72, where I discuss the Homeric and the Pindaric epithets.

[2] The references in the tragic poets are to the following editions: *Aeschylus* ed. P. Mazon (Paris, 1920–5); *Sophocles* ed. P. Masqueray (Paris, 1922–4); *Euripides* ed. G. Murray (Oxford, 1901–9).

[3] *Traces of Epic Influence in the Tragedies of Aeschylus* (Baltimore, 1895), pp. 69–76. The unaltered Homeric phrases are: *Suppliants* 350 πέτραις ἠλιβάτοις (*Π* 35); 663 ἥβας ἄνθος (*N* 484); *Persians* 80 ἰσόθεος φώς (*B* 565). Cf. Max Lechner, *De Aeschyli studio Homerico* (Erlangen, 1862).

[4] *De Sophocle poeta* Ὁμηρικωτάτωι (Erlangen, 1859), pp. 23–5. The unaltered Homeric phrases are: *Ajax* 146 αἴθωνι σιδήρωι (*Δ* 485); 175 βοῦς ἀγελαίας (*Ψ* 846); *Electra* 167 οἶτον ἔχουσα (*I* 563); *Oedipus at Colonus* 706 γλαυκῶπις Ἀθάνα (*A* 206); fr. 432, 1 (Nauck) ἀετὸς ὑψιπέτας (*M* 201).

[5] *De Homeri imitatione Euripidea* (Erlangen, 1864), pp. 17–23. The unaltered Homeric phrases from the lyrics are: *Alcestis* 742 μέγ' ἀρίστη (*B* 82); *Medea* 425 ὤπασε θέσπιν ἀοιδάν (*θ* 498); *Suppliants* 80 ἀλιβάτου πέτρας (*O* 273); *Trojan Women* 193 νεκύων ἀμενηνόν (*κ* 521); *Orestes* 1256 φοίνιον αἷμα (*σ* 97); *Iphigenia at Aulis* 202 θαῦμα βροτοῖσιν (*λ* 287); 175 ξανθὸν Μενέλαον (*Γ* 284). The Homeric phrases in the elegy of the *Andromache* are: v. 103 Ἰλίωι αἰπεινᾶι (*O* 558); v. 109 ἐπὶ θῖνα θαλάσσας (*β* 260); v. 115 περὶ χεῖρε βαλοῦσα (*λ* 211).

half as many of his phrases as he did in all the rest of his dramas. Moreover, all three phrases occur in the hexameters of the distichs—so friendly was this verse to the epic diction, whereas the iambic and trochaic lines rejected it altogether!

But though we have fewer Homeric phrases in tragedy than in choral poetry, we may well look for tragic formulas. Here are poets using more or less the same style, and the same kind of stories, and, finally, giving the first place in their plays to the same verse-form. The irregular rhythms which kept choral verse free from formulas have here a limited place. A. B. Cook,[1] without attempting completeness, but implying that he gives all the more evident cases, cites 23 passages in Euripides's *Trojan Women* which recall the wording of the *Hecuba* which appeared ten years earlier; in nine of these parallels we find expressions which are repeated without change. F. Niedzballa[2] gives a list, which seems to be inclusive, of repetitions within the *Prometheus* of Aeschylus; of these fifteen are unaltered. F. Schroeder, however, furnishes by far the most ample evidence of repetition without change within the work of a tragic poet:[3] he gives 297 different cases within the plays of Euripides, all but six of them in the trimeters. Of these phrases 48 are used three times, 13 four times, 4 five times, one six times, and one seven times. This makes 392 cases in which an expression appears which the poet has employed before. The first appearance of course cannot be counted, since a phrase cannot become a formula until it has been used more than once; and since the greater number of expressions are repeated only once, we can be sure that all but a very few of them are really being used for the first time in the first of the extant plays in which they appear. To this | number of 392 may be added 91 other cases of borrowing from the work of Aeschylus and Sophocles, making a total of 483 repetitions. This may seem at first a very large proportion; certain scholars have cited far fewer repetitions in later verse as a final proof that Homer's use of formulas was no different from that of modern poets. Yet this number straightway loses its importance when one computes the average number of lines between these repetitions, and between those which we find in Homer, for we then see that Euripides is repeating himself, or borrowing, in every fortieth iambic verse,[4] whereas Homer, if we discount likewise the first appearance of the phrase, is doing so in more than every other verse. Nor is the objection at all sound that most of Attic tragedy is lost, and that if we had it all the number of repetitions would be much larger; the 91 phrases which Euripides took from Aeschylus and Sophocles would have to be multiplied many times

[1] 'Unconscious Iterations' in *Classical Review*, XVI (1902), pp. 151–3.

[2] *De copia verborum et elocutione Promethei Vincti q. f. Aeschyleae* (Vratislaviae, 1913), p. 56.

[3] *De iteratis apud tragicos Graecos.*

[4] In the extant plays of Euripides and the fragments given in Nauck's edition are 19,723 whole iambic trimeters.

before they would change our conclusions, and one would also have to suppose other poems for Homer's time. In a stylistic study small statistical differences have little value: one must use the strictest method of search, but the differences found must be large enough to be beyond the reach of any imaginable faults in method. Whether we suppose that Euripides used a repeated phrase in every thirtieth, or every twentieth verse, it could never be more than an expression put into his verses from time to time. There is not the least reason to suppose, as there is for Homer, that he made any considerable part of his poetry out of them. As for the possible conclusion that Homer could have made as many formulas by himself as Euripides, that is, one for every 36 or so that were handed down to him,[1] I do not think that that will please those who dislike the notion that Homer's style is not more or less his own. But it is time at this point to remind ourselves that we are, in these calculations, supposing that the repeated phrases in Euripides are all formulas. We may very well find that they are not at all the regular means of expressing an idea under certain metrical conditions, but phrases which the poet brought into his work a second time because he could obtain some special effect by them. |

We pass now from the mere frequency of the repetitions in tragedy to their nature, and it may be well to say here that our purpose is much more than that of showing that the number of tragic formulas is much smaller even than the number of repetitions, which is already too small to have any bearing on the epic practice. The one thing which we are seeking to know is what the formula is: its higher frequency in Homer cannot in itself have any great value for us until it leads us to see that frequency is a quality of the formula. The study of the character of the repetitions in tragedy, by showing us just why they are not more frequent, will help us to this understanding.

We may begin with the five cases which Schroeder found of a phrase which appears unchanged in the work of all three tragic poets. One of these expressions is no more than a poetic locution: ὑπουργῆσαι χάριν[2] for the prosaic χαρίσασθαι. Δόμων ἐφέστιος[3] is also highly poetic, and πρὸς τὰς παρούσας συμφοράς[4] and τῆς νῦν παρούσης πημονῆς[5] have a more than usual dignity of statement, but besides this the three phrases express ideas which are more than usually striking. The idea of τὸν παρόντα δαίμονα,[6] used by Aeschylus of fate, and by the other two poets of a particular fate, that of death, is of a force which calls for no comment. We find, then, that the repeated phrases common to the three writers are either especially

1 The figure is based on Schmidt's *Parallel-Homer*.
2 Aeschylus, *Prometheus* 635; Sophocles, fr. 314; Euripides, *Alcestis* 842.
3 Aeschylus, *Eumenides* 577, 669; Sophocles, *Trachiniae* 262; Euripides, *Medea* 713.
4 Aeschylus; Sophocles, *Philoctetes* 885; Euripides, *Hippolytus* 483, *Helen* 509.
5 Aeschylus, *Prometheus* 471, 1000; Sophocles, *Electra* 939.
6 Aeschylus, *Persians* 825; Sophocles, *Electra* 1306, *Tyro* fr. 587, 1; Euripides, *Alcestis* 561.

poetic in wording or highly dramatic in thought. To bring out the meaning of this last term we must have more examples. In passing, then, to the phrases found in only two of the poets, there is hardly need of saying that the rarity of the cases we have just quoted disproves the existence of any body of formulas common to tragic poetry, and makes the question of the phrases found in the work of more than one tragic poet purely that of the influence of a dramatist.

Schroeder[1] lists 29 different phrases found both in Aeschylus and | in Euripides, all of which appear once in the work of the older poet, and of which three appear twice in Euripides, two four times, and one six times. He finds 34 different phrases which Euripides took from Sophocles, of which three appear twice in Euripides, two three times, and one four times. These figures check with those of others. Thus F. Niedzballa[2] gives a list of phrases repeated from Aeschylus's *Prometheus*, of which fourteen occur in the work of Sophocles, and fifteen in that of Euripides. M. L. Earle,[3] in a study in which he sought to prove the influence of the *Alcestis* of Euripides on the *Women of Trachis* of Sophocles, found one repetition: *καὶ συνωφρυωμένος*.[4] To this must be added another given by Schroeder: *ἅλις γὰρ ἡ παροῦσα*.[5] Here again the evidence is overwhelming: to judge from the plays which we possess, Euripides uses an expression from Aeschylus or Sophocles in every 215 or so iambic verses.

When one looks at the phrases Euripides has thus chosen, it is straightway clear that almost none of them belong to the more general level of the style: either their wording is more than usually poetic, or their thought highly dramatic. As examples of the first kind one notes *ὥστε ναὸς κεδνὸς οἰακοστρόφος*,[6]—Pindar seems to have been the first to use *οἰακοστρόφος* for *οἰακονόμος*;[7] *πρᾶσσε τἀπεσταλμένα*;[8] *πόλεμον αἵρεσθαι μέγαν*;[9] *συνάψας μηχανήν*.[10] These expressions Euripides took from Aeschylus. From Sophocles he took *μωρίαν ὀφλισκάνω*,[11] and *τοῦτο κηλητήριον*,[12]—he is the only other author to use this poetic adjective. In the greater number of cases, however, the phrase is rather what must be called a specific dramatic device. We must consider here the essential difference between epic and drama. The epic contains a good | deal of speech, which, in its way, comes very near to drama in its direct imitation by action, and often, to make this imitation effective, the epic poet uses

1 *De iteratis apud tragicos Graecos*, pp. 91–101.

2 *De copia verborum Promethei Vincti*, pp. 55–61.

3 'Studies in Sophocles's Trachinians', in *Transactions and Proceedings of the American Philological Association* XXXIII (1902), pp. 5–29.

4 *Alcestis* 777, 800; *Women of Trachis* 869.

5 *Alcestis* 673; *Women of Trachis* 332.

6 *Seven against Thebes* 62; *Medea* 523.

7 *Isthmian Odes* 4, 72.

8 *Libation Bearers* 779; *Trojan Women* 1149.

9 *Suppliants* 439; *Alexander* fr. 51.

10 *Agamemnon* 1609; *Helen* 1034.

11 *Antigone* 470; *Alcestis* 1093; *Iphigenia in the Tauric Land* 488.

12 *Women of Trachis* 575; *Hecuba* 535.

formulas made especially for this end. Such formulas are of various sorts. They may express indignation at some sight:

ὢ πόποι ἦ μέγα θαῦμα τόδ' ὀφθαλμοῖσιν ὁρῶμαι.[1]

They may set forth the clash of opinions.

ποῖόν σε ἔπος φύγεν ἕρκος ὀδόντων.[2]

They sometimes imitate the tone of one threatening:

ἄλλο δέ τοι ἐρέω, σὺ δ' ἐνὶ φρεσὶ βάλλεο σῇσιν.[3]

Less often they may be of a less purely emotional tone, giving the intention of the speaker, as in

σῆμα δέ τοι ἐρέω μάλ' ἀριφραδές, οὐδέ σε λήσει.[4]

Of this dramatic sort too are the verses which comment on a situation, and which Homer, refusing to let himself enter his poem, always gives as the opinion of a character in regard to some certain event:[5]

αἰδομένων ἀνδρῶν πλέονες σόοι ἠὲ πέφανται.[6]

What all these formulas I have quoted have in common is that they are the character's expression of what is going on in his mind, rather than the poet's statement of what a character did, which is the nature of narrative. Now the epic being far more narrative than dramatic, the dramatic formulas have only a very small place beside those which tell the tale. But the dramatic poet, giving us characters who think and feel before us, needs expressions of this sort far more than any other.

Accordingly we find that the repetitions in tragedy which are not stylistic are almost all special devices for supplying the dramatic ele- | ment. In one of the three cases in which Euripides has taken almost a whole line from Sophocles, we have a means whereby a character expresses despair, as Electra does in the play of Sophocles:

ἀπωλόμην δύστηνος· οὐδέν εἰμ' ἔτι.[7]

So Hecuba speaks in Euripides:

ἀπωλόμην δύστηνος· οὐκέτ' εἰμὶ δή.[8]

In another case the repeated verse is one by which, in the rapid give and

[1] *N* 99, *O* 286, *Y* 344, *Φ* 54.

[2] *Δ* 350, *Ξ* 83, α 64, ε 22, τ 492, ψ 70.

[3] *Δ* 39, *E* 259, *Π* 444, 851, λ 454, π 281, 299, ρ 548, τ 236, 495, 570.

[4] *Ψ* 326, λ 126.

[5] Cf. Aristotle, *Poetics* 1460a5 ff.; and T. Stickney, *Les sentences dans la poésie grecque d'Homère à Euripide* (Paris, 1903), pp. 25–49.

[6] *E* 531, *O* 563.

[7] *Electra* 677.

[8] *Hecuba* 683.

take of angry talk, one character bids another ask his question. Sophocles wrote:

λέγ', εἴ τι χρήιζεις· καὶ γὰρ οὐ σιγηλὸς εἶ.[1]

Euripides changed only one word of this:

λέγ', εἴ τι βούληι· καὶ γὰρ οὐ σιγηλὸς εἶ.[2]

Both verses, of course, are found in stichomythy. An example of the phrase by which we know the speaker's intention is this verse from Aeschylus:

βραχεῖ δὲ μύθωι πάντα συλλήβδην μάθε.[3]

In Euripides this becomes:

βραχεῖ δὲ μύθωι πολλὰ συλλαβὼν ἐρῶ.[4]

Very frequent among the phrases Euripides borrowed are those in which a character expresses himself by a nice use of language, as in the words which Euripides took from Sophocles: ἑκόντες οὐκ ἄκοντες,[5] and τά τ' ὄντα καὶ μέλλοντα.[6] Sophocles in turn took a verse from Euripides and did not trouble to change it at all:

ὦ φίλτατ' εἰποῦσ', εἰ λέγεις ἐτήτυμα.[7]

If the only repeated phrases in Homer were those of the dramatic sort which we have quoted, and if they did not appear too often, so that we could be sure that the poet's hearers were always very much | struck by them, we should have no need to seek the difference between epic and tragic repetitions. But in Homer these formulas have only the smallest place beside those which make up the narrative, or even the speeches, and many of them are so frequent that it is doubtful whether their dramatic effect would ever have set them much apart from the more usual level of the style. It is otherwise for Euripides: almost all of his repeated expressions are especially forceful, and, rarely used more than once, they are always sure of their effect. They are, then, not a regular means of expressing the idea but a body of outstanding dramatic artifices. There is almost nothing in them to show that Euripides, in order to make the composition of his verses easier, was limiting his thought to the diction created by others.

Voltaire was doing very much as Euripides had done, when, in his *Oedipe*, he borrowed two verses from the play of that name by Corneille:

[1] *Women of Trachis* 416.
[2] *Suppliants* 567.
[3] *Prometheus* 505.
[4] *Erechtheus* fr. 364, 5.
[5] *Oedipus the King* 1230; *Children of Heracles* 531, *Andromache* 357
[6] *Electra* 1498; *Helen* 14.
[7] *Ion* 1488; *Philoctetes* 1290.

Ce monstre à voix humaine, aigle, femme, et lion. . . .
[Il vit, et le sort qui l'accable]
Des morts et des vivants semble le séparer.

Voltaire felt called upon to give his reasons for thus using the lines of another: "Je n'ai point fait scrupule de voler ces deux vers, parce-qu'ayant précisément la même chose à dire que Corneille, il m'était impossible de l'exprimer mieux; et j'ai mieux aimé donner deux bons vers de lui, que d'en donner deux mauvais de moi."[1] This is the very reasoning whereby borrowing in the Greek orators was justified: τὸ γὰρ καλῶς εἰπεῖν φασιν ἅπαξ περιγίγνεται, δὶς δὲ οὐκ ἐνδέχεται.[2] These, however, are not the grounds for the use of the true formula: Voltaire does not say that the borrowed lines made his verse-making easier; he would have been ashamed to admit any other than purely artistic motives. For him, what comes before all else is the idea to be expressed, and which he has for his own reasons chosen to express. In this case he had found his ideas in Corneille, where they had struck him by their high emotional and dramatic quality. He used the ideas and the words from which he could not separate them; but we may | well suppose that he spent as much thought in borrowing these verses as Corneille did in making one of them out of the lines of Seneca:

quaeratur via
qua nec sepultis mixtus et vivis tamen
exemptus erres.[3]

One only has to think of the number of formulas in Homer, and of how closely they follow one another, to see that Homer's use of borrowed phrases could have been nothing like this. A poet making verses with the greatest care, who sought to put into his poetry all that he had found best in the poetry of others, could never have thus stopped at every other verse to ponder some line he knew, whether that of another or his own. Virgil, it would seem, did this more than any poet we know of, yet he is far from such a practice.[4] The case of Virgil, indeed, bears very directly upon this distinction between the formula and the phrase which expresses an unusually striking idea: far from being led by any consideration of an easy verse-making, he is quite willing to translate his striking ideas from Greek. Virgil is not a writer of plays, of course, to be brought in with regard to the effective dramatic phrase. But it is clear that, as the tragic poet is concerned with the forceful dramatic expression, so Virgil, writing heroic narrative, is seeking the salient epic phrase.

1 *Lettres sur Oedipe* 5; cf. R. C. Jebb, in his edition of *Oedipus the King* (Cambridge, 1893), p. xlii.

2 Theon, *Progymnasmata* 1, 3 (Walz).

3 *Oedipus* 950–1.

4 Cf. A. Cartault, *L'Art de Virgile dans l'Énéide* (Paris, 1926), *passim*.

I do not think it should be said that the element of usefulness is absolutely lacking from the phrases which Euripides borrowed. One case I am very nearly tempted to class as a true formula. It happens to be the one which the poet used most often, namely *ἀλλ' εἰσορῶ γάρ*. This is used once by Aeschylus and six times by Euripides.[1] The words are a means of turning the eyes of the audience towards an actor who is just coming on to the stage. But even here the device is more than ordinarily dramatic, and there is no other case which approaches this. Perhaps one should grant too that the poet was helped somewhat by the poetic locutions he borrowed. But the fact that they fall between groups of words which the poet was using for the first time, and not, as the true formula does, into a pattern of formulas | which were made to fit before and after it in the verse, brings them after all very close to the phrases which Pindar took from the epic and which, as we have seen, were no more or less helpful than any words which were being used for the first time.

The expressions which Euripides repeated from his own works are not very different from those he borrowed, except that they seem at times to be more particularly his own, such as certain forceful but prosaic phrases: *ἁμιλλῶμαι λόγοις*,[2] *ἐς τοσοῦτον ἀμαθίας*,[3] *οὐκ ἐς ἀμβολάς*,[4] *σὸν ἔργον ἤδη*,[5] and the like. But the poet shows his taste in borrowing others as well as in choosing his own words. The best way to show that the repeated phrases within his verses are of the sort we have already seen will be, I think, to take up all the cases of repetition in a certain play. It is of course the later pieces which contain the greater number; the *Orestes* with 36 has most. They may be classed under five headings.

I.—Three phrases of a highly tragic force:

Ὦ Ζεῦ καὶ γᾶ καὶ φῶς.[6] This is one of the rare lyric formulas. It is used by the slave in the *Orestes* to tell his wonder at the vanishing of Helen. It opens the first chorus of the *Medea*, serving to deepen the effect of Medea's lamentation off stage.

Ὥς μ' ἀπώλεσας καὶ τόνδε.[7] In the *Orestes* Electra speaks thus in her outburst of hate for Helen. In the *Phaethon* the words are addressed to Helios by the mother as she leaves the stage following the body of her dead son.

Ἐγὼ δ' ἐπεγκέλευσα. Euripides, dealing with the same characters as in an old play, is making second use of a dramatic play of dialogue. In the

[1] Aeschylus, *Prometheus* 941; Euripides, *Hippolytus* 51, *Hecuba* 724, *Heracles* 138, *Electra* 107, *Orestes* 725, *Bacchanals* 1165.

[2] *Hippolytus* 971, *Hecuba* 271, *Heracles* 1255, *Suppliants* 195.

[3] *Ion* 374, *Trojan Women* 972.

[4] *Children of Heracles* 270, *Helen* 1297.

[5] *Electra* 668, *Iphigenia in the Tauric Land* 1079.

[6] *Medea* 148; *Orestes* 1496.

[7] *Phaethon* fr. 781, 11–12; *Orestes* 130–1.

Electra the words had appeared in the lament between Orestes and his sister after they have slain their mother:

ΟΡ. ἐγὼ μὲν ἐπιβαλὼν φάρη κόραις ἐμαῖς
φασγάνωι κατηρξάμαν
ματέρος ἔσω δέρας μεθείς. |
ΗΛ. ἐγὼ δ' ἐπεγκέλευσά σοι
ξίφους τ' ἐφηψάμαν ἅμα.[1]

In the *Orestes* the phrase is spoken when the brother and sister and Pylades, having resolved the death of Helen, call Agamemnon's spirit to their aid:

ΠΥ. ὦ συγγένεια πατρὸς ἐμοῦ, κἀμὰς λιτάς,
Ἀγάμεμνον, εἰσάκουσον· ἔκσωισον τέκνα.
ΟΡ. ἔκτεινα μητέρα . . . ΠΥ. ἡψάμην δ' ἐγὼ ξίφους . . .
ΗΛ. ἐγὼ δ' ἐπεγκέλευσα κἀπέλυσ' ὄκνου.[2]

The grasping of the sword is here shifted from Electra to Pylades. One can see that Euripides was repeating a complex dramatic grouping of ideas in a different verse-form, though only in the case of three words could he keep the same language.

II.—Five phrases which, though not so purely dramatic, contain an idea more than usually striking either in itself or in the way in which it is expressed:

Ὦ τλῆμον Ἑλένη.[3] This is used three times by Euripides. There is no need of explaining 'unhappy Helen,' nor the thought of Helen unhappy in the sorrows she has caused, which is that found in two of the passages:

ὦ τλῆμον Ἑλένη, διὰ σὲ καὶ τοὺς σοὺς γάμους
ἀγὼν Ἀτρείδαις καὶ τέκνοις ἥκει μέγας . . .[4]

ὦ τλῆμον Ἑλένη, διὰ σ' ἀπόλλυνται Φρύγες.[5]

Ἅλις τὸ κείνης (μητρὸς) αἷμα. Orestes speaks thus in the *Iphigenia in the Tauric Land* and in the *Orestes*; both when he refuses to endanger the life of one sister for the sake of his escape, and when his | other sister asks for her death at his hands rather than at those of the Argives.[6]

Ταύτηι γέγηθα κἀπιλήθομαι κακῶν.[7] The verse is both very pathetic and very nicely put. The same thing may be said of δυστυχοῦντί σοι φίλος.[8]

[1] v. 1221 ff.

[2] v. 1233 ff. Murray prints, but daggers, the reading ἐπεβούλευσα. Musgrave's reading, however, based on ἐπεκέλευσα of *B*, is almost certain, in view of the many other cases where Euripides utilizes the same words for the second expression of a striking idea. Nauck's reading ἐπενεκέλευσα is less good, since the source of the corruption in the manuscripts was probably the absence of the augment, which is rare in the dialogue of tragedy.

[3] *Orestes*, 1613.

[4] *Iphigenia at Aulis* 1253–4.

[5] *Helen* 109.

[6] *Iphigenia in the Tauric Land* 1008, *Orestes* 1039.

[7] *Hecuba* 279, *Orestes* 66.

[8] *Electra* 605, *Orestes* 1096.

Τοῖς μὲν λόγοις ηὔφρανε, τοῖς δ' ἔργοισιν οὔ.[1] The verse upon which this was modelled is the following: *τοῖς πράγμασιν τέθνηκα, τοῖς δ' ἔργοισιν οὔ.*[2] One thinks of the verse of the *Hippolytus* which Aristophanes ridiculed: *ἡ γλῶσσ' ὀμώμοχ', ἡ δὲ φρὴν ἀνώμοτος.*[3] Euripides was writing for the same Athens which, nineteen years before, had listened in grave wonder to the balanced style of Gorgias, in whose work we read such sentences as the following one from the *Praise of Helen*: *τὸ γὰρ τοῖς εἰδόσιν ἃ ἴσασι λέγειν πίστιν μὲν ἔχει, τέρψιν δ' οὐ φέρει;*[4] and one is not surprised to find in this author's *Defence of Palamedes* the same play of words as in the verse quoted from the *Orestes: ὑμᾶς δὲ χρὴ μὴ τοῖς λόγοις μᾶλλον ἢ τοῖς ἔργοις προσέχειν τὸν νοῦν.*[5]

Οὐκ ἔστιν οὐδὲν κρεῖσσον.[6] This is a phrase of purest gnomic tone.

III.—Six phrases found in dialogue, either in stichomythy or at the beginning of a longer speech, always at the beginning of the verse, and with one exception the first words in the speech. They are a device by which a character who has just come upon the stage can begin his speech, or by which the thought can be carried back and forth between actors in the give and take of dramatic conversation:

Ὦ χαῖρε καὶ σύ. This is said in three cases by a character who returns the greeting made him as he enters.[7] In the *Hippolytus* they are put to a more dramatic use as the words of the dying hero to his father.[8]

Ἔα, τί χρῆμα;[9] This cry of surprise is uttered in three different plays by characters who, entering the stage, have come upon some startling sight. |

Ὦ φίλτατ', εἰ γὰρ τοῦτο.[10] This emotional expression is used to begin a wish suggested by the previous speaker's words.

The other three cases are found in stichomythy: *κἀγὼ τοιοῦτος,*[11] 'I too'; *ἐς ταὐτὸν ἥκεις· καὶ γὰρ οὐδέ,*[12] 'We agree, for . . .'; *τί χρῆμα δρᾶσαι;*[13] 'What must we do?'

IV.—Thirteen phrases in which the diction is more than usually poetic. There are those in which the words themselves are of the sort not used in prose:

συμφοραὶ θεήλατοι[14] *τάλαιναν καρδίαν*[17]
λεύσιμος . . . δίκη[15] *θεοῖς στυγούμενον*[18]
λευσίμωι πετρώματι[16]

[1] *Orestes* 287. [2] *Helen* 286.
[3] *Hippolytus* 612; cf. Aristophanes, *Frogs* 1471.
[4] § 5 (Baiter and Sauppe). [5] § 34.
[6] *Andromache* 986, *Orestes* 1155.
[7] *Medea* 665, *Children of Heracles* 660, *Orestes* 477.
[8] *Hippolytus* 1453. [9] *Hippolytus* 905, *Heracles* 525, *Orestes* 1573.
[10] *Cyclops* 437, *Orestes* 1100.
[11] *Children of Heracles* 266, *Orestes* 1680. [12] *Hecuba* 748, *Orestes* 1280.
[13] *Helen* 826, *Orestes* 1186, 1583. [14] *Andromache* 851, *Orestes* 2.
[15] *Children of Heracles* 60, *Orestes* 614. [16] *Orestes* 50, 442.
[17] Fr. inc. 900, 6, *Orestes* 466.
[18] *Alcestis* 62, *Iphigenia in the Tauric Land* 948, *Orestes* 19.

In others it is the way the words are used which is poetic:

ἀρίστας θυγατέρας σπείρας[1]	*ὑπὲρ γῆς Ἑλλάδος*[4]
κἀνεκουφίσθην δέμας[2]	*ἀθλίως πεπραγότα*[5]
συμφορὰς κεκτημένη[3]	*ἔργον ἀνοσιώτατον*[6]

In two cases the expression, by calling up the legend, brings into the style what may be called a romantic note:

Ὀρέστην παῖδα τὸν Ἀγαμέμνονος . . .[7]
ἣν . . . ἔλιφ' ὅτ' ἐς Τροίαν ἔπλει.[8]

These last two examples might have been put in the second class. |

V.—There remain of the 36 repeated phrases nine which seem hardly striking enough in themselves to have been used for much else than their usefulness, though here too there are poetic words and word-order, and forceful ideas:

ἔσω στείχοντες[9]	*Κλυταιμήστρας τάφον*[14]
ὧν δ' οὕνεκ' ἦλθον[10]	*χρηστὰ βουλεύουσ' ἀεί*[15]
ἐγὼ θήσω καλῶς[11]	*κτενεῖν σου θυγατέρ'*[16]
πάσης ὑπὲρ γῆς[12]	*ἔκτεινα μητέρα*[17]
οὐκέτ' ἂν φθάνοις ἄν[13]	

It is to this extent of nine short expressions in a play of almost sixteen hundred lines that Euripides used what would seem to be more or less true formulas. In all but one of these cases he was repeating himself for the first time, and in four of them he was repeating words which had been used earlier in the same play, but had not yet faded from his mind, which would be likely to hold for any length of time only the most remarkable. Moreover four of the six expressions whose first and second appearance occur within the play fall in this fifth class: the poet could not well use any very noticeable phrase twice in the same drama. Yet there remains a final reason why even these cases should not be classed unhesitatingly as formulas: there are quite as many repeated expressions in the prose of most writers, where the factor of the verse, essential to the formula, plays no part. Even here it is doubtful how often Euripides was

1 *Orestes* 750, *Bacchanals* 1234.
2 *Hippolytus* 1392, *Orestes* 218.
3 *Iphigenia in the Tauric Land* 1317, *Orestes* 865.
4 *Hecuba* 310, *Orestes* 574, *Iphigenia at Aulis* 1456.
5 *Heracles* 707, *Orestes* 87.
6 *Medea* 796, *Hecuba* 792, *Orestes* 286.
7 *Orestes* 371, 923.
8 *Electra* 14, *Orestes* 63.
9 *Iphigenia in the Tauric Land* 470, *Orestes* 1222.
10 *Andromache* 1238, *Ion* 332, *Helen* 144, *Orestes* 611.
11 *Hippolytus* 521, *Hecuba* 875, *Orestes* 1664, *Iphigenia at Aulis* 401.
12 *Suppliants* 1190, *Orestes* 574.
13 *Trojan Women* 456, *Orestes* 1551.
14 *Orestes* 114, 1185.
15 *Orestes* 773, 909.
16 *Orestes* 1578, 1609.
17 *Orestes* 935, 1235.

guided by any other motive than that of the prose author who uses his words over purely for the sake of their thought or their fitness.

It is clear from this analysis that one would not be far wrong in saying that the formula does not exist in tragedy. The dramatic poet, working at ease into the mould of his verse those words he carefully chose for his very own thought, used from time to time some idea or poetic expression which had proved effective in the past and which he remembered | for that reason. Since he was using a regularly recurring verse-form, the metre did not prevent him, as it had prevented Pindar, from using the words which had already expressed the idea, or had even given it some of its value. In one sense the verse-form has influenced his style, in that it did not keep him from repetition, though it did not push him on to it as it had Homer. But in this last distinction lies all the difference between a traditional and an individual style.

We have learned the nature of the repetitions in tragedy. Looking now to see whether there are any traces of schematization in the style of the tragic poets we find a very few, such as the following:

In Aeschylus	*In Euripides*
τί δῆτ᾽ ἐμοὶ ζῆν κέρδος[1]	*τί δῆτ᾽ ἐμοὶ ζῆν ἡδύ*[2]
τῆς νῦν παρούσης πημονῆς ἀπαλλαγῶ[3]	*τῆς νῦν παρούσης συμφορᾶς αἰτήσομαι*[4]
δυοῖν λόγοιν σε θατέρωι δωρήσομαι[5]	*δυοῖν δὲ μοίραιν θατέραι πεπλήξεται*[6]
	δυοῖν ἀνάγκη θατέρωι λιπεῖν βίον[7]
κεκύρωται τέλος[8]	*κεκυρῶσθαι σφαγάς*[9]
πᾶσαν συνάψας μηχανὴν δυσβουλίας[10]	*κοινὴν συνάπτειν μηχανὴν σωτηρίας*[11]

Within the Work of Euripides

καινὸν ἀγγελεῖ κακόν[12]	*καινὸν ἀγγελεῖς ἔπος*[13]
	καινὸν ἀγγελῶν λόγον[14]
οὐχ ὁρᾶις ἃ χρή σ᾽ ὁρᾶν[15]	*οὐ φρονοῦσ᾽ ἃ χρὴ φρονεῖν*[16]
ὑπὲρ γῆς Ἑλλάδος[17]	*ὑπὲρ γῆς Δαναιδῶν*[18]
οὐδ᾽ ἄκραντ᾽ ἠκούσαμεν[19]	*οὐδ᾽ ἄκρανθ᾽ ὡρμήσαμεν*[20] |

The systems in Euripides are always made up as here of two or three expressions. There is hardly need of pointing out that they are of the same sort as the phrases repeated without change. The poet is usually modifying some striking idea or some forceful use of words to fit a new

1 *Prometheus* 747.
2 *Andromache* 404.
3 *Prometheus* 471.
4 *Helen* 509.
5 *Prometheus* 778.
6 *Hippolytus* 894.
7 *Andromache* 383.
8 *Libation Bearers* 874.
9 *Electra* 1069.
10 *Agamemnon* 1609.
11 *Helen* 1034.
12 *Medea* 1120.
13 *Trojan Women* 55.
14 *Trojan Women* 238.
15 *Phoenicians* 713.
18 *Bacchanals* 1123.
17 *Hecuba* 310, *Orestes* 574, *Iphigenia at Aulis* 1456.
16 *Suppliants* 1190.
19 *Iphigenia in the Tauric Land* 520, *Bacchanals* 1231.
20 *Bacchanals* 435.

situation. One could rarely say that he was guided in any way by the wish for an easy versification. Yet this, we shall see, was the regular motive for the epic poet.

Since there are no systems of any length in tragic diction, there is, of course, no question of the thrift of the system. The lack of thrift in the diction is made clear, however, by the large number of expressions which could replace one another, that is to say, expressions in which the essential meaning and the metrical value are the same, but the words different. Such examples are the following:

In Aeschylus	*In Euripides*
λέγων τὰ καίρια[1]	λέγειν ἵν' ἀσφαλές[2]
πάντα συλλήβδην μάθε[3]	πολλὰ συλλαβὼν ἐρῶ[4]
τῶν ὑπερκόμπων ἄγαν[5]	τῶν ἄγαν ὑπερφρόνων[6]

Within the Work of Euripides

δεσπότης γάρ ἐστ' ἐμός[7]	ἀλλ' ἄναξ γάρ ἐστ' ἐμός[8]
οἲ ἐγὼ τῶν ἐμῶν τλήμων κακῶν.[9]	οἴμοι τῶν ἐμῶν ἐγὼ κακῶν[10]

Equivalent phrases of this kind are not lacking in Homer, but they are always due to the play of analogy which underlies the diction, and they are never phrases of more than a few words.[11] In tragedy, however, whole equivalent verses are very common, and we shall do well to consider some of them for what they show us of the working of the poet's mind. Aeschylus wrote the following verse:

εἰ δ' αὖθ', ὃ μὴ γένοιτο, συμφορὰ τύχοι.[12] |

In Euripides this became:

ὃ μὴ γένοιτο δ', εἴ τι τυγχάνοι κακόν.[13]

We read in Sophocles:

ἐλπὶς γὰρ ἡ βόσκουσα τοὺς πολλοὺς βροτῶν.[14]

This same idea had been expressed before by Aeschylus in a trochaic verse:

οἶδ' ἐγὼ φεύγοντας ἄνδρας ἐλπίδας σιτουμένους.[15]

Rather than use the line of Sophocles, Euripides blended the two verses, and made:

αἱ δ' ἐλπίδες βόσκουσι φυγάδας, ὡς λόγος.[16]

[1] *Prometheus the Firebearer* fr. 204. [2] *Ino* fr. 417, 2. [3] *Prometheus* 505. [4] *Erechtheus* fr. 364, 5. [5] *Persians* 827. [6] *Children of Heracles* 388. [7] *Medea* 83. [8] *Electra* 1245. [9] *Helen* 1223. [10] *Phoenicians* 373. [11] Cf. TE, pp. 173–89. above. [12] *Seven against Thebes* 5. [13] *Ion* 731. [14] Inc. fr. 863. [15] *Agamemnon* 1668. [16] *Phoenicians* 396.

Finally, the scholiast on this verse quotes another with identical thought from some unnamed poet:

αἱ δ' ἐλπίδες βόσκουσι τοὺς κενοὺς βροτῶν.

Euripides varies the terms of his own statement:

κράτιστον εἶναι φημὶ μὴ φῦναι βροτῶι . . .[1]
τὸ μὴ γενέσθαι κρεῖσσον ἢ φῦναι βροτοῖς . . .[2]

ἦ πόλλ' ἀνήρου μ' ἐνὶ λόγωι μιᾶι θ' ὁδῶι . . .[3]
ὡς πάνθ' ἅπαξ με συλλαβοῦσ' ἀνιστορεῖς.[4]

Possibly the most curious case of equivalent verses is to be found in the following passages, one from the *Helen*, the other from the *Iphigenia in the Tauric Land*:

ΕΛ. ἦλθες γάρ, ὦ ξέν', Ἰλίου κλεινὴν πόλιν;
ΤΕ. καὶ ξύν γε πέρσας αὐτὸς ἀνταπωλόμην.
ΕΛ. ἤδη γὰρ ἧπται καὶ κατείργασται πυρί;
ΤΕ. ὥστ' οὐδ' ἴχνος γε τειχέων εἶναι σαφές . . .[5] |

ΙΦ. Τροίαν ἴσως οἶσθ', ἧς ἁπανταχοῦ λόγος.
ΟΡ. ὡς μήποτ' ὤφελόν γε μηδ' ἰδὼν ὄναρ.
ΙΦ. φασίν νιν οὐκέτ' οὖσαν οἴχεσθαι δορί.
ΟΡ. ἔστιν γὰρ οὕτως οὐδ' ἄκραντ' ἠκούσατε.[6]

Not only do these equivalent verses show the lack in the poetry of any factor which would have urged the writer to a thrift of diction; they show clearly how the idea could lie in the mind of the poet without being bound to any certain words. Euripides, when he made verses, looked for terms to express his ideas, but the epic poet, we shall see, thought in terms of his formulas, and did not separate the idea from the words with which it went. It is not the place here to show this fully, but in passing I would quote certain Homeric lines and ask if one should not be much surprised to find the same ideas expressed in verses of different wording:

διογενὲς Λαερτιάδη πολυμήχαν' Ὀδυσσεῦ . . .

ἀλλ' ἄγε μοι τόδε εἰπὲ καὶ ἀτρεκέως κατάλεξον.

The first of these verses occurs 21 times, the second 17 times.

Poetry after the Fifth Century

Leaving tragedy to go on to later poetry one sees straightway that we have very little to learn about the formula outside the epic itself. We may even be charged with having followed thus far a very laborious

[1] *Bellerophon* fr. 287, 2. [2] Inc. fr. 900, 1. [3] *Helen* 765.
[4] *Iphigenia in the Tauric Land* 528.
[5] *Helen* 105 ff. [6] *Iphigenia in the Tauric Land* 517 ff.

course to prove what is clear enough anyway, namely, that the repeated phrase in poetry, unless it be poetry very different from our own, is an ornament of verse, not a means of making it. The repetitions in later verse have long been put to their proper use as a ready means of studying the influence of one author upon another, either upon his thought or upon some aspect of his style. As far as our understanding of Pindar or of Euripides goes, there is almost no value in the distinction we have been making between the phrase which, taken without change from another poet, might be helpful, and that which he took and changed for his own needs. The influence of ideas shown by the borrowed phrase is very real, but no more so than is that of the altered phrase, while its metrical help is too small to deserve note. | More than that, unless we consider the repetitions as showing this influence of ideas, we cannot know why they come more or less closely together in the verses of a poet. We took care to see just how many repetitions there were in tragedy, supposing that the exact difference in number between those in Attic poetry and those in Homer would have some bearing upon the problem of the formulas in the *Iliad* and in the *Odyssey*. But the truth is that only the absolute difference thus proved has any bearing on Homer's practice. The contrast between a vast number of repetitions in Homer and a comparatively very small number in the work of the tragic poets at once suggested that repetition could not be due to the same causes in both cases. Then a study of the nature of the repetitions in tragedy showed that almost none of them, or even none of them at all, are true formulas, and so we reached that important point where we know surely that Homer's poetry is governed by factors unknown to later Greek poetry. Just what those factors are we shall go on to see; yet our essay would not be complete if we did not pause here a moment to point out what sort of causes, special to a certain poet, or to the poetry of a certain period, have determined the frequency of repetitions in poetry outside the early epic.

If we find almost no Homeric formulas in Apollonius, for example, it does not at all mean that they would not have helped his verse-making, but that he wanted very much to avoid them.[1] If Theocritus, on the other hand, used twelve in his little epic *The Infant Heracles*, it means that he was seeking, in a rather amusing way, for the epic note, and that the use of the twelve formulas was in no way different from that of the ten which he changed metrically.[2] Indeed, one misses the point if one does not see the pains which the poet has spent upon them. Likewise the three hundred phrases of his own which, as we just saw, Euripides used over again, have nothing at all to do with the number of formulas which Homer might have made himself, but they do show the high point to which

[1] Cf. G. Boesch, *De Apollonii Rhodii elocutione* (Göttingen, 1908), p. 7; DE, p. 260–1 above.
[2] G. Futh, *De Theocriti poetae bucolici studiis Homericis* (Halis Saxonum, 1876), pp. 7–8.

Euripides carried the artifices of his dramatic technique, and, if one will study them along with the other | cases in which he expresses the same ideas but changes his words, one will find them an excellent means of learning the nature of his tragic art. The number of repeated phrases in Virgil is high. The lists of E. Albrecht[1] give 372 cases from the *Aeneid*, as follows: 44 in which the expression had been used in the *Eclogues* or the *Georgics*; 248 in which the expression appears three times within the *Aeneid*; 47 in which it is found four times; 22 in which it is found five times; and 11 in which it is used even more often. This makes, not counting the first appearance, a repetition for every twentieth verse. The number is high, but it shows only two things. The phrases from the *Eclogues* and *Georgics* are a measure of the endless care which Virgil gave to his style, and of the need he felt of using again some of the best expressions he had made in his earlier years. The repetitions found in the *Aeneid* show this also, but far more they show that he was trying to make a poem like Homer's. As in the case of the Homeric formulas in Theocritus we must see, if we are to understand the poet, how much toil these repetitions must have cost him. When we turn to our own poetry and to our own language, the nature of the borrowed phrase in written poetry becomes very clear. Charles Crawford,[2] after writing a concordance to the works of Kyd and the play *Arden of Feversham*, whose authorship is doubtful, was able to show 47 places where that play recalls Kyd's *Soliman and Perseda*; of these there are thirteen where the same phrase is used, though never more than once. But it will do to quote a few of the repetitions: 'to everlasting night', 'leave protestations now', 'vengeance light on me', 'this melancholy mood'. I give one more example because it should make clear how little effect the loose form of Elizabethan blank verse could have had upon the choice of a certain word-group. We read in *Soliman and Perseda*:

> *Lucina.*—What ailes you, madam, that your colour changes?
> *Perseda.*—A sudden qualm.[3]

In *Arden of Feversham* we find:

> *Franklin.*—What ails you, woman, to cry so suddenly?
> *Alice.*—Ah, neighbours, a sudden qualm came o'er my heart.[4] |

To find repetitions which could be said to help the verse-making one must rather go to the tradition of Milton's style. Here the strictness of the verse, and the demand for form in style, come much nearer to the practice of the Greek and Roman poets. Yet when one finds Pope copying 'the

[1] *Wiederholte Verse und Verstheile bei Vergil* in *Hermes*, XVI (1881), pp. 393–444.
[2] *The Authorship of Arden of Feversham* in *Shakespeare Jahrbuch*, XXXIX (1903), pp. 74–86.
[3] II, 1, 49–50. [4] V, 1, 308–9.

glowing violet', or 'rough satyrs danced', or 'tufted trees', or 'dropt with gold', one sees the utter vainness of thinking one will find a true formula in the remaining 51 pages of parallels to Milton which R. D. Havens collected from English verse.*

It would seem, indeed, that those who wished to show that Homer, in his formulas, was not really different from any other poet, were not altogether logical. Thinking that the use of formulas as a means of easy verse-making might damage Homer's good name, they cited the examples of repetition in later verse, where they themselves would be the first to deny any but purely artistic motives. It may be, though, that Homer was not such a bad poet even if he did make verses in a way which some have found not quite right.

5. THE FORMULA IN HOMER

The easiest and best way of showing the place the formula holds in Homeric style will be to point out all the expressions occurring in a given passage which are found elsewhere in the *Iliad* or the *Odyssey*, in such a way that, as one reads, one may see how the poet has used them to express his thought. I have put a solid line beneath those word-groups which are found elsewhere in the poems unchanged, and a broken line under phrases which are of the same type as others. In this case I have limited the type to include only those in which not only the metre and the parts of speech are the same, but in which also at least one important word or group of words is identical, as in the first example: *μῆνιν . . . Πηληιάδεω Ἀχιλῆος* and *μῆνιν . . . ἑκατηβόλου Ἀπόλλωνος.* |

ΙΛΙΑΔΟΣ Α

Μῆνιν[1] *ἄειδε θεὰ Πηληιάδεω Ἀχιλῆος*[2]
οὐλομένην ἣ[3] *μυρί'*[4] *Ἀχαιοῖς ἄλγε' ἔθηκε,*[5]
πολλὰς δ' ἰφθίμους ψυχὰς Ἄϊδι προΐαψεν[6]
ἡρώων, αὐτοὺς δὲ[7] *ἑλώρια τεῦχε κύνεσσιν*
οἰωνοῖσί τε πᾶσι, Διὸς δ' ἐτελείετο βουλή[8]
ἐξ οὗ δὴ[9] *τὰ πρῶτα διαστήτην ἐρίσαντε*
Ἀτρεΐδης τε[10] *ἄναξ ἀνδρῶν*[11] *καὶ δῖος Ἀχιλλεύς.*[12]
Τίς τ' ἄρ σφωε θεῶν ἔριδι[13] *ξυνέηκε μάχεσθαι;*[14]
Λητοῦς καὶ Διὸς υἱός·[15] *ὁ γὰρ βασιλῆι χολωθεὶς*
νοῦσον ἀνὰ στρατὸν ὦρσε[16] *κακήν, ὀλέκοντο δὲ λαοί,*[17]
οὕνεκα τὸν Χρύσην ἠτίμασεν ἀρητῆρα
Ἀτρεΐδης· ὁ γὰρ ἦλθε θοὰς ἐπὶ νῆας Ἀχαιῶν[18]

* *The Influence of Milton on English Poetry* (Cambridge, Mass., 1922), pp. 571–624.

λυσόμενός τε θύγατρα φέρων τ' ἀπερείσι' ἄποινα[19]
στέμματ' ἔχων ἐν χερσὶν[20] ἑκηβόλου Ἀπόλλωνος[21]
χρυσέωι ἀνὰ σκήπτρωι·[22] καὶ λίσσετο πάντας Ἀχαιούς,[23] = *Α* 372–5
Ἀτρείδα δὲ μάλιστα[24] δύω κοσμήτορε λαῶν·[25]
Ἀτρείδαι τε καὶ ἄλλοι[26] ἐυκνήμιδες Ἀχαιοί,[27] = *Ψ* 272, 658.
ὑμῖν μὲν θεοὶ δοῖεν Ὀλύμπια δώματ' ἔχοντες[28]
ἐκπέρσαι Πριάμοιο πόλιν,[29] εὖ δ' οἴκαδ' ἱκέσθαι·[30]
παῖδα δ' ἐμοὶ λύσαιτε φίλην, τὰ δ' ἄποινα δέχεσθαι,
ἁζόμενοι[31] Διὸς υἱὸν ἑκηβόλον Ἀπόλλωνα.[32]
Ἔνθ' ἄλλοι μὲν πάντες[33] ἐπευφήμησαν Ἀχαιοί[34]
αἰδεῖσθαί θ' ἱερῆα καὶ ἀγλαὰ δέχθαι ἄποινα·
ἀλλ' οὐκ[35] Ἀτρείδηι Ἀγαμέμνονι[36] ἥνδανε θυμῶι,[37] = *Α* 376–9
ἀλλα κακῶς ἀφίει, κρατερὸν δ' ἐπὶ μῦθον ἔτελλε.[38] |

[1] Cf. *μῆνιν ἀλευάμενος ἑκατηβόλου Ἀπόλλωνος Π* 711. [2] *Πηληιάδεω Ἀχιλῆος Α* 322, *Ι* 166, *Π* 269, 653, *Ω* 406, *λ* 467, *ω* 15. [3] *οὐλομένην ἧι Ε* 876, *ρ* 287, 474. [4] Cf. *μυρί' Ὀδυσσεὺς ἐσθλὰ ἔοργε Β* 272. [5] *ἄλγε' ἔθηκε Χ* 422. [6] *πολλὰς ἰφθίμους κεφαλὰς* (v.l. *ψυχὰς*) *Ἄιδι προιάψειν Λ* 55; *Ἄιδι προιάψει Ζ* 487. [7] Cf. *ἡρώων τοῖσίν τε Ε* 747, *Θ* 391, *α* 101. [8] *Διὸς δ' ἐτελείετο βουλή λ* 297. [9] *ἐξ οὗ δή ξ* 379. [10] *Ἀτρείδης δέ Γ* 271, 361, *Ι* 89, *Ν* 610, *Τ* 252, *δ* 304. [11] *ἄναξ ἀνδρῶν Α* 172, 442, *Β* 402, 441, 612, *Γ* 81, 267, 455, *Δ* 148, 255, 336, *Ε* 38, *Ζ* 33, 37, 162, 314, *Θ* 278, *Ι* 114, 672, *Κ* 64, 86, 103, 119, 233, *Λ* 99, 254, *Ξ* 64, 103, 134, *Σ* 111, *Τ* 51, 76, 172, 184, *Ψ* 161, 895, *θ* 77. [12] *καὶ δῖος Ἀχιλλεύς Α* 7, *Υ* 160; *δῖος Ἀχιλλεύς Α* 121, 292, *Β* 688, *Ε* 788, *Ζ* 414, 423, *Ι* 199, 209, 667, *Λ* 599, *Ο* 68, *Π* 5, *Ρ* 402, *Σ* 181, 228, 305, 343, *Τ* 40, 364, 384, *Υ* 177, 386, 388, 413, 445, *Φ* 39, 49, 67, 149, 161, 265, 359, *Χ* 102, 172, 205, 326, 330, 364, 376, 455, *Ψ* 136, 140, 193, 333, 534, 555, 828, 889, *Ω* 151, 180, 513, 596, 668. [13] *θεῶν ἔριδι Υ* 66. [14] *ξυνέηκε μάχεσθαι Η* 210. [15] *καὶ Διὸς υἷι Χ* 302. [16] Cf. *ἀνὰ στρατόν εἰσι Κ* 66. [17] Cf. *ἀρετῶσι δὲ λαοί τ* 114; *δαινῦτό τε λαός Ω* 665; etc. [18] *ἦλθε θοὰς ἐπὶ νῆας Ἀχαιῶν Α* 371; *θοὰς ἐπὶ νῆας Ἀχαιῶν Β* 8, 17, 168, *Ζ* 52, *Κ* 450, 514, *Λ* 3, *Ω* 564; *θοὴν ἐπὶ νῆα γ* 347, *κ* 244. [19] *λυσόμενος . . . φέρω δ' ἀπερείσι' ἄποινα Ω* 502; *ἀπερείσι' ἄποινα Α* 372, *Ζ* 49, 427, *Ι* 120, *Κ* 380, *Λ* 134, *Τ* 138, *Ω* 276, 502, 579. [20] *ἔχων ἐν χειρί Θ* 221, *Ξ* 385. [21] *ἑκηβόλωι Ἀπόλλωνι Α* 438, *Π* 513, *Ψ* 872. [22] *χρυσέωι ἐν δαπέδωι Δ* 2; *χρυσέωι ἐν δέπαι Ω* 285. [23] *πάντας Ἀχαιούς Α* 374, *Γ* 68, 88, *Η* 49, *Θ* 498, *Ι* 75, *Ξ* 124, *Ψ* 815, *γ* 137, 141, *δ* 288, *ω* 49, 438. [24] Cf. *Αἴαντι δὲ μάλιστα Ξ* 459. [25] *κοσμήτορε λαῶν Γ* 236. [26] Cf. *Ἀτρείδη τε καὶ ἄλλοι ἀριστῆες Παναχαιῶν Η* 327. [27] *καὶ ἄλλοι ἐυκνήμιδες Ἀχαιοί Ξ* 49; *ἐυκνήμιδες Ἀχαιοί Β* 331, *Δ* 414, *Ζ* 529, *Η* 57, 172, *Μ* 141, *Ν* 51, *Σ* 151, *Τ* 74, *Ψ* 721, *Ω* 800, *β* 72, *γ* 149, *σ* 259. [28] *Ὀλύμπια δώματ' ἔχοντες Β* 13, 30, 67, *Ε* 383, *Ο* 115, *υ* 79, *ψ* 167. [29] *Πριάμοιο πόλιν Σ* 288, *Χ* 165, *γ* 130, *λ* 533, *ν* 316. [30] *οἴκαδ' ἱκέσθαι Ι* 393, 414, *Ω* 287, *ι* 530, *ο* 66, 210, *φ* 211, *χ* 35. [31] Cf. *εὐχόμενος δ' ἄρα εἶπεν ἑκηβόλωι Ἀπόλλωνι Π* 513. [32] *Διὸς υἷι ἑκηβόλωι Χ* 302; *ἑκήβολον Ἀπόλλωνα Α* 438, *Π* 513, *Ψ* 872. [33] *ἔνθ' ἄλλοι μὲν πάντες Ω* 25, *α* 11, *β* 82, *δ* 285, *ε* 110, 133, *θ* 93, 532, *ρ* 503. [34] Cf. *ἀφορμηθεῖεν Ἀχαιοί Β* 794; *ἐφοπλίζωμεν Ἀχαιοί Δ* 344; etc. [35] Cf. *οὐδ' ἄρ' ἔτ' Αἴαντι μεγαλήτορι ἥνδανε θυμῶι Ο* 674. [36] *Ἀτρείδεω Ἀγαμέμνονος Β* 185, *Λ* 231, *ι* 263. [37] *ἥνδανε θυμῶι Ο* 674, *κ* 373. [38] *κρατερὸν δ' ἐπὶ μῦθον ἔτελλε Α* 326, *Π* 199. |

ΟΔΥΣΣΕΙΑΣ Α

Ἄνδρα μοι ἔννεπε Μοῦσα[1] πολύτροπον ὃς[2] μάλα πολλά[3]
πλάγχθη ἐπεὶ Τροίης ἱερὸν[4] πτολίεθρον ἔπερσε·[5]
πολλῶν δ' ἀνθρώπων[6] ἴδεν ἄστεα καὶ νόον ἔγνω,[7]

πολλὰ δ' ὅ γ' ἐν πόντωι πάθεν ἄλγεα[8] ὃν κατὰ θυμόν[9]
ἀρνύμενος ἥν τε ψυχὴν[10] καὶ νόστον ἑταίρων.[11]
ἀλλ' οὐδ' ὧς[12] ἑτάρους ἐρρύσατο[13] ἱέμενός περ·[14]
αὐτῶν γὰρ[15] σφετέρῃσιν ἀτασθαλίῃσιν ὄλοντο,[16]
νήπιοι οἳ[17] κατὰ βοῦς Ὑπερίονος Ἠελίοιο[18]
ἤσθιον· αὐτὰρ ὁ τοῖσιν[19] ἀφείλετο νόστιμον ἦμαρ.[20]
τῶν ἁμόθεν γε θεὰ θύγατερ Διὸς[21] εἰπὲ καὶ ἡμῖν.
Ἔνθ' ἄλλοι μὲν πάντες[22] ὅσοι φύγον αἰπὺν ὄλεθρον[23]
οἴκοι ἔσαν[24] πόλεμόν τε πεφευγότες ἠδὲ θάλασσαν·[25]
τὸν δ' οἶον[26] νόστου κεχρημένον[27] ἠδὲ γυναικὸς[28]
νύμφη πότνι' ἔρυκε Καλυψὼ δῖα θεάων[29]
ἐν σπέσσι γλαφυροῖσι[30] λιλαιομένη πόσιν εἶναι.[31] = ι 30
ἀλλ' ὅτε δὴ[32] ἔτος[33] ἦλθε[34] περιπλομένων ἐνιαυτῶν[35]
τῶι οἱ ἐπεκλώσαντο θεοὶ[36] οἶκόνδε νέεσθαι[37]
εἰς Ἰθάκην,[38] οὐδ' ἔνθα πεφυγμένος ἦεν ἀέθλων[39]
καὶ μετὰ οἷσι φίλοισι. θεοὶ δ' ἐλέαιρον ἅπαντες[40]
νόσφι Ποσειδάωνος·[41] ὁ δ'[42] ἀσπερχὲς μενέαινεν[43]
ἀντιθέωι Ὀδυσῆι[44] πάρος ἣν γαῖαν ἱκέσθαι.[45]
Ἀλλ' ὁ μὲν Αἰθίοπας μετεκίαθε[46] τηλόθ' ἐόντας,[47]
Αἰθίοπας τοὶ διχθὰ δεδαίαται ἔσχατοι ἀνδρῶν,[48]
οἱ μὲν δυσομένου Ὑπερίονος, οἱ δ' ἀνιόντος,
ἀντιόων ταύρων τε καὶ ἀρνειῶν ἑκατόμβης. |

[1] μοι ἔννεπε Μοῦσα *B* 761. [2] πολύτροπος ὃν κ 330. [3] μάλα πολλά *E* 197, *I* 364, *Π* 838, *X* 220, *Ω* 391, δ 95, θ 155, ν 90, ο 401, ψ 267; cf. ὅς μοι πολλά *X* 170. [4] Cf. Τροίης ἱερὰ κρήδεμνα *Π* 100. [5] Cf. Κικόνων ἱερὸν πτολίεθρον ἑλόντες ι 165. [6] Cf. ἄλλων ἀνθρώπων δ 34, etc.; πάντων ἀνθρώπων *Π* 621, etc. [7] Cf. θεὸν ἔγνω α 420. [8] ἐν πόντωι πάθετ' ἄλγεα κ 458; πάθεν ἄλγεα *Ω* 7. [9] πάθ' ἄλγεα ὃν κατὰ θυμόν ν 90; ὃν κατὰ θυμόν *N* 8, *Ψ* 769, υ 59, ψ 345. [10] σὴν δὲ ψυχήν *X* 257. [11] Cf. καὶ νόστον Ἀχαιῶν κ 15. [12] ἀλλ' οὐδ' ὧς 16 times. [13] Cf. ἀλλ' οὐδ' ὧς σχεδίης ἐπελήθετο τειρόμενός περ ε 324; cf. τὸν νεκρὸν ἐρύσομεν *P* 635, 713. [14] ἱέμενός περ κ 246, ξ 142. [15] Cf. τούτου γὰρ . . . ἀτασθαλίῃσιν ὄλοντο κ 437. [16] σφετέρῃσιν ἀτασθαλίῃσιν ὄλοντο *Δ* 409. [17] Cf. ἀτὰρ Δαναοῖσί γε πῆμα | νήπιοι οἳ *Θ* 176–177. [18] Ὑπερίονος Ἠελίοιο *Θ* 480, μ 263. [19] αὐτὰρ ὁ τοῖσι *H* 383. [20] ἀφείλετο νόστιμον ἦμαρ τ 369; νόστιμον ἦμαρ α 168, 354, γ 233, ε 220, ζ 311, θ 466, π 149, ρ 253, 571, τ 369. [21] θεὰ θύγατερ Διός *E* 815, υ 61. [22] ἔνθ' ἄλλοι μὲν πάντες. See above on *A* 22. [23] Cf. ὅπηι φύγοι αἰπὺν ὄλεθρον *Ξ* 507, *Π* 283, χ 43; αἰπὺν ὄλεθρον *Z* 57, *K* 371, *Ξ* 507, 859, *Σ* 129, α 37, ι 286, 303, μ 287, 446, ρ 47, χ 67. [24] Cf. οἴκοι ἔχειν *A* 113. [25] ἠδὲ θάλασσαν β 407, δ 428, 573, θ 50, λ 1, μ 391, ν 70. [26] τὸν δ' οἶον ω 226. [27] Cf. νόστον πευσόμενον α 94, β 360. [28] ἠδὲ γυναικῶν *I* 134, 366, *Σ* 265, *Ψ* 261, ι 199, λ 403, φ 86, 323, ω 113. [29] ἔρυκε Καλυψὼ δῖα θεάων ι 29; Καλυψὼ δῖα θεάων ε 78, 85, 116, 180, 202, 242, 246, 258, 276; δῖα θεάων *E* 381, *Z* 305, *Ξ* 184, *Σ* 205, *T* 6, *Ω* 93, δ 382, 398, ε 159, 192, κ 400, 455, 487, 503, μ 20, 115, 143, 155, σ 190, 197, υ 55. [30] ἐν σπέσσι γλαφυροῖσι α 73, ε 155, ι 114, ψ 335. [31] λιλαιομένη πόσιν εἶναι ι 32, ψ 334. [32] ἀλλ' ὅτε δή 106 times. [33] Cf. πόστον δὴ ἔτος ἐστίν ω 288. [34] ἀλλ' ὅτε . . . ἦλθεν β 107, τ 152, ω 142. [35] περιπλομένους ἐνιαυτούς *Ψ* 833, λ 248. [36] ἐπεκλώσαντο θεοί *Ω* 525. [37] οἶκόνδε νέεσθαι *B* 290, 354, 357, *Γ* 390, *Δ* 397, *Ψ* 229, ζ 110, ξ 87, π 350. [38] Cf. ἐς πατρίδ' ἔπεμπον | εἰς Ἰθάκην τ 461. [39] Cf. πεφυγμένον ἔμμεν ὄλεθρον ι 455. [40] Cf. θεοὺς δ' ὀνόμηνεν ἅπαντας *Ξ* 278. [41] Cf. ἄντα Ποσειδάωνος

Φ 477. [42] Cf. ὁ δ' ἐπιζαφελῶς μενέαινεν ζ 330. [43] ὅ τ' ἀσπερχὲς μενεαίνεις *Δ* 32, *X* 10. [44] ἀντιθέωι Ὀδυσῆι *Λ* 140, β 17, ν 126, χ 291. [45] γαῖαν ἱκέσθαι δ 558, 823, ε 15, 26, 144, 207, 301, ζ 191, 202, 331, η 193, θ 301, κ 39, ν 426, ο 30, ρ 144, ω 281. [46] ἀλλ' . . . μετεκίαθον *Λ* 71. [47] τηλόθ' ἐόντι λ 439. [48] Cf. ἔσχατοι ἄλλων *K* 434.

The expressions in the first twenty-five lines of the *Iliad* which are solidly underlined as being found unchanged elsewhere in Homer count up to 29, those in the passage from the *Odyssey* to 34. More than one out of every four of these is found again in eight or more places, whereas in all Euripides there was only one phrase which went so far as to appear seven times. If we had chosen our verses from the end of the *Odyssey*, one could not possibly have objected that the twelve expressions in the passage from the *Iliad*, which are repeated only once, are perhaps being used there for the first time. But there is no real need of judging this point. Without these expressions the difference between the repetitions in Homer and those in the work of later poets is very great; but more than that, we are looking for the difference not in repeated phrases but in formulas.

It is important at this point to remember that the formula in Homer is not necessarily a repetition, just as the repetitions of tragedy are not necessarily formulas. It is the nature of an expression which makes of it a formula, whereas its use a second time in Homer depends largely upon the hazard which led a poet, or a group of poets, to use it more than once in two given poems of a limited length. We are taking up the problem of the Homeric formulas from the side of the repetitions, but only because it is easier to recognize a formula if we find it used a second or third time, since we can then show more easily that it is used regularly, and that it helps the poet in his verse-making. We have found that formulas are to all purposes altogether lacking in verse which we know was written, and we are now undertaking the first step in showing the particular character of Homeric style, which is to prove that Homer's verse, on the contrary, has many. We are establishing the difference between many formulas and none. But when that is done we shall still be left to decide the nature of the Homeric diction as a whole.

It is straightway clear that only a very few of the repeated expressions which are underlined in the two passages have anything either in thought or in style which could possibly set them apart in the poet's mind as particular devices for making his verses effective. There is nothing unusual about ἀλλ' ὅτε δή (107 times), γαῖαν ἱκέσθαι (18 times), οἰκόνδε νέεσθαι (10 times), ἔνθ' ἄλλοι μὲν πάντες (10 times), nor in ἥνδανε | θυμῶι (4 times), κρατερὸν δ' ἐπὶ μῦθον ἔτελλεν (3 times), ἔχων ἐν χερσίν (3 times). Nor are the expressions made up of a noun and an epithet or a patronymic more noticeable than those just quoted, though some may have wrongly thought them so. Πηληιάδεω Ἀχιλῆος might seem to one who has not read much Homer, fully as forceful as the phrase *Ὀρέστην παῖδα τὸν Ἀγαμέμνονος*, which Euripides, we said,[1] used to call up the legend, and this is the way that students just beginning the *Iliad* in Greek read the word. But when one has read the two poems, and has met the expression seven times more, usually in a context which gives us not the least idea of why Homer wished to mention the father of Achilles, one becomes indifferent to the patronymic, and ceases to look for a special meaning in its use. Besides that, one has found *Λαερτιάδεω Ὀδυσῆος* eleven times, *Ἀγαμέμνονος Ἀτρείδαο* thirteen times, *Νέστορ Νηληιάδη* seven times, *Ἕκτωρ Πριαμίδης* eight times, *Τυδέος υἱός* thirty times, *Ἀτρέος υἱός* eleven times, not to speak of *Πηλείδης* or *Πηλείων*, patronymics which are used 93 times in the place of the hero's name. After that it is very hard to remember, each time one begins the *Iliad*, to find in *Πηληιάδεω* the meaning which one gave it in its newness. What has just been said of the patronymic is likewise true of the epithet *ἄναξ ἀνδρῶν*, which is used not only 48 times elsewhere in the *Iliad* and the *Odyssey* of Agamemnon, but also of Anchises, Aeneas, Augeias, Euphetes, and Eumelos, none of whom is any more a king of men than is any other of the chief heroes; but all of them have names of the same metrical value as that of Agamemnon. *Δῖος*, the epithet of Achilles, appears again in *Α* 145 with the name of Odysseus. Even here the beginner in Homer may still believe that these two heroes share the honor of being 'divine', whatever that may mean. But when he has found the word used for Nestor (*Β* 57), for Agamemnon (*Β* 221), for Paris (*Γ* 329), and, before he has finished reading the two poems, for thirty-two different characters, many of them of no very great legend, and when he has met it as an epithet of some noun once in about every seventy verses, he at length forms the habit of scarcely heeding the word as he reads. Finally, if he ever found a sinister meaning in *ἑκηβόλου*, the epithet of Apollo in *Α* 14, he will have to make very much of an effort to find it again after he has heard the god called by that word, or by *ἑκατηβελέταο*, | *ἑκάτοιο*, *ἑκάεργος*, or *ἑκατηβόλου*, in twenty-nine other places. The fixed epithet in Homer is purely ornamental. It has been used with its noun until it has become fused with it into what is no more, so far as the essential idea goes, than another metrical form of the name. The reader knows the epithet and likes it, but it is the liking for what is familiar. He would be surprised if in a given passage the epithets were lacking, or were missing in certain known phrases; but when he does meet them he passes over them, scarcely heedingt heir meaning. The noun–epithet expressions are thus no more striking, if read rightly, than any other part of Homer's diction.[2] The case

[1] HS, p. 295 above.

[2] I have shown more fully in TE, pp. 118–72 above how the reader, through familiarity, becomes indifferent to the meaning of the fixed epithet. One will also find there other proofs

of ἐπεκλώσαντο θεοί in α 17, with its metaphor of spinning, is similar. The same verb is used in seven other places in the poems of the lot assigned to a man, and like ἕρκος ὀδόντων, 'the barrier of the teeth' (10 times), πολέμοιο γεφύρας 'the bridges of war' (5 times), or ὀλέθρου πείρατ' ἐφῆπται 'the cords of ruin are fastened' (4 times), and the fairly numerous other Homeric metaphors, its newness must have been lost long before Homer used it. This does not mean that the poetry has suffered either here or in the case of the fixed epithets; it is only a short-sighted judgment which would think of that. It means simply that the expression has found its place in the even level of this perfect narrative style, where no phrase, by its wording, stands out by itself to seize the attention of the hearers, and so stop the rapid movement of the thought, or, if one wishes, where every phrase has its perfection of style, so that the evenness of the diction comes not from its lack of what is striking, but | from its lack of any phrase which has not been accepted finally as the one best means for stating the idea.

It does not follow, because the style of Homer is even, that all the ideas of his poetry are equally forceful. There is hardly any need of pointing out the varying intensity of the thought within the fifty lines we are studying. Yet that intensity, where it appears, usually comes from the thought of the passage at that point, rather than from any certain expression. Very often, as one reads, the thought of some group of words will stand out, but it is usually the way in which they are used that makes them do so. The line which Homer uses in *A* 33 does not seem notable as one reads:

ὣς ἔφατ'· ἔδδεισεν δ' ὁ γέρων καὶ ἐπείθετο μύθωι.

But when it appears again, in the scene between Priam and Achilles (*Ω* 571), it becomes one of the very pathetic verses in Homer. The words ἔνθ' ἄλλοι μὲν πάντες in α 11 bring us to the moment when the *Odyssey* opens, and to the situation with which the poem begins, and does so with an ease which leaves us wondering; in *A* 22 this same expression is used for a more ordinary transition. Likewise the half-verse Διὸς δ' ἐτελείετο βουλή is highly forceful in the prologue of the *Iliad*, but in λ 297, where it concludes Melampus's adventure with the cattle of Iphicles, it is in no way remarkable. Besides this last repeated phrase there are six others, of the 63 found in the fifty verses we are considering, which express what

for which there is no place here: the use of the fixed epithet in a contradictory context (ἀμύμονος Αἰγίσθοιο), the use of epithets of vague connotation (δαίφρων, δῖος, μεγάθυμος), the invariable use of epithets in certain type-verses (τὸν δ' ἠμείβετ' ἔπειτα in 251 cases out of 254 is followed by a noun-epithet formula), the restriction of certain epithets to certain grammatical cases (Odysseus is δῖος 99 times in the nominative and only once in an oblique case) the limitation of an epithet to nouns of the same metrical value (as in the case of ἄναξ ἀνδρῶν just mentioned, p. 305). In my paper HG, above, I added still another proof, showing that the survival and the use of the epithet-glosses (e.g., αἰγίλιψ, ἀργειφόντης) was to be explained only by the traditional inattention of the poet and the public to their meaning.

seem to be more than ordinarily effective ideas: οὐλομένην ἥ (*A* 2), ἰφθίμους ψυχάς (*A* 3), Ἄϊδι προΐαψεν (*A* 3), ἔννεπε Μοῦσα (α 1), πολύτροπον ὅς (α 1), νήπιοι οἵ (α 8). Ἴφθιμος and πολύτροπος, it should be noted, are not ornamental epithets, but are used as an essential part of the thought.[1] It is then only to this extent of one out of every nine or ten that the repeated phrases of Homer are in any way like those which are found in later verse.

Having shown that the repeated phrases in Homer are only for a very small part to be classed as striking phrases, we must now go on to see if they are useful, since utility was a quality of the formula as we defined it. |

The technique of the formulas in Homer is vastly complex, but its general principle can be stated briefly. The Singers found and kept those expressions which without change, or with slight change, fall into that part of the hexameter which is determined by the role they play in the sentence. Since the problem of the poet is not only that of making a verse of six dactylic feet, but of fitting his words between the pauses within the verse, the formulas which express the most common ideas fall exactly between one pause in the verse and another, or between a pause and one of the verse-ends. The ways in which these formulas fit into the parts of the verse and join on to one another to make the sentence and the hexameter are very many, and vary for each type of formula. A full description of the technique is not to be thought of, since its complexity, which is exactly that of the ideas in Homer, is altogether too great. One must either limit oneself to a certain category of formulas, and describe their more frequent uses, as I have done in my study of the noun–epithet formulas, or one must take a certain number of formulas of different sorts which can be considered typical. We must choose the latter course. I shall thus consider the metrical usefulness of the first five repeated expressions which appear in the *Iliad* and in the *Odyssey*.

I.—Πηληιάδεω Ἀχιλῆος is one of a series of noun-epithet formulas, in the genitive, for gods and heroes: Λαερτιάδεω Ὀδυσῆος, πατρὸς Διὸς αἰγιόχοιο, Διομήδεος ἱπποδάμοιο, Μενελάου κυδαλίμοιο, ἀγαπήνορος Ἰδομενῆος, Ἀγαμέμνονος Ἀτρείδαο, Θηβαίου Τειρεσίαο, Ὑπερήνορος ἱπποδάμοιο, and so on. The usefulness of these formulas lies in the fact that they can finish the verse with a clause which is complete but for the genitive of a character's name; or that, if they do not finish it, they can bring the poet at any rate to the beginning of the next line where he can use formulas which regularly begin the verse. In the two cases where ἑκατηβόλου Ἀπόλλωνος, a formula of this type, is used with μῆνιν, the sentence ends with the verse:

E 444 = *Π* 711 μῆνιν ἀλευάμενος ἑκατηβόλου Ἀπόλλωνος.

[1] For the particularized epithet see TE, pp. 153–65 above, where the sense of πολύτροπος, and other epithets whose uses are not fixed, is discussed.

In λ 387 another formula of the same type brings the clause as far as the verse-end, so that the poet can use the common device of beginning the next verse with a middle form of the participle:

> ἦλθε δ' ἐπὶ ψυχὴ Ἀγαμέμνονος Ἀτρεΐδαο
> ἀχνυμένη. |

The formula in the first line of the *Iliad* renders a like service. It would be very hard at the best to put οὐλομένην ἥ in any other place in the verse than at the beginning, where it is found all of the five times it is used.[1]

II.—Very common in Homer is the device of using an adjective followed by a relative clause to continue a sentence which might have come to an end with the preceding verse. This type of enjambement is found four times in the first hundred verses of the *Odyssey*: νήπιοι οἵ (v. 8), δυσμόρῳ ὅς (v. 49), μακρὰς αἵ (v. 54), ἀμβρόσια χρύσεια τά (v. 97).[2] One should compare with *A* 2 two passages from the Odyssey:

> ρ 286 γαστέρα δ' οὔ πως ἔστιν ἀποκρύψαι μεμαυῖαν
> οὐλομένην ἣ πολλὰ κάκ' ἀνθρώποισι δίδωσι . . .

> ρ 473 αὐτὰρ ἔμ' Ἀντίνοος βάλε γαστέρος εἵνεκα λυγρῆς
> οὐλομένης ἣ πολλὰ κάκ' ἀνθρώποισι δίδωσιν.

The verse which is repeated in these two cases differs in meaning from *A* 2 only in the word ἀνθρώποις. The formula which follows the trithemimeral caesura in *E* 876:

> οὐλομένην ᾗι τ' αἰὲν ἀήσυλα ἔργα μέμηλεν

is of the same type as that found in ε 67:

> εἰνάλιαι τῇσίν τε θαλάσσια ἔργα μέμηλεν.

Indeed the play of formulas in this device of the appositive adjective extending to the middle of the second foot, followed by a relative clause which finishes the verse, seems so easy that one is tempted to make verses for oneself. Thus the line ξ 289:

> τρώκτης ὃς δὴ πολλὰ κάκ' ἀνθρώποισιν ἐώργει

becomes the following verse by the omission of δή, which is clearly used here to fill in the half-foot:

> οὐλομένην ἣ πολλὰ κάκ' ἀνθρώποισιν ἐώργει. |

III.—Ἄλγε' ἔθηκε in *A* 2 is of the very common type of formula which is made up of a verb and its direct object and falls after the bucolic diaeresis. To give only a few of the formulas which are directly like it

[1] For the use of noun-epithet formulas in the genitive see TE, pp. 55–63 above.

[2] For the relation between the forms of unperiodic enjambement and the need of the Singer for an easy versification, see DE, p. 262 above.

there are *τεύχε' ἔθηκε*, *εὖνιν ἔθηκε*, *κῦδος ἔθηκε*, on the one hand, and on the other *ἄλγε' ἔδωκε*, *ἄλγε' ἔπασχον*, *ἄλγε' ἔχουσιν*, and the like. The uses of these formulas are much more varied than those of the noun–epithet formulas which serve to expand the simple name to a certain length, or than those of the longer types of formulas, such as the one just discussed, which make up an entire clause. For a shorter group of words such as *ἄλγε' ἔθηκε* expresses an idea which will be used with many kinds of formulas to make many different sentences. This formula thus belongs to the less obvious part of the technique; yet it would be false to suppose that it is any less helpful to the poet than the longer ones: it is chiefly in the formulas of these shorter types that lie the suppleness and the range of the diction, and their usefulness is to be measured by the many different kinds of other short formulas with which they combine, as in *Κρονίδης Ζεὺς ἄλγε' ἔδωκεν* (three times), *ἀλώμενος ἄλγεα πάσχων* (twice), and so on. *A* 2, however, is not the only verse where this type of formula is preceded by a dative. We find *ἐπ' αὐτῶι κῦδος ἔθηκε* (twice), and *τῶι δευτέρωι ἵππον ἔθηκε*. In *X* 422 *ἄλγε' ἔθηκεν* follows *περὶ πάντων*. This last expression falls very often before the bucolic diaeresis: *περὶ πάντων ἔμμεναι ἄλλων*, *περὶ πάντων τῖον ἑταίρων*, and the like. It should be noted that the poet has another formula of the same meaning as *ἄλγε' ἔθηκε*, but beginning with a single consonant, so that it can be used after a final vowel: *κήδε' ἔθηκε* (*Φ* 525, *ψ* 306). Such pairs of formulas are frequent: *ἄλγεα θυμῶι* and *κήδεα θυμῶι*, *αἴσιμον ἦμαρ* and *νηλεὲς ἦμαρ*, *εὖχος ἀρέσθαι* and *κῦδος ἀρέσθαι*, and so on.

IV.—In *A* 3 we have a formula which, but for the change of a word, fills a whole line and is itself a complete sentence. Verses of this kind are outdone in usefulness only by those used unchanged, and one would have such a line here if one wished to adopt *ψυχάς*, the variant reading to *Λ* 55, for *κεφαλάς*. But the difference after all is very slight, as one can judge by the many other verses in which the poet has shifted only a word, or two words such as:

Π 186 *Εὔδωρον πέρι μὲν θείειν ταχὺν ἠδὲ μαχητήν*

δ 202 *Ἀντίλοχον πέρι μὲν θείειν ταχὺν ἠδὲ μαχητήν.* |

V.—*Διὸς δ' ἐτελείετο βουλή* in *A* 5 is of the type of numerous other formulas which form a complete sentence in one half of the verse. It happens that the words which precede it here have no direct parallel, but *θέσφατα πάντ' εἰπόντα* which goes before it in *λ* 297 is like *ἀγγελίην εἰπόντα* in *π* 467. The formula appears in an altered form in *Διὸς δ' ἐξείρετο βουλήν* (twice). Other formulas which are used in this way as half verses are *κρατερὸν δ' ἐπὶ μῦθον ἔτελλε* (four times), *παλάμηι δ' ἔχε χάλκεον ἔγχος* (twice), *νεμεσσήθη δ' ἐνὶ θυμῶι* (three times), and so on.

VI.—*Μοι ἔννεπε Μοῦσα* is one of the rare cases of a formula of any length which is found in more than one place in the verse. One can see how its place was determined by the play of the other formulas which have taken up their regular position in the line. It appears also in *B* 761:

τίς τ' ἄρ τῶν ὄχ' ἄριστος ἔην σύ μοι ἔννεπε Μοῦσα.

The beginning of the verse is that of *A* 8, which is likewise addressed to the Muse. Ὄχ' ἄριστος and the related μέγ' ἄριστος fall regularly at this place, and ὄχ' ἄριστος ἔην is found three times. In the first verse of the *Odyssey* μοι ἔννεπε Μοῦσα falls before πολύτροπον ὅς which begins a series of formulas each of which has its fixed position.

VII.—Πολύτροπος ὅς, the first of these, appears again in κ 330:

ἦ σύ γ' Ὀδυσσεύς ἐσσι πολύτροπος ὅν τέ μοι αἰεί
φάσκεν ἐλεύσεσθαι χρυσόρραπις ἀργειφόντης.

Ὅν τέ μοι αἰεί appears in six other places at the verse-end. It is one of a numerous class of formulas made up of relative words, particles, pronouns, and adverbs, which begin a clause of which the principal words will be found in the next line. Examples are εἴ ποτε δὴ αὖτε, εἴ ποτε δή τι, οὐδέ νυ σοί περ, καί ἑ μάλιστα, and the like. In the verses just quoted the formula of this sort leads up to φάσκεν ἐλεύσεσθαι, which is of the same type as φῆισιν ἐλεύσεσθαι (α 168). In α 1 we find ὅς μάλα πολλά followed by πλάγχθη, which brings the sentence to the end of the clause. A like use of πλάζομαι, as a run-over word, occurs in ε 389:

ἔνθα δύω νύκτας δύο τ' ἤματα κύματι πηγῶι
πλάζετο.

The use of a simple verb at the beginning of the verse, measured – ⏑ and followed by ἐπεί, is found, for example, in σ 174: ἔρχευ ἐπεὶ . . . This brings us by an unbroken chain of formulas to our next case. |

VIII.—Τροίης ἱερόν reappears in *Π* 100:

ὄφρ' οἶοι Τροίης ἱερὰ κρήδεμνα λύωμεν.

The line, after the first foot and a half, is no more than a variation of α 2, made necessary by the fact that λύωμεν, beginning with a consonant, cannot be joined to ἱερὸν πτολίεθρον. There is yet another variation of the verse in ν 388 where the metrical value of the verb does not allow it to be placed at the verse-end:

οἷον ὅτε Τροίης λύομεν λιπαρὰ κρήδεμνα.

IX.—In κ 458 the poet used the fixed epithet of πόντος rather than the intensifying ὃν κατὰ θυμόν which is found in α 4:

ἠμὲν ὅσ' ἐν πόντωι πάθετ' ἄλγεα ἰχθυόεντι.

Πάθεν ἄλγεα ὃν κατὰ θυμόν is one of a long series of formulas, all of which express in the different persons, numbers, moods, tenses, and cases of the participle the essential idea 'to suffer woes,' but each of which has its unique metrical value. A list of the formulas of this kind which fall at the end of the verse will give us some idea of the extent to which Homer had a formula for each metrical need:[1]

After the fifth foot and a half:	πάθεν ἄλγεα (twice)
After the fourth foot:	ἄλγεα πάσχει (10 times)
	ἄλγε' ἔχουσιν (4 times)
	πήματα πάσχει (7 times)
	πῆμα πάθῃσιν (3 times)
After the third foot and a half:	πάθον ἄλγεα θυμῶι (6 times)
	χαλέπ' ἄλγεα πάσχῃι
	κρατέρ' ἄλγεα πάσχει (4 times)
	κρατέρ' ἄλγε' ἔχοντα (4 times)
	κακὰ κήδε' ἔχουσιν
	κακὰ πολλὰ παθόντα (4 times)
	κακὰ πολλὰ μογήσας (4 times)
After the third foot:	ἄλγεα πολλὰ μογήσας (4 times)
	ἄλγεα πολλὰ πάθοιμεν |
After the trochaic caesura of the third foot:	πάθ' ἄλγεα ὃν κατὰ θυμόν
	ἔχοντί περ ἄλγεα θυμῶι (twice)
	κακῶς πάσχοντος ἐμεῖο
	ὀιζύομεν κακὰ πολλά
After the second foot and a half:	πάθεν ἄλγεα ὃν κατὰ θυμόν
	χαλεπὸν δέ τοι ἔσσεται ἄλγος

The help given the poet by these formulas is that each of them completes his verse, leaving him free to continue his thought by the formulas that begin the verse. One should not judge from this that the technique of formulas aims altogether at bringing the thought to a close at the end of the verse. It does do this often enough to bring it about that the thought comes to end in three out of every four verses in Homer, whereas in Apollonius and in Virgil it does so in only two out of every four verses.[2] But the technique also has its formulas which run the clause over into the following line. We have just studied in the case of πολύτροπον ὃς μάλα πολλά and πολύτροπος ὅν τέ μοι αἰεί two formulas of this kind.

X.—ἱέμενός περ is of the type of a large number of formulas: ἀχνύμενός περ, κηδομένη περ, ἐσσύμενόν περ, γιγνόμενόν περ, οὐτάμενοί περ, τειρόμενοί περ, and so on. These formulas can be joined to the large number of clauses whose thought is brought to a point of completion at the bucolic

[1] The list of course omits the variation of endings. Thus ἄλγε' ἔχουσιν (once) represents also ἄλγε' ἔχοντα (twice) and ἄλγε' ἔχητον (once).

[2] Cf. DE, p. 254 above.

diaeresis, where they usually end with a verb, for the fourth foot of the hexameter is very well suited to the verb by its measure and its position.[1] One may see this in ε 324, which is a verse very much like α 6:

ἀλλ' οὐδ' ὣς σχεδίης ἐπελήθετο τειρόμενός περ.

The verse ξ 142:

οὐδέ νυ τῶν ἔτι τόσσον ὀδύρομαι ἱέμενός περ

should be compared with *X* 424:

τῶν πάντων οὐ τόσσον ὀδύρομαι ἀχνύμενός περ. |

We have now found that there are formulas in Homer, one at least to every verse or so, for we have seen that the repeated expressions in the *Iliad* and the *Odyssey* are really formulas. They express only for a small part ideas which are more than usually striking, and they form a part of a highly developed technique for making hexameters. What we have done then is to prove that the style of Homer, so far as the repeated expressions go, is altogether unlike that of any verse which we know was written.

But we have also seen a difference between Homer and the later poets which is not confined to the repetitions. We found only the slightest traces of schematization in the diction of Euripides, but we have had it continually before us in our study of Homer. First, we have had one measure of it in the simple number of the repetitions, and in the large number of times many of them appear. For, as was said at the beginning of our search, whenever a poet uses his words over, he is limiting his thought to a fixed pattern on the one hand, and on the other he is casting aside all the other possible ways in which the idea could be expressed. Secondly, we have seen, by the broken line used in the passages taken from the *Iliad* and the *Odyssey*, the large number of expressions which, though not repeated, are related to others of the same type. Finally, in showing the usefulness of the repeated expressions we did nothing more than find the systems of formulas to which they belonged. One must not overlook this fact that the schematization of the diction is always due to the fact that the poet is using, to express an idea, the same device which he had used to express one more or less like it. The role played by analogy as a guide to the poet in his choice of terms is one which, we shall see, can be fully understood only when one sees the relation between the play of sound and the thought of the poet, but at no moment should one forget that the use of like formulas is a direct means of overcoming the difficulty of expressing ideas in hexameters.

The systems which were given to show the utility of the repeated expressions in Homer were often made up of phrases found only once in the two

[1] Cf. TE, pp. 40 ff. above.

poems. That these expressions were formulas, however, was clear. We could not observe them in different places, and thus prove their regular usage, but we saw that they belong to particular | artifices of versification which have a fixed place in the diction. We have thus brought into the category of formulas not only the repeated expressions, but those which are of the same type as others. In the two passages analyzed above I marked with a broken line only those formulas which were like others in rhythm, in parts of speech, and in one important word; but there are more general types of formulas, and one could make no greater mistake than to limit the formulaic element to what is underlined. *Γιγνώσκω σε θεά* in *E* 815 is like *μῆνιν ἄειδε θεά* in *A* 1, since in both cases one has a complete clause of the same length, followed by the vocative *θεά*. The similarity between *Ἀχαιοῖς ἄλγε' ἔθηκε* and *ἐπ' αὐτῶι κῦδος ἔθηκε* has been noted. *Πολλὰς δ' ἰφθίμους ψυχάς* in *A* 3 is an accusative phrase of the same length as *πολλὰς δὲ δρῦς ἀζαλέας* (*Λ* 494), and *πολλὰς δὲ στίχας ἡρώων* (*Υ* 326). If one excepts the change from accusative to nominative, the formula *ψυχὰς Ἄιδι προίαψεν* is paralleled by *ψυχαὶ δ' Ἄιδόσδε κατῆλθον* (*H* 330, *κ* 560, *λ* 65). The use of *ἡρώων* at the beginning of a verse, followed by a new clause, appears in *I* 525, and *Ἀργείων* is often used in the same way. *Τεῦχε κύνεσσιν* is like *δῶκεν ἑταίρωι* (*P* 698, *Ψ* 612). Often one finds the same verse-pattern where the words are different:

A 10 *νοῦσον ἀνὰ στρατὸν ὦρσε κακήν, ὀλέκοντο δὲ λαοί*
A 20 *παῖδα δ' ἐμοὶ λύσαιτε φίλην, τὰ δ' ἄποινα δέχεσθαι*

α 23 *Αἰθίοπας τοὶ διχθὰ δεδαίαται ἔσχατοι ἀνδρῶν*
O 526 *Λαμπετίδης ὃν Λάμπος ἐγείνατο φέρτατος ἀνδρῶν.*

Even in the very limited amount of poetry in which we are searching for like expressions there are, with the exception of those phrases used more or less often to express some special idea, as, for example, *ἐπ' ὀνείαθ' ἑτοῖμα προκείμενα* quoted above,[1] very few which do not fall into some closer or more general system; and one must never forget that the results of any analysis of this sort are conditioned by the hazard that has given us under the name of Homer not quite twenty-eight thousand verses. If we had a greater or a smaller number, we should have underlined either more or fewer expressions when we analyzed the first verses of the *Iliad* and of the *Odyssey*. If we had even twice as much of Homer's poetry as we have, the proportions | between the repeated expressions, the closer types of formulas, and the more general types, would be much changed, and we should very often find that Homer was using a formula a second time where, as far as our evidence goes, he is only using a formula which is like another. But as it is we have verses enough to show us the vast difference between the style of Homer and that of poetry which we

[1] HS, p. 275. For the special formula see TE, pp. 76–9 above.

know was written: we have found that the schematization, of which there were only the faintest traces in later poetry, reaches almost everywhere, if not everywhere, in the diction of the *Iliad* and the *Odyssey*.

6. THE TRADITIONAL ORAL STYLE

Having shown this difference we must now look for its causes. Did this style of Homer's come into being through one poet or many, in a short time or over many years? And why should Homer have wished to use a formulaic diction?

The direct proof that the style of the *Iliad* and the *Odyssey* is traditional is, of course, the schematization of the diction itself, and the number of artifices of verse-making which make up this schematization. It is not possible, for example, that one man by himself could work out more than the smallest part of the series of formulas of the type Πηληιάδεω Ἀχιλῆος. We may make ourselves believe that the one poet who composed both the *Iliad* and the *Odyssey* first used οὐλομένην ἥ, which is found three times in the first poem and as often in the other, yet we cannot go on endlessly adding νήπιοι οἵ (5 times), δύσμορος ὅς (6 times), σχέτλιος ὅς (4 times), νηλεὲς ὅς (Π 204), and so on. One cannot grant the same poet ἱέμενός περ (10 times), ἀχνύμενός περ (13 times), κηδομένη περ (11 times), οὐτάμενοί περ (4 times), and yet more. Virgil, striving to do as Homer, was able to repeat in the *Aeneid* 92 verses. How many of the 1804 repeated verses in the *Iliad* and the *Odyssey* can we then give to one poet, for whom we shall have to find I know not what reasons to repeat himself, since he could scarcely have had those which led Virgil to do so? Finally, how could one man even have made a beginning of the technique of the diction as a whole in which the various types of formulas accord with one another so well? Indeed, the more one studies the formulas in Homer and the artifices of their use, the more one sees what efforts have gone to their making. One may well say that the single series of formulas πάθεν ἄλγεα, ἄλγεα | πάσχει, and so on, is by itself alone far beyond the power of any one man. For the formulas are not only too ingenious to be the work of the one poet of the *Iliad* and the *Odyssey*; they are also too good. The epithets, the metaphorical expressions, the phrases for the binding of clauses, the formulas for running the sentence over from one verse into another, the grouping of words and phrases within the clause and within the verse, all this is many times beyond whatever supreme creative genius for words one could imagine for the poet Homer.

Moreover, we know that the Homeric diction was centuries making. The linguists have shown us that the language of the Homeric poems, which was once given the mistaken name of Old Ionic, is an artificial language, made up of words and forms taken from the current Ionic, from Aeolic, even from Arcado-Cyprian dialects; and along with these are artificial forms which could never have existed in the speech of any people.[1] The epic poets kept the older or foreign forms and words, and adopted or created new ones, in order to have a language which would suit the hexameter. The scholars who have thus finally given us the answer to the ancient question of Homer's dialect have, however, not seen clearly enough that the survival of the older forms is due not to their metrical value alone, but also to the fact that they occur in traditional formulas. There is no reason, for example, why the Aeolic prefix ἐρι- should not have been changed to the Ionic ἀρι-.[2] Yet beside ἀριδείκετε λαῶν (6 times), and ἀριδείκετος ἀνδρῶν (twice), and so on, we find: ἐρίηρες ἑταῖροι (20 times), ἐρίγδουπος πόσις Ἥρης (7 times), ἐριαύχενες ἵπποι (5 times), Τροίην ἐριβώλακα (5 times), Θρήκης ἐριβώλακος (twice), Τάρνης ἐριβώλακος, and so on. Since the presence of ἀρι- in the poems shows that the epic poets were not consciously archaizing in their use of the Aeolic prefix—and they archaize knowingly only when the metre leads them to it—we know that the series of formulas just given goes back to a time before the Ionians had learned the traditional formulaic style from the Aeolic Greeks. More | usually, however, the older forms are kept because the epic poets would otherwise have had to give up the formula altogether. The presence in the *Iliad* and in the *Odyssey* of Κρόνου παῖς ἀγκυλομήτεω (8 times), and θεοὶ δόσαν ἀγλαὰ δῶρα (4 times), warns us not to seek to change Πηληιάδεω Ἀχιλῆος (8 times), with its Ionic ending, to Πηληιάδα' Ἀχιλῆος, though there is no doubt that the Aeolic poets used it thus. But in μητίετα Ζεύς (19 times),[3] Διὸς αἰγιόχοιο (19 times), Διὸς νεφεληγερέταο (6 times), μελαινάων ἀπὸ νηῶν (7 times), μακάρεσσι θεοῖσι (7 times), the Ionic poets had to keep the Aeolic endings or lose the formulas. Likewise we have Aeolic ἄλλυδις in ἄλλυδις ἄλλῃ (8 times), περιπλομένων ἐνιαυτῶν (3 times) beside its Ionic form περιτελλομένων ἐνιαυτῶν (3 times), ἀνὰ πτολέμοιο γεφύρας (3 times) beside ὁμοιίου πολέμοιο (8 times), which falls at the verse-end where the poetry did not allow a syllable to contain a long vowel and be followed at the same time by two consonants.[4] It is certain in this last case that the formula represents an older ὁμοιίοο πτολέμοιο. But we also have στυγέρου πολέμοιο (twice) which must remain.[5] Κακομηχάνου ὀκρυοέσσης (*Z* 344),

[1] Cf. Kurt Witte, *Homer, B) Sprache* in Pauly-Wissowa, XVI (1913), coll. 2213–38; K. Meister, *Die Homerische Kunstsprache* (Leipzig, 1921); TE, pp. 5–8 above.

[2] For the Aeolic forms in Homer cf. K. Witte, *op. cit.* coll. 2214–2223; A. Meillet, *Aperçu d'une histoire de la langue Grecque*[2] (Paris, 1920), pp. 120–7; C. Buck, *Greek Dialects*,[1] pp. 135–40.

[3] Μητιέτης would cause overlengthening, for which see the following note.

[4] On overlengthening in the last two and a half feet of the hexameter, see TE, pp. 41, 93, 188.

[5] The genitive in -οο is probably not the older Ionic form of -ου, but the original of the Arcado-Cyprian -ω. The retention of ι in the original ending -οιο, is confined to Thessalian.

however, can only stand for an earlier *κακομηχάνοο κρυοέσσης*. The epic poets preserved the formula by creating the strange but easily understood *ὀκρυοέσσης*. But the antiquity of certain parts of the formulaic diction goes back even before the time when the Aeolic Greeks either learned this diction for the first time, or fused the lays of another Greek people with their own. We find in Homer a number of words which, in historical times, occur only in the dialects spoken in Arcadia or in the island of Cyprus: *αἶσα, ἆμαρ, ϝάναξ, ἀνώγω, εὐχολά, κέλευθος, οἶϝος*, and so on.[1] To these Arcado-Cyprian dialects has been given the name of Achaean, since it would seem that they are the remnant of the language spoken by those Greeks who were powerful in Greece | and the Aegean before the Dorians came. If E. Forrer's translations of the Hittite tablets found at Boghaz-Keui is correct, an Achaean chief of the thirteenth century went by the title of *κοίρανος*.[2] There is of course no need to suppose that all the formulas in Homer which contain Achaean words go back to a time before the coming of the Dorians, since it is very possible that the later poets may have used one of the old words in a new formula, but in many cases it is easier to accept the antiquity of the formula than explain it by such a hazard. *Αἴσιμον ἦμαρ* (4 times), for example, is made up of two such Achaean words: *ἤματα πάντα* (27 times) appears in fifth-century prose inscriptions from Mantinea and Tegea. One can only guess at the age of *νηλεής*, in which appears the prefix *νη-* which had disappeared from spoken Greek before the historical period: this word is found nine times in *νηλεὲς ἦμαρ*. Most important, perhaps, of all the Achaean words is *αὐτάρ*, found only in Cyprian. The use of this word, of which we have given one of the systems above,[3] is so far-reaching in Homeric style that we must either accept the high antiquity of many of the most common phrases for joining clauses in the hexameter, or say that the later Greeks just happened to seize upon what was to them no more than a helpful poetic word to use in many of their most common formulaic devices. It is hard to believe in such a curious chance. Finally, the age of certain parts of the diction, as well as of the form of the hexameter, is shown by the great number of noun–epithet formulas in which the meaning of the epithet has been lost to us, as it must have to Homer also, for otherwise we must suppose a rapidity of change in spoken Ionic which would be without a linguistic parallel.[4]

The form *πτόλις*, found in Cyprian, Arcadian, and Cretan, and *πτόλεμος* glossed as Cyprian, are Achaean, unless one wishes to accept the Thessalian *οἱ ττολίαρχοι* as evidence of a possible Aeolic origin. Cf. Buck, *op. cit.*, pp. 57, 81.

[1] Cf. Buck, *op. cit.*, p. 132; C. M. Bowra, 'Homeric Words in Arcadian Inscriptions', in *Classical Quarterly*, XX (1926), pp. 168–76.

[2] E. Forrer, 'Die Griechen in den Boghazköi-Texten' in *Orientalische Literaturzeitung*, XXVII (1924), pp. 114–8.

[3] HS, p. 276 above.

[4] Cf. HG, above.

It may still seem to some at this point that the schematization of the diction, and the age of parts of it, prove that most of Homer's style is traditional, but still leave room for the creation of phrases by the single poet. One could answer simply that the expressions created within the systems, by following the fixed types, would have none of | the newness which the term 'originality' suggests to us, and that those created outside the systems, if there are any besides the special formulas, are too few to call for much thought. But in treating of the oral nature of the Homeric style we shall see that the question of a remnant of individuality in Homeric style disappears altogether.

It is of course the pattern of the diction which, as in the matter of the authorship of the style, proves by its very extent that the Homeric style is oral. It must have been for some good reason that the poet, or poets, of the *Iliad* and the *Odyssey* kept to the formulas even when he, or they, had to use some of them very frequently. What was this constraint that thus set Homer apart from the poets of a later time, and of our own time, whom we see in every phrase choosing those words which alone will match the color of their very own thought? The answer is not only the desire for an easy way of making verses, but the complete need of it. Whatever manner of composition we could suppose for Homer, it could be only one which barred him in every verse and in every phrase from the search for words that would be of his own finding. Whatever reason we may find for his following the scheme of the diction, it can be only one which quits the poet at no instant. There is only one need of this sort which can even be suggested—the necessity of making verses by the spoken word. This is a need which can be lifted from the poet only by writing, which alone allows the poet to leave his unfinished idea in the safe keeping of the paper which lies before him, while with whole unhurried mind he seeks along the ranges of his thought for the new group of words which his idea calls for. Without writing, the poet can make his verses only if he has a formulaic diction which will give him his phrases all made, and made in such a way that, at the slightest bidding of the poet, they will link themselves in an unbroken pattern that will fill his verses and make his sentences.

This necessity which oral verse-making sets upon the poet shows its force most clearly, as has been said, in the simple number of formulas found in the *Iliad* and in the *Odyssey*; but there are also many cases in which that force can be measured by its effect upon the single phrase. The greater number of metrical irregularities in Homer come in the play of the formulas, either from a change within the formula, as when *υἱὸς Πετεῶο* (3 times) becomes *υἱὲ Πετεῶο* (*Δ* 338), or from the | grouping of formulas which will not join to one another without fault, as in the following example. Homer makes a large number of verses by joining to different predicates, which fill just one half of the verse, subjects of the type πατὴρ ἀνδρῶν τε θεῶν τε, ἄναξ ἀνδρῶν Ἀγαμέμνων, and so on. By this pattern he made τ 59 and τ 102:

ἔνθα καθέζετ' ἔπειτα περίφρων Πηνελόπεια

ἔνθα καθέζετ' ἔπειτα πολύτλας δῖος Ὀδυσσεύς.

He could have made just as many verses of this sort as he had noun-epithet formulas in the nominative, falling after the trochaic caesura of the third foot, and beginning with a simple consonant. But for Telemachus, whose name has a measure which bars it from forming in the latter part of the hexameter any formula save the little-used type *Τηλέμαχος θεοειδής* (5 times), he had only *Ὀδυσσῆος φίλος υἱός* (9 times), which begins with a vowel. Nevertheless, the force of the formulas and the pattern of the verse was so strong upon him that he made π 48:

ἔνθα καθέζετ' ἔπειτα Ὀδυσσῆος φίλος υἱός.

In the same way, on the type of formula found five times in the following verse:

τέκνον ἐμόν ποῖόν σε ἔπος φύγεν ἕρκος ὀδόντων;

and on Δ 350 = Ξ 83:

Ἀτρείδη ποῖόν σε ἔπος φύγεν ἕρκος ὀδόντων;

he made γ 230:

Τηλέμαχε ποῖόν σε ἔπος φύγεν ἕρκος ὀδόντων;

The type of formula found in the first verse of the *Iliad* has entered into the making of *T* 35:

μῆνιν ἀποειπὼν Ἀγαμέμνονι ποιμένι λαῶν.

It is not until we have read forty verses farther in the poem, however, that we find the direct model of this incorrect line:

μῆνιν ἀπειπόντος μεγαθύμου Πηλείωνος.

This verse in turn belongs to the system in which falls *E* 444 = *Π* 711:

μῆνιν ἀλευάμενος ἑκατηβόλου Ἀπόλλωνος. |

One should note especially that in this case as in that of π 48, just quoted, the incorrect verse occurs before its correct model. In neither place was the poet altering a line he had just used, but was composing after the pattern which he had in his mind. Now it is not possible that the metrical irregularities of the sort which have been given, and they are very numerous in the *Iliad* and in the *Odyssey*,[1] could occur in any but an oral poetry. The poet who makes verses at the speed he chooses will never be forced to leave a fault in his verse, but the Singer, who without stopping

[1] For other examples see FM above, which is devoted to a study of such cases.

must follow the stream of formulas, will often be driven to make irregular lines. In such cases it is not the poet who is to blame, but his technique, which is not proof against all fault, and which, in the unhesitating speed of his composition, he cannot stop to change.

But there is more to show the oral nature of Homer's diction than the need of explaining why he limited his thought to the formulas and made faulty verses. There is also the diction itself. First, there is a fairly large number of cases where the pure sound of one expression has suggested another which is altogether unlike it in meaning. Thus some Singer, whether Homer or another, when he had to express the idea 'along with the clouds', thought of the words ὁμοῦ νεφέεσσιν (*E* 867), simply because his mind was guided by the echo of ὁμοῦ νεκύεσσι (*O* 118), 'among the dead'; or perhaps it was the latter phrase which was the model. The only examples of this sort that I have found in Euripides are ἀξένου πόρου,[1] made after Εὐξείνου πόρου,[2] and αὐτὸς ἀνταπωλόμην,[3] made after αὖθις ἀνταπώλετο.[4] One case at first sight seems to come near what we find in Homer: we read in the *Andromeda*: ἔα· τίν' ὄχθον τόνδ' ὁρῶ,[5] and in the *Cyclops*: ἔα· τίν' ὄχλον τόνδ' | ὁρῶ.[6] This would be no more than a faint parallel to the Homeric verses:

Θ 395 ἠμὲν ἀνακλῖναι πυκινὸν νέφος ἠδ' ἐπιθεῖναι
λ 525 ἠμὲν ἀνακλῖναι πυκινὸν λόχον ἠδ' ἐπιθεῖναι.

Here, by the change of four letters, the verse 'to throw ajar the thick cloud, or set it to', becomes 'to open the door of our shrewd ambush, or set it to'. But the source of the Euripidean phrase becomes clear when we find Aristophanes using it in a ridiculous scene in his comedy *The Women at the Thesmophoria*,[7] which means that Euripides was answering

[1] *Iphigenia in the Tauric Land* 253, 1388.
[2] *Andromache* 1262. [3] *Helen* 106. [4] *Suppliants* 743.
[5] Fr. 124:
ἔα· τίν' ὄχθον τόνδ' ὁρῶ περίρρυτον
ἀφρῶι θαλάσσης; παρθένου τ' εἰκώ τινα
ἐξ αὐτομόρφων λαίνων τυκισμάτων
σοφῆς ἄγαλμα χειρός.

[6] Vv. 222 ff.:
ἔα· τίν' ὄχλον τόνδ' ὁρῶ πρὸς αὐλίοις;
λῃσταί τινες κατέσχον ἢ κλῶπες χθόνα;
ὁρῶ γέ τοι τούσδ' ἄρνας ἐξ ἄντρων ἐμῶν
στρεπταῖς λύγοισι σῶμα συμπεπλεγμένους
τεύχη τε τυρῶν συμμιγῆ γέροντά τε
πληγαῖς πρόσωπον φαλακρὸν ἐξῳδηκότα.

Vv. 1105 ff.:
ἔα· τίν' ὄχθον τόνδ' ὁρῶ καὶ παρθένον
θεαῖς ὁμοίαν ναῦν ὅπως ὡρμισμένην;

Aristophanes and the Athenian public, it would seem, found the use of 'Lo! I see . . .' very ridiculous upon the stage. So far as I know, no editor has noted the relation of these verses to the lines in the *Cyclops*, nor used it to date this play, which we may suppose to have been written in the year following that of the comedy of Aristophanes, when it was still fresh in the mind of the Athenians. If we accept 410 (Rogers) as the date of *The Women at the Thesmophoria* the *Cyclops* would belong to 409. R. Marquart, in *Die Datierung des Euripideischen Kyklops* (Halle

Aristophanes' mockery by mocking himself. Thus only by a planned comic use of words does the Attic dramatist do what the epic poets did without thinking.[1] Other examples in | Homer in which the sound of words has suggested the terms of statement for an unlike idea are the following. The likeness of νήεσσι to νήσοισι has given us the verses *K* 214 and α 245 = π 122 = τ 130:

ὅσσοι γὰρ νήεσσιν ἐπικρατέουσιν ἄριστοι

ὅσσοι γὰρ νήσοισιν ἐπικρατέουσιν ἄριστοι.

The likeness of ἠδέ to ἦλθε has suggested one or the other of these two verses:

Υ 34 ἠδὲ Ποσειδάων γαιήοχος ἠδ' ἐριούνης Ἑρμείας

θ 322 ἦλθε Ποσειδάων γαιήοχος, ἦλθ' ἐριούνης Ἑρμείας.

The line *B* 581:

οἳ δ' εἶχον κοίλην Λακεδαίμονα κητώεσσαν

was the model of δ 1, in which the relative οἵ becomes a demonstrative:

Οἱ δ' ἷξον κοίλην Λακεδαίμονα κητώεσσαν.

Apollo and Athena both take the form of a man named Mentes:

P 73 ἀνέρι εἰσάμενος Κικόνων ἡγήτορι Μέντηι

α 105 εἰδομένη ξείνωι Ταφίων ἡγήτορι Μέντηι.

Of shorter expressions we find ἀμφήλυθεν ἡδὺς ἀυτμή (μ 369) and ἀμφήλυθε θῆλυς ἀυτή (ζ 122), ἄναξ ἀνδρῶν Ἀγαμέμνων (37 times), and ἄναξ ἐνέρων Ἀιδωνεύς (*Υ* 61), and so on.[2] There is in most of these cases nothing to

1912), concluded, on the grounds of language, meters, dramatic technique, scenery and costuming, and possible reminiscences of other works, that the play, commonly assigned to the poet's earlier years, was to be placed after the *Iphigenia in the Tauric Land* (414–412 according to Murray) and the *Helen* (412), and before the *Phoenicians* (411–409) and the *Orestes* (408).

[1] The only unusual case of this sort which I know outside the epic is in English poetry. Twice in *Paradise Lost* Milton uses the forceful line

The serpent, subtlest beast of all the field . . .

(VII, 495 and IX, 86). Then once more he writes:

Thee, Serpent, subtlest beast of all the field
I knew . . .

(IX, 560). It may be that the poet's dependence upon his hearing had something to do with this. He may even have made the verse thinking of those he knew in Homer:

καί μιν φωνήσας ἔπεα πτερόεντα προσηύδα (29 times)

καί μιν φωνήσασ' ἔπεα πτερόεντα προσηύδα (9 times).

[2] For other cases of this sort, and a discussion of the artistic value of such a method of creation, see TE, pp. 71–4 above.

show us which of the expressions is the model and which the copy, nor do we know that it was Homer who was thus guided in his language by the play of sound, since it is more likely that he knew both original and copy as separate formulas. This, however, affects | our conclusions in no way; we are merely saying that the traditional style which Homer used was oral, and not that Homer's style was so.

It is largely chance that has given us these expressions in which we find likeness of sound without likeness of idea; yet we would have known just as well without them that Homer's style was oral. For there is a simple, almost too obvious, fact to show it: namely, that there is no memory of words save by the voice and the ear. We who have lived our lives with books, and have read much, often reach a point, at least for prose, where the words upon the printed page are more symbols for ideas than the record of speech; and it is our eyes which carry to our minds the author's thought, rather than our ears. Yet if we would remember any sentence, even any phrase, we must say it to ourselves either aloud or beneath our breath, until the organs of our voice will repeat, at our bidding, the gesture of its utterance. There are some, they say, who can recall whole sentences or even passages because they can picture to themselves the way they look in print. In the same way schoolboys remember the place of Greek accents, being unable to make with their voices any sound for which they would stand; and we also know that one can learn a foreign language in a way by learning to tell the idea from the printed image of the words and phrases, and that one can even write sentences of a sort by grouping together such images by a purely visual process. But as there is no real knowledge of a language thus learned, so is there no real memory without sound. As a rule we are unable to recall a single phrase of the book we have read silently. The poet who is repeating his own phrase, or that of another, is doing so by ear. To deny this for any poet is to suppose impossible things. The repeated phrases in Virgil, then, would become, as it were, labels which the poet fitted into his verse in the same way that one pieces together a puzzle, and not, as we know they were, expressions which were judged in every part by his sensitive feeling for sound. And would one dare to say that Pope had never heard the phrase he took from Milton: 'thick as autumnal leaves'?

We know Virgil's practice of dictation, and of reading his verses to his friends, but we do not have to suppose that he spoke aloud every phrase which he had used over; nor did Pope necessarily have read to him all the poems of Milton from which he borrowed. He may | have muttered the words, or have spoken them to himself beneath the hearing of any other person. But memorizing under one's breath is possible only up to a certain point. Pope may thus have learned all the phrases of Milton which he knew by heart, and Virgil most of what he repeated, though it is hard to believe that. But when we come to Homer such a thing is beyond reason. Would he, by the conning of long manuscripts of epic poetry, have learned the thousands of whole verses, the thousands of verse-parts, which make up the traditional diction? And we must suppose that the authors of all those manuscripts in turn had learned just as faithfully in the same way the countless mass of formulas, and so on back. But the argument has reached the absurd, and we are trying to suppose an oral poetry in an undertone. Homer could only have learned his formulas by hearing them spoken in the full voice of those poets to whom he listened from his childhood.

Homer learning his formulas from manuscript is no harder to imagine than Homer using his formulas to write verses. He is then keeping his thought to them not because he has to, but because he wants to. His is a strange game in which he must fit into his written lines only those phrases which have been used by others. Each one of the eighty-eight times he uses τὸν δ' αὖτε προσέειπε, followed by a noun–epithet formula, or the hundreds of times he uses αὐτὰρ ἐπεί at the beginning of the verse, or whenever he uses any formula whatsoever, he is showing his skill in choosing the old expression, his stern disregard of all the new groups of words which, since his writing materials gave him time to pause, must have crowded annoyingly about his head. And this is the way we must suppose him to have made almost all, if not all, of his poetry. If one wishes to think that Homer composed his poems orally, and then sat down and wrote them out, there is little that can be said in disproof, and little that needs to be said, since the question ceases to be one of the oral style, and becomes that of the way in which the spoken poetry was recorded.

So far we have said only that the formula itself must be a thing of sound and not of sight. We now come to the last of proofs that the diction of the *Iliad* and the *Odyssey* is oral, and to the one which is most precious for our understanding of Homer: the technique of the formulas is one which could only be created and used by oral poets.

Each system of formulas comes, in the last analysis, from some single expression. The simple fact that two phrases are too closely alike to be due to chance implies that one of them imitates the other, or that they go back to a common model. There was one formula, what one we shall never know, from which comes all the system found in Homer: δῖος Ἀγήνωρ, δῖος Ἀλάστωρ, δῖος Ἀχιλλεύς, δῖος Ἐπειγεύς, δῖος Ἐπειός, δῖος Ἐχέφρων, δῖος Ὀδυσσεύς, δῖος ὑφορβός. More than that, there was one noun–epithet formula which was the beginning of all the larger system δῖος Ἀχιλλεύς, μητίετα Ζεύς, πότνια Ἥρη, φαίδιμος Ἕκτωρ, and so on. Likewise, all the formulas of the system αὐτὰρ ἐπεί ῥ' ἵκοντο, αὐτὰρ ἐπεί ῥ' ἤγερθεν, and the like, go back to one source, as does the type of verse we see in the two following lines:

A 121 τὸν δ' ἠμείβετ' ἔπειτα ποδάρκης δῖος Ἀχιλλεύς

B 402 αὐτὰρ ὁ βοῦν ἱέρευσεν ἄναξ ἀνδρῶν Ἀγαμέμνων.

When one multiplies these cases by the number of the systems in the Homeric diction, one sees that the formation of the style was of a very special sort. The Singers, ever seeking to reduce the terms of their expression to the simplest pattern, used for this end the means of analogy.[1] That is to say, wherever they could obtain a new formula by altering one which was already in use, they did so, and this they did up to the point where the complexity of the ideas which must be expressed in their poetry put a stop to this making of systems. This means of forming the system is quite different from that which would have been followed if it were the usefulness of the formula alone which led the poets to make it and keep it, for then we should find a diction in which there would be formulas, but few of them would have the same words as another. Instead of ἄναξ ἀνδρῶν Ἀγαμέμνων and ἄναξ ἀνδρῶν Αἰνείας, we should have had formulas with different epithets. We should not find τὸν δ' ἠμείβετ' ἔπειτα joined with twenty-seven different noun–epithet formulas, but many different kinds of lines for announcing a character's answer. But such is not the nature of the epic diction, which so much preferred to use the same words where it could that there are in all the *Iliad* and the *Odyssey* only forty fixed epithets that are used for single heroes, beside sixty-one that are used for two | or more.[2] Thus we have δῖος in the nominative used of twelve characters, θεοειδής of fourteen, ἥρως of ten, δουρικλυτός of eight, and so on. In these cases, and in all others, we see the sound of the words guiding the Singers in their formation of the diction. Nor is the factor of sound limited to the formulas where the same words appear; it appears equally in the more general types where the likeness of sound consists in the like rhythm. The sound of the words has not acted so willfully in the creation of the systems as it has in the case of those formulas which we noted above, in which it has gone so far as to give the poetry its ideas. Here it has followed the thought which the Singers wished to express, though it imposed rigorous limits for that thought; yet whereas in the one place it created only a certain number of isolated phrases, it here has had an influence as far-reaching as the schematization of the style.

This formation of the traditional diction belongs, of course, to a time far earlier than that in which Homer lived, but the making of the diction is in no way different from a single poet's use of it. One can say that the

1 On the place of analogy in the formation of the Homeric diction, see TE, pp. 68–74 above.

2 Cf. TE, pp. 83–96 above.

Singer, in a recitation of a few hours, repeats the history of his style, for it is the play of sound which guides him in his grouping of the formulas, quite in the way that it had guided the poets of an older time in their making of them. As they had made for him *οὐδέ με πείσεις*, *οὐδέ με λήσει*, *οὐδέ ἕ φημι*, and so on, to be used at the verse-end, even so, when he has ended a sentence at the bucolic diaeresis, he is led by the habitual movement of his voice to these formulas. Or at the beginning of a verse, when he has another sort of transition to use and a certain act to tell, he will be guided by his feeling for what there is in common in the sound of such a system as *νῦν δ' ἐθέλω*, *νῦν δ' ἔχομαι*, *νῦν δ' ἦλθον*, or *οἱ δ' ὅτε δή ῥ' ἵκοντο*, *οἱ δ' ὅτε δὴ σχεδὸν ἦσαν*, and so on. And it is here, finally, that we can see why we should not seek in the *Iliad* and in the *Odyssey* for Homer's own style. The poet is thinking in terms of the formulas. Unlike the poets who wrote, he can put into verse only those ideas which are to be found in the phrases which are on his tongue, or at the most he will express ideas so like those of the traditional formulas that he himself would not know them apart. At no time is he seeking words for an idea which has never before found expression, so that the question of originality in style | means nothing to him. It may here occur to some to ask how the diction was ever made if one thus grants the Singer no power to change it. It is to be answered that the years of its first making belong to a very dim past, and were also those of its least perfection; then, that we may well suppose for the single poet a very few cases where the play of words has suggested some new epithet, or phrase, or verse, which the other Singers found worth using and keeping, but that there could never be more than a few such creations for any one Singer, and they could win a place in the diction only as they were in accord with what was traditional, and fitted the habits of verse-making of the other poets. Indeed, in certain places in the poems we can see how certain very effective phrases or verses were made. The wondrously forceful line:

Π 776 = *ω* 40 *κεῖτο μέγας μεγαλωστὶ λελασμένος ἱπποσυνάων*

is made up of verse-parts found in other parts of the poems: *κεῖτο μέγας* (*M* 381); *μέγας μεγαλωστί* (*Σ* 26); *λελασμένος ὅσσ' ἐπεπόνθει* (*ν* 92); *λελάσμεθα θούριδος ἀλκῆς* (*Λ* 313). There is a striking play on the name of Odysseus in *α* 62: *τί νύ οἱ τόσον ὠδύσαο, Ζεῦ*; which is made after *ἐπεὶ μέγας ὠδύσατο Ζεύς*, which is found in *Σ* 292. There are in all the poems only two other places where *Ζεῦ* is found at the verse-end: *μητίετα Ζεῦ* (*A* 508) and *εὐρύοπα Ζεῦ* (*Π* 241). That Homer might, by a like new play of formulas, have added to the great wealth of the traditional style is possible, but we shall never know, since if he did so he was guided by the same play of words and phrases as all those other poets who, bit by bit, and through the many years, had made this best of all styles.

6

Studies in the Epic Technique of Oral Verse-Making. II. The Homeric Language as the Language of an Oral Poetry.*

1. THE HOMERIC LANGUAGE AND THE HOMERIC DICTION

WITHIN the last twenty years Homeric scholars have shown that the language of the *Iliad* and *Odyssey* is a poetic language made to suit the needs of the verse, and they have thereby done away with a whole number of hypotheses which were no longer needed. A brief account of these earlier theories of Homer's language will serve to set forth the subject of the present pages. The reader should bear in mind that we are speaking here at the beginning about language, and not about diction or style. All three have to do with the sum of words, word-forms, and word-groupings used by a man. As *language*, however, we look at them as used by a certain people, at a certain time, and in a certain place; as *diction*, as the material by which thought is expressed; and as *style*, as the form of thought.

Older Theories of the Homeric Language

The common view of Homer's language in antiquity was that which, while it seems the simplest, is likewise the furthest from the truth: | Homer himself chose various forms and words from the dialects which

* First published in *Harvard Studies in Classical Philology* 43 (1932), 1–50.

he had heard in his travels about Greece.[1] Such a view could of course be held only in the lack of any careful study of the Greek dialects and of Homer's language, for we now know that some of the forms in the *Iliad* and *Odyssey* are much older than others, while some could never have been a part of the everyday speech of any Greek. Also Homer's use of the forms and words of different dialects follows a fixed rule and no varying chance of memory.[2] The gravest fault of such a theory, however, is that it supposes that one man could all by himself create a poetic language. Such a thing has been seen nowhere. No single poet could ever have such powers; and a poetic language, it is clear, is poetic only by a convention shared by the poet and his hearers, so that the growth of a poetic language must be gradual.

The ancients, since they had no rigorous historical method of literary criticism, may be excused for such a mistake, but not so the authors of a recent theory who hold that Homer was the native of a city wherein a mixed population of Aeolians and Ionians had come to speak a language having the same variety of forms as that found in the Homeric poems.[3]

[1] [Plutarch], *Life and Poetry of Homer* 2, 8; cf. Dio Chrysostom, *Orations* 11, 23.

[2] See p. 328.

[3] The latest critic to hold this idea is T. W. Allen in his *Homer: the Origins and Transmission* (Oxford, 1924), pp. 98–109, where he claims to be developing the views of P. Giles (cf. *Proceedings of the Cambridge Philological Society*, 1916, pp. 7–9), whose very sensible view, however, he has failed to understand. He did not know, it would seem, that the theory had already been set forth by Wilamowitz (*Sitzungsberichte der Akademie der Wissenschaften, Berlin*, 1906, pp. 52–75, and *Die Ilias und Homer*, Berlin, 1906, pp. 356 ff.), and straightway disproved (cf. E. Drerup, *Das Homerproblem in der Gegenwart*, Würzburg, 1921, p. 110). For the views of a linguist on such a theory see A. Meillet, *Aperçu d'une histoire de la langue grecque*[3], p. 171. There is scarcely any need of giving further warning against the theory, but one finds even so good a critic as C. M. Bowra falling into the error in a milder way. In his *Tradition and Design in the Iliad* (Oxford, 1930), pp. 139–40, he compares Homer's Ionic and Aeolic with Chaucer's English and French — the comparison shows that the author is thinking of Homer in terms of written literature: 'Chaucer wrote for a class who knew both English and French, and for whom his mixed language was intelligible. But it was essentially his own creation. His predecessors wrote in the Anglo-Saxon tradition, but he created a new language for English verse. If we press the analogy, it would follow that Homer lived in a world where different dialects, though existing separately, impinged on each other and were mutually intelligible. Out of this situation Homer or his predecessors created a poetical speech.' Bowra, however, somewhat misses the nature of Chaucer's language, as one may judge by the following statement of A. W. Pollard ('Chaucer' in the *Encyclopaedia Britannica*, 14th ed.): 'The part played by Chaucer in the development of the English language has often been overrated. He neither corrupted it, as used to be said, by introducing French words which it would otherwise have avoided, nor bore any such part in fixing it as was afterwards played by the translators of the Bible. The practical identity of Chaucer's language with that of Gower shows that both merely used the best English of their day with the care and slightly conservative tendency which befitted poets.' Moreover the French part of Chaucer's language, as of English, is of a very certain kind, namely abstract words without which the pattern of European, as opposed to Anglo-Saxon, thought could not be kept, and names of objects brought in by French culture. It could be held only in the rarest cases that the Aeolic element in Homer thus represented any contribution of thought or culture foreign to Ionic.

As this article goes to press I find that Allen's unlucky theory is accepted by B. F. C. Atkinson (*The Greek Language*, London, 1931, p. 201): 'We shall not be far wrong in regarding it

Such a view altogether overlooks the nature of Greek poetic diction as it is to be seen everywhere in the poetry of the historical period; by the same reasoning the population of Attica was partly Dorian. Nor has anyone anywhere found a spoken language which shows even faintly such a variety of forms current side by side.

A third theory, which found many believers at the end of the last | century, held that Homer's language was altogether Ionic and that the variety of forms was due to a simple literary conservatism which kept the older forms from age to age for purely stylistic reasons.[1] This view, like the next which will be mentioned, is much better than the first two, since it has a part of the truth in it. Its authors, however, had insufficient linguistic knowledge when they held that all of the Aeolisms in Homer had at one time been used in earlier Ionic, since many of the forms in question are the creation of a later period than that of common Greek. Yet their greatest faults were those of giving no | good reason for so strong a conservatism and of failing to see that the different forms are used under fixed conditions.

The last of the earlier theories is one of the oldest of all, since it was already held by Zopyrus and Dicaearchus at the end of the fourth century B.C.: *τὴν δὲ ποίησιν ἀναγιγνώσκεσθαι ἀξιοῖ Ζώπυρος ὁ Μάγνης Αἰολίδι διαλέκτωι· τὸ δ' αὐτὸ καὶ Δικαίαρχος.*[2] This hypothesis as developed by A. Fick won both more favor and more scorn than it deserved.[3] The favor it should not have had because Fick in putting it into practice used a method far too arbitrary, and those who scorn it now do not see that it first brought into prominence the two facts on which the whole problem of Homeric language hinges, namely that Homer's poetry can with no very great change be turned from Ionic into Aeolic, and that the non-Ionic forms are kept as a rule only when Ionic itself has no forms which could take their place. K. Witte, when he wrote that the Homeric language is the work of the Homeric verse, gave the better reason for this, but it was Fick nevertheless who made the needed if false step, and we shall see what a large amount of truth there was after all in his views.

[i.e. the Homeric language] as in the hands of the poet of the epics a living language against whose everyday use in the island of Chios earlier than the ninth century we know no valid reason.' It is criticism enough to have quoted the statement.

1 The theory was first set forth by K. Sittl ('Die Aeolismen der homerischen Sprache' in *Philologus*, XLIII, 1884, pp. 1–31), and answered by G. Hinrichs (*Herr Dr Karl Sittl und die homerischen Aeolismen*, Berlin, 1884); cf. his *De Homericae elocutionis vestigiis Aeolicis* (Berolini, 1875). It was developed in English chiefly by D. B. Monro (*Journal of Philology*, IX, 1880, pp. 252–65; XI, 1882, pp. 56–60; *Homeric Grammar*², Oxford, 1891, pp. 386–96). See below HL, p. 345.

2 F. Osann, *Anecdotum Romanum* (Gissae, 1851), p. 5; cf. p. 280.

3 August Fick, *Die homerische Odyssee in der ursprünglichen Sprachform wiederhergestellt* (Göttingen, 1883); *Die homerische Ilias* (Göttingen, 1886); *Die Entstehung der Odyssee* (Göttingen, 1910).

The Homeric Language as a Poetic Language

Witte was able to show long lists of words from the *Iliad* and *Odyssey* in which Aeolic or older forms stood beside Ionic forms, always with a difference of metrical value, and he was further able to show that these different forms were suited for use in different places in the verse.[1] As we shall see,[2] he failed to consider Arcado-Cyprian, and had no notion of an Aeolic poetic language, and so was wrong in thinking that some of these Ionic forms were only Ionic and so could not have been used by Aeolic poets. But this misunderstanding in no way affects the soundness of the principle which he drew from his evidence: | the Homeric poems were composed in a poetic language wherein old and foreign forms had been kept and new forms brought in by reason of the help they gave the epic poets in making their hexameters. These poets ever sought a language which was easier to handle, and for that reason ever made use of the fact that the older or foreign form of a word was to a Greek, as Aristotle tells us, more poetic than the form used in everyday speech.[3]

The Homeric Language as an Oral Poetic Language

In one way, however, the theory of Witte, even with the further work done on it by Meister, is unfinished: they have logically proved that the language of Homer is the work of the Homeric verse, but they have not at all shown how the verse in this case could have such power. It did not have it in the later Greek epic, nor in Roman hexameter verse, nor in short do we find elsewhere in ancient or modern literature (with the very notable exception, however, of the early poetry of the nations) any but the slightest traces of the verse-form acting on the language of the poetry. Clearly a special language for the hexameter could come into being only when poetry was of a very different sort from that which we ourselves write, and which we know to have been written throughout the history of European literature. To say that the Homeric language was the work of the Homeric verse thus implies a poetry which is, at least to our way of thinking, of a very special kind, so that while the theory may be proved it cannot really be understood until we know just what this poetry was.

It is my own view, as those who have read my studies on Homeric style know, that the nature of Homeric poetry can be grasped only when one has seen that it is composed in a diction which is oral, and so formulaic, and so traditional.[4] So it is for the language of the *Iliad* and *Odyssey*: if we know what an oral diction is we shall have the larger | background which the theory of a language made to fit the hexameter calls for. At the

[1] K. Witte, *Homeros B) Sprache* in Pauly–Wissowa, VIII (1913), coll. 2213–47. The subject has been further developed by K. Meister, *Die homerische Kunstsprache* (Leipzig, 1921).

[2] HL, pp. 344–5, 349, 32.

[3] *Rhetoric* 1404^{b}10.

[4] TE; FM; HG; DE; HS, above. TM, below.

same time the Homeric language when thus explained by the diction will in turn give us the history of that diction.

2. THE TRADITIONAL POETIC LANGUAGE OF ORAL POETRY

The Formula

In a society where there is no reading and writing, the poet, as we know from the study of such peoples in our own time, always makes his verse out of formulas. He can do it in no other way. Not having the device of pen and paper which, as he composed, would hold his partly formed thought in safe-keeping while his unhampered mind ranged where it would after other ideas and other words, he makes his verses by choosing from a vast number of fixed phrases which he has heard in the poems of other poets.[1] Each one of these phrases does this: it expresses a given idea in words which fit into a given length of the verse. Each one of these fixed phrases, or formulas, is an extraordinary creation in itself.[2] It gives the words which are best suited for the expression of the idea, and is made up of just those parts of speech which, in the place which it is to fill in the verse, will accord with the formulas which go before and after to make the sentence and the verse. Each formula is thus made in view of the other formulas with which it is to be joined; and the formulas taken all together make up a diction which is the material for a completely unified technique of verse-making.[3] Finally, the formulas of an oral poetry are not each one of them without | likeness to any other; in that case the technique would be far too unwieldy. They fall into smaller groups of phrases which have between them a likeness of idea and words, and these in turn fall into groups which have a larger pattern in common, until the whole diction is schematized in such a way that the poet, habituated to the scheme, hits without effort, as he composes, upon the type of formula and the particular formula which, at any point in his poem, he needs to carry on his verse and his sentence.[4]

[1] Cf. A. van Gennep on the Serbian epic (*La question d'Homère*, Paris, 1909, p. 52): 'Les poésies des guslars sont une juxtaposition de clichés, relativement peu nombreux et qu'il suffit de posséder. Le développement de chacun de ces clichés se fait automatiquement, suivant des règles fixes. Seul leur ordre peut varier. Un bon guslar est celui qui joue de ses clichés comme nous avec des cartes, qui les ordonne diversement suivant le parti qu'il en veut tirer.' Cf. also F. S. Krauss, *Slavische Volksforschungen* (Leipzig, 1908), pp. 183–4, and John Meier, *Werden und Leben des Volksepos* (Halle, 1909), pp. 17–19.

[2] For a fuller definition of the formula see TE, pp. 13–15 above; HS, pp. 272–5 above.

[3] For the technique of composition by formulas see TE, pp. 8–16, 37–117 above; FH, pp. 197–9, 202–6, 225–9 above; HS, pp. 275–9, 319–24 above.

[4] For the schematization of the formulaic diction see TE, pp. 17–20, 68–75 above; HS, pp. 275–9, 319–24 above. W. Radloff (*Proben der Volkslitteratur der nördlichen Türkischen Stämme. V. Der Dialect der Kara-Kirgisen*, p. xvii) gives the words in which an oral poet tells of the ease with which he composes: 'Ich kann überhaupt jedes Lied singen, denn Gott hat mir diese Gesangesgabe ins Herz gepflanzt. Er giebt mir das Wort auf die Zunge, ohne dass ich

A single man or even a whole group of men who set out in the most careful way could not make even a beginning at such an oral diction. It must be the work of many poets over many generations. When one singer (for such is the name these oral poets most often give themselves)[1] has hit upon a phrase which is pleasing and easily used, other singers will hear it, and then, when faced at the same point in the line with the need of expressing the same idea, they will recall it and use it. If the phrase is so good poetically and so useful metrically that it becomes in time the one best way to express a certain idea in a given length of the verse, and as such is passed on from one generation of poets to another, it has won a place for itself in the oral diction as a formula. But if it does not suit in every way, or if a better way of fitting the idea to the verse and the sentence is found, it is straightway forgotten, or lives only for a short time, since with each new poet and | with each new generation of poets it must undergo the twofold test of being found pleasing and useful. In time the needed number of such phrases is made up: each idea to be expressed in the poetry has its formula for each metrical need, and the poet, who would not think of trying to express ideas outside the traditional field of thought of the poetry, can make his verses easily by means of a diction which time has proved to be the best.

Actually, of course, this birth of a diction is beyond observation, and unless it can really be shown that a people reverting from written to oral poetry created anew a formulaic diction we must suppose that it took place in a very distant past, since the poetry of an unlettered race has as much claim to age as have any of its other institutions. But if the birth of a formulaic diction is only to be described theoretically, we can see in living oral poetries how such a diction is passed on from one age to another, and how it gradually changes.

The young poet learns from some older singer not simply the general style of the poetry, but the whole formulaic diction. This he does by hearing and remembering many poems, until the diction has become for him the habitual mode of poetic thought.[2] He knows no other | style, and he is

zu suchen habe, ich habe keines meiner Lieder erlernt, alles entquellt meinem Innern, aus mir heraus.' This is a commentary on two passages in Homer:

θ 44 τῶι γάρ ῥα θεὸς πέρι δῶκεν ἀοιδήν
τέρπειν ὅππηι θυμὸς ἐποτρύνηισιν ἀείδειν,

χ 347 αὐτοδίδακτος δ' εἰμί, θεὸς δέ μοι ἐν φρεσὶν οἴμας
παντοίας ἐνέφυσεν.

For the meaning of αὐτοδίδακτος cf. *Kalevala*, I, 36 ff.; Radloff, *op. cit.*, pp. xx–xxi; H. Basset, *Essai sur la littérature des Berbères* (Algiers, 1920), pp. 330–1.

[1] Greek ἀοιδός, Serbian *pjevač*, Finnish *laulaja*.

[2] Cf. Mathias Murko, *La poésie populaire épique en Yougoslavie au début du XXe siècle* (Paris, 1929), p. 12: 'Les chanteurs commencent à apprendre à jouer des *guslè* et à recueillir la tradition épique dès leur tendre enfance, sur les genoux d'un père ou d'un aïeul, ou d'autres parents, ou de familiers, puis dans le public, la plupart du temps entre dix et douze ans, mais

ever kept from quitting the traditional diction and using phrases of his own make because he could not find any as pleasing or as useful as the old ones, and moreover, since he is composing by word of mouth, he must go on without stopping from one phrase to the next. Since his poetry has being only in the course of his singing, and is not fixed on paper where it can show itself to him verse by verse, he never thinks of it critically phrase by phrase, but only faces the problem of its style when he is actually under the stress of singing. Thus whatever change the single poet makes in the traditional diction is slight, perhaps the change of an old formula, or the making of a new one on the pattern of an old, or the fusing of old formulas, or a new way of putting them together.[1] An oral style is thus highly conservative;[2] yet the causes for change are there, and sooner or later must come into play.

These causes for change have nothing to do with any wish on the part of the single poet for what is new or striking in style. They exist above the poets, and are two: the never-ceasing change in all spoken language, and the association between peoples of a single language but of different dialects.

The Archaic Element

As the spoken language changes, the traditional diction of an oral poetry likewise changes so long as there is no need of giving up any of the formulas. For example, a change in the sound of a vowel or consonant which calls for no change in the metrical value of a word soon | makes its

toujours en général jeunes, "alors qu'ils ne pensent encore à rien", jusque vers l'âge d'environ vingt-cinq ans. Il leur suffit d'ordinaire d'entendre chanter un chant une seule fois, et, quand ils sont plus âgés, plusieurs fois.' Cf. also the same work, p. 42, paragraph 18, and D. Comparetti, *Traditional Poetry of the Finns* (English translation, London, 1898), p. 20. In countries where the art of the singer is a paying profession there is a more formal apprenticeship; cf. James Darmesteter, *Chants populaires des Afghans* (Paris, 1888–90), p. cxcii: 'Le *ḍum* novice va auprès d'un *ḍum* célèbre qui est devenue maître, *ustâd*; il devient son *shâgird*, son disciple. Le maître lui enseigne ses propres chansons, puis les chansons des grands chanteurs passés ou présents, et les chansons les plus populaires de Khushhâl Khân. Il l'emmène à la *ḥujra*, où l'on se réunit tous les soirs pour causer des nouvelles du jour et écouter quiconque a un conte à conter ou une chanson à chanter. . . . Quand le *shâgird* commence à se sentir assez fort pour voler de ses propres ailes, il quitte son maître, compose en son propre nom et devient *ustâd* à son tour.' Cf. also H. Basset, *Essai sur la littérature des Berbères* (Algiers, 1920), p. 331.

[1] Cf. HS, pp. 317–24 above.

[2] A. Dozon, *L'épopée Serbe* (Paris, 1888), pp. lxxiii f.: 'L'âge des pesmas n'est pas une question facile à résoudre. En présence de l'uniformité de style et de langue qui les caractérise, on n'a pour guide, afin de constater du moins leur ancienneté relative, qu'un reste de couleur plus antique ou plus barbare . . . pour ces sujets mêmes qu'une célébrité exceptionnelle maintient dans la tradition vivante et qui peuvent tenter quelque chanteur, on y trouvera à la vérité certains anachronismes: la composition, le style et l'esprit de la pesma ne varieront pas. Pour s'en convaincre, on n'a qu'à lire, par exemple, la pièce des *Adieux de Karageorge*, qui date de 1813, et la comparer avec les plus anciennes. Rien, sinon l'incident qui en forme le fond, ne vous avertit qu'il y a entre elles un espace de plusieurs siècles.' It should be added, however, that this uniformity of style is due as well to the fact that the language of the older poems changes along with the language of the diction as a whole; cf. HL, below, pp. 332–3.

way into the poetic language: the singer naturally pronounces the word as he usually does, and there is not the least thing to keep him from doing so. But when a change in the form of a word must also change its metrical value it is far otherwise, for the poet, if he then wished to keep up with the spoken language, would have to put up with a phrase which was metrically false, or give it up altogether and make himself a new one. But neither of these two choices is at all pleasing. The rhythm must be kept fairly regular,[1] and the oral verse-making makes it very hard for him to find new words; it is even doubtful if with all the good will and time in the world he could do so in any great number of cases. Each formula, as it was said above, is the long-proven choice of a long line of singers, and it is not possible that a phrase which is useful in oral composition could be made in any other way than by a singer who, making his verses through his sense of the scheme of the formulaic diction, created, in the stress of the moment, a new phrase more or less like an older one. For otherwise the new phrase would not fit into the scheme of the diction, and since it could be used only with an effort it would not be used at all.[2] Finally the change in the spoken language would very likely be such that a phrase to express the same idea in words of the same metrical pattern would be out of the question. The new phrase must be shorter or longer, or begin or end differently. Then the formulas to which it would be joined must also be | changed, and so on. Thus by no wilful choice, but by the constraint of his technique of verse-making, the singer keeps the formula though its language has become archaic.[3]

As it happens, this archaic language does not at all displease him. His style is thus lifted above the commonplace of daily speech and made distant and wondrous. But though the old words and forms are thus desirable, they are never wilfully sought after. When the formula can be changed it sooner or later will be, and the cleavage between the old and the new in the style depends on whether it is easy or hard to change the formula.[4] An oral diction may thus in time become very archaic, since

[1] It often happens, however, that oral poets will change a formula under the influence of the current language and yet keep it despite the false verse which is the result. Kaarle Krohn has noticed this in Esthonian oral poetry ('Kalevalastudien I. Einleitung' in *F*[*olklore*] *F*[*ellow*] *Communications*, XVI (1924), pp. 56 f.: 'Bei der feststellung der urform eines altestnischen liedes durch vergleichung der verschiedenen varianten kann somit die forderung aufgestellt werden, dass sie sowohl der älteren sprachform als den metrischen gesetzen der rune entsprechen muss. Für die beurteilung der in den varianten vorkommenden verse und ihrer variierenden formen ist diese doppelte forderung ein ausgezeichnetes kriterium. Ein scheinbar fehlerhafter vers kann, wenn er in die ältere sprachform zurückgedacht metrisch regelrecht wird, der urform angehört haben. Als spätere interpolation muss dagegen ein scheinbar fehlerfreier vers angesehen werden, der in die ältere sprachform zurückgedacht eine überzahl von silben aufweist.' For the same thing in Greek epic poetry see FM, pp. 222–34 above; and see below, HL, pp. 350 n. 1, 352–9 n. 1. Such cases show how the usefulness of the formula overtops all else in oral verse-making.

[2] Cf. HS, p. 324 above.

[3] For this strong conservatism of the formulaic technique cf. FM, pp. 222–39 above.

[4] It should be added here, however, that a form or word easily changed may nevertheless

even though a word has been lost altogether from the spoken language its context in the poetry will teach the poet and his public its meaning. In the case of words which are not a needed part of the thought, such as the ornamental epithets, the meaning of the word may even be lost altogether.[1] In time, however, a point must be reached in the case of each formula where its meaning, needed for the thought, is lost, and here an even heavier constraint than ease of | verse-making comes into play: the formula must be given up cost what it may, and the singers must do the best they can to find another one to take its place. Thus the language of oral poetry changes as a whole neither faster nor slower than the spoken language, but in its parts it changes readily when no loss of formulas is called for, belatedly when there must be such a loss, so that the traditional diction has in it words and forms of everyday use side by side with others that belong to earlier stages of the language.[2] The number of new words and old words varies, of course, from one oral poetry to another as different factors have force: a complex verse-form, a fondness for tales of an heroic past rather than of the present, and the practice of poetry by a class of professional singers all tend toward a greater conservatism, whereas a short verse without enjambement, a change in the way of living of a people, and the lack of a class whose gain it is to keep the best poetry of the past all allow a quicker change. But the principle of change and conservatism of language is the same in all cases.

The Art of Traditional Poetry

I have written so far, in telling of how the language of oral poetry comes to be archaic, as if the formula were the unit of diction, and such

be kept for a long time because it is bound with the words which go before or after into a larger word-group which the singers feel as a single whole; but such survivals are not apt to be common. Cf. HL, below, pp. 351–3 ff.

[1] Cf. HG, pp. 247–8 above; A. Rambaud, *La Russie épique* (Paris, 1876), pp. 18–19: 'Les chanteurs ne comprennent pas toujours ce qu'ils chantent: la langue a vieilli et plus d'un vers s'est altéré. Si on leur demande compte d'une expression singulière ou d'un passage obscur, ils répondent invariablement: "Cela se chante ainsi", ou bien: "Les anciens chantaient ainsi; nous ne savons ce que cela veut dire" . . . Ce qui prouve la ténacité de la mémoire populaire, c'est que le paysan de l'Onéga continue à chanter les "chênes robustes", et "la stipe de la prairie" et "la plantureuse campagne", bien que ces traits de la nature kiévienne ne répondent en rien à la nature qu'il a sous les yeux, et que de sa vie il n'ait vu un chêne. Il parle de casques, de carquois et de massues d'acier, bien qu'il n'ait même pas une idée de ces sortes d'armes, de "l'aurochs au poil brun" et du "lion rugissant", bien que ces animaux qui ont pu exister dans l'ancienne Scythie, lui soient aussi inconnus que les quadrupèdes australiens. . . . Ces scrupules n'ont pas empêché qu'il ne se glissât parfois dans les bylines des détails étrangement modernes. . . . C'est ainsi qu'on voit des héros écrire sur du papier timbré, ou encore, sur le point d'attaquer un dragon ou un géant, braquer sur lui une lunette d'approche.' Cf. also, Basset, *op. cit.*, p. 319.

[2] For numerous examples of the conservatism of the oral poetic diction see O. Böckel, *Psychologie der Volksdichtung* (Leipzig, 1913), pp. 59–63. Böckel himself altogether misses the nature of the poetic language; witness his use of the term *Schriftsprache*.

it is in the end. But in practice the oral poet by no means limits his borrowing to the single formula; rather he uses whole passages which he has heard. This is, indeed, his whole art: to make a poem like the poems he has heard.[1] I know only too well that this is sure to suggest | the thought of plagiarism to those not familiar with oral poetry, but it must be understood above all that plagiarism is not possible in traditional literature. One oral poet is better than another not because he has by himself found a more striking way of expressing his own thought but because he has been better able to make use of the tradition. He strives not to create a new ideal in poetry but to achieve that which everyone knows to be the best. This is true even of the poetry which may tell of happenings of the singer's own day: the event may be new, but it will be told in the traditional way on the pattern of passages from other poems, and in more or less the same phrases as were used in those passages, so that the only difference between the poem made about the present and that which tells of the past is that the former will be made from the memory of a larger number of different poems.[2] For if the tale | is old, and, as is usually the

[1] Cf. W. Radloff, *op. cit.*: 'Man glaube nun nicht, dass dieses Improvisiren ein jedesmaliges Neudichten ist. Es geht dem improvisirenden Sänger gerade, so wie dem Improvisator auf dem Klavier. Wie der letztere verschiedene ihm bekannte Läufe, Uebergänge, Motive nach der Eingebung des Augenblicks in ein Stimmungsbild zusammenfügt und so das Neue aus dem ihm geläufigen Alten zusammenstellt, so auch der Sänger epischer Lieder. Er hat durch eine ausgedehnte Uebung im Vortrage, ganze Reihen von Vortragstheilen, wenn ich mich so ausdrücken darf, in Bereitschaft, die er dem Gange der Erzählung nach in passender Weise zusammenfügt. Solche Vortragstheile sind die Schilderungen gewisser Vorfälle und Situationen, wie die Geburt eines Helden, das Aufwachsen eines Helden, Preis der Waffen, Vorbereitung zum Kampf, das Getöse des Kampfes, Unterredung der Helden vor dem Kampfe, die Schilderung von Persönlichkeiten und Pferden, das Charakteristische der Bekannten Helden, Preis der Schönheit der Braut, Beschreibung des Wohnsitzes, der Jurte, eines Gastmahles, Aufforderung zum Mahle, Tod eines Helden, Todtenklage, Schilderung eines Landschaftsbildes, des Einbrechens der Nacht und des Anbruchs des Tages und viele Andere. Die Kunst des Sängers besteht nur darin, alle diese fertigen Bildtheilchen so aneinander zu reihen, wie dies der Lauf der Begebenheiten fordert und sie durch neu gedichtete Verse zu verbinden.' Cf. also Murko, *op. cit.*, p. 18; Basset, *op. cit.*, p. 307.

[2] Cf. G. Gesemann's account of the composition in 1914, in the military hospital of Kragujevac, of a poem on the death of the son of one of the hospital surgeons (*Studien zur südslavischen Volksepik*, Reichenberg, 1926, p. 66): 'Der Sänger sang sofort drauf los, das erstemal bezeichnenderweise mit Einkleidung des Ganzen in einem der häufigsten traditionellen Kompositionsschemata. Natürlich, er war ja nicht dabei gewesen, als der junge Mann fiel. So stilisierte er das Ereignis in einer Weise, die es ihm ermöglichte, etwa hundert Verse herzusingen und seiner Aufgabe zu genügen, ohne sich auf reale Einzelheiten einlassen zu müssen: Da liessen sich zwei Raben auf dem Dache der Kaserne nieder mit blutigen Flügeln und blutigem Schnabel, da fragt sie der Oberst, von wo sie kommen. Sie kommen aus der Mačva, wo grosse Kämpfe sind. Sie werden gefragt, ob die Serben gesiegt haben, ob Šabac noch in Feindes Hand ist usw., nein die Stadt ist befreit, die Serben haben gesiegt. Ob der Sohn nun bald auf Urlaub kommt, mit einem Orden geziert? Einen Orden trägt er, aber heim kommt er nicht mehr. — Ein paar Tage später hörte ich denselben Sänger in einer anderen Krankenstube dasselbe Lied singen, und siehe da, er hatte nicht nur das eben angeführte Kompositionsschema aufgegeben, indem er es nur noch als Einleitung benutzte, dann aber gleich nach der ersten Frage an die Raben zur Schilderung einer Schlacht überging, die sich durch ziemlich viel realistische Züge auszeichnete und auch das Bild des Gefallenen

case, regarded as more or less true, the singer may tell it just about as he heard it.

Yet no graver mistake could be made than to think the art of the singer calls only for memory. Those who have sought to record oral poetry in lands where it still lives have straightway found that the same poem, that is to say, a poem on the same subject, could be sung badly or well, and that the people carefully set apart the poor singers from the good.[1] Still the fame of such a singer comes not from quitting the tradition but from putting it to the best use. The poorer singer will repeat a poem with the loss of its most pleasing lines or its most dramatic moments, but the good singer will keep what is striking, and even add, on the pattern of other poems, lines which he knows will please, and new incidents, or give a fuller tale with many such borrowings. He may even have heard the same tale told by a singer living at a distance who inherited from a different tradition; then he will fuse the poems, using the best in each. Thus the highest sort of oral verse-making achieves the new by the best and most varied and perhaps the fullest use of the old. This is the meaning of what Telemachus says: |

> *τὴν γὰρ ἀοιδὴν μᾶλλον ἐπικλείουσ' ἄνθρωποι*
> *ἥ τις ἀκουόντεσσι νεωτάτη ἀμφιπέληται.*[2]

It is the same in all thriving oral poetries. The good singer wins his fame by his ease and versatility in handling a tradition which he knows more thoroughly than anyone else and of which his talent shows him the highest use, but his poetry remains throughout the sum of longer and shorter passages which he has heard.[3]

irgendwie persönlicher zu zeichnen versuchte. Er hatte offenbar die Führung durch ein festes Schema der Erzählung nicht mehr nötig, er hatte wahrscheinlich auch von Kameraden irgendwelche Einzelheiten inzwischen gehört, die er jetzt verwandte. Aber eins blieb erhalten: die episch-heroische, feudale Stilisierung der Einzelzüge und des Gesamtgehalts.' Cf. also M. Murko, 'Neues über südslavische Volksepik' in *Neue Jahrbücher für das klassische Altertum*, XLIII (1919), p. 294; John Meier, *Werden und Leben des Volksepos*, pp. 11–17.

[1] Cf. Murko, *op. cit.*, p. 21: 'Un bon chanteur peut faire d'un poème médiocre un poème remarquable, et un mauvais chanteur gâter le meilleur poème. Ce n'est pas à tort que, souvent Vuk Karadžić cherchait un chanteur de qualité pour se faire dicter tel chant qui ne lui avait plu. Les auditeurs apprécient, eux aussi, cet art du chanteur. Un bey m'exprima un jour son admiration en ces termes: "Moi, je ne saurais même pas faire une composition de trois mots." En Herzégovine, on m'a parlé de paysans qui auraient donné le meilleur boeuf de leur étable pour savoir chanter un seul chant.

'Les chanteurs sont des artistes, le fait qu'ils se montrent extrêmement jaloux l'un de l'autre le prouve encore. Un jour, à Sarajevo, après avoir recueilli des phonogrammes de trois chanteurs, je donnai à tous trois la même récompense. L'un d'entre eux refusa de l'accepter. Je flairai aussitôt que je l'avais froissé de quelque manière. Les personnes présentes me prévinrent en effet qu'il se considérait comme un bien meilleur chanteur que les deux autres.'

[2] α 351–2.

[3] Cf. Gesemann, *op. cit.*, p. 68: 'Ein Improvisator muss improvisieren können. Er muss nicht nur ein Dichter sein, um unter Umständen ein neues Lied singen zu können — das war besonders bei Višnjić der Fall — er muss als Haupterfordernis seines Dichterberufes nicht

The formula thus is by no means the unit of the singer's poetry, but it nevertheless ever tends to become so, for no singer ever tells the same tale twice in the same words. His poem will always follow the same general pattern, but this verse or that will be left out, or replaced by another verse or part of a verse, and he will leave out and add whole passages as the time and the mood of his hearers calls for a fuller or a briefer telling of a tale or of a given part of a tale. Thus the oral poem even in the mouth of the same singer is ever in a state of change; and it is the same when his poetry is sung by others.[1] His great name and the | fame of his verse may

nur einem alten, überlieferten Liede sein "adäquate" Form geben, d. h. die höchsten künstlerischen Möglichkeiten, die ein Stoff in sich trägt, herausarbeiten Können — er muss also nicht nur im Rahmen traditionellen Fühlens und mit traditionellen Stilmitteln eine von der eigenen künstlerischen Persönlichkeit durchwärmte Leistung hervorbringen können, sondern er muss, um alles dieses zu können, eine vollkommene Beherrschung über die Formenelemente seines Kunststils fertig mitbringen, wenn ihm eine Improvisation oder ein teilweise improvisierter Vortrag gelingen soll.'

[1] The researches of M. Murko on this point will long remain a model of method for students of oral poetry (*op. cit.*, pp. 16–17): 'On a longtemps cru, et l'on croit encore, que les chanteurs ne modifient pas les poèmes. . . . J'ai déjà dit qu'au contraire il peut à volonté raccourcir ou allonger ses chants et que le même poème peut être très différent, quant au fond, dans les versions de divers chanteurs. Il est bien certain que dans de telles conditions un texte ne peut demeurer immuable. Deux fois, j'ai emporté avec moi le phonographe perfectionné de l'Académie de Vienne. Je n'ai pu enregistrer avec cet appareil les longs chants épiques, mais il m'a suffi de fragments de moins de 30 vers pour constater quelque chose d'inattendu. Comme il était prescrit de noter chaque texte avant l'enregistrement phonographique, je demandais au chanteur de s'exercer, au préalable, une fois devant le pavillon, tandis qu'un sténographe notait le texte. J'avais ainsi à la fois trois textes, et j'en ai même eu quatre dans un cas. La comparaison a montré que ce ne sont pas seulement des mots isolés ou l'ordre des mots, mais des vers entiers qui apparaissent sous une forme entièrement nouvelle ou disparaissent, si bien que sur 15 vers dictés, par exemple, il n'en reste plus que 8 chantés. Un bon chanteur musulman du nord-ouest de la Bosnie modifiait a chaque fois le premier vers lui-même.

'Il dicta une première fois:

Beg Osman beg rano podranio (figure étymologique)
"Le bey Osman bey s'est levé de bon matin";

puis en s'exerçant:

Beg Osman beg na bedem izidje
"Le bey Osman bey est monté sur les remparts";

et puis il chanta:

Beg Osman beg niz Posavlje gleda
"Le bey Osman bey regarde la plaine de la Save."

. . . Dans le monastère orthodoxe de Duži près de Trebinje, en Herzégovine, nous avons entendu les chants d'un paysan attaché au monastère. . . . Un des moines et l'instituteur avaient écrit le commencement du chant sous sa dictée. Je les priai de noter les variantes au cours du chant, mais ils furent contraints d'y renoncer dès le second vers. . . . Il est désormais bien clair pour moi que les chants que nous possédons aujourd'hui imprimés n'ont tous été qu'une seule fois chantés, ou plus exactement dictés, et cela, lors de leur mise par écrit. C'est pourquoi aussi toutes les tentatives faites pour reconstituer un chant dans sa forme originelle sont vaines. Le comparaison des différentes variantes ne peut nous permettre de déterminer que le contenu primitif ou encore des parties ou des vers.' The bibliography of these phonographic studies is given *op. cit.*, p. 7, and the author has given a summary of them, 'Neues über südslavische Volksepik', in *Neue Jahrbücher für das klassische Altertum*, XLIII (1919), pp. 273–96. Cf. also Radloff, *op. cit.*, pp. xvi–xxviii; Basset, *op. cit.*, pp. 306–7.

urge those who have learned from him to a more careful and more faithful use of memory than that which they would show for the poetry of a lesser singer. But the memory of the hearer depends after all on his being habituated to the diction as a whole, rather than on the learning of the poem word by word, so that he too must change and add and leave out verses and parts of verses, and this process will go on until all that is left of the poem are its single formulas and shorter passages which are the final units in the traditional diction. It should be added here that an oral poetry practiced by guilds of singers with masters and apprentices would tend to a more faithful | keeping of poems which had won fame, and that one singer might win such a name that his disciples would find their profit in keeping his poetry as nearly without change as they could; but then they are no longer singers but rhapsodes, their task is not that of creation but only of memory, and they are merely keeping from age to age the verse which was first composed by a singer who made his poetry, in the way that we have seen, by an ever varying use of what he had sung and heard others sing.

The Foreign Element

When poems thus pass from one singer to another in the same region the language of the poetry undergoes no change other than that which time may set upon it. But when the poets of one locality hear the poetry of a singer who speaks another dialect of their language their own traditional poetic language may undergo a much more rapid change. One must suppose that the two dialects are enough alike for their speakers to understand each other fairly well, and that the poems from abroad are such as to please. The fame of some singer may have spread until other singers came from afar to hear him; or the way of life in one region may have brought about a great liking for poetry, so that it was practiced more intensely and carried to a higher point; or the singers may have made their living by carrying their songs abroad.[1] In some way, then, the foreign poems are heard by the local singers and repeated more or less as they have been heard, and just as they have brought into their poetic language new words and forms of their | spoken language, so do they make the foreign poetry fit their spoken language in so far as they can do

[1] For the way in which the poetry is spread cf. A. Hanoteau, *Poésies populaires de la Kabylie* (Paris, 1867), p. iv: 'Ces poésies sont répandues parmi le peuple par des chanteurs de profession qui parcourent les villages et vivent des offrandes du public. Cette profession est ordinairement héréditaire et se transmet de père en fils, souvent pendant plusieurs générations. . . . Quelques-uns néanmoins . . . vivent retirés dans leurs villages. Leurs vers ne restent pas dans l'oubli pour cela. Dès qu'ils ont acquis une certaine réputation, les chanteurs qui n'ont pas reçu le don poétique viennent, souvent de fort loin, enrichir auprès d'eux leur répertoire. Moyennant une rétribution assez légère, mais toujours proportionnelle aux succès déjà obtenus par l'auteur, celui-ci leur répète ses chansons jusqu'à ce qu'elles soient gravées dans leur mémoire. Ils vont alors les répandre dans le public et les apprennent, par le même procédé, à leurs collègues.' Cf. *Hymn to Apollo*, vv. 173–6.

so without any too great loss. The new poems thus take on straightway a local color, but they keep those foreign forms which cannot be changed without harm to the verse, as well as words whose meaning may be known only from the context or which may be meaningless.[1] In time these poems, by the unending process of change which has been told of above, become fused with the local poetry, yet even when they have been lost as poems they leave their mark upon the poetic language. Coming from a tradition which has developed separately, the foreign poems have in them many pleasing| and useful formulas which are kept even after the poems which brought them to the new land have been lost, and in these formulas live the forms and words of the foreign dialect. Then on the pattern of these formulas others will be made which, while they are foreign in their language, are nevertheless native work. Even as the poets kept archaic formulas and made new formulas with archaisms, so do they keep foreign formulas and make formulas with foreign forms, so that a foreign word or form may show that a passage in a given poem was made abroad, or may prove no more than a contact at one time between the poetry of two regions. The poet and his hearers, it should be noted, in no way think of these words and forms as the words of a certain locality: like the archaic elements, they simply serve to carry the style above the commonplace of everyday speech.[2]

[1] Cf. K. Krohn, 'Kalevalastudien I' in *F*[*olklore*] *F*[*ellows*] *Communications*, XVI (1924), pp. 76–7: 'Dass noch in der neuesten zeit estnische lieder über die Narova nach Ingermanland gewandet sind, beweist am klärsten ein ausläufer des estnischen liedes von der freierei der himmelslichter, der auf der insel Lavansaari in der nähe der westingermanländischen küste aufgezeichnet worden ist. In diesem finden wir nicht nur einzelne wörter, die in ihrer estnischen form und bedeutung beibehalten, wie z. b. *opunen* (fi. *hevonen*) "pferd", *soittamaan* = *sõitamaie* "fahren" (fi. bedeutung "spielen"), oder durch ein ähnlich lautendes finnisches wort verschiedener bedeutung ersetzt worden sind, wie z. b. *poikinensa* "mit seinen söhnen" < *poisikene* "söhnchen", *lassa* "als kind" < *las* "lasse", *sängyn* "des bettes" < *särgi* "des hemdes", *vilu* "kälte" < *Viru* "Wierland". Auch ganze sätze sind bis zur unverständlichkeit und zu reinem unsinn verdreht worden. Der estnischen aufforderung zum tanze, bis eine mark aus dem boden, ein ferding zwischen den zehen, aus der drehung des schuhabsatzes hervorspringt (*marko maasta, veerik varvaste vahelta, kinga kanna kierämistä*), entspricht in dem finnischen abklatsch: *marka* (statt *markka*) *maasta, verikorvat ei vaella* "die blutigen ohren wandern nicht", *kimmi kammi kieremästä* (unverständlich). Weiter wird im estnischen geschildert, wie die schlafende jungfrau; *Hebemesta keitas kieltä* "aus dem federbette warf die zunge", *kõneles kivikojasta* "sprach aus dem steingebäude"; diese zeilen sind im finnischen ohne rücksicht auf den gedanken lautlich nachgeahmt worden: *hedelmästä heitä kiellä* wörtlich: "von der frucht sie verbiete", *kojota* (?) *kivi* "stein" *kovasta* "aus dem harten". Ähnliche sinnlose übertragungen aus dem finnischen finden wir in den zauberliedern Nordostestiens. Fi. *maito* "milch" ist einfach als *maidu* übernommen, obgleich ihm im estnischen *piim* entspricht. Das in Ingermanland in *Tyrnän koski* verdrehte *Tyrjän koski* "wasserfall von T". (= stürmischer Tiberiassee) ist mit den worten *türna kaske* wiedergegeben, die im estnischen "zwergbirke" und "birke" bedeuten. Der finnischen zeile: *suonia sovittamahan* "um die adern zusammenzupassen", entspricht in einer estnischen handschrift: *Sohvia ei soovita Maie* "Sophia empfiehlt nicht Marie", ein unsinn, der nicht nur vom sänger, sondern auch vom aufschreiber herrührt.' Cf. also Meier, *op. cit.*, p. 18; Böckel, *op. cit.*, pp. 59–63; Basset, *op. cit.*, pp. 314–5.

[2] Cf. above, HL, p. 328 n. 3.

The Artificial Element

Finally, to the archaic, the new, and the foreign elements must be added a fourth and last: the artificial. Since the language of an oral poet is already far removed from daily speech, his public will not wonder at him if he should use a form which has never really been used anywhere. A whole new word no poet could make, since no one could understand him if he did, but he may make a form like another. That is to say, he may make the artificial by analogy with the real. The reason for such a creation is of course the same which leads the singers to keep the old and foreign forms, namely the need of a formula of a certain length which can be gotten only by this means. One poet, driven by this need, and making his verses under the sense of analogy which binds together the whole technique of his diction, will hit upon such a phrase, another will take it up, and it too will win its own place in the traditional poetic language.[1] Another kind of artificial form is due to the only partial adaptation of old or foreign forms. In certain cases the meter will allow part of a word to be modernized but force the singers to keep the rest of the word unchanged.[2] |

3. THE STUDY OF A TRADITIONAL POETIC LANGUAGE

Such is the making of the language of an oral poetry. That the Homeric poems were oral is shown by their diction, which, being formulaic, can only be traditional and oral. Putting the two sets of facts together, we see that the variety of words and forms which so long puzzled Homeric scholars is the natural and necessary condition of the Homeric diction. Being oral it must be traditional, and being traditional it must have in it old words and forms, and it could be without foreign words and forms only if the people among whom it was developed had been cut off from the rest of Hellas. Until very lately scholars have started with the study of the forms and words in the *Iliad* and *Odyssey*, and have sought in them an answer which could not be true because, though they were not aware of it, they were basing their search on their belief that they were written in just the same way they themselves would write poetry. But the sounder way, it is now clear, is first to learn the oral nature of the Homeric poems—this is shown us by the diction quite apart from the language—and then to turn to other poetries of the same kind, where we learn, besides

[1] For the part played by analogy in an oral style cf. TE, pp. 68–74 above; HS, pp. 322–4 above.

[2] The present article discusses only the second of these two kinds of artificial forms (pp. 350–1). For the first kind see K. Meister, *Die Homerische Kunstsprache* (Leipzig, 1921); such forms, to give a few examples from many, are ἠνιοχῆες beside the nominative ἡνίοχος, προσώπατα as a plural to πρόσωπον, the subjunctive in -ῃσι, δῶ, σέθεν, θέαιναι, all the forms with lengthening of a normally short vowel, and so on.

many other things, that the language of Greek heroic poetry could not have been any other than it is.

Even more, the knowledge that the Homeric diction is traditional gives us the method we need for the study of the Homeric language, and shows us what we may hope to learn from it.

I.—*The spoken dialect of the author of an oral poem is shown by his poetic language, which will tend to be the same as his spoken language wherever he has no metrical reason to use an older or foreign word or form or construction.* Many scholars, when forced to show why the language of an oral poem follows a given dialect wherever the meter will allow, have supposed the text to be due to a scribe who, in copying a poem from another dialect, changed it to his own language where he could. To the bookish mind such a process may seem quite natural; yet it is hard to see why a scribe should have wanted to do such a thing. | If he was merely copying the poem for other readers, why should he think that they would find it harder to read the original than he found it? If it was in order that the poem might be read to local hearers, why should he change only single forms or small groups of words? The foreign words and forms where the metrical value was different from that of his own dialect would be quite as puzzling to his hearers, and since he had writing materials to aid him at his task he should not find it much harder to change the language of the poem from beginning to end. When one does away with the factor of oral verse-making and its ever-present check on change there is nothing left to show why the change of language in a poem should be only partial. Further, the change of dialect which one thus finds in an oral poetry is so regular in its smallest points that one would have to suppose that such a scribe kept card indexes. But all such theories, after one has grasped the notion of traditional oral poetry, are seen to be forced.[1]

II.—*On the other hand an oral poet, composing in a diction which follows his own language where it can, may be using phrases and passages which are neither his own work nor that of other poets of the same dialect, whether of his own or of an earlier time, but borrowings from the poetry of another dialect.* Thus one cannot say that a given phrase or passage in a poem is the work of the author, or of another poet of the author's linguistic group, just because it has forms of the author's language. Such a phrase or passage may have been taken from another dialect and changed only where the forms had the same metrical value. Thus the proof that a given phrase or passage is the original work of the author's dialect calls for the same demonstration by metrical value as the proof that it is the work of a foreign dialect.[2]

[1] Cf. above, HL, pp. 331–3, 377–9 and below HL, pp. 342–3.
[2] HL, Cf. pp. 358–61.

III.—*A given word, form or group of words can be proved to be the original work of poets speaking a given dialect only when it can be shown that no other dialect which had had a part in the history of the poetry had, in either its spoken or its poetic language, the same word or form or group of words with the same metrical value.* That the poetic as well as the spoken language of another dialect must be taken into account is a fact which is usually overlooked. But it is clear that the poetic language of one region is as subject to change under the poetry of its | neighbors as is that of another region, and just as likely to show the same variety of forms. Thus the form which may seem to be the work of the author's dialect may instead be taken from abroad, where it was a foreign form taken from still a third dialect.[1]

IV.—*Conversely, a word or form or group of words which is metrically false, or fails to make sense, must be the work of a dialect whose words and forms when used would make the verse correct, or give it meaning.* In making use of this principle, however, the critic must be quite sure he has to do in a given case with a word or phrase which is really metrically false and meaningless.[2]

V (exception to I).—*A foreign or older form may be kept in the poetic language even when the poet's own language has a form which could take its place, but such a keeping, apart from metrical reasons, will be due to the regular use of the form along with other words which are always used as a group and which the poet feels as such, or to the poetic character of the word, or to some other such special reason.* This is most apt to be so when the words or forms used with it are themselves foreign or especially poetic, thus making a larger word-group which the singer feels as a whole, so that he changes none of its parts.[3]

VI (exception to IV).—*The working of a formulaic diction may itself be the cause of metrical faults.* These will be of two sorts: those which are due to the

[1] In the paragraph from Krohn quoted above (p. 338) mention was made of the passage of poems from Esthonia to Finland and from Finland to Esthonia. On page 61 of the same work the author gives a comprehensive diagram of the poetic influences between the different regions of Finland and Esthonia:

West-	→	Sa-(Österb.)	→	Hinterkarelien
				↑
Finn-	→	vo-	→	Finn.-Ost- u. Nordk.
				↑
land	→	lax	→	Finn.-Südkarelien
				↓ ↑
Es-	←	West- u. Mittel-	←	Nordingermanland
				↑
tien	→	Ingermanland	→	→

Cf. below, HL, pp. 349–50, 353–4.

[2] Cf. HL, above, pp. 331 n. 1, 332–3, 337–8, and below, pp. 349–50, 353–4.

[3] Cf. HL, pp. 351–3.

joining of formulas which do not fit, and those | which come from changing a correct formula to fit the needs of a sentence.[1]

VII (exception to III).—*A form which seems old or foreign may be a creation by analogy from forms which are really so.* The form, however, still stands to show that the poetry was at one time influenced by another dialect or that the tradition of the language is old.

VIII.—*A word, form, or group of words which is old or foreign is not in itself proof that the verse or passage in which it is found is the work of an older or foreign singer.* One must ever be ready to admit that a given poem may be made by putting together anything from single traditional words or phrases to whole traditional passages.[2]

4. THE HOMERIC LANGUAGE AS A TRADITIONAL AND ORAL POETIC LANGUAGE[3]

Any attempt to localize the traits of Homeric language must be largely balked by the conditions of the search: the lateness of the inscriptions, their small number which allows us to know only a part of the words and forms of any one dialect, and our complete, or almost complete, lack of them for many regions. The evidence quoted by the ancient grammarians is simply by itself untrustworthy because they had no sound linguistic or textual method, and so must be left aside unless it happens to agree with the evidence of the inscriptions. The manuscripts of the Ionic prose writers likewise give us little help, since they have suffered from the ignorance, and even more from the mistaken linguistic notions, of their editors and copiers. The remains of Ionic and Aeolic verse are more helpful, though they too have suffered | from copiers and mistaken theories of language, and their evidence, as we shall see, bears on the poetic rather than on the spoken language. Thus the study of Homeric language must be based above all on the inscriptions.

The Ionic Recording

The language of the *Iliad* and *Odyssey* has at least one very common sound and one very common form which, as the prose inscriptions show us, were used only in Attic and Ionic speech, but which might have been replaced without harm to the meter by the sound and form of the other

[1] On this point cf. FM, pp. 197–220 above, HS, pp. 317–19 above. These types of metrical fault are not discussed in the present article.

[2] Cf. HL, above, pp. 333–7, and below, HL, pp. 358–61.

[3] Save where other sources are named, the dialectal evidence used in the following pages is taken from one of the following works: C. D. Buck, *Introduction to the Study of the Greek Dialects*[2] (Boston, 1928); F. Bechtel, *Die Griechischen Dialekte* (Berlin, 1921–4); O. Hoffmann, *Die Griechischen Dialekte* (Göttingen, 1891–8).

dialects: η for original ᾱ, and the third singular of the imperfect ἦν. Original ᾱ is found in inscriptions of all the other dialects, and ἦς is found where that form of the verb occurs outside Attic and Ionic,[1] namely in West Greek, Boeotian, Lesbian, Arcadian, and Cyprian. Neither η for ᾱ nor ἦν could be the archaism of another dialect.[2] These traits of Attic–Ionic, though only two, play such a part in the language that they are more than enough to show, in view of what was said above,[3] that the singer (or singers), or rhapsodes, who composed, or gave final form to, the *Iliad* and *Odyssey*, spoke either Ionic or Attic. These traits of language do not, however, necessarily show whether the recording was due to Ionic singers, whose verse-making was a constant creation, or to Ionic rhapsodes, who were mere reciters, although all the evidence of contemporary oral poetry which I know points to the singer, and none to the rhapsode. Nor do they show in what measure the diction of the poem —words, phrases, verses, or passages—was the original creation of Ionic rather than foreign singers.

That the spoken language in question was Ionic and not Attic is shown by the following sounds and forms: η for original ᾱ even after ε, ι, ρ, where Attic would have ᾱ-; -σσ-, ἤν (εἰ+ἄν), ἤνεικα, ἱστίη for Attic -ττ-, ἄν, ἤνεγκα, ἑστία. Of these Ionic traits at least three—η | after ε, ι, ρ, -σσ-, and ἤν—could not be Attic archaisms.[4] The various Ionic dialects are not well enough known to allow a more exact localization.[5]

Arcado-Cyprian, Aeolic, and Ionic

The various elements of the Homeric language are drawn from three dialects—Ionic, Aeolic, and Arcado-Cyprian. As we have just seen, the language was last affected by Ionic, and we have the following evidence to show us that the Arcado-Cyprian element was not brought into the language by any direct contact between Arcado-Cyprian and Ionic poetry, but came in along with the Aeolic element. The Homeric poems

[1] Since there is no evidence that the language of the Homeric poems has any other elements than those of Ionic, Aeolic, and Arcado-Cyprian, the other dialects are referred to under the general term of West Greek.

[2] ἦς is for *ἦστ, cf. Vedic Sanskrit ā̆ḥ.

[3] HL, pp. 331–2.

[4] Even though -σσ- and -ττ- (cf. Buck, *op. cit.*, p. 65) be only different writings for the same sound, -σσ- nevertheless proves an original Ionic recording of the poems. The relation of ἤνεικα to ἤνεγκα, and of ἱστίη to ἑστία, is disputed. On η after ε, ι, ρ cf. W. Ridgeway, *Origin of Tragedy* (Cambridge, 1910), p. 3.

[5] West Ionic -ττ- and -ρρ- would show that the recording was not Euboean. The use of ὅποι, ποτε, etc., is attested by inscriptions of Amorgos, Thasos, and Ceos, while the single form in κ so far brought to light is ὁκοῖα from Erythrae. This might show that the last singer (or singers) or rhapsodes spoke island Ionic, but the evidence is slight (cf. Bechtel, *op. cit.*, III, pp. 87–8; H. W. Smyth, *Sounds and Inflections of the Greek Dialects*. I. *Ionic* (Oxford, 1894), pp. 289–93). The use again of such forms as ὄκως, δέκομαι, etc., in Ionic prose would show that literary prose was developed by a different linguistic group (Miletus?) from that to which the recording was due. More cannot be said on the grounds of language.

have Aeolic αἰ for Ionic εἰ when the next word is κε, αἴ κε being felt more or less as one word because of the foreign κε. The Arcado-Cyprian form of the phrase, however, has εἰ (Cyprian ἔ κε, Arcadian εἰκ ἄν), and had this phrase ever been known to the Ionic poets it must, because of the greater likeness to the Ionic form, have straightway taken the place of αἴ κε.[1] Likewise, the poems have Aeolic ἄμμες, ὔμμες, etc., whereas the knowledge of the Arcado-Cyprian forms ᾱμές, ῡμές, etc., would have brought about their use because of their greater likeness to Ionic ἡμεῖς, ῡμεῖς, etc., ᾱμές doubtless becoming *ἡμές. Δόμεναι and φήρ, where Arcado-Cyprian has δοϝέναι and θήρ, point the same way; otherwise one must be willing to grant the bare possibility that δόμεναι might have taken the place of δοϝέναι by analogy with other non-thematic infinitives in -μεναι, and that the legend of the Beasts (cf. below, p. 353) might not have been known in Arcado-Cyprian | poetry. The history of the Homeric language is thus seen to follow the order Arcado-Cyprian, Aeolic, Ionic, whatever may have been the influence back from Aeolic to Arcado-Cyprian and from Ionic to Aeolic.

The Arcado-Cyprian Element

The following Homeric forms are found, as far as the evidence of the inscriptions goes, neither in Ionic nor in Aeolic, but in Arcado-Cyprian; if they are found elsewhere it is in West Greek:[2] the infinitive of contract verbs in -ῆναι (Arcadian κατυφρονῆναι, Cyprian κυμερῆναι, Homeric φορῆναι, ἀῆναι, and also, therefore, βιῶναι); the declension of ηϝ-stems in -ης, -ην (Cyprian ἰjερής, γραφής, Arcadian hιερήν, Homeric ζαῆν, Ἄρην, Μέγην); the suffix -τερος in the sense of one of a pair of things (Arcadian τὠρρέντερον γένος, Homeric θηλύτεραι, θεώτεραι, ἀγρότερος, etc.); Arcadian δῶμα, ἀέλιος, ἔσχεθον, ἄματα; Arcadian and Cyprian πτόλις (Homeric πτόλις, πτόλεμος, cf. Eustathius ὁ δὲ πτόλεμος Κυπρίων).[3]

The following Homeric words are found in neither Ionic nor Aeolic inscriptions, but in Arcado-Cyprian; they occur in the Greek literature we know only as poetic words:

In Arcadian and Cyprian αἶσα, ἕρπω, εὐχωλά, οἶϝος.

In Cyprian ϝάναξ, ἀνώγω, ἀρτύω, αὐτάρ, ἕλος, ἰδέ, πόσις, σπέος, χραύω.

In Arcadian ἀπύω, ἀσκηθής, δέαμαι, κέλευθος, λεύσσω.[4]

[1] Cf. below, HL, p. 5.

[2] On Arcado-Cyprian in Homer see H. W. Smyth, 'The Arcado-Cyprian Dialect' in *Transactions of the American Philological Association*, XVIII (1887), pp. 59–133; C. M. Bowra, 'Homeric Words in Arcadian Inscriptions' in *Classical Quarterly*, XX (1926), pp. 168–76; Hoffmann, *op. cit.*, I, pp. 276–83.

[3] It is hard to see what sure conclusions can be drawn from the Arcadian name of a festival Ἑκοτόνβοια. Arcado-Cyprian βόλομαι is also found at Oropus and Eretria. Of the forms given above the following are found in West Greek: ἀέλιος; ἄματα (in Aetolian); the pairing -τερος (in Elean).

[4] Ἕρπω and ἀρτύω occur also in West Greek. *Νυ* is found in Arcadian, in Cyprian, and in

If we consider how small a part of Arcado-Cyprian vocabulary it is which we know from the inscriptions, this number of poetic Homeric | words which we find in current usage in Arcadia and Cyprus is highly significant. It can be understood only by assuming that the Homeric diction comes, for a large part at least, from Arcado-Cyprian poetry. The most stable part of an oral diction is its vocabulary, since it is usually easier for a singer to change a form on the model of his own language than it is for him to give up one word and find another, and his art of verse-making is chiefly the art of using the traditional poetic words. The Aeolic element in the Homeric language seems indeed to have been more one of morphology than of vocabulary.

The Aeolic Element

The belief was held at one time that the Aeolisms in Homer were really only older forms of Ionic, but this was due to a misunderstanding of the nature of linguistic change, since most of the forms in question are due to two separate treatments of one original form. Thus the dative in -εσσι was formed on the analogy of the εσ- stems (γένεσ-σι, βέλεσ-σι); the first aorist in -σσ- on the analogy of σ-stems (ἔθλασ-σα, ἐτέλεσ-σα); the perfect active participle in -ων, -οντα, was formed after the present participle; πίσυρες for Ionic τέσσαρες, and Φήρ for Ionic θήρ, show different treatments of *qu̯ and *g̑u̯h; ἴα for Ionic μία shows a complete absence of the initial *sm; ἀργεννός and ἄμμες show different treatments of *-σν- and *-σμ- from those which gave Ionic φαεινός and ἡμεῖς. Ὄππως, ὄππoι, etc. is an innovation of Lesbian, seemingly made after ὄττι (original *ὅδτι). In view of the number of these certain Aeolisms it is clearly better to take also as Aeolisms those forms which might be earlier forms of Ionic, e.g. the genitives in -ᾱο and -άων and in -οιο. Indeed the number of Homeric forms which are not Ionic but are found in other dialects is such that it seems to outweigh that of the archaic and artificial forms.

The following traits of the Homeric language are Aeolic:

(1) In Lesbian (Aeolic of Asia Minor), Thessalian, and Boeotian, the dative in -εσσι; θερσ- instead of θαρσ- (Homeric Θερσίτης, Θερσίλοχος, cf. Thessalian Θερσίτας, Θερσιλόχειος, etc.); ἴα instead of Ionic μία; the patronymic adjective instead of the genitive of the father's name (Homeric Τελαμώνιος, Νηλήιος, etc.); the treatment of labio-velars as labials even before front vowels (Lesbian πέσσυρες according to Hesychius, cf. Balbilla πέσυρα, Sappho πήλυι, Boeotian πέτταρες, | Thessalian πέμπε,

Boeotian, but its use in no one of these three places is that found in Homer. Hesychius glosses οὖνον . . . Κύπριοι δρόμον, which is some reason to take ἐριούνιος, the epithet of Hermes, as Arcado-Cyprian. If E. Forrer's translation of the Boghaz-Keui tablets (*Orientalische Literaturzeitung*, XXVII, 1924, pp. 114–18) is correct they show κοίρανος to be an 'Achaean' word.

πεφειράκοντες, Homeric *πίσυρες*, *πεμπώβολα*, *περιπλόμενος*, *ἔπλε*, *ἔπλετο*, *πέλομαι*, etc., *πέλωρ*, *πελώριος*, *Φήρ*, and the variant reading *φλίψεται* for *θλίψεται* in ρ 221); declension of *ηϝ*-stems in -*ῆος*, -*ῆι* (Lesbian *βασίληος*, Thessalian *βασιλεῖος*, Boeotian *βασιλεῖι*); *ἄμμες*, *ὔμμες*, etc. (Lesbian and Thessalian, no evidence for Boeotian); the apocopated forms of the prepositions; the dual (Thessalian *δείμενε*, *ἀδ*[?]*άτοιν*, Boeotian *ἐποιεστάταν*, *ἀνεθέταν*, Lesbian [*ἄν*]*δρε*, *τὼ ἐπιστάτα*).[1]

(2) In Lesbian and Thessalian the development of σ followed by a liquid or nasal into double liquids or double nasals respectively (Lesbian *ἔμμεναι*, *Ζοννύσω*, *Ἄλληκτος*, Thessalian *ἔμμεν*, *Διοννύσοι*, Homeric *ἔμμεναι*, *ἔμμεν*, *φιλομμειδής*, *ἔμμορε*, *ἐρεβεννός*, *ἀργεννός*, *ἀγάννιφος*, *ἔννεον*, *ἄλληκτος*, *ἔλλαβε*, *ἔρρεον*, *ἐύρροος*, *καταρρέω*); the change of *τι̯ and *θι into σσ (Lesbian and Thessalian *ὅσσος*, etc., Lesbian *μέσσος*, Homeric *ὅσσος*, *μέσσος*, etc.); *κάλλος* instead of Ionic *καλός* in compounds, and in the comparative and superlative (Lesbian *Καλλίκληι*, etc., Thessalian *Καλλιφρούντειος*, etc., cf. Boeotian *καλϝός*, Homeric *Καλλιάνασσα*, *κάλλιον*, *καλλιγύναικα*, etc.); *κε* instead of *ἄν*.

(3) In Lesbian *ὄππως*, *ὄπποι*, *ὄττι*, etc.; the infinitive of non-thematic forms in -*μεναι* (Lesbian *ἔμμεναι*, *ἔδμεναι*, *θέμεναι*, *δόμεναι*, Homeric *ἔμμεναι*, *ἔδμεναι*, *θέμεναι*, *δόμεναι*, etc.); *ἀμβρότην* (Homeric *ἤμβροτον*, *βροτός*, *ἀμβρόσιος*); *ζα*- from *δια*- (cf. Lesbian *Ζοννύσω*, Sappho *ζὰ δ' ἐλεξάμαν*, Homeric *ζάθεος*, *ζατρεφής*, etc.).

(4) In Lesbian and Boeotian the aorist in -*σσ*-.

(5) In Thessalian and Boeotian the thematic and non-thematic infinitive in -*μεν* (Thessalian *ἔμμεν*, *θέμεν*, *δόμεν*, Boeotian *δόμεν*, etc., Thessalian *κρεννέμεν*, *πρασσέμεν*, Boeotian *φερέμεν*, etc., Homeric *ἔμμεν*, *θέμεν*, *δόμεν*, etc., *ἀγέμεν*, *φερέμεν*, etc., and the variant readings *πολεμιζέμεν* *Π* 834, *ἀκουέμεν* *Τ* 79, etc.); the genitive in -*οιο* (Thessalian of Pelasgiotis and Perrhaebia *Πανσουνείοιο*, *πολέμοιο*, etc.).

(6) In Boeotian the genitive in -*ᾱο* (Boeotian *Ἀριστέαο*, etc.); the genitive in -*άων* (Boeotian *δραχμάων*, etc., cf. Thessalian *κοινάουν*, etc.); *τοί*, *ταί* instead of *οἱ*, *αἱ*.[2] |

Of all these Aeolic traits the only ones which are found in other dialects are the following: in Cyprian *κε*; in Arcado-Cyprian the declension in -*ῆϝος*, -*ῆϝι*, etc.; in West Greek the non-thematic infinitive in -*μεν*, *μέσσος*, etc., *τοί*, *ταί*; and in Arcadian and West Greek apocope in the prepositions. *Ἀπ*, *ἐπ*, and *ὐπ*, however, are Thessalian only.[3] The only cases of apocope in Ionic inscriptions are two occurrences of *παρ*. The Homeric words which have Aeolic (and original) *ᾱ* where one would

[1] Cf. A. Cuny, *Le nombre duel en grec* (Paris, 1906), pp. 454–66, 487–505.

[2] The vocative in -*ᾰ* is attested only in Lesbian verse, which also has -*ᾱ*, so that there is nothing to show us which was the common form. The evidence for -*φι* as Aeolic is too slight to be given much weight (cf. Bechtel, *op. cit.*, I, p. 269).

[3] One might add -*ᾱϝυ* in Cyprian as equivalent to Boeotian -*ᾱο*.

look for Ionic η are dealt with below (p. 346). The traces of the digamma in Homer are likewise Aeolic, and allow us to say from which of the three Aeolic groups the poetry passed to the Ionians, but before dealing with this sound we must understand the nature of the Lesbian poetic language.

The Traditional Language of Lesbian Lyric Poetry

The same forces which created the poetic epic language of Homer created the poetic lyric language of Sappho and Alcaeus. The scant remains of these two poets do not allow us to show, as we can do for Homer, that their diction is formulaic, and so oral and traditional. We do know, however, that Solon and Theognis were still following an oral tradition of iambic poetry,[1] and that they lived at that time, always so precious for our own knowledge of oral poetries of the past and present, when verse-making was oral but writing known and used as a means of recording and keeping.[2] All that we know of the use of writing in Greece at the beginning of the sixth century points to the same thing for Sappho and Alcaeus. Yet while we may still feel some doubt as to the way in which they made their verses, there is not the least doubt that their poetic language was drawn from an oral tradition: | only in an oral poetry does one ever find such a variety of forms that have each one its own metrical value.[3]

Thus Sappho and Alcaeus use the endings of the spoken language, that is of the inscriptions, -ω, -ᾱ, -ᾱν, -εσσι, -οισι, -οντες (perfect active participle), but they also use -οιο, -ᾱο, -άων, -σι, -οις, -ότες; although the forms with -σσ- were the current forms, they also have ὄσος, μέσος, ὐπίσω, and first aorists such as ἐσκέδασ', ὤλεσαν; beside Lesbian πόλις, ἔδωκαν, ἔσχον, ἶρος, ἄλιος, δόμος, they have πτόλις, ἔδοσαν, ἔσκεθον, ἴερος, ἀέλιος, δῶμα; beside παρ, which we always find in the inscriptions, they have the longer παρά, and where their speech used ἀπύ they shorten to ἀπ; they have the uncontracted νόος beside νῶ.

The foregoing forms are either archaic or found in other dialects than Lesbian; the following are artificial forms: ἄμμεσιν beside Aeolic ἄμμιν; the genitives ἔμεθεν, σέθεν, ἔθεν; Νηρήιδες beside Νηρέιδες; the transfer of endings from one declension or conjugation to another, as in πόλληος, τεμένηος, ἔχηισθα; the use of ν-movable which, in verb-forms at least, was

[1] Cf. HS, pp. 280–1 above.

[2] Cf. Murko, *La poésie épique en Yougoslavie* '. . . Mujo Selimotić, paysan, ne sait pas lire, chante des poèmes qui durent jusqu'à des quatre heures' (p. 46). '. . . Ilija Gašljević, riche meunier, qui a dicté un gros recueil de chants populaires au curé catholique' (p. 34). 'Mais le plus grand ennemi du chanteur, c'est l'instruction moderne. Les recueils ont fait perdre l'intérêt aux chants populaires (je n'ai gagné la confiance de nombreux chanteurs qu'en leur assurant que je ne prendrais pas note de leurs poèmes)' (p. 30).

[3] For the language of Sappho and Alcaeus cf. E. Lobel, *Σάπφους Μέλη* (Oxford, 1925), pp. xxviii–lxxvi; *Ἀλκαίου Μέλη* (Oxford, 1927), pp. xxviii–xciv.

foreign to Lesbian; artificial forms such as ὠράνω, ποικιλόδειροι, ὤρεσι, πωλυανάκτιδα, ὠλομέναν, beside ὀράνω, δέραι, ὄρεσι, πόλυ. In all these cases there is a difference in the metrical value of the forms; the language is the work of the verse.

It is my own view[1] that initial digamma had been altogether lost in Lesbian by the time of Alcaeus and Sappho. Where it still seems to be called for to prevent hiatus or make position, it is not the sound itself, but its one-time presence, which is felt, much in the same way that the French feel the one-time presence of *h-aspiré*. It was likely that even in everyday speech certain word-groups that had had an initial digamma were long kept without elision, as the combination of the unelided article before *h-aspiré* keeps the traces of that sound in French (δέ οἱ may be such an instance), but the greater number of cases in Lesbian poetry, as in Homer, must have been due to the keeping of the poetic formula. The poets and their hearers, being used to these formulas, would feel no fault where there was hiatus or failure to make position, while on the other hand, if they were using newer phrases, they were free to treat the word as if it had never had the | sound. Thus we find in Sappho γλῶσσα ἔαγε, φαίνεταί οἱ,[2] and in Alcaeus πνεύμονα οἴνωι, ὐπά ἔργον (beside ἀμύστιδος ἔργον), λῦσ' ἄτερ ἔθεν (– ⏑ – ⏑ ⏑); likewise the trace of the initial digamma is seen in Sappho's ἔειπε, and in Alcaeus' ἀ]πυείπη[ι and ἐάνασσε, where the meter kept the unshortened form beside εἶπον and ἤλ̣π̣[in Sappho and εἶπε and ἤλπετο in Alcaeus. There are in the two poets some 33 places where an initial digamma would spoil the meter.

The keeping of ϝρ- in some form which is noted in our manuscripts as βρ- (Sappho βρόδον, βράδινος, βράκεα)—how it was sounded is doubtful —was a poetic device to keep for these words the power of lengthening the foregoing syllable. Had such a treatment ever been a part of the spoken language the poets would have used it when the second element of a word began originally with *ϝρ-, and Herodian would have quoted from Lesbian poetry *ἐβράγη and *ἄβρηκτος (*ἐ-ϝράγη, *ἄ-ϝρηκτος), and not εὐράγη and αὔρηκτος, as he did. These two forms are beyond doubt, because they show the treatment which the spoken language gave to the group vowel-digamma-consonant-vowel, as in δεύω (*δέϝσω), ναῦος (*νᾶϝ-σος), and Εὐρυσίλαος (*'Ε-ϝρυσί-λαϝος) of the inscriptions. Nevertheless such forms as εὐράγη and αὔρηκτος could never have been a part of the

[1] On ϝ- in Homer cf. FM, pp. 222–32 above and TD below.

[2] The reading of a papyrus fragment of Sappho (Lobel ᾱ 3, 6) is without value, since antiquity, no less than our own times, had its grammarians who, failing to understand the hiatus, wished to restore the digamma, e.g. Apollonius Dyscolus, who quotes λῦσαι ἄτερ ϝέθεν to show that the third personal pronoun began with a digamma. Likewise John the Grammarian (Hoffmann, *op. cit.*, II, p. 217) states that the Lesbians wrote ϝοῖνον, but Aulus Gellius wrote the quotation from Alcaeus πνεύμονα οἴνωι, while others emended πνεύμονα to πνεύμονας. Balbilla has no more authority than the grammarians.

spoken language, since -ϝρ- would then have been treated as an initial and not an intervocalic sound-group, and they would have become *ἐράγη and *ἄρηκτος. *Εὐράγη* and *αὔρηκτος* can only be understood as poetic forms made to keep the metrical value of *ἐϝράγη and *ἄϝρηκτος. The following forms in Homer show this Lesbian treatment of the digamma: δεύω beside Ionic δεῖ; χεύω, ἔχευαν, etc., beside Ionic χέει, ἔχεαν, etc., ἀπούρας (*απόϝρας), ἀπηύρας (*ἄπεϝρας), ταλαύρινος (*ταλά-ϝρινος), καλαῦροψ (*κάλαϝροψ). A like treatment was given in Aeolic to the group vowel-consonant-digamma-vowel. *Εὔαδε* (from *ἔσϝαδε) is cited by Choeroboscus as | Aeolic. Homer has εὔαδε beside ἅδε, αὐίαχοι (*ἀσϝίαχοι),[1] αὐερύοντα (*ἀνϝερύοντα). Of these words ἀπούρας, ἀπηύρας, ταλαύρινος, καλαῦροψ, εὔαδε, αὐίαχοι, αὐερύοντα, could have come only from the poetry of the Aeolians of Asia Minor. They are the proof that the Aeolic in Homer was brought into the Ionic epic from the Lesbian epic language at a time when spoken Lesbian had lost the digamma.[2] Likewise poetic and Lesbian is the treatment of a short vowel followed by digamma when the short vowel is followed by two more short syllables. The glossographers quote as Lesbian καυαλέον, φαυοφόροι, etc.; the same treatment is seen in Homer's ἀλευόμενοι, etc., beside ἀλέοντο, etc. To this same source belongs the artificial treatment of intervocalic -δϝ- as -δδ- in ἔδδεισας, ἔδδεισεν, etc.[3]

There is no sure case of a form borrowed by the Lesbian singers from some other Aeolic dialect: wherever the Aeolic form in Homer differs from that of the Lesbian inscriptions the form may be archaic Lesbian. Yet the readiness with which the Ionic singers took over the Aeolic forms would rather point to just such an exchange between the Aeolic groups before the migration to Asia Minor. The Lesbian lyric language offers the same difficulty of deciding between forms which are Thessalian or Boeotian but might also be archaic Lesbian; nor is the source of the non-Aeolic forms always altogether sure. Ἀέλιος, δῶμα, ἔσκεθον, ἴερος, and πτόλις, however, are Arcado-Cyprian and not Ionic; moreover, the non-Aeolic endings of the dative -οις and -αις, which are the only ones found in Arcado-Cyprian inscriptions, are later in Ionic than -οισι, -ηισι, which were not altogether supplanted until well into the fourth century. *N*-movable, which is generally classed as an Ionic trait, is nevertheless found in the dative plural of consonant stems in Thessalian and in verb-forms in some Cyprian inscriptions. There is thus nothing to show that the foreign element of the Lesbian lyric language was not drawn wholly from Arcado-Cyprian. This is a point to remember when we seek for

1 That ἰάχω began with a double consonant is proved by 23 cases where the word makes position after a short final vowel, e.g. σμερδάλεα ἰάχων, 8 times.

2 Lesbian is used here, of course, in the sense which it bears as a linguistic term.

3 I shall discuss more fully in another article the traces of the digamma in Aeolic and Ionic verse.

forms in Homer | which could only be Ionic: if the form is also Arcado-Cyprian, we must grant that it may have been a part of the Lesbian epic language.

The Artificial Element

There are in the Homeric language a number of artificial forms which can be understood only as Aeolisms which were changed by Ionic singers to forms nearer those of their spoken language, though they could not make them altogether Ionic. The change in each case was brought about by a purely oral process. Thus the Lesbian poems which the Ionic singers learned had in them a number of perfect active participles in -ων, -οντος. Where the forms of the Ionic participle had the same metrical value these were put in their place, save in a few words where the Aeolic ending and the meaning of the word led the Ionic singers to mistake the forms for presents, as in κεκλήγοντας, τετρίγοντας.[1] Usually, however, the Ionic singers, when the forms of the two dialects were metrically different, were drawn by their habit of using different endings for the present and perfect to the endings -ότος, -ότι, which the rhythm forced them to lengthen to -ῶτος, -ῶτι. Thus we find τεθνηῶτα beside τεθνηότος, πεπτηῶτες beside πεπτηότα, κεκμηῶτα beside κεκμηότας, etc. This same struggle of the Ionic singer between the foreign form and the habit of his daily speech is likewise the source of ἑήνδανε. He had heard on the one hand the Aeolic poetic *ἐάνδανε, but all the usage of his speech tended to ἥνδανε, so that, speaking the two forms as it were at once, he made ἑήνδανε. This form, it should be noted, shows that the initial digamma had been lost in Ionic.

The so-called 'distracted' forms were the work of singers who, torn between their desire to keep the metrical value of the genuine uncontracted forms on the one hand, and their habits of daily speech on the other, in which they used the contracted forms, made such artificial forms as μνωόμενοι, ὁρόω, ὁρόωντες, δρώωσι, etc. Thus the poet who had heard μνᾱόμενοι in verse, but said μνώμενοι in talk, would tend to begin the word with μνω-, whereupon the rhythm would force him to | keep without change the latter part of the poetic form and make μνωόμενοι. When faced with a verb of the Aeolic -άω conjugation, such as ἡβάωσα, where he would usually say ἡβῶσα, he would be drawn into using the first two syllables of the spoken word ἡβω-, and then when forced by the rhythm to supply two more syllables would use the ending of the spoken word -ωσα, thus using the ω twice and making ἡβώωσα. When faced with the poetic ὁράω beside the spoken ὁρῶ the singer would be drawn to the spoken form, but the rhythm would force him to shorten the

[1] Κεκλήγοντες was a variant reading of Aristarchus at ξ 30, and is also found as a variant reading at μ 256, Μ 125, Π 430. It is found in all the manuscripts at Ρ 756 and 759. At Β 314 Zenodotus read τιτίζοντας, which can only be an attempt to Ionize τετρίγοντας.

ω-syllable to ο, which would be felt only as a poetic sound to fill in the verse until the real last syllable could be given, making ὁρόω. The same thing happened in certain nouns: φάος, where the spoken form was φώς, became φόως; πρᾱονες, where the spoken form was πρῶνες, became πρώονες; σάος, where the spoken form was σῶς, became σόος; etc. Another way in which the uncontracted forms were brought nearer to the usual contracted forms was by lengthening a short root-vowel and making τρωπᾶσθε from τροπάεσθε, πωτῶντο from ποτάοντο, etc. That this change was a purely oral process is shown by the fact that when the root had an α there was a tendency to keep the genuine uncontracted forms, as in ἀοιδιάει (the voice repeating in -άει the movement of ἀοι-), κραδάων, ναιετάουσι, etc.

A like oral creation of artificial forms is found in such forms as Ἰῐ́λου, ἀγρῐ́ου, ὁμοιῐ́ου, ὅου, etc., found always before a double consonant, which can have come only from *Ἰλίοο, *ἀγρίοο, *ὁμοιίοο, *ὅο, etc. In another case the loss of the ending *-οο led to the making of the poetic form ὀκρυόεις in the phrases ἐπιδημίου ὀκρυόεντος (*I* 64) and κακομήχανου ὀκρυοέσσης (*Z* 344) for *ἐπιδημίοο κρυόεντος and *κακομηχάνοο κρυοέσσης. Van Leeuwen is doubtless right in thinking the poets were guided by the model of the adjective ὀκριόεις,[1] but of far more weight in each instance was the need of keeping the formula, and wherever the former presence of the *-οο ending is found there is a marked formulaic device. Thus the form Ἰλίου is found only in the phrase Ἰλίου προπάροιθε (3 times); ὅου is found only in a special type of clause, ὅου κλέος οὔ ποτ' ὀλεῖται (*B* 325, *Hymn to Apollo* 156), ὅου κράτος ἐστὶ μέγιστον (α 70). Ὁμοιίου, which is found only in the phrase ὁμοιίου πολέμοιο for *ὁμοιίοο πτολέμοιο, is used six times in the *Iliad* and twice in the *Odyssey*, and | here the Arcado-Cyprian πτόλεμος might show that the ending *-οο belonged to the Arcado-Cyprian poetic language. But we cannot be sure, since a Lesbian poet might have used the foreign πτόλεμος in a new phrase.[2] But whether *-οο is the original of Arcado-Cyprian -ω, or a middle stage between Aeolic -οιο and -ω, the creation of the artificial forms in question can have been due only to singers who had to keep the formulas.

Equivalent Aeolic Forms

It is likewise only the theory of oral verse-making which can show why certain Aeolic forms were kept when an Ionic form might have been used. In at least one case it was only because there was no such form in Ionic: θεᾱ́ was kept because Ionic used θεός for both masculine and feminine. But usually the Aeolic form was kept for less simple reasons, which could be only those of a poet who was drawn more towards the

[1] *Enchiridium dictionis epicae*[2], (Lugduni Batavorum, 1918), p. 176 n. *o*.

[2] A Thessalian inscription gives οἱ πτολιάρχοντες.

foreign form he found in poetry than towards the form which was habitual with him in his daily speech. An equivalent Aeolic form might be kept for one or more of the following reasons: the form was used along with other words, so that the poet felt the group as a unit and sought to change none of its parts; the form was known to him more from poetry than from speech, so that the habit of the poetic language was greater than that of his spoken language; the syntax of the form was foreign, and thus set it apart from the current form.

Aeolic *αἰ* for Ionic *εἰ* is regularly found in the phrases *αἴ κε*, *αἰ γάρ*, and *αἴθε*. In the phrase *αἴ κε* it has been kept because of the foreign *κε* with which it was felt more or less as a single word, like *ἤν* for *εἰ ἄν*. So soon as a single word is put between *αἰ* and *κε*, however, the motive for keeping the Aeolic form is lost and we have *εἰ δέ κε*, *εἰ μέν κεν*, *εἰ γάρ κεν*, etc. The use of *αἰ γάρ*, and its metrical variant *αἴθε*, is foreign to Ionic speech, being found only in Ionic and Attic prose in highly emotional passages where the author meaningly assumes the tone of poetry.

Ἐρι-, which seems to have come first from Arcado-Cyprian,[1] tended in the Ionic vocalization to become *ἀρι-*. The form *ἐρι-* was kept in | certain fixed phrases: e.g. *ἐριαύχενες ἵπποι* (5 times); *ἐρίηρες ἑταῖροι* (22 times); *ἐρίγδουπος πόσις Ἥρης* (7 times); *ἐρικυδέα δαῖτα* (5 times); *ἐρικυδέα δῶρα* (twice); *ἐρικυδέα τέκνα* (once).[2] It was these formulas that kept the prefix, but it was kept unchanged for another reason: where the radical of the word is a noun *ἐρι-* is used, while *ἀρι-* was brought in where the radical is a verb or adjective and thus properly calls for an adverbial prefix. Thus we find *ἐριβῶλαξ*, *ἐρίγδουπος*, *ἐρικυδής*, *ἐρίμυκος*, *ἐρισθενής*, *ἐριστάφυλος*, *ἐρίτιμος*, *ἐρίωπος*, but *ἀρίγνωτος*, *ἀριδείκετος*, *ἀρίζηλος*, *ἀριπρεπής*, *ἀριφραδής*, *ἀρισφαλής*. In *ἐριούνιος* and *ἐρίηρος* the meaning of the radical is so vague that the prefix is scarce felt as such, and in *ἐριθηλής* it was the poetic *θηλ-*, for the prosaic *θαλλ-*, which kept the whole poetic word unchanged.

There is no need, if we would understand why *λαός* was not changed to **ληός* whereas *νᾶος* became *νηός*, to argue that there was no word *λεώς* in Ionic. Indeed two names in the *Iliad* and *Odyssey* prove an Ionic *λεώς*: *Λειώκριτος* and *Λειώδης* are artificial forms which have been made from **Λαόκριτος* and **Λαώδης* (**Λαϝοϝάδης*) after the spoken **Λεώκριτος* and **Λεώδης*. *Ἀγέλεως* in *τοῖς δ' Ἀγέλεως μετέειπε* (χ 131, 247), where the Aeolic would be **τοῖς δ' Ἀγέλαος ἔειπε*, shows that there must have been many names of this type in early Ionic (cf. *Ἀναξίλεο*, *Ἀρχέλεος*, *Θερσίλεω*, *λεωφόρον*, of the Ionic inscriptions), for the form *ἔειπε* was common enough in the Homeric poetic language and *Ἀγέλαος* is found in other verses where the change would not have been so simple. The foreign *λαός* was kept simply because it was more common in poetry than *λεώς* was in

[1] Cf. p. 344 n. 4. [2] Cf. K. Witte in Pauly-Wissowa, *s.v.* Homeros, col. 2121.

speech, so that the singers were more habituated to the poetic than to the prosaic word. Each time a singer met *νᾱος* in verse he would tend to modify it in the direction of the spoken *νεώς*. But *λαός*, which figured in so many poetic phrases—*ποιμένα λαῶν* (56 times), *κοίρανε λαῶν* (11 times), *λαὸν Ἀχαιῶν* (19 times), etc., in the epithet of gods *λαόσσοος* (6 times), in heroic names—and was moreover a word which by its meaning had a special dignity, won a place for itself far beyond the reach of *λεώς*. Where on the contrary a word had no such special place in the poetic language, but differed only in form from the common prose word, the singers would be drawn to the current form. Thus *ᾆος* and *τᾶος* became *ἕως* and *τέως*, contrary to the usual laws of | the heroic meter.[1] It is wrong, however, in the case either of these words or of the words which make hiatus through a lost digamma, or in such phrases as *ἡμεῖς δὲ δείσαντες, μάλα δήν, σμερδάλεα ἰάχοντες*, to speak of metrical faults, for these irregularities of the rhythm are constant and accepted, and so are rightly to be felt as the correct rhythmic usage.

The Aeolic form *φηρ-* wherever it was used in the common sense of 'hunting' or 'game' appears as *θηρ-* in Ionic (*θήρη, θήρ* etc.), but when the word was used of the Centaurs the Ionic singers very naturally failed to translate the word into their own dialect, but left it to be a proper name, *Φῆρες*, 'the Beasts,' and so we find it in *A* 268, *B* 743.

Ἑρμείας was kept beside *Ἑρμῆς*, though *Ἀθηναία* became *Ἀθηναίη*, and *Ῥεία* became *Ῥείη*, because the non-Ionic ending *-ειᾱς* was well fixed in other heroic names such as *Αἰνείας* and *Αὐγείας*. *Ναυσικάα* and *Φεία* were not changed because the names were not Ionic.

Πίσυρες kept its initial consonant because the whole word differed in form from *τέσσαρες*. *Ἐρεβεννός* and *ἀργεννός* were unchanged because there was no like word in *-εινός* in Ionic.

The Ionic Element

We may now turn to the forms of the Homeric language which are Ionic.

The greater number of sounds and forms which are Ionic and not Aeolic are metrically equal to the Aeolic sounds and forms. They can in no way be looked on as an Ionic addition to the traditional diction, but are the work of Ionic singers changing the Aeolic epic language to suit the habit of their own speech. Thus, save for the few unusual forms just noted, Homer has *η* where Aeolic kept original *ᾱ*; *ευ* from *εο* where

[1] The overwhelming reading of the manuscripts is *ἕως* where the scansion should be – ᴗ, and *εἵως* where it is – –. *Εἵως* is an artificial form made by lengthening *ἕως* under the force of the rhythm. There is no real ground for the **ἧος* with which, as with the *ϝ*, some modern editors have disfigured their texts. Here, as elsewhere, the seeming vagaries of the manuscript tradition accord with the processes of oral poetry and thus bear witness to their faithfulness.

Aeolic had εο; ἦν for Aeolic ἦς; -ου, -ους, -ᾱς, -εω, -ν, εω in | the noun where Aeolic has -ω, -οις, -αις, -ᾰ, -ᾱν; -ειν -ουσι, -ουσα, in the verb where Aeolic has -ην, -ωσι, -οισα; φᾱσί, Μοῦσα, ξεῖνος, εἰμί, ἕτερος, θάρσος, etc., where Aeolic has φαῖσι, Μοῖσα, ξέννος, ἔμμι, ἄτερος, θέρσος, etc. Each one of these sounds and forms is a sign of the thorough Ionization of the traditional epic diction.

A number of Homeric forms which are Ionic and not Aeolic are found in the Lesbian lyric language. Some of these are also found in Arcado-Cyprian, which seems to be their source. These forms are: the noun-endings -οις, -αις, -σι; the first aorist in -σ-; the perfect participle in -ώς, -ότες; μέσσος, ὅσσος, etc.; and ν-movable in verb-forms.

The non-thematic infinitive in -ναι is not found in the remains of Lesbian poetry, but was used in Arcado-Cyprian (Arcadian ἀπειθῆναι, ἦναι, ἐξῆναι). We are thus unable to say surely that these infinitives are an Ionic addition to the Homeric language. Likewise we are unable to claim an Ionic source for ἄν in Homer. Cyprian has κε, but Arcadian has ἄν, and for εἰ followed by ἄν it has εἴ κ' ἄν; in one case in Arcadian we find εἴ κ' used without ἄν followed by the subjunctive.[1] The tendency in Aeolic would have been to change ἄν in Arcado-Cyprian formulas to κε(ν), as it was in Ionic to change Aeolic κε(ν) to ἄν. There are in the *Iliad* and the *Odyssey* some 43 out of 156 cases where ἄν cannot be changed to κε(ν), and some 747 cases of κε(ν), but even this small portion of sure cases of ἄν may have come over from the Lesbian epic.

The Lesbian lyric language also has the artificial (or Arcado-Cyprian?) ἄμμεσιν, which is metrically equal to ἡμῖν scanned ⏖ –, and ἄμμες,[2] which can usually take the place of the Ionic accusative ἡμέας. *Eo* in Lesbian poetry can be scanned as a single syllable, and is thus the equal of Ionic ευ (Lesbian βέλεος scanned ⏑ –). Synizesis of ε with a diphthong, and so we may suppose with a long vowel, is common to Ionic, Aeolic, and Arcado-Cyprian verse (Lesbian θέοισ', ἀργάλεαι, Cyprian θεοῖς, 144, 2 in Hoffmann, *op. cit.*, I, p. 76).[3] |

Once we have set aside the Ionisms cited in the foregoing paragraph we find that there are left almost no forms in the *Iliad* and *Odyssey* which have not equivalents in the Lesbian poetic language. We find δοῦναι

[1] 29, 21 in Hoffmann, *op. cit.*, I, p. 23.

[2] For the accusative ἄμμες cf. Hesychius *s.v.*; *Etymologicum Gudianium* 45, 18.

[3] -ατο, -αται, for -ντο, -νται, in the optative and certain non-thematic forms, are often called Ionic, but the ancient grammarians called the endings Aeolic (cf. Hoffmann, II, p. 568), and as it happens we have no inscriptional evidence for the third plural middle of the optative in either Aeolic or Arcado-Cyprian. Πολυκτήμων may have taken the place of a πολυππάμων. The third plural of the non-thematic aorist in -σαν is found in Cyprian (κατέθισαν, cf. κατέθιjαν); the ending -σαν is also used in Aeolic in the aorist passive. -εων is said to be disyllabic in three places (πυλέων *H* 1, *M* 340, θυρέων φ 191), but the Aeolic singers may have lengthened the υ in these words in the way that gives us ὕδωρ in Lesbian verse with both short and long υ. Ἴδεω in *I* 558 may be for *Ἴδοο.

twice at the end of the verse, beside three places within the verse where δόμεναι could be used just as well; but we lack evidence on this form for Arcadian which might have a form *δῶναι (cf. Arcadian θῆναι).

Out of 25 uses of ἕως 23 call for the scansion of Aeolic ἆος; ἕως in *P* 727 is monosyllabic, leaving only β 78 where ἕως has a definitely Ionic scansion.

The Ionic forms of the first and second personal pronoun plural likewise give us almost no grounds for believing in Ionic changes in the diction. Ἄμμες is found in Homer 37 times within the verse, and never where the Ionic form could take its place. On the other hand ἡμεῖς, in 73 of its 81 occurrences, could be replaced by ἄμμες, and of the 8 remaining cases 3 occur in the phrase ἡμεῖς ἴδμεν, that is ἄμμες (ϝ)ἴδμεν. Beside ἄμμι (18 times) ἡμῖν is used 72 times: in 55 of these cases ἄμμιν could be used instead, in 16 where ἡμῖν is used at the head of the verse before a vowel ἄμμεσιν could take its place, and the single remaining case is ἡμῖν ἑκάεργον, that is *ἄμμιν (ϝ)ἑκάεργον. The accusative ἄμμε is used 13 times, always within the verse, while ἡμέας appears 3 times at the verse end, which shows that the Ionic singers felt ἡμέας as disyllabic. Where ἡμέας is found elsewhere it is 8 times followed by a consonant, including one case of the digamma, so that the poetic Lesbian could just as well be used, leaving only 8 cases for which we have no Lesbian equivalent.

Out of 35 occurrences of ὑμεῖς there are only 4 where ὔμμες could not be used. Out of 38 occurrences of ὑμῖν there are only 5 where ὔμμιν could not take its place, and in 2 of these 5 places ὔμμεσιν could be read. Out of the 5 times that ὑμέας occurs, ὔμμες could be used in 3. |

There are thus only 21 verses of Homer where the meter seems to be warrant for the Ionic form of the personal pronouns: *Γ* 104 ἡμεῖς, *Δ* 246 ὑμεῖς, *H* 194 ὑμεῖς, *I* 528 ὑμῖν, *I* 649 ὑμεῖς, *K* 211 ἡμέας, *Λ* 695 ἡμέας, *M* 223 ἡμεῖς, *Ξ* 369 ἡμεῖς, *O* 136 ἡμέας, *Ψ* 495 ὑμεῖς, α 76 ἡμεῖς, β 75 ὑμέας, 86 ἡμέας, 210 ὑμέας, 244 ἡμέας, γ 81 ἡμεῖς, π 387 ὑμῖν, χ 264 ἡμέας, ψ 138 ἡμέας, 224 ἡμέας. Even these few cases, however, are not sure. The larger number of accusatives might point towards an artificial (or originally Arcado-Cyprian?) *ἄμμεας in Lesbian verse, and in some cases the metrical fault caused by using the Lesbian form might be like the numerous other faults we see resulting from the formulaic technique. For instance, *ἄμμες ὀτρυνώμεθ' in *Ξ* 369 might be due to the modification of a common *ἄμμες δ' ὀτρυνώμεθ'; cf. at the beginning of the verse ἡμεῖς δὲ φραζώμεθ' (*Δ* 14).[1]

5. CONCLUSIONS

We have seen in our study that both Arcado-Cyprian and Aeolic singers had used the epic diction and left the mark of their language

[1] Cf. FM, pp. 202–21 above.

upon its words and phrases in such a way that we know the epic diction was more or less altogether their creation; whereas we have found only very slight traces of Ionic work besides the mere change in pronunciation. There are two possible conclusions, either that the *Iliad* and *Odyssey* as we have them are, save for the Ionic pronunciation, the work of an Aeolic singer or singers, or that they are the work of an Ionic singer or singers who made their verses out of a traditional diction which had undergone almost no change from the time when the Ionians had learned it from the Aeolians.

The Theory of an Aeolic Homer Rejected

According to the first explanation, this Aeolic Homer would have lived at the moment when the oral poetry was most creative—for of course every oral poem has its moment of creation, however long it may have lived merely by recitation—and would have made his verses from an oral diction which was very ancient, which may even in some parts have gone back to the time before Greek broke up into the dialects in which we find it. But whatever may be the age of the diction, | it had, in the period before Homer's time, been used and highly developed by Arcado-Cyprian and Aeolic singers. Whether there was a period of mutual exchange between Arcado-Cyprian and Aeolic, or whether Aeolic took over an Arcado-Cyprian tradition and greatly changed it, we cannot know. Homer would then have composed in this Arcado-Cyprian and Aeolic diction, and his poems would have won such fame that his followers found their profit in merely reciting them. Now recitation is not the natural practice of oral poetry, which, as was seen above (pp. 335–7), is ever in a state of change, so that one must suppose the formation of a guild, not of singers, but of rhapsodes, who made their living by faithfully keeping and reciting the poems which Homer had composed as a singer. We must then suppose further that this guild was fixed in a city which in Homer's time was Aeolic but later became Ionic, so that the daily speech of the reciters changed from Aeolic to Ionic. This change in their spoken language would have brought about a change in their pronunciation of the *Iliad* and *Odyssey*; while the tradition of their craft may have kept the poems line for line, they would have changed the sounds and forms to suit the habits of their speech in so far as that called for no change in the words of the line. Then finally, at some moment well along in the Ionic period of the city, when the Ionic speech had had time to Ionize completely the pronunciation of the poems, they would have been recorded in writing.

Simple as such a theory may seem—Fick, who had not the notion of an oral poetic language, gave himself needless trouble, since he need almost never have changed more than the form of the single word[1]—it is without any sound basis, and there is much to be said against it. First, such a close keeping of the words in a way quite foreign to the natural functioning of an oral diction must necessarily have made for a keeping of the older pronunciation; in any case the complete Ionization of the equivalent sounds and forms can be understood only by an utterly free handling of the diction by Ionian singers. | Secondly, we must then suppose that all the poems of the epic cycle, the greater Homeric Hymns to Apollo, Aphrodite, and indeed all the fragments we have of the older poetry, had likewise been kept by some guild from the Aeolic period, with just the same change in their own speech from Aeolic to Ionic; for the language of these other poems, as their diction, differs in no point from that of Homer. In the case of the *Hymn to Apollo* one would have to reason most ingeniously about the lines wherein the man who sang it makes mention of his hearers and of himself:

> *Ἀλλὰ σὺ Δήλωι Φοῖβε μάλιστ' ἐπιτέρπεαι ἦτορ*
> *ἔνθα τοι ἑλκεχίτωνες Ἰάονες ἠγερέθονται*
> *αὐτοῖς σὺν παίδεσσι καὶ αἰδοίηις ἀλόχοισιν.*
> *οἱ δέ σε πυγμαχίηι τε καὶ ὀρχηθμῶι καὶ ἀοιδῆι*
> *μνησάμενοι τέρπουσιν ὅταν στήσωνται ἀγῶνα.*
> *φαίη κ' ἀθανάτους καὶ ἀγήρως ἔμμεναι αἰεί*
> *ὃς τότ' ἐπαντιάσει' ὅτ' Ἰάονες ἀθρόοι εἶεν.*
>
> . . . .
>
> *Ἀλλ' ἄγεθ' ἱλήκοι μὲν Ἀπόλλων Ἀρτέμιδι ξύν,*
> *χαίρετε δ' ὑμεῖς πᾶσαι, ἐμεῖο δὲ καὶ μετόπισθε*
> *μνήσασθ' ὁππότε κέν τις ἐπιχθονίων ἀνθρώπων*
> *ἐνθάδ' ἀνείρηται ξεῖνος ταλαπείριος ἐλθών·*
> *ὦ κοῦραι, τίς δ' ὔμμιν ἀνὴρ ἥδιστος ἀοιδῶν*
> *ἐνθάδε πωλεῖται, καὶ τέωι τέρπεσθε μάλιστα;*
> *ὑμεῖς δ' εὖ μάλα πᾶσαι ὑποκρίνασθε ἀφ' ἡμέων·*
> *τυφλὸς ἀνήρ, οἰκεῖ δὲ Χίωι ἐνὶ παιπαλοέσσηι,*
> *τοῦ πᾶσαι μετόπισθεν ἀριστεύουσιν ἀοιδαί.*
> *ἡμεῖς δ' ἡμέτερον κλέος οἴσομεν ὅσσον ἐπ' αἶαν*
> *ἀνθρώπων στρεφόμεσθα πόλεις εὖ ναιεταώσας·*
> *οἱ δ' ἐπὶ δὴ πείσονται ἐπεὶ καὶ ἐτήτυμόν ἐστιν.*[2] |

[1] It is impossible to build any theory of either multiple or single authorship on the basis of the language. Such attempts as that of Fick are based upon the purest of *a prioris*; *e.g.* he changed *ἡμέας αὐτούς* in *Θ* 529 to **ἄμμεας αὐτόυς*, assuming that Aeolic had such a form, but in *K* 211 he claimed *ἡμέας ἔλθοι* as proof of an Ionic redaction.

[2] Vv. 146–52, 165–76. The great majority of the manuscripts read *ὑποκρίνασθε* in v. 171, which is correct, the metrical fault being a guarantee of the text (cf. FM, pp. 199–201 above). The reading *ἀφ' ἡμέων* of some nine manuscripts, instead of *ἀφ' ὑμέων*, which is given by the other manuscripts and modern editors, is exactly suited to the pride which oral poets everywhere have in their own skill; likewise the variant *ἡμέτερον* in v. 174 is to be preferred to *ὑμέτερον*. The variant reading was due to the feeling of the scribes—which has also been that of modern editors — that Homer could not have been so immodest.

Here we clearly have to do with a singer and no reciter; he is singing to Ionians; and he says that there are many other singers and that each of them has his own songs. One is forced to grant that this Hymn, in which we find the very same poetic language as in the *Iliad* and *Odyssey*, was the work of an Ionian, in the diction common to all other heroic poets of his time, at a moment when the tradition of epic poetry was still that of creation and not of recitation.

The Theory of an Aeolic Diction Accepted

Moreover the theory of an Aeolic *Iliad* and *Odyssey* rests altogether on one supposition, which is false, namely that the ease with which the poems can be turned into Aeolic proves they must have been more or less entirely as they stand the work of an Aeolic poet: really it proves only that the formulaic diction was Aeolic. As was said above (p. 329), oral poetry is altogether made up of traditional formulas and series of formulas, each of which is an artifice for making the verse and the sentence. The singer has learned these formulas by hearing them in the mouths of older singers, and he makes his own poetry out of them from beginning to end, since the only way he can compose is by thinking in terms of the formulas. Thus while the poems of an oral poetry are ever each one of them in a never-ceasing state of change, the diction itself is fixed, and is passed on with little or no change from one generation of singers to another. This is why we find that even those Ionic words which in themselves are metrically different from the Aeolic words are used in the *Iliad* and *Odyssey* in such a way that the change to Aeolic is still possible: in each case the word is used in fixed formulas and types of formulas which are traditional artifices of verse-making. Ἡμεῖς, for example, can be changed to ἄμμες in 73 out of the 81 times it occurs, which could by no means be due to hazard, and could not happen in the verse of any poet who was making each verse out of his own new words. Homer, however, was using the word in fixed phrases; so we find ἡμεῖς δ(έ) 41 times as the device for beginning a sentence, and in 34 of these 41 it is a device for beginning the verse as well. Ἡμεῖς μὲν accounts for 9 other occurrences of the word, falling 8 times at the beginning of the verse. Ἀλλ' ἄγεθ' ἡμεῖς περ begins the verse twice. This, when we have set aside the 13 cases | of ἡμεῖς at the verse-end, leaves ἡμεῖς before a consonant in only 8 places where the phrase is not clearly fixed in the diction. It is of course largely hazard and the length of the *Iliad* and *Odyssey* which bring it about that we can observe the use of a fixed phrase in a number of places and so analyze the technique of its use.

Ἡμεῖς δ(έ) is itself often used to make up longer formulas. One of the most needed artifices of the singer is that of ready phrases of different metrical values to join his sentences on to one another. Homer's technique of the conjunctional formula is vast and complex, and, as in the case of the epithet, easily permits analysis into systems of great length and great simplicity. One such series of formulas is that for expressing the essential idea *but we*: ἡμεῖς δ' (20 times), ἡμεῖς δέ (9 times), ἡμεῖς δ' αὖ (3 times), ἡμεῖς δ' αὖτ' (once), ἡμεῖς δ' αὖτε (3 times). Each of these phrases expresses the same essential idea but has a different metrical value. These formulas are then in turn used in other formulas. We find at the beginning of the verse ἡμεῖς δ' ἐμμεμαῶτες (*N* 785, *ψ* 127), ἡμεῖς δ' ἑσταότες θαυμάζομεν (*B* 320, *Ω* 394), ἡμεῖς δὲ φραζώμεθ' ὅπως (*Δ* 14, *Ξ* 61, *ψ* 117). Twice we have the pair of verses

> ἡμεῖς δ' οὔτ' ἐπὶ ἔργα πάρος γ' ἴμεν οὔτε πηι ἄλληι
> πρίν γ' αὐτὴν γήμασθαι Ἀχαιῶν ὧι κ' ἐθέληισι,

(*β* 127–8, *σ* 288–9). We have the system ἡμεῖς δὲ δείσαντες (*ι* 236, 396), ἡμεῖς δὲ κλαίοντες (*ι* 294), ἡμεῖς δὲ ἰάχοντες (*δ* 454).[1] Among the nine uses of ἡμεῖς μέν we find ἡμεῖς μὲν τὰ ἕκαστα διείπομεν (*Λ* 706, *μ* 16), ἡμεῖς μὲν γάρ (*γ* 262, 276).[2] Nor are the 13 cases of ἡμεῖς at the verse-end due wholly to chance: the word is regularly used there as a means of filling in the last foot of a verse in which the fifth foot has ended with -ομεν, -ομεν ἡμεῖς, making, as it were, merely a longer personal ending. Thus we find ἐπέφνομεν ἡμεῖς (*K* 478), εἴπομεν ἡμεῖς | (*α* 37), κατελείπομεν ἡμεῖς (*λ* 53, 447), ἔκταμεν ἡμεῖς (*μ* 375), ἐπιέσσαμεν ἡμεῖς (*υ* 143). We also find ἡμεῖς at the end of the verse in the formulaic passage

> οὐ γάρ μοί ποτε βωμὸς ἐδεύετο δαιτὸς ἐίσης
> λοιβῆς τε κνίσης τε, τὸ γὰρ λάχομεν γέρας ἡμεῖς,

(*Δ* 48–9, *Ω* 69–70). We are sometimes unable to analyze so exactly the artifice of verse-making which carries in itself the possibility of changing Ionic ἡμεῖς to Aeolic ἄμμες, but we may be sure, nevertheless, that it is only because the small remnant of Greek heroic poetry which we still have does not let us follow everywhere the vastly varied technique of the diction.

Such an analysis as we have just made for the use of ἡμεῖς in Homer could be made for any other form or word in the traditional diction

[1] Ἡμεῖς δὲ δείσαντες and ἡμεῖς δὲ ἰάχοντες when δ' αὖ and δ' αὖτ', which in the heroic style are equal in meaning to the simple δέ, might have been used, show how keenly the singers felt the accepted irregularities as positive features of the epic versification. They are among the many Homeric phrases which bear witness to the oral nature of the diction at the same time that they prove the soundness of the traditional text.

[2] The repetition of a more or less uncommon formula at a short interval, as in the case of ἡμεῖς δὲ δείσαντες and ἡμεῖς μὲν γάρ above, is a constant feature of the Homeric diction, and is another sign of its oral nature: a phrase or type of phrase will linger in the mind of the singer, and in the speed of his verse-making, where his thought largely follows for its expression the habitual vocal gestures of his poetic diction, it will come to the fore and be used again.

which is used at all often, and since each form and word, save for the few Ionisms we have noted, is either Aeolic, or equal in metrical value to Aeolic, we should thus be analyzing an Aeolic technique of verse-making. There thus ceases to be anything surprising in the fact that the *Iliad* and *Odyssey* can be turned into Aeolic almost word for word: the formulaic diction was learned by the Ionians from the Aeolians, and though under the stress of habit of their own speech they made it Ionic wherever that could be done without harm to the technique of its use, they otherwise kept it almost without change, since the way in which verse is orally made forced them to do so. The few Ionic forms which we were able to point out above are, for all they are few and some of them doubtful, a precious proof that the Ionic singers had made at least some slight changes in the diction. Far from showing, by their rarity, that Homer could not have been an Ionian, they are, in view of the little change made in an oral diction from generation to generation, just about what one might look for in a tradition of Aeolic heroic poetry which was being carried on by Ionic singers. |

The History of the Greek Heroic Style

The study of the Homeric language has thus given us the outlines of the history of the heroic style. From a high antiquity it was carried on in the Greek peninsula by peoples who spoke Arcado-Cyprian and Aeolic. Just what part each of these two peoples had in keeping and developing heroic poetry is not clear. If it was the work of Arcado-Cyprian singers, they must have made an ample use of Aeolic poetry with its Aeolic forms; if it was the work of Aeolic singers, they drew largely on Arcado-Cyprian words and phrases. A long period with mutual exchange of poetry seems most likely. Why the Ionians while in Greece proper had nothing to do, so far as we know, with the formation of this heroic diction, and why when they migrated to Asia they brought with them no heroic poetry, must remain matters for conjecture. It was only in Asia Minor that they met with peoples of Aeolic speech and learned from them to practice the epic. Just how they learned must likewise stay in doubt. The art of the Greek heroic poetry is so far above that of any other oral narrative verse that one might, perhaps, conclude that it was the work of a more highly professional class than that which usually practices oral poetry. In that case we might suppose, as others have, that Ionic heroic poetry was due to the tradition of poetry in some city or cities where the speech of the people had once been Aeolic, and then, because of their defeat at the hands of Ionians, Ionic. However that may be, the new way of life which the Ionians took up in their new land gave a great impulse to the practice of their new poetry, and brought forth all the countless poems which were heard and forgotten, as well as the *Iliad* and *Odyssey*. Here again we are in doubt. Were the two poems put in writing during the lifetime of their author, and kept by some group who recited them? Or were they kept by some such guild of reciters as that which was described above? Or were they passed in manuscript among many singers who, while they still practiced creative oral poetry, found this way of getting for their repertory the poems which had the greatest fame?[1] One thing is plain: our manuscripts cannot | all go back to a manuscript of Homer's time; for their variant readings, while some are due to copyists, are for the greater part the variants of an oral tradition, which means that the manuscripts which the Alexandrians used came from different oral traditions.

Nor, because of any evidence which the language gives us, may we say that the *Iliad* and *Odyssey* are single poems, nor show how the singer, or singers, of the poems have put smaller poems and whole passages together. The answer to these problems is not to be found in the language, which, like the diction of which it was a part, merely shows that the whole of the two poems, with perhaps a few rare verses excepted, are the work of one or a number of Ionic singers using, at about the same time, the same traditional style, which was itself an Arcado-Cyprian and Aeolic creation. For on the one hand the same diction is common to all singers, and on the other its tradition is so conservative that even the complete unity of language which we find in the poems and in some of the *Homeric Hymns* might have been kept over a fairly long period. To prove that there were one or many poets, and to show what passages were taken whole from the tradition and which were made anew out of single formulas or verses, we must turn to the study of other oral poetries where the processes of composition can be studied in actual practice and in a greater body of poetry than we have for the Greek epic. When, by the exact analysis of oral poems in reference to their tradition, we have grasped in detail just how the oral poet works, and what it is that makes a poem good or bad in the judgment of himself and his hearers, we shall then, but only then, be able to undertake to study the authorship of the *Iliad* and *Odyssey*, and to try to apportion that which is due to the tradition and that which is due to the author. |

[1] Murko (*La poésie épique en Yougoslavie*, pp. 12–13) describes such a state of poetry, half oral, half written, as is conceivable in a general way for the preservation of the Homeric poems: 'Janko Ceramić, agé de 68 ans, m'a assuré qu'il pouvait répéter le lendemain toute chanson entendue la veille au soir. Cependant, les chants de la poésie dite orale ou traditionnelle ne sont pas toujours transmis de bouche en bouche; ils sont très souvent, et de plus en plus, pris dans des livres et des brochures, et cela même en Herzégovine, terre classique du chant épique. . . . Le chanteur qui apprend un chant qu'on lui lit doit se le faire répéter plusieurs fois pour le savoir.'

[HP *Editors' note:* For the convenience of the reader there is appended (pp. 362–4) an index of Greek words and forms discussed in this article.]

INDEX OF GREEK WORDS AND FORMS

[references are to original page numbers]

7

The Traditional Metaphor in Homer*

ARISTOTLE tells in his *Poetics* of the kinds of words which make for a poetic diction, then he adds: 'It is a great thing to make a fitting use of each one of these devices [i.e., of poetic word-forms], as well as of compounds and glosses, but the greatest thing of all is being metaphorical. This alone can be gotten from no one else, and is the sign of born talent, since to use metaphors well is to have a sense for likenesses. Compounds best suit the dithyramb, glosses heroic verse, and metaphors iambic verse. In heroic verse, finally, all the devices which I have named are useful. . . .'[1] Further on he says: 'The heroic meter is the steadiest and the fullest, so that it is the readiest to take glosses and metaphors.'[2] Now if we take the term 'heroic', as we usually do, as meaning most of all the *Iliad* and *Odyssey*, Aristotle has said in so many words that Homer's metaphors will show us as nothing else in his style can just why he is great. What, then, are we to make of it when modern scholars tell us that the metaphor has only a small place in Homer, and that it is usually put to no striking use?[3] That it was Aristotle who was mistaken is clear, but we must learn why he thus fell into error. In doing so we shall find we have to deal with that principle of criticism on which at the present time, more than on any others, depends the true understanding of Homeric poetry. |

Aristotle's statement does not hold for all Greek heroic poetry because he had in mind as he wrote not so much Homer as the epics of his own age. We may even be sure he was thinking of the two chief epic poets of the fifth century, Choerilus and Antimachus.[4] We know how much Plato liked the verse of Antimachus, and how he defended him against the

* First published in *Classical Philology* 28 (1933), 30–43. Reprinted by kind permission of the editor.

[1] *Poetics* 1459 a 4: *ἔστιν δὲ μέγα μὲν τὸ ἑκάστωι τῶν εἰρημένων* [i.e., *ἐπεκτάσεις, ἀποκοπαί, ἐξαλλαγαὶ τῶν ὀνομάτων*] *πρεπόντως χρῆσθαι, καὶ διπλοῖς ὀνόμασι καὶ γλώτταις, πολὺ δὲ μέγιστον τὸ μεταφορικὸν εἶναι. μόνον γὰρ τοῦτο οὔτε παρ' ἄλλου ἔστι λαβεῖν εὐφυίας τε σημεῖόν ἐστι· τὸ γὰρ εὖ μεταφέρειν τὸ τὸ ὅμοιον θεωρεῖν ἐστιν. τῶν δ' ὀνομάτων τὰ μὲν διπλᾶ μάλιστα ἁρμόττει τοῖς διθυράμβοις, αἱ δὲ γλῶτται τοῖς ἡρωικοῖς, αἱ δὲ μεταφοραὶ τοῖς ἰαμβείοις. καὶ ἐν μὲν τοῖς ἡρωικοῖς ἅπαντα χρήσιμα τὰ εἰρημένα* . . . Cf. *Rhetoric* 1405 a 8: *καὶ τὸ σαφὲς καὶ τὸ ἡδὺ καὶ τὸ ξενικὸν ἔχει μάλιστα ἡ μεταφορά, καὶ λαβεῖν οὐκ ἔστιν αὐτὴν παρ' ἄλλου.*

[2] *Ibid.* b 34: *τὸ γὰρ ἡρωικὸν στασιμώτατον καὶ ὀγκωδέστατον τῶν μέτρων ἐστίν. διὸ καὶ γλώττας καὶ μεταφορὰς δέχεται μάλιστα.*

[3] Cf. A. L. Keith, *Simile and Metaphor in Greek Poetry from Homer to Aeschylus* (Chicago dissertation, 1914), pp. 33, 49; Karl Meister, *Die Homerische Kunstsprache* (Leipzig, 1921), p. 244, n. 1.

[4] Fragments in G. Kinkel, *Epicorum Graecorum fragmenta* (Leipzig, 1877).

vogue which Choerilus was having.[1] Aristotle often quotes both of them and does so in a way which shows he took for granted a very common knowledge of their work. In one place he says briefly: 'In the way Homer does, not Choerilus', and in the *Rhetoric* he quotes only from the first line of a passage in Antimachus, though it is only in the following lines that the artifice of which he is treating is illustrated.[2] Now the two poets had very bad names for their use of metaphor. Proclus must be giving a critical commonplace when he says: 'If the grand manner has anything artificial about it, it becomes very forced and bombastic. The fault usually lies in the use of metaphor, as in the case of Antimachus.'[3] Choerilus on his side had called stones 'the bones of the earth', and rivers 'the arteries of the earth', and though it must be partly through chance, his few fragments show a straining of metaphor far beyond anything to be found in what we have of Antimachus.[4] In his *Perseid* a noble Persian, brought low in defeat, is forced to drink from a broken clay cup: 'Here in my hands, all my fortune, is the shard of a cup broken in twain, a timber from a shipwreck of banqueters, such as oft the gale of Dionysus doth cast up on the coast of pride.'[5] This, indeed, | is what one might look for after his prologue, which Aristotle quotes: 'Happy the man who in those times was skilled in song and comrade of the Muses, when the meadow was unmowed. Now, when all has been allotted and the arts have their outcomes, we are left last in the race, and though we gaze everywhither there is no chariot newly yoked to which we may win.'[6] One sees straightway that the very thing might be done for Choerilus which was done by a critic of modern poetry who made a study of the metaphors of Guillaume Apollinaire, the French symbolist poet, because he could find in them the essence of the poet's thought.[7]

[1] Plutarch, *Lysander* 18; Proclus, *Commentary on the Timaeus* i. 28; Suidas, *s.v.* *Χοιρίλος*.

[2] Aristotle, *Topics* 157 a 14: *εἰς δὲ σαφήνειαν παραδείγματα καὶ παραβολὰς οἰστέον, παραδείγματα δὲ οἰκεῖα καὶ ἐξ ὧν ἴσμεν, οἷα Ὅμηρος, μὴ οἷα Χοιρίλος· οὕτω γὰρ ἂν σαφέστερον εἴη τὸ προτεινόμενον.* *Rhetoric* 1408 a 1; cf. E. M. Cope, *Aristotle's 'Rhetoric'* (Cambridge, England, 1877), III, 68.

[3] *Op. cit.* I. 20: *καὶ γὰρ εἴ τι τεχνικόν ἐστι παρά τινι τῶν ποιητῶν ὕψος, πολὺ τὸ μεμηχανημένον ἔχει καὶ στομφῶδες, μεταφοραῖς χρώμενον ὡς τὰ πολλὰ καθάπερ τὸ Ἀντιμάχειον.*

[4] Tzetzes, in Walz's *Rhetorici Graeci*, III, 650: *ὥσπερ ποιεῖ Χοιρίλος καλῶν τοὺς λίθους γῆς ὀστᾶ, τοὺς ποταμοὺς γῆς φλέβας.*

[5] Athenaeus xi. 464 A:

> *χερσὶν δ' ὄλβον ἔχω κύλικος τρύφος ἀμφὶς ἐαγός,*
> *ἀνδρῶν δαιτυμόνων ναυάγιον, οἷά τε πολλὰ*
> *πνεῦμα Διωνύσοιο πρὸς ὕβριος ἔκβαλεν ἄκτας.*

[6] *Rhetoric* 1415 a and Scholiast *ad. loc.*: *Ἆ μάκαρ, ὅστις ἔην κεῖνον χρόνον ἴδρις ἀοιδῆς, Μουσάων θεράπων, ὅτ' ἀκήρατος ἦν ἔτι λειμών· νῦν δ' ὅτε πάντα δέδασται, ἔχουσι δὲ πείρατα τέχναι, ὕστατοι ὥστε δρόμου καταλειπόμεθα, οὐδέ πηι ἔστι πάντηι παπταίνοντα νεοζυγὲς ἅρμα πελάσσαι.* [M. Parry evidently thought Choerilus the tragic poet and Choerilus the epic poet one and the same.—A. P.]

[7] P. B. Rice, 'A Modern Poet's Technique: Guillaume Apollinaire' in *The Symposium* II, (1931), 470.

But what is true of Choerilus and Antimachus, and of Aristotle's friend Aeschrion who called the new moon 'heaven's fair new letter—*s*',[1] and of modern verse, is not true of Homer.

It is not that metaphors are lacking in Homer, or that when taken by themselves they are not striking enough. The rhetoricians usually took their examples from the *Iliad* and *Odyssey*. Aristotle has the highest praise for Homer's metaphors 'from living to lifeless', such as that in which he says of Sisyphus' punishment, 'back to the bottom rolled the shameless stone', or speaks of spears which, having fallen short, 'stood in the ground, yearning to sate themselves on flesh'.[2] Demetrius dwells at length on 'the ruinous battle quivered with spears',[3] and Byzantine writers are still quoting 'unquenchable laughter', 'shepherd of the people', and 'the seed of fire'.[4] When | thus weighed alone, however, these phrases are not at all what they are in their place in the poems. There the way they are used and their use over and over have given them a sense which is utterly lost when they are torn from the poetry. They are fixed metaphors.

The true fixed metaphor has not existed in English poetry since the days when Anglo-Saxon was spoken. Nevertheless some idea of its nature can be gotten if we consider the use of metaphor in the English Augustan age. This was the one time in English literature when poets used a diction which was at all fixed.[5] Dr. Johnson sets forth its theory thus:

Every language of a learned nation necessarily divides itself into diction scholastick and popular, grave and familiar, elegant and gross; and from a nice distinction of these different parts arises a great part of the beauty of style. But if we except a few minds, the favourites of nature, to whom their own original rectitude was in the place of rules, this delicacy of selection was little known to our authors. . . . There was therefore before the time of Dryden no poetical diction: no system of words at once refined from the grossness of domestick use and free from the harshness of terms appropriated to particular arts. Words too familiar or too remote defeat the purpose of a poet. From those

[1] Tzetzes, *loc. cit.*: *μήνη τὸ καλὸν οὐρανοῦ νέον σίγμα.*

[2] *Rhetoric* 1411 b 31: *καὶ ὡς κέχρηται πολλαχοῦ Ὅμηρος, τὸ τὰ ἄψυχα ἔμψυχα ποιεῖν διὰ τῆς μεταφορᾶς. ἐν πᾶσι δὲ τῶι ἐνέργειαν ποιεῖν εὐδοκιμεῖ, οἷον ἐν τοῖσδε, "αὖτις ἐπὶ δάπεδόνδε κυλίνδετο λᾶας ἀναιδής"* (λ 598) *καὶ "ἔπτατ' οἰστός"* (*N* 587) *καὶ "ἐπίπτεσθαι μενεαίνων"* (*Δ* 126) *καὶ "ἐν γαίηι ἵσταντο λιλαιόμενα χροὸς ἆσαι"* (*Λ* 574) *καὶ "αἰχμὴ δὲ στέρνοιο διέσσυτο μαιμώωσα"* (*O* 542).

[3] *On Style* 82: *ἔνια μέντοι σαφέστερον ἐν ταῖς μεταφοραῖς λέγεται καὶ κυριώτερον ἤ περ ἐν αὐτοῖς τοῖς κυρίοις, ὡς τὸ "ἔφριξεν δὲ μάχη". οὐ γὰρ ἄν τις μεταβαλὼν διὰ κυρίων οὔτ' ἀληθέστερυν εἴποι οὔτε σαφέστερον.*

[4] *ἄσβεστος γέλως* (*A* 599), *ποιμένα λαῶν* (*A* 263), *σπέρμα πυρός* (ε 490), etc. Cf. Cocondrius, 'On Figures of Speech', in Boissonade, *Anecdota Graeca*, III, 291; Tryphon, 'On Figures of Speech', in *ibid.*, p. 273.

[5] Cf. Thomas Quayle, *Poetic Diction: A Study of Eighteenth Century Verse* (London, 1924); R. D. Havens, "Poetic Diction of the English Classicists", in *Kittredge Anniversary Papers* (Boston, 1913), pp. 435–44; Myra Reynolds, *The Treatment of Nature in English Poetry between Pope and Wordsworth* (Chicago, 1909), pp. 1–57.

sounds which we hear on small or on coarse occasions, we do not easily receive strong impressions or delightful images; and words to which we are nearly strangers, whenever they occur, draw that attention on themselves which they should transmit to things.[1]

Such an idea of poetic diction is of course far too small to be true: Johnson has merely put into words his feeling that only a very certain class of words and phrases were 'appropriate' to poetry. There is no need here to question his notion of the proper. The thing to mark is that almost every other writer of the time shared the notion, so that most of the poetry was written in a style which largely used the same words and types of phrases, and very often even the same phrases. The verse form also had no small part in this fixation of the poetic diction, since the close form of the heroic couplet often prompted the | repeated use of certain types of phrases. Pope, in his *Essay on Criticism*, is all without knowing it, his own critic:

> Whene'er you find the 'cooling western breeze',
> In the next line it 'whispers through the trees';
> If crystal streams 'with pleasing murmur creep'
> The reader's threaten'd, not in vain, with 'sleep'.[2]

A certain diction, in short, became the style, and the words and phrases which made it up came to have not only the meaning which they would naturally have, but also the quality of 'propriety', which in time tended to do away with the meaning. Phrases and types of phrases came to be used with less thought for what they said and more for the sake of their correctness.

In this fixed diction the metaphor has a large place. It was one of the most elegant ways of keeping away from the commonplace word, so that certain correct and pleasing metaphors were used until their meaning was quite lost. Shakspere had written of

> The watery kingdom, whose ambitious head
> Spits in the face of heaven—[3]

and one feels in the verses all the violence of Elizabethan thought. Milton likewise had lamented Lycidas

> Sunk though he be beneath the watery floar.[4]

Here, it might seem to the casual reader, the meaning of the metaphor cannot be forced; but Milton had in mind Virgil's lines:

> vastis tremit ictibus aerea puppis
> subtrahiturque solum,[5]

[1] *Lives of the English Poets: Dryden*, ed. G. B. Hill, III, 420.

[2] Ll. 350–53. Cf. G. Saintsbury, *History of English Prosody* (1908), II, 449.

[3] *Merchant of Venice*, Act II, scene vii, l. 44.

[4] L. 167.

[5] *Aeneid* v. 198 f. Milton's commentators usually give *aequor* as the source of the metaphor and find in it the thought of the level sea; but it is not possible that *aequor* ever meant 'floor' to Milton.

and in his close-packed thought the metaphor means that the ship sunk in the very element which ships are built to float on. It is far otherwise with the poets who followed and used this sort of metaphor for the sea. *Aequor* of the Latin poets came over into English verse | as 'plain', which Dryden already used until the word has been emptied of its meaning:

> Ocnus was next, who led his native train
> Of hardy warriors through the watery plain,[1]
>
> . . . .
>
> he skims the liquid plains
> High on his chariot,[2]

and so on. But the metaphor only had all the more charm for Pope, who likewise used it over and over:

> Pikes, the tyrants of the watery plains,[3]

and

> Meanwhile our vessels plough the liquid plain,[4]

and so on. Indeed, the phrases are to be found in almost every poet of the age. Even Falconer, who was a sailor, must speak of the sea in the same fixed way. Of a ship he says:

> Thus like a swan she cleaved the watery plain,
> The pride and wonder of th' Aegaean main,[5]

and of dolphins:

> Awhile beneath the waves their tracks remain,
> And burn in silver streams along the liquid plain.[6]

There is scarce need of giving further examples of the fixed metaphor in English Augustan poetry: Dryden also calls the sea a 'watery desert', 'watery deep', 'watery way', 'watery reign'; Pope has 'wat'ry waste', 'wat'ry way', ''watr'y world', 'watr'y glass'; and Falconer 'watery world', 'watery path'. Two special types of metaphor, however, should be noted which are common at this time, since they are very common in Homer. The first of these is the fixed metaphor which is limited to the single word and is little more than a poetic synonym. Thus in Pope's *Homer*—to take examples from the | work which more than any other set up this fixed diction—a voyage is 'crowned' with success,

[1] *Aeneis*, X, 261 (Virgil's *Aeneid* x. 198). The Latin says merely: 'Ille etiam patriis agmen ciet Ocnus ab oris'.

[2] Dryden, *op. cit.*, I, 223 (Virgil's *Aeneid* i. 147). Here, too, the Latin has nothing of the sort: 'atque rotis summas levibus perlabitur undas.'

[3] *Windsor Forest*, l. 146.

[4] Pope, *Odyssey*, X, 54. The Greek has nothing of the sort:

κ 54 αἱ δ' ἐφέροντο κακῇι ἀνέμοιο θυέλληι
αὖτις ἐπ' Αἰολίην νῆσον.

[5] *Shipwreck*.

[6] *Ibid.*

a cape with a temple, the sky with clouds, and a conquest is simply 'crowned'; men 'burn with rancour', ships 'plough' the sea, Philoctetes is 'taught to wing the dart', oars 'cut th' immeasurable way', Hermes' wand 'seals the wakeful eye', cares are 'lulled', woes 'banished', and so on. Second, there is the fixed metaphor in the epithet. To Pope and Dryden anything white is 'snowy' or 'silver', anything colored 'enamel'd' or 'painted', anything that had a yellow gleam 'golden'.[1]

Many moderns, following the Romantics, still feel the greatest scorn for such a way of writing and for that state of mind which would rather call the sea a 'glass', 'way', 'main', 'desert', 'wave', 'waste', 'foam', 'tide', 'flood', 'deep', or 'billow' than give it its own name.[2] The reaction to the so-called age of classicism brought in the view which is still held that each word a poet uses should be the word of his very own thought and never simply a word that other poets had used. For our own poetry such an opinion is altogether sound, but to condemn the diction of the English Augustan age on the same principle is a sort of criticism which is too simple to be true, for it fails to see that what the words lost in meaning they gained in charm of correctness. We must judge not the device in itself but the state of mind which found pleasure in the device, and, more largely, the society which set up such a state of mind as the most desirable one. The men of that time were agreed that certain words and phrases were more noble than others. We must not then condemn the language of their poetry before we have condemned their entire way of life, since their fixed diction, of which we have taken the fixed metaphor as an example, is a valid and finished sign of their common outlook.

Many times greater, however, in reading Homer is the need of thus understanding that what a diction loses through common use it gains in the kind of charm which suits the times, for the diction of the *Iliad* and *Odyssey*, being altogether traditional, is fixed to a point of which English poetry can give us only a faint notion, and is filled with | phrases emptier of meaning than any in Pope or Falconer. I have written elsewhere about the traditional diction of the Homeric poems, but there is no need here of giving the results of other studies. The metaphor, being typical, will give us knowledge enough of the diction as a whole.

When one has set aside the phrases in which the metaphor is not real, being only the tangible term used for the intangible thing, as in νοῦσον ὦρσε, 'he roused up a plague';[3] λοιγὸν ἀμῦναι, 'to ward off the bane';[4] or a poetic shift of the parts of speech, as in πολύστονα κήδεα, 'unhappy woes';[5] πολυάικος πολέμοιο, 'violent warfare',[6] there are left only

[1] All these examples are taken from Books IV and V of Pope's *Odyssey*.
[2] All in the same two books of *ibid.* [3] *A* 10. [4] *A* 67. [5] *A* 445. [6] *A* 165.

some twenty-five metaphors in the six hundred and eleven lines of the first *Iliad*.[1] This is a small-enough number in itself, but in reality the place of the metaphor is far more limited than the mere number would show, because only two of these metaphors bear on more than the single word. In the other cases it lies either in an epithet or on a word which merely takes the place of the κύριον ὄνομα, the 'regular word', with what force of metaphor we must see.

The 'watr'y way' of English verse doubtless goes back in some way or other to Homer's ὑγρὰ κέλευθα, which is one of the two cases in the first book where the metaphor goes beyond the single word; the loss of meaning in the phrases, however, is of course due in each case to the way it has been used in each of the two languages. Were ὑγρὰ κέλευθα found only once in the Greek epic we might perhaps give the phrase all its force, and the English use would have no bearing on it, but by the time one has read the *Iliad* and *Odyssey* one has met the same phrase four more times, always with ἐπιπλέω, 'sail over', and once indeed the same whole verse of the first *Iliad*:

A 312 = ο 474	οἱ μὲν ἔπειτ' ἀναβάντες ἐπέπλεον ὑγρὰ κέλευθα,
δ 842	μνηστῆρες δ' ἀναβάντες ἐπέπλεον ὑγρὰ κέλευθα,
γ 71 = ι 252	ὦ ξεῖνοι, τίνες ἐστέ; πόθεν πλεῖθ' ὑγρὰ κέλευθα; |

Moreover, one then finds the verse γ 71 = ι 252 without change in the Homeric *Hymn to Apollo*, so that not only does the use over and over of the metaphor wear out its force, but the use with it of other words which are always the same, and which always bring back the phrase with the same rhythm at the same place in the verse, act strongly in making it habitual: Homer's formulaic diction is in this much like the chant of ritual. But if the phrase can thus lose its meaning for us, how much more must it have lost for the Greeks who lived when epic poetry flourished; for we know from Thucydides that the verse was used 'everywhere in the same way by the old poets'.[2] Nor is this all. The reader has likewise found seven times in Homer and once in the *Hymns* ὑγρή, 'wet', used all by itself for the sea; and itself is used as often in its metaphorical as in its real meaning: Homer also calls the sea ἰχθυόεντα κέλευθα, 'the fishy ways';[3] ἠερόεντα κέλευθα, 'the misty ways';[4] and speaks of ἀνέμων λαιψηρὰ κέλευθα, 'the speedy ways of the winds'.[5] By this time the reader would think of the meaning of the metaphor only if he stopped and tried to.

The metaphors which lie in the fixed epithers are of the same sort, and there is no need of going so fully into the background of their

[1] Achilles' insults to Agamemnon—κυνὸς ὄμματ' ἔχων, κραδίην δ' ἐλάφοιο (*A* 225)—are not metaphors, since Achilles means that Agamemnon really has the eyes of a dog and the heart of a deer. Nor is κυνῶπα (*A* 159) metaphorical. Here, as doubtless in the foregoing case, much use has worn down the meaning. The word means only 'shameless', but if it did mean 'dog-faced' there would even so be no transfer of terms.

[2] i. 5. 2. [3] γ 177. [4] υ 64. [5] *Ξ* 17, *O* 620.

thought in the diction. Going on with the metaphors of the first *Iliad*, ἔπεα πτερόεντα, 'winged words',[1] is used by Homer one hundred and twenty-three times; ῥοδοδάκτυλος Ἠώς, 'rosy-fingered dawn',[2] twenty-seven times; Ἀχαιοὶ χαλκοχίτωνες, 'bronze-shirted Achaeans',[3] twenty-four times; ἀργυρόπεζα Θέτις, 'silver-footed Thetis',[4] thirteen times; βοῶπις Ἥρη, 'ox-eyed Hera',[5] eleven times; νῆες ὠκύποροι, 'swift-faring ships',[6] eleven times. θοαὶ νῆες, 'fleet ships',[7] is used four more times in the first book and a hundred times altogether. ἄσβεστος γέλως, 'laughter unquenchable',[8] is found only three times, and the phrase has been much admired in English chiefly because of | the English words, but the phrase could not have had such vividness for Homer, who uses ἄσβεστος, 'unquenchable', over and over for the shouting of men, and also speaks of ἄσβεστον μένος, 'might unquenchable', and ἄσβεστον κλέος, 'fame unquenchable'. Φθίῃ βωτιανείρῃ, 'nourishing Pthia', where the idea of the metaphor is that of men tending beasts at pasture, is not found outside the first book of the *Iliad*, but the same metaphor is found sixteen times in χθὼν πουλυβότειρα, 'the nourishing earth', and in Ἀχαιὶς πουλυβότειρα, 'nourishing Achaea'.

It is clear to anyone reading the *Iliad* and *Odyssey* that these epithets are used by the poet largely for the help they give him in making his verses. Pope, in the verses quoted above, pointed out the same thing in the poetry of his own time, but where the English poets would from time to time pause and pick out an elegant epithet to fill out their couplet, having a large choice of such words and usually making the choice more or less in view of the thought at that point, Homer had usually only one epithet which he used, one might say, without thinking, and he had moreover for any noun that he used at all often a whole set of such epithets, each one made to fulfil a different metrical need. This technique of Homer's epithets can be analyzed into whole systems, as I have shown elsewhere.[9] Here it will be enough to give a few examples from the phrases we have just studied. Homer, to simplify his verse-making, has a system of verses which expresses the idea such and such a person said, answered, asked, and so on, giving also the tone of voice when the poet wishes, or some other detail. One special line of this type which is needed is that in which the character who is to speak has been the subject of the last verses so that the use of his name in the line would be clumsy. The one verse that will do this is καί μιν φωνήσας ἔπεα πτερόεντα προσηύδα, or, when the tone of voice is to be given, καί ῥ' ὀλοφυρόμενος ἔπεα πτερόεντα προσηύδα, and so on. Homer has this one line for this one frequent need,

[1] *A* 201. [2] *A* 477. [3] *A* 371. [4] *A* 538. [5] *A* 568. [6] *A* 421.

[7] *A* 12, 300, 308, 371, 389. This epithet and the foregoing may hardly seem to deserve the name of metaphor, but the Greeks were more sensitive here than we are. Aristotle quotes as an example of metaphor Homer's νηῦς δέ μοι ἥδ' ἕστηκεν, 'Here stands my ship' (α 185; cf. *Poetics* 1457 b 10).

[8] *A* 599.

[9] TE, above.

and its use always brings in ἔπεα πτερόεντα. Likewise, the formulaic line which expresses the idea 'at dawn' always brings in the epithet ῥοδοδάκτυλος. The metrical purpose of the other phrases could likewise be shown. Now the bearing of the practice on | the meaning of the metaphor is clear: a phrase which is used because it is helpful is not being used because of its meaning.

There remain thirteen metaphors from the first *Iliad*: all but one of them bear only on the single word, which is thus no more than a word used in the place of some words which would have more usually been used. Pope's use of the word 'crowned' for 'topped', which was referred to above, was such a word. Here too the word is generally used by Homer alone often enough to wear out even for a modern reader the force of the metaphor. κάρηνα, 'heads', for 'peaks';[1] a ship 'running'—ἔθεεν;[2] a wave 'howling'—ἴαχε;[3] a god, 'standing over' a city—ἀμφιβέβηκας;[4] the 'crowning' of bowls with wine—ἐπεστέψαντο,[5] 'a wall against war'—ἕρκος πολέμοιο;[6] 'clothed in shamelessness'—ἀναιδείην ἐπιειμένε;[7] even the curious and untranslatable ἔχετ' ἐμπεφυυῖα,[8] have all lost their meaning. Χόλον καταπέψηι, 'he shall swallow his wrath';[9] πλοῦτον ἀφύξειν, 'to pour out wealth';[10] δημοβόρος βασιλεύς, 'a ravening king';[11] and θυμὸν ἀμύξεις, 'thou shalt rend thy heart',[12] may, for a while, keep the force of their metaphor because they are not found elsewhere in Homer. But because there is nothing outside the word to show the reader that Homer had the notion of the metaphor in his mind, and because he soon ceases in reading Homer to seek for any active force in such single words, they too finally become for him simply epic words with no more meaning than the usual term would have.

The last metaphor of the first book is that which praises the speech of Nestor: τοῦ καὶ ἀπὸ γλώσσης μέλιτος γλυκίων ῥέεν αὐδή,[13] 'from his tongue flowed voice sweeter than honey'. Here, there can be no doubt, the metaphor was meant to be felt, but even here there is nothing which one could wish to take as the work of Homer's own new thought. First, the metaphor lies only in the words 'sweeter than honey' since 'flow' is used too often elsewhere of speech to carry here | the idea of 'flowing honey'. Then the same idea is found twice in the *Theogony*:

τῶι μὲν ἐπὶ γλώσσηι γλυκερὴν χείουσιν ἐέρσην,
τοῦ δ' ἔπε' ἐκ στόματος ῥεῖ μείλιχα.[14]

ὁ δ' ὄλβιος ὅντινα Μοῦσαι
φίλωνται· γλυκερή οἱ ἀπὸ στόματος ῥέει αὐδή[15]

[1] *A* 44. [2] *A* 483. [3] *A* 482. [4] *A* 37. [5] *A* 470. [6] *A* 284. [7] *A* 149. [8] *A* 513. [9] *A* 81. [10] *A* 171. [11] *A* 231. [12] *A* 243. [13] *A* 249.

[14] Vss. 83–4: '. . . On his tongue they pour sweet dew and honeyed words flow from his mouth.'

[15] Vss. 96–7: 'Happy is the man the Muses love: sweet voice flows from his mouth.'

And finally the same metaphor is used again by Homer, this time, and here, as it happens, the following line shows clearly how little Homer felt its force, unless one should wish to make Homer mix metaphors with all the ruthlessness of an Elizabethan. The metaphor is of anger:

> *ὅς τε πολὺ γλυκίων μέλιτος καταλειβομένοιο*
> *ἀνδρῶν ἐν στήθεσσιν ἀέξεται ἠύτε καπνός.*[1]

So even the one active metaphor of the first *Iliad*—and the rest of Homer is in no way different—fails to do what Aristotle said the metaphor must do—that is, show why Homer was like no other poet.

At least, it fails to do so in the way that Aristotle meant, for really these metaphors that have been emptied of their meaning do show just what the natural talent of Homer was: it was a talent that worked not in the new but in the traditional. A careless reader of the foregoing pages may have thought that each one of the fixed metaphors which had lost its force was so much to be counted against Homer, but the example of fixed diction in English poetry should have shown him that what the words and phrases lost in meaning they had gained in kind of charm which pleased the poet and his hearers. As the fixed diction of the Augustan age can only be understood as the expression of a whole way of life which we may call the proper, so Homer's traditional diction is the work of a way of life which we may call the heroic, if one will give that word all the meaning it had for the men of Homer's time. It is a term which can only be understood in the measure that one can think and feel as they did, for the heroic was to them no more | or less than the statement of all that they would be or would do if they could. To give form to this heroic cast of thought they had the old tales that had come down in time, and they had a rhythm in which to tell them, and words and phrases with which to tell them. The making of this diction was due to countless poets and to many generations who in time had found the heroic word and phrase for every thought, and every word in it was holy and sweet and wondrous,[2] and no one would think of changing it wilfully. The Muses it was truly who gave those poets voices sweeter than honey. And those parts of the diction which did not carry the story itself, since their meaning was not needed for understanding, lost that meaning, but became, as it were, a familiar music of which the mind is pleasantly aware, but which it knows so well that it makes no effort to follow it. Indeed, poetry thus approaches music most closely when the words have rather a mood than a meaning. Nor should one think that since the

[1] Σ 109–10: 'Sweeter than trickling honey it waxes in the breasts of men like smoke.'

[2] As one might say in Greek: *τὸ σεμνὸν καὶ τὸ ἡδὺ καὶ τὸ ξενικὸν οὗ τὸ θαυμάσιον πλεῖστον μετέχει.*

meaning is largely lost it ceases to matter if the meaning is good. Though the meaning be felt rather than understood it is there, as it matters whether music idly heard be bad or good. Of such a kind is the charm of the fixed metaphor in Homer. It is an incantation of the heroic.

Aristotle did not understand this. Between the final vanishing of the old oral poetry and his own time two hundred years or more had already passed, and, thinking of Homer as he thought of the epic poetry of his own age, he failed to see that the metaphor was one thing for Antimachus and another for Homer. Modern critics, on the other hand, whose study was more careful, have found that Homer used the metaphor quite otherwise than Aristotle thought, and we ourselves have seen how utterly right they are, so that we are forced to choose between Aristotle's view of the nature of metaphor, in which case we must condemn Homer as mere copier, and the view that a traditional poet is good not because of the new that he brings into verse but because he knows how to make use of the traditional. If we do this we have found a charm far beyond any which can be found by men who wilfully wish to read Homer as they would any poetry of their own day. Indeed, the Greeks were not the men to carry the | historical method of criticism to any such point. For that there had to come a new world which did not know the old by birthright but which, seeking rules of art for itself in times past reasoned much about that art, and more and more closely. In literary criticism generally this was the growth of the historical spirit. In Homeric criticism it was first the growing scorn for Homer's art in the sixteenth and seventeenth and eighteenth centuries in Italy, France, and England; then the period of Wolf and his followers who, however much they may have failed to grasp the meaning of what they did find, left no doubt that the *Iliad* and *Odyssey* were not such poems as we would ever write, or as Virgil and Dante and Milton wrote; and lastly of our own days in which, through a study of the oral poetries of peoples outside our own civilization, we have grasped the idea of traditional poetry. There is not a verse in Homer that does not become clearer and greater when we have understood that he too was a traditional poet. This way lies all true criticism and liking of his poems.

8

Whole Formulaic Verses in Greek and Southslavic Heroic Song*

οὕτω καὶ τῶν πρόσθεν ἐπευθόμεθα κλέα ἀνδρῶν

In this essay on the method to be used in the comparative study of early poetries the view is set forth that the essential feature of such poetry is its oral form, and not such cultural likenesses as have been called 'popular', 'primitive', 'natural', or 'heroic'. As an example of method those numerous cases are considered where we find both in Homer and in South-slavic heroic song a verse which expresses the same idea. The explanation is as follows. Oral poetry is largely composed out of fixed verses. Especially will ideas which recur with any frequency be expressed by a fixed verse. Thus where the two poetries express the same frequent idea they both tend to do it in just the length of a verse. Knowing this common feature in the oral form of the two poetries we can conclude that the extraordinary hold which heroic poetry has on the thought and conduct of the Southern Slavs provides us with an example of what heroic poetry must have been for the early Greeks.

THE ancient poetries of Europe—Greek, Saxon, Welsh, Irish, Norse, and German—have lately been studied together as common examples of heroic poetry,[1] and certainly no reader can help being struck by the fact that all these poetries have chiefly to do with the prowesses of men of strength and courage, whom the poets believed to have lived in a more or less distant past when human powers were greater, and whom they called by a special term which we translate as 'hero'. It is wrong, however, to go on and suppose that heroic poetry (in this exact sense of the term) is due to any law in the growth of literature. The poetry is heroic only because it is created by people who are living in a certain way and so have a certain outlook on life, and our understanding of the heroic will come only as we learn what that way of living is, and grasp that outlook. | We find, for example, that cattle-lifting is a common theme in the ancient European poetries, but it is found there because of no law of poetry, but because these peoples happened to live in a way which led them to the stealing of cattle on the one hand and to the practice of poetry on the other. It may seem far-fetched to say that any

* First published in *Transactions of The American Philological Association* 64 (1933), 179–97.

[1] H. M. and N. K. Chadwick, *The Growth of Literature: I, The Ancient Literatures of Europe* (Cambridge, 1932).

one has gone so far as to suppose a law of poetry which makes cattle-lifting a common theme at a certain stage in the growth of poetry, and which results in reaving, but still that is implied by those who study the heroic element in early poetry as primarily a literary problem. Its proper study is even more anthropological and historical, and what Doughty tells us about cattle-lifting among the Bedouins[1] is more enlightening, if we are reading Nestor's tale of a cattle raid into Elis,[2] than is the mere knowledge that the theme occurs elsewhere in ancient poetry.

The critics, groping for the rules by which they should group and separate the varied works of the world's literature, have come to see more or less clearly that literature falls into two great parts, but they have not yet agreed upon the real nature of these two parts, nor upon the terms which should be applied to them. 'Heroic' is one of the attempts to find the term for the first part. Others have chosen 'popular', or 'primitive'. 'Natural' was one of the first tries, and was given up largely because of the romantic notions of those who sought to apply it (though it has been revived in a much sounder way in a late study of the psychological processes of poetry).[3] There is surely much truth in each one of these names, but I think that no one of them goes deep enough: in each case there is the failure to see that literature falls into two great parts not so much because there are two kinds of culture, but because there are two kinds of *form*: *the one part of literature is oral, the other written.* Until this is grasped we cannot hope for any sound | method whereby we could use *Beowulf*, for example, for the better understanding of the *Iliad.*

The 'primitive', the 'popular', the 'natural' and the 'heroic', all hang upon a poetry's being oral. This is not only because of the negative reason that the use of writing is the great cultural happening and brings on a new way of life. That does account for the loss of the *primitive* (though that tells us little, since the term means only the lack of the new way of life). It also accounts for the growth of a new form of society in which there is no longer any place for the old heroic ideal. But there is also the positive reason why the oral quality is more basic than the other qualities named: *oral poetry is formulaic and traditional.* The poet who habitually makes his poems without the aid of writing can do so only by putting together old verses and old parts of verses in an old way. Since the verses, and the parts of the verses, and the schemes by which they are put together, are beyond the power of any one man to make, but must be the common creation of a people who all have a right to them, the poetry can well be called *popular*. The Romantic opinion that the poetry in question was more natural than other poetry was, as we can now see with our greater anthropological knowledge, little more than first fancies about the

1 *Arabia Deserta*, index *s.v. ghrazzu.*

2 *Λ* 670 ff.

3 M. Jousse, *Le Style oral rhythmique et mnémotechnique chez les Verbo-moteurs* (Paris, 1925).

thought of uncivilized man. When Jousse, however, after dividing poetry into the oral and the written, explains his reasons for thinking the thought of oral poetry the more spontaneous, he is working on much sounder ground: those phrases and verses are kept from one oral poet to another, and from one generation to another, which are most easily remembered and most easily grouped together. In this sense oral poetry really is more *natural* than written poetry.

Not all oral poetry is *heroic*. The careful use of this term must exclude not only a great part of the lyric poetry which we usually find side by side with an heroic narrative poetry, but also such a popular and traditional narrative poetry as the Finnish, which rather is magical. These reasons alone make | the term unsuitable as the term for one of the two great parts of poetry; but it is my wish, in the following pages, to go further and show how the heroic quality of a poetry also hangs upon its being oral, and I shall follow a method which makes use of more than one poetry that I may show how, by starting from the form, we can surely use one poetry for the understanding of another.

When one hears the Southern Slavs sing their tales he has the overwhelming feeling that, in some way, he is hearing Homer. This is no mere sentimental feeling that comes from his seeing a way of life and a cast of thought which are strange to him, nor from the fact that the man who is singing to the four notes of a horsehair string calls himself a *singer—pjesnik*, as the blind poet of the *Hymn to Apollo* called himself an ἀοιδός, and that he calls his songs *heroic songs—junačke pjesme*. When the hearer looks closely to see why he should seem to be hearing Homer he finds precise reasons: he is ever hearing the same ideas that Homer expresses, and is hearing them expressed in phrases which are rhythmically the same, and which are grouped in the same order. The verse forms, of course, are different. The rhythm is falling in both cases, but the Greek has a verse of six feet which are either dactyls or spondees, while the Southslavic has a verse of five feet which is sung either as a spondaic or trochaic whole. Moreover, the rhythmic break in the Greek verse can fall in several places—after the strong syllable of the third or the fourth foot, or after the second syllable of a third dactylic foot, or after the fourth foot; whereas the Southslavic verse has a single break after the second foot. Yet this difference in the verse form is only a surface difference in the rhythmic likeness of the thought: in both the poetries we find the same idea being stated in just the length of a verse, or in the part of the verse which stretches just from one of the rhythmic breaks to one of the verse ends. I shall deal here chiefly with those cases in which Homer and | the Southslavic singers say what is after all the same thing in just the length of the verse. I might have chosen my Southslavic examples from any part of the large number of printed texts, or even from those which I have collected myself. It seemed better, however, to limit myself to the most famous collection, that which Vuk Stefanov Karajitch made at the beginning of the last century.[1]

VERSES BEGINNING AND ENDING DISCOURSE

Like Homer, the Southslavic singer, save in rare and fixed cases, always states the idea *so and so answered* in just the length of a verse, and in both poetries the verses are made in the same way. The first part is fixed and holds the verb, the second part holds the name of the speaker, which is fitted in with the aid of an epithet. The likeness extends even to the way in which, in the first part of the verse, the pronouns for the two numbers and genders change places. Thus in Homer we have the long series:

τὸν *to him* τὴν *to her* τοὺς *to them* (m.) τὰς *to them* (f.)	δ' αὖτε προσέειπε *again spoke*	πολύτλας δῖος Ὀδυσσεύς (8 times) *much enduring divine Odysseus* θεὰ γλαυκῶπις Ἀθήνη (14 times) *the goddess grey-eyed Athene* μέγας κορυθαίολος Ἕκτωρ (thrice) *great flashing-helmed Hector* ἄναξ ἀνδρῶν Ἀγαμέμνων (5 times) *the king of men Agamemnon* Γερήνιος ἱππότα Νέστωρ (*K* 168) *the Gerenian horseman Nestor*

and so on. Altogether there are in the *Iliad* and *Odyssey* verses of this sort for 28 different characters.[2] Indeed, the only characters who have not such a verse are those who do not appear often enough for there to be the occasion or need for such a verse, or those whose names cannot, even with the | epithet, be fitted into the last half of the verse. I now give the like series in Southslavic poetry:

Veli *Said*	njemu *to him* njojzi *to her* njima *to them*	nahod Simeune (II, 13, 54) *the foundling Simeon* Todore vezire (II, 28, 19) *Theodore the high counselor* Miloš čobanine (II, 28, 158) *Milosh the shepherd* srpski car Stjepane (II, 28, 382) *the Serbian emperor Stephen* Kraljeviću Marko (II, 55, 277) *the king's son Mark*

[1] *Srpske Narodne Pjesme*. Volumes II–IV, which contain the heroic poems which Karajitch himself edited, were first published in 1823 and 1824 at Leipzig and in 1833 at Vienna. There have been a number of later editions. The latest is that printed by the Jugoslavian state at Belgrade, 1932. The references in the text are to the volume, the poem, and the verse.

[2] *Cf.* TE, pp. 12 f., above.

In giving the Greek series I stated the number of times the verse is found in Homer, and mentioned the number of such verses for different characters. There is no point in doing so for the Southslavic system, for here we are not limited as in Greek heroic poetry to a small vestige. It is possible to find in the Serbian texts, and if not in them, in the poetry as it is still sung, as many examples as one wishes of any given verse, and as many different verses of the type as one wishes.[1]

Both poetries have more than one verse for the idea in question. Homer, for example, has another series:

τὸν / *him* / *τὴν* / *her*	*δ' ἠμείβετ' ἔπειτα* / *answered then*	*πολύτλας δῖος 'Οδυσσεύς* (thrice) / *much suffering divine Odysseus* / *ποδάρκης δῖος Ἀχιλλεύς* (twice) / *swift-footed divine Achilles*

and so on for 27 other characters. The Southslavic poets have:

Al' govori / *But spoke*	Boško Jugoviću (II, 44, 58) / *Boshko Yugovitch* / sluga Milutine (II, 44, 154) / *the squire Milutin* |

These different verses are needed to provide variety in the style as the talk passes back and forth, and both Homer and the Southslavic poets have still others of the same form.

But the poets must also have a way of beginning a conversation. This must be done in a much greater variety of ways, since the way in which the statement is made must depend largely upon the way in which the action leads up to the speaking. If both the speaker and the person spoken to are clear in the hearer's mind Homer uses the verse:

καί μιν φωνήσας ἔπεα πτερόεντα προσηύδα (49 times)
And addressing him he spoke winged words

This in Southslavic is:

Pak mu poče tiho govoriti (II, 44, 50)
And quietly she began to speak to him.

The word *quietly* in the one poetry has become as conventional as *winged*

[1] This does not mean to say that the same verses could be found in an identical form in any desired number. While this is true of a great number of the whole formulaic verses in the texts of Karajitch, other such verses have more or less different forms in different regions, and to a less extent, at different times: a study of these differences will furnish us with conclusions which will bear directly on early Greek heroic poetry. In the present pages, however, we are concerned only with the existence of given types of verses, and these are common to the Southslavic poetry as a whole.

in the other. If the speaker is known, but not the person spoken to, we find such a series as:

	ἄρ' Εὔμαιον	
αἶψα δ'	*to Eumaeus*	*ἔπεα πτερόεντα προσηύδα* (twice)
And straightway	*Ἀθηναίην*	*he spoke winged words* (thrice)
	to Athena	

and so on. This is like the Southslavic:

	svoj gospodi srpskoj (ii, 49, iii, 14)
Pa govori	*to his Serbian nobility*
And he spoke	srpskom car Stjepanu (ii, 28, 677)
	to the Serbian emperor Stephen

Or the poet may wish to tell both who speaks and to whom he speaks:

	ἄρ' Ἰδαῖον		*κρείων Ἀγαμέμνων* (*H* 405)
καὶ τότ'	*to Idaeus*	*προσέφη*	*royal Agamemnon*
And then	*Ἀπόλλωνα*	*spoke*	*νεφεληγερέτα Ζεύς* (twice)
	to Apollo		*cloud-gathering Zeus* |

	Simo gospođi kraljici (ii, 13, 143)	
	Simeon to the royal queen	
Reče		ostariloj majci (ii, 55, 79)
Said	Marko	*to his aged mother*
	Mark	Ljutici Bogdanu (ii, 38, 108)
		to Lyutitsa Bogdan

Homer has a type of verse in which he tells the mood of the speaker:

	πόδας ὠκὺς Ἀχιλλεύς (4 times)
τὸν δ' ἄρ' ὑπόδρα ἰδὼν προσέφη	*swift-footed Achilles*
To him, scowling, spoke	*κρατερὸς Διομήδης* (thrice)
	mighty Diomede

Here there is a certain difference. The shortness of the Southslavic verse does not allow it to say so much. The thought of the Homeric verse will be stated simply as

Ražljuti se Miloš Voinovič (ii, 28, 419)
This angered Milosh Voïnovitch

or more fully in two verses:

Ražljuti se Kraljeviću Marko,
Pa govori Novaku kovaču (ii, 66, 152–3)

This angered the king's son Mark,
And he spoke to Novak the smith

But the rhythmic effect of the verses is the same in both languages. The thought still begins and ends with the verse, and the rhythmic pattern of the Homeric verse with its two clauses separated by the verse-break is little different from that of the two clauses separated into two verses.

The verses which begin speech are by far the most common type of verse in the two poetries, but the likeness in the style of discourse goes even further. Homer very often begins the speech itself with a set verse of address:

Ἀτρεΐδη κύδιστε, ἄναξ ἀνδρῶν Ἀγάμεμνον (8 times)
Son of Atreus, most glorious king of men Agamemnon!

Τυδεΐδη Διόμηδες, ἐμῶι κεχαρισμένε θυμῶι (thrice)
Son of Tydeus, Diomede most pleasing to my heart! |

ὦ πάτερ ἡμέτερε Κρονίδη, ὕπατε κρειόντων (4 times)
O our sire, Cronus' son, loftiest of monarchs!

The Southslavic singers follow the same practice:

Car Lazare, srpska kruno zlatna! (II, 44, 4)
Emperor Lazarus, Serbia's crown of gold!

Pobratime, Kraljeviću Marko! (II, 73, 21)
My comrade, Mark the king's son!

O naš babo, stari Jug Bogdane! (II, 31, 122)
O our father, old Yug Bogdan!

Of a like sort is the following type of verse:

κέκλυτέ μευ / *Hear me* {
Τρῶες καὶ Δάρδανοι ἠδ' ἐπίκουροι (4 times)
you Trojans and Dardanians and allies!
πάντες τε θεοὶ πᾶσαί τε θέαιναι (twice)
all you gods and all you goddesses!

Čujete li / *Hear me* {
sva srpska gospodo! (II, 34, 53)
all you Serbian lords!
gospodo latinska (II, 36, 102)
you lords of the Latins!

Finally, the poets in both languages have verses which they use when speech is ended, either to tell the effect of the speech, or what was done right afterwards:

αὐτὰρ ἐπεὶ τό γ' ἄκουσε / *But when this was heard by* {
πολύτλας δῖος 'Οδυσσεύς (θ 446)
much enduring divine Odysseus
Ποσειδάων ἐνοσίχθων (twice)
Poseidon the earth-shaker

Kad to začu / *When this was heard by* {
Pecirep Lazare (IV, 7, 300)
Lazarus Petsirep
bego Zotovića (IV, 22, 29)
beg Zotovitcha

ὣς ἔφατ' εὐχόμενος, τοῦ δ' ἔκλυε Φοῖβος Ἀπόλλων (thrice)
So he spoke in prayer, and he was heard by Phoebus Apollo

Boga mole, i umoliće ga (IV, 8, 163)
They prayed to god, and won their prayer

ἦ ῥα, καὶ ἀμπεπαλὼν προίει δολιχόσκιον ἔγχος (9 times)
He spoke, and brandished and hurled his long-shadowing spear |

To mu reče, bojno koplje pušti (II, 43, 617)
So he spoke to him, and hurled his battle spear

ὣς ἄρα μιν εἰπόντα τέλος θανάτοιο κάλυψεν (twice)
So he spoke, and the end of death came over him

To izusti, laku dušu pusti (II, 32, 64)
So he spoke, and gave up the lightsome soul

As a last example of the verses used in discourse I would call attention to a certain formal manner of putting and answering questions:

ἀλλ' ἄγε μοι τόδε εἰπὲ καὶ ἀτρεκέως κατάλεξον (α 169+16 times)
But come, tell me this, and relate it to me truly
. . . .
τοιγὰρ ἐγώ τοι ταῦτα μάλ' ἀτρεκέως ἀγορεύσω (α 179+3 times)
Indeed I shall relate this to you truly

Što te pitam, pravo da mi kažeš (II, 31, 8)
What I ask you, truly do you tell me
. . . .
Kad me pitaš, pravo da ti kažem (II, 31, 23)
When you ask me, truly I must tell you

VERSES TELLING OF THE MOVEMENT OF TIME

After the verses beginning and ending speech the like verses in the two poetries which are most noticeable are those which mark the progression of time. Most frequent of all is the following:

ἦμος δ' ἠριγένεια φάνη ῥοδοδάκτυλος 'Ηώς (21 times)
When appeared the early-born rosy-fingered dawn

Kad u jutru jutro osvanulo (II, 5, 54)
When on the morn the morning dawned

Each verse in Homer which tells the time of day could be paralleled from the Southslavic. I quote only the following:

δύσετό τ' ἠέλιος, σκιόωντό τε πᾶσαι ἀγυιαί (7 times)
And the sun set, and all the ways grew dark

Danak prođe, tavna noćca dođe (II, 42, 138)
The day passed, the somber night came on |

ἦμος δ' ἠέλιος κατέδυ καὶ ἐπὶ κνέφας ἦλθε (7 times)
But when the sun had set, and darkness had come on

A kada je tavna noćca došla (II, 28, 51)
But when the somber night had come

Whole fixed verses likewise mark the passage of the years:

ἀλλ' ὅτε τέτρατον ἦλθεν ἔτος καὶ ἐπήλυθον ὧραι (thrice)
But when the fourth year had come, and the seasons had come on

Kad nastala godina četvrta (II, 25, 13)
When the fourth year had set in

VERSES TELLING OF THE MOVEMENT OF THE CHARACTERS

A third notable group of like verses in the two poetries is that in which the poet moves his characters about the scene of his story:

αὐτὰρ ἐπεί ῥ' ἵκοντο δόμους εὖ ναιετάοντας (thrice)
But when they had come to the pleasant palace

Kad su bili pred bijele dvore (II, 33, 86)
When they had come before the white palace

αἶψα δ' ἔπειθ' ἵκοντο Πύλου αἰπὺ πτολίεθρον (ο 193)
Quickly then they came to the sheer city of Pylos

Kada dođe bijelu Prizrenu (II, 28, 66)
When he had come to white Prizren

ἀγχίμολον δέ οἱ ἦλθε Βοηθοΐδης Ἐτεωνεύς (ο 95)
And there drew near to him Boethus' son Eteoneus

Dolazi mu otac igumane (II, 13, 49)
There drew near to him the reverend abbot

ὄρνυτ' ἄρ' ἐξ εὐνῆφι Γερήνιος ἱππότα Νέστωρ (γ 405)
Rose from his bed the Gerenian horseman Nestor

Uranio starac kaluđere (II, 13, 1)
Rose up an aged monk

VARIOUS OTHER LIKE VERSES AND GROUPS OF VERSES

It would be possible to draw up a very long list indeed of the various other like verses in Homer and Southslavic heroic poetry. They are of all kinds: |

δῆσε δ' ὀπίσσω χεῖρας ἐυτμήτοισιν ἱμᾶσι (Φ 30)
He bound his hands in back with well-cut thongs

Svezaše mu ruke naopako (III, 21, 113)
They bound his hands behind him

αὐτοκασιγνήτη ὀλοόφρονος Αἰήταο (κ 137)
The very sister of the baleful-hearted Aeetes

Mila seka Frpce Ibrahima (III, 26, 38)
The dear sister of Ibrahim Ferptsa

σπασσάμενος τανύηκες ἄορ παχέος παρὰ μηροῦ (3 times)
Drawing his sharp-edged sword from beside his stout thigh

On poteže sablju od bedrice (II, 24, 164)
He drew his sword from beside his thigh

ᾤμωξεν δ' ἄρ' ἔπειτα καὶ ὢ πεπλήγετο μηρώ (3 times)
He groaned then, and smote his thighs

Udari se rukom po koljenu (III, 24, 40)
He smote his hand upon his knee

When, as happens in many cases, the action of the poetry is alike even in its details, we may find whole groups of like verses:

Kad se pobre nakitile vina
Onda reče Tanković Osmane (III, 24, 5 f.)
When the comrades had sated themselves with wine
Then spoke Osman Tankovitch

αὐτὰρ ἐπεὶ πόσιος καὶ ἐδητύος ἐξ ἔρον ἕντο,
τοῖς ἄρα μύθων ἦρχε Γερήνιος ἱππότα Νέστωρ (γ 67 f.)
But when they had sent from them desire for drink and food
Then began to speak the Gerenian horseman Nestor

Pa pripasa sablju okovanu,
I prigrnu ćurak od kurjaka,
A na glavu kapu od kurjaka,
. . . .
Pa uzimlje koplje ubojito (II, 41, 75–7, 79)
And he belted on his sharp sword,
And put on a coat of wolfskin,
And on his head a cap of wolfskin,
. . . .
And he grasped a spear of battle |

ἀμφὶ δ' ἄρ' ὤμοισιν βάλετο ξίφος ἀργυρόηλον, (4 times)
ἕσσατο δ' ἔκτοσθεν ῥινὸν πολιοῖο λύκοιο, (*K* 334)
κρατὶ δ' ἐπ ἰφθίμωι κυνέην εὔτυκτον ἔθηκεν (4 times)
εἵλετο δ' ἄλκιμον ἔγχος ἀκαχμένον ὀξέι χαλκῶι (4 times)
About his shoulders he slung his silver-studded sword,
And he put on over all the hide of a grey wolf,
And on his mighty head he set a well-made helm,
And took a strong spear pointed with sharp bronze

Njim dolazi Blažena Marija,
Roni suze niz bijelo lice.
Nju mi pita gromovnik Ilija:
'Sestro naša, Blažena Marija!
Kakva ti je golema nevolja,
Te ti roniš suze od obraza?'
Al govori Blažena Marija:
'A moj brate, gromovnik Ilija!
Kada neću suze proljevati?' (II, I, 10–17)

Unto them drew nigh blessed Mary,
Weeping tears down her white face.
Her questioned the thunderer Elijah:
'Our sister, blessed Mary!
What is your great sorrow
That you weep tears adown your cheeks?'
Answered him blessed Mary:
'O my brother, thunderer Elijah!
How may I not pour forth my tears'?

Πάτροκλος δ' Ἀχιλῆι παρίστατο ποιμένι λαῶν
δάκρυα θερμὰ χέων ὥς τε κρήνη μελάνυδρος
. . . .
τὸν δὲ ἰδὼν ᾤκτιρε ποδάρκης δῖος Ἀχιλλεύς
καί μιν φωνήσας ἔπεα πτερόεντα προσηύδα·
"*τίπτε δεδάκρυσαι, Πατρόκλεες, ἠύτε κούρη*
. . .;"
τὸν δὲ βαρὺ στενάχων προσέφης, Πατρόκλεες ἱππεῦ·
"*ὦ Ἀχιλεῦ Πηλῆος υἱέ, μέγα φέρτατ' Ἀχαιῶν,*
μὴ νεμέσα· τοῖον γὰρ ἄχος βεβίηκεν Ἀχαιούς" (*Π* 2 f., 5–7, 20–2)

But Patroclus stood beside Achilles the shepherd of the people,
Pouring forth warm tears like a spring of dark water
. . . . |
And when he saw him, swift-footed Achilles pitied him,
And spoke and addressed him winged words:
'Why are you in tears, Patroclus, like a girl
. . . .?'
With a groan you spoke to him, horseman Patroclus:
'O Achilles, Peleus' son, far the mightiest of the Achaeans!
Be not angry: such grief has come upon the Achaeans'

Finally, there are the many cases in which the thought which Homer expresses in one line will be expressed by the Southslavic singers in two full lines:

τίς πόθεν εἰς ἀνδρῶν; πόθι τοι πόλις ἠδὲ τοκῆες; (*α* 170)
Who are you, and whence? Where is your city and where your parents?

Otkle li si, od koje l'krajine?
Kako l' tebe po imenu viču (III, 21, 73 f.)
Whence come you, from what land?
What is the name by which they call you?[1]

In other cases there will be some small difference in the essential meaning of the verses:

Posadi ga u stolove zlatne,
Ugosti ga vinom i rakijom
I gospodskom svakom đakonijem (II, 24, 267–269)
She placed him at the golden tables,
Guested him with wine and brandy
And all manner of lordly delicacies

εἷσε δέ μ' εἰσαγαγοῦσα ἐπὶ θρόνου ἀργυροήλου
. . . .
σῖτον δ' αἰδοίη ταμίη παρέθηκε φέρουσα,
εἴδατα πόλλ' ἐπιθεῖσα χαριζομένη παρεόντων (κ 366, 371 f.) |

And she led me and sat me down upon a silver-studded seat
. . . .
And a grave housekeeper set food before me,
Giving me many dishes generously from her store

In such cases as these, though the number of verses is not the same, or the thought is somewhat different because of differences of idiom in the two languages or because of differences in customs, the hearer still has the feeling of a like rhythmic mould of the thought, and we find at work the same forces which tend to make the whole verse the dominating unit of the poetic style.

This rhythmic likeness of the thought of the two poetries also is found, though to a somewhat less striking degree, when the different lengths of verse have made it necessary for the Southslavic singers to use two verses where Homer uses one, or when Homer uses only a half-verse where the

[1] One of my own texts, dictated by Perkachin Shtyepan of Stolats in Hertsegovina, contains an even fuller expression of this thought:

Odaklen si, od koga si grada?
Cijega si roda i plemena?
Kako li se po imenom vičeš?
Whence come you, from what city?
Of what family and race are you?
What is the name by which you call yourself?

These verses contain not only the thought of α 170, but also of θ 550:

εἴπ' ὄνομ' ὅττι σε κεῖθι κάλεον μήτηρ τε πατήρ τε

Southslavic poets have a whole verse. An example of the first kind is this:

> Vidosava, moja vjerna ljubo!
> Ja sam noćas čudan san usnio (II, 24, 137–138)
> *Vidosava, my true wife,*
> *In the night I dreamed a wondrous dream.*

> κλῦτε, φίλοι· θεῖός μοι ἐνύπνιον ἦλθεν ὄνειρος (twice)
> *Hear me, friends! In my sleep there came a wondrous dream.*

In such a case as this, where the thought begins and ends with a verse, though not the same verse in the Southslavic poetry, the verse is still felt as the unit. In cases of the second kind, however, it is a part of the verse which corresponds with the whole verse:

> Ono reče, na noge ustade (II, 2, 19)
> *So he spoke, and rose to his feet*

> ὣς εἰπὼν ἀνόρουσε, [τίθει δ' ἄρα οἱ πυρὸς ἐγγύς] (ξ 518)
> *So he spoke, and leaped up* [*and set up for him near the fire*]

> A on ode uz bijelu kulu (II, 13, 103)
> *But he went through the white palace* |

> βῆ δ' ἴμεναι διὰ δώμαθ' [ἵν' ἀγγείλειε τοκεῦσι] (ζ 50)
> *And she went through the palace* [*that she might tell her parents*]

Even in such cases as these, however, the verse break in the hexameter is strong enough to keep much of the rhythmic likeness.

As a matter of fact, instances of these two sorts are not nearly as common as one might expect from the difference in the length of the Southslavic and the Homeric verse, because the Greek singers, instead of adding to the thought of a verse, tend to fill it out instead with ornamentation. The greater number of examples quoted from above will show this tendency of the Southslavic to simpleness, of the Homeric to fullness of style. Thus we find the tendency of the two poetries to express the same idea in the like rhythmic form of the whole verse so strong as even to counteract differences of idiom and verse form. The differences of thought, of course, are much stronger: as many as are the points of likeness between these two heroic ages, the differences of customs, religion, warfare, private, social, and political life are more frequent, if not more profound, and such differences make it useless to look in the one poetry for most of the verses of the other. But wherever that thought is the same we find it tending to be expressed in the like form of the whole verse which is also a whole sentence.

There is nothing strange in this common tendency of the two poetries. Indeed, to the person who has actually seen the practice of a living oral poetry it seems the most natural of things: the easiest formula for the oral poet to handle is that which is both a whole sentence and a whole verse. This is the only formula which is complete in itself both in rhythm and thought. It is only formulas of this kind which can be joined on to one another, and be joined together in any number to make a shorter or longer passage. Formulas of other kinds | can fill only a given part of the verse, and they must be preceded and followed by formulas which are different in rhythm and which contain other parts of the sentence. Thus the art of the oral poet is largely that of grouping together whole fixed verses. These fixed verses themselves are, of course, no work of the single singer, but the gradual work of time and of countless singers ever seeking to cast their thought into the easiest mould. When any one of them hits upon the formula which is poetically good, and which expresses an idea which other singers would wish to use, and expresses it in a form which is easy to use, that formula is kept, and becomes a part of the tradition. In the measure that the idea to be expressed is a common one in the poetry, so is there need for the formula which is easily handled, and since the sentence-verse is most easily handled, the most common ideas will be cast into this form. Also the thought of the poetry will be largely shaped in this process: it is only when the thought of a verse is of the simplest sort that it can be used over and over for different stories and different situations. Thus the singers of an oral poetry ever seek and keep for the common ideas of their poetry the whole verses which give the simple statement of those ideas. Now to a very great degree the common ideas of Southslavic heroic poetry are the same as those of early Greek heroic poetry: it therefore follows that both poetries will often express the same idea in just the length of a verse.[1]

The diction of Southslavic heroic poetry we know to be oral and traditional. The diction of Greek heroic poetry, which has those features which in the Southslavic poetry are due to that traditional and oral nature, such as the feature of whole formulaic verses which we have looked at in these pages, must therefore also be oral and traditional. But we need not stop here at the form: understanding it we can go on to see | the hold which heroic poetry, by its *oral and traditional* forms, has on the life of men of an heroic age.

In the summer of 1933 I met in Gatsko, in Hertsegovina, Mitcho Savitch, a man then eighty-two years old. He had never learned to write. He dictated to me a number of poems which told of the uprising against the Turks in 1876, in which he took part, and he also dictated to me the story of his life. It began: 'I was twenty-two years old when I took part

[1] Cf. DE, above.

in my first battle at Ravno above Gatsko. . . .' The account goes on in a prose which keeps falling into verse, thus: 'My fourth battle was in the Valley of the Wolves. Two pashas attacked King Nicholas, the Montenegrins and us men of Hertsegovina, in the Valley of the Wolves. King Nicholas met them heroically. There were three pashas, by God:

> Dvije paše bismo i ubismo,
> A Selima živa ufatismo.
> *Two pashas we fought and overcame,*
> *And Selim we took alive.*'[1]

The first of these two verses is a very common one in all the poetry. It is used very often, for example, in the poems which tell of the battle of Kosovo in 1389, about which has been built one of the greatest cycles of Southslavic poetry. Thus in the poem which tells of how Musitch Stephan went to that battle we have the verse (II, 46, 162):

> Tri je paše bio i ubio
> *Three pashas he fought and overcame*

The verse appears in Vuk's volumes in the poems of different singers, and from different regions. It must have been a very | old verse in his day. A hundred years later it is still the form in which an old man casts the thought of his own life. It is no verse that he has made, but has come down to him from the past. For the people as a whole who created the verse and kept it, it is an ideal; for this man it has become a boast. And as we can see in the case of this one verse, so the whole body of traditional poetry from the past brought with it the ideal of life as a whole for these men of Gatsko who have ever been renowned for their singing. So in the Greek heroic age did they sing the κλέα ἀνδρῶν—*the high deeds of men.*

[1] Bilo mi je 22 godine kad sam prvi put bio u boju na Ravnom više Gacka. . . . E četvrta bitka na Vučji dol. Udariše na Kralja Nikolu dvije paše, na Crnogorce i na nas isto Ercegovce, na Vučjem dolu. Kralj Nikola junački dočeka. Tri su Bogami paše bile.

9

The Traces of the Digamma in Ionic and Lesbian Greek*

RICHARD BENTLEY has won only blame for wishing to change α 29 from μνήσατο γὰρ κατὰ θυμὸν ἀμύμονος Αἰγίσθοιο to μνήσατο γὰρ κατὰ νοῦν ἀνοήμονος Αἰγίσθοιο;[1] whereas his plan of writing the digamma into the Homeric text[2] is still cited as one of his claims to fame. Yet in both cases he did much the same thing: he was unable to see why the traditional text was as it was, he was unwilling to grant a simple lack of understanding on his own part, and so he changed the text. Had he known Homer better, however, or known more about other early poetries, he would have seen that the unreasoned use of the fixed epithet is so common that we must explain it, not try to do away with it. First, the analysis of Homer's diction might have shown him that the poet had, to help him in his verse-making, many fixed phrases in which there was an epithet, and that he used these phrases so often that he forgot to think about the meaning of the epithets in them.[3] Or second, the study of oral poetries might have shown him that the use of the fixed epithet is common there, and this would have led him on to the cause of metrical usefulness.[4] It is the same for the digamma. Had Bentley, or any of all those scholars who have corrected Homer or printed the digamma in their editions been willing to grant that there might be some force acting on the Homeric language which they did not see, they would not have fought so fiercely against the stubborn text. But they had | seen a part of the truth, and they were beguiled by the complexity of what they had seen. Yet a fuller knowledge of Homer's poetry and of oral poetry shows

* First published in *Language* 10 (1934), 130–44. Reprinted by permission of the Linguistic Society of America.

1 Cf. R. C. Jebb, *Bentley*, 149–154 (London, 1882).

2 Cf. J. W. Donaldson, *The New Cratylus*³, 219–25 (London, 1849).

3 Cf. TE, pp. 118–72 above.

4 E.g. *rusa*, 'blond', in Southslavic heroic poetry as an epithet of the head. In one of the Bulgarian poems (36, v. 45 in A. Dozon, *Chansons populaires bulgares inédites*, Paris, 1875) a 'black negro', as he has constantly been called, is killed. The words of the singer are *Otseče mu nemu rusa glava*, 'he cut off his blond head'. The verse is one which occurs often both in the Serbo-Croatian texts of Karadžić (1823–1833), and in those which I myself collected in Hertzegovina in 1933. In the same way the 'hyacinthine' locks which Athene had given Odysseus (ζ 231, cf. ψ 158), are later called 'blond' (ν 399, 431).

us why Homer's language has traces of the digamma, but not the digamma itself.

The poet who has no writing materials to aid him can make his poetry only out of fixed phrases, verses, and passages which have come down to him from the past, and which are the gradual work of generations of countless poets.[1] The phrase which will easily fall into the mould of the verse in the right place to make the sentence is a hard thing to create, as is the verse which forcefully expresses a given idea in just its length. One poet might make a few such phrases and verses, but he could not make many, let alone the vast system of them needed for free composition. Really he does not even think of making them. He has learned the poetic diction by hearing many poems which had been composed out of it, and his art lies in putting that diction to its best and fullest use, not in changing it or adding to it.

He does, however, without thinking, change it in one way. If phrases in the diction have come from the people of another dialect, or if they have come down from a time when the spoken language was different, he will tend to change the language of such phrases to suit his own spoken language. He will usually make such changes only if he can do so without damaging the rhythm, but he may even do so if the damage is only slight. Beowulf, for example, has such forms as *frēa*, *gān*, *doð*, where the meter calls for an older or Anglian dissyllabic form.[2] Old Norse poetry has such verses as *en at virði rekaz* (*Hávamál* 32), *þess mun Viðarr reka* (*Vafþrúðismál* 53) which depart from the rule of alliteration through the loss of the older forms *vrekaz* and *vreka*.[3] Krohn has pointed out such cases in Finnish poetry as that in which the singers of Savolax have turned the Tavastland form *orasta* into *oraasta*, though the resulting | verse has one too many syllables.[4] In the same way he gives the metrical irregularity as one of the chief means of finding the older verses in Esthonian poetry.[5] The editors of Beowulf and of the Norse poetry have in many cases followed the same reasoning as Bentley, and changed the text; but the mere fact that we find this same thing in a number of early poetries so far removed from one another, and that the thing is unknown in the manuscript

[1] Cf. HS, pp. 269–79, 301–24 above; HL, pp. 329–42 above.

[2] Cf. *Beowulf* ed. A. J. Wyatt and R. W. Chambers xxiii (Cambridge, 1925); Eduard Sievers, *Altgermanische Metrik*, 122 f. (Halle, 1893). On the language of Beowulf as a poetic language cf. O. Jespersen, *Growth and Structure of the English Language*, 55 f. (Leipzig, 1905); H. Collitz, *The Home of the Heliand*, in Publications of the Modern Language Association 16. 123–40 (1902).

[3] This parallel was first pointed out by O. W. Knös, *De digammo Homerico*, 9–10 (Upsala, 1872); cf. also S. H. Grundtvig, *Om nordens gamle literatur*, 71 (Copenhagen, 1867); *Er nordens gamle literatur*, 69–73 (Copenhagen, 1869).

[4] Cf. K. Krohn, *Kalevalastudien*, in Folklore Fellows Communications 16.44 (1924).

[5] Ibid. 56–7.

tradition of any poet for whom we can be sure that writing was the normal means of composition, shows that we have here a true feature of oral poetry, and no scribe's changes. Moreover the Finnish and Esthonian poetry show that the faults really do occur.

Similarly the digamma was lost in the diction of early Greek heroic poetry neither sooner nor later than it was lost in the daily speech, but the singers who had to compose in a rigorous and therefore highly conservative verse-form, still used the old phrases and verses because that was their way of making poetry, because to have given up the traditional phrase wherever the loss of the digamma now caused hiatus or failure to make position, would have been to destroy the diction almost entirely.

The traces of the lost digamma were not maintained simply by the regular failure to avoid hiatus or to make position within certain often used phrases, such as the following which show by the number of the times which they occur in the short space of the *Iliad* and *Odyssey* the fixed and helpful place which they had in the diction: ὧδε δέ τις (ϝ)εἴπεσκεν (24 times), ἄνδρα '(ϝ)έκαστον or ἀνδρὶ '(ϝ)εκάστωι (12 times), εἵματα '(ϝ)έσσε or '(ϝ)έστο, etc. (17 times), ὅπως ἔσται τάδε (ϝ)ἔργα (7 times), πολεμήια (ϝ)ἔργα (7 times), σμερδαλέα (σϝ)ἰάχων (8 times), βόας καὶ (ϝ)ἴφια μῆλα (10 times), ὧι ἐνὶ (ϝ)οἴκωι (11 times), αἴθοπα (ϝ)οἶνον (16 times), μελιηδέα (ϝ)οἶνον (5 times), ἐπὶ (ϝ)οἴνοπα πόντον (8 times), and so on. It is not enough merely to point out how many phrases, often used, have kept the trace of the digamma, nor even to show how many different repeated phrases a single word of the sort can occur in, such as (ϝ)ἰδεῖν: θαῦμα (ϝ)ἰδέσθαι (8 times), ὑπόδρα (ϝ)ἰδών (23 times), ἐπεὶ (ϝ)ἴδεν ὀφθάλμοισιν (6 times), τὸν δέ (ϝ)ἴδε or (ϝ)ἰδών, etc. (20 times), οἱ δὲ (ϝ)ἰδόντες (6 times), ὄφρα (ϝ)ἴδηι or (ϝ)ἴδηαι, etc. (17 times), ἄντα (ϝ)ἰδών (7 times), ἐσάντα or εἰσάντα (ϝ)ἰδών (7 times), and so on. To understand fully why the traces of the digamma are so firmly fixed in the epic | diction we must understand the technique of formulaic verse-making. In this way alone can we grasp the nature of the fixed phrases which have just been quoted.

The easiest unit of diction for the poet to handle is the sentence which fills just a verse. Such a formula is complete in itself both in meaning and rhythm; it carries the poem on from the end of one verse, where most formulaic phrases or groups of phrases end, to the beginning of another verse, where they mostly begin; and it is the one kind of formula which can be followed by another of the same kind.[1] The technique of all oral poetries is more or less simply that of grouping together whole formulaic verses. The traces of the digamma are found in a large number of formulaic Homeric verses:

ἀλλ' ἄγε μοι τόδε (ϝ)εἰπὲ καὶ ἀτρεκέως κατάλεξον (17 times)
οἱ μὲν κακκείοντες ἔβαν (ϝ)οἶκονδε '(ϝ)έκαστος (4 times)

[1] Cf. WF, above.

ἀλλ' ἄγε δεῦρο, πέπον, παρ' ἔμ' ἵστασο καὶ (ϝ)ἴδε (ϝ)ἔργον, (*P* 179 χ 233)
Ἀτρείδη κύδιστε, (ϝ)ἄναξ ἀνδρῶν Ἀγάμεμνον (8 times)

and so on.[1]

The next easiest formulas to handle are those which fall into the verse between one of the rhythmic breaks and one of the verse-ends, such, for example, as the noun–epithet formulas which just fill the last half of the verse and supply a grammatical subject for any predicate which just fills the first half of the verse:[2]

τὸν δ' ἠμείβετ' ἔπειτα	} (ϝ)ἄναξ ἀνδρῶν Ἀγαμέμνων	(thrice)
ῥίγησεν δ' ἄρ' ἔπειτα		(twice)
ὤρνυτο δ' αὐτίκ' ἔπειτα		(*Γ* 267)
λῦσε δέ '(ϝ)οι θώρηκα (ϝ)ἄναξ Διὸς υἱὸς Ἀπόλλων		(*Π* 804)
καί νύ κεν ἔνθ' ἀπόλοιτο (ϝ)ἄναξ ἀνδρῶν Αἰνείας		(*E* 311)

This formulaic device of the predicate-subject verse divided at the trochaic caesura of the third foot regularly supposes that the predicate will end with a short vowel, as for example, τὸν δ' ἠμείβετ' ἔπειτα, which is used in 62 verses of this type, or ὣς φάτο, μείδησεν δὲ, which | is used in 10 verses of this type. The device also supposes that the subject phrase will begin with a simple consonant, as in πολύτλας δῖος 'Οδυσσεύς (38 times), or θεὰ γλαυκῶπις Ἀθήνη (51 times).[3] *ϝάναξ ἀνδρῶν Ἀγαμέμνων served at one time in this way without fault until the digamma was lost, when the poets were faced with three choices: (1) to find a new subject formula, (2) to give up this type of verse for Agamemnon, (3) to use the verse in spite of the hiatus. An epithet of the metrical value of *ϝάναξ ἀνδρῶν could not have been an easy thing to find; in any case there is no epithet of this sort in Homer.[4] If the poet were to give up the type of verse he would find himself greatly hampered whenever he was telling about Agamemnon, and forced to avoid the phrases which he regularly used for his other characters; indeed it is doubtful if he had other phrases which he could have used instead. Therefore he simply followed the age-long habit of the diction and committed a fault, which was scarcely a fault, since he and his hearers had been used to it from their earliest days.

In the complex play of the formulaic technique the device is not always as simple as that of the predicate-subject verse. The oblique cases of (ϝ)ἄναξ, for example, came down from the older poetry as

[1] Cf. the number of whole verses showing trace of the digamma which are to be found in H. Dunbar's list of the verses found in both the *Iliad* and *Odyssey* (*Concordance to the Odyssey and Hymns of Homer*, 393–419 (Oxford, 1880)).

[2] Cf. FM, pp. 192, 202–21 above, on the fallacy of distinguishing between 'legitimate' and 'illegitimate' hiatus.

[3] On the Homeric formulas for the predicate-subject verse cf. TE, pp. 10–16, 38–55 above, and Table I.

[4] TE, Table III, p. 90, metre XIV.

the word which could be used to finish the verse after a proper name ending in a vowel and in the rhythm: . . . ⏕ – ⏕:

. . . . *Πριάμοιο*	(ϝ)*ἄνακτος*	(8 times)
. . . . *Ἑλένοιο*		(3 times)
. . . . *Ἡφαίστοιο*		(twice)

and so on for nine other different names;[1]

. . . . *Διὶ Κρονίωνι*	(ϝ)*ἄνακτι*	(4 times)
. . . . *Ποσειδάωνι*		(9 times)

and so on. These genitive and dative phrases in turn have their fixed uses. Thus, for example, they allow the poet to make a subject phrase with *βίη* where the metrical value of a name does not allow the poet to use the nominative of the name with an epithet:

ὣς ἔφατ'· ὦρτο δ' ἔπειτα	*μέγας Τελαμώνιος Αἴας*	(twice)
	βίη Τεύκροιο (ϝ)*ἄνακτος*	(*Ψ* 859)[2] |

The two dative phrases quoted, on the other hand, are used chiefly in a type of verse which expresses the essential idea of praying or sacrificing to a god:

ὣς ἔφαθ'· οἱ δ'	*εὔχοντο*	*Διὶ Κρονίωνι*	(ϝ)*ἄνακτι*	(*H* 200)
ὣς οἱ μέν ῥ'		*Ποσειδάωνι*		(*ν* 185)[3]

Least of all should we think that the smaller words are freer from the traditional fixity of the diction than the longer words. If anything, it is the other way. The vast number of fixed phrases in Homer in which we find *δέ* ʽ(ϝ)*οι*, *ὄφρα* ʽ(ϝ)*οι*, *γάρ* ʽ(ϝ)*οι*, *πέρ* ʽ(ϝ)*οι*, *ἄρα* ʽ(ϝ)*οι*, and so on, show that the traces of the digamma are probably more firmly fixed in this word than in any other. There are not only the many longer formulas, such as

ἐν δ' ἄρα ʽ(ϝ)*οι φῦ χειρὶ* (ϝ)*ἔπος τ' ἔφατ' ἐκ τ' ὀνόμαζε* (10 times)

There are also the many simpler series, such as the following, which gives the poet a complete sentence to finish his verse after the verse-break of the third foot:

νεκρὸς	*δέ* ʽ(ϝ)*οι ἔκπεσε χειρός*	(*Δ* 493)
τόξον		(twice)
δαλὸς		(*O* 421)
σκῆπτρον		(*ξ* 31)
σκῦτος		(*ξ* 34)
δέπας		(*χ* 17).

[1] Cf. TE, p. 86 above.
[2] Cf. *H* 194, *γ* 43, 54, *ι* 412, *λ* 130, *ψ* 277.
[3] Cf. *N* 758, 770, 781; *Ψ* 836, *ξ* 499; *Θ* 409, *Ω* 77, 159.

When one multiplies this one series of formulas by all the others in which ʽ(ϝ)οι seemingly causes hiatus, or seemingly fails to make position, we can see how firm a hold the older use of the word has upon the diction.

The few examples which have been analyzed in the foregoing paragraphs differ in no way from any of the other phrases in the Homeric poems where the writing in of the digamma would make the rhythm more regular. When the phrase is often used, or is of a type which is often used, we can most easily see the part which it plays in the formulaic technique; but even a phrase which Homer uses only once, and which has no close counterpart elsewhere in the diction, is also to be taken as traditional. Either the phrase as a whole is traditional, and it is only the scantiness of the remains of Greek heroic poetry which does not allow | us to show its place in the formulaic diction;[1] or it is a later creation by analogy,[2] which is much the same thing. It is probable that in some cases a poet who himself did not know the digamma made a new phrase in which he used a word as though it still had the sound; this means merely that he is following the traditional use of the word, though he is not using one of the older phrases which maintained that use. Cases, however, in which any one poet, such as the poet of the *Iliad*, would use one of the words we are considering in a new phrase, are so few as to be negligible: with the oral poet the making of the new phrase is very rare, and almost always due to the chance play of traditional phrases.[3]

We find constantly that the better understanding of Homer's formulaic diction confirms the soundness of the traditional text. Thus even as we should not try to restore the digamma where the rhythm is seemingly irregular, so we should not touch those places in which, while there is no irregularity, the digamma can be very easily restored. There was, however a certain soundness in the emendation of the text which was practiced for two centuries: the editors in most cases really did establish the older form of the phrase. For example our texts have

τὸν δ' αὖτε προσέειπεν ἄναξ ἀνδρῶν Ἀγαμέμνων (5 times)
ὣς ἔφατ'· οὐδ' ἀπίθησεν ἄναξ ἀνδρῶν Ἀγαμέμνων (twice)

By removing the ν-movable of προσέειπεν and ἀπίθησεν, and restoring the digamma we get what must have been the older form of the verse. Certainly the sense of *Ω* 154 is better when we read *ὅς ʽϝ' ἄξει, and μειλιχίοις ἐπέεσσιν (10 times) was surely made from *μειλιχίοισι ϝέπεσσιν. These changes, however, were made by the later singers themselves, drawn on by the habit of their spoken language, but held back by the constraint of the formulaic diction.

[1] Cf. TE, pp. 102–5 above. [2] Cf. TE, pp. 68–74 above.

[3] Cf. HS, pp. 322–4 above. I have been able to observe in Southslavic heroic poetry, in its actual practice, this complete absence on the part of the oral poet of any thought of making original phrases.

This does not mean that we can use the digamma to establish an older form of the *Iliad* and *Odyssey*. We can say that certain phrases and verses are the creation of an older time when the digamma was pronounced (though even here we must admit that certain forms may have been made later by analogy), but such phrases and verses will be only the older parts of the diction which the singers used side by side with later phrases and verses. Just as we can show the metrical usefulness | of the older phrase, and the fixed place which it holds in the diction, so can we do for phrases with newer forms.[1] For instance, before the digamma was lost, the singers were able to use the following verse only in the masculine:

*καί μιν φωνήσας ϝέπεα πτερόεντα προσηύδα

But by Homer's time the verse could not only be used in the masculine, as it appears 30 times in the *Iliad* and *Odyssey*, but also in the feminine:

καί μιν φωνήσασ' ἔπεα πτερόεντα προσηύδα (9 times)

In the same way, after the example of μελιηδέα (ϝ)οἶνον (5 times), the singers made μελιηδέος οἴνου (twice); after the series given above, Ἡφαίστοιο (ϝ)ἄνακτος (twice), etc., they made Ποσειδάωνος ἄνακτος (twice). They could now begin verses with

τὸν δ' ἴδεν (ἴδον) { Αἰνείας (*E* 166) / Ἀντίλοχος (*E* 565) / ἐν νήσωι (δ 556) }

The following verse should be particularly noted, since it shows the early use of (ϝ)εἶπεν (or ἔϝειπεν), and the late use of ὅν side by side in the same formula:

ὀχθήσας δ' ἄρα (ϝ)εἶπε πρὸς ὃν μεγαλήτορα θυμόν

(*Λ* 403, *P* 90, *Σ* 5, *Υ* 343, *Φ* 53, 552, *X* 98; ε 298, 355, 407, 464).[2] We |

[1] Cf. D. B. Monro, *Homeric Grammar*, § 401 (3) (Oxford, 1882; second edition, 1891).

[2] Knös (215) admits the impossibility of emending this verse. Bentley wished to read ἔφη πρὸς ϝόν, but such a use of ἔφη is not Homeric. Fick corrected to ἔϝειπε πρὸς ἕον, but the contracted ἕον supposes the earlier loss of an intervocalic digamma in a form *σέϝος. There was probably never any form *σέϝος, but only *σϝός. The form ἑός is the classic modification of ἕος which in Lesbian is itself an artificial creation, on the analogy of ἔων and ἔμος, to compensate for the loss of position in arsis. Thus τοὺς μὲν ἑοὺς ἠρύκακε μώνυχας ἵππους (*E* 321) is probably for an older *τοὺς μὲν σϝοὺς ἠρύκακε; παιδὸς ἑοῖο is for an older *παιδὸς σϝοῖο, etc. In those cases where *σϝός had made position for a final short vowel in thesis, however, the metrical fault could not be corrected, and Homer uses θυγατέρα ἥν (4 times), πόσει ὧι (*E* 71), τέκει ὧι (twice), etc. The actual existence at some time of a form *ϝϝός may be doubted. The dissyllabic forms of the word which are cited from Aeolic (Bechtel, *Griechische Dialekte*, 1.277) are all poetic and are evidence that the Homeric ἑός dates from the Aeolic period of the poetry, when it was adapted either from an old Aeolic or an Arcado-Cypriote *σϝός. Cf. HL, pp. 347–50 above.

can see how this verse was made. The singers had inherited on the one hand such verses as (1)

εὐξάμενος / *ὀχθήσας*	*δ' ἄρα* (ϝ)*εἶπεν*	*ἰδὼν*	*εἰς οὔρανον εὐρύν*	(*T* 257)
			ἐπὶ (ϝ)*οἴνοπα πόντον*	(*Ψ* 143)
		ἔπος τ' ἔφατ' ἐκ τ' ὀνόμαζε		(*φ* 248)

and on the other hand such verses as (2)

ὣς φάσαν· ἀλλ' οὐ πεῖθον ἐμὸν μεγαλήτορα θυμόν (*ι* 500)
πόλλ' ἀπομυθεόμην· σὺ δὲ σῶι μεγαλήτορι θυμῶι (*I* 109)

They also had such verses as (3)

εὐξάμενος δ' ἄρα (ϝ)*εἶπεν ἑκηβόλωι Ἀπόλλωνι* (*Π* 513)

And finally, one of their most common words for 'speak to' was *προσειπεῖν*. By the natural play of phrases which is the essential process of oral composition, the words of the first two types of verses combined to give a verse which is syntactically like the third type; *προσέ*(ϝ)*ειπε* gave (ϝ)*εἶπε πρός*, and the third person *ὅν*, losing the trace of the digamma, took the place of the first person *ἐμόν* in such a verse as *ι* 500, or of the second person *σῶι* in such a verse as *I* 109. The verse thus made proved so useful that it won the fixed place in the diction which led Homer to use it 11 times. It is an example of the stability of the diction as a whole and of the fluidity of the diction in the grouping of its elements, and as such it shows that while there are older and newer phrases in Homer they are not necessarily the mark of older and newer passages in the poems. It should be fully understood, however, that the number of outstanding formulaic phrases which refuse the digamma is small;[1] this merely shows how little the Greek heroic style changed over a long period of time.[2]

The traditional formulaic diction must have trained the ears of the singers and their hearers to feel the traces of the lost initial digamma much in the way that the French feel the traces of *h-aspiré*, so that, while they say *l'herbe*, *l'homme*, they say *la hache*, *le hêtre*. In the French it is the feeling for the rhythm of the close group of the word with the article which has kept the feeling for the lost sound; in the Greek heroic poetry it was a feeling for the equally fixed word group. It has been objected to this that the keeping of *h-aspiré* is largely due | to formal education,[3] and to the fact that it occurs in regular combination of article and substantive, whereas in Homer hiatus occurs between all sorts of words.[4] The answer in both cases is that the feeling for the digamma was maintained by the altogether artificial constraint of the diction. Nevertheless the parallel of

[1] Cf. Knös 50–146. [2] Cf. HL, pp. 358–60 above.

[3] Monro, *Homeric Grammar*, § 402.

[4] A. Meillet, *Aperçu d'une histoire de la langue grecque*³, 154–5 (Paris, 1930).

h-aspiré should not be pushed too far, because the singer was also habituated by his spoken language to the use of the words in question without any trace of the digamma: he had not one, but two conventions. For this reason we should not insist too much on the feeling for the lost consonant as an acting factor, but only as a factor which justified the irregularities which the diction imposed.[1] The ever increasing use of the words without regard for the lost digamma, which we can trace in Hesiod and the Homeric hymns, shows on the contrary that the habit of the spoken language was constantly wearing down the habit of the song. Nevertheless the latter habit should not be overlooked, since we find it lasting well on into Greek poetry. Thus we have in Archilochus Ἐνυαλίοιο (ϝ)ἄνακτος (1.1 Diehl), in Solon καλὰ (ϝ)ἔργα (1.21), in the epic poet Antimachus μέλανος (ϝ)οἴνοιο (19.1 Kinkel), and in Apollonius of Rhodes καταφθιμένοιο (ϝ)ἄνακτος (1.411), ἄνδρα ‘(ϝ)έκαστοι (1.399), etc.[2]

It has also been objected that while hiatus resulting from the lost digamma might be bearable, the fault of the short syllable in the first part of the foot is too grave to be possible.[3] *Μέλανος* (ϝ)*οἴνοιο* of Antimachus, which was just quoted, shows that this is not so, but of much more weight than this is the great number of short syllables in the first part of the foot in Homer which come not from the loss of the digamma, but from the faulty putting together of formulas.[4] For example, verses such as

ἐντροπαλιζομένη, θαλερὸν κατὰ δάκρυ χέουσα (Z 496)
πυκνὰ μάλα στενάχων ὥς τε λὶς ἠυγένειος (Σ 318)

may combine to make such a verse as

ἐντροπαλιζόμενος ὥς τε λὶς ἠυγένειος (P 109) |

Similarly the poet may change the case of a formula with a resulting failure to make position, as when after μερόπων ἀνθρώπων (9 times) he makes μέροπες ἄνθρωποι (Σ 288).[5] It should also be remembered that we have to do here with song, and not with speech, so that the poet would be allowed a freedom in treatment of vowel or consonant which would not be possible in spoken verse.[6]

Those cases in Homer in which the use of an uncontracted form might seem to show a survival of intervocalic digamma are to be explained in the same way as the seeming use of initial digamma. A single example will suffice. The uncontracted ἔ(ϝ)ειπε occurs in a whole series of fixed phrases, from whole verses such as

στῆ δ' ὀρθὸς καὶ μῦθον ἐν Ἀργείοισιν ἔ(ϝ)ειπεν (7 times)
αἰνότατε Κρονίδη, ποῖον τὸν μῦθον ἔ(ϝ)ειπες (6 times)

[1] This was the mistake of G. Curtius (*Grundzüge der griechischen Etymologie*[5], 560, Leipzig, 1879), who first adopted this explanation.

[2] Cf. *Argonautica*, ed. G. W. Mooney 416–421, Dublin, 1912.

[3] Meillet, loc. cit.

[4] Cf. FM, p. 215 above.

[5] Cf. FM, pp. 10–11 above.

[6] Cf. Krohn, 56.

to shorter phrases such as *κατὰ μοῖραν ἔ(ϝ)ειπες* (10 times), or *οἶον ἔ(ϝ)ειπες* (7 times). One notable series is the following:

ἔπος	νηκερδὲς	ἔ(ϝ)ειπε(ς)	(ξ 509)
	θυμαλγὲς		(twice)
	ὀλοφυδνὸν		(twice)
	νημερτὲς		(Γ 204)
	κατὰ μοῖραν		(4 times)

The problem of the digamma in Lesbian poetry is very similar to that of this sound in Homer: we find cases where the digamma would correct a seemingly faulty rhythm and others where its introduction on the contrary would harm a rhythm which has no fault. The only difference is that whereas in Homer the number of words which refuse the sound is small in comparison with those which call for it, or take it by an easy change in the text, this proportion is reversed in Sappho and Alcaeus. The natural conclusion is that the Lesbian poets, like Homer, were following a tradition of poetic diction in which certain phrases had kept the trace of the digamma, but that they were further away than Homer, either in time or in evolution of style, from the time when this sound had its natural place in the poetic language. Now this is not the prevailing critical opinion. Modern editors, with the exception of Lobel,[1] follow the line of reasoning which, we have seen,[2] is usual in such cases, | and restore the digamma, and even emend the text to take it, and they support their view, which is also that of the writers on Greek dialects,[3] by a certain amount of ancient evidence. That evidence, however, is less sure than is generally supposed.

The form *ϝοῖσι* in a papyrus text (Sappho α′ 3.6 Lobel, reproduced in photograph in *Oxyrhyncus Papyri* I, plate II), and *ϝόν* in a text from Herculaneum (Alcaeus 120.2[4] Lobel) actually show us the digamma, but aside from these two cases there is no other example of initial digamma in the papyri or in the literary quotations of Sappho and Alcaeus; all other evidence comes from the grammarians or from Balbilla, a Roman lady poetess of the second century A.D.[5] The correction of *τ' εἴπειν* to *ϝείπειν* in the fragments of Sappho and Alcaeus quoted by Aristotle is uncalled for, since elision of the dative of the pronouns is regular in Lesbian poetry, and we have *τάδ' εἴπην* elsewhere in Alcaeus (48.2

[1] E. Lobel, *Σάπφους Μέλη* (Oxford, 1925), *Ἀλκαίου Μέλη* (Oxford, 1927).

[2] Cf. above, TD, p. 393.

[3] O. Hoffmann, *Griechishe Dialekte*, 2.454–9 (Göttingen, 1893); F. Bechtel, *Griechische Dialekte*, 1.11–15 (Berlin, 1921); R. Meister, *Griechische Dialekte*, 1.103–6 (Göttingen, 1882).

[4] Cf. A. Vogliano, 'Herculanensia', in *Atti della reale accademia delle scienze di Torino* 47.91 (1911).

[5] Lobel alone of all the editors has seen the weakness of the evidence for initial digamma before a vowel (*Σάπφους Μέλη* xxx). For a contrary view see J. M. Edmonds in *Cambridge Review*, 47.211 (1926).

Lobel), and *τόδ' εἴπῃ*[elsewhere in Sappho (α′ 8.12).[1] Similarly *ἄχει δ' ἐκ πετάλων τάδε ἂν τέττιξ* quoted by Proclus has been corrected to *ϝάδεα τέττιξ*, but the reading of the text is too bad to be the work of any but the latest time and of a scribe with the haziest ideas of classical syntax whose ear was led astray by the *τ*'s of the following word. The *ϝ* before *ἄδεα* is no surer than the *ν* after it, and Lobel is right in reading simply *πετάλων ἄδεα τέττιξ*.[2]

When the ancient grammarians give a certain form as 'Aeolic' we cannot be at all sure that they mean Lesbian. Their studies of dialect were rudimentary; they never grasped the rigorous notion of dialectal subdivisions; and the forms they quote may come not only from Lesbian poetry, but also from Boeotian poetry or the spoken dialects of Thessaly.[3] Thus we have the 'Aeolic' glosses *γάλλοι* (*ἧλοι*), *γέμματα* | (*ἱμάτια*), *γοίδημι* (*ἐπίσταμαι*), *γόλαμος* (*διωγμός*), *γρῖνος* (*δέρμα*), in which the initial *γ* is supposed to be a miswritten *ϝ*.[4] We have, however, another gloss: *τὸ γὰρ οἶδα οἴδημι φασὶν οἱ Αἰολεῖς*,[5] and our texts of Sappho and Alcaeus show us that where *ϝρ*- survived it became *βρ*-, as in *βροδοδάκτυλοι* and *βρόδα* of a papyrus of Sappho (ε′ 5.8 and 13). The easier explanation is that the grammarians had found, or rather heard of, some regional Aeolic dialect in which the digamma had survived in a velarized form, and that they concluded that this was the actual sound which had been used in Lesbian poetry. It must have been in accordance with such a doctrine that Balbilla, as we know from the inscription of her poem on the colossus of Memnon in Egypt, actually wrote *γοι* and *γε* as what she thought was Sappho's language,[6] and that our texts of the grammarians almost always show us the digamma as *γ* in the words which are given as examples. *Βροδοδάκτυλος*, etc., however, show that where the sound did survive in Lesbian it was labialized. If John the Grammarian really states that *ϝοῖνον* was Aeolic for *οἶνον*,[7] we nevertheless know from the fact that Aulus Gellius quoted the phrase of Alcaeus (108.1) as *πνεύμονα οἴνωι*, while Athenaeus and Plutarch quoted the obvious correction of this reading *πλεύμονας οἴνωι*, that he did not find this form in the text of one of the Lesbian poets. Terentianus Maurus says: 'Quamque *ἴτυν*

[1] *Rhetoric* 1376 a 9, 12; cf. F. Bechtel, *Griechische Dialekte* 1.12; Edmonds, *Lyra Graeca*[2] 1.266 (London, 1928); on elision in Lesbian poetry cf. *Σάπφους Μέλη* lxi.

[2] Cf. Edmonds, *Cambridge Review*, loc. cit.

[3] Cf. Hoffmann 2.223. Edmonds (loc. cit.) is wrong in saying that John the Grammarian identifies 'Aeolic' with Sappho and Alcaeus. He merely gives his confused description of the 'Aeolic' dialect, and then says that Alcaeus and Sappho used it. The correct statement could be that the grammarians associated everything 'Aeolic' with these poets.

[4] Hoffmann 2.236–7.

[5] Choeroboscus, *Scholia in Theodosium*, 342.1 (ed. Hilgard, Leipzig, 1889).

[6] Hoffmann 2.125, vv. 7, 15.

[7] Hoffmann 2.217, § 21. The text has *ἔοινον* which is itself not an impossible form, but may actually have come into the poetry as a form to correct the rhythm, as *ἔος* (see above, note 21) was made from **σϝός*.

dicunt Achaei, hanc vitym gens Aeolis'[1] which goes no further than the vague term 'Aeolic'. Trypho the Grammarian really does refer by name to a Lesbian poet: "ἅπαξ δὲ παρ' Ἀλκαίωι τὸ ῥῆξις οὔρηξις λέγεται",[2] where the spelling seems to be the survival of some attempt at a phonetic explanation. Finally Apollonius Dyscolus says:

σαφὲς ὅτι καὶ τὸ Αἰολικὸν δίγαμμα ταῖς κατὰ τὸ τρίτον πρόσωπον προσνέμεται, καθὸ καὶ αἱ ἀπὸ φωνήεντος ἀρχόμεναι δασύνονται. Ἀλκαῖος (110)·

ὤστε θέων μηδ' ἔν' Ὀλυμπίων
λῦσαι ἄτερ γέθεν.[3] |

His remark explains all the confusion of forms under which the grammarians refer to the digamma, and the discrepancy between their remarks and the tradition of the poetic text itself: Apollonius is not basing his view upon the evidence of the texts, but is arguing for a reading of the text from metrical evidence. The last part of his statement refers to a view set forth more fully by Velius Longus,[4] according to which the sound *h* was a consonant and could make position in such a verse as

ἦ ὀλίγον οἷ παῖδα ἐοικότα γείνατο Τυδεύς (*E* 800).

The ancient critics had observed the similarity between Lesbian and the other Aeolic dialects, and they had found somewhere in these other dialects in some form or other the digamma which would correct what they thought were the metrical faults of Sappho and Alcaeus. They thus practiced emendation on exactly the same grounds as the modern critics do. Indeed, the source of the modern practice lies entirely with the ancient grammarians, for it was by reading the Latin grammarians that Bentley got his whole notion of the restoration of the digamma. In view of this it is reasonable to suppose that the two cases where the papyri show us the digamma are also due to the work of ancient editors. That they seem to have limited their correction to the third personal pronoun and possessive adjective would be indicated by the fact that Apollonius Dyscolus, in the three passages where he deals with the 'Aeolic' digamma,[5] is concerned only with these words, and it would be explained by the large number of cases in which these words must have invited emendation, even as they do in Homer. The fixity of the older use of these words in the diction is further indicated by the fact that we find even in Ionic poetry ἤ δέ ʽ(ϝ)οι in Archilochus (25.2 Diehl), and οὐδέ ʽ(ϝ)οι in Simonides (7.79 Diehl).

[1] *De Syllabis*, v. 658, text vitem (Keil 6.344).

[2] Πάθη Λέξεων 11.

[3] Περὶ Ἀντωνυμίας 761.32, ed. Schneider and Uhlig (Leipzig, 1878); text λυσεατερ γεθεν.

[4] Keil 7.52.

[5] The second case is φαίνεταί (ϝ)οἱ κῆνος (p. 82, l. 17). The third case, in which the text of Apollonius reads τὸν ἔον παῖδα κάλει (p. 107, l. 12), cannot be corrected to τὸν ϝόν because Apollonius is discussing precisely forms in -εο-.

When we have thus removed from the problem the confusing theoretical forms of the grammarians and editors, both ancient and modern, we find that the Lesbian lyric poetry conserved traces of the digamma in just the way that the Ionic heroic poetry did. There are some fourteen cases in which Sappho and Alcaeus elide before words which had once had an initial digamma, and some seventeen cases in which the introduction of the digamma would lengthen a vowel which must be metrically| short. Side by side with this neglect of the digamma we find five cases where the phrase shows the traces of the digamma: *ἄτερ* (ϝ)*ἔθεν* considered above; *φάινεταί* (ϝ)*οἰ* (Sappho, inc. lib. 48), also quoted as an example by Apollonius; *πλεύμονα* (ϝ)*οἴνωι*; *ὑπὸ* (ϝ)*ἔργον* (Alcaeus 108.1) beside *ἀμύστιδος* (ϝ)*ἔργον* (Alcaeus 36.19); and the famous *γλῶσσα* (ϝ)*ἔ*(ϝ)*αγε* (Sappho α′ 2 App., 9).[1] Similarly we find the traces of the digamma in such forms as *ἔ*(ϝ)*ειπε* (Sappho ϵ′ 3.3) beside *εἶπον* (Sappho ϵ′ 4.8), *α*]*πυ*(ϝ)*ειπη*[(Alcaeus 64.4), and *ἐ*(ϝ)*άνασσε* (Alcaeus 118). We have not enough of the early Lesbian poetry to be able to show, as we can for Homer, fixed phrases in the diction which must be traditional. *Φαίνεταί μοι κῆνος* (α′ 2 App., 1) and *φαίνεταί οἰ κῆνος* of Sappho may, or may not, be such examples. We do know, however, that the two poets lived at the beginning of Greek poetry, and that if they were not following an oral tradition of lyric poetry as completely as Homer followed the oral tradition of heroic poetry, they must anyway have been more or less closely bound up with the popular tradition which had brought down from the past phrases which had in them traces of the digamma.[2]

[1] Confronted by these last three cases Lobel, who by rigorously keeping to the evidence of the texts had saved himself from the error of restoring the digamma, commits an even worse fault: he marks two of the three passages as corrupt and attempts emendation of them, while he reads *πλεύμονας οἴνωι* after the quotations by Plutarch and Athenaeus. One can understand how *πλεύμονα* (ϝ)*οἴνωι* became plural but not how the plural could ever become the singular.

[2] I have dealt in HL, pp. 347–50 above with those cases in Aeolic and Ionic poetry where the loss of the digamma has modified the form of the word itself.

10

On Typical Scenes in Homer*

THERE are certain actions which tend to recur in the *Iliad* and *Odyssey*, and which, each time they do recur, are told again with many of the same details and many of the same words. Arend calls such passages 'typical scenes,' inasmuch as they have a common 'type.' The greater part of his book is made up of his analysis in turn of the most striking sets of such scenes, namely, those which recount arrival, sacrifice and eating, journeys by sea or land, arming and dressing, sleep, hesitation before decision (μερμηρίζειν), assembly, oath, and bath. In each case he starts from those passages which are most alike, and shows by charts how nearly they have the same stages of the action in the same order, and how nearly they use the same verses and verse parts. He then goes on to other places where the course of the tale has changed or shortened or lengthened the action, and here he shows how Homer, far from quitting his usual pattern, uses it as the base and framework for scenes which may be even among the most unique in the poems. For example, Arend first fixes (p. 28) the simple type of an arrival scene on the basis of the passages where Athena, at Hera's order, seeks out Odysseus (*B* 167–72), where Nestor and Odysseus go to waken Diomed (*K* 150–8), where Thetis brings Achilles the divine weapons (*Σ* 616–*T* 7), and where Nestor recounts how he and Odysseus had visited the home of Peleus (*Λ* 769–81). Then taking up again the last two of these passages, he shows for the one (p. 29) how like it is to the other three scenes where Thetis comes to her son (*A* 359–63, *Σ* 65–74, *Ω* 121–7), and for the other (pp. 34–6) how like it is to other scenes where the arrival takes the form of a visit, as when Patroclus calls at the tent of Nestor (*Λ* 617–47), or when Achilles receives the embassy (*I* 182–223). Finally we see how Priam's visit to the tent of Achilles, for all the uniqueness of its telling, yet follows the pattern of the type (*Ω* 322–484, pp. 37–9). Arend elsewhere brings out the same 'typical' treatment in other parts of the story of Hector's ransoming, namely, for Priam's *journey* from Troy to the Achaean camp (*Ω* 189–469, pp. 88–9), for Hermes' *arrival* on the Trojan plain (*Ω* 333–48, pp. 54, 58–61), and for Priam's *eating*

* Review of Walter Arend, 'Die typischen Scenen bei Homer', *Classical Philology* 31 (1936), 357–60. Reprinted by kind permission of the editor.

in Achilles' tent (*Ω* 625–8, pp. 69–70), and he thus makes plain how Homer builds his tale by joining and interworking the traditional schemes of composition. The book closes with a like analysis of the practice of Apollonius and Virgil, who, however, as later poets, make use of the 'typical' only in so far as they set out to copy Homer. Here as elsewhere the analysis is fine and thorough. To some readers it may seem tiresome, but it is chiefly | to those who, like Arend, join to a real feeling for Homer's song the sober work needed to make clear with exactness wherein it differs in form from more modern poetries that we can look for a real advance in Homeric studies.

Yet for all that he so clearly sees the schematization of Homer's composition, Arend fails almost altogether to understand the reasons for it. For this he is not greatly to be blamed, since there is still so little general knowledge of the way in which oral narrative poetry is composed, and it is only with this knowledge that we can understand the very simple reasons why Homer uses a fixed diction and follows a fixed pattern for the telling of his story. Having nothing better, Arend outlines a philosophic and almost mystic theory, to which he seems to have been inspired (cf. p. 2, n. 3) by Nietzsche's oracular utterances about Homer dancing in chains. Arend writes (p. 26), referring to Priam's *journey* from Troy to the battlefield (*Γ* 259–65):

> To sum up, the Greek sees right through to the essential, and brings it out in the presentation: the structure, the form, the εἶδος. But the essential of an incident is that which is constant in all the repetitions. And therefore this type of *journey by land* can and must recur whenever a like happening comes up.

repetition

On the other hand (p. 27):

> Yet we find scenes which have almost nothing in common with *Γ*. But it is just this little bit which counts. What counts is that all the particular cases result either from the toning down or the embellishing of a single type. All the variations, extreme as they may be, especially in the *Odyssey*, yet have not broken down the fixed form. So arises the peculiar and unique nature of the Homeric art, the play between fixed form and varying embellishment (εἶδος and ποικιλία in the language of the old commentators), between the necessary and the chance, between the typical and the individual, between repetition and variation, and it has preserved for us a picture of the peculiar Greek comprehension of reality, which in manyness saw the one and yet by reason of oneness did not forget the many.

Now all that may or may not be true—it does not matter much, but it is surely simpler to say that Homer relates the same action in more or less the same way because that was the only way he had learned. The singer of tales, unlike the writer of poetry, is never free of his tradition. He has not learned his art from a varied reading, but only from listening to older singers. He has no pen and ink to let him slowly work out a novel way of recounting novel actions, but must make up his tale without pausing, in the speed of his singing. This he can do only by telling each action as it comes up in more or less the usual way, and in more or less the usual verses which go with that way. That there are not many of these ways is because the singers, even as they tended, for reasons of easier verse-making, to keep only the one best and easiest formula for expressing a given idea in a given length of verse, so tended also to keep only a single set of details for a given action. The fixed action-patterns and the fixed formulas, of course, depend on one another: an action which | each time took a new form would call for new words, and in the same way the formulas are useful only inasmuch as the singer uses the schemes of composition in which they are meant to serve.

Arend points out that Homer likes to relate an action from beginning to end, and to treat each principal stage of the action in its proper order. But in this there is nothing strange or particularly Greek. The singer, like anyone who is telling a story aloud, finds it easiest to lead his action straight ahead. Where Homer, however, must have differed from the ordinary singer of his day, was in his being able to tell the action more fully. A highly developed oral poetry differs from one which is less developed because its singers have a more ample art. The song which has only a few hundred verses in the hut of some hard-working tiller of the soil, whose time for such sport is short, will run into thousands of verses when it is sung before some noble by a singer who, raised among men with great leisure for talk and song, has had time to become fully practiced in a highly developed art. The difference between such long and short versions of the same song lies in what singers call the 'adornment.' The finished singer will boast that he knows 'how to saddle a horse', or 'dress a hero', or 'plan a battle', and whereas one less skilful might spend only a verse or two on these actions, he himself will give twenty or fifty or more verses to them. This great difference is never due in any more than a small part to the singer's own making up things. It comes instead from his having been trained in a richer tradition, and, as a singer of talent, from his having been able to grasp all the richness of the tradition. When asked how he has learned to caparison a horse so well, he will say briefly that as he has heard so he sings. But if one is able to point out that the singer from whom he learned his song has nothing of that sort in his version, he will then say that the other had shortened the song (which among singers is the most rankling of all accusations), and that he himself had known how to put it right. Questioned further, he will explain that bad singers leave this out and leave that out, but a good singer knows how to put it back in, even though he has never heard that particular song. What he means, though never having reasoned about his art he cannot say it, is that he has listened to so many songs and stored away in his mind ready for use such a vast stock of details of heroic action, in the form of the verses and verse parts whereby they are expressed in song, that at no point in his story is he forced to give up telling his story in all its fulness.

It is along such lines as these that Arend might have planned his analysis, not aiming to bring out a meaningless play of norm and variation, but rather to show how Homer, with his overwhelming mastery of the traditional epic stuff, enriches the course of his story now with one group of details, now with another, though each group for a given action will tend to center about certain key verses and to follow a certain general pattern. Happily the theory of 'type' and variation is so tenuous a thing that it has had almost no effect at | all upon Arend's analysis itself, which thus remains good. He is also to be praised for going to other early poetries for parallels to Homer's style, though such parallels are likely to be idle when we know as little about how the poetry was really composed as we do for the Assyrian-Babylonian poem of Gilgamesh, which Arend is most fond of citing. The healthy result of this reading of early poems shows itself in his not finding falsely subtle meanings in the repetitions, as meant to recall an earlier scene where the same words are used, and in his forceful refutation of the practice of those older critics who, setting up an unhomeric conciseness as the Homeric standard, threw out at will such repeated passages as did not suit them or their theories.

II

The Historical Method in Literary Criticism*

I DO not think that it is generally well enough understood how great a change has taken place in the last hundred years in the way in which we see the writing of past times. The change of which I speak has gradually been going ahead from the very beginning of the tradition of European reasoning, though now faster and now slower, and again with long set-backs, but in our own time the speed of that change has quickened and in the space of a very few years has created a critical point of view which is having, and will have, very far reaching results on human institutions in general, and particularly on the institution with which we are here concerned, the University.

I refer to nothing more than that which is familiarly known as the historical method in literary criticism, a point of view which is so obvious to us, or rather so much a part of us, that for that very reason we fail to see how much it sets our own intellectual times off from the past. Yet it is really a very new thing. Those who know Greek and Latin literature know that the principle was already stated in the fifth century before Christ, notably by Thucydides, but that classical literature as a whole either pretty well ignores it, or makes, at the best, rare and rudimentary attempts to apply it. The first exact statement of it in modern times seems to be that of Francis Bacon in his *Advance of Science* (*De augmentis scientiarum*). There we have what seems to be the first statement of the concept of literary history: 'General history without literary history is like a statue of blinded Polyphemus: what is lacking is just that which best shows the particular genius and character of the person.' And then on the next page he goes on: 'In the study of these things I wish that instead of passing our time like the critics in assigning praise and blame we should give a frankly historical account, and reserve our personal judgments.' And we can see that we should not reject this statement as nothing more than the now much questioned notion of so-called 'objective history', for he continues on the next page as follows: 'It is not by a mere exhaustive reading, which would really have no end, but by the

* An address delivered by Milman Parry, as Assistant Professor of Greek and Latin, before the Board of Overseers of Harvard College at a meeting on 15 May 1934; first published in *Harvard Alumni Bulletin* 38 (1936), 778–82, and reprinted by permission.

assimilation of the subject, the style, the method, that we must, as it were, call up from the dead the literary spirit of those times.'

It is only at the beginning of the last century, however, that this historical method of literary criticism suddenly begins to become a common point of view which we find frequently either assumed or expressly stated, and ever more and more, in critical writing. I shall mention only its statement by Ernest Renan who at least as much as any other man, if not more, moulded European thought in the last hundred years: 'How can we seize the physiognomy and the originality of early literatures if we do not enter into the moral and intimate life of a people, if we do not place ourselves at the very point in humanity which it occupied, in order to see and to feel with it, if we do not watch it live, or rather if we do not live for a while with it?'

Now I believe that the remarkable thing about that point of view is that it is one which can never reach completely, but only | come nearer to its attainment. The work upon it will never be done. The students of each generation, approaching the literature of some past period with the clearer sight which has been won for them by the earlier generation, will find in the best opinions on that past elements which jar with one another, or things which have been left out, or things which have been given too much place; and if they have head enough not to become befuddled by details—which is the great hazard—they will in their turn give a truer picture. I myself can see at present no current in the best modern thought which goes counter to this historical trend. The notion of relativity surely lies in this direction: if I say that Grote's account of democracy at Athens is more revealing of the mind of an English Liberal of the nineteenth century after Christ, than it recalls what actually took place in Athens in the fifth century before Christ, and then go on to admit that the opinion which I have just expressed about Grote may in turn reveal even more my own state of mind than it does that of Grote—(indeed, I know that I am expressing this thought here because I came across it about two weeks ago in one of the essays submitted for the Bowdoin prize essay contest and it struck me)—even in that case I am still doing no more than to try to attain a more perfect method for the historical approach to the thought of the past. And then apart from method, there are all the other fields of learning which concern themselves with man as he lived in the past, or lives in forms of society other than our own—history itself, anthropology, sociology, philosophy, the study of the plastic arts, of music, indeed, every field of learning right down to the physical sciences, is moving in this direction, and each subject lends knowledge to each other. So, gradually, we learn to keep ourselves out of the past, or rather we learn to go into it, becoming not merely a man who lived at another time than our own, but one who lived in a certain nation, or city, or in a certain social class, and in very certain years, and sometimes—when we are concerned with a writer in that whereby he differs from his fellow men—we must not only enter into the place, the time, the class—we must even become the man himself, even more, we must become the man at the very moment at which he writes a certain poem.

I can then see nowhere in the critical study of literature anything to check this ever accelerating concern with the past as the past. But when one trained in this method (and I speak very particularly about myself, for the quotation which I gave above from Renan was once quoted by me in one of my own writings; indeed they were the first words in the first book which I ever published)—when one trained in this method, while still staying in the past, turns his eyes back to his own time, he cannot prevent a certain feeling of fear—not for the fact that he has become a ghost in the past, but because of what he sees in the person of his living self. For in the past, where his ghostly self is, he finds that men do the opposite of what he has been doing: they by their literature turn the past into the present, making it the mirror for themselves, and as a result the past as it is expressed in their literature has a hold upon them which shows up the flimsiness of the hold which our past literature has upon ourselves.

I shall try to show what I mean by an example drawn from the field which I myself teach, that of classical literature, and particularly from the Homeric poems on which I have done most of my writing. There is a famous passage in the twelfth book of the *Iliad* in which Sarpedon, the ally of the Trojans, calls upon his friend Glaucus to follow him to the assault on the Greek Wall: "If after escaping this war we were to become ageless and deathless, then would I not fight myself in the front ranks, nor urge you into the battle which gives men glory. But there are hazards of death beyond counting which stand above us, and which no man can escape or dodge. So let us go | forward: we shall give glory to some man, or some man will give glory to us." Now there is a passage in Matthew Arnold's essay *On Translating Homer* in which he relates an incident concerning this passage; the story originally comes from Robert Wood's *Essay on the Genius of Homer*, written in the eighteenth century, and one of the first books to bring into existence the well-known and so-called 'Homeric Problem'. Robert Wood says that in 1762, at the end of the Seven Years' War, being then Under-Secretary of State, he was directed to wait upon the President of the Council, Lord Granville, a few days before he died, with the preliminary articles of the Treaty of Paris. 'I found him so languid that I proposed postponing my business for another time; but he insisted that I should stay, saying it could not prolong his life to neglect his duty, and repeating the following passage out of

Sarpedon's speech, he dwelled with particular emphasis on the third line, "Then would I not fight myself in the front ranks", which called to his mind the distinguished part he had taken in public affairs.' And then Lord Granville recited to himself in Greek the lines which I just gave you in translation.

Now I myself, because of the particular training in historical method, read those verses with an understanding which Lord Granville could never have had. I keep in mind, beyond doubt in a way which he never did, certain earlier lines in this same speech of Sarpedon in which that hero states the moral grounds which oblige them to high deeds: because their fellow countrymen give them at banquets the best cuts of meat, and keep their cups filled with wine, and have given them broad farm-lands. And then from my understanding of the speech of Sarpedon as a whole, from my knowledge of other early heroic poetries, from the general picture drawn of men of the heroic age by such scholars as Ker and Chadwick, and from what I myself have observed of traditional heroic poetry as it is still sung in the mountains of Hertzegovina, I see that this speech of Sarpedon is really a statement of the rewards and the responsibilities of prestige in the society of Homer's time—a society in which men were fewer in number, the social group smaller and its members known to one another, the mechanic arts still undeveloped, and warfare of a certain sort the constant condition of life. And so I make for myself a picture of great detail.

That is what that speech of Sarpedon must be to the scholar. To Homer and to the men who sat before him with their different cuts of meat, and their varyingly filled cups of wine, and their different recognized positions of importance in the community, it was another matter. It was the statement in heroic terms of their own way of life. More than that, it was a sanction and an ideal for that way of life. There was no separation there between what Sarpedon said and what they did and saw and admired every day. By not seeking to find out the past as it was (such a thought could not possibly even occur to them because they had never conceived that the past could be essentially different from the present), but making it the heroically magnified reflection of their own life, that past had become a very part of their being. The hold which Homer had on later centuries, though weaker, was of much the same sort. In one of the dialogues of Plato we find the *Iliad* praised because of the pointers it gives for chariot racing. Lord Granville was still reading Homer in this way, but there must have been few in his day, and how few now! And of those few who do, certainly the smallest part are the scholars.

Now the situation which I have described with relation to Homeric studies cannot be very different from that which applies to any other field of literary study, and to the whole body of the humanities as they are taught in universities; and this is what cannot keep me from a certain feeling of uneasiness as to the future not | only of classical studies, but also for the very existence of all our study of the literature of the past, whether in our own or in any other language. For men—even those few who study the literatures in universities, and those, even fewer and rarer, who reach the point where their familiarity with the literature of a certain period allows them to speak soundly about it—must, as they always have, attach their action to some emotional body of ideas which provides them with a moral code. They have always done this, presumably they always will, and one has only to look anywhere to see that they are doing it now. The chief emotional ideas to which men seem to be turning at present, as the older ones fade, are those of nationality—for which they exploit race—and class, and for these ideas they create a past by a fictitious interpretation. Anyone who has followed the history of the use of propaganda for political purposes, with its extraordinary development of intensity and technique in the last fifty years, cannot but have been struck by the many occasions on which those who were directing that propaganda expressed their lack of concern, or even contempt, for what actually was so, or actually had been so. Particularly the conception of relativity which I mentioned a while ago has been misused as a justification for this disregard of what truth we have.

To the student of literature, to myself as a student of Homer, this should be no surprise. The general process of early poetry, whereby what begins as an historical poem inevitably becomes a fictitious tale to idealize the present, is only repeating itself in its particular modern form, and must continue to do so until men again have a stable way of life in accord with a stable body of emotional thought. In the meanwhile the critical study of the past is finding itself in an ever more and more uncertain position. While it perfects its method and learns more about the past, the true understanding of what knowledge it has or gains is limited to a smaller and smaller number; and from the standpoint of people in general it is probably now having a greater influence as a source of material for propaganda than as a source of real understanding of what is and has been. By its very method it is setting itself apart from human movements and advancing ahead to what may be its own destruction. In times of social changes and confusion, a bewildered people will seize with explosive suddenness upon some emotional idea and in a matter of months create a past for itself without bothering about the verity of details.

There is, so far as I can see, only one alternative to such a future. It is that the universities and the scholars must provide, and even impose upon a people, a sense of the nobility and the importance of their own search for knowledge. I can see no substitute for Plato's belief that there is nothing at the same time finer or more practical than the truth. In the field with which I have been particularly concerned here, that of the literatures of the past, unless we can show not only a few students, but all those people whose action will determine the course of a whole nation, that, by identifying one's self with the past, with the men, or with a man of another time, one gains an understanding of men and of life and a power for effective and noble action for human welfare, we must see literary study and its method destroy itself. I have seen myself, only too often and too clearly, how, because those who teach and study Greek and Latin literature have lost the sense of its importance for humanity, the study of those literatures has declined, and will decline until they quit their philological isolation and again join in the movement of current human thought.

There is no question here of sacrificing the search for a fuller knowledge of the past. We surely can never know too much about what people have done, and how they came to do it; nor can one compromise with the truth. But the scholars must see that they must impose their truths | before others impose their fictions. They must create their heroic legend—or rather they must make it known—for the European humanistic tradition which we of the universities follow is no inglorious thing. Otherwise they will be choosing a future in which they must see themselves confined not by choice, but by compulsion, to be forever ineffective, if they would not be untruthful.

12

About Winged Words*

PROFESSOR CALHOUN's study of the Homeric formula ἔπεα πτερόεντα shows, as has so much of his late work, that he is one of the very few scholars with a real understanding of the nature of Homer's style.[1] Nevertheless—and it is the first time, I believe, that we have not rather generally agreed—he has failed to make me believe that I was mistaken in holding that Homer uses this phrase just because it is useful, and without thought for any particular meaning which the epithet 'winged' might have. I stated my reasons for thinking this in an earlier number of this journal, but only in a single sentence, and I should now like to give my view more fully.

The various ἔπεα πτερόεντα verses, I believe, are used to bring in speech when 'the character who is to speak has been the subject of the last verses, so that the use of his name in the line would be clumsy'.[2] Thus Homer could not have used at α 122 such a verse as τὸν δ' αὖ Τηλέμαχος πεπνυμένος ἀντίον ηὔδα, as can be seen by reading from verse 113. The name of Telemachus is given in this verse, and it serves as the grammatical subject of all the following sentences in such a way that the second use of the name at 122 would break the style badly; what Homer wants to say is essentially 'and he said', not 'and Telemachus said'. Likewise it cannot be only Homer's wish to get πτερόεντα in at ε 172 which keeps him from using some such verse as τὸν δ' ἄρ' ὑπόδρα ἰδὼν προσέφη πολύμητις Ὀδυσσεύς. He has just given the name of Odysseus in the verse before, and could not do so again. It is the same in all the other 124 ἔπεα πτερόεντα verses in the *Iliad* and the *Odyssey*: the hearer already has the speaker in mind as the natural subject of the sentence which introduces the speech, and there is no place for the second use of the name. Only in some five or six cases, where subordinate clauses with another subject have come between, might we again use the name without spoiling the style. Of course, if Homer had some other whole verse or verses without πτερόεντα in them whereby he could say 'and he said', there would be no purpose in pointing this out; but there is no other verse. If he wishes to express this idea in just the length of a verse, he is bound to use the

* First published in *Classical Philology* 32 (1937), 59–63.

[1] 'The Art of Formula in Homer—ἔπεα πτερόεντα', *Classical Philology*, XXX (1935), 215–27.

[2] TM, pp. 372 f. above.

words *ἔπεα πτερόεντα*. On the other hand, the phrase is never found in the same verse with the name of a character. |

Thus, in order to hold that Homer uses the phrase only when he has in mind speeches of some given sort, one has to argue both that Homer never wanted to say in just a verse 'and he said' and also that, when he wants to use *πτερόεντα*, he plans the syntax ahead in such a way as not to have to give the name of the speaker when he introduces the speech. This would be a very complex sort of verse-making and quite foreign to the way in which such traditional and oral song as that of Homer is composed. The singer of oral narrative rarely plans his sentence ahead, but adds verse to verse and verse part to verse part until he feels that his sentence is full and finished. The poet, with writing materials, can think leisurely ahead, but the singer, in the speed of his song, must compose straight on out of fixed verses and verse parts until he comes to the point where one of his characters is to speak. Then he must have straightway at hand a verse or verse part to introduce the speech. This the common oral style has given him, as it has given him his diction as a whole; and it has given him not one or two formulas which he must in some way work in, but a whole living system of them which allows him each time to express just the right idea in a phrase of just the right words and length and rhythm. He has formulas to bring in a first speech in dialogue, or an answer, or to bring in monologue. He has formulas where there is place for the speaker's name, and others where the name, already understood, is implied in the verb. He has also formulas which simply bring in the speech, or which also state the tone, or which give the name of the person spoken to, or give some circumstance about the speaking. Finally, within these categories of meaning he has formulas of different grammatical form to fit the grammatical sequence of the passage, and of different metrical forms to fit into his verse at the different points where he may find himself. However, he usually has only one formula to suit a particular need, since the earlier singers in their natural and never ceasing search for the easiest means of verse-making had usually kept and passed on to him only as many fixed phrases as were really useful. Thus Homer, when he has just a verse to fill and wishes to express the idea 'and he said', will use the simple formula *καί μιν (σφεας) φωνήσας (φωνήσασ') ἔπεα πτερόεντα προσηύδα (προσηύδων)* 54 times. Or, if he wishes also to give the tone of the speech, he will use a formula of the type:

[11 times] *καί ῥ' ὀλοφυρόμενος*
[4 times] *καί μιν λισσόμενος* } *ἔπεα πτερόεντα προσηύδα*

Or he may state some circumstance:

[13 times] *ἀγχοῦ δ' ἱστάμενος*
[thrice] *τοὺς ὅ γ' ἐποτρύνων* } *ἔπεα πτερόεντα προσηύδα*

Finally, there are times when he finds himself ready to announce speech though he is only halfway through a verse. He then says, simply, ἔπος τ' ἔφατ' ἔκ τ' ὀνόμαζε (45 times). It is for purely grammatical reasons that we have ἔπος τ' ἔφατ' ἔκ τ' ὀνόμαζε and not ἔπεα πτερόεντα προσηύδα in such a | verse as ἔν τ' ἄρα οἱ φῦ χειρὶ ἔπος τ' ἔφατ' ἔκ τ' ὀνόμαζε (11 times). Now to find in πτερόεντα and ὀνόμαζε some meaning which would limit the use of these formulas to speeches of some one sort is to take away a whole part from the system and say that Homer has no speech formulas for the verse and the half-verse—the most common measures of the formula—which simply mean 'and he said'.[1]

When Professor Calhoun gives the particular meaning which he finds in ἔπεα πτερόεντα and ἔπος τ' ἔφατ' ἔκ τ' ὀνόμαζε, he says that the range of the two expressions overlap, and that they express 'myriad facets of the human spirit', and finally that 'the one usually connotes animation or urgency, the other earnestness or affection'.[2] Is it not possible, however, that he has here for once fallen into somewhat the same line of reasoning as that so often followed by the so-called 'Unitarians'? This school of critics thought that the only way to defend Homer against the disintegrators' charge of inconsistencies in the text was to show that there were really no inconsistencies at all. They accordingly gave their ingenuity full play and looked for subtle beauties of thought which had escaped the dull understanding of Homer's belittlers, who through their lack of poetic feeling had seen inconsistencies where there was only poetic refinement. Professor Calhoun, of course, is far beyond this; yet is it not, perhaps, a like unwillingness to believe that Homer might have used common formulas, and used them without thinking about what the words in them meant, which has led him to find in all the speeches introduced by ἔπεα πτερόεντα προσηύδα an emotion and intensity which would set them off from the other speeches of the poems? Certainly when he paints for us in his own words the circumstances and the substance of each one of these speeches he sets vividly before us its intensity and emotion. But here I must fall back on the somewhat questionable charge of δεινὸς λέγειν, because I believe that the fallacy of the method lies in the fact that another critic, if he knew how to write as well as Professor Calhoun, could paraphrase in the same lively way the speeches introduced by any other group of formulas. Is there not everywhere in the *Iliad* and the *Odyssey* enough of the simple force of Homer's heroic style to allow a writer of talent to bring forcibly before us the intensity and emotion of any given passage? Professor Calhoun thus places his readers

[1] No small part of my knowledge of ἔπεα πτερόεντα I owe to my former students, J. P. Cooke and M. V. Anastos, who made a study of the length of the speeches introduced by the different speech formulas. This they did to disprove an explanation of ἔπεα πτερόεντα more improbable even than Professor Calhoun's—namely, that the phrase is used to introduce short speeches.

[2] Pp. 225 f.

in the plight of having to agree with him before they can disagree, save perchance in the few cases where one can argue against the sort of intensity and emotions which he finds. Thus he tells us that Eteoneus (δ 20 ff.) has his hands so full with the banquet that the sight of Telemachus and Pisistratus, two new and uninvited guests, | is for him 'the last straw', and he 'momentarily loses his head' and announces their arrival in winged words, but I do not believe that every reader of the *Odyssey* will be willing to find this comedy between the lines for it. Likewise I myself do not like to think of Zeus as being "eager and brisk" when he gives orders to the baneful dream (*B* 7). Such a Zeus seems to me too little Phidian.

Professor Calhoun uses as one of his arguments the fact that 'out of somewhat more than 120 instances of *ἔπεα πτερόεντα* more than 70 are preceded by explicit allusions to emotion or its symptoms',[1] but is it not also true that the speech formulas of the type ending in *προσέφη πόδας ὠκὺς Ἀχιλλεύς*, *προσέφη πολύμητις Ὀδυσσεύς*, and so on (if one puts aside verses of the type *τὸν δ' ἀπαμειβόμενος προσέφη πόδας ὠκὺς Ἀχιλλεύς*, which is limited to answers) show an equally high number of cases where there is some word which we could class as emotional? What difference is there between *καί μιν ὑπόδρα ἰδὼν ἔπεα πτερόεντα προσηύδα* (twice) and *τὸν δ' ἄρ' ὑπόδρα ἰδὼν προσέφη πολύμητις Ὀδυσσεύς* (9 times) save the presence of the name in the one case and its absence in the other, and the difference for grammatical reasons of the conjunction? We can, perhaps, see here what has led Professor Calhoun to his conclusions: having found in the text, either in the same verse as *ἔπεα πτερόεντα* or very near it, a large number of such words as *νεμεσσήθη*, *ῥίγησεν*, *γήθησεν*, and so on, has he not supposed that the meaning of these words must accord with the meaning of the epithet *πτερόεντα*? By the same reasoning, however, we could argue equally well for an emotional connotation of *ἔπεα* and of *προσηύδα*. One can be somewhat surer that he has thus reasoned his way to his understanding of *ὀνόμαζεν* as connoting "earnestness or affection'. This half-verse is most often found in the following whole verse formulas:

[6 times] *χειρί τέ μιν κατέρεξεν* } *ἔπος τ' ἔφατ' ἔκ τ' ὀνόμαζε*
[11 times] *ἔν τ' ἄρα οἱ φῦ χειρὶ* }

and in these verses there are doubtless earnestness and affection. However, we also have

[4 times] *Ἀντίνοος* }
[π 417] *Ἀντίνοον* } *δ' ἐνένιπεν ἔπος τ' ἔφατ' ἔκ τ' ὀνόμαζεν*
[τ 90] *ἀμφίπολον* }
[ψ 96] *Τηλέμαχος* }
[O 552] *τόν ῥ' Ἕκτωρ ἐνένιπεν ἔπος τ' ἔφατ' ἔκ τ' ὀνόμαζε.*

[1] P. 225, n. 1.

Is there not, therefore, as much reason to say that ὀνόμαζε connotes dislike as to say that it connotes affection? Have we the right to suppose, in the one case more than in the other, that the meaning of the first half of the verse has anything to do with the meaning of the second half?

These are the particular reasons I have for thinking that Homer used πτερόεντα and ὀνόμαζεν without thinking of their special meaning; but the | issue at stake here is one which probably stands beyond such minute arguing. It seems to me to be the whole issue of whether we should read Homer as we read written poetry, which is for us the natural form of poetry, or whether we should not rather try to gain for our reading the sense of style which is proper to oral song. I know from my own mistakes that this is no easy thing. In some measure we may gain this sense by our mere feeling for the diction of the Homeric poems, but there is still then the danger of looking too closely and finding beauties where they are not. The reading of the *Iliad* and the *Odyssey* must be abetted by much reading of the other early European heroic poetries, and by the study of some of the many oral narrative poetries which still thrive in those places of the world where reading and writing have as yet gained no hold. The Homeric student who does this will come back to the *Iliad* and the *Odyssey* better able to feel their conventional wording as the usual heroic language of a tale which ever sweeps ahead with force and fineness, but also with an obviousness which is so utter that it may deceive, as I believe has been the case for Professor Calhoun, even the best of critics.

13

The Homeric Metaphor as a Traditional Poetic Device*

In contrast with the simile, which finds its most complete expression in the *Iliad* and *Odyssey*, the metaphor has in Homer (and the early epic) a more limited place than anywhere else in Greek poetry: metaphors are rare in Homer, are usually confined to the single case, and in only a very few cases receive any development. This is curious to begin with, in view of Aristotle's opinion that the epic poet could make as free a use of metaphor as he chose, and that it is this poetic device more than any other which shows the particular talent of a poet. But a further study of the Homeric metaphor shows even more: (*a*) it is almost never used as any but a casual poetic device—that is to say, one rarely finds it used to heighten a specifically emotional instant, or to bring out some crucial point in the narrative; (*b*) in almost no case is the metaphor such as to suggest the working of a mind seeking to express its unique kind of thought, which is the case, for example, for the Pindaric metaphor; (*c*) a very large proportion of the extended metaphors have a meaning which is vague, and at times problematic; (*d*) a large number of them are used so often that it is difficult, after reading any amount of Homer, to find in them a force greater than that of the ordinary word; (*e*) bound up with all the foregoing considerations are the facts that the metaphors are in many cases a part of the technique of composition by formulas, and that they are found elsewhere in the early epic. All these circumstances force us to the conclusion that the Homeric metaphor is traditional, and not the original work of the poet, and thus we are brought face to face with the need either of condemning Homer, or of judging him by standards other than those applicable to a poet using an individual style. The aim of the paper is less that of describing the Homeric metaphor than of bringing to a crystallization this need of oral standards in Homeric criticism.

* An abstract from *Transactions of the American Philological Association* 62 (1931), xxiv.

14

Homer and Huso: I. The Singer's Rests in Greek and Southslavic Heroic Songs*

THE traditional heroic songs which are still sung by the Bosnian Moslems, particularly by those on the old Montenegrin border (and of which I have made the first and only collection) commonly run in length to four or five thousand verses, and sometimes to as many as sixteen thousand verses. We thus have in them, for the first time, a body of songs, composed and transmitted orally, which generally equal in length the early Greek heroic songs, and so may be expected to throw much light upon them. We can thus see, for example, how the singer of a traditional song breaks his narrative, both when he needs to rest himself from the effort of his singing and when he needs to put off the rest of his song until another session. The circumstances of the singing of the long Southslavic songs are then described in so far as they bear upon the rests: the places, the occasions, the audience, and the time at the singer's disposal; also the differing length of the various songs and the singer's ability to lengthen or shorten a song. The bearing of these circumstances on the actual practice is then shown, and the practice is described both in the terms of my observations and of the explanations given by the singers when questioned. A comparison is then drawn with the early Greek heroic singing to see how far we can apply our knowledge gained from the observable Bosnian singing to the Greek songs where such external evidence is scanty. The conclusions of the comparison bear very definitely on the theories which seek to divide the *Iliad* and *Odyssey* into books or chants.

* An abstract from *Transactions of the American Philological Association* 66 (1935), xlvii. This abstract was submitted by the author before his death on 3 December, 1935. It may not have been intended for publication in its present form.

15

A Comparative Study of Diction as one of the Elements of Style in Early Greek Epic Poetry*

I

JUST as the story of the Fall of Troy, the tale of the House of Labdakos, and the other Greek epic legends were not themselves the original fictions of certain authors, but creations of a whole people, passed through one generation to another and gladly given to anyone who wished to tell them, so the style in which they were to be told was not a matter of individual creation, but a popular tradition, evolved by centuries of poets and audiences, which the composer of heroic verse might follow without thought of plagiarism, indeed, without knowledge that such a thing existed. This does not mean that personal talent had no effect on style, nothing to do with the choice and use of the medium whereby an author undertook to express his ideas: Aristotle points out Homer's superiority to other writers of early epic verse in the organization of his material. It does mean, though, that there were certain established limits of form to which the play of genius must confine itself.

This is very clearly seen when we consider the unrestricted range of style in contemporary letters. An audience of the period of epic poetry would have been dumbfounded had they heard a rhapsodist recite a piece whose story was altogether his own invention. They would probably have been more amazed if he had used a new method of telling, say having some minor character tell the story so that everything is seen through his eyes, a method often adopted by modern writers. And if he had made the theme of his story a study of the mental processes of the main character—. But it was not done. As a matter of fact, they could no more imagine such things than they could modern machinery. Homer, the authors of the *Hymns*, the composers of the *Thebais*, the *Afterborn*, the *Kypria*, the *Returns*, the *Telegony*, had to take their stories from legend, from no place else. They had to tell them in the grand manner, in which almost all the characters are eminently noble and speak as beautifully as the poet can contrive. They had to tell them in straightforward narrative,

* Master of Arts Thesis, 'A comparative study of diction as one of the elements of style in early Greek epic poetry', University of California, 21 December 1923.

which seldom allowed speeches shorter than half a dozen lines. And while the psychology of the characters might be treated with the greatest subtlety, it was always subordinated to the principal interest, which was the story itself.

Probably there are few things more necessary to the appreciation of Greek epic poetry than an understanding of the quality and value of this traditional element in the style, this necessity of the composer to follow certain very definite lines. Explanations of it have often been taken for granted, or vaguely guessed at, especially in discussions of the 'Homeric question'; it has never been properly explained. And yet it is the very point where modern critics must change their attitudes if they would understand the epics as their original audiences understood them. It is in this respect that epic poetry differs diametrically from modern poetry which lays so great a value on individuality and uniqueness of style.

Now any complete discussion of epic style must take into consideration the larger subjects of epic psychology, society, even religion. For since the proper study of style is the study of the ability with which an artist has expressed his ideas, the first thing is to know the nature of the author's thought. The element of diction, however, the *choice of words* for the expression of ideas, which is one of the constituents of style, is at once a more limited and a more tangible matter, and it is from the study of this that we shall attempt to gain some understanding of the broader field of style. We cannot be unsuccessful. It would be like studying the heart without learning anything about the body.

II

As might be expected, the character of the diction reflects the character of the style. Its most striking feature is its traditional, almost formulaic quality, its regular use of certain words and phrases in a certain way. The actual extent to which this quality enters into epic language is seen only upon investigation. We shall see how far it enters into the make-up of the *Iliad* and the *Odyssey*.

The reader of the *Iliad* and the *Odyssey* first perceives this traditional use of language in the more obvious instances. He notices that the name Ἀθήνη, whatever the case, whatever the thought, comes with very few exceptions at the end of the line.[1] The line may end, for instance,

. . . ἦλθε δ' Ἀθήνη
. . . ὅν ποτ' Ἀθήνη
. . . καὶ Ἀθήνης
. . . εἴσιδ' Ἀθήνην.

This is the beginning of an inexhaustible search. He next notices that the line often ends γλαυκῶπις Ἀθήνη. Investigation shows that it ends this

[1] For the exact figures as to the positions of Ἀθηνη and Ἀθήναίη see Appendix I.

way more than one third of the time.[1] Further inquiry shows that γλαυκῶπις, in its oblique cases occurs only in two positions, although the lines where they occur would seem unusual enough to have escaped any formulaic impress; that is, their thought seems to have been created only for the situation in hand. The form Ἀθηναίη also has its very definitely assigned place, beginning with the third syllable of the first foot. There is, for instance,

ὣς φάτ', Ἀθηναίη δέ . . .
ὣς φάτ' Ἀθηναίη . . .
χαῖρε δ' Ἀθηναίη . . .
ὃς μετ' Ἀθηναίης . . .

This is its position four-fifths of the time; the other fifth it occurs in another very specific position, where its use is even more obviously formulaic, since it occurs only in a formulaic line and two set phrases:

αἲ γὰρ Ζεῦ τε πάτερ καὶ Ἀθηναίη καὶ Ἄπολλον,
. . . Ἀθηναίη καὶ Ἄπολλον,
. . . Ἀθηναίη καὶ Ἥρη.

Investigation of phrases shows the same quality of prescribed position and order. There are lines ending θοὴν ἀνὰ νῆ' ἐρύσαντο or θοῆς παρὰ νηὸς ἐΐσης, θοῇ σὺν νηὶ μελαίνῃ. There are lines beginning ἀκταὶ δὲ προβλῆτες, ἀκταὶ ἀπόρρωγες, and ἀκτῇ ἐπὶ προβλῆτι.

Once begun, the search for traditional or formulaic words and phrases is endless. The word μῆνις, which one would suppose uncommon enough to have escaped the lot of having its position assigned to it, we find has two definite places, either at the beginning or the end of a line, and twice it occurs in the formulaic line

μῆνιν ἀλευάμενος ἑκατηβόλου Ἀπολλῶνος.

(It occurs fourteen times at the beginning and end of the line.) The three exceptions where it is used in other positions seem to have been made necessary by the use of other formulaic words and phrases.[2]

So far we have considered only the *Iliad* and the *Odyssey*. We find the same traditional diction in the Homeric *Hymns*, in Hesiod, and in the fragments of the Epic Cycle. To think that it would soon disappear from epic poetry would be as foolish as to think that a technique so elaborate, so complex, and so much the very essence of the epic, could have been evolved by one man or even by a single generation. In the *Hymn* to Dionysos, written at least three hundred years after the *Iliad*, probably

[1] For the positions of γλαυκῶπις see Appendix II.

[2] For the position of μῆνις see Appendix III, especially the conclusion. There is much corroborative material in these first three appendices which has not been used in the discussion. Its use would be superfluous to any but scholars with particular doubts.

more, we find the same words, the same phrases, and the same formulaic quality of position.

III

Such is the character of epic diction. Now what is the significance of the use of language of such a nature? What are its advantages? What are its drawbacks?

A reader, asked to describe this epic diction, might liken it to a school of sculpture which taught that all figures were to be modelled by the piecing together of certain ready-made arms, legs, heads, torsos, fingers, and so on. There is quite a variety to select from, and the parts in themselves are very beautiful. Moreover they fit with a perfection made possible only by centuries of constant experiment. But there are doubts as to the merits of this school. It may be that these parts are of such variety that the skilful artist can make a figure as subtle and individual as his own imagination, with every curve and line as he would wish. It may be, though, that the material is not so pliable, and that the best work must be much like all the other work of the school, and at the most, only an approximation of the author's conception. Then there is another drawback. Would it not be an art which could be learned with little genius? Why could not anyone make a statue by fitting together the various pieces; since they fitted so easily it would be a task requiring little ability in the handling of the material? And even the greatest artist, might he not, sometimes, when at a loss, use a piece just because it fitted and would make little difference in the finished work? We must learn the merits of this sort of art.

Now we have drawn our analogy from standards of modern sculpture. Is this valid? Can we apply to the art of one period the criterion of the art of another? Should we not rather have drawn our analogy from not modern, but Greek sculpture? And Greek sculpture immediately gives us the clue to the significance of this traditional element in the epic. For in Greek sculpture, too, convention, tradition, plays a large part, a part which has been recognized and appreciated.

Like the Greek painter the Greek sculptor worked in fixed schemes. He was dependent upon the manner in which his subject had been represented in earlier art. So, Furtwängler[1] points out, Phidias, in his Lemnian Athene, followed the traditional design of the peaceful Athene—an Athene with uncovered head and closely-bound hair circled by a festal fillet, who holds a spear in one hand and a helmet in the other, and wears the aegis in unwarlike fashion aslope her breasts. Moreover, the expression of the statue, a repose of body and face which by its very quietness indicates a divine strength and intellect, was an expression which, at the time, any carver of divinity must represent to the best of his abiltiy. By

[[1] See *Introduction*, pp. xxiv f.—A. P.]

following this tradition of design and expression Phidias has filled his work with the spirit of a whole race: he has not only followed its conception of the nature of the goddess, he has also represented her in the position and with the attributes which the race had chosen and approved as the most fitting to represent the beauty, the strength, the calmness of her nature. In a sense it might almost be said that the statue was produced by the Greeks in collaboration with Phidias. Nor, by accepting these broader lines, has he hampered the strength or subtlety of his own personality. He has used them for the further perfection and purification of the popular ideal. He has blended his own genius with that of his race, so inextricably that the two are hard to distinguish: they can only be realized in the perfection of the result.

Such is the role of convention in Greek sculpture, and we can now see that its role in epic poetry is much the same. We realize that the traditional, the formulaic quality of the diction was not a device for mere convenience, but the highest possible development of the hexameter medium to tell a race's heroic tales. The poetry was not one in which a poet must use his own words and try as best he might to utilize the possibilities of the metre. It was a poetry which for centuries had accumulated all such possibilities—all the turns of language, all the words, phrases, and effects of position, which had pleased the race.

We were obviously wrong in applying to the diction of this verse the standards of modern art which made it seem a patchwork technique. We cannot speak here of making a figure subtle and individual as the artist's imagination; for the artist's subtlety was a sort which expressed itself not in individuality but in refinement of the popular conception. We cannot speak disparagingly of the fact that all the work of the school was much the same; it was similar only in kind, not in the degree of perfection. And while it was a technique which might be learned parrot-like by men of little genius who added nothing to their inheritance, it was also a technique which furnished inexhaustible material for genius: the work of bringing to perfection is never finished.

We must keep these things in mind if we would understand the values of epic diction, if we would understand the epics at all. We must not look upon this poetry as we would upon our own contemporary, individualistic art. Rather it is Phidian; for it may be said that like the Lemnian Athene it was produced by the Greek race in collaboration with the artist, whose proper task was the perfection and refinement of the popular ideal.

IV

As the Platonic philosophy so keenly realized, abstractions are necessary but dangerous things. They are easily made, and they are easily made falsely. Yet they are indispensable to the understanding of the particular, the concrete, the indubitable fact. Now reasonable as our generalizations about the nature of epic diction may seem, we can be sure of their truth only by seeing how they conform to the actual facts. We must fit them to some phase of the poetry, which, you might say, is solid enough to be taken and held in the hand. Such a particular phase is the use of adjectives. This is also an especially convenient field for study; for here in the use of ornamental adjectives we have a traditional element which can be evaluated from a literary viewpoint. Thus we shall be able to determine how much the constraint of formulaic use has actually contributed to or detracted from the merits of the poetry.

An ornamental adjective is one which mentions some characteristic of an object without regard or reference to the special condition of that object in the narrative. One of the most striking instances of ornament occurs with the word 'ship' in the *Iliad.* There are twenty ornamental adjectives used with this noun:[1] hollow (κοίλη and γλαφυρή), swift, black, well-decked, sea-faring, trim, many-tholed, curved, huge, famed, well-built, many-benched, vermilion-cheeked, prowed, swift, straight-horned. In more than a third of the cases where Homer uses this noun in the *Iliad* he affixes one of these adjectives. There is in the whole poem only a single use of a specialized adjective with this word, that is, an adjective which contributes to the direct thought: 'There are revilings in plenty for both of us to utter, a *hundred-thwarted* ship would not suffice the burden.'

There is little difference in the use of ornament with objects animate or inanimate. The mention of Athene is nearly half the time accompanied by some word which describes the goddess, not on that particular occasion, but as she is immutably.[2] She is grey-eyed, the driver of the prey, fair-haired, Alalcomenean, she of the spoil, the saviour of the folk, protector of cities, lady, she of many counsels, great-hearted. In not a single case is she described by a specialized adjective.

Although in most cases not so marked, the tendency prevails throughout the poem. The sea is loud-sounding, echoing, broad, restless, boundless, grey, green, wine-dark, teeming. Kine are shambling, well-horned, wide-browed, straight-horned, of the field. The account could be lengthened indefinitely. In all, about half[3] of the adjectives in the *Iliad* and in the *Odyssey* are of this nature.

How utterly regardless of the situation this use of ornament is can be seen from such instances as these: Polyphemos lifts his hands to the starry heaven in broad daylight; ships are swift, even when drawn up on land; and raiment is gleaming, although it is ready for the wash.

The first impression which this use of ornamental words makes upon the reader is one of utter loveliness. They flow unceasingly through the

[1] See Appendix IV. [2] See Appendix V. [3] See Appendix VI.

changing moods of the poetry, inobtrusively blending with it, and yet, by their indifference to the story, giving a permanent, unchanging sense of strength and beauty. They are like a rhythmic motive in the accompaniment of a musical composition, strong and lovely, regularly recurring while the theme may change to a tone of passion or quiet, of discontent, of gladness or grandeur.

Then may come a disappointment, a suspicion that we are possibly reading into the epic poetry a beauty which is not really there. For it is clear that these words are often used for convenience' sake. There is nothing, it would seem, especially admirable in this: Athene is called 'grey-eyed' over one third of the time her name is used in the nominative with the form *Ἀθήνη*. A good proportion of these times she is called 'the goddess grey-eyed Athene'. Evidently the composer, wishing to tell something done by Athene, and finding it inconvenient to use the form *Ἀθηναίη*, managed his sentence or clause so that Athene would be named as the subject at the very last; he knew her name was a metrical line-ending. Now if his sentence or clause was so long, not including the subject, that it filled all but the very end of the line, Athene had no adjective. But if there was not quite so much to be said, and there was some space left, then she was called grey-eyed Athene. And if there happened to be even more space at the end, then she was called 'the goddess grey-eyed Athene', which ended the line very neatly.

This need for filling space in the metrical pattern seems to have entered invariably into the use of ornamental adjectives. For instance, we find (*A* 200)

αὐτίκα δ' ἔγνω
Παλλάδ' Ἀθηναίην·

Athene was not called Pallas here, as some might wish to believe, for the sake of introducing her in emphasized augustness. She was called Pallas because there was space which had to be filled in so that *Ἀθηναίη* could fall into its natural place and the hexameter flow smoothly on. And anyone who doubts the truth of this is welcome to refute us by rewriting that sentence, either with the omission of *Παλλάδ'* or with the substitution of other words.

Finally, if there is still any hesitation in believing that the use of these words was dictated by convenience, we may observe this fact: of eleven different adjectives used in the Iliad to describe Athene, only two (*πολύβουλος* and *μεγάθυμος*), each of them used only once, have the same metrical value. Homer had to hand a particular word for each of ten metrical exigencies that might arise.

So, we may ask ourselves, are we not overzealous in finding such beauty as we first described in words whose use is determined not by careful choice for the sake of their meaning, but by pure metrical convenience?

If we are judging by modern individualistic standards, yes; but not if we consider them in the light of what has been observed with regard to the influence and value of the racial artistic tradition.

These ornamental adjectives are really the practice of an artistic principle of unquestionable value, the principle that the medium should be blended to the ideas which the medium is to express, and conversely, the blending of the ideas to the medium. The desire for smoothness, that even flow of verse which Matthew Arnold described as 'rapidity of movement', made filling-in, padding, if you want to call it by that name, a necessity. There is no other poetry in the world as smooth and rapid as this epic poetry, in which the ideas of the particular passage seem fitted so perfectly, and yet so compactly, to the hexameter framework. And this smoothness is due, of course, to the use of a traditional diction which for centuries had experimented for words and phrases which would most perfectly fit the framework of the verse, and it is especially due to the use of ornamental words which eliminated even more completely any discrepancies in the pattern. The process of composition for the epic poet was much like of that of the worker in mosaic, who, having made his outline by the use of set pieces fills in whatever odd spaces may be left by pieces which fit exactly and yet blend inobtrusively with the pattern.

Such is the need of filling-in, and Greek epic poetry took that need not as a necessity, but as an opportunity. The words which they chose for the filling were those which generations of poets and audiences had selected as producing the highest artistic effect, as being most beautiful and appropriate to the subject. The fact that every epic poet used them is nothing to disparage: in their case the race was the artist, and the artist satisfied an artistic need and made of that need an opportunity for extraordinary beauty.

V

And now, by way of conclusion, we may discuss the merits of the various epic poems in the light of what has been discussed, we may see how the various poets have made use of this tradition of diction, and as a tangible means of judging we may see how they have made use of this tradition of conventional adjectives. Since our chief interest, of course, is to see how well Homer has made use of his medium, we will do best to study not Homeric usage first, and then compare our findings with later epic poetry, but rather to bring to the earlier poetry what we may learn from the later. We must reverse our chronology. We shall deal in order with Quintus of Smyrna, Apollonius of Rhodes, the later Hymns, the earlier Hymns, Hesiod, and the *Iliad* and the *Odyssey*.

The first impression of the reader of 'Matters Omitted by Homer' is one of extreme stiffness. It seems pompous, least of all, heroic. It is soon seen that, writing in the sixth century after Christ, in a society not altogether Homeric, he has out-epicked the epic. He has exaggerated what he mistook for the heroic to a degree of caricature. This is especially clear in his misunderstanding of ornament, which he mistook for grandiloquence, evidently believing that an epic adjective should be as lofty and uncommonplace as it could be made. For instance, he describes the boar at bay wrought upon a shield as 'grim-eyed', 'with woeful teeth' in a 'loud-gnashing jaw'. The boar that wounds Odysseus is meek by comparison: 'And forth from his lair he sprang forward with crest well bristled (φρίξας εὖ λοφιήν) and stood at bay before them.' An analysis of his adjectives shows hardly a simple word. He uses only about half as many purely ornamental adjectives as does Homer,[1] yet one hesitates to class hardly any of the rest as used specifically for the sake of the narrative. They are poor half-caste things. Indeed, there is little to observe in this author except the misunderstanding of the nature of ornament. For ornament could have no proper place in a diction that knew the traditional style and diction only by literary imitation; the traditional element was essentially a part of an oral poetry, a poetry that was learned by the ear, not by the eye. Quintus does, however, do us a real service in helping us appreciate the real merit of Apollonios.

Apollonius swings us from imitation to originality. Just as the mood of his *Argonautica* is his own, a romantic tale of the demigods, a story of the race of men half-divine, filled with the spirit of his own Hellenistic age—consider, for instance, his description of the toilet of Aphrodite—so his diction is his own. He affects ornament, along with epic forms and words, only enough to produce a pleasantly archaic impression,[1] an atmosphere much like that which the prose tales of William Morris have given our own time. There are no formulaic lines, few formulaic phrases, and the formulaic quality of position is noticeably absent. His work has every mark of originality and can in no way be criticized as a mere imitation of Homer, as the emulation of a literary form evolved by an altogether different stage of society. In this respect, at least, Callimachos and the Alexandrians were very much mistaken.

In turning, now, to the later Homeric *Hymns* we go back into the field of epic poetry proper, where the formulaic tradition was a natural and a vital part of an oral poetry. The best of the later hymns are those to Dionysos and to Pan, and there is in these poems, neither more than sixty lines long, a richness, a life, besides which even Apollonios at his best is a pauper of genius. This must be attributed to the use of the traditional diction, an inheritance so rich that its lesser partakers were richer than the greater men of later years. Compare, for instance, the first four lines of the *Hymn* (vii) *to Dionysus*,

[1] Appendix VI.

> Ἀμφὶ Διώνυσον Σεμέλης ἐρικυδέος υἱόν
> μνήσομαι, ὡς ἐφάνη παρὰ θῖν' ἁλὸς ἀτρυγέτοιο
> ἀκτῆι ἐπὶ προβλῆτι νεηνίηι ἀνδρὶ ἐοικώς
> πρωθήβηι·

with the first four lines of the *Argonautica*:

> Ἀρχόμενος σέο, Φοῖβε, παλαιγενέων κλέα φωτῶν
> μνήσομαι, οἳ Πόντοιο κατα στόμα καὶ διὰ πέτρας
> Κυανέας βασιλῆος ἐφημοσύνηι Πελίαο
> χρύσειον μετὰ κῶας εὔζυγον ἤλασεν Ἀργώ.

By comparison the poetry of Apollonios seems poor, halting, and clumsy; in the hymn there is hardly a phrase or position which cannot be paralleled over and over again in other epic poetry. One may notice too, the beauty and grace of the two ornamental adjectives ἐρικυδέος and ἀτρυγέτοιο.

Yet by comparison with the earlier hymns these later hymns use comparatively little formulaic diction or ornament. In the *Hymn to Dionysus* about a third of the adjectives are ornamental, in the *Hymn to Pan* about a sixth; but in the *Hymn to Apollo* this proportion is increased to almost two-thirds.[1] The relative merits of the poems are clear. The later poems are graceful, charming, but they have not the greatness of the earlier hymn, which, losing nothing in grace or charm, has added to them a grave reverence and a spirit of universality. For this result the diction is largely responsible: it has been to a great extent the means of submerging the poet's consciousness in that of his race. The later hymns have allowed a definite impress of personality to creep in. We may be sure that the author of the *Hymn to Dionysus* was a man who above all delighted in phantasy, in wonders, a fairy-tale mind. The composer of the *Hymn to Pan*, like Theocritus, whose verse is in certain respects strikingly similar, was a genial soul who carried the love of nature to a very high point. But the one who would sketch the personality of the author of the *Hymn to Apollo* would have to delineate the characteristics of the Greek people.

Matter-of-fact Hesiod in his *Works and Days* has gone as far as the late hymns in his abandonment of ornament,[1] but it is in a different respect that we feel the lack of it. For in robbing his verse of the beauty which ornament gives he did not substitute for it his own sense of charm. He said only what he had to say, and as a result he will never be too interesting, though that was probably no concern of his. He wished to teach, not to please. Yet his *Theogony*, which uses an Homeric proportion of ornament,[1] and whose diction as a whole seems to follow the tradition as much as Homer's, is little, if any, better. And this failure of the *Theogony* is probably our best evidence that, despite the native richness of the

[1] Appendix VI.

tradition, it required a great poet to turn it into great poetry. Both Homer and Hesiod followed the set scheme, but while one breathed a divine life into it, the other could hardly make it open its eyes.

For the *Iliad* and *Odyssey*, just as their conception and thought are the most perfect, have made the most perfect use of this tradition of words. They have used it to gain a depth and universality which the later poetry lost, to express a beauty which Hesiod in his moral strain could not hope for, and to fill it with a sense of life which the *Theogony* hardly hints at. As in the sculpture of Phidias the genius of the artist has blended with that of his race so inextricably that the two are hard to distinguish: they can only be realized in the perfection of the result.

APPENDIX I

Position of the words Ἀθήνη and Ἀθηναίη in the Iliad *and* Odyssey

α. Ἀθήνη[1]

In the nominative this word occurs 193 times at the end of the line (*Iliad* 86, *Odyssey* 107). The nominative form elsewhere in the line occurs three times:

Ε 260	*αἴ κέν μοι πολύβουλος Ἀθήνη κῦδος ὀρέξῃι*
Ο 123	*εἰ μὴ Ἀθήνη πᾶσι περιδείσασα θεοῖσιν*
π 260	*καὶ φράσαι ἤ κεν νῶιν Ἀθήνη σὺν Διὶ πατρί.*

In 41 of these instances the line ends *Παλλὰς Ἀθήνη* (*Iliad* 23, *Odyssey* 18), in 49 *θεὰ γλαυκῶπις Ἀθήνη* (*Iliad* 19, *Odyssey* 30), in 28 *γλαυκῶπις Ἀθήνη* (*Iliad* 10, *Odyssey* 18).

In the genitive it occurs 4 times at the end of the line (*Iliad* 3, *Odyssey* 1), and twice elsewhere:

Ζ 297	*αἱ δ' ὅτε νηὸν ἵκανον Ἀθήνης ἐν πόλει ἄκρῃι*
ζ 291	*δήεις ἀγλαὸν ἄλσος Ἀθήνης ἄγχι κελεύθου.*

In the dative it occurs 13 times at the end of the line (*Iliad* 6, *Odyssey* 7), and thrice elsewhere:

Ζ 301	*αἱ δ' ὀλολυγῇι πᾶσαι Ἀθήνηι χεῖρας ἀνέσχον*
τ 2 = *τ* 52	*μνηστήρεσσι φόνον σὺν Ἀθήνηι μερμηρίζων*

In the accusative it occurs 12 times (*Iliad* 4, *Odyssey* 8), always at the end of the line.

β. Ἀθηναίη

In the nominative this word occurs 34 times in a position beginning with the third syllable of the first foot (*Iliad* 14, *Odyssey* 20). Its only other position is

[1] These figures are compiled from Ebeling's *Lexicon Homericum*, Leipzig 1885.

beginning with the third syllable of the third foot. Its use in this position is purely formulaic, for it occurs 9 times (*Iliad* 4, *Odyssey* 5) in the formulaic line

αἴ γὰρ Ζεῦ τε πάτερ καὶ Ἀθηναίη καὶ Ἄπολλον,

7 times in the phrase Ἀθηναίη καὶ Ἥρη (*Iliad*), twice in the phrase Ἀθηναίη καὶ Ἄπολλον (*Iliad*), and nowhere else.

In the genitive it occurs only in these two positions, in the first 10 times (*Iliad* 8, *Odyssey* 2), and in the second 3 times:

Ζ 269 . . . πρὸς νηὸν Ἀθηναίης ἀγελείης
Ζ 300 τὴν γὰρ Τρῶες ἔθηκαν Ἀθηναίης ἱέρειαν.
π 207 . . . τόδε ἔργον Ἀθηναίης ἀγελείης.

In the dative it occurs 5 times in the first position (*Iliad* 4, *Odyssey* 1), and thrice in the second position:

Δ 64 . . . σὺ δὲ θᾶσσον Ἀθηναίῃ ἐπιτεῖλαι
Φ 392 . . . καὶ πρῶτος Ἀθηναίῃ ἐπόρουσεν.

In the accusative it occurs 11 times in the first position (*Iliad* 9, *Odyssey* 2), and once in the second:

Ε 765 ἄγρει μάν οἱ ἔπορσον Ἀθηναίην ἀγελείην.

APPENDIX II

Position of the word γλαυκῶπις *in the* Iliad *and* Odyssey[1]

The nominative of γλαυκῶπις occurs only in the line-ending γλαυκῶπις Ἀθήνη. It occurs thus 29 times in the *Iliad* and 38 times in the *Odyssey*.

The genitive, which appears three times (*Iliad* 2, *Odyssey* 1) shows a new position, beginning with the second syllable of a spondaic third foot.

In the dative it appears twice in the first position (*Iliad* 1, *Odyssey* 1) both times in the phrase γλαυκώπιδι κούρῃ, and four times in the second position (*Iliad* 3, *Odyssey* 1).

There are two forms of the *accusative*, γλαυκῶπιν and γλαυκώπιδα, each occurring once in the first position.

[1] The following figures are compiled from Prendergast's *Concordance to the* Iliad, London 1875, and Dunbar's *Concordance to the* Odyssey, Oxford 1880.

APPENDIX III

Position of the word μῆνις in the Iliad *and* Odyssey[1]

The nominative of this word occurs only in the *Iliad*, once at the end of the line and twice at the beginning of the fifth foot.

The genitive occurs only once, in the *Odyssey*, at the beginning of the line.

In the accusative the word with one exception occurs at the beginning or end of the line, 7 times at the beginning (*Iliad*), and 5 times at the end (*Iliad* 2, *Odyssey* 3). The exceptional line occurs in

I 517 οὐκ ἂν ἔγωγέ σε μῆνιν ἀπορρίψαντα κελοίμην.

It is also significant that the word appears three times in a formulaic line:

A 75 μῆνιν Ἀπόλλωνος ἑκατηβελέταο ἄνακτος
E 444 = *Π* 711 μῆνιν ἀλευάμενος ἑκατηβόλου Ἀπόλλωνος.

CONCLUSION: This word probably gives a more significant idea of the prevalence of the formulaic element than do the other words we have discussed. For it is by the exceptions as well as by the agreements to position that this must be learned. The word is sufficiently uncommon, and yet in five-sixths of the instances its position is prescribed. Those three exceptions would seem to be an original use of diction, yet there is another factor, the use of other formulaic phrases which render the new position necessary. In the first two exceptions,

O 122 πὰρ Διὸς ἀθανάτοισι χόλος καὶ μῆνις ἐτύχθη
Φ 523 ἄστεος αἰθομένοιο· θεῶν δέ ἑ μῆνις ἀνῆκε,

is the phrase πὰρ Διός, which like πρὸς Διός and ἐκ Διός occurs regularly in this position; the word ἐτύχθη, which never appears in any other position, and the word ἀνῆκε which appears only three times elsewhere in the line. The third exception (*I* 513) contains the word κελοίμην which is always final, and the whole line bears a striking similarity to another:

Ω 297 οὐκ ἂν ἔγωγέ σ' ἔπειτα ἐποτρύνουσα κελοίμην
I 517 οὐκ ἂν ἔγωγέ σε μῆνιν ἀπορρίψαντα κελοίμην.

It would seem that there is almost no purely original diction, the use of most words is seen to be exactly prescribed, and the most individual lines are found to be only the result of more unique combinations of these prescribed words and phrases.

[1] The figures are compiled from Prendergast and Dunbar.

APPENDIX IV

The following observations may be made upon the use of adjectives with the noun νηῦς in the *Iliad*:[1]

Case		times used without an adjective	times used with an adjective	Total
Sing.	Nominative	0	2	2
	Genitive	14	10	24
	Dative	5	16	21
	Accusative	7	5	12
Plur.	Nominative	14	36	50
	Genitive	104	21	125
	Dative	116	55	161
	Accusative	97	68	165
		357	213	560
		62%	37%	

Twenty-one different adjectives are used with νηῦς. Of these twenty are ornamental and seem in no place to be used with specialized significance. They are:

adjective	times used	adjective	times used
γλαφυρή	48	ἀμφιέλισσα	6
θοή	48	μεγακήτης	3
μελαίνη	33	εὐκλείης	1
ἐυσσελμός	16	εὐεργής	1
κοίλη	15	πολύζυγος	1
ποντόπορος	12	μιλτοπάρηος	1
κορωνίς	15	εὔπρυμνος	1
ὠκύπορος	9	κυανόπρωιρος	2
ἐίση	8	ὠκεῖα	1
πολυκληίς	7	ὀρθόκραιρος	1

In a single case the adjective used with this word bears a specialized sense—οὐδ' ἂν νηῦς ἑκατόζυγος ἄχθος ἄροιτο.

[1] These figures are compiled from the account of νηῦς in Ebeling's *Lexicon Homericum*.

APPENDIX V

The following observations may be made upon the use of adjectives with the name Ἀθήνη or Ἀθηναίη in the *Iliad*:[1]

(The figures in the left-hand columns are for the form Ἀθήνη, those in the right-hand columns for the form Ἀθηναίη.)

Case		times used without an adjective		times used with an adjective		Total
Sing.	Nominative	32	23	55	5	115
	Genitive	3	4	—	6	13
	Dative	10	3	—	4	17
	Accusative	—	9	6	3	18
	Vocative	3	—	—	—	3
		48+39 = 87		61+18 = 79		166
		52%		48%		

The adjectives used are these:

Adjective	Times used		Total
γλαυκῶπις	29	3	32
Παλλάς	24	5	29
ἀγελείη		4	4
ἠυκόμος		3	3
Ἀλαλκομενηΐς	3		3
ληῖτις		1	1
ἐρυσίπτολις		1	1
πότνια		1	1
λαόσσοος		1	1
πολύβουλος	1		1
μεγάθυμος	1		1

In no instance do we find a specialized adjective applied to the description of this goddess.

[1] These figures are compiled from Ebeling's *Lexicon Homericum*.

APPENDIX VI

Proportion of Ornamental and Specialized Adjectives in the Epic Poems

The lines chosen for investigation were the following.

Iliad 200 lines: *Α, Δ, Η, Κ, Π, Τ, Ν, Ω* 1–25
Odyssey 200 lines: α, γ, ε, θ, ξ, ρ, φ, ω 1–25
Works and Days 100 lines: 1–25, 101–25, 201–25, 301–25
Theogony 100 lines: 1–25, 201–25, 401–15, 601–15
Hymn to Apollo lines 1–100
Hymn (vii) *to Dionysus* entire
Hymn to Pan entire
Argonautica 200 lines: *Α, Β, Γ, Δ,* 1–50
Matters Omitted by Homer: *Α, Γ, Ε, Ζ, Θ, ΙΑ, ΙΔ* 1–25.

The proportion of ornamental adjectives was found to be as follows:

	per cent
Iliad	43
Odyssey	52
Works and Days	18
Theogony	48
Hymn to Apollo	64
Hymn to Dionysus	33
Hymn to Pan	17
Argonautica	5
Omitted by Homer	24

These figures make no aim at being ultimately exact: a comparatively small part of the poetry was investigated, and some adjectives border undecidedly between the two classes. They are doubtless, however, near the exact proportion, which is all that is necessary for the purposes of our discussion.

16

Ćor Huso: A Study of Southslavic Song

(Made in the years 1933 to 1935 under the auspices of Harvard University aud the American Council of Learned Societies, and with the gracious favour of H.M. the King of Yugoslavia)

EDITOR'S NOTE

Ćor Huso *is an unfinished work; it is largely concerned with Serbo-Croatian poems, and some of these of low quality. Moreover, it is a long work, and would have strained the limits of this volume. Hence excerpts only from it have been printed here. Passages were chosen which are of direct interest to the Homeric scholar and which do not require a knowledge of Serbo-Croatian to be understood. None the less, it will be seen from these excerpts how much Parry's general insights derived from close observation of specific poetic texts. In order to assemble his best general remarks, it was sometimes necessary to include references to texts and discussions which themselves could not be printed here.*

Nikola: From whom did you learn your first Bosnian songs?
Salih: I learned Bosnian songs from One-Eye Huso Husović from Kolašin.
N: Who was he? How did he live? What sort of work did he do?
S: He had no trade, only his horse and his arms, and he wandered about the world. He had only one eye. His clothes and his arms were of the finest. And so he wandered from town to town and sang to people to the *gusle*.
N: And that's all he did?
S: He went from kingdom to kingdom, and learned, and sang.
N: From kingdom to kingdom?
S: He was at Vienna at Franz's court.
N: Where was he?
S: At Vienna, at the court of Franz Joseph.
N: Why did he go there?
S: He happened to go there, and they told him about him, and went and got him, and he sang to him to the *gusle*, and King Joseph gave him a hundred sheep, and a hundred Napoleons as a present.
N: How long did he sing to him to the *gusle*?
S: A month.
N: So there was a Dutchman who liked the *gusle* that much?
S: You know, he wanted to hear such an unusual thing. He had never heard anything like it.
N: All right. And afterwards, when he came back, what did he do with those sheep? Did he work after that, or did he go on singing to the *gusle*?
S: He gave all the sheep to his relatives, and put the money in his purse, and wandered about the world.
N: And went on with his *gusle* and arms from kingdom to kingdom?
S: And went on again, the same way, from kingdom to kingdom.
N: Was he a good singer?
S: There could not have been a better.

—*Talk on Discs: Text Number 652*

[1]

FOREWORD

I HAVE planned the following volumes both for myself and for any other students of Southslavic oral literature as the full record of the way in which I gathered Southslavic oral prose and song. These volumes are in no way meant to be a finished work, but first a source of material for the author for a finished work of a very certain sort, and then a source for other students who may either wish to use the material for their own ends or to better the conclusions which I myself have drawn.

Those who consult these volumes should fully understand with what end in mind I gathered my material. It was least of all for the material itself that I planned the study. What I wished to learn was in general what an oral poetry was, and in particular what the Southslavic poetry was. The brief tale of how I was led to this poetry will make this clearer.

My first studies were on the style of the Homeric poems and led me to understand that so highly formulaic a style could be only traditional. I failed, however, at the time to understand as fully as I should have that a style such as that of Homer must not only be traditional but also must be oral. It was largely due to the remarks of my teacher M. Antoine Meillet that I came to see, dimly at first, that a true understanding of the Homeric poems could only come with a full understanding of the nature of oral poetry. It happened that a week or so before I defended my theses for the doctorate at the Sorbonne Professor Mathias Murko of the University of Prague delivered in Paris the series of conferences which later appeared as his book *La Poésie populaire épique en Yougoslavie au début du XXe siècle*. I had seen the poster for these lectures but at the time I saw in them no great meaning for myself. However, Professor Murko, doubtless due to some remark of M. Meillet, was present at my *soutenance* and at that time M. Meillet as a member of my jury pointed out with his usual ease and clarity this failing in my two books. It was the writings of Professor Murko more than those of any other which in the following years led me to the study of oral poetry in itself and to the heroic poems of the South Slavs.

I did not at once give myself up to the study of oral poetries, I was still too absorbed in following the method which I had worked out in the writing of my theses, and of which I shall shortly say something, but I gradually found myself obliged to clear up certain points, to seek what I could find in the works of students of the different oral poetries. Finally, when my study of the Homeric language led me to see that such a language could be created only by a long tradition of oral poetry I found myself in the position of speaking about the nature of oral style almost purely on the basis of a logical reasoning from the characteristics of Homeric style, whereas what information I had about oral style as it could be seen in actual practice was due to what I had been able to gather here and there from the remarks of different authors who, save in a few cases—that of Murko and Gesemann for the Southslavic poetries, and of Radloff for the Kirgiz-Tartar poetry—were apt to be haphazard and fragmentary—and I could well fear, misleading. Of the various oral poetries for which I could obtain enough information the Southslavic seemed to be the most suitable for a study which I had in mind, to give that knowledge of a still living oral poetry which I saw to be needed if I were to go on with any sureness in my study of Homer.

The purpose of the present collection of oral texts has then been made not with the thought of adding to the already vast collections of that poetry, but of obtaining evidence on the basis of which could be drawn a series of generalities applicable to all oral poetries; which would allow me, in the case of a poetry for which there was not enough evidence outside the poems themselves of the way in which they were made, to say whether that poetry was oral or was not, and *how* it should be understood if it was oral. In other words the study of the Southslavic poetry was meant to provide me an exact knowledge of the characteristics of oral style, in the hope that when such characteristics were known exactly, their presence or absence could definitely be ascertained in other poetries, and those many large and small ways in which the one oral poetry differed from written poetry for its understanding could be carried over to the Homeric poems.

A method is here involved, that which consists in *defining the characteristics of oral style.* I believe this method to be the essence of whatever I may have been able to add to our understanding of early poetries, and while my earlier studies gave too little place to the nature of oral poetry as such, nevertheless, they gave me the method which I have followed in my study of Southslavic oral poetry. There is nothing especially new in the method itself, only in the measure to which it has been used and the purity of its use. Thus my first work on the formulas of Homer thoroughly developed a familiar enough theme, since it was generally said that the Homeric style was formulaic, but no one had yet tried to see just to what extent the style was formulaic, nor to show how the technique of the formulas functioned for the composition of poetry, nor to show how such a technique of formulas by its complexity must be the work not of one man, but of many, and of many years. The method of the present investigation is essentially the same—that of obtaining the necessary knowledge which allows as exact and sound a description as possible of the style of the Southslavic poetry. Here, however, we can go much further than is possible in the case of the *Iliad* and the *Odyssey*, or of any of the other early poetries of Europe: the actual practice of the poetry itself suggests the hypothesis, and that hypothesis can be verified by the observation of the actual practice of the poetry. We can learn not only how the singer puts together his words, and then his phrases, and then his verses, but also his passage and themes, and we can see how the whole poem lives from one man to another, from one age to another, and passes over plains and mountains and the barriers of speech,—more, we can see how a whole oral poetry lives and dies.

And this stylized method, unless I am altogether mistaken, is at the same time the most rigorous and the most living of the methods of literary study. Style, as I understand the word and use it, is the form of thought: and thought is shaped by the life of men.

That particular form of thought which is sung or told—and in our own time written—and which we call literature, is only a more finished kind of thought, and is equally shaped by the character of the man and his times. Then to fully seize the style of a piece of literature would be to know everything about the author and the world in which he lived. For the Southslavic oral literature we can see how the form of life is mirrored in the form of style. For Homer we have only the form of style and the working backward to the form of thought—for so many elements enter into the problem—can only be partly done. The Southslavic poetry, however, can show us in many ways—just how many remains to be seen—how points of style in the Homeric poetry can be grouped together in a pattern which can be followed back to that moment which criticism must seek to create—the instant when the thought of the poet expressed itself in song.

[2]

Poetically this poem [which tells of the assassination of Franz Ferdinand] is negligible, whatever its value may be as a document of the popular thought. A popular poetry rises to greatness only in the measure that it shows a full understanding of the life which is portrayed or symbolized in its verses (and then, of course, only as that life itself is admirable), and it is the natural ability of oral poetry to show such an understanding that explains the high quality of so much of it. But when the civilized world, with complexities which can only be grasped by the educated mind as we understand it, encroaches upon the earlier life, the result is naïvety of different degrees. The theme of the seven kings in the Moslem poetry causes one to smile, yet such a poem as that of *Džanan buljuk-baša i Rakocija* (Hörmann I, 2), in which this theme appears, can still be one of the best Moslem poems, since after all the seven kings do effectively typify the enmity of Christian Europe; but the scene in Jugins's poem in which the Austrian Emperor calls for the telephone and telephones to the Kaiser, to the King of Bulgaria, and to the Sultan is only ludicrous. Notable in this poem are certain cases where the older phrases of the poetry have been adapted to an original use, such as

Evo tebi sigurna fermana.

or Jevo ti šarovite guje?

(Nikola, who is sitting just behind me working at the transcription of discs, when he heard me reading to the dictaphone the verse of Princip's speech went on and recited the line which follows them,

Puče strašno, ču se na nebesa.

When I asked him to recite the poem from the beginning he was able to do so only for twelve verses, and then lost himself in making the rhymes (doubtless had he been playing the *gusle* he would have had time to think of his verses as he sang or played the *gusle* between the verses). His explanation which, in its way, is doubtless true, was that it is very easy to forget poems that are rhymed. With this should be compared the statement which he made a week ago at Novi Pazar when Đemail Zogić remarked that no two singers ever sing the same songs alike. He then stated that the one exception was with rhymed poems. All this means that the song without rhyme heard in the manner habitual to the traditional poetry is recreated by each singer in his own verses more or less as an improvisation each time. The poem in rhyme, however, must be learned by heart, and when forgotten it cannot be re-improvised on the instant, since the rhymes present too great an obstacle to such improvisation. Corroborating this is Milovan's statement of last year that one could not improvise in rhyme to the *gusle* but must have the time provided by writing materials if he would compose a rhymed poem.)

[3]

All my observations of the poetry so far have, without exception, pointed to the conclusion that a singer who learns a song from another singer makes his own version more or less from the same themes (of the theme much must be said further on and a suitable classification of them devised) but almost altogether out of his own verses. There are, it is true, certain cases where the verses will be identical:

First, the first two or three lines of the poem to which the singer will listen with special attention, and which he can memorize;

Second, verses which are remarkable by an inner play of sound, particularly by rhyme at the caesura and the verse end;

Third, verses which are highly striking in some dramatic way, and will thus particularly force the attention of the singer who is listening;

Fourth, in the case of singers of the same region, those verses which may be called common verses, that is to say, which are used more or less by all the singers of a given region (the distinction between the common verse and the verse which is the singer's own is one of degree, and is dependent upon the function of the verse. Of this much more must be said later on);

Fifth, in the case of a singer who has learned to sing, that is to say, who has learned his equipment of verses, from a certain other singer there will be a larger number of identical verses common to his poem and to the poem as his master sings it;

Sixth, the greater number of times that one singer hears another singer sing the same song will make for a proportionately greater number of identical lines.

In the cases of the songs which have been learned from the books, the degree of identity between the text and the poem as it is sung will also vary for reasons similar to those just given. The primary factor of variation here is the proficiency of the singer who reads. In the extreme case, if the singer knew himself no other song he could only memorize the printed text. Such a case, however, is purely hypothetical, since the acquisition of the melody and the ability to play the instrument necessarily go side by side with the acquisition of verses; that is, the singer as he practices to sing to the *gusle* must necessarily sing verses.

[4]

A point is involved here which is one of the most difficult to get at, but which must definitely be cleared up, to wit, to what extent, and how, singers practice by themselves. Nikola, on occasions when we have had long drives, has amused himself by singing to himself beneath his breath parts of certain of the heroic songs we had heard. Another indication of the process is furnished by Nikola's statement, when I asked him about whether a singer who is dictating thinks of the verses to himself as sung or spoken, that he can think of them only as sung. I have not yet, however, met any case of a singer who came to the printed texts without first having a sufficient equipment of verses of his own, and it may be that, at the present, there exists in the Southslavic region no such singer, so that this factor of the previous proficiency may be discounted. It is, however, an important one from the point of view of the distinction between written and oral poetry, and it will become important for the Southslavic poetry if the time arises when the natural oral tradition is lost and the songs merely sung in the ancient manner. Such may or may not have been the case of the Homeric rhapsodes.

[5]

I have thus up to the present time found no evidence at all which would permit the conclusion that similarity of verses between a printed text and the same song as sung by a singer could be due to a natural oral transmission.

This conclusion is one which, I believe, has a great bearing upon the question of the authorship of the Homeric poems. There is, so far as I have been able to observe (*L'épithète*, Chapter V [TE, pp. 173–90], particularly the last three pages. Of course, before anything can be done in applying the conclusions of the Southslavic poetry to Homer there must be a thorough investigation of this problem of identity of style. None of the comparisons yet made by anyone are really worth much since none of them proceeded on the basis of the technique of oral composition) an entire identity of formulas—that is, of the parts of verses, of the verses, and even of the groups of verses which express a given idea—between the different parts of the *Iliad* and the *Odyssey* and between the *Iliad* and the *Odyssey*,—and this similarity can be observed in certain of the Homeric *Hymns*, certain of which, however, show evidence of dissimilarity of formulas, as do the Hesiodic poems. Two conclusions only seem to be possible, either first, that both the *Iliad* and *Odyssey* in their entirety, with perhaps some small exception, as well as some of the Homeric *Hymns*, are all the work of a single singer, or else, secondly, that for some reason, that does not exist for the Southslavic poetry, there existed for the Greek heroic songs a fixity of phrasing which is utterly unknown in the Southslavic. Such a fixity, as I see it, could be due to one or the other of two factors, or to both. First, it might possibly be due to the existence of a closed professional organization which gave to the young singer a long apprenticeship in which he must steep himself in the poems which the members of that association sang. The fact that the organization must have been closed is as important here for the reasoning as the fact of the apprenticeship. The reasoning is as follows: if there was in the group a singer who had not received the same identical training as the other singers of the group, and if the *Iliad* and the *Odyssey* and those of the *Hymns* which are identical in style are all the work of a single period, then that singer could have had no part in the poems as we have them since, coming from a different background, his phrasing must be different, and would thus reveal itself. If, on the other hand, the poems in question are not the work of the same period, and in the interval singers entered the group from outside, they would have influenced the style of the younger singers and would thus have destroyed the similarity of style. Thus, if we limit ourselves to identity and similarity of style, the evidence of the Southslavic poetry indicates that the poems are all either the work of a single singer or of a single closed professional group of singers. There is also, however, a second possible factor to consider: the far greater rigour of the hexameter as a verse form might have imposed a highly rigorous conservatism of phraseology whereby the poets one and all were obliged to have recourse to the traditional phrases, which only with the greatest difficulty could they alter or replace.

There is much still to be learned before we can pronounce with any sureness as to the exact place to be given to one or the other of these two factors. This much, however, I can see at present. The explanation of the uniformity of style of the *Iliad* and the *Odyssey* and certain of the *Hymns* on the grounds that they are the product of the work of different members of a closed corporation of singers will not satisfactorily be proved or disproved on the single evidence of the Southslavic poetry. We must have an exact account of the functioning of some oral poetry which is practiced in a far more professional way than is to be observed in the Southslavic region, where the nearest approach to professionalism exists among the Moslem singers, for whom at one time, to judge by what Luka Marjanović tells us, it was a definitely lucrative profession, that is in the days of the old Bosnian aristocracy. Jousse in his *Procédés orales* makes reference to an African tribe in which a priestly group has maintained without change songs composed at an earlier stage in the language, since the penalty of the change of any syllable was death. The conclusions to be drawn from that statement, however, are very doubtful. If they are songs preserved merely by fixed repetition they are similar to the song of the Arval brotherhood in Latin and have no bearing on the problem of the composition (since the problem is not that of preservation) of narrative poetry. On the other hand, what the Lomax's have told me about variations in the same song by the same singer among the southern Negroes would indicate that certain ballads in that poetry exist in a far more fluid state than is ever to be found in the case of the Southslavic. This might furnish evidence for a principle whereby a poetry as it was more intensely practised and more fully elaborated became more fixed in its verses and in its themes (the Macedonian and Bulgarian regions may furnish more definite evidence on this point). Finally, I add that there is another way of getting at the problem of the authorship of the Homeric poems through the Southslavic epos, to wit, on the basis of the construction of the large as opposed to the shorter poems. This is the problem of the technique of the themes, of which much must be said later. Briefly the principle may be stated in the form that what the shorter Serbian song is to the larger Moslem song, the Moslem song is to the still larger Homeric song.

[6]

Line five of Nikola is to all effects the line four of Podrugović. Such simple substitution or rearrangement of the words in the line as are found in the case of these two verses are inevitable. No singer who memorizes a text would ever think of doing so with an exactness which extended to the precise word and the ordering of words.

[7]

Now even as the verse may be evidence of influence, so may the simple theme, and for similar reasons. The great fluidity of the poetry, which makes it almost impossible for any given verse in a poem to remain unchanged for any great length of time or through any great number of singers also makes it difficult for any given simple theme to maintain itself for any great time in any given poem. Indeed, it is obvious that the distinction between the verse and the simple theme is only one of degree, and that even as the verse and the theme might be called formulas, so the simple verse might be designated as one of the types of simple themes. (Of the simple themes in a given song some are *stable* or *essential*, and others are *momentary* or *decorative*; this distinction will be developed later on).

[8]

Nikola's present version (text 2) of the poem seems to me even finer than that of Vuk. The details of the escape give a fullness to the poem as a whole which raises it above the barren statement of its classical version. Indeed, as I see it now, it is almost altogether this difference of barrenness or fullness which makes for the weakness or the strength of the poetry; and in such fullness more than in anything lies the superiority of the Moslem songs and of such of the greater Serbian songs as *Banović Strahinja* (Vuk II, 43) or as *Musić Stefan* (Vuk II, 46). (There is also, of course, an *empty fullness*, of which we shall find examples enough, but here I am speaking only of *real fullness*.)

[9]

However, here, as in so many places, one must resign oneself for the moment to uncertainty and wait patiently until an abundance of evidence provides knowledge enough of the processes of composition and transmission to make it possible to tell certainly by the stylistic characteristics of a given poem just what are the circumstances of its composition and transmission. The direct and simple method of asking the singer for the necessary information, though it is in general a good one, is nevertheless apt to be unsatisfactory in the case of any given question. The singer is, of course, completely unable to grasp the purpose of the sort of question designed to bring out the information about composition and transmission. In the first place, he has never thought very much about it, and what ideas he has about it are not exact and are influenced by certain vague conceptions of what is the ideal process of composition and transmission. Moreover, far transcending any desire to speak the truth is his desire to give the answer which will please the most and will place himself in the most favourable light. The soundest information which the singer thus gives is apt to be that which he gives by hazard or which he gives naturally at the beginning of the questioning before he has had time to formulate any theories about what one is trying to get at. The seeker after information will himself be at fault here unless he is careful. For instance, it is clear from the conversation in general of Salih Ugljan at Novi Pazar (spoken texts 652, 654–6, 658–9) that he was himself unable to remember in a great many of the cases where, and from whom, he had learned a certain song. Nevertheless, since he was asked in each case where he had learned a song he felt it incumbent upon himself to give an answer, which was in many cases far from consistent with what he had said elsewhere. In the case of Nikola self-interest always is and has been very much at stake. It was only gradually and by circumstances arising here and there which actually put him to the proof that I learned the smallness of his repertory and the fact that in the case of a good number of the songs of that repertory he did not know them to the end.

[10]

Because of a certain degree of professionalism, indeed, it is easier to locate the best Moslem singers in a given region than the best Christian singers. But even in the case of the Moslem singers the difficulty is great enough: the execution of the singer is apt to outweigh the intrinsic merit of his songs, and the repertory of any given singer is due so much to hazard that it is only in rare cases that his favourite poem would give the treatment of a theme which one was seeking. So in the case of all the poetry, but particularly in the case of the Christian, and even more so in the case of the short song, one must see that the odds are overwhelming against the possibility that any poem could be the best version. One can only say of the best version of a given poem that it was the best that could be collected.

[11]

The variations between the texts of Podrugović and that of Nikola, while considerable from the point of view of the number of verses affected, are nevertheless not very deep. The long passage of lines 67 to 141 which tell how Toša travelled over hill and dale to Prilip to the tower of Marko and came at the happy moment just as the day was dawning, and how he went up to the door and knocked upon it with the ring, that the ring was heavy and could be heard afar, and Marko in the summit of the tower heard it, and Marko had just arisen, and so on, is a passage made up of a great number of the so commonplace simple themes. Prkaćin Šćepan who, as we shall see, is like Nikola a singer of a most limited repertory, generously helped himself to themes of this precise nature in composing what poems he knew, and I know myself from my experience in telling the stories from various poems for my children that themes of this sort are the very easiest to repeat and the very easiest to remember. A bad singer will use them to excess, while a good singer, like Salih Ugljan, will use them sparingly.

[12]

Skurić came, a small man with a large sense of importance, and after many formalities of speech, remarks of such a sort that Nikola was the standard-bearer who must carry on the art of song when the older singers such as himself had passed away, he consented to sing. He was the first whom I met of the class of singers who give themselves the designation of *narodni guslar*, a kind who, from the point of view of one interested only in the genuine tradition, are only an inconvenience, but who are, nevertheless, definitely interesting by the fact that they represent one of the final stages in the disappearance of the tradition of oral song. Konavle is a community with some vestiges of Dalmatian oral song, and on the other hand by its contact with Dubrovnik it has a certain sophistication; it has accordingly followed the example set, I take it, by Belgrade, and then by Sarajevo, of holding *guslar* competitions, 'utakmice'. Such competitions are necessarily held under conditions which from any critical point of view must be considered the worst possible. They are public affairs and their organization is due to those political elements in the community which are precisely most closely in contact with the newer cultural and social points of view, and the farthest removed from the older life which produced the poems as a natural thing, and likewise understood them naturally. The critical point of view, on the other hand, of the completely sophisticated person of education, which carefully tries to reconstruct for its judgement the older point of view must obviously be a rare enough thing even in the most highly educated communities. The Guslar Competitions are necessarily demonstrations judged by notables (one account which I had of the competition at Belgrade, gave governors and generals among the judges) and since they attract an audience with no idea of what the true old songs would be, the singers are usually men with operatic voices and a stupendous style of song, and their songs are either the classical ones,—usually the shorter ones, because an audience of the sort is not patient for longer songs—or the new songs of the type of that of Guzina mentioned above. There is thus not the least requirement that singers in such competitions should be in any sense the inheritors of a genuine tradition, and from the point of view of anyone concerned with the poetry as it exists naturally, such singers have no worth.

But they enjoy no small fame in the communities from which they come (in the more educated communities where they give their performances they attract little attention) and the more so in the measure that their natal district has still maintained the true tradition of the oral song. Thus at Gacko, half an hour after my first arrival in the place, I was told of Ilija Vuković, shown his postcard, and listened to an admiring account of the cash value of his costume and the hitherto unheard of ornateness of his *gusle*. Even as the very communities which produced the finest songs (and as we shall see, Gacko has as much claim to distinction in this respect as any other place in the Southslavic area) utterly fail to have any idea of what are the true poetical values of the singing, so they are unable to understand that the simple lines of the older *gusle* with its simplified stylization of the goat's head is a finer thing than a *gusle* which bears upon it the carved head of the ancient kings and heroes, the sovereign, and Vuk Karadžić.

[13]

The question of original verses is a fundamental one and one which, because of the distinction involved between oral and written poetry, must be established with great exactness and completeness. There is probably already in the collection material enough from the region of Stolac to make possible an investigation in which one would seek in the poems of singers of other regions as many verses as possible of any poem or of all the poems of Petar; provided, of course, that we had from other singers versions of the same poems that Petar sang, so that it would be possible to have the essential verses of the different poems and the verses containing the different names of each poem. My impression is that it will be possible to find elsewhere almost every single verse of Petar's. Further effort must be made at Stolac to obtain a complete collection of such material. But more important than this mere demonstration by analysis of accumulated material, is the establishing on logical grounds of the reason why such a singer as Petar has no original lines in his poems: the verses and the themes of the traditional song form a web in which the thought of the singer is completely enmeshed; there is some strand of words to bind his lightest thought. His major theme can be made up only of minor themes, his minor, only of lesser, and his lesser, only of the verses and phrases which he has heard from other singers. The old romantic notion of the poetry as a thing made by the people is by no means a completely false one. The poetry does stand beyond the single singer. He possesses it only at the instant of his song, when it is his to make or mar. Make it or mar it he will as he is able or unable to tell a story well, but well told or poorly told a song must be made of the traditional themes and traditional verses.

[14]

We saw above *that these two themes are precisely two of the four which are possessed in common by the eighteenth-century short-line version of the poem and Vuk's version*: and in the one case where there is an identical verse in the two older versions the verse is the same as Petar's I, 100 = II, 25. In other words, we find that those parts of the poem which are the most exactly fixed in the mind of a single singer are precisely the parts which are most fixed in the tradition as a whole. From our literary point of view this is almost a startling thing: *the singer embodies the tradition, and what is true of the one is true of the other*. Petar, when he learned his poem, learned the larger themes in a general way; the unessential themes he learned or forgot or introduced as the occasion of each singing prompted; but the essential simple themes of the poem he learned with exactness and repeated faithfully. The tradition is, of course, only the sum of such singers as Petar. One might symbolize it by the idea of a singer who is at once all singers.

[15]

One of the faults to which the singers are most prone is that of diluteness, and the characteristics of concision and diluteness, and the rôle which they play in the Southslavic song, must be discussed fully in their place.

[16]

The faults which have been discussed thus far are all of them dependent upon the circumstances of singing, that is to say upon the constraint which the speed of the song sets upon the singer, and accordingly they are such faults as would not be found in a dictated text. In dictating the singer has ample time to think about the next verse, and if the verse is not a good one the writer will not accept it. But dictation also makes for faults of its own kind. I am not thinking at this point of the relative *narrative* merits of the song and the dictated version, which will be discussed shortly, but of faults which arise when a singer lacks the powers of concentration which would enable him to hold in mind exactly the train of thought, while he is waiting for the last verse to be written, and at the same time compose to himself the verse which he will dictate next, and which will carry that train of thought ahead as it should be carried. The necessary slowness of dictation is itself trying in the singer's attention; the pause for the writing gives place for distraction; and finally, the singer, as in the pause for writing he thinks ahead, may more or less forget just how he dictated the last verse, and may even skip some verse which he has thought of in his own head, and thinks he has dictated.

[17]

DIGRESSION: NOTES SUGGESTED BY THE READING OF THE *ODYSSEY*

1. *Tempo and Length of Narrative Song*

The more I understand the Southslavic poetry and the nature of the unity of the oral poem, the clearer it seems to me that the *Iliad* and the *Odyssey* are very exactly, as we have them, each one of them the rounded and finished work of a single singer; though whether they are both the work of *one* singer I do not yet know. I even figure to myself, just now, the moment when the author of the *Odyssey* sat and dictated his song, while another, with writing materials, wrote it down verse by verse, even in the way that our singers sit in the immobility of their thought, watching the motion of Nikola's hand across the empty page, when it will tell them it is the instant for them to speak the next verse. The reasons I have for such an opinion are many, some of them still very vague, some very exact. I have mentioned above the line of arguing by the principle of the elaboration of themes, which produces the longer oral poem. This will probably be the most convincing, and also the most objective method of taking up the problem. There is also the line of argument by unity of style, which has been mentioned above, and which bears on the question, not only of the unity of each poem, but also on the question of whether they are both the work of the same singer. Also the problem of the characteristics of oral style and the language of oral poetry still has many phases other than those on which I have already touched: I have already in my Homeric studies dealt with the oral character of the formula and the oral character of certain metrical irregularities; but still untouched are the matters of irregularities of syntax due to oral composition, and of contradictions of detail in the narrative as indication of oral composition, that is to say, the use of Lachmann's material to this very different end. The arguments by the characteristics of oral style (of which the most important is probably the theme) will prove only the oral nature of the Homeric poems, which, of course, does not necessarily establish the unity of the poems; but the whole problem involves two steps: the demonstration of the oral character of the poems from beginning to end, and then the demonstration of the unity on the basis of the unity of the oral poem.

The whole problem of the transmission of the poems once composed is also one which must be considered in detail. In view of what the Southslavic poetry shows us about the history of the poems when they have been written down, and when singers have begun to take advantage of writing, there is good reason not only to be patient, but inquisitive with the *narodni guslari* and such young singers as the nephew of Hasan Čustović, who on Christmas Day, when we were questioning him about the songs which he had learned from his uncle, stated in a burst of frankness, 'Najviše znam od pjesmarica.'[1] Much also will be learned from the alterations made to the Southslavic texts by such unscholarly collectors and editors as Šaulić. A methodical study along such lines will probably show us much about the sources of the variants of the texts such as Ludwig and Allen give them in their editions, about the longer and shorter papyrus texts, and the action of the early editors.

Date of writing, January 20, 1934

The particular point, however, which prompted the writing of these pages is what may be called the tempo of the narrative. As I have become familiar with the tempo of the narrative of the Moslem poems, and in single cases with the tempo of the narrative of such a good Moslem singer as Salih Ugljan at Novi Pazar, I have come to have enough knowledge of the style of the narrative to see that certain shorter passages of the poems imply by their nature a long poem. Thus, in Salih Ugljan's *Kraljišnici Turci izbavljaju Bega Mustajbega iz sužanjstva* (dictated text 649), the story moves ahead with such a full and unhurried movement of the exposition that it is clear that the poem will be a long one before the poet, at the same detailed rate of utilization of the oral material, has developed the possibilities of the chief theme which he has exposed; the poem, indeed, runs on to 1,297 verses. The opening theme of the poem in itself implies length. Its function is highly pathetic. I have mentioned above how deficient the Southslavic epic is in pathos, as compared with the Greek. In the same way the Christian poems, with certain notable exceptions, are more lacking in pathos than the Moslem poems, and the principle may be stated that the length of the poem in an oral poetry is generally in proportion to the place which the pathetic has in the poetry as a whole, and in individual cases in the work of each poet. Even in the Moslem

[1] ['Most of what I know is from the songbook.'—A. P.]

poetry, however, such pathetic opening themes as that of this poem of Salih's are rare enough; an outstanding case is that of the opening theme of III, 1 of the *Matica Hrvatska.*

Even more, however, than the indications of length which are given by the way in which such a theme as the opening theme is developed, one may deduce such length from shorter passages whose presence in the poem indicates on the part of the singer the intention of developing his story with all fullness, and without hurry. Such a passage in the poem of Salih in question is that of verses 41–50, where the singer relates how, on this morning of Bajram on which the poem opens, Beg Osman Beg, after hearing from his mother how Mustaj Beg and the agas of Osijek were lost, performs the ritual of ablution and goes to the mosque for the ceremony of Bajram. The passage is in no way essential to the story of the poem, but more than anything, here at the beginning, it adds to that sense of fullness which is one of the finest characteristics of the *Iliad* and *Odyssey*. Another such passage in the work of Salih indicative of fullness of story and corresponding length of song is that of the verses 110–80 of text 270: *Ženidba Đerđelez Alije.* The Sultan's Tartar arrives at Kaniđa at Alija's tower with the message of the Sultan, and the singer, had he wished, might have said immediately in the next verse that he gave the message to Alija. Instead, the poet relates at length how, Alija not being at home, the Tartar is directed to go on to the mosque where Alija has gone, and there is then a long and very fine scene wherein is related how the Tartar finds Alija seated in the garden before the mosque with the nobles, how Alija is pointed out to him in verses which describe his appearance (165–8), and how Alija, with the proper actions of noble fealty, receives the message from the hands of the Tartar. The fullness of the detail in this passage is very like that of the fullness and leisure of Homer's account of the arrival of Hermes at the isle of Calypso with the orders of Zeus for the sending of Odysseus. The description of the island and the cave, the details of the entertainment, and the talk which leads up to the words of the actual message, all [date of writing, January 21, 1935] show the oral poet in full command of all the traditional material, leisurely building theme on theme to make the fullness of detail.

For it is the construction *by themes* which makes this comparison of the Greek and the Southslavic poetries different from a comparison in the field of written literature. It is true, for instance, that a person well read in modern novels, and with the other works of, say, Jane Austen and Tolstoy, could tell by reading not very many pages of *Sense and Sensibility* or *War and Peace* that the work as a whole must run to considerable length, but he could not determine the fact in anywhere nearly the short space that he can in the case of the oral poetry, nor with nearly the same sureness: almost all the themes of the modern authors are completely new to him, and he is not able to distinguish between the essential themes and the unessential themes, nor to see to what fullness comparatively the author has chosen to develop a given traditional theme.

Recent Homeric criticism generally recognizes that the narrative of the first four books of the *Odyssey* is not of a sort which could stand by itself. Its interest disappears so soon as it loses its relation with the later part of the poem, and in its detail it shows itself clearly to be the narrative preparation for that later part. Calhoun's article on the legal liabilities of the suitors brings this out very well. (G. M. Calhoun: 'Télémaque et le plan de l'Odyssée', *Revue des études grecques* 47 (April–June 1934), 153). Moreover, Bérard's assumption of a *Telemachy* supposes a type of oral poem of a very special sort, which has no chief theme, and of which the only unity must be either the interest of the epic detail, or the interest attached to the person of Telemachus by his relationship to Odysseus. Neither of such interests could be sufficient to create a special type of poem. In regard to the first, there is no example in oral narrative poetry of detail being interesting by itself. In regard to the second, it is true that relationship by blood of the hero to a yet greater hero can to a great extent provide the interest of a poem, but the deeds of the son must be of the same high sort as those of the father. Thus, in the Southslavic poetry a cycle has developed about the young Omer, the son of Mujo Hrnjica, and for a Homeric audience the deeds of Diomed must have gained no small part of their interest from the fact that he was the son of Tydeus of the Afterborn. The character of Telemachus, however, is of a very different sort from that of these two heroes. There is thus abundant enough evidence on the mere basis of plot for the reader of the first books of the Odyssey to suppose a long poem to follow. The completely different sort of evidence of elaboration of theme points to the same end.

II. *The Falsity of the Notion of the Chants of the Homeric Poems*

The habit of chapters which our general reading has given us is a strong one, and for a long time, even as Bérard, I believed that a proper analysis of the poems would furnish a proper division of the Homeric poems into their chants. The imposition by the Alexandrians of all the letters of the alphabet was obviously, by its arbitrariness, false, and I looked for some unit in the poems which would correspond to the length of song suited to the regular length of time which a singer would sing. I was, of course, unable to figure to myself the exact details of life in Homer's time which would have made a certain length of time a normal one for a gathered company to listen to heroic song; I probably had in the back of my head some reflex of critical thought which came from the modern actuality of the theatre.

The mind, since it cannot think in a vacuum, must necessarily carry over to its comprehension of the past the notions of the present, unless a man has actually been able to build up from the very details of the past a notion which must necessarily exclude the application of his habitual notions. Here lies that tremendous difficulty of making clear to the modern reader of written literature the nature of oral literature: until he has got a fairly complete idea of oral literature, he will comprehend the explanation of what oral literature is in accordance with the standards of written literature, and will be almost sure to misunderstand what seems to the explainer a most simple thing. So, for a long time I expected that I would find some day the sections of his song which Homer had planned for the successive days of his singing, although I at no time in my reading of the poems ever came upon the slightest indication of such divisions. It was only when the Southslavic poetry showed me the actual practice of a sung poetry that I saw how foolish my notions had been.

Date of writing, January 22, 1935

Each household where there is a *guslar* with any claim to his art, or which has any tradition of song, has its *gusle*; and so has each *kafana* in the community where songs still thrive. To these two places of (*a*) the singer's home, or (*b*) the *han* or *kafana*, are to be added (*c*) the wedding, and (*d*), in the case of the Moslem poetry and in the days of the old Moslem aristocracy, the home of the nobles, who invited singers for the entertainment of themselves and their guests. No one of these four places provides for circumstances of singing which would make for any fixed length of time as the ordinary one for a single continuous singing. In every case the singer himself has himself almost no control over the time of his performance, which, on the contrary, is subject to the conveniences of his listeners. The irregularities of the comings and goings, and the tasks and different interests of the members of a household leave no fixed moment for singing; there are no regular moments for arrival and departure at the tavern; and weddings are notoriously boisterous and eventful. The nobleman's entertainment provides by far the best circumstances for the singer's performance, but it is obvious that even here there will be no fixed moment for a singer's beginning or ending his song, or for the moment when some circumstance will interrupt the performance, or bring the gathering to its end. The *general* length of time which the singer can generally count on has indeed a far reaching effect, in that it produces a comparatively longer song; but it is better to state this fact by saying that an audience which has greater leisure and greater interest in singing than another audience is ready to give more time to the singing, knows more about the songs, and so demands a fuller tale.

The instances in which Homer gives us scenes in which there is singing of the heroic songs show us in almost every case how the length of the singing is subject to the circumstances of the moment, quite as are the Southslavic singers. Achilles in the *Iliad* (*I* 186 ff.) is singing for himself the high deeds of men, quite like some man of the Black Mountain, while Patroclus listens. The arrival of the embassy necessarily puts an abrupt end to his song. Thus the one example which the Homeric songs give us of informal singing properly shows us the uncertainty of its length; which, of course, if one thinks about it at all, is an only too obvious thing. The passages in which the professional *aoidoi* sing also conspire to show this. In the first book of the *Odyssey* the singer Phemius starts to sing to the suitors the Return of the Achaeans. He cannot have gotten very far before he is stopped by Penelope, who begs him to sing some song less painful to herself. There follows the conversation between Telemachus and his mother and between Telemachus and the suitors, and when that is done there seems to be no more thought of Phemius. The suitors turn to dancing and to singing themselves. When Telemachus and Peisistratus arrive at the palace of Menelaus they find a marriage in progress, and as a part of the marriage entertainment there is a singer, but there are also acrobats, whose presence can hardly have made for an undivided attention to the songs, and the general boisterousness which their presence implies can hardly have made for a very sustained narrative. I take it that Homer, in this passage (δ 15 ff.), means that Menelaus had provided a minstrel and acrobats for the entertainment of his guests, and not that the singer and acrobats performed at the same time, or had any relation to one another in their performance. At any rate, the arrival of the new guests must have broken into whatever singing there was, although Homer is thinking so little about the singer that he makes no more than the simple mention of his presence as part of the entertainment. In the verses following *θ* 62 Homer tells how, at the banquet which the Phaeacians give in honour of the wanderer, after the meal is over, the singer Demodocus strikes up the song of the Strife of Odysseus and Achilles. (Note that Demodocus, like Phemius, does not seem to have been an actual member of the household in which we see him singing, but rather a member of the community who through his art has won a certain place in the life of the household, that is to say, there is no evidence that the singers in question were men whose sole concerns and means of livelihood was their song, or that they were attached exclusively to a single household.) The song makes Odysseus weep, and then Alcinous considerately suggests that his guest had had enough of food and song, and that it is now time for the sports. There is no question of the end of the song: when one has had enough of singing no more is served. At the games Demodocus sings the Loves of Aphrodite and Ares. It is a short song, and its comprehension calls for the solution of two problems: whether it is one of an accepted type of short and amusing oral songs; and whether, for the Greeks, a pure hexameter rhythm could be a dance rhythm. At any rate, the song is of a different type than that which the singers sing elsewhere in the poems, and the fact that the song itself is given as a song within a song removes it from all relevancy in the present discussion. (The ending of this song is worth noting (*θ* 361–6), because the manner of its ending is like the manner of ending of both the *Iliad* and the *Odyssey*.) When they return to the halls of Alcinous Odysseus himself asks Demodocus to sing the Wooden Horse. Again the song is too much for him. He breaks down in tears, and again Alcinous bids the singer stop (*θ* 537):

Δημόδοκος δ' ἤδη σχεθέτω φόρμιγγα λίγειαν.

(Note in passing the subject of the evidence within the Homeric poems on the character of the singer in Homeric times, on the repertory of heroic songs of Homer's time, and on the technique of the construction by shortened themes as it is shown in the shortened version of the Calydonian Hunt in *I*, and of the Wooden Horse and Odysseus Spies Out Troy in δ.) It may of course be argued with reason that the difficulty which the singers in the Homeric poems thus experience at every point in getting very far with their songs could hardly be typical of the actual practice, since in all the cases but one Homer is making use of the theme of the interrupted song. What is important, of course, is the picture of the Homeric gathering, which plainly shows what is obvious enough anyway, that the poet is at the convenience of his hearers.

Or it might be thought that the length of a chant could be determined by the length of time which the singer could sing at a stretch, but here again there is absolutely no element making for fixity. Fine singing for the Greeks must have been very like fine singing for the Southern Slavs: a voice as strong as possible singing to as high a pitch as possible, a clear-cut and forceful delivery of the words, and a vigorous accompaniment upon the instrument. It takes the full strength of a man to sing this way. The movement of the body in playing the instrument, the labouring of the lungs for the breath needed for the volume of song, the strain on the muscles of the throat and mouth that go to forming the words, make the singing a toil, and a good singer after a half hour of his song is drenched in sweat. The length of time which any singer will sing at a stretch is thus largely determined by the stamina of his physique, and since it is the singer who sets the pause for his song when he feels that he can say that he can sing no further, the amount of singing before that pause will depend upon the strength of the man, which again largely depends upon his youth or age, on the way he is feeling, on the condition of his voice, and finally, upon how much he feels spurred on by the particular audience to which he is singing.

Date of writing, January 23, 1935

Thus Ćamil Kulenović at Kulen Vakuf, a young man of 25 years, sang at a single stretch the song *Vrhovac Alija u sužanjstvu* (text 523), a song of over 1,300 lines, at a single stretch and in over two hours of continuous singing. Such a sustained singing is quite unique in my own knowledge, and I have never heard nor read of anything which approaches it. The singing was done in the open air *kafana* that stands by the great spring. It was a very pleasant summer day, and no small portion of the town were there to see the making of the discs. The excitement of the moment led Ćamil to outdo himself. Sulejman Hrnjica, who sang after Ćamil, sang a song of 828 lines in 3 pieces of 287, 352, and 189 verses, which represent about 20 minutes, 26 minutes, and 12 minutes of singing respectively. The usual length of time for singing at a stretch is somewhere between 20 and 40 minutes. It is not much use trying to give a more exact figure, since in almost every case there is some varying circumstance, such as those which have been mentioned, which is the determining factor, or anyone of a thousand thoughts which may suggest to the singer when he has sung enough.

The singer then stops and rests, and gives the audience to understand that his strength will let him go no further, and no 'Goni, goni' from his audience obliges him to go on unless he so wishes. He at this point has some ethical claim to some form of entertainment—almost always a cigarette, and very often something to drink, and his listeners must wait until he is ready to go on. The length of such a pause is also necessarily variable, depending upon the patience or impatience of the audience, the extent of weariness of the singer, or rather upon the extent which he has made his weariness apparent to the audience, upon the time taken to allow him to consume his entertainment, upon the course of the conversation which has sprung up in the interval, and so on.

Still another fundamental factor of variability in the amount that is sung at a stretch and in the space of a given time is that of the different rate of singing of singers. To begin with, the singer does not always sing at the same rate of speed. The verses at the beginning of the song are usually sung more slowly than those of the middle and the end of the poem, when the singer has warmed to his work. Thus, Salih Ugljan in the *Ženidba Đerđelez Alije* (text 277a) is singing at the beginning of his song at the rate of about 13 verses to the minute, but between lines 538 and 608 he is singing at the rate of about 18 verses to the minute. Then the singers vary greatly between themselves in the speed of their singing. The calculation which Murko has made (*La Poésie populaire épique en Yougoslavie*, 20) that singers vary between 13 and 28 verses a minute, and have an average variation of 16 to 20 verses a minute seems to be a good one. Finally, the fact is very certain that the singer has no exact idea at all how long his song will take him. Almost always when we have tried to get from a singer some indication of how long relatively his song will be, or how much of it is still left, he has been mistaken. The song which he has described as a very long song will not be particularly long, and on the contrary his longest song will be one which he gave as one of his shorter poems. Very often a singer has told us during a pause that his song will finish in a very few moments, when, in fact, there were still many hundreds of verses for him to sing. Such uncertainty is, of course, bound up with the great variability in the length of the song, and in most cases the factors for this variability are unconscious ones as far as the singer himself goes.

Thus, from beginning to end there is not a single thing in the circumstances of singing which would tend to the development of a song or part or a song of fixed length and occupying a fixed time. The tendency there is, however, to the longer or shorter poem according to the comparative length of time which the singer's general public has to give, and to the interest which it has in singing. Thus the far greater length of the Moslem poems must be set down to the longer period for amusement which the Moslems had or wished to give to the singing. Frequent in the Moslem songs is the verse:

Na Udbini u begluk mehani,[1]

and the *begluk mehana*, the tavern where the nobles of the Turkish border sit and drink and boast of their prowess (such is a common opening theme of the Moslem songs) may be taken as symbolic of the conditions which have made for length in the Moslem poems, as well as for their form, and the many other qualities which set them off from the Christian songs. It is clear that there must have been an even greater interest and leisure for song among the Greeks of Homer's time, for the circumstances of singing do impose this limitation in the case of the Southslavic Moslem songs: none of them is longer than may be sung in an afternoon or a long evening, whereas the *Iliad* and the *Odyssey*, or the long epics which we hear about point rigorously to a performance by the singer to the same audience on a number of successive days, which implies a *very* leisurely aristocratic audience.

The idea accordingly might suggest itself that this necessity of the Homeric singer of dividing his poem between successive days renders inapplicable to the Homeric poems the parallel example of Southslavic song, but this only makes the circumstances even more against any fixed division of the poems: to all the elements of variability mentioned for the Southslavic which make for the uncertainty of the singer's singing any exact length of song at a given meeting must then be added the new necessity of the singer's having to complete each day the fixed portion of

[1] ['at Udbina, in the tavern'—A. P.]

his song in order to be able to go on the next day from the beginning of the new section. While we can well suppose that Homer could count on his audience for a comparatively long period, and probably on successive days, it is obvious that the circumstances of each day must be different and the mood of his audience changing.

[18]

One particular circumstance of the practice of the Southslavic singers will conclude this array of evidence against the notion of the chant. It happens constantly that there is not time for a singer to finish his song. It is then simply abandoned. This is particularly frequent for songs sung in the *han* or *kafana* as opposed to those sung at home, when they will be sung over a number of days. Thus Đuro Vujnović, who had heard most of his songs while living as a *kiridžija*, knew more songs only part way than he knew whole songs. Hajdar Đozo of Bare had learned his songs in the *han* which his father kept for the caravan drivers on the caravan route from Sarajevo to Foća, and so knew most of his songs only half way. Salih Ugljan at Novi Pazar told us once how he knew only part of a certain song because he had heard it sung at some *han* by a singer who had had to go on before his song was finished. There is in all this far more than the mere very inconvenient interruption of a song as we would understand it. The song for the oral audience has an interest of its own apart from the plot. The song is usually known already. If it is not known, other songs of the same theme are most sure to be familiar to the listeners. On the other hand, each verse and each one of the shorter themes as they are sung is itself relished, so that a singer's beginning a song in no way obliges him to finish it if his audience is to have any pleasure in it at all. Accordingly, the risk of not being able to finish a long song, or the insufficiency of a short song to fill up an entire evening, has in no way operated to the creation of songs of any standard length. The length of song depends on factors altogether other than the probable length of time for which the singer will have an audience at his disposal: it will depend on the type of chief theme—for instance the *ženidba* in the strict sense of the term, that is the poem in which the inviting and the arrival of the wedding guests must be told in detail for each guest, is necessarily a long poem: it will depend on the extent to which the tradition of the region has created a fuller or shorter version of a poem; on whether the singer has inherited a poem in a fuller or shorter version; on how much the singer himself is given to the elaboration of the theme; and so on. Now if, in the case of the Southslavic poetry, where the song must be sung in its entirety or left usually forever incomplete, the length of time for singing has in no way ever affected the length of the song, it is evident that it would do so even less in the case of the Greek. For the Greek song is such that it must be sung anyway over many evenings, and, in view of all that there is still left to be sung on other days before the end of the poem is reached, the singer could always put off until the morrow any hundreds of verses which might remain before any particular part of the action could come to an end.

The *Iliad* and the *Odyssey*, like the Southslavic songs, have only the single unity of their whole story. No part of them has a unity of its own, and in both the poetries, when his time is at an end, the singer breaks off his narrative at any one of the points of progression in the narrative. Since that narrative is continually progressive such points are abundant. Accordingly, the Alexandrians were able to make no bad division of the poems, and those which modern editors have proposed are usually neither better nor worse than those of the Alexandrians.

[19]

The oral song is made up on the one hand of the essential theme, which may in itself be a bare enough thing, and on the other hand of the traditional oral material which furnishes its elaboration. That oral material, if properly applied, is good in itself, and accordingly whether more or less of it is used is not the deciding factor in the quality of a song, but rather the appropriateness of its use. Thus one can say little more than that Petar's version I is good for a shorter poem, and his version IV is good for a longer song. The good or bad song is due to no mere accident of length, but to the singer's narrative ability, which is in turn limited by the quality of the tradition, which is to say, by the quality of the themes which make the texture of his song. This brings us into the fundamental but large problem, to be treated later on, of the social conditions which have made for a more noble or a less noble tradition.

[20]

All this would point to the conclusion that the poems of a flourishing tradition which were constantly being sung would be comparatively fixed, and that in a professional tradition with an intense apprenticeship a certain poem would preserve a fixed form for a longer period. Factors in this relationship must be the extent to which the apprentice singer felt himself inferior or superior to the singer to whom he was listening. However, an oral tradition which has a large number of long songs must, in the most extreme circumstances which one can imagine of exact transmission and constant practice, nevertheless involve a more or less imperfect transition between singers, and for each singer long periods without practice in which any given song must largely revert to its verbal fluidity. Also the accumulation of small changes in a constant singing of the same song must in time amount to major changes. The fundamental point to remember in connection with this problem is that without writing there is no fixity of the model, and a singer can never know exactly just how his master sang, nor even just how he himself sang the last time. Thus, while the fluidity of Petar's song seems by its circumstances to provide an extreme example, it is nevertheless an example which must be to some extent typical of all narrative song.

[21]

Prkačin himself, however, claimed to have learned the poem from his father, but since time proved him to be a particularly great liar, no certainty on this point is possible.

[22]

DIGRESSION: ENJAMBEMENT AND THE PUNCTUATION OF THE VERSE END IN NARRATIVE SONG

The singing of narrative in verses of equal length with a pause between each verse necessarily makes for an adding or, as it is usually called, an unperiodic style. The poet, thinking of his story verse by verse, will only to a small extent be led to look further ahead than the verse end, and as a result, unless the sentence is to be limited in its length to the verse, that part of the sentence which comes after the first verse will be of such a kind that while it carries on and develops the thought of the first verse of the sentence, it is nevertheless not particularly indispensable to that first verse. This may be stated simply by saying that in narrative song the narrative can be broken off at almost any point and brought to a close with a period. This is, however, very far from saying that each verse in such a style can stand by itself. The first verse of the sentence can, but the following verses are dependent on the foregoing verses for their meaning.

The first lines of the *Iliad* give an example of this type of oral narrative poetical syntax. The first verse of the poem could stand by itself. The second verse, however, is syntactically dependent on the first, as likewise is the third verse; and the fourth is dependent upon the third, the fifth upon the fourth, and the sixth upon the fifth. Yet it would be possible in the case of any one of these first five verses to bring the verse to an end with a period, and thus make a sentence which, to anyone who does not already know the text, must seem in every way complete.

The sixth verse, on the contrary, relies on the seventh verse to give it its grammatical subject. Even here, however, the break in the syntax is largely of the same sort as that at the end of the foregoing verses. The verse will be read by anyone who has the habit of Homeric syntax: 'From the time when *they* first parted in strife, Atrides, the king of men, and divine Achilles.' Verse nine likewise would not bear a period at the end, but there is still a sharp break in the thought, caused by the division at this point between a participle clause and its finite clause. The enjambement is essentially like that in Southslavic song when the dependent clause precedes its principal clause:

> Kad je rana zora udarila
> Gospođica pa se razbudila.[1]
> (Sulejman Makić, dictated text 683, vs. 9–10)

A good deal of the difference in the poetries is due to the role which the participle plays in the one language, and the tendency of the other language to parataxis. From verse nine one goes on to verse 18 before finding another sentence where a period could not close the verse. Here definitely is a kind of enjambement which has no parallel in the Southslavic song: the verse end is reached and the verb is still without its object. It is to be noted, however, that Ὀλύμπια δώματ' ἔχοντες is a purely ornamental phrase of the epithet type. Homer here used the phrase since, when he reached δοῖεν and the middle of his verse, he realized that the thought of his ἐκπέρσαι Πριάμοιο πόλιν would not fit into the last half of the verse but could find its place at the beginning of the following verse. A point to be exactly investigated in the Homeric technique is that of the ornamental device for filling the last half of the verse, so that the thought of the first half of one line can be carried on from the beginning of the following line. Verses 39 and 40 are the next examples of verses which would not bear the period: they are of the same type of preceding dependent clause that has been noted above in the case of the Southslavic. The enjambement after ἐφιείς of 51 is like that after χολωθείς of 9; 66, however, provides a true case of enjambement, since the κνίσης of 66 has no place in the syntactic pattern until the participle ἀντιάσας of the next verse is reached.

It is thus to be seen that while the Homeric poetry is for the greater part like the Southslavic in its adding of verses to the already potentially completed sentence, there are nevertheless a certain number of verses where the syntactic pattern is divided between two verses. We must thus seek in the Homeric verse some factor making for enjambement which is absent in the Southslavic. That factor must be one of three sorts: either rhythmic, or syntactic, or both. The rhythmic explanation would be that the Homeric rhythm is such that the verse is not the rigid unit of the rhythmic phrase, but is divisible into sub-phrases of various lengths, and

[1] ['And when early dawn appeared,
Then did the lady awaken.'—A. P.]

that a sub-phrase of a verse end may be combined with a sub-phrase at the beginning of a following verse in such a way as to constitute a longer single phrase, which would be sung as a unit. A final answer to this question must depend upon a fuller knowledge of the nature of the rhythms of Greek song than is possessed at present, but against it can be mentioned the *syllaba anceps* of the verse end and the fact that all the cases of really close enjambement, that is to say where the essential words of a single clause are divided between two verses, all seem to be due to an unusual functioning of the technique of formulas which, not grouping themselves within the verse, have made necessary the enjambement. The syntactic explanation seems more satisfactory, and in itself is enough to account for the differences of enjambement we know between the Greek song and the Southslavic song.

17

Homer, Parry, and Huso*

ALBERT B. LORD

MILMAN PARRY began his first study of Homeric style[1] with a quotation from Ernest Renan which epitomized the method which he was later to follow so scrupulously. Renan's words have become familiar to all of Parry's students. 'Comment saisir la physionomie et l'originalité des littératures primitives, si on ne pénètre la vie morale et intime de la nation, si on ne se place au point même de l'humanité qu'elle occupa, afin de voir et de sentir comme elle, si on ne la regarde vivre, ou plutôt si on ne vit un instant avec elle?'[2] 'La littérature de chaque pays et de chaque époque', Parry continued, 'n'est comprise comme elle doit l'être de façon naturelle que par l'auteur et son public contemporain. Il existe entre eux un fonds commun d'expérience qui permet à l'auteur de mentionner tel objet, ou d'exprimer telle idée, tout en étant sûr que son public se représente bien le même objet et saisit les nuances de l'idée. L'auteur, et c'est là une partie de son génie, tient compte à tout instant des idées et du savoir de ceux auxquels il soumet son oeuvre; donc la tâche de celui qui, vivant à une autre époque, veut apprécier cette œuvre avec justesse, consiste précisément à retrouver le savoir varié et les groupes d'idées que l'auteur supposait appartenir naturellement à son public . . . si le principe n'est que trop apparent, son application rigoureuse est des plus rares, étant complexe au point d'être impossible à réaliser de manière tout à fait satisfaisante: la critique se propose là un but qui est la perfection même.'[3] This was the goal which Parry set for himself from the very beginning and it was this which led him by logical steps from the painstaking analysis of Homeric style to the investigation of the oral nature of the South Slavic epic, from Homer to Huso.

In *L' Épithète traditionnelle* [TE, above], he showed that the noun–epithet combinations in the Homeric poems were part of a vastly intricate pattern of formulas which the poet (or poets) had available to enable him (or them) to express a given idea within the limits of the verse.

* First published in *American Journal of Archaeology* 52 (1948), 34–44. Reprinted by kind permission of the editor and Dr. Lord.

[1] TE, above.

[2] *L'Avenir de la science*, p. 292; TE, p. 2 above.

[3] TE, p. 2 above.

Because of the lack of extant Greek material it was impossible to prove that all of the noun-epithet combinations were formulas, but the proportion which were demonstrably so was great enough that it was obvious that such a style could not be the work of a single poet. It must have been years in the making and it must have required the efforts of many poets. Hence this style was traditional and was thus set apart from the style of other epic poets such as Apollonius or Virgil. They were imitating Homer, but they were composing in a different way. With them the epithet was a literary device used to impart an 'epic' flavor to their verses, but in the Homeric poems the traditional, or ornamental, epithet was forced on the poet by the exigencies of the verse and was an integral and necessary part of the style. The requirements of the verse-making created the formulaic, traditional, style.

When approached from this angle many of the difficultiems in the poes were solved, or at least were readily understood, without any departure from the critical method which Parry ever had before him. In his supplementary thesis[1] he considered two types of metrical irregularities from this point of view: the hiatus and the short vowels which had to be given the value of longs because of their position in the verse. In putting the formulas together to form verses the poet sometimes found that a metrical irregularity occurred at the point of | juncture; a formula ending with a vowel, for example, had to be joined to a formula beginning with a vowel and to elide would leave the verse short a syllable; or a formula ending with a short vowel followed by a single consonant was to be joined to a formula which began with a vowel. But the poet would rather ignore this irregularity than change the formula, which was for him the proper way of expressing the idea. He was not willing to depart from the traditional phrase. Another cause of such metrical irregularities, Parry pointed out, was the construction of formulas by analogy with others. This is important, because it illustrates the way in which formulas are created. The most common examples, and the most obvious, arise from a change of case in a noun and its adjective. *Μέροπες ἄνθρωποι* occurs at the end of *Σ* 288 and the last syllable of the adjective must be considered long. To understand how this happened the verse should be compared with the several instances where a line ends with the formula *μερόπων ἀνθρώπων* (*Σ* 342, *Σ* 490, *Υ* 217).[2] The modification of the formula caused a metrical irregularity, which the singer was willing to overlook in favor of the formulaic pattern.

One could continue in this way to show how Parry applied the touchstone of the traditional style to the apparent inconsistencies which critics had found in Homer,[3] but it is not the intention of this brief article to

[1] FM, above. [2] FM, pp. 1978 above.
[3] See HG, and DE, above.

review in detail the writings of Milman Parry. What I would like to point out is that in his early works he was thinking of a traditional style which was created by the poet's need for an easy way of making verses. The oral nature of that style had not yet occurred to him. He did not yet realize that this need for an easy versification arose from the fact that the poems were composed orally.

The first expression of this is found in his article on enjambement in Homeric verse. '. . . Homer was ever pushed on to use unperiodic enjambement. Oral versemaking by its speed must be chiefly carried on in an adding style. The Singer has not time for the nice balances and contrasts of unhurried thought: he must order his words in such a way that they leave him much freedom to end the sentence or draw it out as the story and the needs of the verse demand.'[1] The idea had been sown in fertile soil and it grew rapidly. Parry's two articles in the *Harvard Studies*[2] show an amazing development. He had in the meantime been delving into other heroic poetries, as even a cursory glance at the footnotes in the second of the two articles shows. These two articles, together with his French theses, present fully his theories and convictions about the Homeric poems up to the time of his research on the Yugoslav epic.

The first of these two studies deals with style and the second with language. Since style is concerned with the form of thought, the basis for a discussion of Homeric style is the formula. Parry showed that the formula and the systems of formulas are peculiar to Homeric style. 'It is of course the pattern of the diction which, as in the matter of the authorship of the style, proves by its very extent that the Homeric style is oral. It must have been for some good reason that the poet, or poets, of the *Iliad* and the *Odyssey* kept to the formulas even when he, or they, had to use some of them very frequently. What was this constraint that thus set Homer apart from the poets of a later time, and of our own time, whom we see in every phrase choosing those words which alone will match the color of their own thought? | The answer is not only the desire for an easy way of making verses, but the complete need of it. Whatever manner of composition we could suppose for Homer, it could be only one which barred him in every verse and in every phrase from the search for words that would be of his own finding. Whatever reason we may find for his following the scheme of the diction, it can be only one which quits the poet at no instant. There is only one need of this sort which can even be suggested—the necessity of making verses by the spoken word. This is a need which can be lifted from the poet only by writing, which alone allows the poet to leave his unfinished idea in the safe keeping of the paper which lies before him, while with whole unhurried mind he seeks along the ranges of his thought for the new group of words which his idea

[1] DE, p. 262 above. [2] HS, above; and HL, above.

calls for. Without writing, the poet can make his verses only if he has a formulaic diction which will give him his phrases all made, and made in such a way that, at the slightest bidding of the poet, they will link themselves in an unbroken pattern that will fill his verses and make his sentences.'[1] This is an enlargement of the brief statement I have already quoted from Parry's article on enjambement. When he came to study the Homeric language as the language of an oral poetry he gave a much fuller description of this style, and then proceeded to show by the same type of reasoning that the language of an oral poetry is made up of archaic elements, foreign elements, and artificial elements, and he applied this to the Homeric language. In this paper, too, he was thinking for the first time not only of formulas but of whole traditional passages.[2] This is a point which was later to assume even greater importance in his thinking, although he did not live long enough to set his ideas down on paper. I know, however, that he had formulated them pretty exactly.

But at this point in 1932 he had reached a crisis. He wrote: 'To prove that there were one or many poets, and to show what passages were taken whole from the tradition and which were made anew out of single formulas or verses, we must turn to the study of other oral poetries where the processes of composition can be studied in actual practice and in a greater body of poetry than we have for the Greek epic. When, by the exact analysis of oral poems in reference to their tradition, we have grasped in detail just how the oral poet works and what it is that makes a poem good or bad in the judgment of himself and his hearers, we shall then, but only then, be able to undertake to study the authorship of the *Iliad* and the *Odyssey*, and to try to apportion that which is due to the tradition and that which is due to the author.'[3] Up to this point he had been talking of oral poetry from a theoretical basis and from accounts of others who had done field work. With rare exceptions (for example, the research of Murko and Gesemann in South Slavic poetry and Radloff in Turkish) Parry had no great faith in the reports of these investigators. He was too thorough a scholar (as anyone will attest who has taken the trouble to follow the close reasoning and careful analyses in his writings) and too devoted to method to rely upon the observations of others when it was possible for him to observe the phenomena of oral poetry himself. There was nothing else to do then but to learn Serbo-Croatian (he chose the Yugoslav field because in those days it was the most accessible of the still living oral epics), to have a recording apparatus built which would satisfy the needs of continuous recording, and to go to Yugoslavia. With the financial assistance of the American Council of Learned Societies and

[1] HS, p. 317 above.
[2] HL, p. 334 above. [3] HL, p. 361 above.

of the Milton Fund and Clarke Bequest of Harvard, and with the cooperation of the Yugoslav government, he surmounted all the difficulties of such an undertaking and returned in the fall of 1935 with one of the most remarkable collections of oral poetry ever made. |

We all know that he did not have the opportunity to commit the results of his field studies to writing. However, in the fall of 1935 he did begin a book to which he gave the title 'The Singer of Tales'. Seven typewritten pages of the first chapter of that book, typically entitled 'Aim and Method', are still in my possession and, obviously unfinished though they be, they are published here for the first time. They are the last words which he wrote on the subject of oral poetry.

'This book is the report of a study which I made in the years 1933–1935 of the heroic songs of the Slavic speaking peoples of the Balkan peninsula. It happened at the time that I gathered much lore and music of many sorts, and made beginnings of what I hope may be in time a full and much needed work on Southslavic heroic and lyric song, but the study reported here was planned and carried out with no such large end in view: its business was to find out how the singers of the heroic tales learn and practice their art. But if I thus narrowed the scope of the search it was because I believed that we needed a very particular kind of knowledge before we could go much farther in our understanding of a whole vast and often very famous body of poetry, namely of what is properly to be called the *song of unlettered peoples*, but has been variously named as *folk*, or *popular*, or *primitive*, or *traditional*, or merely *early poetry*. Briefly, the aim of the study was to fix with exactness the *form* of oral story poetry to see wherein it differs from the *form* of written story poetry. Its method was to observe singers working in a thriving tradition of unlettered song and see how the form of their songs hangs upon their having to learn and practice their art without reading and writing. The principles of *oral form* thus gotten would be useful in two ways. They would be a starting point for a comparative study of oral poetry which sought to see how the way of life of a people gives rise to a poetry of a given kind and a given degree of excellence. Secondly they would be useful in the study of the great poems which have come down to us as lonely relics of a dim past: we would know how to work backwards from their form so as to learn how they must have been made. Thus this book is meant not only for the Slavist but as well for the folklorist or anthropologist who has to do with the songs of any unlettered people, and even more for the students of such "early" poems as the *Iliad* and *Odyssey*, or the *chansons de geste*, or *Beowulf*.

'I am not of course the first to try to find out how an oral poem comes into being and passes from one singer to another, and what changes it undergoes in the course. No more am I the first to try to use living unlettered song for better understanding of "early" poetry. Indeed, no small part of my faith in the method I have followed has come from my belief that the work of other scholars has tended ever more and more towards this method, until the time had come for someone to attempt a rigid formulation and use of it. It is even more than likely that someone else would have done this before had it not been for the lack of the mechanical means: it has only been in the last few years that the science of electrical sound recording has given us an apparatus of such a sort that it can record songs of any length and in the large numbers needed before one can draw conclusions, and finally which can make records which are so good that the words on them can be accurately written down for the purpose of close study.

The Oral Form of Unlettered Song

'The critics, groping for the rules by which they should group the varied works of the world's literature, have come to see more or less clearly that literature falls into two great parts, but they have not yet agreed upon the real nature of these two parts, nor upon the terms which should be applied to them. Such names as *folk-literature*, or *popular*, or *primitive* | *literature* have much truth in them but they are not finally good because, not to speak of the strange use of the word "literature", they are purely negative terms and mean at the best nothing more than the talk and song of men who have not the education of a self-styled civilized people, while at the worst they either betray a scorn which it would be hard to justify for certain ranks and forms of society, or else a wistful belief in questionable theories which make of the "common" man and the "simpler" stages of society the springhead of art. With our great anthropological knowledge we can now see that such terms get us little further than the point men reached in the seventeen hundreds when they believed that savages had a poetry which was more "natural" than their own. We are readier, now that we know more, to set *lore* against *literature*. These two words entangle us in no doubtful theories, but they do suppose that the use of writing brought about the one greatest change in man's artful use of words. It would seem true, however, that learning the use of writing is the one greatest cultural happening in the life of a people.

'If we put *lore* against *literature* it follows that we should put *oral poetry* against *written poetry*, but the critics so far have rarely done this, chiefly because it happened that the same man rarely knew both kinds of poetry, and if he did he was rather looking for that in which they were alike. That is, the men who were likely to meet with the songs of an unlettered people were not ordinarily of the sort who could judge soundly how good or bad they were, while the men with a literary background who published oral poems wanted above all to show that they were good as literature. It was only the students of the "early" poems who were brought into touch at the same time with both lore and literature. Early poems come from the time debatable between the lack and the use of writing, and if the pride of the nations in the genius of their past has led above all to the vaunting of these poems for the same sort of merits in them as one finds in great literary poetry, the little that is known about how they were made keeps pointing the other way to poets who made little or no use of writing. So from the start the songs which men gathered in modern times from unlettered peoples were likened to the early poems. The theories which resulted, for good or for worse, have been of any number of sorts, but broadly they may be put under the headings of those which stressed *origins*, *content*, or *practice*.

'We can see now that the critics began working from the wrong end when they leaped upon the oral poems to wrest from them the answer to the question which had so long vexed them: who was their author? Their question, unhappily, was the wrong one, because in it they failed to see that an oral poem undergoes two kinds of creation, that of the man who first makes it and that of the man who sings it each time. We are able to get pretty fully at the creation of the *singer*, but we are slapped at every turn when we try to get our hands upon the creation of the *maker* (and very properly, for it is the only way we will learn that we are looking for the wrong thing), but it was nevertheless the creation of the maker which the first critics of the oral poems were sure they had found. It was simply that they had never heard or dreamed of a poem being otherwise than *fixed*, so they left the factor of the *fluidity* of the oral poem altogether out of their equation and got the answer that whereas the author of a written poem is so-and-so, the author of the oral poem is the people. The solution to the age-long problem they then set forth in a pleasant setting of ideas on the genius of the folk, which were then prompted largely by the democratic faith in man, but which have since, not without a certain irony, become the heart of the various doctrines of nationalism. The view which came belatedly, because it is only by careful study that we can work away from habitual ideas, that uneducated and uncivilized man is not really very unlike the man of the modern world, and that the genius of the oral poet is not really any different from the | genius of the written poet, is still so rare that it is limited almost to the experts. Nevertheless it was this first great eagerness to know the origins of the oral poems which turned men to them and brought into being the work of such great collectors as Karajitch and Radloff whose work with true singers led them to see for the first time the true nature of creation in unlettered song.

'It was soon seen that there was much against the theory of folk-origin in such a simple form and further work was carried on along two lines. First, the method of comparative linguistics was carried over into the field of early and oral poetry, and a great deal of sound study showed how parts of stories, or even the whole story, keep turning up in poems of different regions of a country, and in different centuries, and even in different countries. It was a method which could not be used as rigorously as in the field of linguistics for fixing the "common" form from which all the other forms must have come in the course of time and travel, because the material was too varied, and there was no way of telling whether two poems with the same story came from a common source, or whether one of them came from the other. Nevertheless the search itself was of a sort which kept to the songs themselves, and even though it failed to give us a body of Aryan ballads it showed much about the life of the theme in oral poetry, though the reasons for that life can be well understood only when one has seen the use of it by the singer in making up his song. The second line of study which sought to get at the origins of oral poetry took up more carefully the practice of the poetry itself as a way to this end, but it will be better, before looking at what was done by scholars along this right road, to glance at what was done along another.

'The students of the early European poetries, as these became better known, were struck by the great likeness in their thought, in such a way that passing over their oral nature, which they were more or less ready to grant, they came more and more to treat them as common examples of *heroic* poetry. This was very good as far as it went. Certainly no reader of these ancient poetries can help being struck by the fact that they have chiefly to do with the prowesses of men of strength and courage, whom the poets believed to have lived in a more or less distant past when human powers were greater, and whom they called by a special term which we translate as "hero". These critics were wrong, however, when they went on and supposed that heroic poetry was one of the necessary stages in the growth of literature. They failed to keep apart history and poetry. Poetry is heroic only because it is created by a people who are living in a certain way, and so have a certain outlook on life, and our understanding of the heroic will come only as we learn what that way of living is and grasp that outlook. We find, for example, that cattle-lifting is a common theme in the ancient European poetries, but it is found there because of no law of poetry, but because these people happened to live in a way which led them to the stealing of cattle on the one hand and to the practice of poetry on the other. The heroic element in early poetry is not a problem of lore, but one of anthropology and history, and the students of heroic poetry have done a very great deal in showing how the social background is mirrored in the poetry, but far less in showing us the nature of the poetry itself. The same is true for a number of other works which follow what is usually called a sociological method: inasmuch as they explain the content of the poems by the social life of the people they show us nothing about oral poetry which could not also be true of literary poetry. When, however, such works point out the *function* of song in a given society, that is another matter, for they are then beginning to get at social factors which bear upon the form of song. But to this I shall shortly return.

'To get back now to the critics who worked further along the line of origin: these were | chiefly the students of the English and Danish ballads, that is, of poems which were written down fairly lately, and which even now are sung in such out of the way regions as the Faroes Islands and the mountains of Kentucky.'

When we were still in the field in Dubrovnik during the winter of 1934–5 Parry began to dictate a running narrative account of his two Yugoslav trips, inserting each text into the narrative in its chronological order and providing each text with a commentary. He covered only eight texts (the last unfinished) and a period from the fifth to the twenty-second of July, 1933. These are only field notes, but they are far from rough. I believe he intended some time to complete them. The present plan is to include them in the introductory pages to volume one of the published collection. I mention them here because Professor Parry gave to them the title *Ćor Huso*.

Ćor Huso Husein was a blind singer whom we never met because he had already gone to his reward in 1935, but who had become a legendary figure among the singers in the Sandzak of Novi Pazar, where we first heard of him, and in Montenegro. A full account of what we know about him will be given in its proper place, but to Parry, I believe, he symbolized the Yugoslav traditional singer in much the same way in which Homer was the Greek singer of tales par excellence. Some of the best poems collected were from singers who had heard Ćor Huso and had learned from him.

The Parry Collection of South Slavic Texts, now the property of the Harvard University Library, contains over 3,580 twelve-inch phonograph records and more than 12,500 texts, of which approximately 750 are recorded. Generally speaking, there are four types of text: (1) Instrumental; there are a few records illustrating the music of various instruments used in the Balkans; (2) Women's Songs; lyric and short narratives sung, usually unaccompanied, by the women and young people for their own entertainment or at social gatherings; about 11,000 of the total number of texts in the collection are of this type and some 250 are on records;[1]

[1] The music of many of the recorded women's songs has been transcribed by the late Prof. Béla Bartók, who, with the permission of Harvard University, was commissioned by Columbia University to do this work. Seventy-five of these, together with a detailed analysis by Prof.

(3) Narrative poems of adventure sung to the accompaniment of the one-stringed *gusle*; these are the core of the collection and, although the actual number of texts is smaller than that of the women's songs, they are much longer; (4) Conversations held before the microphone with the singers, who tell of their lives and of how they learned to sing. The interest of the Homeric scholar naturally centers around the third group of texts.

It would seem that the best way to determine what oral form is and to analyze the oral technique of composition and transmission is to take the songs of a given singer and relate every formula and passage in them to the songs of other singers first in the same district and then in other districts. If the material were abundant enough one would thus be able to show exactly what elements in that singer's songs are the common traditional property of all the singers and what elements are 'original'. It was with this in mind that a plan of publication for the Parry Collection was laid down several years ago. The material is to be published by districts and by singers within a district, and correspondences between the poems within the district and those outside are to be noted in an appendix. The first volume is nearing completion. It will contain, beside a lengthy introduction which will give an account | of the collecting, a representative selection of poems gathered from the region of Novi Pazar.

It is obvious that before publication could be undertaken the words had to be transcribed from the phonograph records and a series of indices had to be devised so that the twelve thousand odd texts could be handled readily. Some of the transcription was done in Yugoslavia during 1934 and 1935 by Mr. Nikola Vujnović, himself a singer from Hercegovina, who had been Professor Parry's chief assistant in the field. In the spring of 1937 approximately 500 records were copied at Harvard and I took them to Dubrovnik that summer where Mr. Vujnović transcribed them. But there were still many records left untranscribed, and in 1938, with the combined assistance of the American Council of Learned Societies, the Society of Fellows, and Harvard University, Vujnović was brought to Harvard for a period of eighteen months. By the spring of 1940 all the records of the collection, with the exception of a handful in Albanian and Turkish and one or two which Vujnović could not understand either because of poor recording or of dialect differences, had been transcribed.

During the period in which the transcription was going forward a set of

Bartók and texts edited and translated by myself are soon to be published by the Columbia University Press. The reader is referred to this forthcoming volume for a fuller account of these songs. Several of the women's songs were also transcribed musically by Prof. Samuel P. Bayard of State College, Pa. and it is planned to publish six of these in the not too distant future.

practicable indices was devised and completed. Up to that time there had been only a rough log of each text as it was collected: a number was assigned to each in the field and an entry made of the name of the singer, the place and date of recording, and the numbers of the records. There are now four separate indices, on three-by-five cards. One is a master index of texts listed numerically; another is a master index of recorded texts arranged numerically, with guide cards for the centers in which the texts were collected; a third is an index of singers with the songs gathered from each entered on the card; and the fourth is an index of the first lines of the songs giving the text number of each version, the name of the singer, and the place of collection. With this apparatus one can readily review the songs contributed by any singer, or survey the songs collected in a single district, or study all the variants of any given song.

There was also a third task of a clerical nature which had to be done. This was typing the texts so that one could work from a typed copy, thus leaving the original manuscripts to be handled as little as possible. This work was started in Dubrovnik and continued later in Cambridge, Mass. There are still a large number to be typed, but this can be done as their turn for publication comes up. It can be done properly only by somebody who has at least an elementary knowledge of Serbo-Croatian.

Within the framework of the larger study of oral form are two related problems the investigation of which will add immeasurably to our understanding of those poems which have come down to us from the past. In the Parry Collection there are many instances of the same song from a single singer both in a recorded and in a dictated version. The process of dictating was unnatural for most of the singers. Accustomed to compose their verses rapidly to the rhythm of the instrumental accompaniment the majority of the singers found it difficult to dictate good lines. In fact, some of them found it impossible and it was necessary to give them the *gusle* and ask them to sing a line and then stop and wait for the scribe to record it before passing on to the next. Since the collector was seeking a normal ten-syllable line, the dictated version tends to be more perfect metrically than the sung version, because in the heat of normal oral composition metrical irregularities are frequently glossed over in the singing by adding an extra grace note or drawing out another for two beats. With the material at our disposal in the Parry Collection we shall be able to determine very exactly what the differences are between the sung and the dictated versions of a song.

The second problem is of peculiar interest to Homeric scholars. Most of the songs taken | down from unlettered peoples are short, usually only a few hundred lines, in rare instances reaching two thousand lines. This is far from the sixteen thousand lines of the *Iliad* or the thirteen thousand of the *Odyssey*. During the summer of 1935, while collecting at Bijelo Polje, Parry came across a singer named Avdo Međedović, one of those who had heard Ćor Huso in their youth, whose powers of invention and story-telling were far above the ordinary. He was encouraged to take all the time which he wished, to rest whenever necessary, and to sing as long a song as he could. He sang for a week and our turntables rolled for about two hours in the morning and two hours in the afternoon, with short breaks every twenty minutes or half hour for a cup of Turkish coffee or some stronger refreshment. At the end of a week the song was still unfinished, but the singer's voice had gone, so medication was ordered and after a week's rest Avdo continued. Another week sufficed to complete the song, which ran to 13,331 lines.[1] Another song from the same singer, this time in a dictated version, runs to about the same length.[2] One should not seek the same type of excellence in these long songs as one finds in the *Iliad* and the *Odyssey*, yet in spite of repetition of incident and lengthy catalogues (it will be noted that these are characteristic also of the Homeric poems) Avdo's songs are well above the average. We must posit for the Homeric poems, I believe, a more flourishing tradition than the one which prevailed in Yugoslavia in 1935, and a much richer one. But it is the length of Avdo's poems and the way in which that length was obtained which are of particular value. To illustrate the leisurely style of these songs I quote from a translation of the dictated 'Song of Meho, Son of Smail' which Professor Parry began. After a brief introduction the story begins:

Now to you, sirs, who are gathered here I wish to sing the measures of a song, that you may be merry. It is a song of the olden time, of the deeds of the great men of old and the heroes over the earth in the time when Suleyman the glorious held empire. Then was the empire of the Turks at its highest. Sixty provinces it had and Bosnia was its lock, its lock it was and its golden keys, and a place of all good trust against the foe.

Now they gathered together in Kanija in the gay tavern as the custom long had been. At that gathering were thirty barons, the chief men of all the city of Kanija, and four and twenty of the Emperor's lords. At the head of the gathering was the Duke Hasan Tiro with his fifty men of war and beside the Duke at his left side, Count Omer of Kanija, the old man. Beside the old man were two of the Emperor's marshals, and beside the marshals was Sifrich lord Hasan. Next to Hasan was his nephew lord Mehmed, the dear son of Smail the Pilgrim, and brother's son to Sifrich Hasan. . . .

Two squires served the wine, one the squire of Kanija's count, the other of their marshal, even the warriors Hasan and Huseyin. Beneath their arms each held a goatskin of wine, and in his right hand a great measuring cup. Ever in order did they serve their chiefs, Duke Hasan and the great men of the realm. When they had served every man then did they thrust their hands behind their

[1] Parry Collection, Texts nos. 12389 and 12441. [2] Ibid. Text no. 6802.

sashes and stood at homage to their lords, that their lords might find their drink the sweeter.

Now when the lords had drunk of their wine they put the wine glasses aside, for the wine had flushed their faces, and took up the brandy bowls. Brandy is ever a talker, and of those barons and those lords of the Emperor not one was a man who had to borrow. . . .[1]

Among the projects which Professor Parry had set for himself was a series of articles for the American Philological Association under the general title 'Homer and Huso'. He published an abstract of the first of these,[2] which he called 'Homer and Huso I: The Singer's Rests in Greek and South Slavic Heroic Song'; and I later followed the pattern of the abstract and | wrote an article on the subject.[3] This and two later articles[4] were modelled along the general lines of Professor Parry's earlier paper entitled 'Whole Formulaic Verses in Greek and South Slavic Heroic Song.'[5] They were intended to illustrate the ways in which the two poetries could be most profitably compared.

While in Novi Pazar Parry had recorded several Albanian songs from one of the singers who sang in both languages. The musical instrument used to accompany these songs is the *gusle* (Albanian *lahuta*) but the line is shorter than the Serbian decasyllabic and a primitive type of rhyming is regular. It was apparent that a study of the exchange of formulas and traditional passages between these two poetries would be rewarding because it would show what happens when an oral poetry passes from one language group to another which is adjacent to it. However, there was not sufficient time in 1935 to collect much material or to learn the Albanian language. While in Dubrovnik in the summer of 1937 I had an opportunity to study Albanian and in September and October of that year I travelled through the mountains of northern Albania from Shkodre to Kuksi by way of Boge, Thethi, Abate and Tropoje, returning by a more southerly route. I collected about one hundred narrative songs, many of them short, but a few between five hundred and a thousand lines in length.[6] We found out that there are some songs common to both Serbo-Croatian and Albanian tradition and that a number of the Moslem heroes of the Yugoslav poetry, such as Mujo and Halil Hrnjica and Đerđelez Alija, are found also in Albanian. Much work remains to be done in this field before we can tell exactly what the relationship is between the two traditions.

Milman Parry has already been assigned a place in the history of Homeric scholarship among the great. Bassett, although he disagreed

[1] I have continued the translation of this song as far as line 9000.

[2] HH, above.

[3] *TAPhA*, lxvii (1936), pp. 106–13.

[4] *TAPhA*, lxix (1938), pp. 439–45, and lxx (1939), p. xxxix (abstract only).

[5] WF, above.

[6] This collection is now in the Houghton Library at Harvard University.

with the implications of Parry's discoveries, asserted: 'Thus far Parry seems to me to have made one of the most important contributions of recent years to our understanding of Homer's poetry.'[1] And Carpenter, in discussing American Homeric scholars like Calhoun, Scott, and Bassett, added: 'But perhaps the most brilliant of this distinguished company has probably remained the least heeded. Milman Parry suffered the tragic and untimely death of those whom the old Homeric gods love, but not before he had completed and published his unanswerable and unassailable proof that *Iliad* and *Odyssey* belong to the class of oral literatures. . . . His work—only a few pamphlets in all—will not be read, like that of Scott, by the general student of literature. But whether or not it is read at all, its truth abides almost as surely as Euclid's demonstrations abide whether or not anyone chooses to retrace their close-knit reasoning.'[2] Actually, however, a true appraisal of the value of Milman Parry's work must wait until the full import of his collection of South Slavic texts is understood. Through it he will have added not only to our appreciation of the real merit of the Homeric poems but to our knowledge and comprehension of all oral traditional poetry.

[1] Samuel Eliot Bassett, *The Poetry of Homer*, Sather Classical Lectures, vol. 15, Berkeley, 1938, p. 15; see also my review in *AJP*, vol. lxviii, 2, April, 1947, pp. 219–22.

[2] Rhys Carpenter, *Folk Tale, Fiction and Saga in the Homeric Epics*, Sather Classical Lectures, vol. 20, Berkeley, 1946, p. 6.

INDEX OF NAMES AND SUBJECTS

In names the following index is reasonably complete; in subjects it is highly selective, both in the entries chosen and in the page references given for them, which might otherwise have been too numerous. The reader is advised to look also at the analytic tables of contents on pp. 2, 24, 37, 118, 173, 266, and 325. Where a subject entry is in italics, the reference is usually to a passage where the word in question is defined.